ELLIS ISLAND – WHEN AMERICA DID IMMIGRATION RIGHT

by Kevin Sherlock

Author of <u>Ellis Island Scrapbook</u>

BRENNYMAN BOOKS
AKRON, OHIO
UNITED STATES OF AMERICA

ELLIS ISLAND – WHEN AMERICA DID IMMIGRATION RIGHT by Kevin Sherlock
Copyright © 2010 by Kevin Sherlock

Published by Brennyman Books
PO Box 3988
Akron, Ohio 44314

Send direct inquiries or orders to the above address.

Printed in the United States of America.

Cataloging in Publication Data

Sherlock, Kevin
    ELLIS ISLAND – WHEN AMERICA DID IMMIGRATION RIGHT
    Includes footnotes, bibliography, and index.

ISBN 978-0-9654036-3-4

1.   United States -- History.
2.   United States – Culture
3.   Genealogy -- United States
4.   Heritage – United States
5.   Immigration – History – United States.
6.   Ellis Island
7.   Current Events -- Non-Fiction -- United States

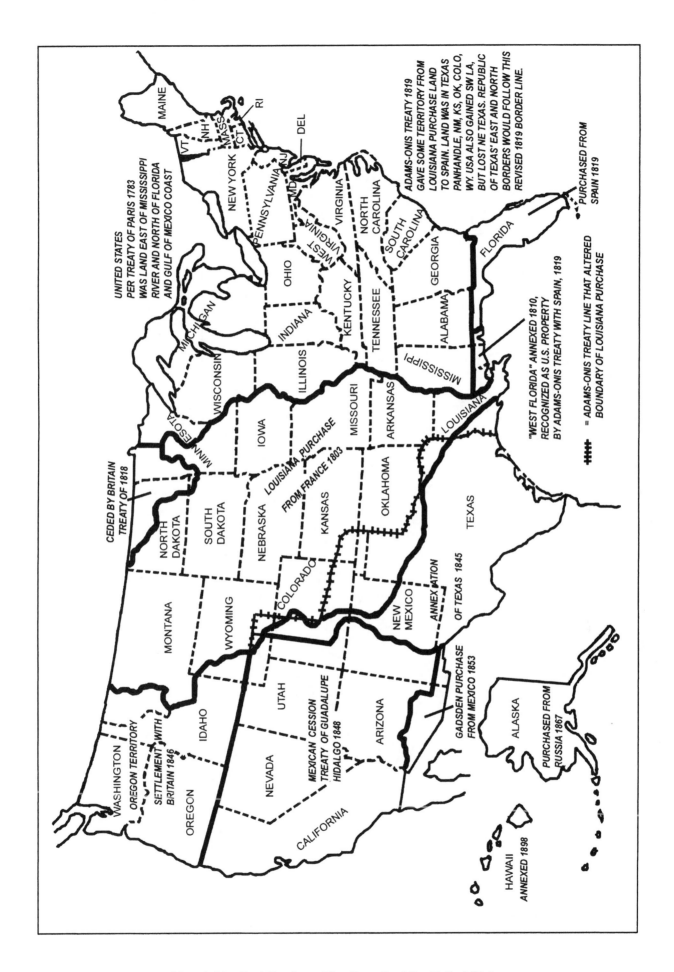

Map 1. Manifest Destiny – The Growth of the United States

Map 2 (left). Europe in 1871, after the Franco-Prussian War and Italian Unification

Map 3 (below). Europe in 1914, just before the start of World War One

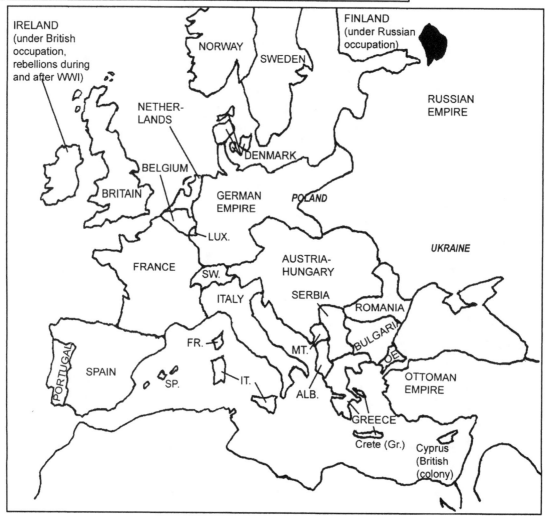

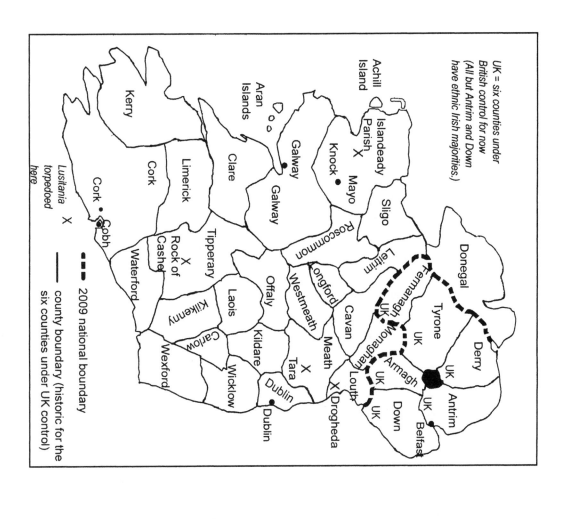

Map 4. Ireland's 32 Counties

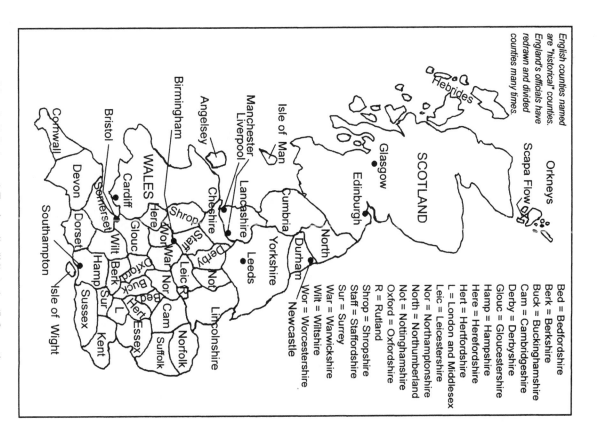

Map 5. Britain and England's "Historical" Counties

Map 6 (top). Spain's Historical Regions and Portugal

Map 6 (top) labels

Santiago, Santander, Basque Lands, FRANCE, ANDORRA, Asturias, Covadonga, Bilbao, Cantabria, Navarre, La Rioja, Galicia, Burgos, Leon, Castile (Old Castile), Zaragoza, Catalonia, Aragon, Oporto, Salamanca, Madrid, Madrid, Barcelona, PORTUGAL, Fatima, Toledo, Castile - La Mancha (New Castile), Valencia, Estremadura, Valencia, Lisbon, Andalucia, Murcia, Seville, Cadiz, Granada, MOROCCO

- - - 2009 national boundary
—— regional boundary

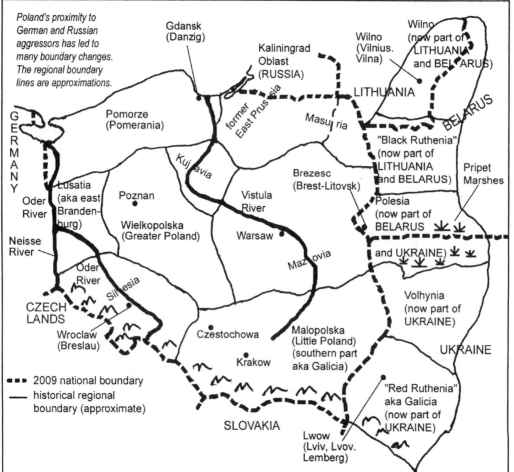

Map 7 (left). Poland's Boundaries and Historical Regions

Poland's proximity to German and Russian aggressors has led to many boundary changes. The regional boundary lines are approximations.

Map 7 labels

Gdansk (Danzig), Kaliningrad Oblast (RUSSIA), Wilno (now part of LITHUANIA and BELARUS), Wilno (Vilnius. Vilna), LITHUANIA, BELARUS, GERMANY, Pomorze (Pomerania), former East Prussia, Masuria, "Black Rutheria" (now part of LITHUANIA and BELARUS), Pripet Marshes, Kujavia, Lusatia (aka east Brandenburg), Poznan, Vistula River, Brezesc (Brest-Litovsk), Polesia (now part of BELARUS and UKRAINE), Oder River, Wielkopolska (Greater Poland), Warsaw, Neisse River, Oder River, Mazovia, Volhynia (now part of UKRAINE), CZECH LANDS, Silesia, UKRAINE, Wroclaw (Breslau), Czestochowa, Malopolska (Little Poland) (southern part aka Galicia), Krakow, "Red Ruthenia" aka Galicia (now part of UKRAINE), SLOVAKIA, Lwow (Lviv, Lvov. Lemberg)

- - - 2009 national boundary
—— historical regional boundary (approximate)

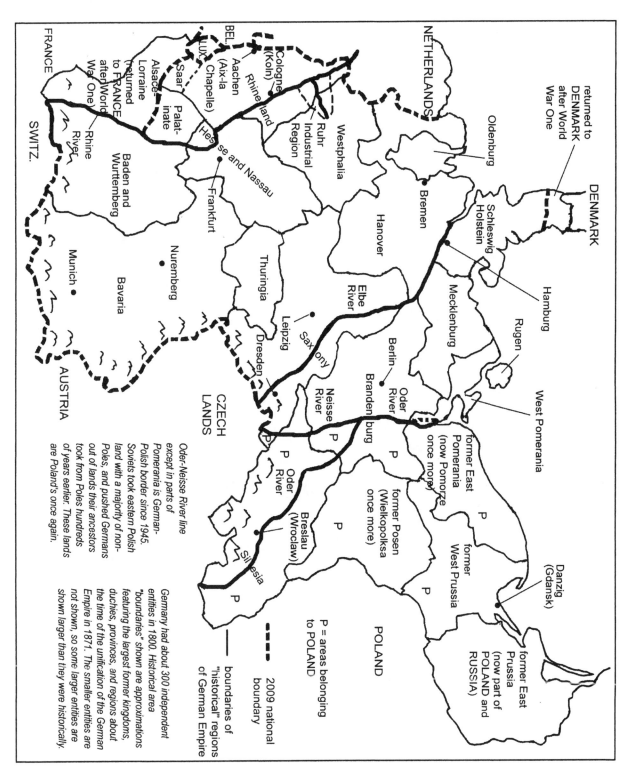

Map 8. Germany's Boundaries and Historical Regions

FRANCE

SWITZ.

AUSTRIA

FRANCE

BEL.

LUX.

NETHERLANDS

DENMARK

returned to
DENMARK
after World
War One

Oldenburg

Schleswig
Holstein

Hamburg

Rügen

West Pomerania

Mecklenburg

Bremen

Hanover

Thuringia

Leipzig

Dresden

CZECH
LANDS

Nuremberg

Bavaria

Munich

Baden and
Wurttemberg

Rhine
River

Palat-
inate

Saar

Alsace-
Lorraine
(returned
to FRANCE
after
World
War One)

Hes-
se and Nassau

Frankfurt

Aachen
(Aix-la
Chapelle)

Cologne
(Köln)

Rhine-
land

Ruhr
Industrial
Region

Westphalia

Elbe
River

Saxony

Neisse
River

Berlin

Branden-
burg

Oder
River

Oder
River

Silesia

Breslau
(Wroclaw)

P

P

P

P

P

P

P

former East
Pomerania
(now Pomorze
once more)

former Posen
(Wielkopolksa
once more)

former
West Prussia

Danzig
(Gdansk)

former East
Prussia
(now part of
POLAND and
RUSSIA)

POLAND

P = areas belonging
to POLAND

boundaries of
"historical" regions
of German Empire

2009 national
boundary

Oder-Neisse River line
except in parts of
Pomerania is German-
Polish border since 1945.
Soviets took eastern Polish
land with a majority of non-
Poles, and pushed Germans
out of lands their ancestors
took from Poles hundreds
of years earlier. These lands
are Poland's once again.

Germany had about 300 independent
entities in 1800. Historical area
"boundaries" shown are approximations
featuring the largest former kingdoms,
duchies, provinces, and regions about
the time of the unification of the German
Empire in 1871. The smaller entities are
not shown, so some larger entities are
shown larger than they were historically.

Map 9. France and its Regions

Map 10. Italy and its Regions

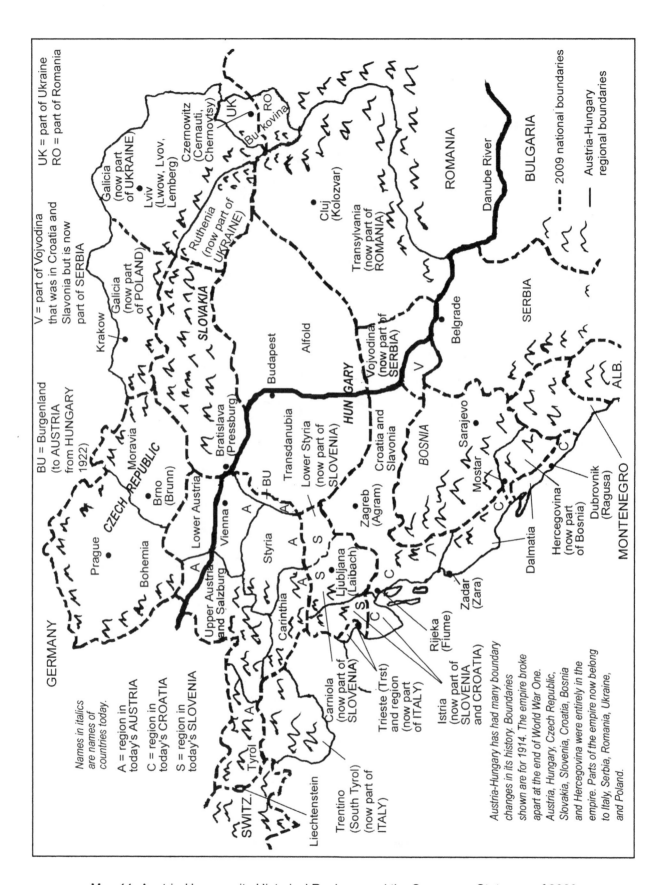

Map 11. Austria-Hungary, its Historical Regions, and the Successor States as of 2009

Map 12. The Balkans

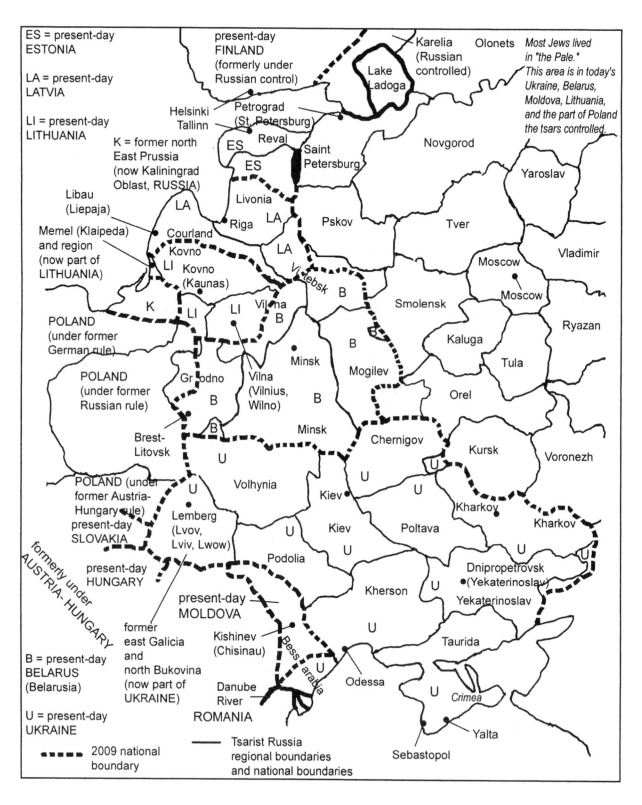

Map 13. Tsarist Russia, and Boundaries of the Successor States
to the Former Soviet Union as of 2009

ALB = Albania
B = Bosnia
CRO = Croatia
CZECH = Czech Republic
H = Hercegovina
LX = Luxembourg
MC = Macedonia
MT = Montenegro
SERB = Serbia
SLOVAK = Slovakia
SL = Slovenia
SW = Switzerland

ICELAND

Ulster (marked UK) is becoming
an Irish majority land. Most of its
counties have Irish majorities.

Faeroes
(Denmark)

Shetlands
(UK)

Murmansk

Archangel

FINLAND

NORWAY

SWEDEN

EST-
ONIA

RUSSIA

LATVIA

LITHU-
ANIA

IRISH
REPUBLIC

UK

UNITED
KINGDOM

NETHER-
LANDS

BELGIUM

DENMARK

RUS.

BELARUS

GERMANY

POLAND

LX

FRANCE

CZECH

SLOVAK

UKRAINE

MOLDOVA

SW

AUSTRIA

HUN-
GARY

SL

CRO

ITALY

H

B

SERB

ROMANIA

CRO

MT

ALB

MC

BULGARIA

GEORGIA

UR

PORTUGAL

SPAIN

Corsica
(Fr.)

Sardinia
(It.)

Balearics
(Sp.)

Sicily (It.)

MALTA

TURKEY

ARMENIA

GREECE

Hercegovina is a long-
recognized Christian
majority region of
Moslem plurality Bosnia.

Crete and other islands shown
around Greece belong to Greece.

Crete

Cyprus
(divided between
Greeks and Turks)

Map 14. Europe as of 2009

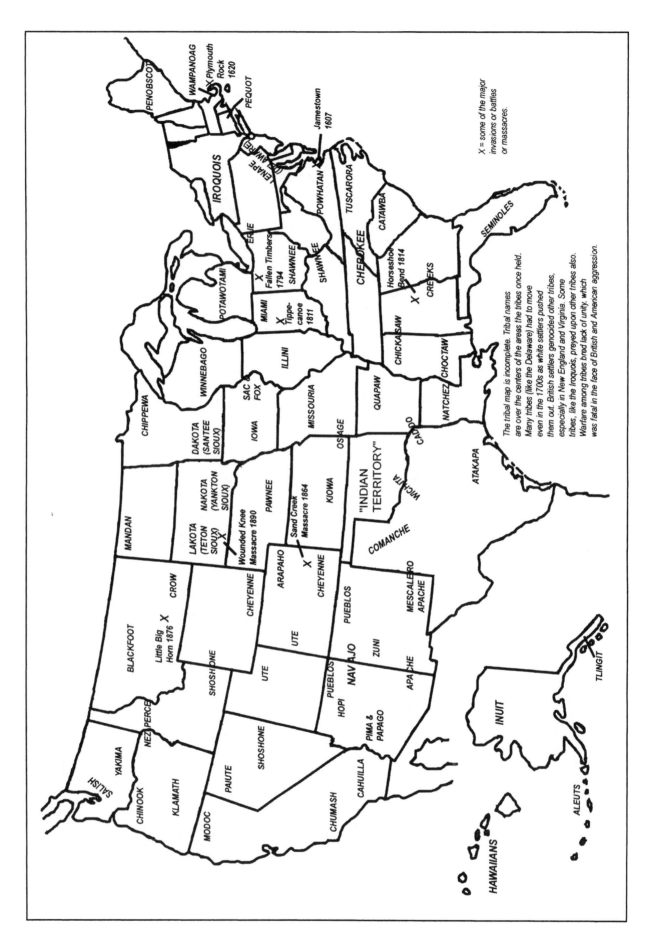

The tribal map is incomplete. Tribal names are over the centers of the areas the tribes once held. Many tribes (like the Delaware) had to move even in the 1700s as white settlers pushed them out. British settlers genocided other tribes, especially in New England and Virginia. Some tribes, like the Iroquois, preyed upon other tribes also. Warfare among tribes bred lack of unity, which was fatal in the face of British and American aggression.

X = some of the major invasions or battles or massacres.

Map 15. Native Americans and the Lands They Lost

TABLE OF CONTENTS

DISCLAIMER

The purpose of this book is to inform and entertain. The author and publisher sell this book with the understanding they do not render legal advice. Neither the author nor the publisher assumes any responsibility for the misuse of info contained in this book. Neither the author nor the publisher assumes responsibility or liability for any damage or loss caused or alleged to be caused directly or indirectly by the info contained in this book.

Although the author and publisher have researched all sources to ensure the accuracy of information presented in this book, there is the possibility that typographical errors and content errors have gotten into the book. No human is perfect.

Since books and documents available to the public within the life span of the author form the backbone of this book, the author and publisher have cited them in the text so you the reader will know where the information came from. The author and publisher assume no liability or responsibility for any possible inaccuracies in the sources quoted ... in any case, each strove within the limits of his abilities to be as accurate as the sources used

If you see an error, let the author know about it and he will correct it. The author and the publisher each can make errors despite diligence to keep the text accurate. Only Our Lord is perfect – and look how He has been resented for that through the centuries!

The author and the publisher assume no liability or responsibility for any possible damage caused or claimed to have been caused to those whose questionable behavior is mentioned in this book.

Most of those criticized in this book are dead. Nothing in this book can objectively hurt them; they have answered for their sins before God. The living who are criticized in this book are mostly politicians, bureaucrats, and media figures, people who tend to deserve criticism. The public assumes the first group is often a criminal class. The public assumes the second group has many people who out of incompetence or out of a slew of personal failings or both tend to make people's lives miserable. The public assumes the third group largely consists of shallow-self-absorbed and often untruthful and unfaithful people who are essentially idiot savants ... they can act or sing or look pretty or dispense propaganda as alleged journalists, but they usually don't have other skills.

Writing the truth about members of these three groups, no matter how much it offends them or their flunkies, is absolutely a defense against libel. And freedom of speech and libel laws guarantee the right to satire and fair comment on the character and job performance of these individuals. No one put a gun to their heads to make them act the way they do!

The author and publisher are familiar with laws regarding nuisance lawsuits, malicious prosecution, and RICO ... and will protect their rights and exact just retribution to the fullest extent of the law if unjustly challenged in court by anyone they fairly criticized ... or one of his allies or flunkies.

MAP NOTES

In America, the citizens of the 13 states made the Union, and American settlers organized the land of the other 37 states (often over the protests of the Mexican, Spanish, American Indian, and Hawaiian first settlers) and later applied for admission to the Union. In Europe, they didn't do it this way.

Because of the threat posed by Moslem, Asian, and Viking invaders, local strongmen set up local governments and made agreements with stronger regional lords. These lords made agreements with national leaders known as kings or emperors. The stronger helped the weaker, and drew labor and food and raw materials from the weaker. This series of agreements was known as feudalism. It was the only way at the time the people of Europe could defend themselves against the bloodthirsty vermin arrayed against them.

Regional governments often started as the holdings of a powerful lord who swore allegiance to a less-than-all-powerful king. In many cases, the people and leaders of these regions had rights as well as responsibilities, and they guarded their rights zealously.

The people of Europe tried to keep as much authority local as possible, but the rulers of Europe wanted all the power in their slimy hands. Wars, revolutions, and government dictates, almost always driven by someone's greed, continually changed the regional and national boundaries of Europe.

The maps of European nations in this book are an attempt by the author to show the historical regions of most of the countries of Europe. The maps of Europe, unless otherwise specified, tend to show regional boundaries from the 1870s, after the unification of Germany and Italy, and the reorganization of Austria-Hungary, to the eve of World War One in 1914. These maps also show 2009's boundaries.

The author is a better historian than he is a cartographer. However, these maps he drew are reasonable representations of the organization of Europe in the time of the Ellis Island Era.

His map of the growth of the United States does not show all the details of the Webster-Ashburton treaty that fixed the Maine boundary and other disputed parts of the American boundary with British-owned Canada in the 1840s. However, it accurately shows the growth of the nation. And the American Indians' map shows, by and large, the areas of the larger tribes the British and the Americans fought, defeated, and stripped of their land.

INTRODUCTION

One of the best reasons for the study of history is to learn how people have faced problems over time. The purpose for this book is to give the American public a perspective of how the people who came before us rationally dealt with the issue of immigration. We The People need to know what our officials tried in an earlier time, why their methods worked, and how they could apply to today. We The People need to make sure our elected officials understand this too.

The vast majority of the immigrants who came to America in the Ellis Island era wanted to become Americans and did so. They became real Americans in thought and in action. They assimilated. Many of them served in our nation's armed forces in World War One and their sons answered the nation's call in World War Two.

In the Ellis Island era, America didn't import Europe's welfare recipients or Latin America's underpaid or Asia's slave laborers or the Middle East's jihadists. The people who came here in the Ellis Island era had to support themselves, not come in on labor-undermining contracts, not have communicable diseases that threatened the American public, not come in illegally, and not have an attitude that was at odds with the American way of life. Those who couldn't or wouldn't meet these reasonable standards couldn't get in or were shipped back to where they came from.

The heyday of Ellis Island – from the 1890s through the 1920s – was a time when American officials *did* care about the good of Americans in regards to immigration. This is an approach our public officials ought to try now, since their current approaches are miserable failures.

The book lays out like this:

This first chapter of this book gives a short sketch of Europe in the late 1800s.

The second chapter explains how America got to be so big, and why America could accommodate immigrants.

The third chapter covers how Americans tried to regulate immigration from the time of George Washington to the presidencies of Theodore Roosevelt and William Taft. It mixes in sketches of American history during those times to give a frame of reference for the regulations.

The fourth chapter explains how Ellis Island operated from the 1890s to the Great Depression.

The fifth chapter covers "white slavery" – the trafficking of females for the sex trade in America in the Ellis Island Era. It also covers how resolute American officials tried to fight the vermin who trafficked and exploited immigrant girls and American girls.

The sixth chapter covers two tragedies that killed hundreds of immigrants within a year of each other – the *Titanic* sinking and the Triangle Fire. It covers how two politicians made lasting reforms in the wakes of these preventable tragedies to protect the lives and health of America's people.

The seventh and eighth chapters cover how Americans tried to regulate immigration from the time of World War One through the Roaring Twenties. They mix in sketches of history from that terrible war, and from the Roaring Twenties to give a frame of reference for the regulations. The eighth chapter also covers the slowdown in immigration that led to the closing of Ellis Island as an immigration station.

The ninth chapter analyzes the Ellis Island Era. It displays statistics and debunks false legends. It explains why the "Ellis Island Approach" worked.

The tenth chapter discusses solutions to the immigration problems of today in light of the wisdom our earlier leaders acquired from their experiences in the Ellis Island Era.

The final chapter is a wrap-up of the book.

In this post 9/11 era, immigration enforcement is now no longer a Cheech Marin joke a la "Born in East L.A." It's serious business ... and many Americans wonder whether or not the Department of Homeland Security and the FBI know what they're doing. Some Americans have even taken it upon themselves to watch sections of the border with Mexico.

The Canadian border and the Mexican border and our own airports are leaking in Middle Easterners and others who intend Americans no good.

Suicidal terrorism committed by Moslem fanatics sneaking past asleep-at-the-switch officials isn't the only immigration issue that is wounding America.

About 800,000 foreign nationals are studying in our nation's universities. Besides draining grant money and class space that our own kids could use, many of these students are learning military and industrial technology and are taking it back to the dictators of their homelands.

China sends us tens of thousands of students every year, and we send China back young professionals trained in the kinds of advanced engineering and computer sciences they will need to undercut our industries, build weapons of mass destruction, and build the missile systems to deliver them. Likewise, tens of thousands of students from India and Islamic countries have been able to pick up everything from illegal technology transfers to information on making nuclear weaponry.

American business leaders are also importing thousands of doctors, engineers, and programmers who work for much less than their American counterparts. American industry suffers as many bright American engineers are driven from the field and less capable ones from Asia take their places. American medicine dips as HMOs and other medical businesses recruit alien doctors and nurses with lesser skills and more problems talking with patients.

Then there is the sheer cost of paying for immigrants who view America as a bottomless barrel of welfare benefits. American taxpayers whose own ancestors would have been deported if they ended up on public assistance are paying billions of dollars a year for immigrants who can't work or choose not to. Hospitals are collapsing under the weight of uninsured immigrants who freeload off the health system.

And there is one other ugly facet of the "new immigration" – the wholesale enslavement and smuggling of young women and teenage girls into America for degradation in the sex trade.

Huge global corporations and many other companies in the United States have parasitical chiefs who want the market of the United States and the quality of life of the United States, but have no shame in hiring illegals because they work cheap and are afraid to complain about being exploited. These same corporate quislings have no qualms about sending much of their work out to China, India, and other places with virtual slave labor. They contribute to many politicians' campaign coffers, so the politicians are more prone to do their bidding instead of serving the public. Otherwise, our politicians would impose tariffs on foreign products at least high enough to reflect the costs of labor, safety, and environmental standards our manufacturers and farmers have to abide by, thus keeping millions more Americans employed.

There are many politicians and bureaucrats whose incomes and power depend on having ignorant and dependent voters to keep them in office. These individuals also support the influx of illegals, then giving them welfare, schooling, health care, and other perks that American workers have to pay for with their taxes. They want these illegals to be given American citizenship, anticipating these illegals will vote for the politicians who gave them so much money they confiscated from American taxpayers.

Professional immigration pimps call those who argue for American political leaders to make and enforce laws that protect the American public "racists." And when that doesn't work, they go to the Ellis Island card. Since roughly 40 percent of all Americans born in this country have at least one ancestor who was processed at Ellis

Island, the professional immigration pimps say, "The new immigrants are no different than the people who came through Ellis Island."

If the "New Immigration" people are the moral equivalent of the "Ellis Island Era" immigrants, then wouldn't it be fair to subject them to the same kinds of screening the earlier immigrants had to undergo?

Using the Ellis Island set of standards, the following would apply today:

Any immigrant unwilling or unable to earn a living would be barred or deported. Also, immigrants would not be able to daisy-chain in old relatives and ask the American taxpayers to give them benefits.

Trying to enter illegally would earn an illegal a trip home.

Criminal conduct would force the deportation of hundreds of thousands of immigrants, legal and illegal. Not only street crime, but white collar crime, industrial espionage and regular espionage would send criminals home.

The ban on immigrants with labor contracts (with a few exceptions) would drastically drop the number of immigrants looking to displace Americans in the technical fields.

The ban on polygamy would ban Moslems and others who practice this relic of barbarism.

Enforcing "inimical (hostile or harmful) attitude" laws would ban a very large number of people from the Middle East and a large proportion of other Asians. It would also ban other aliens who disagree with American institutions and are unwilling to adjust to them.

Also, Ellis Island era officials made sponsors and others put up bonds in the thousands of dollars apiece for questionable immigrants whose causes they advocated. Applying that law to today and adjusting for inflation to about $40,000 per bond could break many immigrant advocacy groups and individuals, thus stopping the flow of questionable immigrants further.

Millions of European immigrants had to play by these rules. Fairness calls for making today's immigrants play by the same rules. The immigrants of today are no more special than those who came in steerage to this nation and helped _build_ this nation instead of bombing it, or spying on it, or leeching off its taxpayers.

Without question, much of this nation's foundation is from British dissenters who wanted freedom from the Crown. But much of the work on the foundation was also done by Spaniards and Mexicans and Frenchmen and Creoles who built cities in America before the American Revolution. St. Augustine, Florida, and Santa Fe, New Mexico are older than Boston and New

York City. San Diego, San Francisco, and Los Angeles are older than Cincinnati, Cleveland, and Chicago. French-founded Detroit, New Orleans, and St. Louis also date back to the early and mid 1700s.

There were other builders of America. Despite American bigotry against Catholics, roughly 30 percent of the Continental Army was Irish. And roughly 5% to 10% of the soldiers and sailors in the ranks of the Patriots were black men whose ancestors were kidnaped and exiled from Africa to be sold and worked as slaves. The sad truth is many of our Patriots were slaves also.

The peoples of Europe who didn't want to bow to an inbred king or nobility or to a crooked parliament came to this nation and built it up. Many slaves were forced to come here, and they and their descendants added their own labor and intellect and talents to the national culture. It was this amalgamation of European, American Indian, American Hispanic, and African cultures under a common belief in God and a sense of the rights and responsibilities of the people that made America into the greatest nation on earth.

History is not about forces, but about people. I try to give you sketches of some of the great and some of the infamous who led this nation for better or worse. Learning what makes leaders tick gives people a better understanding of why they acted the way they did.

Plus, history is a story. It's fun to read about the foibles of the famous, and it's interesting to get a glimpse of how our ancestors lived. When you put yourself in the shoes of these people, your ancestors, you begin to understand why they did what they did.

This book is proudly America-centric, without restriction, without exception, and without apology. It is a reasonably detailed examination of immigration, but in a conversational tone, not in an academic tone. I'm not trying to impress you with what I know, but I am trying to give you a frame of reference.

The maps provided show the jumbled state of affairs in Europe in the 1800s and early 1900s. They also show the regions of the countries so you can find them readily. If your ancestors came from Galicia (in Spain) or Galicia (in Poland or Ukraine), from Lorraine or Lombardy, Bavaria or Bohemia, or Mayo or Montenegro, you will be able to find these regions. The maps aren't fancy but they get the job done.

By the way, don't skip the footnotes. Many of the best anecdotes in this book are in the footnotes.

This book and its sister book Ellis Island Scrapbook cover the growth of America, the history of immigration regulation to the Ellis Island Era, and immigration processing. This book has chapters on American history from World War One up to World War Two, a chapter on the fight against "white slavery," and a chapter on two immigrant tragedies that happened a year apart – the Triangle Fire and the *Titanic* disaster. This book also focuses more on the problems of immigration today.

The other book also has a short chapter on steerage, a large chapter on the lives of the peoples of Europe, and a huge chapter of true stories of Ellis Island people that this book does not have.

Virtually no other country on Earth has leaders who favor diluting their culture or ethnicity or identity out of a misguided sense of inclusion or political correctness. Favoring the legal and controlled immigration of Europeans and Latin Americans and sub-Saharan Africans over the people of the Middle East and the rest of Asia to preserve the essential cultural makeup of this nation is the right of Americans who actually have to live and work and go to school with the people who our politicians decide to let in. The people of America, as do the people of every nation, have the right to try to preserve their culture.

The purpose of this book, again, is to inform you how we as a nation used to handle immigration successfully. We need to study history to learn how people dealt with problems, and why they failed or succeeded. Our predecessors figured out a way to admit foreigners and ensure they would be productive Americans. There is no reason we should not demand our officials do likewise now. We The People have a stake in making sure our leaders regulate immigration to benefit America.

And there's a more fundamental reason for knowledge.

Government's greatest enemy is a public with intelligence, memory, and courage. An informed and determined public, with the help of God, is this nation's best defense against the abuses of the rich, the powerful, and the greedy.

Kevin Sherlock
Washington's Birthday, 2010

NOTES ON TERMS IN THIS BOOK

The "Ellis Island Era" is basically the four decades from the start of the 1890s through to the end of the 1920s. In this four-decade span came most immigrants of the "old immigration" before the 1960s. The term "modern era" of immigration or the "new immigration" era generally refers to legal immigration since LBJ's disastrous Immigration and Nationality Act of 1965.

The term "Native American Indian" or "American Indian" refers to the people who settled and populated the Americas before Columbus, the Vikings, or even Brendan the Navigator. This distinguishes them from the people from India in South Asia. I extend similar respect to the Inuit ("Eskimos") who first settled Alaska and the Polynesians who first settled Hawaii.

The term "Orthodox Jew" refers to Jews who practice Orthodox Judaism. The terms "Jew" and "Jewish" refer to people who practice one of the various forms of Judaism, and those who by blood (if not always observance) consider themselves Jewish.

The term "Christian" refers to Catholics, Orthodox Christians, and Protestants. Too many people incorrectly use the term "Christian" to refer to Protestants only. Catholics and Orthodox Christians believe in the divinity of Christ and His mission as Redeemer of mankind. Protestants got these beliefs (and the Bible) from Catholics and Orthodox Christians.

The term "Orthodox Christian" or "Orthodox" refers to the Christian churches which serve the majority of believers in Russia, Ukraine, and the Balkans, and some other lands. There are Orthodox Christians in America, also. Most of them have roots in the above-mentioned countries.

Some statistics I present in this book were reported by 12-month calendar years and others were reported by 12-month fiscal years. Unless there was an important reason to do so, I tended not to say which was a calendar year statistic and which was a fiscal year statistic.

I don't write or speak "the King's English." I write and speak somewhere between the county sheriff's English and the county coroner's English. In other words, I proudly think, write, and speak in _American_. I trust you my reader do also. I hope my terms, figures of speech, slang, and popular cultural references will help make this book more readable and enjoyable for you. I care much more about talking plainly than I care about impressing some stuck-up reviewer with my vocabulary.

I realize the term "corrupt politician" is redundant, but I use the term in this book anyway. I apologize for the extra ink used in printing this term.

WHY DID PEOPLE LEAVE EUROPE?

Why would more than 30 million people leave Europe to come to America in the 1800s and 1900s? Why would they pull up roots and leave loved ones and come to a far away and unknown land? In order to understand the immigrants' mindsets, you have to understand what the conditions were in the lands they left behind. This chapter is a sketch of Europe in those times.

A SNAPSHOT OF EUROPE AT THE START OF THE 1800s

The wars of Napoleon – the heir of the French Revolution – took up the first 15 years of the continent's calendar in the 1800s. After the British locked the Little Corporal on St. Helena, Europe quieted down some, but it was never truly at peace from the end if the Napoleonic Wars to the start of another general war in Europe – World War One – a century later.

At the end of the Napoleonic Wars, the French were free but resentful, a nation held in check only by the combined efforts of peoples with nowhere near the liberties they had. France had been the strongest power in Europe for almost 200 years. Losing this position (and losing the hundreds of thousands of strong young men who kept them in this position) galled and grieved the French greatly.

Here's how the rest of the continent looked at the end of the Napoleonic Wars in 1815:

The British government ruled England, Wales and Scotland. They occupied Ireland and treated the justifiably hostile Irish little better than slaves. Britain's navy was strong enough to fight and beat any other two nations' navies, and Britain's sailors proved it during the Napoleonic Wars. However, Andrew Jackson, William Henry Harrison, Winfield Scott, Jean Lafitte, Isaac Hull, Stephen Decatur, Oliver Perry, and other American heroes beat them on land and on water in the War of 1812.

Germany was a 39-entity puzzle; Prussia was its biggest piece. Kinglets and princelings ruled postage stamp sized storybook realms elsewhere in the Fatherland. Prussians also wrongfully held much Polish land.

Russian soldiers occupied Finland (which they took from the Swedes during the Napoleonic Wars), Ukraine, Belarusia (Belarus), Moldova (then called Bessarabia), the Baltic lands (Estonia, Latvia, Lithuania), the Caucasus land of Georgia and some of Armenia, and most of Poland. Many Russian soldiers and civilians lay dead; the people of their homeland had suffered greatly during the wars against Napoleon.

Austria's emperor ruled Austria, Hungary, the Czech and Slovak and Ruthenian lands, southern Poland, Galicia (southeastern Poland and northwestern Ukraine), Transylvania and Bukovina (northwestern and northern Romania), Vojvodina (northern Serbia), Croatia, Slovenia, and much of northern Italy (including Venezia, Lombardy and Tuscany).

The Turks occupied the rest of Serbia, Bosnia and Hercegovina, Albania, Greece, Macedonia, Bulgaria, and most of Romania. The Turks also occupied Armenian land, Cyprus, much of the Arabian peninsula, and present-day Iraq, Kuwait, Syria, Lebanon, Israel, and Jordan. Egyptian leaders would break their land free from the Turks in the 1800s, only to lose it to the grasping British later in the century. The local rulers of present-day Algeria, Tunisia, Morocco, and Libya were basically Moslem bandits, pirates and slavers. The Turks had loose control over or affiliations with all these areas except Morocco. American sailors and Marines fought some of these human vermin in the early 1800s. The French would occupy and rule Algeria and Tunisia later in the 1800s. The French (with Spanish help) would take over Morocco in the early 1900s. Likewise, the Italians would take Libya from the Turks a few years before the start of World War One.

Denmark and Sweden were free. So was poor and isolated little Montenegro. Switzerland was free once again, after a few years of French occupation.

Spain and Portugal were two proud but poor and battered nations after the Napoleonic Wars. Their royals and nobility had fled or had connived with Napoleon, and many of their "enlightened" had collaborated with him. In short, the countries' elites had sold out. The priests and people had waged guerrilla warfare against the French oppressors. The Iberian Peninsula was full of ruined towns and families mourning their dead. Meanwhile, Spain and Portugal's own colonists in Latin America were rebelling or soon would rebel and would throw out the Iberian noblemen who had ruled them.

Italy was a jumble of territories ruled by Austria, the Pope, and a number of comic opera local rulers. Many wanted to run Italy, therefore no one could.

The European powers took Belgium from France after the Napoleonic Wars and united it with the

Netherlands, which they also pried out of Napoleon's grip. The Dutch held Belgium until the Belgians forced their way out of the unhappy union in 1830.

The European powers took Norway from Denmark (a French ally) after the Napoleonic Wars and assigned Norway to Sweden (an enemy of France). The Swedes held Norway until the Norwegians got a divorce similar to Belgium's in 1905. The Danes still held Iceland and would do so until World War Two.

Throughout the 1800s, British soldiers forcibly held Ireland in the British Empire. Poland's people lost their freedom in the partitions of the 1770s and the 1790s. Poland lay dissected and divided between three greedy empires – Prussia, Russia, and Austria – throughout the 1800s. The Irish and the Poles would not take these oppressions passively.

The major countries during the 1800s and early 1900s fought each other, and so did the minor countries. Major countries fought minor countries, and once several minor countries took on a major country that was a threat to all of them.

Italy and Germany would each become united countries in the 1860s and 1870s, with considerable bloodshed.

The Serbs, Greeks, Romanians, Bulgarians, Macedonians, and Albanians would gain their freedom from the Turks by revolt and by warfare in the 1800s and the years of the early 1900s before World War One. The Turks slaughtered most of the Armenians under their control during World War One.

The Hungarians could not throw off the rule of the Austrian emperor, but they made so much trouble for him he left them as masters in their own house until they eventually separated from Austria at the end of World War One. The Poles would not regain their freedom until after World War One. World War One made it possible for the Czechs and Slovaks and Ruthenians and many Poles and Romanians to gain their freedom from the Austrians and Hungarians at war's end. World War One also made it possible for the Slovenes and Croats to leave the crumbling Hapsburg empire and join with the Serbs and the people of Montenegro and Bosnia and Hercegovina and most of the people of Macedonia to form Yugoslavia at war's end.

Most of the Irish won their freedom from Britain in a successful guerrilla war after World War One. The newly-free Poles would have to fight the Russians – now under Communist rule – for similar stakes and win in the same time period. Likewise, the people of Lithuania, Latvia, Estonia, and Finland were able to secure their freedom from the Soviet Union in the wake of Russia's slide into Communism toward the end of World War One.

The Communists would continue the oppression of the many in Russia and Ukraine and Belarusia after they overthrew the democrats who overthrew the Tsar. Many Poles, and the people of the Baltic states would escape the Reds' grasp until World War Two. Then the Poles would suffer German and Russian invasion and partition, while the Baltic peoples would suffer Soviet occupation and later Nazi occupation. Eventually the Poles and the Balts would suffer re-occupation by the troops of the Soviet Union.

Most countries convulsed at least once during the 1800s and early 1900s due to a rebellion, a dynastic struggle for power, a revolution, the struggle of patriots for independence, or some or all of the above. No matter who won, the people almost always lost.

This was the civilized and progressive Europe many of our ancestors would flee from in the 1800s and early 1900s. Thank the Good Lord they came here to America.

WARS AND RUMORS OF WAR

There was an overall threat of war that hung over Europe from the 1870s to the start of World War One in 1914. The people called the build-up of tensions around Europe the "Dry War" – in much the same way people called the decades of tension between the Soviet Union and the United States the "Cold War." Unlike Ronald Reagan, Pope John Paul II, Lech Walesa and Solidarity, and Lane Kirkland and the AFL-CIO, the leaders of Europe were unable to win the "Dry War" without a cataclysmic bloodbath.

The scramble for colonies in Africa and Asia pitted Britain against other nations. Since the British grabbed for by far the most colonies, they had more squabbles with the natives and with other European rivals. Britain nearly went to war with France, Germany, Russia, and the United States during this period ... all because of British greed for land.

By the end of the 1800s, the British had grabbed one-fifth of earth's surface. The British systematically plundered Africa, India, and China. British settlers overran Australia, New Zealand and Canada; British businessmen also took over South Africa with the help of the British army.

In 1900, the British held Egypt, Sudan, a strip of present-day Somalia, Uganda, Kenya, the land that would become Zambia, Zimbabwe, and Nyasaland (Malawi), Bechaunaland (Botswana), Nigeria, Gold Coast (Ghana), Sierra Leone, and Gambia in Africa. They were also in the process of taking all of South Africa, and after World War One, they would take over most of Germany's colonies in Africa (Tanganyika, Southwest Africa, and Togo). In Asia in 1900, the British held "India" (which then included, besides India, today's Pakistan, Bangla Desh, and Burma), Ceylon (Sri Lanka), part of New Guinea, and Malaya and Sarawak (Singapore and today's Malaysia). In the Western Hemisphere, the British held British Guiana, British Honduras (Belize), Jamaica, and some other islands in the Caribbean Sea. The British also held a number of islands and enclaves at key points along the shipping routes of the world; the most well-known of these were Hong Kong, Gibraltar, Malta, Cyprus, Aden, and Zanzibar. Canada, Australia, and New Zealand were more or less voluntary parts of the British Empire; the people of Ireland were very involuntary subjects.

The total land mass of the world is not quite 58 million square miles. This includes Antarctica and all the islands, as well as the other continental masses. The British, whose home island is about the size of Minnesota (less than 90,000 square miles), ruled an empire of more than 11 million square miles in size. By comparison, the United States (including Alaska and Hawaii) are less than 3.7 million square miles in size.

The British had disputes with the French over territory in Africa. The British had disputes with the Russians over territory in Central Asia, and desired to keep Russia from ever gaining solid naval access to the Mediterranean Sea, because Britain's leaders thought the Russian navy might interfere with their plunder of India. To that extent, the British would rather allow the Turks to commit repeated atrocities against the peoples of the Balkans instead of letting Russian troops punish the fez-wearing murderers for their crimes against humanity. The British clashed with the Germans in a number of areas, mostly colonial, naval, and trade issues.

The British tried to bully nations in Latin America, but at least here the United States invoked the Monroe Doctrine and made the British back off. Theodore Roosevelt also made the British back off when they tried to claim the Alaska Panhandle for their colony Canada in the wake of the 1898 Yukon gold rush. The posturing militaristic Germans might have posed the greatest threat to peace in Europe, but the greedy grasping British clearly posed the greatest threat to world peace.

Saying the British posed a greater threat to world peace than the Germans is like saying Hitler was more evil than Stalin. Understand Germany's leaders were not contestants for the Nobel Peace Prize themselves. Germany, a recently re-assembled nation, started competing with Britain and France for colonies and with

Britain for naval superiority under the aggressive Kaiser Wilhelm II. German leaders built up the army into the continent's best, and intimidated all their neighbors by threatening to unleash their soldiers against them. German leaders also built up a navy powerful enough to provoke quarrels with other European powers, and with American naval officers too.

German propaganda stressed German military might in an attempt to cow the other European leaders. Kaiser Wilhelm II on occasion personally pointed out to foreign dignitaries who visited him the top German officers designated to lead the planned assault on France. Because the Germans were so dominant and domineering, the French and Russians had to keep large standing armies to be ready for them.

Kaiser Wilhelm, judging by some his public utterances, was an unbalanced meglomaniac. The Kaiser routinely said things that made other European heads of state worry about his intentions and sometimes his sanity. But compared to the Junkers and the chief military officers, he was mild.

Kaiser Wilhelm was more like the Wizard of Oz than the spiritual father of Adolf Hitler. He had considerable power as a ruler, but he kept it by being a royal demagogue. The Kaiser had to appear tough and crazy and arrogant to overcome his physical handicaps and to keep the army and the Junkers from undermining him or overthrowing him.

The Germans, by comparison with the British, got into the colonial business very late. They managed to grab Tanganyika, Southwest Africa, Cameroon, and Togo in Africa. They grabbed part of New Guinea and some islands in the Pacific Ocean, and they thought about grabbing the Philippines after the Spanish-American War. American leaders sent a large enough number of soldiers, sailors, marines, and ships to the Philippines to keep the Germans (and the equally militaristic and greedy Japanese) at bay. Teddy Roosevelt's rise to the Presidency did much to make the Germans behave.

Germany's colonies weren't exactly garden spots. More Germans "colonized" New York City, Chicago, St. Louis, Milwaukee, and "Zinzinnati" than any of the lands in Africa or Asia the Kaiser's men grabbed.

The French hated the Germans for taking Alsace and much of Lorraine from them. But the French also had a long hatred of the British, going back as far as Norman baron William the Conqueror, and extending through the ages of the Hundred Years War, Joan of Arc, Louis XIV, the French Revolution, and Napoleon ... roughly 800 years. Even Joan, the girl saint, personally called the English "Godons" – French for "God-damned."

The behavior of the British and German leaders was evil, but sadly not too much worse than those of other European powers.

The French, though less powerful than the British or the Germans, were world-class in their greed for colonies. The French colonial empire was larger than that of any other European nation except for the British Empire. The French, whose country is about the size of the states north and east of the Potomac River – Maryland, Delaware, Pennsylvania, New Jersey, New York, and New England (about 200,000 square miles before they regained Alsace and all of Lorraine), ruled an empire of about 5 million square miles in size.

The French colonized Algeria in the 1830s. By 1900, the French also gained control of Tunisia and most of Morocco in North Africa, the areas of west and central Africa that form today's countries of Mauritania, Mali, Niger, Chad, Senegal, Guinea, Ivory Coast, Upper Volta aka Burkino Faso, Dahomey aka Benin, Central African Republic, Gabon, and Congo (Brazzaville), an enclave on the Red Sea next to Ethiopia they called French Somaliland, and the large island of Madagascar. After World War One, they would take over Germany's African colony of Cameroon (Kamerun). The French also took Indochina (today's Laos, Cambodia, and Vietnam) in Asia, and some other islands in the Indian Ocean and the Pacific Ocean. They held French Guiana (which had the truly evil penal colony on Devil's Island) and some islands in the Caribbean Sea.

The leaders of Austria-Hungary and Russia had rival designs on the Balkans. Russia's leaders wanted Constantinople and with it access to the Mediterranean Sea. Some of the leaders of Austria-Hungary wanted Serbia and Macedonia down to the port of Salonika for better access to the Mediterranean Sea; Franz Ferdinand opposed this lust because he felt the empire had too many rebellious Serbs as it was.

The leaders of France and Britain and Italy also had designs on the Turks' Middle East possessions. Germany pushed for control of the Turks' economy. Russia and Britain had rival spheres of influence in Persia (present-day Iran). The major European colonial powers and Japan lusted for control of China.

Even lesser states like Italy, Spain, Portugal, Denmark, Belgium, and the Netherlands had colonies. The Italians held most of present-day Somalia and Eritrea. In the 1890s, the Italians tried to subjugate Ethiopia, but the African Christian people of that land slapped down the Italians in humiliating fashion. In a war with Turkey in 1911 and 1912, the Italians did manage to take Libya away from the Turks.

The Portuguese held Angola and Mozambique in southern Africa, and also held some other small strips of land and islands in and around Africa, India, the East

Indies, and China. The Spanish held Cuba, Puerto Rico, the Philippines, and some Pacific islands until the United States took away the first three possessions after the Spanish-American War and Spain's leaders sold the Pacific islands to the Germans. The Spanish held onto a strip of Morocco, some desert land called Spanish Sahara south of Morocco, Equatorial Guinea in central Africa, and some islands off the African coast.

The Belgians held a huge piece of Africa consisting of the land of the Congo River basin; at the time it was called the Belgian Congo. On independence, this land would be called Congo, then Zaire, and once again Congo. They also held what is now Rwanda and Burundi. The Dutch held Surinam in South America, some islands in the Caribbean Sea, and the so-called "Dutch East Indies" (today's Indonesia). The Danes held Iceland, Greenland, and those Virgin Islands that the British hadn't grabbed. American officials would buy Denmark's Virgin Islands during World War One.

At the start of World War One, the Turks still held the lands that make up present-day Iraq, Syria, Lebanon, Israel, Jordan, and much of Saudi Arabia and the other states of the Arabian peninsula.

The greedy Europeans treated the Africans as little more than slaves. German chancellor Otto von Bismarck convened the Berlin Conference in late 1884 and early 1885 as a way of playing off the various colonial nations against each other. (At the time, 80% of black Africa was under black African rule.) The European delegates divided Africa like a pie, drawing borderlines across areas that divided tribal groups from each other and lumping rival tribal groups into proposed colonies to serve the desires of European politicians and colonial corporations, not the people of Africa. Shortly, in all of Africa, the Christian king of Ethiopia and the freed resettled American slaves who ran Liberia would be the only blacks running independent African countries.

So much of the ethnic strife that has plagued Africa throughout the 20th Century and into this century is due to that three-month conference of greedy Europeans.

By the way, when I say "tribal groups" and "ethnic strife," I could be talking about Europe as well. Their hatreds and greeds weren't any more civilized than those of the Africans; only their means of murdering other people were more up-to-date.

A rival series of alliances pitted Germany and Austria-Hungary against England, France, and Russia. Italy played the prostitute, seeking to couple with the countries which would pay the most. Italy's leaders had an open treaty with Germany and Austria-Hungary, and a secret treaty with France.

Militarism and blind nationalism also helped rise the specter of war. After the Prussians won three quick wars in the 1860s and 1870s, other nations raised their military spending and increased their drafts, hoping to get results like Bismarck. Politicians wrapped themselves in their nations' flags in part to gain popularity and in part to deflect public view from their many failures. The rival nations' presses were only too happy to demean other nations as a way of building up their own nations. Politicians and media figures preached quasi-pagan worship of the state instead of worship of God Who demands the politicians and the people of all states to live by the Ten Commandments.

How did this affect the people of Europe?

In the countryside, a common scene was the hated local sheriff notifying young peasant men they were drafted. These young men knew they would be little more than cannon fodder for unjustifiable wars.

In Austria-Hungary, the Austrians and Hungarians ruled Slavs and Romanians, so naturally the subject peoples were not enthused about fighting for their despised masters. Likewise, Poles, Balts, Jews, and Ukrainians under Russian rule had no desire to die for the Tsar. Nor did Poles under German control want to die for the Kaiser. Nor did Irish peasants want to further the cause of their British oppressors.

Wars hit the peasants hardest. Most peasants were poor. All they had of value were their sons and daughters. The state wanted their sons as cannon fodder. The state wanted their daughters as uniform makers or munitions makers ... and all too often the state wanted them as the spoils of war.

The wars took the sons immediately. Many of them died on distant battlefields, or they limped home crippled or blind or otherwise too weak to do serious farmwork anymore.

But the rest of the peasants suffered too. The young women lost men who should have been their husbands.

Governments raised taxes, which cost the peasants more and more of their crops and livestock. Large landlords either evaded the taxes or transferred them to the backs of their tenants.

Think of the poor peasants who lived in the paths of the armies. Soldiers confiscated the peasants' livestock and grain, bivouacked in their fields and barns, raided the houses, and fornicated with the peasant girls – either with the girls' consents, or against the girls' wills. Farms, livestock, crops, daughters, all ruined.

On their way home, the soldiers repeated the process. And these were the soldiers of the same country, of the government supposedly protecting their peasants!

Soldiers of an invading army naturally behaved much worse. What they couldn't loot, they destroyed. The girls who wouldn't give in they raped and often killed.

They grabbed teenagers off the streets of the villages and made slave laborers of them. Their leaders had officers who took inventory of the wealth of a conquered area, and they ordered the local people to hand it over. They vandalized homes and barns, they burned churches, and they desecrated graveyards. Even the bones of the dead were not safe.

On their way home, these soldiers repeated the process.

The constant upheavals throughout Europe, and the wars and rumors of war hit the average people the hardest. If the loss of farms or the danger and drudgery of mine or factory work couldn't make them leave, certainly the oppression and warfare could.

Tensions increased as Europe went deeper into the 1900s. Nearly every year would see some sort of "crisis" that would bring Europe to the brink of general war. Finally general war – the war they called the Great War and the war we know as World War One came in 1914. This four-year war would kill millions of soldiers, sailors, airmen, and civilians. This war would feature the use of poison gas, submarine warfare, starvation blockades, air combat and aerial city bombing, machine guns, modern artillery, and tanks. This war would topple the emperors of Germany, Austria-Hungary, Russia, and the Ottoman Empire. This war would spawn the Communist takeover of Russia, and the Nazi takeover of Germany.

Does it surprise you at all that the heaviest period of European immigration to America came during the years 1900 to the summer of 1914?

WHY DID SO MANY PEOPLE LEAVE EUROPE?

Why did so many people leave Europe?

Leaving your homeland, traveling in a leaky overcrowded wooden ship teeming with vermin and eating wormy food and drinking bad water for weeks – or upgrading a few decades later to an overloaded stinking steamship packed like a city bus – only to come to a strange land and deal with people who more often than not don't speak your language and all too often treat you like dirt on the surface doesn't sound like a rational choice to make.

However, almost 38 million people made that choice from 1820 (when American officials started keeping detailed immigration statistics) through 1930, when American immigration laws and the Great Depression slowed the flood of immigrants to a trickle. **(1)**

Were the immigrants crazy? Were they overly optimistic? Or did they know what they were dealing with at home and decide to take a chance on a life in a foreign land that might turn out better? If Europe was so special, why did so many people leave it?

Every adult and every unaccompanied teenager who got on a boat for America had his or her own special reason for leaving the homeland.

The inability to earn a living in the home country was as big a reason as any. If there was not enough land to farm, or if there were not enough jobs in the cities and towns to go around, then immigration sure beat starving or living like a beggar. Many husbands and wives made the difficult decision to leave behind their loved ones and start anew because they had to.

Many young adults left because their parents were good-hearted and wanted to help their children as they reached adulthood, but were desperately poor. They couldn't afford a dowry, or an inheritance for all of their children, and the unlucky daughters and sons would have to make their own starts in life. With few chances in their home villages and towns, they often left their homelands altogether.

The spreading of the news about the opportunities in America gave many Europeans the dream of becoming better off in America. Many hoped to become rich in America. Many others dreamed of earning enough money in America to come home and buy a nice sized farm or start a business in the home country. Still others with talent wanted to try their luck in America because they foresaw themselves being unable to rise in the homeland, where rank and privilege all too often crowded out energy and talent.

Certainly many people came because of oppression against them for religious or ethnic or political reasons.

Huge numbers of Irish, Poles, and Jews left Europe for these reasons. So did many Czechs, Slovaks, Ruthenians, Romanians, Slovenians, Croatians, Serbs, Greeks, Balts, Armenians, and Ukrainians. Many of the German immigrants in the mid 1800s left for these reasons also. In the 1800s and early 1900s, many people who were part of an ethnic or religious minority in their homelands felt the pressure to leave because the authorities and the people in the majority felt free to abuse them.

Many young people fled from their abusive parents and relatives. In the old country, many parents treated their sons and daughters like indentured servants once they were old enough to earn their keep, and then earn their parents extra money as workers. Many parents farmed out their teenage children to greedy relatives who took advantage of them. Many of these young men and women mistreated in these ways escaped to America.

Other young people ran to escape arranged marriages to people they didn't want for spouses. Too many parents in the old country tried to live off the generosity a rich son-in-law might show them. For money too many parents were willing to condemn their daughters to unhappy marriages.

Many young men fled for a related, but less noble reason. They got their girlfriends pregnant, and they ran away like cowards to escape their obligations, while their girlfriends were stuck with the shame, the abuse of their neighbors, and the cost of raising a child without a man to help her. Many pregnant girls and young women had to leave because their parents banished them or they were unwilling to face the unfriendly scrutiny of other villagers.

Many young men fled to escape another kind of embrace – that of the state. Draft-age young men often left their villages a step ahead of the officers whose job it was to get them into uniform to fight the peasants and proletarians of other countries, or to oppress other farm workers and city laborers in their own countries.

Many people fled because they were common criminals, as opposed to those who had to flee because they committed illegal but not immoral political offenses. Many Americans of British ancestry who brag their ancestors were here before the American Revolution would not be pleased to know their illustrious forebears were pickpockets or prostitutes. Likewise, there were those from all countries of Europe who came to America in the 1800s and 1900s whose criminal behavior would not make their descendants proud. Once Ellis Island and other federal immigration stations were in operation, the number of criminals escaping to America dwindled as the inspectors started screening them out.

All the desires to leave would be wasted emotions if there weren't places that were easy and cheap for people to move to. The mid to late 1800s had a number of factors that allowed many millions of people to leave Europe.

The advance of technology enabled people to make good livings as farmers and ranchers in the vast lands of the United States, Canada, Brazil, Argentina, and Australia. Farming machinery improved crop yields per farmer, railroads made it easier for farmers to get their crops and animals to market, and refrigeration and steamships even allowed growers and ranchers in these countries to export meat and produce to Europe. The Spanish had introduced ranching and farming practices to the New World that would help build Texas and California into agricultural powerhouses.

Officials in the United States gave huge amounts of land to the railroad companies when they built railroads into the Great Plains states and the western states. The railroad companies wanted passengers and freight to haul, so they were willing to sell the land to American "pilgrims" (think Jimmy Stewart in the movie "The Man Who Shot Liberty Valance") and immigrants at reasonable rates. The railroads made it relatively easy for people to settle in the American West.

In many of these countries there were precious metal and precious stone strikes that fired the imagination of the world. There was a gold rush in California in the late 1840s and 1850s, a silver strike in Nevada in the early 1860s, gold rushes in Alaska and in the nearby Canadian Yukon region in the 1890s, and several other smaller "rushes" in the other western states in the late 1800s and early 1900s. There were also major mining booms in places like South Africa, Australia, and Brazil in the late 1800s and early 1900s.

The Industrial Revolution began in Britain, whose practical scientists and businessmen were able to turn scientific discoveries into cash. But fueled by the railroad industry, the steel industry, the oil and coal industries, and the Civil War, the Industrial Revolution went farther in the United States. The United States was a young big country that was not held in check by tradition like Britain was. Its cities needed building, not renovating. American entrepreneurs soon found ways to turn inventions into money, and they needed people to work in the mills and factories to make the goods that made them big money.

The development of mass steelmaking techniques made it possible to build ships of steel and propel them with steam engines. Steel steamships started replacing wooden sailing ships in the late 1800s. The new steamships were faster and more reliable than the sailing ships, and they could haul more cargo – and more huddled masses of people.

Shipping companies made a great deal of money hauling bulky cargoes like grain, sugar, hides, cotton, timber, and metal from North America and Latin America to Europe. However, they sailed with virtually empty holds from Europe to the Western Hemisphere. Then the shippers hit on the idea of hauling people in the holds of their ships on the voyages from Europe to America. Other steel ships, while built exclusively to handle passengers, were still designed to move large numbers of people in cramped quarters for very little cost.

Steamship companies could now offer people passage to the New World at a price they could afford, and still make the steamship companies good money.

What helped the steamship companies further (besides the desperation of many to leave Europe and the desire of some government leaders and industrial leaders in the New World to get cheap labor to build their countries) was the development of two other fields – education and communications.

In the United States, Catholic priests, nuns, brothers, and laypeople established schools for their children. Some Protestant ministers and laypeople did likewise. Others without major ties to religion pushed the idea of compulsory school attendance, and taxpayer funding for schools. The spread of religious schools and government-run schools improved the literacy of the American public. **(2)**

Advances in communications shrunk the time it took for news to travel between continents. Samuel Morse invented the telegraph in the late 1830s. Cyrus Field in 1866 put telegraph wires under the Atlantic Ocean to provide speedy communication with Europe. Alexander Graham Bell invented the telephone in 1876, which sped communications further. Marconi would make the first trans-Atlantic wireless telegraph transmission in 1901. This would lead to radio. A free press in the United States, bolstered by energetic reporters, almost instantaneous communication, and the support of many people who could now read, spread the word about what it was like to live in the United States.

Reliable mail service between the New World and Europe, supported by steam-powered trains and ships, also spread the word about the opportunities on the west side of the Atlantic Ocean. Europeans learned that America was free, safe, and unhindered by nobility. They learned a person born poor could rise to be president, like Andrew Jackson, or Honest Abe Lincoln.

People in Europe learned land was there for the taking if they wanted to homestead. People in Europe learned American factories paid better wages than the factories of Europe, because there was more work to do than skilled hands to do it, and because many American workers – who had never been as servile as European workers – quit jobs, moved, or started their own companies if they didn't like their bosses. Many millions of people started thinking about saving some money and coming to the United States. They knew the building of railroads in Europe made it easier to get to port cities, and steamships made it cheaper to sail across the Atlantic Ocean.

Not all the immigrants came to the United States. Most of the immigrants from Spain and Portugal emigrated to Latin America, where they knew the language. Many of those who emigrated from Italy likewise landed up in Latin America, especially in Argentina.

Some English and Scottish and Welsh emigrants moved to Canada, which was still a British possession almost until World War Two. So did settlers from colder portions of Europe, like Scandinavia, Ukraine, and Russia. Still, more of the people from these countries chose to come to the United States, because it was a more free and less harsh place to live than Canada.

The word also got to the villages of Europe that America was safe from war. Except for the Civil War, and except on the frontier, white people were safe from war and the corresponding pillage, arson, and rape. In the Civil War, the women and girls in the paths of the armies were essentially safe from rape. This was due in large part to the discipline exerted by the military leaders on both sides, but it was also due in huge part to the innate decency of the Union and Confederate soldiers alike.

In fact, during the Civil War, Union authorities court-martialed and dismissed from service General John Turchin, for reportedly urging his soldiers to burn and loot an Alabama town and rape some of the women. Turchin, a Russian native, was disciplined for playing by European rules. Abraham Lincoln eventually restored Turchin to rank, after Turchin's wife traveled to Washington and pleaded his case personally. General Turchin did get told not to play war that way again.

Lincoln's people scoured Europe for talented military officers early in the Civil War, because most of the best American officers had defected to the Confederacy. Many veterans of the wars and rebellions in Europe, especially German and Irish refugees, did serve in the Union Army. Lincoln offered the great Garibaldi himself command in the Union Army during the Civil War, but the Italian patriot turned him down. Lincoln's army did include a regiment called the Garibaldi Guard (the 39th New York), which was as diverse as Europe in miniature. Their colonel was a Hungarian. The soldiers were natives of Italy, Hungary, Croatia, Ukraine, Switzerland, Germany, Portugal, Spain, France, and England. (3)

In America, some bigotry against Catholics and Jews was standard practice and sometimes was government policy, but pogroms against Europeans were not. Of course, the leaders of the U.S. government ordered many acts of genocide committed against the native

American Indians during this time. Also, lynchings of blacks in the South were common, race murders of Mexicans in the West and Southwest happened all too frequently, and the killings of Chinamen out West all too often got little police attention. Likewise, "Jim Crow" laws codified discrimination against blacks, and members of the Ku Klux Klan and other organized bigots abused the blacks in a manner similar to the pogroms against the Jews in the Russian Empire.

A desire to leave, a good place to go to, and a reasonable way to get there all contributed to the decisions of millions of Europeans to start anew in the United States. Now you see why your ancestors left. They wanted to leave, and they were able to do so.

America was light-years ahead of Europe politically and socially when it came to having a level society where people of talent and drive could rise. In 1829, most people in Russia, Ukraine, the Baltic lands, and Poland were serfs. Many in Central Europe, though formally not serfs, lived in conditions not much better. Most people in France, Germany, and Italy were only one or two generations out of serfdom. The Balkans were under Turkish enslavement. Most Irish were landless tenants exploited by British landlords. Most Spaniards and Portuguese lived in grinding poverty. Life wasn't a bowl of cherries for the people of Scandinavia, Switzerland, Britain, or the Low Countries either.

By comparison, in 1829 America, Andrew Jackson, the son of an impoverished hillbilly widow, became president of the United States. He made his fortune in Tennessee, the first state where poverty did not keep a man from voting. And about 100,000 mountaineers, rednecks, and other proud Americans of less than genteel upbringing descended upon Washington and cheerfully trashed the White House while drunkenly celebrating Jackson's inauguration day. Why? Because one of theirs had become president, he was taking up residence in their house, and the whisky was free.

In the Europe of the 1800s, those called "liberals" paid lip service to the workers and peasants and servants but usually wanted to limit the right of workers and peasants and servants to vote because they looked down on them. They were willing to let the less educated (rebelling peasants and other farm workers, tradesmen, and laborers) get shot for them in rebelling while they reaped the benefits of redistribution of power. They also wanted to limit the power of the nobility because most of them were not nobles. Most liberals were atheists, agnostics, or tepid Christians who believed the state should rule the church. Many liberals wanted to deny women the right to vote because women tended to practice religion more than men. Liberals from that era tended to come from the classes of lawyers, bureaucrats, and professors. Many capitalists, hoping for free trade legislation and laws to break the economic power of skilled tradesmen so they (the capitalists) could increase their profits, also were liberals. Liberals of course supported reforms, as long as these wouldn't cost them money or power. Liberals opposed kings and dictators because they wanted power for themselves, not because they intended to share power with the downtrodden. In short, there was no great philosophical difference between these people and those who call themselves liberals who hold power in Europe (and America) today.

In the Europe of the 1800s, those called "conservatives" were usually those who held power and didn't want to give it up. They wanted to limit the right of workers and peasants and servants to vote because they looked down on them. They were willing to let the less educated (the soldiers and policemen) get shot for them resisting rebellions while they reaped the benefits of power and money. They wanted to limit the rights of people like lawyers and professors because most of them were not lawyers or professors. Most conservatives were agnostics or tepid Christians who believed the state should rule the church. Conservatives from that era were estate holders or large businessmen or nobility or career military people. Some clergymen were conservatives because they thought the rulers would support their churches, or at least wouldn't confiscate what they had. Conservatives of course opposed reforms that would cost them money or power. Conservatives supported kings and dictators as long as these men protected their rights and their property, but could switch sides on a dime if kings or dictators wanted to take their rights or property. In short, there was no great philosophical difference between these people and those who call themselves conservatives who hold power in Europe (and America) today.

The main difference between "liberals" and "conservatives" in Europe was that "conservatives" were usually more honest about their selfishness than "liberals" were.

By comparison, America was a nation without nobility, or without a white serfdom, or without an upper crust of lawyers or businessmen scheming to stir the masses to rebel so they could misrule in the place of the nobility. The American Revolution, the Constitution, and later reforms had put power into the hands of a much greater percentage of Americans than any revolution and aftermath had done for people in any European country. Blacks in Southern States before the Civil War were mostly slaves, and after the Civil War they were definitely treated like dirt, but the average landless peasants in Europe were not much better off, and some were worse off. America had more than its share of shysters and snake-oil salesmen and thieves and petty tyrants, but most of the men who governed the country were essentially patriotic and committed to democracy, regardless of party.

How else can we compare America to Europe? In the early 1900s, Americans had the freedom and the cussedness to elect a man like Teddy Roosevelt – a man so gung-ho he lost an eye in a White House boxing match with one of his Secret Service men – to lead them, in no small part because this cowboy, police commissioner, war hero, outdoorsman, and hard-driving reformer was the type of man Americans were proud of and wished they could be. By comparison, most of Europe still called some morbidly inbred king or emperor or kaiser or tsar or sultan their boss. And in the "democracies" of France and Britain, a clutch of greasy debauched inbred bribetakers ran things.

For many of you, thanks to those who passed through Ellis Island, you, your parents, your grandparents, and maybe your great-grandparents missed out on living in the way of World War One, World War Two, Nazi occupation, and/or Soviet occupation. The descendants of these immigrants, you included, have lived in the greatest nation on earth because of them. Thank God for their willingness to give America a try, and the resulting better life you have now.

END NOTES

1. Statistics come from the Annual Report of the Commissioner General of Immigration, 1931, listed on Page 195 of the Historic Research Study, Statue of Liberty – Ellis Island National Monument, by Harlan D. Unrau, National Park Service, 1984.

Figures for estimate of the rural population of Europe come from European Historical Statistics 1750-1970 by B.R. Mitchell. Of special interest are the following reported statistics for the occupations of employed adult males in "agriculture, fishing, and forestry" in these countries:

Britain (1871)	20% of 8.23 million
Ireland (1871)	54% of 1.74 million
France (1866)	47% of 11.07 million (not counting Alsace-Lorraine, lost in 1870)
Belgium (1866)	45% of 1.58 million
Netherlands (1859)	41% of 0.94 million
Switzerland (1890)	46% of 0.89 million
Sweden (1870)	62% of 1.13 million
Norway (1875)	39% of 0.53 million
Finland (1880)	72% of 0.36 million
Denmark (1870)	48% of 0.85 million

Germany (1882)	43% of 13.37 million (and occupied Poland and Alsace-Lorraine)
Poland (1897)	48% of 2.24 million (Russian occupied Poland only)
Russia (1897)	63% of 23.96 million (includes Ukraine, Baltics, Belarusia, Moldova, Georgia, Armenia, Turkestan, Siberia also)
Austria-Hungary (1880)	59% of 11.61 million (includes rest of Poland, Slovenia, Croatia, Czech., Slovakia, Ruthenia, Galicia, Vojvodina, Bukovina, and Transylvania)
Italy (1871)	61% of 9.26 million
Spain (1877)	72% of 5.73 million
Portugal (1890)	68% of 1.58 million

The vast majority of these men worked on farms. (Statistics for women were more spotty, so I used stats for males ... and if a man was in agriculture, his wife was almost always in agriculture also.)

Since nations reported as late as 1897, my estimate of at least 60% for 1870 Europe comes from the higher rural percentages from before 1870, and from the absence of statistics from the Balkans, where the people were overwhelmingly rural.

2. Horace Mann, considered the father of public school systems in America, talked Massachusetts officials into getting into the public school business by claiming they would counteract Catholic influences in the state. Mann unwittingly helped cause the founding of many Catholic schools, because many Catholic parents wanted to shield their children from the anti-Catholic bigotry of many public school faculty members. From Mann's time until the 1960s, America's public schools had a nondenominational Protestant bent. Now they are bent against Catholics and Protestants alike.

A source of information about Horace Mann is in The Persistent Prejudice by Michael Schwartz (pages 188-189). Mann was also a temperance freak and a believer in phrenology, which is like "palmistry of the skull" (a great quote by Schwartz) in that its quacks claim they can determine character based on head shape. These people, in other words, are pinheads.

3. The source for the Turchin incident is The Civil War: Strange & Fascinating Facts by Burke Davis (page 229). The source for the Garibaldi Guard is The Civil War: Strange & Fascinating Facts (page 93).

MANIFEST DESTINY, MAGNIFICENT DESTINATION

Very few people want to leave their homelands if they are content. Many Europeans were not content. They gave up lifestyles they knew and made a crapshoot on what life would be like in a strange continent. More than 30 million people came from Europe to America from the century or so between the end of the War of 1812 and the start of the Great Depression.

In order to take on that many people, America had to live up to its billing as a much better place to be than crowded, poverty-stricken, war-torn, and oppressive Europe. America also had to be able to accommodate all the new arrivals.

This chapter will cover how the Spanish, French, English, and others settled America, how the English and their descendants wiped out the American Indians, and how Americans increased the size of the United States to its present boundaries.

This chapter will also cover the story of America's Mormons, who effectively seceded from the Union and got away with it for decades. Their story is in this chapter to explain what our leaders finally had to do to a quasi-militarily organized group of people who violated American law behind the guise of religion. It is an object lesson and precedent for what we might have to do as a nation against militant Islamists.

This chapter will also give a roundup of where America's immigrants came from in the Ellis Island era. And this chapter will explain how America's economy expanded so rapidly that America was able to put all these immigrants to work.

THE FIRST SEVERAL MILLION PEOPLE JUST SHOWED UP

In the beginning there were no immigration laws. People just showed up.

The first Americans, the people we call American Indians and Eskimos, settled the American Hemisphere from north to south thousands of years before the white man. Meanwhile, Polynesians settled on the Hawaiian Islands.

The Vikings were the next to show up, sort of. They tried to colonize Greenland. They sailed south, along the Canadian and American coast. American Indians along the Atlantic seaboard drove them off.

People from Iberia were the next to show up. The Portuguese pretty much kept to Brazil. The Spanish settled elsewhere in South America, and in Mexico, in Central America, on the Caribbean Islands, and in the present-day United States, long before the English came. (Santa Fé, New Mexico is 50 years older than Boston. St. Augustine, Florida is 65 years older than Beantown.)

The English showed up next, but briefly at first. The first English settlers tried North Carolina in the 1580s, but disappeared. They were supposedly killed or enslaved by the native American Indians.

The French showed up next. They would settle first in Quebec in the early 1600s, and later in Acadia (now called Nova Scotia), some islands in the Caribbean, Louisiana, along the Great Lakes, and along the Mississippi River and the Ohio River.

The English showed up again, in Virginia in 1607, and in Massachusetts in 1620. In the area that became the 13 Colonies, religious fanatics populated New England and massacred the American Indians who had helped them. English adventurers and lowlifes settled Virginia, and treated the American Indians likewise. Even the gentle Quakers who first settled eastern Pennsylvania in the late 1600 had no trouble cheating the American Indians or hiring those who would resort to violence to expel the American Indians.

Lord Baltimore, one of the few Catholics who was a friend of the king of England, got the right to establish Maryland as a colony for Catholics. His brother did so in 1634. Lord Baltimore's relatives tried to ensure the settlers lived peaceably with the American Indians, and they allowed Protestants and Jews to come to Maryland. The Anglican governor of Virginia formed a war party, and invaded Maryland in 1644. He had priests arrested and sent to England in chains. Those he couldn't catch his minions drove out. Eventually the more numerous Protestant immigrants voted to strip Catholics in Maryland of many of their civil rights. Catholics could not inherit land, educate their children as Catholics, attend Mass in public, serve as lawyers, or serve as public officials. **(1)**

The Dutch showed up in the 1620s, and settled in New York. The Swedes showed up in the 1630s and settled in Delaware, then the Dutch took Delaware over in 1655. The English took New York over from the Dutch in the 1660s ... and Delaware, too, while they were at it.

New Jersey started out as wealthy businessmen's colonies. Puritans and their enemies also settled in New Jersey. Controversies involving who had authority and valid title to the land (and the associated massive fraud involved) set the pattern for official corruption in New Jersey for centuries to come.

The Carolinas also started out as wealthy businessmen's colonies. Soon malcontents from New England and Virginia came there. So did small farmers from Britain's holdings in the West Indies. Rich British landowners had forced them out, and they turned the islands they stole from the small farmers into sugar cane plantations, which they brought slaves to work on.

Georgia started as a debtor and penal colony for poor whites from England. Many other pickpockets and prostitutes were forced to come to the other colonies; their descendants would eventually lord it over non-English immigrants because their dissolute ancestors were "early Americans."

What happened to the American Indians in the Eastern United States?

They lost because they didn't unite to fight the European invaders. And the American Indians along the Eastern Seaboard had the bad luck to be in land the English coveted.

The English settlers brought over with them the entitlement mentality. If they wanted the land, they killed or ran off the people who were living on it, and used the natives' different religion as an excuse to rob them and kill them. The English first tried this approach against the Catholic Irish in the 1500s, under Henry VIII and his bastard daughter Elizabeth, the Pirate Queen. English leaders King James I and Oliver Cromwell and William of Orange in the 1600s, in their theft of Irish land and the killing of the Irish people, would give the colonists of America a pattern to follow.

Purists point out William of Orange was not totally English, but a half-breed Dutchman who got the English throne when Parliament overthrew James II – a Catholic convert – and put William's business-arrangement wife Mary (James II's still-Protestant daughter) and himself on the English throne. William, also a Protestant, was height challenged and posture challenged — a polite way of saying he was a short hunchback. William's mother was James II's sister Mary. William was James II's son-in-law and nephew. In other words, for a wife of convenience, William married his first cousin. Did inbreeding lead to their failure to produce heirs? Probably not. William of Orange and Mary had no children because William preferred buggery with males to sexual intercourse with females.

The English applied the smash-and-grab tactics that they perfected in Ireland to the American Indians. The English in Virginia kidnaped and raped Pocahontas to gain leverage against her tribe. Tobacco entrepreneur John Rolfe was sexually attracted enough to Pocahontas to force marriage on her and show her off in England, where she died at the age of 21. Rolfe's countrymen stole enough from Pocahontas' people that the natives finally had enough and killed several hundred English settlers. The English responded by killing men, women, and children of her tribe and other tribes in the area for years, and burning them in their villages after signing peace treaties with them. **(2)**

Likewise, the Pilgrims and their rival Puritans killed American Indians in New England and praised God for the land they could steal. These godly buckle-hatted men sold the surviving Indian captives into slavery ... they even sold American Indians they could capture as slaves to the Moslems in North Africa! By the 1700s, there would be only few more American Indians in New England than members of Teddy Kennedy's family in Mothers Against Drunk Driving. **(3)**

Coming from the land of tulips and windmills didn't make the Dutch any less bloodthirsty. The Dutch killed peaceable American Indians in today's New York and New Jersey. The Dutch, by the way, were the first Europeans to bring blacks from Africa to the present-day United States to be sold as slaves. The Dutch sold slaves to the English colonists as well as to their own people. **(4)**

All the colonial nations of Europe would allow enslavement and transportation of Africans to the New World as slaves. Queen Isabella of Spain (Columbus' sponsor) forbade slavery, but her successors didn't have her morality.

French colonists tended to treat American Indians with dignity, while Spanish colonists wrongly tended to treat American Indians like peons. But at least the Spanish tried to teach the American Indians European ways so they could make it in Spanish New World society. The different Latin approach in part came from the different religious mindset of the French and Spanish. Catholic religious leaders – reinforced at different times by people like Queen Isabella and the Jesuits – determined American Indians had immortal souls and were children of God also. This meant – on paper, at least – that the French and Spanish colonists were not supposed to slaughter the Indians but to try to convert them, and introduce them to European ways. The missions that dot the Spanish-settled parts of America are proof they spent plenty of time and money doing so.

The French and Spanish certainly did not look down on Indian women but married them (and fornicated with them) readily. The proof is in the pudding; in Mexico and many other countries in Latin America, most people are mestizos – people of mixed Spanish and American Indian blood. In Canada, there are métis – people of mixed French Canadian and American Indian blood.

Spanish rule in the Western Hemisphere proved to be much easier on the American Indians than rule by those of British blood. In the Spanish-settled American states, there tend to be a higher proportion of American Indians than there are in most of the rest of the Lower 48 United States, or in English-speaking Canada. (Oklahoma has a large number of American Indians because white Americans exiled many of their ancestors to the place – then known as "the Indian Territory" – after taking their land.) This doesn't even count the huge number of American Indians in Mexico or elsewhere in Latin America.

In 1763, after winning the French and Indian War, the British took Quebec, Acadia (which the British renamed "Nova Scotia"), and France's other holdings in Canada. They also took French-settled land between the Appalachians and the Mississippi River. The British forcibly exiled most of the French settlers of Acadia during the French and Indian War. Many Acadians made their way to Louisiana, which would remain under French control until the end of the war, when the French ceded the Louisiana Territory to Spain. The descendants of these unfortunates would bear the nickname of "Cajun" after the land they were exiled from. The British also took Florida and the eastern Gulf Coast from the Spanish.

In the century before the American Revolution, people from Germany, Switzerland, Ireland, Scotland, and Wales would also come to the 13 colonies. So would the Huguenots – French Protestants escaping a milder persecution in Catholic France than the harsh persecution by the Protestant English that the Irish were escaping. Enough of these people – and enough of the descendants of the jailbirds, holy rollers, shady ladies, con artists, and malcontents from England – would rebel against English authority and develop the best experiment in liberty the world would ever see.

Protestantism had an unintended but positive impact on the people of English, Scot, Welsh, Huguenot, Dutch, and German blood in America in the 1700s which led to the American Revolution, and to the American way of life. The Puritans, Anglicans, Baptists, Presbyterians, Methodists, and other Protestant colonists all thought theirs was the only true faith. But even within these churches, there was no unanimity among the people over what the tenets of their faiths should be. Many believers figured their own views on the precepts of their faith were as good as anyone else's. Since all these churches recognized individual interpretation of the Bible, people could and did dissent from the teachings of ministers and often started their own congregations. There developed among the people a lack of respect for formal religious authority if they believed this authority conflicted with their own consciences ... or often merely their own desires.

This mindset transferred over to politics. The American colonists would in time have no problem with disputing the regulations and commands that came from the royal governors or from Parliament if they didn't agree with them. In a society where everyone could be his own pope spiritually, it was only natural that people in time came to believe they could rule themselves without any help from an inbred king, a debauched nobility, or a grasping Parliament. This mass realization of the people led to the founding and the building of the finest nation the world has ever seen.

George Washington and other American officers and enlisted men, and with aid from French, Irish, German, and Polish officers, French, Spanish, and black Haitian troops, French and Spanish seamen, French priests, and French, Spanish, and Dutch foreign aid, fought a war against Britain from 1775 to 1781. The Americans, aided with the foreign help, most of it coming from Catholic people of Catholic lands, beat the British and won freedom from Britain.

Roughly one-third of the Continental Army was of Irish blood, although less than 10 percent of the people of the 13 colonies were of Irish blood. People from the Emerald Isle percentagewise were much more patriotic for America than WASP Americans because they understood better than anyone else how oppressive the British could be, and they didn't want any more of it in America. Many of the WASPs favored the continuation of British rule; these native traitors were called Tories. Many would flee to Canada or England after the war. Some say the spiritual descendants of the Tories would ensconce themselves in Ivy League schools and in the State Department.

Many Americans of Irish ancestry who were Protestants – some as the descendants of those forcibly converted in Ireland, and others who turned to the Protestant denominations because the British and American Anglicans and Puritans kept Catholic priests out of most of the 13 colonies -- had not lost their distrust of the British. A large proportion of these people – to include a 13-year-old Andrew Jackson – also were in the ranks of the Patriot forces.

Also, 5 to 10 percent of all soldiers and sailors who fought for America's liberty were blacks. Many who were slaves gained their freedom after the war. In some horrible cases, these black patriots were returned to slavery, gypped and betrayed by the men they helped liberate from the British.

HOW AMERICA GOT TO BE SO BIG

At the time of the American Revolution, there were about three million people living in the 13 colonies plus today's Vermont and Maine. By comparison, there were about nine million people living in Britain (England, Scotland, and Wales).

Ben Franklin and his fellow diplomats made a favorable agreement with the British after the American Revolution which enabled the Americans to take most of the land between the original 13 states and the Mississippi River. The states of Kentucky, Tennessee, Alabama, Mississippi, Ohio, Indiana, Illinois, Michigan, and Wisconsin – and some of Minnesota -- would arise on these lands. (In New England, Vermont became a state in 1791 and Maine would become a state a generation later.) The Spanish, as practical allies of the Americans, recovered Florida and the eastern Gulf Coast from the British.

If it hadn't been for the anti-Catholic bigotry of the people of New England, America might have gotten Canada as well. England's rulers, who were militant anti-Catholics themselves, had during the French and Indian War exiled the French living in Acadia. There were too many French settlers in Quebec to exile, so the British left them in place. The British were at least smart enough to grant some religious toleration to the Catholic French of Quebec in 1774, a year before the American Revolution. They knew the French settlers of Quebec distrusted the bigoted New Englanders nearby, so they hoped to enlist the French to fight the New Englanders. The French in Quebec would not help their British masters suppress the American Revolution. But they would not respond to American overtures to join them in throwing off England's yoke during the American Revolution either, because they thought the Americans would persecute them for their religion. **(5)**

American settlers and American troops ran the American Indians off of the land they got from the British. In the Great Lakes region, British agitators armed American Indians to try to slow the advance of the Americans. Mad Anthony Wayne's troops beat warriors of the Miami tribe at Fallen Timbers in Ohio in 1794. William Henry Harrison's troops beat Shawnee warriors under the Shawnee Prophet at Tippecanoe in Indiana in 1811. Harrison and his Americans invaded Ontario in 1813 during the War of 1812, beat the British at Thames, and killed the great chief Tecumseh in the battle. Tecumseh, the Shawnee Prophet's brother, was the Shawnee chief who tried to organize the tribes (and secure cynical British help) against the American settlers and soldiers. In the South, Andrew Jackson's militiamen would crush Creek warriors at Horseshoe Bend in Alabama in 1814, also during the War of 1812. Both Jackson and Harrison would later become presidents largely due to their military prowesses.

Americans weren't stopping at the Mississippi. In 1800, Napoleon invaded and occupied Spain. He forced the Spanish to give up the Louisiana Territory. When Thomas Jefferson was president in the first decade of the 1800s, he sent envoys to France to try to buy New Orleans and the surrounding area so the settlers in the Mississippi, Tennessee, and Ohio valleys could send their goods to Europe and to the eastern United States through the port of New Orleans. In those days, there were no railroads. River boats and ocean-going ships were the cheapest and most reliable forms of freight transportation. Napoleon, in need of cash for his wars in Europe, and grimly aware France had no effective access to American colonies as long as rival Britain ruled the seas, in 1803 offered to sell the American government New Orleans, and all the land France claimed west of the Mississippi River. In exchange for $15 million and the promise of religious tolerance and citizenship for Catholic French and Spanish residents of the land, Jefferson's envoys brought home serious bacon – the title to land for the United States that would include most of present-day Louisiana, all of present-day Arkansas, Missouri, Iowa, and Nebraska, virtually all of South Dakota, much of Minnesota, most of North Dakota, Montana, Wyoming, Oklahoma and Kansas, and a large chunk of Colorado.

About the time of the War of 1812, American settlers started squatting on the strip of Gulf Coast territory that Spain owned, which now is part of Alabama, Mississippi, and eastern Louisiana. Napoleon, still lord of Spain, chose to do nothing about it, because he was still at war all over Europe.

After the War of 1812 (which Andrew Jackson and his militiamen and Jean Lafitte's privateers ended successfully by soundly thrashing the British at New Orleans in early 1815), British agitators armed American Indians in Spanish-held Florida. The tribesmen attacked settlers in Alabama and Georgia. Andrew Jackson and his men invaded Florida in 1818, defeated the American Indians, took Pensacola, and hanged two Britishers who had been selling the natives firearms. This created a row with Britain and Spain; John Quincy Adams turned it to America's advantage. He proposed since the Spanish government couldn't control the British or the American Indians in Florida, Americans would be happy to pay $5 million to take Florida off their hands. The Spanish sold Florida to the United States in 1819. Americans also got formal title to the Spanish Gulf Coast land they had been squatting on. Adams and his Spanish counterpart made some border adjustments between the Louisiana Territory, the Oregon Territory, and Spanish holdings in Texas, the Rocky Mountains, and California. Spain would lose these holdings two years later when the Mexicans revolted successfully.

Deportation and massacre of the remaining American Indians in the Southeast accelerated during Jackson's presidency (1829-1837) and continued into the 1840s.

A gold rush on Cherokee land in Georgia sped up the theft of Cherokee land – which the literate and politically savvy Cherokees held by valid American title – and the exile of the Cherokees. American settlers, backed by president Andrew Jackson and his successor Martin Van Buren, forced the Creek, Choctaw, Chickasaw, and Cherokee people to take the "Trail of Tears" to the "Indian Territory" in present-day Oklahoma.

Some Seminoles also went under force to the Indian Territory. But many of the Seminoles refused to move from Florida. American troops butchered most of them where they lived. Some remained in Florida, retreating deep into the swamps; others belatedly joined the exile.

In the Old Northwest, American settlers and soldiers forced out the Shawnee, the Miami, the Delaware, and smaller tribes. American settlers and soldiers in the 1830s forced tribes in Illinois to move across the Mississippi River into Iowa. They also beat Chief Black Hawk's braves when they tried to defend their homes.

American politicians, by negotiating with the British who held Canada, won a treaty that settled the northern boundary of the country along the 49th Parallel from Minnesota to the Rocky Mountains in 1818. By threat of seizure of land in what is now British Columbia, American president James Polk in 1846 got the British to settle the northern boundary of the country from the Rocky Mountains to the Pacific Ocean along the 49th Parallel. Thus, by these two agreements, the land that forms today's states of Washington, Oregon, and Idaho, portions of Minnesota, North Dakota, Montana, and Wyoming, and a small piece of South Dakota became American property. American negotiators settled Maine's boundary with the British in 1842.

American politicians were ruder to Mexico. Mexicans overthrew Spanish rule in 1821 and took over Spanish-held land from California to Colorado to Texas. The new Mexican government invited Americans to settle in Texas as long as they obeyed Mexican laws. American settlers in Texas revolted in 1835 after the Mexican government outlawed slavery and outlawed further American immigration to Texas. The Americans lost at the Alamo but won at San Jacinto in Texas in 1836. They formed the temporarily independent country of Texas, which was populated largely by Americans from the Southern states.

Polk brought Texas into the United States in 1845, and tried to buy California, and all the land between California and Texas from the Mexicans. Mexican leaders would not sell. The Mexicans also had issues as to what constituted Texas. Americans said the Rio Grande was Texas' southern border, and that Texas also should include the eastern half of present-day New Mexico, a large chunk of Colorado, a piece of Wyoming, a corner of Kansas, and what is now the Oklahoma Panhandle. The Mexicans said the boundary should be the Nueces River, farther north into Texas, and they thought Texas should be much smaller in the west also.

Mexican troops crossed the Rio Grande in early 1846 and attacked American soldiers under the command of General Zachary "Rough and Ready" Taylor. The Mexican War was on. Brave and well-led American soldiers beat the brave but poorly-led Mexican troops. Americans took California. General Taylor led his army into northern Mexico. General Winfield "Fuss and Feathers" Scott led another army into central Mexico and they captured Mexico City in 1847.

Ironically, the best Mexican outfit was the San Patricio brigade – a unit composed of Irish and Irish-American deserters from American units. Some Americans had been looting Mexican churches – Catholic churches, of course – and some of these animals raped Mexican women and girls, and the chain of command did nothing about it. So some of the American soldiers of Irish blood who were disgusted with the anti-Catholic bigotry of many of their comrades deserted and fought for Mexico. The Americans hanged or whipped and face-branded the few "Patricios" ("Patricks") whom they captured.

American politicians harvested the fruits of victory against Mexico, bringing into the United States California, and land that would become Nevada, Utah, most of Arizona and New Mexico, much of Colorado, and some of Wyoming, Kansas, and Oklahoma. Texas' border would be the Rio Grande. Americans paid the Mexican government $15 million for all this land. American officials purchased some more land from Mexico in 1853 for $10 million, which would give the southern boundaries of Arizona and New Mexico their final shape. This piece, known as the Gadsden Purchase, offered the easiest route for a railroad from the South to California, because the Rocky Mountains are relatively low in this area and there is a good pass through the mountains.

Certain Southerners weren't satisfied with this haul. General Taylor became President Taylor in 1849. Despite owning a large plantation and many slaves, Taylor opposed the extension of slavery in the West. He encouraged American settlers in California and New Mexico to apply for statehood, knowing their state constitutions would ban slavery. California's gold miners and gold seekers loathed slavery, not because of any early call to brotherhood with blacks, but because allowing slavery in California meant wealthy slaveholders could put slaves to work in the creeks of California to compete with them in panning for gold. Mexicans and Spaniards in the Golden State also opposed slavery.

Leading Southerners opposed statehood for these areas because there would be more free states than slave states in the Union, which would cost the pro-slavery southerners their deadlock in the Senate. Some threatened rebellion and secession. Taylor said he would crush secessionists and hang captured rebels.

Congressmen tried to bypass Taylor with the so-called Compromise of 1850. Taylor opposed them, but he died in July 1850. His replacement, the nonentity Millard Fillmore, allowed the Compromise of 1850 to become law. It allowed California in as a free state, barred New Mexico, and pushed a meaner Fugitive Slave Act that allowed assorted peckerwoods and other white trash to become federal slave catchers.

Some Americans, fearing the eventual statehood of more free states, talked of gaining Latin American land for slave empires suited for tropical plantation agriculture. (Minnesota and Oregon would become free states in the late 1850s. Pro-slavery Democrats failed in their ploy to bring Kansas into the Union in the late 1850s as a slave state.) The Spanish refused to sell Cuba, so some of these men made attempts to take Cuba by force in the 1840s and 1850s, and they also tried to grab Central America from the natives in the 1850s and in 1860. Spanish and Central American soldiers shot some of the adventurers when they caught them. The South's loss of the Civil War and the outlawing of slavery in America ended further American attempts to grab territory for slavery in the Caribbean islands and Central America.

After the Civil War, Russian officials offered to sell Alaska to the United States. Russia was the only major country in Europe whose leaders favored the Union in the Civil War. They had used the friendship to hide some of their warships in American ports when British naval officers considered attacking them. Russian authorities knew they didn't have the sea power to hold Alaska, so that's why they made the offer.

William Seward, Secretary of State for Andrew Johnson, successor to martyred Abraham Lincoln, convinced Johnson and Congress to make the deal. In 1867, Americans bought Alaska from Russia for $7.2 million.

Critics called Alaska "Seward's Folly" or the "American Icebox." But it was a wise deal for America that paid off many times over, in oil, gold, timber, and fishing. The purchase of Alaska also has paid off in protecting America from Japan and the Soviet Union.

The acquisition of Hawaii was less honorable, but was a good idea. American evangelizers had been coming to Hawaii to do good; they gave the natives Bibles and took their land, so they did well. American businessmen didn't even give the natives Bibles, but in 1893 brought about the overthrow of Hawaiian leader Queen Liliuokulani, a Hawaiian patriot who resented the commercial domination of her island by American sugar and pineapple plantation owners. President William McKinley engineered the annexation of Hawaii in 1898, the year of the Spanish-American War.

Hawaii has served since then as a naval base for American military men to protect America's West Coast. Of course, the money the islands have generated in sugar, pineapples, coffee, and tourism haven't hurt America either.

In the late 1800s, American diplomats tried to buy some Caribbean islands, but failed. In the Spanish-American War, American servicemen did take Cuba, the Philippines, and Puerto Rico from Spain, but later freed Cuba and gave Puerto Ricans American citizenship in 1917. American officials granted the peoples of the Philippines independence after World War Two. (They had earlier paid Spain $20 million for taking the Philippines.)

In 1917, American officials purchased some of the Virgin Islands from Denmark for $25 million. We bought the islands to protect the Carribean Sea approaches to the newly-open Panama Canal. Teddy Roosevelt had obtained the Canal Zone during his first term, and the American-built canal was open for business in 1914. The inept Jimmy Carter signed away the Panama Canal in the late 1970s; the canal turnover actually took place during Bill Clinton's corrupt administration. (6)

HOW THE WEST WAS WON, OR LOST

Americans didn't expand their country in a vacuum. Sadly, they crushed people who were already there. As Americans won the West, other people lost it. This section discusses this achievement and human tragedy.

By the end of the Mexican War, the United States government held about three million square miles ... much larger than Europe if you don't count the part of Europe that the Russian czar ruled. Much of the western part of the United States was mountainous, or barren desert, or high plains which were unbearably cold and snow-drifted in the winter. American Indians ruled the Great Plains, making overland trips from the eastern side of the country dangerous.

However, the land was there for the taking, if you were brave enough, or hardy enough, or greedy enough, or crazy enough. Spanish-style ranching was possible. So was Spanish style orchard and vineyard farming, if you and other settlers near you had the endurance to build irrigation ditches. So were mining and logging. So was regular commerce, if you wanted to sell guns, gear, and grub to the miners and would-be cattle barons and would-be timber barons who came west to seek their fortunes. People could farm quietly in the West, as they had done in the East, South, and Midwest, and many would do so. Other people chose to sneak out of town ahead of their debts or the local lawmen back East and start life anew.

The Gold Rush drew thousands of fortune seekers to California in the late 1840s and early 1850s. A large silver strike drew others to Virginia City, near Lake Tahoe in Nevada in the late 1850s. Further discoveries of precious metals and not-so-precious but worthwhile metals like copper, lead, and zinc would draw thousands more westward to work in the mines throughout the West.

American settlers stole the land of many Spaniards and Mexicans living in California. Even though the Treaty of Guadalupe Hidalgo, which ended the Mexican War, guaranteed citizenship and property rights to the people living in the territories Americans took from Mexico, American judges and lawmen found ways to invalidate the land titles of the Spaniards and Mexicans, and then steal their land. They even stole land from Hispanics who helped the American cause in the Mexican War, much like some Americans re-enslaved blacks who fought as Patriots in the American Revolution.

Kansas drew settlers to farm its soil. Kansas also drew big-time trouble. Proslavery settlers (with the connivance of leading Southern Democrats and doughface Democrat presidents Franklin Pierce and James Buchanan, and with the armed help of proslavery white trash from Missouri) attacked antislavery settlers, hoping to overpower them and bring Kansas into the Union as a slave state. This would give slaveholders help in the Senate. Vicious partisan warfare, combining some of the worst elements of the coming Civil War with Wild West banditry, erupted between Southerners and Northerners in the state. Lincoln's Senate race opponent Stephen Douglas and some Northern Democrats joined Republicans in Congress to smash the proslavery Democrats' ploy to make Kansas a slave state.

Eventually the far more numerous freesoilers beat back the slavery boosters, and "Bleeding Kansas" joined the Union as a free state in 1861, the first year of the Civil War. The Civil War brought more bloodshed to Kansas, as units of Southern guerrillas and outlaws operating out of refuges in the counties of western Missouri bordering Kansas raided the new state and killed hundreds of its settlers.

Union general Thomas Ewing and his men eventually forcibly removed most people from four proslavery counties of Missouri after William Quantrill and his Rebel raiders burned Lawrence, Kansas and killed most of the men in town in 1863. A year later, Ewing's brother-in-law General William T. Sherman would do the same thing to the people of Atlanta. How did Kansans feel about the situation? Many Kansas counties now bear the name of Sherman and other Union generals and Northern political figures.

The Civil War caused a real need for gold from California and silver from Nevada. The precious metals helped pay for the Union's war effort. Silver-rich Nevada came in as a free state (and anti-Mormon state) in 1864. Back east, in 1863, mountaineers loyal to the Union seceded their counties from Virginia and entered their counties into the Union as West Virginia.

Abraham Lincoln, besides running the Civil War to a successful conclusion, had the energy to put into place the Homestead Act, the Morrill Act, and the Pacific Railroad act. The Homestead Act, which allowed people to claim title to certain types of government-owned land if they lived on it and farmed it for five straight years, made it possible for many poorer Americans to move west, especially after the Civil War. The Morrill Act started the land grant colleges, which greatly advanced American agriculture and industry. The Pacific Railroad Act helped railroad companies build the cross-country railroads to the Pacific Coast. All of these measures benefited the West in particular and the country in general. They definitely helped open the West to more settlement.

Americans missed a chance to increase the size of the country even more after the Civil War. The British helped the South during the Civil War by building many ships which Rebel navy men used to attack Union commercial and military ships. These ships caused so much damage that some American leaders, after the Civil War, decided to ask for Canada as compensation from the ever-devious British. And if the Brits refused, some Americans argued, maybe America should take Canada by force.

Meanwhile, Civil War veterans of Irish blood plotted to seize Ontario and Quebec to hold them for ransom to free Ireland from British tyranny. Irishmen from both North and South banded together, bought weapons and gear from the War Department for pennies on the dollar, and moved into Ontario. These Irish natives, and Americans of Irish blood, known as "Fenians," beat Canadian militiamen and British regulars in two small battles in 1866.

The Irishmen's "Fenian Raid" into Canada was now a complication to American diplomacy. So Andrew Johnson, who succeeded the martyred Abraham Lincoln as president, had Ulysses Grant and George Meade (the general who won over Lee at Gettysburg) lead troops to seal the Canadian border to keep more Irishmen from joining the Fenians already in Canada. The Fenians, cut off from their American bases, had to return to America.

Eventually the British paid $15.5 million to settle American claims in the early 1870s. The British also gave Canadian settlers more of a say in how Canada was being run ... to hold the loyalty of the locals to the Crown in case Americans decided they wanted Canada in the future.

Andrew Johnson helped the Mexicans instead of trying to seize the rest of Mexico. During the Civil War, France's Napoleon III overthrew Mexico's government and installed a puppet regime under Archduke Maximilian Hapsburg of Austria, the brother of Austrian emperor Franz Josef. This was a violation of the Monroe Doctrine, but Abraham Lincoln was in no position to do anything about it during the Civil War. After the Civil War, Johnson sent general Phil Sheridan and 50,000 troops to Texas to prepare to run the French out.

The move worked. The French left Mexico, and Benito Juárez regained power as Mexico's president. He had Maximilian captured and shot. Maximilian's widow Carlota made it back to Europe but died insane.

After the Civil War, railroad barons opened up the American West for further settlement. Laborers from Ireland and many veterans of the Civil War pushed a railroad west from Omaha through Nebraska and Wyoming and into northern Utah. Meanwhile, laborers including many Chinese blasted through the Sierra Nevada mountain range and built rails east from Sacramento through Nevada and to the linkup with the westbound railroad in Utah in 1869.

Other railroad men built lines which linked Minnesota with Seattle and Tacoma by way of North Dakota, Montana, and Idaho. Others built a line that connected southern California with New Orleans by way of Arizona, New Mexico, and Texas, and still another line that connected southern California with Kansas City by way of Arizona, New Mexico, Colorado, and Kansas. Others built track that linked the three states of the Pacific Coast.

The railroad men usually got title to thousands of square miles of land along their rights of way from the government; they usually also received payments for each mile of track they laid. Some land they sold to settlers, from very cheap to very high, depending on how close to a railroad town the land was. Other land the railroad men sold to speculators and government officials, who charged other settlers exorbitant prices for land they themselves had bought cheaply.

The West, especially California and Nevada, would have developed faster if railroad barons hadn't bled many of their customers dry. Collis Huntington, an owner of the Central Pacific Railroad, (which he and his partners later renamed the Southern Pacific) would make farmers and businessmen show railroad officials their books. Huntington would have his minions charge the farmers and businessmen so much for shipping they had barely enough profit left over to stay in business. Huntington bought politicians and judges to protect his company's piracy. The plundering of Huntington and partners Leland Stanford, Charles Crocker and Mark Hopkins retarded growth of industry and agriculture in the areas the Southern Pacific traveled as long as they controlled the railroad. (7)

However, in the long run, the railroads did more good than harm. Expansion of the railroads provided a fast and cheap way to bring settlers west, bring manufactured goods the settlers wanted west, and bring cattle, grain, minerals, and timber the settlers provided back east.

The railroads also made it possible for more farming people from Europe to settle in the Plains states and further west. Germans, Scandinavians, and Slavs could and did form farming communities in Kansas, Nebraska, the Dakotas, and Minnesota. Skilled miners and laborers who were willing to work in the mines found their way west from Europe to the Rocky Mountain states. Loggers from Europe came to anyplace out west where there was logging to do.

People coming west brought about the near-extermination of the American Indian communities. It didn't have to be that way, but that's how it turned out.

American policy toward the American Indians was the natural descendent of British policy toward the American Indians. American policy was to move red people off of land white people wanted to settle.

American soldiers forced the American Indians to move repeatedly. American soldiers and settlers massacred American Indian communities repeatedly. In the Great Plains, where American Indians were the strongest, the soldiers, settlers, commercial hunters, rich men on hunting excursions, and railroad company hunters killed millions of buffaloes. This deprived the American Indians of buffalo meat and hides, which weakened them severely.

Here are a few red-letter years in the genocide of red men and red women:

In the 1850s, settlers in California virtually wiped out the peaceable local American Indians. They sold thousands of surviving children into slavery, and gang-raped and forced into prostitution many of the best-looking young women and older girls. In 1850, when California entered the Union, there were about 100,000 American Indians in the Golden State. By the end of the decade, there were about 30,000. **(8)**

In 1855, government agents tried to force American Indians in Washington onto various reservations. The American Indians rose after settlers and prospectors started stealing their land. After a three-year campaign, U.S. troops beat the American Indians.

In 1862, Santee Sioux Indians, restricted to reservations in Minnesota, suffered a crop failure. The government owed money to the Sioux but the agents had not paid it, Army officers would not give the Sioux food, and white merchants would not give them credit. The Sioux rebelled, swarmed off the reservations, and killed hundreds of whites, including the merchants who intended to starve them. Union Army soldiers eventually beat the braves at Wood Lake. Many Santee fled to the Dakotas, but about 2000 surrendered. The soldiers hanged 40 of the Santee warriors before Abraham Lincoln could put a stop to the hangings.

In 1864, Colorado militiamen under a minister named Reverend J.M. Chivington sneak-attacked 450 Cheyenne and Arapaho men, women, and children who – at the invitation of the U.S. government – were camping at Sand Creek, Colorado. They killed about 300 American Indians, mostly women and children. Indian fighter Kit Carson called Chivington and his men cowards. Their despicable act did bring American Indian retribution on whites in Colorado for several years.

General Sherman had his soldiers blast Captain Jack and his Modoc tribe out of the lava beds of far northern California. The settlers had wanted his tribe's land, and Captain Jack was brazen enough to try two white man's tricks – he killed settlers and he sprung an ambush during a peace negotiation. He killed General Edward Canby in the process, and Sherman said the Modocs deserved "utter extermination." The Modocs surrendered to Sherman's subordinate General Jefferson Davis (ironically he was a Union general in

the Civil War by the same name as the leader of the Confederacy) in 1873; he had Captain Jack hanged.

Roughly 2000 Sioux and Cheyenne led by Sitting Bull, Crazy Horse, and Gall killed General George Custer and his entire group of about 250 soldiers in battle at Little Big Horn River in Montana in 1876. This victory over Custer and his cavalry encouraged federal officials to step up their efforts to wipe out American Indians on the northern plains.

Crazy Horse and a band of Sioux surrendered in 1877. Four months later, a soldier bayoneted Crazy Horse to death. After years of guerrilla warfare and living on the lam as fugitives in Canada, Sitting Bull and the few braves under his command surrendered to U.S. Army officers in 1881. Sitting Bull toured with Buffalo Bill Cody's Wild West Show in 1885 (nine years after Little Big Horn), and was a huge draw. In his tribal regalia, the great chief inspired fear and admiration among the palefaces who came to see the shows. Sitting Bull also gave fellow Cody star Annie Oakley her nickname of "Little Sure Shot." She would grow fond of the old warrior. But Sitting Bull was disgusted by the neglect of the poor he saw in the cities back East. He said American Indians would never treat their own that way. Sitting Bull gave away most of his earnings to poor people and returned to his tribe. U.S. government officials would never allow him to tour with Buffalo Bill in America again.

Government agents in 1877 ordered the Nez Percé tribe out of their land in the area where Oregon, Washington, and Idaho meet. As the Nez Percé prepared to leave, white settlers stole hundreds of their horses. The enraged Nez Percé killed about 20 settlers, which gave the U.S. Army the excuse to attack them. Chief Joseph decided to take the Nez Percé into Canada to escape. The tribe fought several battles with the soldiers, and they almost made it into Canada, but soldiers finally cut off their escape route in northern Montana just miles from the Canadian border. Chief Joseph had to surrender.

The "last stand" of the Sioux tribe came in 1890. Wovoka, a Paiute tribesman, preached to American Indians that they should go back to their old ways and reject the white man's way of life. Wovoka said this would help bring the dead American Indians back to life and make the white men go away. Many American Indians believed Wovoka's message, which was a mixture of Christian and American Indian beliefs. Whites called Wovoka's religious ceremony the "Ghost Dance."

The revival made the soldiers and settlers in the Great Plains nervous. American authorities shot and killed Sitting Bull while arresting him in mid-December 1890. Two weeks later, at the end of December 1890, American cavalrymen surrounded and arrested a band of several hundred Sioux, and forced them to stop at

Wounded Knee Creek, South Dakota. The Sioux camped overnight, and then the soldiers disarmed them the next morning. The troops then started firing on the Sioux, who defended themselves with their bare hands and any weapons they could grab. When the smoke cleared, 29 soldiers and more than 200 Sioux men, women, and children lay dead, including their chief Big Foot.

In Arizona, settlers took thousands of Apaches as slaves .... and forced the prettiest women and older girls into prostitution. Army officers ambushed Apache leaders who came to meet with them. It was only natural that Cochise and other Apache chiefs would rise against this sort of treatment. In 1871, whites in Tucson showed their good will by massacring about 100 Apaches who had turned themselves in at a nearby Army fort; this made the Apaches even more determined to hold out. General George Crook, an Indian fighter who actually dealt honestly with American Indians, finally convinced Cochise and most of the Apaches to go to reservations. Cochise died of natural causes in 1874.

Crook worked to keep the settlers and government swindlers from taking advantage of the Apaches. Crook's superiors removed him from his post after Apache leader Geronimo failed to surrender to him, and replaced him with Indian fighter (and Indian hater) General Nelson Miles. In 1886, Apache scouts whom Crook recruited talked Geronimo into quitting the warfare and going to a reservation, but Miles had Geronimo and his men (and the Apache scouts too) imprisoned in Florida. General Crook died in 1890 while trying to get the Apaches released, or at least resettled as free men in the Indian Territory.

It might have depressed the Apaches to go even to the Indian Territory. For in 1889, American politicians showed how low they could go when they allowed American settlers to steal even the Indian Territory from the American Indians who had to live there because generations of American politicians had decided to make them go there. By 1907, the Indian Territory would become the state of Oklahoma. **(9)**

Those who romanticize the American Indians do not mention the American Indians were often inhumane to each other before the white man's coming. Ritual torture and cannibalism were part of many tribes' way of life. The tortures they practiced on each other would nauseate all but the most psychopathic among you. The Aztecs were bloodthirsty people who preyed upon weaker Indian tribes. They publicly butchered and ate many thousands of other Indians. Members of these victimized tribes were willing to help Cortes against the Aztec oppressors. But the admitted savagery of American Indian tribes toward each other does not excuse the behavior of the whites — usually British and later American settlers and officials – who as Christians were presumably not supposed to cheat, steal from,

murder, or rape the American Indians.

In 1600, there were roughly two million to perhaps five million American Indians in what is now the Lower 48 states of America. There were maybe 100,000 to 200,000 American Indians and Eskimos in what is now Canada and Alaska. Some claim there were many times this number of natives; if that was true the English settlers and their descendants the Americans would have had much more trouble beating them. Also, there would have been more tangible evidence of the presence of so many natives, like more settlements, burial grounds, or other places showing human habitation or use. There would also be many more Americans who could legitimately claim American Indian blood.

Even with three centuries to increase their numbers, the native peoples of what is now America did not do so. That's because the diseases and the weapons of the whites killed them much faster than they could reproduce. By 1900, there were only about 250,000 native American Indians and Eskimos. Most of these lived in the American Southwest, where the first white settlers were Spanish. Some American Indians died at the hands of rival tribesmen, but most died due to the attacks and the diseases of the European colonists and their descendants. Even counting the intermarriage of American Indian and white people through these centuries (which usually involved people of Spanish or French blood), the drop in the numbers of American Indians was spine-chilling.

By comparison, Mexico's population was perhaps 9 to 11 million American Indians before Cortes landed in the early 1500s. The American Indian population nosedived dramatically, then started to recover by 1900. Of the 13 million or so people in Mexico that year, about a million were of European ancestry, and of the other 12 million, half were pure-blood American Indians, and half were mestizos.

The trends of American Indian and Eskimo numbers in British-controlled Canada paralleled those in the United States. There was a drastic drop in the numbers of these peoples in the 1800s, and then a recovery in numbers of natives by the 1960s. The United States' American Indian and Eskimo (Inuit) population in 1960 was 600,000 to 700,000.

Figures for the rest of Latin America are sketchier. But most of the people of Bolivia are American Indians, and in Paraguay, Peru, Ecuador, and Colombia, American Indians and mestizos far outnumber people of European origin. In Chile and Venezuela, Indians and mestizos are large minorities. In Argentina and Uruguay, whites predominate to a larger extent than whites do in the United States, and in Brazil, whites barely outnumber blacks and mulattoes. The whites of these lands killed off or intermarried with the relatively few American Indians who they found when they colonized these lands. Most of the people of the countries of Central America are American Indians and mestizos. **(10)**

This book doesn't have room to list all the crimes American government officials, military leaders, settlers, and businessmen committed against the American Indians. Nor does it have enough space to identify each treaty violation the whites committed against the American Indians from the time of the Cavaliers and the Pilgrims until the massacre of the Sioux at Wounded Knee in 1890, the year after the Sooners and others stole the Indian Territory itself from the American Indians. We mention some of the more important events of the struggle between the red man and the white man to show what it cost in lives and suffering to make the country open for American-style settlement.

Americans would also find other types of native people to dispossess in the 1800s. In 1867, America bought Alaska from Russia for $7.2 million and inherited a few thousand Eskimos and American Indians.

The first generations of Russian explorers and Siberian pioneers (from the 1740s through the 1790s) killed most of the natives on the Aleutian Islands. In 1799, one Russian entrepreneur won the fur monopoly, and he and his key people obeyed the Russian government's command to treat the natives better. Orthodox missionary priests came from Russia to work among the Eskimos and the American Indians, and won many converts to their faith. The Russian priests and company authorities treated the Eskimos and American Indians firmly but paternally, somewhat like the way the Spanish treated the American Indians in the lands they occupied. Alaska is the only state where the Orthodox Christian faith is among the leading faiths of the residents. **(11)**

When the Russians left, the Eskimos and American Indians had little protection. Owners of a monopoly granted by the U.S. government for seal hunting let their hunters decimate the seal herds, leaving Eskimos little to hunt. They likewise nearly eliminated the walrus and caribou herds. Other Americans likewise cheated the Eskimos and weakened them with bad whisky, infected prostitutes, and other diseases such as tuberculosis. Some Eskimo men took to summer-long drunks instead of hunting to stock up for the winter; their families starved. Some Eskimo women took to prostitution. The Eskimo population dropped dramatically again.

Protestant minister Sheldon Jackson tried a novel approach for Americans – he tried to keep Christ in Christianity in his dealings with the Eskimos. He set up schools for the Eskimos in their settlements, sought medical and legal help for them, and even had them taught how to herd and raise reindeer so they could make a living to replace their old trade of hunting.

A gold rush in the 1890s in the Nome area on Alaska's west coast made "America's Icebox" very profitable all of a sudden. Other gold strikes along the Yukon River in Alaska and in the Klondike district, in Canada's nearby Yukon Territory, brought more gold rushers to the Far North and made the Alaska Panhandle boundary an issue between Britain and America. Teddy Roosevelt used a little gunboat diplomacy to back off the British (who still basically ran Canada) and retain the Panhandle for America.

Meanwhile, Manifest Destiny was hitting the Hawaiian Islands with tidal wave force. American whaling crews had been sailing to Hawaii for almost a century, looking for provisions and looking for female companionship. American missionaries followed, bringing Bibles, a professed disgust over the sexual morals of the locals and the sailors, and a yen for profitable government office with the Hawaiians' king. Behind them came the sharpies, who would complete the conquest of the Hawaiians. Everyone brought diseases, venereal or otherwise, and decimated the native Hawaiians. The population of the natives dropped from about 300,000 in the late 1700s to about 70,000 in the 1850s. **(12)**

The sharpies conned the Hawaiian king into allowing foreigners to own land. The sharpies became sugar and pineapple plantation owners, and they imported Chinese and Japanese laborers to work their estates. Soon the Hawaiians were minorities in their own islands. The sugar barons forced the king and his legislature to give up power. When he died in 1891, his sister Liliuokulani ruled as queen. She tried to regain the monarchy's power and reduce the influence of the sugar and pineapple barons.

In 1893, at the request of greedy American sugar barons, American official John Stevens ordered American Marines on an American warship in Hawaiian waters to take part in a coup to overthrow Queen Liliuokulani. Sanford Dole, the son of a missionary, and a relative to pineapple baron James Dole, managed the coup that booted Queen Liliuokulani off of her throne. The American businessmen petitioned for the United States to annex Hawaii. Being part of America would give the sugar barons tariff-free benefits in the American sugar market. President Grover Cleveland sent an emissary to Hawaii to investigate, and learned most Hawaiians wanted Queen Liliuokulani to continue ruling them. He refused to annex Hawaii, but did nothing to throw the piratical Americans out of power. President William McKinley engineered the annexation of Hawaii in 1898, the year of the Spanish-American War.

Not all white people in Hawaii coveted the Hawaiians' land. Belgian priest Joseph De Veuster, aka Father Damien, ran a leper colony on Molokai. Father Damien, like Rev. Sheldon Jackson in Alaska, tried to serve instead of lording it over those he came to serve.

When Father Damien died of leprosy himself in 1889, a self-satisfied Protestant minister in Honolulu named Hyde libeled him in a letter to another minister, claiming Father Damien got the disease from having sex with the lady lepers. The great author Robert Louis Stevenson lambasted Hyde in public because Father Damien had set an example of Christian charity that was all too rare. Stevenson also predicted Hyde would only be remembered for suffering a written scourging at his (Stevenson's) hands. He was right.

What was the result of the growth of America at the expense of the American Indians, the Spanish, the Mexicans, the Eskimos, and the Hawaiians?

In 1840, Europe (including Russia west of the Urals) had about 250 million people on roughly 3.8 million square miles of land. The United States (which included America east of the Mississippi River, Louisiana, Arkansas, and Missouri – the three states west of the Mississippi River in 1840, and the rest of the Louisiana Purchase) had 17 million blacks and whites on 1.8 million square miles of land.

In 1900, Europe (including Russia west of the Urals) had about 425 million people on the same 3.8 million square miles of land. The 45 American states (and the territories of Oklahoma, Arizona, and New Mexico, which would soon become states) had 76 million people (including American Indians) on about 3 million square miles of land. **(13)**

The bottom line? America had plenty of land for Europe's huddled masses to come to. And now you have a thumbnail sketch of how we got it.

THE RELICS OF BARBARISM

The emptiness of the American West had drawn other members of Protestant America – the Mormons – westward in the 1840s. The Mormons were industrious, thrifty, and well-organized, on paper the perfect WASPs. However, their acquisitiveness and their perceived oddball beliefs led many Americans to loathe them.

Joseph Smith started the Mormon religion in upstate New York in 1830. He claimed he dug golden tablets from the ground, deciphered them, and determined they said one of the lost tribes of Israel migrated to America. Some people believed him and followed him. Smith led his followers to Missouri, where they alienated the locals by discriminating against non-Mormons. They also befriended free blacks in this slave state, but held slaves themselves. The locals ran the Mormons out of Missouri; they eventually started a settlement in Nauvoo, Illinois.

Smith decided to exclude blacks from the Mormon hierarchy, possibly to curry favor with the locals. However, he openly started to preach in favor of polygamy. This truly angered other Christians against the Mormons. Non-Mormons considered polygamy, along with slavery, one of the "relics of barbarism."

Smith and other elders had been practicing polygamy secretly before he made his desires, errr, doctrine public. Dr. John Bennett allegedly helped cover up the sexual use of many of the publicly single females in Nauvoo who were privately in polygamous setups with Smith and other Mormon elders by performing abortions on them. Smith ran out Bennett after they quarreled over who would get possession of a 19-year-old cutie named Nancy Rigdon.

In 1844, Smith tried to destroy the printing press of an opponent who exposed the sect's polygamy. Lawmen arrested Smith and his brother and held them in a nearby jail. Vigilantes, angered at the grasping ways of the Mormons in mammon and mates, broke into the jail and killed them.

After the death of Joseph Smith, the leaders of this now-openly polygamous sect sought to build a state away from other Americans, who hated them. Most Mormons, under the lead of Brigham Young, decided to head west. Using U.S. Army maps, good scouting, and solid planning, they moved to present-day Utah in the late 1840s. Brigham Young started the settlement in the Salt Lake area in the summer of 1847. This took place during the Mexican War; Utah went from nominal Mexican control to nominal American control and definite Mormon control.

Other Mormons in a rival sect led by James Strang (which by now included reputed abortionist John Bennett) didn't go west but instead headed north. They first settled in Wisconsin, but then took over Beaver Island – an aptly named place for the practice of polygamy – in Lake Michigan in 1848. When they became a majority, the Mormons took control of local government and looted the county treasury for "tithes", tried to beat (literally) tithes out of the Irish-American fishermen and their families who were already living on the island, and eventually forbade non-Mormons from fishing in the waters around the island. They ran the non-Mormons off of the island in a couple of years, and tried to spread their tentacles to the mainland of Michigan.

Strang had himself crowned "king" of Beaver Island. The Mormons under his leadership committed the federal crimes of timber theft, mail interference, and counterfeiting to supplement their earlier state crimes of land theft, fishing rights theft, assault and battery, and tax money theft (not to mention polygamy), but federal prosecutors as inept as some of those today could not win any convictions on the federal charges they brought against the Strangites.

When the government fails to protect the people, the people have to protect themselves. And in the 1850s, they weren't afraid to do so. So the people who Strang and his followers had abused planned to evict them from Beaver Island in 1856. Their plans were aided by a fatal row over females among some of the Strangite menfolk just before the non-Mormons attacked.

One of the disgruntled Strangites was a man who couldn't get enough action even in a cult that allowed polygamy. So he committed old-fashioned adultery and Strang ordered him whipped for his sin. Another had married a girl who Strang evidently got the hots for. (There were also insinuations this girl had a crush on one of Strang's "plural wives.") The young husband feared losing his pretty young wife and being castrated at Strang's orders. (Mormon elders under Joseph Smith and Brigham Young who wanted pretty young wives from time to time resorted to ordering their followers to castrate young men who would not give up their cute sweethearts.) So the vengeful adulterer and the man afraid of losing his wife and his manhood shot and beat Strang and left him for dead.

Within days, anti-Catholic journalists of the day noted, "a mob" of "drunken vigilantes" from Mackinac Island (code words for the Irish-American fishermen, some of them distant relatives of the author) drove the Mormons off of Beaver Island. Strang died of his wounds in Wisconsin shortly after the Irish-Americans repossessed the island and the fisheries he and his followers had stolen from them. His five wives, four of whom were pregnant at the time of his demise, eventually hooked up with other men, some of whom were non-Mormons.

Meanwhile, Mormons in Utah were safe from federal justice and other Americans for awhile, because there were very few Americans settled around them for awhile. This didn't mean Americans respected them. Many Americans viewed the Mormons in Utah as freaks of nature. Mormon leader Brigham Young, virtually a dictator over the lives of his flock, had 27 or 28 "wives" but who's counting? Non-Mormons nicknamed him "Bring 'em in Young" for his lechery. The one "wife" who sued Young for divorce wrote an exposé about him titled "Wife No. 19." Young won the suit because the U.S. government didn't recognize the polygamous "marriage." Federal authorities essentially considered her and Young's other "wives" to be concubines and Young to be a whoremonger.

Many other members of the Mormon hierarchy also had "plural wives". Most Mormons had only one wife, but the wealthy Mormons took several. This meant there would be a very high proportion of unmarried young men in Utah unless the church leaders could get females from outside Utah. Church agents even actively "hunted" female game in Britain and Scandinavia to convince them to embrace the Latter Day lifestyle.

The Mormons did make the desert bloom by their hard work, and they made good money selling supplies at high prices to the settlers heading to California. No one has ever denied their energy or their discipline. However, they did harass the non-Mormons heading west through Utah, which made them criminals.

The most brutal incident took place in 1857, when Mormons in southern Utah – probably with the connivance of Brigham Young himself – butchered the men, women, and older children of a wagon train headed to California. They also looted the pilgrims of all their possessions and money. Young's adopted son John Lee – who had close to a score of "plural wives" himself -- commanded the Mormon militiamen who committed the mass murders. Two teenage sisters begged for mercy as about 120 of their fellow wagon train members lay dead; the Mormons raped and murdered them. They escaped punishment for the mass murders (called the Mountain Meadows Massacre) for a number of years by blaming the atrocity on Ute Indians.

The Mormons kidnaped and raised the 17 surviving small children, who were all seven years old or younger, thinking they would be too young to remember the shootings and dismemberments of their parents and older siblings. In 1859, a government agent, two noted frontiersmen, and U.S. Army troops took the 17 surviving children from their Mormon kidnapers and returned them to relatives in Arkansas. One younger child would later testify he saw a Mormon woman wearing the dress of his mother, after another Mormon had stripped her hatcheted corpse of the garment. Other children would recount the horror of watching the Mormons butcher their parents and older

brothers and sisters.

The Mormons confronted and threatened federal troops and law enforcement officials many times from the 1850s through the 1880s. The Mormons tried to colonize Southern California, Nevada, Idaho, Wyoming, Arizona, and Colorado. Brigham Young advocated slavery and at the same time said it wouldn't be profitable in Utah. The Mormons stayed neutral during the Civil War. Young used his militia to murder Mormon separatists during the Civil War.

The Mormons escaped justice during the Civil War because Abraham Lincoln had bigger problems to deal with than a group of deviants who most Americans of that era considered were hiding behind a religion with no more perceived credibility than what Scientology has today. But the Mormons in effect had seceded from the Union and were just as quick to interfere with or threaten federal officers as the Southerners were. Besides, they committed other crimes against the social order besides polygamy .... the worst were the murders of non-Mormons and their own dissidents and their own womenfolk who got too friendly with non-Mormons. Justice demanded a penalty for the Mormons similar to what the Union Army had inflicted on the people of the Confederacy.

After the Civil War, Generals Sherman and Sheridan wanted to crush the Mormons like they had done to the Southerners, because of the Mormons' defiance of laws, their cheating of non-Mormons passing through Utah, and the murders they committed. Mormons shot, stabbed, or beat to death some non-Mormon men who they had legal difficulties with, or who were consorting with Mormon women. Also, Mormons had beheaded some Mormon women, apparently for the "crime" of getting too friendly with American soldiers stationed in Utah. (Soldiers testified to finding two of these women's severed heads.) It made little sense to bring these crypto-jihadists and "honor killers" before a jury of their Mormon peers because Mormon jurymen essentially refused to convict their own when they victimized non-Mormons or Mormons who strayed.

General Sherman sent Young a telegram threatening to allow his soldiers to avenge non-Mormon victims, but received no orders to make good on that threat. General Sheridan set up a base near Provo, Utah, but received no orders to proceed against the Mormons. Neither Andrew Johnson, nor Ulysses Grant, who succeeded Johnson as president, would unleash Sherman and Sheridan on the Mormons. However, neither president would allow Utah to become a state because of polygamy and because of Brigham Young's cultlike control of his followers.

Federal authorities indicted Young and other Mormon leaders on polygamy charges in 1871, but the Supreme Court voided all verdicts against Mormons decided by juries with no Mormon members. Mormons vastly outnumbered non-Mormons in Utah, so the justices ruled a jury in Utah without Mormons would be a violation of the right to jury in front of peers. So the Feds dropped the case against Young and his underlings in 1872, because they knew no Mormon would vote to convict them.

The Supreme Court has always had its share of knucklehead political lawyers. The Dred Scott, Plessy v. Ferguson, and Roe v. Wade decisions are just some of their best-known idiotic rulings. Since the Mormons were essentially an organized group of outlaws who could justify committing violent crimes and crimes of dishonesty against those not of their own kind, and who also advocated a degenerate lifestyle (polygamy) that violated the law of the land, none of them should have been seated on a jury trying people for violating a law they agreed should be violated.

It would be like trying a planter after the Civil War for resuming the practice of slavery; his wealthy Southern peers would not vote to convict him either. It would be like trying a Mob boss before a jury of other organized criminals; they wouldn't convict one of their own. It would be like trying a Saudi national for "honor killing" his daughter in front of a jury of Arabs who believe in that damnable practice; they would acquit him in a heartbeat.

Despite the Supreme Court ruling, some federal officials kept up the pressure on Young and the Mormons. Young essentially gave up his boy John Lee to appease those who were calling for his death for leading the Mountain Meadows Massacre two decades earlier. Authorities shot Lee to death at the scene of his great crime in 1877 after he was convicted. Brigham Young died later in 1877.

Federal lawmakers in 1882 finally passed an anti-polygamy law – the Edmunds Act – that the Supreme Court couldn't overturn. Federal marshals descended upon Utah, located polygamous families, and had the "husbands" prosecuted and sent to prison. The Mormons tried to shield these families, but their willingness to protect their polygamous brethren – who were usually the richest Mormons – weakened as the Feds applied pressure to whole communities. Why should working stiff Mormons who got by honorably with one wife cover for richer elders who kept multiple Mormon mamas?

Eventually Mormon leaders had the "revelation" that polygamy was not essential to their religion. After making the Mormons wait a couple of years to ensure the leaders wouldn't backslide into polygamy again, American officials allowed Utah into the Union in 1896. Mormons – who certainly deserve credit for much hard

work in settling Utah in the American style – have dominated this state ever since.(14)

History repeated itself in a macabre way in 2001. Mormon officials, led by Brigham Young's adopted son, perpetrated the Mountain Meadows Massacre on September 11, 1857. An exact gross of years to the day later, jihadists perpetrated the 9/11 murders. Unlike Brigham Young, the al-Qaeda vermin cheerfully claimed responsibility for the murders their scum committed. Young professed astonishment that his many sermons and directives and other verbal and written orders preaching "blood atonement" and violence against non-Mormons were acted upon by scum under his command like his adopted son. Mormon apologists for Young today admit he ordered his people not to sell food to non-Mormon travelers like the massacre victims that year, and they admit Mormons committed the murders, instead of blaming it on "Injuns."

The reason we are discussing the problems the Mormons posed to the rest of America in the 1800s in a book about immigration is not to make fun of the Mormons today. The reason is to inform the American people of their right to restrict or deport those who import anti-American practices into the country and define these evil acts as part of their religion in order to practice them.

The Mormons learned their lesson. Since the 1890s, when their leaders sued for peace with America and agreed to live under American laws, many Mormons have served this country in war and in peace with honor like those of the Catholic, Orthodox Christian, Jewish, and other Protestant faiths.

Our lawyers and judges seem to work on precedent more than they seem to work on common sense, so at least We The People have a great precedent to present (the treatment of the Mormons) in prosecuting the criminals among us who act according to the dictates of their twisted consciences.

No individual or group has the right to practice crimes like polygamy, honor killings, clitorectomies on little girls, slavery, or jihadist murders of non-Moslems and claim these execrable practices are Moslem practices protected by the freedom of religion clause of the U.S. Constitution. Nor do Hindus have the right to impose a caste system, sacrifice screaming children to false goddesses, or commit dowry murders just because they can get away with it in India. Our public officials understood this in the 1800s and acted accordingly. We need to make the current crop of lowlifes in high places act in similar fashion.

THE ROLL CALL OF IMMIGRANTS BY DECADE

When America's welcome mat was out in the 1800s and early 1900s, who wiped their feet on it?

There are not many people of French blood in the United States. But when the country was young, French people were many of the first immigrants in the early 1800s.

America's first alliance was with France. The French had helped the Patriots in the American Revolution. French thinkers, writers, and speakers admired America's form of government. America remained friendly toward France during the regimes of Louis XVI, the Revolutionary government, the Directorate, and Napoleon without getting involved in the human tragedies of the Reign of Terror and the Napoleonic Wars. America had an undeclared war with France over ship seizures in the late 1790s, but there was more good will by and large between America and France than between America and Britain.

In the 1810s, some French emigrants came after the fall of Napoleon. (Napoleon's own brother Joseph was in this number and settled down for awhile in New Jersey.) They followed many Frenchmen and Frenchwomen seeking to keep their necks from underneath the blade of the guillotine during the French Revolution in the 1790s. The Dupont family came to America around 1800, started making gunpowder in Delaware, and their descendants colonized the tiny state financially.

The French had been in America for a long time. French priests and trappers had explored the Great Lakes and the Mississippi and Ohio Valleys, and a few French settlers lived in the Midwest along these waterways. French colonists and French exiles from Acadia (which the British renamed Nova Scotia – New Scotland – after they deported the French) had settled in New Orleans and surrounding areas in the Deep South. Paul Revere and George Washington had French Huguenot (Protestant) ancestry.

The French, mostly a combination of Catholic and agnostic people, had sided with the Americans against the British in the American Revolution. The French and their black Haitian subjects had fought for America in the American Revolution. Other French people who lived in Louisiana had fought with Andrew Jackson against the British at New Orleans at the end of the War of 1812.

Roughly five million people came to America between 1820 and the start of the Civil War in this, the last era where sail-powered wooden ships hauled the vast majority of passengers and freight.

From **1820 through 1830**, roughly 100,000 people came from Europe. Of these, 54,000 came from Ireland, 27,000 came from Britain (including Scotland and Wales), 9000 came from France, and 8000 came from the various German states.

From **1831 through 1840**, roughly 500,000 Europeans came to America. Of these, 207,000 came from Ireland, 152,000 came from the various German states, 76,000 came from Britain (including Scotland and Wales), and 46,000 came from France. Another 14,000 came from Canada, 7,000 came from Mexico, and 12,000 came from the West Indies.

From **1841 through 1850**, roughly 1,600,000 Europeans came to America. Of these, 781,000 came from Ireland, 435,000 came from the various German states, 267,000 came from Britain (including Scotland and Wales), and 77,000 came from France. Another 42,000 came from Canada, 3,000 came from Mexico, and 14,000 came from the West Indies. This was the decade of the Great Hunger aka the Potato Famine in Ireland, and the decade of the Revolution of 1848, and crop failures in France and in the German states. This was also the decade of the Mexican War and the Gold Rush in California. During this decade Texas joined the Union and Americans took what is today California, Nevada, Utah, most of Arizona and New Mexico, much of Colorado, and parts of Wyoming, Kansas, and Oklahoma from the Mexicans. This land they conquered, along with Texas, contained perhaps 100,000 Mexicans and Spaniards and even more American Indians, none of whom were counted as immigrants. Under the treaty American officials signed with the Mexican government, the Mexican citizens in these lands became American citizens.

From **1851 through 1860**, roughly 2,500,000 Europeans came to America. Of these, 952,000 came from the various German states, 914,000 came from Ireland, 424,000 came from Britain (including Scotland and Wales), and 76,000 came from France. Also 25,000 came from Switzerland and 21,000 came from Norway (which was part of Sweden until 1905). Another 59,000 came from Canada, 3,000 came from Mexico (during the decade the U.S. bought land from Mexico – the Gadsden Purchase – containing a few thousand Mexicans and American Indians not counted as immigrants), and 11,000 came from the West Indies. About 41,000 Chinese came to America, almost all in the wake of the Gold Rush and other developments on the West Coast. The Irish and Germans continued to come in the wake of famine and turmoil in their homelands.

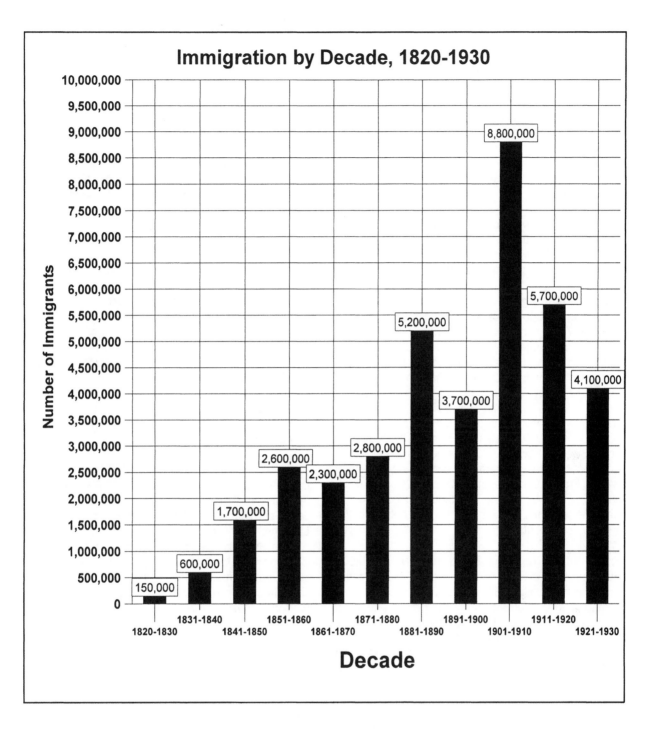

Immigration by Decade, 1820-1930

Number of Immigrants (y-axis): 0 to 10,000,000

Decade	Number of Immigrants
1820-1830	150,000
1831-1840	600,000
1841-1850	1,700,000
1851-1860	2,600,000
1861-1870	2,300,000
1871-1880	2,800,000
1881-1890	5,200,000
1891-1900	3,700,000
1901-1910	8,800,000
1911-1920	5,700,000
1921-1930	4,100,000

Note: Totals include people counted coming from non-European countries as well as European immigrants.

Except for those few who were able to walk or ride from Mexico or Canada, these people sailed to America on sail-powered wooden ships under Spartan conditions. Many others didn't make it because their ships sank, or they died of hunger or disease at sea.

Steam-powered ocean-going vessels were in service before the Civil War, but their use increased dramatically during the 1860s and 1870s. The earliest steamers used paddlewheels to drive them. Then steam-driven propellers replaced the paddlewheels. Finally, steel hulled ships replaced the wooden steamships.

More than 10 million people came to America between 1861 and 1890 ... the last three decades of the pre-Ellis Island era. This was more than double the flow of immigrants of the previous 40 years.

From 1861 through 1870, the decade of the Civil War, roughly 2,100,000 Europeans came to America. Of these, 787,000 came from the various German states, 436,000 came from Ireland, and 607,000 came from Britain (including Scotland and Wales). Also 36,000 came from France, and 23,000 came from Switzerland.

During the 1860s, the first large numbers of people started coming from Scandinavia. From 1861 through 1870, about 72,000 came from Norway, 38,000 came from Sweden, and 17,000 came from Denmark. Another 154,000 came from and through Canada (largely French Canadians), 2,000 came from Mexico, and 9,000 came from the West Indies. About 64,000 Chinese came to America; many would help build the first transcontinental railroad.

From 1871 through 1880, roughly 2,300,000 Europeans came to America. Of these, 718,000 came from the now-unified Germany, 437,000 came from Ireland, and 548,000 came from Britain (including Scotland and Wales). Also 72,000 came from France, 17,000 came from the Netherlands, 7,000 came from Belgium, and 28,000 came from Switzerland. Also 95,000 came from Norway, 116,000 came from Sweden, and 31,000 came from Denmark.

During the 1870s, the first large numbers of people started coming from southern and eastern Europe. From 1871 through 1880, about 56,000 came from the newly-unified Italy, 14,000 came from Portugal, 39,000 came from the Russian Empire (many of these were Poles and Jews, and some were Ukrainians, Finns, Lithuanians, Latvians, and Estonians), 73,000 came from Austria-Hungary (which included Czechs, Slovaks, Ruthenians, Slovenes, Croatians, and some Poles, Ukrainians, Serbs, and Romanians). Also 13,000 others came from Poland who were not counted as subjects of Germany, Russia, or Austria-Hungary.

From 1871 through 1880, another 384,000 came from and through Canada (largely French Canadians), 5,000 came from Mexico, and 14,000 came from the West Indies. About 123,000 Chinese came to America, and another 10,000 came from Australia and New Zealand.

From 1881 through 1890, roughly 4,700,000 Europeans came to America, double the number who came the previous decade.

Why the increase? Many shipping companies put large numbers of steel-hulled vessels into commission during this decade. (Some had done so already in the 1870s.) These newer ships could hold more people and go faster. This rise in shipping capacity made it easier and cheaper to transport people to America. The immigrants didn't need as much food or water per voyage because the ships were faster, and because they could hold more people, the steel ships cut the cost per passenger of carrying people from Europe to America.

Of the Europeans came to America, 1,453,000 came from Germany, 655,000 came from Ireland, and 807,000 came from Britain (including Scotland and Wales). Also 50,000 came from France, 54,000 came from the Netherlands, 20,000 came from Belgium, and 82,000 came from Switzerland. Also 177,000 came from Norway, 392,000 came from Sweden, and 88,000 came from Denmark.

From 1881 through 1890, about 307,000 came from Italy, 17,000 came from Portugal, 213,000 came from the Russian Empire (many of these were Poles and Jews, and some were Ukrainians, Finns, Lithuanians, Latvians, and Estonians), and 354,000 came from Austria-Hungary (which included Czechs, Slovaks, Ruthenians, Slovenes, Croatians, and some Poles, Ukrainians, Serbs, and Romanians). Also 52,000 others came from Poland who were not counted as subjects of Germany, Russia, or Austria-Hungary.

From 1881 through 1890, another 393,000 came from and through Canada (many French Canadians, but also many Europeans who British steamship companies routed through Canada to avoid American taxes and immigration laws), 2,000 came from Mexico, and 29,000 came from the West Indies. About 62,000 Chinese came to America, as the immigration laws cutting down on Chinese immigration began to take effect. Another 7,000 came from Australia and New Zealand.

From 1891 through 1920 – the busiest years of the "Ellis Island era" – more than 18 million people came to America. This was close to double the flow of immigrants of the previous 30 years.

The 1890s saw the opening of Ellis Island and a number of immigration laws aimed at regulating the flow of people to America. The flood of people through Canada and by rail to the United States due to crooked

AMERICAN REVOLUTION

Left: April 19, 1775 was the day armed Americans first stood up to British aggression, at Lexington, Massachusetts. The armed Patriots defended themselves when fired upon, then escaped a much larger British force. American militia stood up to the British at nearby Concord, shown here, and prevented them from seizing American weapons. Patriots harried the Redcoats on their retreat to Boston. Credit: U.S. National Guard.

Below: Washington and Von Steuben made the 8500 or so ragged Americans who survived the Valley Forge, Pennsylvania encampment the winter of 1777-1778 into real soldiers. These men would never again lose to the British in battle. Re-enaction photo by author.

Center left: Tadeusz Kosciuszko, a Polish officer, also aided Washington. So did Lafayette, a French officer. Casimir Pulaski, another Polish officer, died in combat in American service. Roughly 30% of the Continental Army was Irish, and 5% to 10% of America's Revolutionary War soldiers and sailors were blacks. Credit: Kosciuszko Society.

Bottom: American soldiers storm British defenses at Yorktown, Virginia. The Brits surrendered October 19, 1781, 6-1/2 years after Lexington and Concord. Credit: U.S. Army.

SPAIN'S CONTRIBUTIONS TO AMERICA

Left: Crusader Queen Isabella is the mother of the Spanish nation. She united Spain by seeking out and marrying husband King Fernando of Aragon, and letting him mesh his realm in eastern Spain with her realm of Castile in central and northern Spain. They ruled as equals. She and he led and paid for the fighting men who pushed the bloodthirsty Moslems out of Spain. She also bankrolled Columbus' voyage on the chance he might find something of value. She also forbade enslavement of the American Indians. (It happened after her death, shown here in the painting "Testament of Isabella the Catholic," by Eduardo Rosales. King Fernando is by her bedside and Cardinal Cisneros is writing down her orders.) Thanks to the warrior queen, the Spanish beat the British to the U.S. by about half a century.

Center: Queen Isabella ordered the evangelization of American Indians and the integration of American Indians into Spanish American society. Catholic priests built missions, ministered to the Indians, and taught them farming methods and skilled trades. Santa Ysabel Mission, in San Diego County, California, is one of many missions built in the Spanish style. There are far more American Indians in America and elsewhere in the Western Hemisphere where the Spanish ruled than where the British ruled. Photo by author.

Below left: The grounds of San Fernando Mission in Los Angeles County contain a Catholic church, a museum, a seminary, a cemetery, and a park. This Hispanic bride has just been married at the church over Christmastime. Photo by author. Disclosure: The author has visited and participated in many religious services at this great mission over the years. He also has a little Spanish blood, of which he is proud.

Below right: The Mission Bells of San Carlos Borromeo de Carmelo Mission. Better known as "Carmel Mission," this Monterey County mission is where Padre Junípero Serra, founder of the California mission system, is buried. He and his subordinates founded 21 missions along the California coast, each about a day's journey on foot apart. Photo by author.

Top left, top right, and center: The Spanish introduced winemaking, irrigated farming, and cattle and sheep ranching to America. Spanish vaqueros had driven cattle for many years to better pastures in their dry homeland. They applied this method of livestock raising to the dry regions of present-day Texas, New Mexico, Arizona, and California. The Spanish, besides introducing grapes and walnuts (the grove of trees at right), introduced olives, citrus fruit, and various vegetables to California, Texas, and other areas they settled. They also brought horses in large numbers, thus also inadvertently increasing the mobility of the American Indians. The Spanish also helped the Patriots against the British. Photos by author.

Bottom: It took a Spanish ship many many months to sail from Spain around Cape Horn at the bottom of South America to California. Even ships from Peru and western Mexico were rarities. So the appearance of a Spanish ship off the coast of California was a big event for the Spanish settlers of San Diego, Santa Barbara, Monterey, and San Francisco, Spanish towns in California with harbors. Credit: Eileen Sherlock.

FRANCE'S MARKS ON AMERICA

Joan of Arc (seen in the mural Lionel Royer painted for the basilica in her home town of Domremy in Lorraine) was the mother of the French nation. She led men into combat against the English invaders, and had the rightful king crowned. She as a patriot set a great example for America's Patriots.

Joan was backstabbed by her government, and when she was captured in battle, her king didn't try to ransom her. The English abused her in prison, but could not break her. They burned her at the stake on May 30, 1431. Joan was a devout and zealous Catholic, and she was cheerful and kind. She wanted to marry, and she had France's bravest and manliest men at her beck and call ... yet she behaved herself despite her power. That is a sign of heroic virtue!

French explorers and priests like Father Marquette, **left**, explored the Great Lakes and Mississippi Valley. The French founded New Orleans, St. Louis, and Detroit. The Cathedral of St. Louis in New Orleans, **below left**, is a shining example of French architecture. The French also settled Quebec and the Maritime area of Canada. During the French and Indian War, the British exiled the French of Acadia to Louisiana and elsewhere (**below right**, picture by Charles Jeffreys), and renamed the area Nova Scotia. They broke up many families in the process. Americans would call the French exiles from Acadia "Cajuns." George Washington had French ancestry, as did Paul Revere and John Sevier. Lafayette and the French aided the Patriots against the British.

Settlers built towns, and men set up stage coach lines and teamster lines to connect the towns. Eventually men built railroads to link the American West to the rest of the nation. **Top:** Girl admires horses of a stage coach driver in Columbia, California, a gold mining town that is now a state park. **Bottom left:** Workers lay track; California State Railroad Museum. Clueless and alien California politicians want to close this park also. Photos by author.

Center: Pioneers homesteaded from the Great Plains to the Pacific Coast, like the four Chrisman sisters (center), who staked out a piece of western Nebraska and built this sod house. Credit: Library of Congress and Nebraska Historical Society.

Bottom right: The West wasn't truly settled until the ladies came West to civilize the menfolk. Western men gave women the right to vote before the men back East did. Photo by author.

THE CIVIL WAR

Wealthy slaveholders' militant defense of slavery – even at the expense of the Union – was the greatest single cause of the Civil War.

Left: Abraham Lincoln (speaking) and Stephen Douglas (in gray at Lincoln's right) debated slavery in the Illinois senate election of 1858. Thousands rode horses or walked to see these patriots. Douglas won the race; Lincoln beat him and two other rivals in the presidential election two years later. Public domain.

Bottom left: The South's brave men and women rallied gallantly for a bad cause. The vast majority of Southern soldiers owned no slaves. They felt they were defending their homes. Spy Belle Boyd gives Stonewall Jackson key intelligence that helped him win battles against Union troops. Painting by Mark Korolev; sold to raise money for preserving Belle Boyd's home in Martinsburg, West Virginia.

Below: There were free blacks in America, almost all in the North, but they didn't enjoy the same rights as white Americans did. These re-enactors showed this wrong at the Old State Capitol in Springfield, Illinois. Photo by author.

Above: Pickett's Charge at Gettysburg, July 3, 1863, was the climax of the Civil War – and a rare blunder of Robert E. Lee's. Union soldiers shot up his Rebels and broke the attack. Lee had to retreat from Pennsylvania with the men he still had. Credit: gettysburggreenactment.com.

Below: "Strike for God and Country," by Don Stivers. Irish soldiers in Union blue with Old Glory and green flag charge Rebels at Spotsylvania in May 1864. Grant took charge against Lee in Virginia, but there was still no quit in the Southerners. Meanwhile, General Sherman was leading a collateral ancestor of the author and 90,000 other Yankees thru Georgia. The war ended in Union victory (and American victory) in April 1865.

Above: More than 600,000 men in uniform died in the Civil War. Many were married men; there were hundreds of thousands of young widows across America mourning their husbands. Mary Lincoln would mourn her murdered husband too. Honest Abe died on Good Friday, like Our Lord. Photo of this beautiful charming re-enactor by author.

Below: "Home at Last" by Don Stivers. Almost 300,000 free and escaped slave blacks served in the Union Army. Thousands more escaped slaves helped the Union Army in other ways. Surely they deserved to share in the fruits of victory.

AMERICAN INDIANS

lost their lands and often their lives when the settlers came. **Top left**: "Abduction of Pocahontas" by Jean Louis Gerome, summed up British Indian policy: rape, enslavement, and murder. **Bottom:** "Trail of Tears" by Robert Lindneux (courtesy Woolaroc Museum, Oklahoma) shows the forced exile of the Cherokees, Choctaws, Creeks, Chickasaws, and Seminoles from the Southeast to Oklahoma. Sooners would eventually steal Oklahoma from the American Indians, too. **Left:** Geronimo, the Apache on the right, and his warriors fought long and hard against the whites who broke their treaties and abused their people. **Top right:** Catholic Church, San Antonio de Pala Mission, San Diego County, California. American Indians built and decorated this Spanish mission church. Spanish rule was far less brutal than British. Photo by author.

WORK OF THE IMMIGRANTS

Top: Irish immigrants did much of the digging of the canals of America in the first half of the 1800s. They did this work even in the South, because they were expendable, while a worked-out slave would cost his master money. Credit: National Park Service, Ohio and Erie Canal National Corridor.

Center: These Irish workers and other Civil War veterans built the Transcontinental Railroad west through Nebraska and Wyoming to Utah. General William Tecumseh Sherman, who led his men in the destruction of Southern railroads a few years earlier, was an engineer and one of the key leaders in the successful effort to build the rails that tied the West Coast to the rest of the country. Chinese and American workers built the stretch east from California through Nevada to Utah. The woodcut is by Alfred Waud.

Bottom: These Swedes left their snowbound homeland to try their hands at farming in Kansas. Credit: Library of Congress and Kansas Historical Society.

Top: Slavic men were many of the workers in the steel mills – like this one in Pennsylvania – and the coal mines of this nation. Credit: Lewis Hine, New York Public Library.

Center: These Finnish people and other Scandinavians came to places like Minnesota, Wisconsin, Michigan, Washington, and Oregon to work as loggers, like they did in their homeland. Credit: Finland National Immigration Institute.

Bottom right: Mexicans have worked the ranches and farms of California, Texas, Arizona, New Mexico, and Colorado, from the time of Spanish and Mexican settlement of the West to the present. Credit: Library of Congress.

Bottom left: Edward Sherlock, great-grandfather of the author, emigrated from Ireland to Chicago. He was a butcher in Drogheda, Ireland, then a slaughterer in Chicago. He died of TB that he contracted in his trade, like many other poor souls did back in the day. RIP, Great-grandpa Sherlock, RIP.

Bottom line: Immigrants kept some of their customs, but they tried to become real Americans and achievers instead of loafers, criminals, jihadists, spies, and separatists.

EUROPEANS BROUGHT CHRISTIANITY

to America. Some, like Joseph De Veuster, aka Father Damien, a Belgian Catholic priest, heroically practiced what they preached. Living our faith unhypocritically is something we are all called to do.

Left: Father Damien with lepers at Molokai, Hawaii. He died of leprosy in 1889 after ministering to the lepers for many years. Photo courtesy Cathedral of Our Lady of Peace, Honolulu.

Right: "Mayflower Compact" by N.C. Wyeth. Dissident English Protestants who opposed the Protestantism of King James (he of the King James bible) make a citizens' agreement before landing in Massachusetts. Protestants' rejecting Catholic orthodoxy led to arguments with other Protestants, and then to questioning of kings. This questioning of authority and the compromise among equals of different opinions led to American style democracy. Credit: Granger

Below left: Holy Assumption Orthodox Church, Kenai, Alaska. Russian Orthodox priests and other priests from the Balkans brought this faith to America. Credit: National Park Service.

Below right: .San Diego (St. James) Parish, Santa Fé, New Mexico. This is the oldest parish or congregation in the United States; priests have said Mass here since the early 1600s. Photo by author.

British shipping and immigrant screening practices slowed to a trickle due to these laws. Immigration fell to 70% of what it was during the previous decade. However, bigots in America grew angrier as the people from southern and eastern Europe kept coming in even larger numbers, while Anglo-Saxon, Teutonic, and Nordic immigration fell off dramatically.

From 1891 through 1900, roughly 3,600,000 Europeans came to America, more than a million fewer than the previous decade. Part of this was due to the hard times in America in the 1890s; the country's people suffered the worst depression the country had had in its history.

Another reason was the improving standard of living in Germany, Britain, Ireland, the Low Countries, Scandinavia, Switzerland, and France, which up to this point had been the European countries most likely to have immigrants coming to America. In Germany especially, the development of industry, and the German government's policy supporting industry led to many more jobs for Germans and less pressure on them to leave. Nearly a million fewer Germans came to America in the 1890s than had come in the 1880s. The other countries named above all sent many fewer immigrants to America in the 1890s than they had done in the 1880s. These drops more than canceled out a doubling of immigration from Russia and the countries of Southern and Eastern Europe.

Of the immigrants, 505,000 came from Germany, 388,000 came from Ireland, and 272,000 came from Britain (including Scotland and Wales). Also 31,000 came from France, 27,000 came from the Netherlands, 18,000 came from Belgium, and 31,000 came from Switzerland. Also 95,000 came from Norway, 226,000 came from Sweden, and 50,000 came from Denmark.

From 1891 through 1900, about 652,000 came from Italy, 28,000 came from Portugal, 505,000 came from the Russian Empire (many of these were Poles and Jews, and some were Ukrainians, Finns, Lithuanians, Latvians, and Estonians), and 593,000 came from Austria-Hungary (which included Czechs, Slovaks, Ruthenians, Slovenes, Croatians, and some Poles, Ukrainians, Serbs, and Romanians). Also 97,000 others came from Poland who were not counted as subjects of Germany, Russia, or Austria-Hungary. Also 13,000 came from independent Romania, 16,000 came from independent Greece, and 27,000 came from "Turkey in Asia" – almost of these people were Lebanese, Syrians, or Armenians fleeing Turkish oppression.

From 1891 through 1900, another 3,000 came from and through Canada, 1,000 came from Mexico, and 33,000 came from the West Indies. About 15,000 Chinese came to America, and 26,000 came from Japan. Another 3,000 trickled in from Australia and New Zealand.

The first decade of the 1900s was the heyday of Ellis Island. More than double the amount of Europeans came during this decade than had come in the previous decade.

Scandinavian and British immigration increased, and German and Irish immigration fell off. Immigration from Italy, Russia, and eastern Europe mushroomed. In Italy's case, conditions were poor – but Italy's immigration statistics were inflated. Many Italian men would come to America, work, and return to Italy. Then they would come back to America. Pogroms in Russia and constant tensions between Russia, Austria-Hungary, Germany, the Turks, and the Balkans encouraged many in Russia and Eastern Europe to get while the getting was good.

From 1901 through 1910, roughly 8,100,000 Europeans came to America. Of these, 341,000 came from Germany, 339,000 came from Ireland, and 526,000 came from Britain (including Scotland and Wales). Also 73,000 came from France, 48,000 came from the Netherlands, 42,000 came from Belgium, and 35,000 came from Switzerland. Also 191,000 came from newly-independent Norway, 250,000 came from Sweden, and 65,000 came from Denmark.

From 1901 through 1910, about 2,046,000 came from Italy, 69,000 came from Portugal, 1,597,000 came from the Russian Empire (many of these were Poles and Jews, and some were Ukrainians, Finns, Lithuanians, Latvians, and Estonians), 2,145,000 came from Austria-Hungary (which included Czechs, Slovaks, Ruthenians, Slovenes, Croatians, and some Poles, Ukrainians, Serbs, and Romanians). All of those who came from Poland who were counted as subjects of Germany, Russia, or Austria-Hungary. Also 53,000 came from independent Romania, 168,000 came from independent Greece, 39,000 came from Serbia, Bulgaria, and Montenegro combined, 80,000 came from "Turkey in Europe" – almost all of these people were Bulgarians, Greeks, Serbs, Macedonians, and Albanians fleeing Turkish oppression, and 77,000 came from "Turkey in Asia" – almost all of these people were Lebanese, Syrians, or Armenians fleeing Turkish oppression. Even 28,000 people came from Spain – a country whose immigrants almost always went to Latin America – in the decade after the Spanish-American War.

From 1901 through 1910, another 179,000 came from and through Canada, 50,000 came from Mexico, and 108,000 came from the West Indies. Canada was again becoming more of a way station country for European and now Asian immigrants instead of a source country for immigrants, although French Canadians continued to come to New England and the Middle Atlantic states. About 21,000 Chinese came to America, and 130,000 came from Japan. The large amount of Japanese coming to America led president Theodore Roosevelt to get Japan to agree to restrict immigration in the later part of the decade. Another 7000 came from Africa, and another 12,000 came from Australia and New Zealand.

The second decade of the 1900s was the decade of World War One. The Germans and the British, whose merchant fleets carried the most immigrants to America, were in a life-or-death struggle on the high seas. Since Britain's surface fleet was stronger, Germany's ships and Austria-Hungary's ships stayed bottled up in port. British ships, like the *Lusitania*, were targets for German submarines. The Germans and the Turks bottled up Russia's ships. French and Italian ships, like British ships, could sail, but they were also targets for German submarines. Immigrants were rightfully concerned about being aboard ships that could be targets of naval gunfire, submarine torpedoes, or anti-ship mines in the North Sea, so relatively few came to America during World War One, even before America declared war on Germany in 1917.

Other factors held down immigration as well. Just before World War One, troops of the Balkan countries retook Macedonia and surrounding areas from the Turks, and Albania became free. Instead of fleeing frm the Turks, many people in their newly-freed homelands decided to stay put. Because of World War One, millions of young men who were soldiers and sailors – the type of people most prone to come to America – would lay dead on the battlefields and under the waves. After World War One, Germans, Balts, Poles, and Russians fought over the land that became the Baltic countries. Soldiers in these fights died – without much notice, perhaps, like the soldiers in the Balkan warfare – but they were just as dead as the dead in World War One.

Millions of civilians in Germany, Austria-Hungary, Poland, Russia, Armenia, and the Balkans also died, from the British hunger blockade, from crop destructions and seizures by whatever army happened to hold an area, and from Turkish and Communist atrocities. Many of these unfortunates would have wanted to emigrate if only they could have done so.

The net result? **From 1911 through 1920**, only about half as many Europeans came to America as came during the previous decade. Roughly 4,400,000 Europeans came to America. Of these, 144,000 came from Germany, 146,000 came from Ireland, and 341,000 came from Britain (including Scotland and Wales). Also 62,000 came from France, 44,000 came from the Netherlands, 34,000 came from Belgium, and 23,000 came from Switzerland. Also 66,000 came from Norway, 95,000 came from Sweden, and 42,000 came from Denmark.

From 1911 through 1920, about 1,110,000 came from Italy, 69,000 came from Spain, 90,000 came from Portugal, 921,000 came from the Russian Empire (many of these were Poles and Jews, and some were Ukrainians, Finns, Lithuanians, Latvians, and Estonians), 896,000 came from enemy Austria-Hungary (most of whom were Czechs, Slovaks,

Ruthenians, Slovenes, Croatians, and some Poles, Ukrainians, Serbs, and Romanians trying to escape their own emperor and his henchmen). All but 5000 of those who came from Poland who were counted as subjects of Germany, Russia, or Austria-Hungary. Also 13,000 came from independent Romania, 184,000 came from independent Greece, 23,000 came from independent Serbia, Bulgaria, and Montenegro combined, and 79,000 came from "Turkey in Asia" – almost all of these people were Lebanese, Syrians, or Armenians fleeing Turkish oppression. Also, 55,000 came from "Turkey in Europe" – almost all of these people were Bulgarians, Greeks, Serbs, Macedonians, and Albanians fleeing Turkish oppression before the victors of the Balkan Wars limited Turkey in Europe to the area around Constantinople. After the Balkan soldiers liberated their compatriots from the Turks, fewer people from the Balkans would want to flee the Turks because they were free.

From 1911 through 1920, another 742,000 came from and through Canada (mostly through instead of from), 219,000 came from Mexico, 123,000 came from the West Indies, and 59,000 came from Central and South America. About 21,000 Chinese came to America, and 2,000 came from Japan. Another 8000 came from Africa, and another 12,000 came from Australia and New Zealand.

Most of the people listed as coming from Canada were European immigrants and Asian immigrants who came to Canada and tarried a while before coming to America. People from the Indian subcontinent – then under British rule – used Canada as a way to sneak into California. British shipping companies profited from landing foreigners in Canada, where immigrants would not be unduly regulated if they intended to eventually enter the United States. Many Mexicans came to America during World War One to replace American laborers who had gone off to fight in the war.

The third decade of the 1900s was the decade when America's leaders greatly restricted immigration. During this decade, roughly four million people would come to America; a third of these came from and through Canada and from Mexico. Not quite double that amount came from Europe directly.

Even though World War One was over, there were still plenty of reasons for people to want to leave. But due to the immigration quota laws, only about half as many people came from Europe as had done so in the previous decade.

After World War One, the Poles, Czechs, Slovaks, Ruthenians, Croatians, Slovenes, Lithuanians, Latvians, Estonians, Finns, many Romanians and Serbs, and most of the Irish became free. Many people from these lands who might have emigrated if oppression at home had continued would instead try to stay at home and help build their nations.

The Russians dropped out of World War One, suffered some German and later some Allied occupation, endured a civil war, and lost a war to the Poles, all by 1921. Pro-democracy people overthrew the Czar in 1917, and later that year the Communists overthrew the democrats. The Baltic countries became free, as did Poland and Finland. Moldova joined Romania. The Communists retook Ukraine, which was briefly independent. After World War One, the Communists and their rivals fought a horrible internal war in which millions of civilians and soldiers died. The victorious Communists murdered their opponents and locked the country's borders, so immigration from Russia virtually ceased.

From 1921 through 1930, roughly 2,500,000 Europeans came to America. Of these, 412,000 came from defeated Germany, 221,000 came from mostly-independent Ireland, and 330,000 came from Britain (half of whom were Scots). Also 50,000 came from war-ravaged France, 27,000 came from the Netherlands, 16,000 came from war-ravaged Belgium, and 30,000 came from Switzerland. Also 69,000 came from Norway, 97,000 came from Sweden, 32,000 came from Denmark, and 17,000 came from newly-independent Finland.

From 1921 through 1930, about 455,000 came from Italy, 29,000 came from Spain, and 30,000 came from Portugal. From Russia and Ukraine, 61,000 came; 6000 came from newly-independent Lithuania, 3000 came from newly-independent Latvia, and 2000 came from newly-independent Estonia.

World War One killed Austria-Hungary, the "prison of nations." From the lands of the dead empire, 33,000 came from Austria, 31,000 came from Hungary, 102,000 came from newly-independent Czechoslovakia (which included Czechs, Slovaks, and Ruthenians), 49,000 came from the enlarged Yugoslavia (Serbia with Slovenes, Croatians, Montenegrins, Macedonians, and Bosniaks added). From reborn Poland came 228,000 people. Also 68,000 came from Romania (which was enlarged with Transylvania and Moldova), 51,000 came from Greece (whose own people had to give home to a million Greeks fleeing Turkey), and 3,000 came from violence-torn Bulgaria.

World War One also killed the Ottoman (Turkish) Empire. During World War One, the Turks murdered more than a million Armenians. After the war, the British and French grabbed Syria, Lebanon, Jordan, and Israel, and set up Iraq and Arabia and assorted shiekdoms on the Arabian Peninsula as independent and semi-independent states. Turkish officers patriotically overthrew the sultan when he agreed to allow the British, French, and Italians to partition Turkey itself. The Turks beat the Greeks, who were acting as Britain's stooges, and murdered many civilian Greeks living in Turkey. The Turks also went back to genociding the Armenians.

Roughly 15,000 came from "Turkey in Europe" – these people were mostly Bulgarians, Greeks and Armenians fleeing Turkish oppression, or refugees from Russia and Ukraine fleeing Communism by way of Constantinople. Another 19,000 came from "Turkey in Asia" – almost all of these people were Armenians and Greeks fleeing Turkish oppression.

From 1920 through 1930, another 925,000 came from and through Canada (mostly through instead of from), 459,000 came from Mexico, 75,000 came from the West Indies, and 58,000 came from Central and South America. About 30,000 Chinese came to America, and 33,000 came from Japan. Another 6000 came from Africa, and another 8000 came from Australia and New Zealand.

From 1820 through 1930, Europe sent more than 32 million immigrants to the United States. The rest of the world sent another 5 million. Not counted were the hundreds of thousands of blacks who were forcibly seized in Africa and shipped to America. The legal importing of slaves had ended in 1808, but some slave ships still called on American ports without punishment to the captains or the shipowners. After the external slave trade ended, truly depraved slaveowners encouraged black women to have many children, and sold them like livestock.

Most of the people listed as coming from Canada in the early 1900s were European immigrants or Asian immigrants who used Canada as a "prep school" or as a way station to America.

As for Mexico, that unhappy land was in tumult during the 1910s and 1920s. The long-time dictator Porfirio Diaz was overthrown in 1911, and rival groups clashed for almost a decade until Alvaro Obregón wound up winning the revolution in 1920. His hand-picked successor Plutarco Calles in the 1920s instituted one-party rule in Mexico and brutally persecuted the Catholic Church.

Mexico is overwhelmingly a Catholic country, but its government is by law and by practice anti-clerical to this day. This is because government leaders, bureaucrats, and other elites are anti-clerical. Depending on who enforces the law, it was and still can be illegal for priests to wear clerical garb in public, and for nuns to wear their habits (uniforms) in public. Catholic schools and hospitals face discriminatory regulations that secular schools and hospitals escape.

Many Mexicans came to America in the 1910s and 1920s to escape the tumults and persecution. Many others came to seek higher wages. **(15)**

THE ROLL CALL OF IMMIGRANTS BY BLOOD

ENGLISH, SCOTS, AND WELSH

Roughly 2,620,000 people came to America from England from 1830 to 1931. During this time, another 730,000 people came to America from Scotland, and another 90,000 came to America from Wales. Roughly 790,000 people came from Britain in this period whose records didn't specify which part of Britain they came from.

IRISH

Ireland's immigration was huge relative to her population. The impact Irish immigrants have had on America has been huge in proportion to Ireland's population. Between 1820 and 1931, roughly 4,590,000 Irish came to America. Among these were ancestors of mine.

There had to be a reason why so many people were willing to leave such a small country besides the usual desire for a better life that motivated most immigrants to come to America. Ireland ranks – along with Britain, Italy, and Germany – as one of the top four countries of Europe in sending immigrants to America. Ireland at the start of the Great Hunger in 1845 had about 8 million people. Since each of the other three countries had many times more people than Ireland, the British rulers had to be very selfish and hateful to cause so many Irish – including my own ancestors -- to leave their homeland.

GERMANS

From 1820 through 1931, roughly 5,900,000 people came from German ruled lands to America. The vast majority of these were Germans, although some were Poles (even though immigration officials tried to count the Poles separately), and some were other minorities (French and Danes) who were under German occupation. This figure does not count the Germanic peoples of Switzerland or Austria; they are counted elsewhere.

FRENCH

From 1820 through 1931, roughly 580,000 French came to America. This is a very small number compared with the number of people in France in that era. In France, there was inefficiency, yes, but the French took care of their own. The French people would not tolerate the cruelest unsafe and miserable conditions of the factories and mines that the workers of Britain and Germany had to work in. Most of the French were proud of their beautiful country and they thought they had a stake in its success. As a result, very few French left France.

ITALIANS

From 1820 through 1931, roughly 4,660,000 people came from Italy to America. Poverty drove most Italians to immigrate. For every immigrant who came from northern Italy, five came from southern Italy. The numbers may be skewed because many men came back and forth repeatedly before choosing either to stay in America or return home for good.

In 1910, the Italian government claimed Italy had lost up to 5.5 million people permanently to the Western Hemisphere. At first glance, the Italian government's numbers look a little high, but they were probably not too far off the mark. As benchmarks, Italian officials claimed Italy lost 350,000 emigrants in 1900 and 530,000 emigrants in 1910. If this is correct, Italian immigration to Argentina and Brazil and elsewhere in Latin America would have approached 250,000 in 1900 and exceeded 300,000 in 1910, for U.S. immigration officials reported 102,000 immigrants from Italy in 1900 and 223,000 immigrants from Italy in 1910.

From 1857 through 1910, at least one million Italians emigrated to Argentina. As of the 1960s, roughly 40 percent of Argentines reported having at least some Italian blood. In that era, a similar number of Italians emigrated to Brazil. But since Brazil was and is a much more populous country than Argentina, the immigration of the Italians didn't affect Brazil as greatly.

In the 1920s, American officials greatly restricted immigration to the United States. This affected Italians more than any other group of Europeans. Immediately before World War One, the largest numbers of immigrants to America came from the Russian Empire, Austria-Hungary, and Italy. After World War One, the Red slavemasters of the Soviet Union essentially forbade their subjects to leave the workers' paradise. The former Austria-Hungary after World War One broke down into several small countries with shattered economies and millions of dead. Italy still had many people willing and able to leave; most of them wound up emigrating to Argentina and Brazil.

At the end of this section is a discussion on why reported immigration figures from Italy and some other lands may be much higher than net immigration figures.

SPANISH AND PORTUGUESE

The problems of their homelands led many Spanish and Portuguese to emigrate. Most people with power (like those everywhere) believed in little more than rights and enrichment for themselves. The factions in these countries did not believe in compromise, so fighting resulted, and so did repression of those who lost — and harm to those unlucky enough to be in the way.

People from Spain had colonized much of the territory of the United States, but America would come under rule by Anglo-Saxon Americans who openly hated the Spanish. So the immigrants from Spain tended to go to Argentina and other countries in Latin America their countrymen had colonized in previous centuries instead of to the United States. Likewise, immigrants from Portugal tended to go to Brazil instead of to the United States.

Roughly 170,000 Spaniards came to the United States between 1820 and 1931. Roughly 250,000 Portuguese came to the United States in the same period.

By comparison, from 1851 through 1930, roughly four million Spaniards left Spain for the Latin American countries of the New World. And from 1851 through 1920, about 1,400,000 Portuguese came to the New World, almost exclusively to Brazil. From 1921 through 1930, perhaps another 300,000 to 400,000 Portuguese came to the New World, almost exclusively to Brazil.

These numbers may be skewed because many men came back and forth repeatedly before choosing either to stay in Latin America or return home for good.

Perhaps half of the Spaniards and Portuguese returned to their homelands when they could. Most Spanish immigrants to Latin America went to Argentina, the most European in climate and culture of Spain's former possessions. Many Spaniards emigrated to Uruguay and Portuguese-speaking Brazil also. The balance of Spaniards emigrated to Chile, Peru, Mexico, and other countries in Latin America. From 1851 through 1930, roughly one million Spaniards emigrated to Argentina and stayed. This implies at least another million Spaniards stayed in Argentina for awhile – as seasonal workers or as workers seeking to save some money by working overseas a few years – and came home. It is not unreasonable to think a similar proportion of Spaniards and Portuguese did likewise elsewhere. In fact, immigration statistics into Spain during and after World War One indicate almost as many people came into Spain as left Spain.

America's immigration figures did not tabulate Basques. Most of these people came from the Basque lands of northern Spain, and a few came from adjoining territory in southern France. Many Basque sheepherders and their families came to the Rocky Mountain states.

Another 760,000 people from Mexico, Spain's most populous former colony, came to the United States legally in that time span. From Central America and South America came another 160,000 people in this time period; virtually all of these countries had been Spanish or Portuguese possessions. And another 430,000 or so people came to the United States from the West Indies; most of these people came from islands like Cuba, Puerto Rico, and Hispaniola, all of which had been Spanish colonies. (Haiti on the western side of Hispaniola, had later been a French colony. Jamaica, a Spanish colony until the English seized it during the Cromwell dictatorship, was a British colony during the Ellis Island era.)

Of course, this does not count the few thousand Spaniards the United States gained in buying the Louisiana Purchase in 1803, or in buying Florida in 1819. Nor does it count the Spaniards and Mexicans the United States gained in admitting Texas to the Union in 1845, or the Spaniards and Mexicans the United States gained in the Mexican Cession and the Gadsden Purchase (California, Nevada, Utah, Arizona, New Mexico, much of Colorado, and some of Wyoming, Kansas, and Oklahoma). Perhaps 100,000 Spaniards and Mexicans became American citizens after the statehood of Texas and the Mexican War even though they didn't migrate to America. *America migrated to them!*

CANADIANS

British-run Canada was a source of illegal immigrants from Europe and Asia during the Ellis Island era. It was also a conduit for many Europeans who wanted to come to America who avoided the Ellis Island "experience." So of the 2,920,000 or so immigrants listed as coming from Canada from 1820 through 1931, many were not Canadians.

Some Anglo Canadians and French Canadians came to America before the Civil War. From the end of the Civil War to 1890, hundreds of thousands of French-Canadians came to America, primarily to New England and the Mid Atlantic states. The flow stalled in the 1890s, then resumed in the years before World War One and resumed again in the 1920s.

Various estimates say about 900,000 French Canadians emigrated to the United States from 1820 to 1931. Probably an equal number of Canadians with roots in Britain or Ireland emigrated to the United States during this time. This means at least 1.1 million people used Canada as a conduit or a stopover point from Europe or Asia to come to America. Most of these interlopers did so in the 1910s and the 1920s. **(16)**

DANES, NORWEGIANS, SWEDES, AND FINNS

From 1820 through 1931, roughly 330,000 people came from Denmark to America. Another 1,210,000 or so came from Sweden and a further 800,000 or so came from Norway during this period. (Immigration officials noted the difference between the Swedes and the Norwegians even though the Swedes ruled the Norwegians.) Proportionately, Norwegians were more prone to come to America than Swedes, because there were only about half as many Norwegians as Swedes. The Danes, proportionately, were the most prone to stay home of these three groups of Scandinavians.

The Russian tsars ruled the Finns from 1809 through 1917, so the numbers of Finnish immigrants are not documented as well as the numbers of other Scandinavian immigrants. From 1898 – when U.S. officials started counting them -- through 1914, about 190,000 Finns came to the United States. Before 1898, perhaps about another 20,000 Finns came to the United States. From 1915 through 1931, another 40,000 or so Finns came to the United States. This is a total of about 250,000 Finnish immigrants. Perhaps this total counts some people of Estonian blood. The language of the Estonians (and their Lutheran faith) is similar to the language of the Finns, so some immigration officials could have counted them with the Finns.

The best-known Scandinavian immigrant to the United States – a man who came to America as a child from Norway in the 1890s – gained fame in connection with his association with another ethnic group in America. His name? Knute Rockne, player and coach of the University of Notre Dame's Fighting Irish. Also during the Roaring Twenties, "Untouchable" Eliot Ness (whose parents were Norwegian immigrants), and aviator Charles Lindbergh (whose father was a Swedish immigrant and a congressman) would add color to one of America's most colorful decades.

SWISS

Between 1820 and 1931, roughly 290,000 Swiss came to America.

Among these immigrants was John Sutter of California Gold Rush fame. He fled a wife and a Swiss debtor's prison, and wound up in California in 1839. He got a land grant of 76 square miles in the Sacramento area from the Mexican government and started a ranching, wheat growing, and lumber operation.

Sutter and his men built a fort in what is present-day Sacramento, an 18-foot-high wall with cannon towers that enclosed a 150 foot by 500 foot area. "Sutter's Fort," besides giving good protection to his workers, served as their home, storehouse, blacksmith shop, and tannery. Sutter's men rescued what was left of the Donner Party, the people who resorted to cannibalism to stay alive when they got trapped in the snows of the Sierra Nevada range.

Fame doesn't always mean fortune. Sutter lost everything when gold was discovered on his land. His workers left to search for gold and thousands of prospectors and others ran him off of his land. He died in poverty.

I mention Sutter here because most Swiss didn't make the splash he made. Sutter greatly helped the development of America. Sutter bought out the Russians who had colonized land north of San Francisco and acquired their cannons in the transaction. He and his men ran British Hudson Bay Company trappers out of Northern California. They thus played a role in keeping the ever greedy British from stealing California as a colony. For this act Sutter and his men deserve America's eternal gratitude.

DUTCH AND BELGIANS

Between 1830 and 1931, roughly 250,000 Dutch came to America to farm and to work in the cities. Of course, there were those Dutch who came to New York in the 1600s when their flag flew over the New York City area and the Hudson Valley. The Dutch had a long history of making good in America. Three presidents (Van Buren and both Roosevelts, all native New Yorkers) had Dutch ancestry.

Only about 150,000 people from Belgium came to America. There was more land for farming in Belgium, and there were more manufacturing jobs available. However, among the immigrants Belgium sent to America was Father Pierre De Smet, who evangelized American Indians, built schools for them, and pushed (unsuccessfully) for decent treatment for them. Another was Father Joseph De Veuster aka Father Damien, the saint and martyr to leprosy who aided the lepers in the Hawaiian Islands. Like their country's exports of cut diamonds, these immigrants were few in number but very valuable to the people they served.

JEWS

From 1898 – when U.S. officials started counting them -- through 1931, roughly 1,910,000 people they called "Hebrews" came to the United States. Without question, the motivator for most of the Jewish immigrants was flight from oppression.

Of these immigrants, about 1,550,000 Jews came before the end of 1918. Roughly a million of these Jews came from the Russian Empire (mostly from central and eastern Poland, Galicia, elsewhere in Ukraine,

Belarusia, and Lithuania) from 1898 through 1914; another 400,000 came from Austria-Hungary (mostly from Galicia and southern Poland) from 1898 through 1914. The remainder came from Germany and western Poland (which the Germans held), Romania, or other countries before World War One, or came during World War One.

From 1919 through 1931, about 360,000 "Hebrews" came to the United States from Russia, Eastern Europe, Germany, and elsewhere in Europe.

From 1871 (when the first immigrants from Eastern Europe came in quantity) through 1898, about 600,000 people came from Russia, and about 840,000 people came from Austria-Hungary. Also about 160,000 others came from Poland during this time who were not counted as subjects of Germany, Russia, or Austria-Hungary; maybe 40,000 of these people were Jews. And about 10,000 people, mostly Jews, came from independent Romania. Maybe 650,000 of these 1.6 million people were Jews – roughly 500,000 of these were from Russia. Also, from 1871 through 1898, roughly 2.6 million people came from Germany (which owned part of Poland); maybe another 100,000 to 150,000 of these people were Jews. This is a total of about 2,510,000 to 2,560,000 Jews.

The estimates of the numbers of Jews points to problems in estimating the number of immigrants from Eastern Europe and Russia – political instability and divided homelands. There were three large empires in Eastern Europe in the 1800s – Austria-Hungary, Russia, and the Ottoman Empire. Poland was occupied by Russian, Austro-Hungarian, and German troops. The Ottomans held Bulgaria, Greece, Serbia, Montenegro, Albania, and most of Romania at the start of the 1800s. By the start of World War One, all of these peoples would be free of the Turks. But many Romanians were still subjects of Austria-Hungary or Russia. The Turks also held many Armenians and the Lebanese, the Syrians, the peoples of present-day Iraq, the Holy Land, and much of present-day Saudi Arabia. Besides more than half of Poland, the Russian tsars also held Ukraine, some of Armenia, Georgia, Finland, Estonia, Latvia, Lithuania, and present-day Belarusia and Moldova. Franz Josef, the emperor of Austria-Hungary from the end of our Mexican War (1848) until just before we entered World War One (1916) ruled the Austrians, the Hungarians, the Czechs, the Slovaks, the Ruthenians, many Poles, some Ukrainians, many Romanians, some Serbs, the Croatians, the Slovenes, and the people of Bosnia and Herzegovina. He also was the emperor over some Italians. So if the following estimates of peoples seem uneven, this is why.

American immigration officials kept statistics on immigrants by country of residence since 1820 but did not keep statistics by nationality until 1898. Also, immigrant groups tend to inflate the number of their people who came to America. Therefore, the statistics I report on the various peoples who came to America from the lands of Eastern Europe and Russia are estimates on my part, using immigration statistics and other sources.

POLES

From 1898 – when U.S. officials started counting them as ethnic Poles -- through 1914, about 1,400,000 Poles came to the United States. From 1915 through 1931, another 110,000 or so Poles came to the United States. (This includes 85,000 Poles who left the reborn state of Poland for the United States from the end of World War One through 1931. According to the records, 230,000 people came to America from the resurrected Polish state from 1919 through 1931; the other 145,000 or so who left for America were Lithuanians, Ukrainians, Russians and Belarusians, or Jews.)

Before 1898, maybe about 160,000 or so people from the Polish provinces of the German, Austrian, and Russian empires came to the United States. Possibly a quarter of these 160,000 people were Jews living in Poland, and the other 120,000 or more were Poles. Adding these people to the other Poles counted yields a total of about 1,630,000 Polish immigrants.

Of these Polish immigrants, perhaps two-thirds (a million or so people) who came before World War One were from the portion of Poland (Mazovia – the area of central and eastern Poland around Warsaw and Lodz, and Masuria – northeastern Poland) under the rule of the Russian Empire. Perhaps a quarter (400,000 or so people) were from the portion of Poland (western Galicia and Malopolska –the area of southern Poland around Krakow) under the rule of Austria-Hungary. The remainder were Poles from the portions of Poland (Silesia, Pomerania, Wielkopolska) under German rule.

How dissatisfied were the Poles? Despite there being about four Russians for every Pole in the Ellis Island era, Poles provided six times as many immigrants of Slavic blood to the United States as the Russians themselves did. The Poles had more mobility, and more dissatisfaction than the Russians had. (They had three foreign occupier regimes to hate – Prussia's and Austria's as well as Russia's.) They also had the connection with America ideals – their officers helped Americans gain independence, and Kosciuszko in 1794 had tried to bring America's ideals to the fight for liberation to Poland.

RUSSIAN EMPIRE AND SOVIET UNION

Roughly 3,340,000 immigrants came to America from the Russian Empire and the Soviet Union from 1820 through 1931. Besides Russians, this tally also includes Finns and Estonians, Lithuanians and Latvians, some Poles, some Ukrainians, and Belarusians, and a few Romanians, Moldovans, Armenians, and Georgians. It also includes a huge number of Jews.

The Jews and Poles were the people most likely to leave the Russian Empire. The Lithuanians and Finns, proportionately, were similarly dissatisfied. Then came the Ukrainians and Ruthenians. Of all the non-Russian groups who immigrated in large numbers, the Jews suffered most of all in Tsarist Russia, then the Poles and the Lithuanians. The Finns and Ukrainians and Ruthenians suffered less than the Poles and the Lithuanians, but their lives were still hard in their homelands. The pattern was the same in all cases – these people lived on Russia's western edges, they were non-Russian in blood, and they were tired of suffering at the hands of those who ran the Russian Empire.

Those who opted to come to America would escape World War One and/or the Russian Civil War and seven decades of brutal Communist repression. Those who hesitated lost.

Before 1871, fewer than 4000 people came to America from Russia. American officials brought America to about 400 Russians when they bought Alaska from the Russian government in 1867.

From 1871 (when the first immigrants from Eastern Europe came in quantity) through 1898, about 600,000 people came from the Russian Empire. The vast majority of these immigrants were Jews and Poles instead of ethnic Russians.

From 1820 to 1898, about 160,000 Poles came who were counted independent of the three empires which divided Poland; many of these people lived in what was the Russian Empire.

Leaders of the Soviet Union did not prevent 62,000 people from leaving the "workers' paradise" and coming to America from 1921 through 1931. Only about half of these "malcontents" were ethnic Russians. The balance were mostly Jews and Ukrainians.

From the end of World War One to 1931, another 18,000 or so people came from the new Finland, 2000 people came from the new Estonia, 4000 people came from the new Latvia, and 6000 people came from the new Lithuania. All of these people lived in land that had been part of the Russian Empire. Sadly for the people of Lithuania, Latvia, and Estonia, they would enjoy only two decades of freedom. Then they would suffer Soviet and Nazi occupation during World War Two, then they would endure almost five more decades of Soviet slavery until they won their freedom in 1991.

From 1898 through 1914, about 220,000 people who immigration officials called "Russians" came to the United States. Before 1898, hardly any ethnic Russians came to the United States. From 1915 through 1931, another 50,000 or so "Russians" came to the United States. This is a total of about 270,000 immigrants who were Russians and who the immigration officials counted as Russians.

There was no major distinction between the people of Belarusia and Old Russia before the Communist Revolution. (Some Belarusians were Catholics, but most were Orthodox Christians, like the Russians.) Belarusia has had the sad distinction of being the Belgium of Eastern Europe ... several European armies have come through the land to attack Moscow. Likewise, Russian and Soviet armies have used Belarusia as an invasion route to Poland and Germany. The Reds made Belarusia a "people's republic" within the Soviet Union after they seized power. Belarusia became free in the early 1990s and is now known as Belarus, but its retread Communist leaders have kept the new nation in virtual lockstep with Russia. Some people counted as ethnic Russians in the United States are of Belarusian heritage.

Before 1898, perhaps 20,000 people who immigration officials called "Lithuanians" came to America. From 1898 through 1914, about 250,000 people they called "Lithuanians" came to the United States. (Perhaps 20,000 of these people were Latvians; immigration people counted Latvians with the Lithuanians.) From 1915 through 1931, another 13,000 or so "Lithuanians" came to the United States, including 6000 people who came from the new Lithuanian state from 1921 through 1931. Another 4000 people came from the new Latvian state to the United States from 1921 through 1931. This is a total of about 290,000 immigrants from these two Baltic nations; the vast majority of these were Lithuanians.

Virtually all Lithuanians who emigrated left the Russian Empire. (The Germans held Klaipeda (Memel) and the surrounding area until the end of World War One; some Lithuanians came from this area. A few came from Vilnius (aka Wilno or Vilna) and the surrounding countryside after Polish troops took this land – which had large numbers of Poles also -- from Lithuania after World War One.) The Russian leaders had targeted Lithuanians as rebels and as allies of Poland – and as Catholics. (Most Latvians were less rebellious and were Lutherans; their ancestors had converted when Prussian Germans and the Swedes controlled them.)

A small number of Armenians (some of whom were under Russian or Soviet rule until the 1990s) and

Georgians (who were also under Russian or Soviet rule until the 1990s) came to America. Most Armenians who came to America were under Turkish rule; that's why they fled. Besides the Nazis, the Turks had the only government in Europe that made the Russian Empire and the Soviet Empire look somewhat benevolent to ethnic and religious minorities.

Finnish and Estonian immigration is covered with the other Scandinavians. Jewish and Polish immigration is covered previously as well.

UKRAINIANS AND RUTHENIANS

Before 1898, maybe about 5000 or so people who immigration officials called "Ruthenians" came to the United States. (By this name, they meant Ukrainians as well as the Ruthenians tucked up in Ruthenia in the Carpathian Mountains.) From 1898 through 1914, about 255,000 "Ruthenians" came to the United States. From 1915 through 1931, another 15,000 or so "Ruthenians" came to the United States. This is a total of about 275,000 Ruthenian and Ukrainian immigrants.

Of these Ruthenian and Ukrainian immigrants, perhaps 80,000 to 100,000 were Ukrainians from the portion of Ukraine under Russian rule. Perhaps another 30,000 to 50,000 were Ukrainians from the portion of Ukraine (eastern Galicia) under the rule of Austria-Hungary. Perhaps 130,000 to 150,000 people were Ruthenians from their impoverished Carpathian homeland.

Ukraine was briefly independent from early 1918 through the Russian Civil War. The Ukrainians suffered genocidal rule from Soviet commissars until World War Two. The Communists essentially murdered five million to seven million Ukrainians by confiscating their food and starving them during the winter of 1932-1933. The Communists were so hateful to the Ukrainians that many Ukrainian men fought in World War Two on the side of the Germans, and many others fought against the armies of both totalitarian regimes. During World War Two, the Nazis as well as the Communists oppressed the Ukrainian people in some of the most hideous ways imaginable. The Soviets resumed their monopoly of slavery over Ukraine after World War Two and remained as masters of Ukraine until the breakup of the Soviet Union in 1991.

THE FORMER HAPSBURG EMPIRE

Roughly four million immigrants came to America from the Hapsburg Empire (also known as Austria-Hungary) from 1820 to 1914. This includes Slovenians and Croatians, Czechs and Slovaks, some Poles, some Ukrainians, Ruthenians, Bukovinans, some Romanians, some Serbs, some Hercegovinans, and some Bosniaks. (A "Bosniak" is a Bosnian who is

Moslem. Bosnians who are Christians usually count themselves as Croatians or Serbs.) This also includes a large number of Jews. Another 25,000 or so subjects of Austria-Hungary managed to gain entry to America during the four years of World War One.

From 1820 to 1898, about 160,000 people from Poland came who were counted independent of the three empires which divided Poland; some of these people lived in what was Austria-Hungary.

From the end of World War One to 1931, another 110,000 or so people came from the new Czechoslovakia, about 230,000 came from the reborn Poland, 50,000 or so came from the new Yugoslavia, and about 70,000 came from the enlarged Romania. All of the Czechs and Slovaks, some of the Poles, about half of the people in the new Yugoslavia, and some of the people coming from Romania lived in land that had been part of Austria-Hungary. Also, about 65,000 people came from the new ethnic but vastly smaller states of Austria and Hungary. This tallies to about 250,000 to 300,000 people.

HUNGARIANS

Before 1898, perhaps 150,000 to 200,000 Hungarians came to the United States. From 1898 through 1914, about 460,000 people who immigration officials called "Magyars" came to the United States. From 1915 through 1931, another 40,000 or so "Magyars" came to the United States. This is a total of about 650,000 to 700,000 Hungarian immigrants.

CZECHS AND SLOVAKS

Before 1898, perhaps 150,000 to 200,000 Czechs came to America. Among these were ancestors of mine. From 1898 through 1914, about 140,000 people who immigration officials called "Bohemians and Moravians" came to the United States. From 1915 through 1931, another 30,000 or so "Bohemians and Moravians" came to the United States. This is a total of about 320,000 to 370,000 Czech immigrants.

About as many of the earlier Czechs were Protestants and "free-thinkers" (agnostics) as were Catholics. The Czechs tended to come to America much earlier than most of the rest of the minorities of Austria-Hungary. Half of the Czechs took to farming in the Midwest and in Texas; most of the rest of the minorities of Austria-Hungary tended to work in mines in the countryside or work in factories in the cities.

Before 1898, perhaps about 50,000 Slovaks came to the United States. From 1898 through 1914, about 480,000 Slovaks came to the United States. Among these were my wife's ancestors. From 1915 through 1931, another

70,000 or so Slovaks came to the United States. This is a total of about 600,000 Slovak immigrants.

CROATIANS AND SLOVENES, BOSNIANS AND HERCEGOVINANS

Before 1898, perhaps 50,000 Croatians and Slovenians came to the United States. (Immigration officials didn't count people of the two groups separately.) From 1898 through 1914, about 460,000 Croatians and Slovenians came to the United States. From 1915 through 1931, another 30,000 or so Croatians and Slovenians came to the United States. One of these was the father of a former girlfriend of mine. This is a total of about 540,000 Croatian and Slovenian immigrants. Austria-Hungary's rulers ruled these lands until the end of World War One.

This doesn't count Croatians bundled with the roughly 50,000 "Dalmatian, Bosnian, and Herzegovinan" immigrants recorded from 1898 through 1914. Some of these people were Croatians. Austria-Hungary held Dalmatia – Croatia's seacoast – from after the Napoleonic Wars to the end of World War One. Austria-Hungary's leaders sent troops to occupy Bosnia and Hercegovina in 1878 (the Turks had run these areas), and annexed them in 1908. The Hapsburgs would hold these lands until the end of World War One. Virtually all the "Dalmatian, Bosnian, and Herzegovinan" immigrants came from 1898 through 1914. Hardly anyone from these lands came to America before 1898. From 1915 through 1931, another 3000 or so "Dalmatian, Bosnian, and Herzegovinan" immigrants came to the United States. These lands would become part of Yugoslavia -- along with the rest of Croatia, Slovenia, Vojvodina, Serbia, Montenegro, and most of Macedonia -- after World War One. Perhaps 25,000 to 30,000 of these immigrants were Catholic South Slavs, most of whom could count as Croatians, for an overall total of at least 560,000 Croatians and Slovenes.

SERBS, MONTENEGRINS, MACEDONIANS, AND BULGARIANS

From 1898 through 1914, about 145,000 "Bulgarians, Serbs and Montenegrins" came to the United States. Before 1898, hardly any "Bulgarians, Serbs and Montenegrins" came to the United States. From 1915 through 1931, another 25,000 or so "Bulgarians, Serbs and Montenegrins" came to the United States. This is a total of about 170,000 Serb, Montenegrin and Bulgarian immigrants. (This includes Macedonian immigrants, who spoke a language similar to Serbs and Bulgarians, and lived in territory that mostly went to Serbia and later Yugoslavia. Immigration officials did not count Macedonians as a separate ethnic group.)

Since there were about 16 immigrants from Yugoslavia for every immigrant from Bulgaria from 1921 through 1931 (most of these years were "quota years" in which immigrants were admitted to America based on a percentage already in the country), and since Serbs, Macedonians, and Montenegrins made up a little more than half the people of postwar Yugoslavia (and a little less than half the immigrants from the new Yugoslavia to America in this time), I estimate about 150,000 of these immigrants were of Serb, Montenegrin, or Macedonian blood, and about 20,000 were of Bulgarian blood.

Unfortunately, immigration officials lumped the immigration figures from the three kingdoms together. From 1898 through 1918, roughly 60,000 Serbs and Montenegrins and Bulgarians immigrated from territory their respective kingdoms controlled, and another 90,000 or so Serbs and Montenegrins and Bulgarians immigrated from Balkan territory controlled by the Turks before World War One, or from Balkan territory controlled by Austria-Hungary before World War One. Of these 90,000, I estimate more than half were Serbs from Vojvodina or Bosnia, areas which were under the rule of Austria-Hungary until the end of World War One, and fewer than half were Serbs or Bulgarians from areas which were under the rule of the Turks. The ruler of Serbia didn't gain control of Macedonia or Kosovo, or areas of southern Serbia from the Turks until after the First Balkan War in 1913. Likewise, the ruler of Montenegro gained some South Slav land in 1913 that up to that time had been under the rule of the Turks. The ruler of Bulgaria gained Eastern Rumelia from the Turks in 1885, and some of Macedonia and Thrace from the Turks after the First Balkan War in 1913. The Bulgarians lost coastal western Thrace to Greece after World War One.

This doesn't include Serbs and Montenegrins bundled with the 53,000 or so "Dalmatian, Bosnian, and Herzegovinan" immigrants recorded from 1898 through 1931. Perhaps 10,000 to 15,000 of these immigrants were Orthodox South Slavs, most of whom could count as Serbs or Montenegrins, for an overall total of at least 160,000 Serbs and Montenegrins.

GERMANS OF AUSTRIA-HUNGARY

What about the Austrians and the other Germans who were dominant in Austria-Hungary? So what about them, American immigration officials responded.

American immigration officials didn't consider Germans from Austria-Hungary (the Austrians, Sudeten Germans of Bohemia and Moravia, and other Germans in places like Slovakia and Hungary and Transylvania and Bukovina) to be a separate nationality from Germans from the "Fatherland" (the German Empire).

Subtracting the people who emigrated from Austria-Hungary who were not German from the total number of people American officials noted were from Austria-Hungary gives a rough estimate of Austrians and other Germans who emigrated from the Hapsburg Empire. From 1871 through 1890, about 100,000 to 150,000 Austrians and other Germans from the empire came to the United States. From 1891 through 1900, about 150,000 to 200,000 Austrians and other Germans from the empire came to the United States. From 1901 through 1910, about 300,000 to 350,000 Austrians and other Germans from the empire came to the United States. From 1911 through 1918, about 100,000 Austrians and other Germans from the empire came to the United States. From 1918 through 1931, about 30,000 people came from Austria to the United States. In all, maybe around 680,000 to 830,000 Austrians and other Germans from the Hapsburg Empire came to the United States.

THE FORMER OTTOMAN EMPIRE

Very few people from the Balkans were able to come to America. They were too poor, and free to move much too late in comparison with other people in Europe, thanks to the Turks.

From 1881 to 1931, roughly 360,000 people escaped the Ottoman Empire and Turkey and came to the United States. (Hardly anyone came to America from the Ottoman Empire before 1881.) Of these, 155,000 escaped "Turkey in Europe" (the Balkans) and 205,000 escaped "Turkey in Asia" (basically Turkey, Armenia, Syria, and Lebanon).

From the end of World War One to 1931, about 40,000 people came from the severely shrunken Turkey. After the war, Turkey would consist of the Anatolian Peninsula in Asia and Constantinople and the bit of land surrounding it in Europe. About 24,000 of these people came from "Turkey in Asia" – mostly Armenians and Greeks, and another 17,000 of these people came from "Turkey in Europe" – again, mostly Greeks and Armenians.

Lebanon and Syria were under French control after World War One. About 13,000 people left these lands to come to America.

From the end of World War One to 1931, another 55,000 or so people came from Greece, about 4000 came from Bulgaria, about 2000 came from the new Albania, and 50,000 or so came from the new Yugoslavia. In the years before World War One, the villages of many of these people had been under Turkish misrule.

Speaking of the Turks, only 23,000 of them came to America from 1898 to 1931.

GREEKS

Before 1898, about 12,000 Greeks, virtually all from the kingdom of Greece, came to the United States. From 1898 through 1914, about 370,000 Greeks came to the United States. Of these, about 280,000 came from the kingdom of Greece, and most of the rest came from Turkish-occupied land. From 1915 through 1931, another 145,000 or so Greeks came to the United States. Of these, about 115,000 came from the kingdom of Greece, and most of the rest came from Turkish-occupied land.

This is a total of about 530,000 Greek immigrants. Of these, about 410,000 came from the kingdom of Greece and most of the other 120,000 came from Turkish-occupied land. The Turks ruled Epirus (northwestern Greece), most of Thessaly (central and northern Greece), Salonika (Thessalonika) and the surrounding area of southern Macedonia, Thrace (from Salonika to Constantinople), and Crete (nominally), all areas (except Thrace and the city of Salonika itself) overwhelmingly Greek, until after the First Balkan War in 1913. Many Greeks also lived in Constantinople (Istanbul), and Smyrna (Izmir) and other port towns of western Turkey until the Greek government brought the remaining one million or so ethnic Greeks in Turkey to Greece in the 1920s to protect them from retaliatory slaughter by the Turks in the wake of the Greeks' suicidal invasion of Turkey after World War One.

ROMANIANS, BUKOVINANS, AND MOLDOVANS

Romanians were totally independent of the Turks (but not of the Hapsburgs or the Romanovs) when their period of immigration to America really began. In all, about 150,000 Romanian immigrants came to America from 1898 through 1931.

Before 1898, about 10,000 people, mostly Jews, came to America from the kingdom of Romania. Another 10,000 or so people, mostly Jews, came to America from Romania in 1899 and 1900. Hardly any Romanians came to America during that time.

From 1898 through 1914, about 130,000 Romanians — including some from Bukovina -- came to the United States. (Bukovina is tucked into the Carpathian Mountains just east of Ruthenia. Today Bukovina is divided between Romania and Ukraine.) Of these, about 65,000 came from the kingdom of Romania and most of the remaining 65,000 or so came from Transylvania and Bukovina, areas which were under the rule of Austria-Hungary. A small number of Romanians came from Bessarabia (present-day Moldova) which was under Russian rule until 1918, and then was part of Romania until the Russians reseized it in 1940. Since the early 1990s, Moldova has been independent.

From 1915 through 1931, another 20,000 or so Romanians came to the United States. Of these, fewer than 5000 – mostly from outside of the kingdom of Romania – fled during World War One. From 1919 through 1931, about 70,000 people came from the expanded kingdom of Romania, which now also had Transylvania, Bukovina, Bessarabia (present-day Moldova), and southern Dobrujda (a Bulgarian-populated area between the Danube River and the Black Sea that Romania would hold until 1940), besides Wallachia and Moldavia. However, only about 15,000 of these were Romanians. The other 55,000 or so were of Hungarian, Jewish, Ukrainian, or Russian blood.

ALBANIANS

American immigration officials did not count Albanians as a separate ethnic group before the end of World War One. They didn't have to. The mostly Moslem Albanians weren't breaking down doors and gates at Ellis Island. Only about 2000 Albanians came to America from the end of World War One to 1931. Many of these immigrants were Catholics and Orthodox Christians.

ARMENIANS

From 1898 through 1914, about 55,000 Armenians came to the United States. Before 1898, hardly any Armenians came to the United States. From 1915 through 1931, another 30,000 Armenians came to the United States. This is a total of about 85,000 Armenian immigrants. A large number of Armenians lived across the border in the part of Armenia in the Russian Empire, and later the Soviet Union, but hardly any of these Armenians fled their homeland to come to America. Many more Armenians could have come to America if the Turks hadn't murdered so many of them.

LEBANESE AND "SYRIANS"

From 1898 through 1914, about 90,000 people who immigration officials called "Syrians" came to the United States. These were mostly Christian Lebanese and Syrians and Assyrians. Before 1898, hardly any Lebanese or Syrians or Assyrians came to America. From 1915 through 1931, another 20,000 or so "Syrians" came to the United States. This is a total of about 110,000 Lebanese and Syrian and Assyrian immigrants. **(17)**

NET IMMIGRATION (IMMIGRANTS ALLOWED IN MINUS IMMIGRANTS WHO RETURNED HOME)

American immigration officials for many years did not keep track of the number of people who emigrated from America. But the number of people who came to America and then went back to Europe was large.

From 1892 through 1900 – the first nine years Ellis Island was open – roughly 1.9 million males and 1.2 million females emigrated to the United States. From 1901 through 1910, roughly 6.1 million males and 2.7 million females emigrated to the United States. From 1911 through 1920, roughly 3.6 million males and 2.1 million females emigrated to the United States. From 1921 through 1930, roughly 2.3 million males and 1.8 million females emigrated to the United States. These figures include boys and girls as well as men and women. From 1892 through 1930, 6.1 million more males emigrated to America than females; the great majority of the extra males were adults.

Many men and some women went back to their homelands, and many came back to America a second time or more. My wife's Slovak grandmother and my own Irish great-grandmother were two of these many people. Since they already had legal status in America, they were probably counted as travelers instead of departures. Most of those who came to America – except in the first decade or so of the 1900s – did it once and stayed.

Since American women tended to marry American men, the immigrant males had to marry immigrant females in America or in the home country. Of course, not all men and women married ... among the immigrants were groups of priests and nuns whose vows forbade this. Likewise, there were those who chose not to marry, and there were those who couldn't find someone who would have them. And there were many women from time immemorial to almost the present day who never married because they sacrificed their lives to care for parents or relatives. But the math says in the busiest Ellis Island era years there was a surplus of 6.1 million male immigrants. Not all that many wound up living without female companionship for life.

Even with all the deaths working immigrants suffered in industrial accidents and suffered as crime victims, they come nowhere near filling the disparity in numbers between males and females who came to America. *Most of these "extra" men obviously came to America to work for a few years, and then returned to their home countries with their savings.*

Italian males were particularly prone to do this. Many Italians sent money home to help their families. Several records of returns indicate there were far more Italian male immigrants than female immigrants, and more

Italian male returners than men of any other ethnic groups in the Ellis Island era. Some estimates say more than 50% of Italian men who came here returned to Italy, or made more than one immigration here before staying for good. Fewer Spaniards and Portuguese came to the United States, but their percentages were probably similar, based on how many of them went back and forth between Iberia and Latin America.

These sources also indicate 30% or so of Slav and other Eastern European men who came here returned home, or made more than one trip here before staying for good. Many men from places like Poland, Slovakia, Croatia, Hungary, and Greece also returned to their homelands in very high numbers after earning enough money for their plans.

Jews were the least likely to return to Europe, because most of them were fleeing oppression. They had nothing to return to. The Irish were almost as prone as the Jews to be "one and done" in terms of numbers of trips across the Atlantic Ocean as immigrants. Some estimates say about 2% of Jews and about 5% of Irish returned to Europe for good. Also the ratio of women to men was about 1 to 1 for these groups, which indicates family flight and also flight for single adults of both sexes. The Irish, like the Jews, were victims of oppression where they came from.

People from Western Europe (Britain, the Low Countries, Switzerland, Germany, France) and from Scandinavia (Denmark, Norway, Sweden, Finland) were in between these two extremes. Estimates say between 10% and 20% of these people returned to Europe for good or made multiple immigrations.

There are no thorough statistics from the Ellis Island era on immigrant departures because American officials didn't start keeping them until late in the first decade of the 1900s. Before the advent of reliable steamship travel and cheap steerage tickets, there was little returning. World War One and the later quotas and finally the Great Depression put an end to wholesale temporary immigration for work in the Ellis Island era. Estimates indicate about four million Europeans went home for good in the Ellis Island era. This does not count the roughly 160,000 people who American authorities deported for various violations of the law they committed. Nor does it count the 400,000 or so people American authorities barred from entering the country as immigrants. **(18)**

A likely alternative figure is perhaps nine million of the 37 million or so immigrants (32 million from Europe, and 5 million from elsewhere in the world) returned to their homelands. This comes from subtracting the 6 million extra males (most were suspected temporary immigrants) from the 37 million gross immigration figure to get 31 million people, then estimating perhaps 10 percent of all other immigrants returned to their homelands. This much higher estimate still means 28 million people came here for good from 1820 through 1930 – including my ancestors and my wife's ancestors, and many of your ancestors as well.

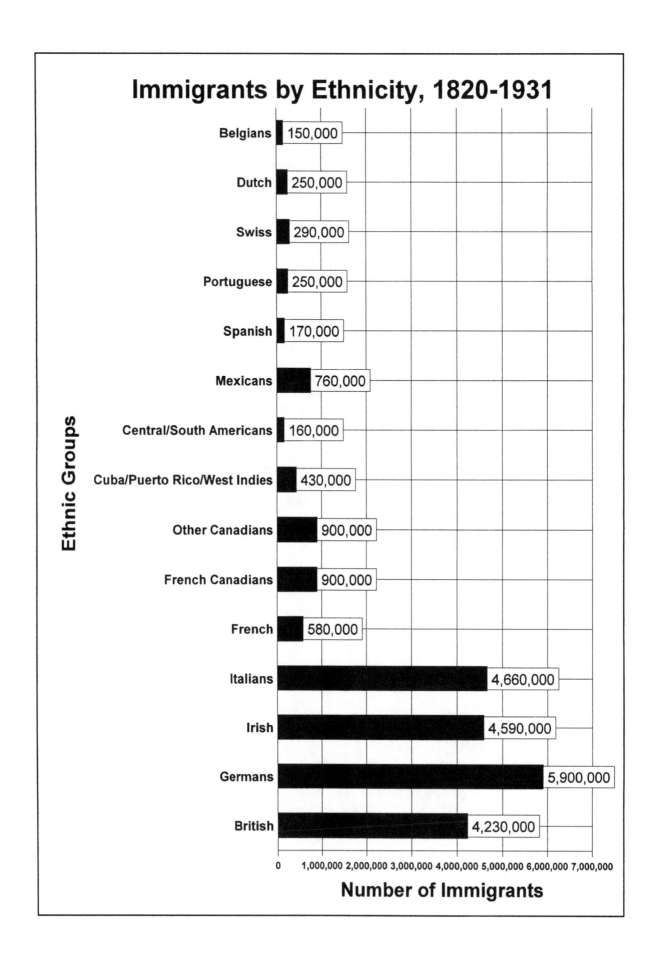

Immigrants by Ethnicity, 1820-1931

Ethnic Groups

- Belgians: 150,000
- Dutch: 250,000
- Swiss: 290,000
- Portuguese: 250,000
- Spanish: 170,000
- Mexicans: 760,000
- Central/South Americans: 160,000
- Cuba/Puerto Rico/West Indies: 430,000
- Other Canadians: 900,000
- French Canadians: 900,000
- French: 580,000
- Italians: 4,660,000
- Irish: 4,590,000
- Germans: 5,900,000
- British: 4,230,000

0   1,000,000 2,000,000 3,000,000 4,000,000 5,000,000 6,000,000 7,000,000

Number of Immigrants

MANIFEST DESTINY, MAGNIFICENT DESTINATION

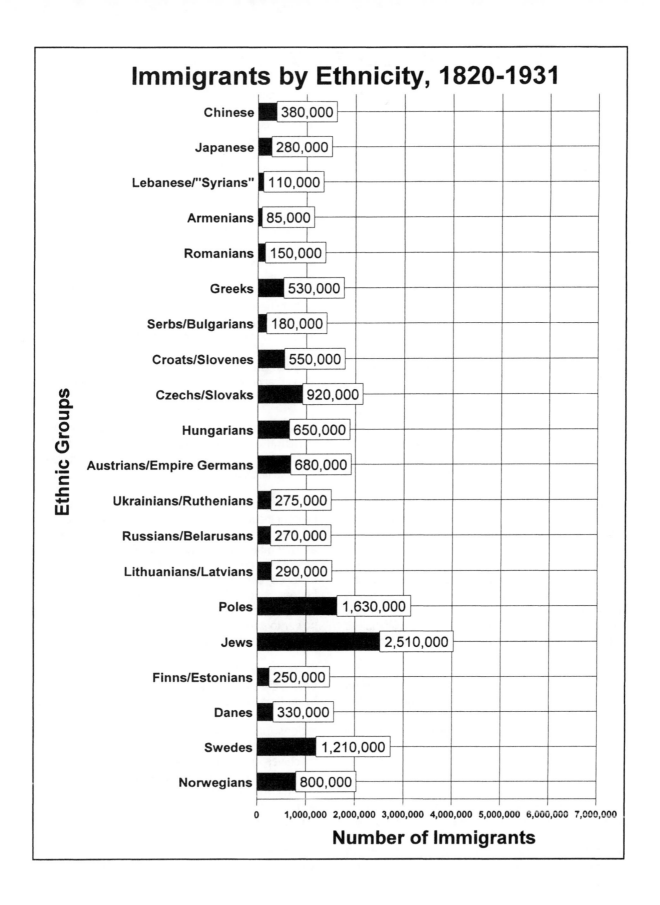

Immigrants by Ethnicity, 1820-1931

Ethnic Groups

Ethnic Group	Number
Chinese	380,000
Japanese	280,000
Lebanese/"Syrians"	110,000
Armenians	85,000
Romanians	150,000
Greeks	530,000
Serbs/Bulgarians	180,000
Croats/Slovenes	550,000
Czechs/Slovaks	920,000
Hungarians	650,000
Austrians/Empire Germans	680,000
Ukrainians/Ruthenians	275,000
Russians/Belarusans	270,000
Lithuanians/Latvians	290,000
Poles	1,630,000
Jews	2,510,000
Finns/Estonians	250,000
Danes	330,000
Swedes	1,210,000
Norwegians	800,000

Number of Immigrants

WHY AMERICA WAS ABLE TO TAKE IN THE IMMIGRANTS

America took in the immigrants because there was plenty of land, and there was plenty of work for the immigrants and everyone else to do.

The Spaniards introduced Spanish-style ranching (men on horses controlling large free-ranging herds of livestock to get the most dollar value out of rangeland that was of poor quality) to the areas that would become present-day California and Texas. They also introduced farming, irrigation, winemaking, mining, schooling, and skilled trades to these areas. The Spanish also taught these skills to American Indians who would learn them. This would "civilize" the areas the Spanish colonized and make the lands easier for Americans to use once they seized them during and after the Mexican War.

The Industrial Revolution had started in England, but people in the Northeastern and Midwestern states would push it much faster.

In the late 1700s, English immigrant Samuel Slater brought the know-how on how to build cotton thread spinning machines to America. At roughly the same time, Eli Whitney invented the cotton "gin," which made cotton a feasible cash crop in America for those who had enough land to plant the crop and enough slaves to pick it. Whitney also hit upon the idea of interchangeable parts to provide muskets on contract to the American government when John Adams was president. *(Despite his brainstorm, he was late in delivering the firearms. This was possibly the first American defense contract overrun.)* Whitney's first idea would make cotton an inexpensive cloth but retard the progress of the Industrial Revolution in the Southern states and lead indirectly to the Civil War. His second idea would make the success of the Industrial Revolution possible.

The power loom made commercial clothmaking feasible. Fabric mills sprung up in New England in the early 1800s using cheap waterpower and cheap farmgirl labor. Eventually steam engines would replace waterpower. Eventually many fabric making companies moved their mills south, where cheaper Southern labor would replace New England labor.

The first practical steam engine was the work of Scotsman James Watt in the late 1700s. In the early 1800s American Oliver Evans developed a steam engine that could power factory machinery. The rise of the steam engine, which engineers and mechanics improved upon all through the 1800s, meant factories didn't have to depend on water power. They could burn coal, wood, or oil and make steam power to weave cloth, mill grain, saw timber, or do other tasks wherever men decided to install them.

The steam engine also made faster travel possible. In the very early 1800s, American Robert Fulton built a feasible commercial steamboat, and soon American state governors and private companies were having canals built to move goods by water. The country needed laborers to dig these canals, and workers to build the boats to travel them.

Britishers invented the steam locomotive and railroads. But Americans laid down many more miles of track to connect their cities. They needed to, for America was a much bigger country ... the island of Britain is only about the size of Minnesota, or smaller than New York, New Jersey, and Pennsylvania put together. The country needed laborers to lay the rails, mine the coal that fed the locomotives, and make the steel that made the locomotives and rails possible.

Shipbuilders would combine steel and steam to build ships that could carry cargos and passengers quicker and safer than wooden ships.

Railroads and ships needed lots of steel. American William Kelly in the late 1840s and Briton Henry Bessemer in the 1850s developed pneumatic converters to make large batches of high-quality steel cheaply.

Iron works and steel mills sprung up in Pennsylvania to be near the supply of high-quality coal that steelmaking required. (It takes much more coal as fuel than iron ore as raw material to make steel.) Railroads and ships brought the coal and the iron ore to the steel mills, and factories rose to build locomotives, rails, rolling stock, bridges, ship hull steel, and steamship parts. Steam-driven pumps kept many coal mines dry and provided power to perform many tasks in these mines, making it easier and cheaper to mine coal.

In the 1840s, John Deere built a steel plow factory in Illinois; the steel plows helped farmers bust prairie sod better than they could with a wooden or cast iron plow. At about the same time, Cyrus McCormick built a factory for horse-pulled reapers in Chicago. This invention cut grain-harvesting time. Threshing machines and mowing machines would follow. These devices made it possible for farmers to raise more crops. Even humble barbed wire made it possible for farmers to retain livestock and protect their fields, especially in the Great Plains.

Steamboats and trains would carry the extra grain, which made it easier and cheaper to feed people who were coming to work in mills and factories in the expanding cities. Eventually steam-powered machinery would find use on many farms.

Steam-driven saw mills and grain mills would make it easier to make lumber and process grain for people.

Steamboats and trains would carry these products also.

Edwin Drake erected the first commercial oil drilling rig in Pennsylvania in 1859. Men built refineries to make crude oil into kerosene and other products. Kerosene would light America's homes and businesses. Refiners would eventually figure out how to make diesel oil and gasoline, which would make the diesel engine and the gasoline engine feasible.

Thomas Edison invented the light bulb in 1879 and introduced the direct-current electric power plant in the 1880s. George Westinghouse, Serb immigrant Nikula Tesla, and German Jewish immigrant Charles Steinmetz developed alternating current and alternating current power plants and transformers, which were more efficient at bringing electricity to businesses and homes. Tesla developed alternating current motors, which were more useful than steam-driven machinery.

Electric motors replaced steam power for driving machines in many factories. Electricity replaced kerosene and candles in homes and businesses. Electricity would make commercial refrigeration feasible, which in turn prolonged the freshness of meat, fish, dairy products, and produce, making it possible to feed more people more nutritiously and more cheaply.

Mining engineers developed techniques for making mines safer to work in and more profitable to operate. Metallurgical engineers discovered processes that made it easier to extract metal from ore. Chemical engineers discovered processes that made it easier to refine oil, and make products from coal. Mechanical engineers and industrial engineers made better machine tools and designed more effective processes to manufacture the goods people needed.

A number of inventors would make internal combustion engines (diesel engines and gasoline engines) practical. Such engines would power locomotives, cars, trucks, and tractors, starting in earnest in the first decade of the 1900s. The internal combustion engine would make it possible for Orville and Wilbur Wright to power their first airplane in 1903.

Charles Goodyear in 1839 discovered vulcanizing, a process to make rubber useable in industry. Rubber would gain use as a waterproof material that could be used to make a number of products. Likewise, chemists discovered how to use coal to make plastics.

American Samuel Morse in the late 1830s invented the telegraph, which helped not only the railroad industry, but other businessmen who needed information quickly. Soon journalists were also using the telegraph to report the news. Cyrus Field in 1866 first put telegraph wires under the ocean to provide speedy communication with Europe.

Better printing presses allowed newspapermen, magazine editors, and book publishers to sell printed matter to people cheaply. Because most people in America could read, and because there was freedom of expression, there was a market for their publications.

Teachers in Catholic schools, other religion-based schools, and public schools taught most Americans reading, writing, arithmetic, and a number of other useful subjects. Americans could understand more ideas, spread them, and make use of them, thanks to these teachers.

Scottish immigrant Alexander Graham Bell invented the telephone in 1876, which sped communications further. Marconi would make the first trans-Atlantic wireless telegraph transmission in 1901. This would lead to radio.

In the mid and late 1800s, Europeans like Frenchman Louis Pasteur, German Robert Koch, and Britisher Joseph Lister studied germs and provided ways to kill them. Pasteur and Koch developed vaccines and treatments to kill germs. Lister is considered the father of antiseptic surgery.

Europeans and Americans developed sewer systems, water processing plants, and other sanitation practices, which made it possible for larger amounts of people to live in cities without regularly dying of epidemics. Electricity made it possible to provide public transportation, lighting, and power to homes and industries in the cities more safely.

These inventions, discoveries, improvements, and applications made it possible to feed vast numbers of people, move raw materials and goods, and make modern industry and modern cities possible. In so many ways these inventions, discoveries, improvements, and applications were interdependent or contingent. In other words, someone had to discover or invent something that would in turn make something else possible, and that advance would in turn lead to other advances. All of these helped make America the leading industrial and agricultural nation on the globe.

The American system did not penalize initiative. This made it easier for people to produce the inventions, discoveries, improvements, and applications that led to the industrialization of America. There were no established cartels or government officials waiting to crush new ideas, or bleed them of profit, like in Europe. A very high proportion of investment capitalists in America were willing to gamble on promising ideas, and cash in on the results. American academia, much less formal than Europe's, was more receptive to ideas. Since America was a new country, there wasn't a strong enough financial establishment and landed aristocracy to hold people back (except for the South, which paid dearly for its wealthiest citizens' fixation on slave-raised cash crops) If someone thought his hometown was too stifling, he could move away and do better elsewhere.

What was the upshot of all of this?

America, from its very beginnings until well into the 20th Century, was going to need extra help. America had room and good land for farmers willing to work and raise food. America needed miners to mine coal, iron ore, and other metals. America needed workers to build the railroads, locomotives, canals, and steamboats to take the minerals to the factories. America needed loggers to provide the lumber to build ships, railroad cars, and houses. America needed laborers to work in the factories and build the cities the factories were in. America needed the trained technical people and the thinkers and entrepreneurs to make things happen.

America back in the day needed immigrants. America had room available for immigrants willing to come, earn their way, and assimilate into American society. And from the 1700s through the Ellis Island era, most immigrants were willing to become real Americans and contribute to the nation.

THE EMIGRANT EMPRESS

In the 1940s, Americans would open their doors to a European empress who came to America as a refugee. For a decade or so she would join the people she had once ruled.

Zita Bourbon-Parma von Hapsburg, the former empress of Austria-Hungary, came to the throne in 1916 with her husband Karl when his great-uncle Franz Josef died. The imperial couple lost their thrones late in 1918, when World War One collapsed their empire. They went into exile, Karl died in the early 1920, and Zita would live in very modest circumstances in European exile with her eight children. But she saw to it that they got schooling and training.

Zita's oldest son Otto, who would have been a ruler if she and her husband Karl hadn't been forced out of Austria and Hungary, was under a sentence of death from Hitler because he publicly opposed joining Austria to Nazi Germany. Otto worked against Hitler's seizure of Austria, and when Hitler succeeded, he moved the family to Belgium, in whose army his uncles Sixtus and Xavier (brothers of his mother Zita) had served in World War One. The family, with the help of Portuguese diplomat Aristides Sousa Mendes, fled to Portugal when Belgium fell to the Germans, and then

to America. Otto also worked with Sousa to help get Jews out of Nazi-occupied Europe.

Zita lived in New York and Quebec throughout the 1940s. In one of her public appearances in the 1940s, she attended the installation of the Byzantine Catholic bishop of Pittsburgh. (The great Catholic preacher Bishop Fulton J. Sheen, then a monsignor, gave the sermon at this event.) The Slovaks and Ruthenians who brought this form of Catholicism to America came from lands that for hundreds of years were under the rule of the Hapsburg family she married into. Zita was of French, Italian, and Portuguese ancestry.

In the 1950s Zita returned to Europe. Otto and some of her other children would rise to prominence in the professions and they were able to make her last four decades of life very comfortable. Zita died in a convent in Switzerland in 1989 and she was given a public funeral in Vienna – the city that she once ruled an empire from – that was more than worthy of a former empress. The sober and solemn rite was a moving spectacle that inspired many people to reflect on the vanity of human life and the reality of eternal life. **(19)**

Unlike many of the immigrants today, Zita and her children and nephews did not show ingratitude to the people who gave them sanctuary. Once he came to America, Otto von Hapsburg worked as a civilian to help America's war effort; American officials would not allow him to serve in the military. His brothers and his cousins fought in the ranks of America's armed forces. Despite being a prominent journalist and a European politician, Otto von Hapsburg tried to be a friend of the United States in his writings and in his political acts.

Ironically, many of the "best and brightest" of Otto von Hapsburg's never-to-be-realized domain and the other lands of Europe left for America because of his ancestors and others in the ruling classes of Europe. So did many, many, many peasants and laborers, who added their own efforts to America.

All of these solid people could have contributed to making Europe stronger, if only the elites and their bureaucrats in their homelands had been willing to provide the people with security and fair treatment. When the leaders failed the people, some people rebelled, and many more simply left to find better lives in America. With their blood, sweat, and tears, and their desire to become real Americans, they would help build their adopted homeland, the United States, into the mightiest nation in the world.

1. The account of the governor of Virginia sending armed invaders into Maryland and jailing and driving out priests, and the account of English officials and Protestant settlers persecuting Catholics comes from Michael Schwartz's book The Persistent Prejudice (pages 25-28). Cardinal James Gibbons, the bishop of Baltimore in the late 1800s and early 1900s, also commented on the laws against Catholics in Maryland in his book The Faith of Our Fathers (pages 192-197).

2. Information on the kidnaping and rape of Pocahontas comes from The American Heritage Book of Indians by William Brandon (pages 165-167), and from The True Story of Pocahontas by Linwood "Little Bear" Custalow, a member of Pocahontas' tribe.

3. Information on the abuses of the Puritans and Pilgrims comes from George Willison's book Saints and Strangers. This book, based on the Puritans' and Pilgrims' own records, and published in 1945, long before leftist and atheist political correctness dominated the history field, noted the Puritans' and Pilgrims' robbery and enslavement and butchery of the Indians (and to a lesser extent their mistreatment of rival Quakers).

Willison noted the Pilgrims' original pastor would not go with them from the Netherlands to New England because of their disagreeableness. Willison also noted these Protestants' hatred for the Catholic-style celebration of the Christmas and Easter holidays; they outlawed the celebration of Christmas for many years. He also reported the treason of many of their descendants who supported the British against the Patriots.

Willison also noted the Puritans' and Pilgrims' many sexual problems. An elder named Studley had to be drummed out before the Pilgrims came to America for serial adultery, incest, and child molesting. Prominent minister John Cotton had to be shipped out for sexually abusing young girls; he was allowed to pastor in South Carolina. Willison reported many bonneted women and buckle-hatted men had problems obeying the commandment against adultery, including one spirited matron who was punished for preferring to go native and cheat with red men. He also noted most weddings were civil weddings in Massachusetts in colonial days because the godly Protestants hated "popery." In other words, most Puritan and Pilgrim men and women wed in front of a magistrate instead of in church under the ministrations of a minister because Catholics had church weddings which priests solemnized. So the Puritans' and Pilgrims' ceremonies were more like a "civil union" than like the Sacrament of Matrimony.

Willison was not trying to tear these people down. He admired their guts, their hardiness, and their zeal. But as a good historian, he researched the truth and reported it.

4. Information on the Dutch abuse of American Indians comes from The American Heritage Book of Indians (pages 167-170), and from the book The Gateway States (page 33).

5. Ben Franklin, Jesuit priest John Carroll, and Maryland Catholic Charles Carroll visited Quebec's French leaders and priests in early 1776 to try to get them to join the American cause. They failed, in large part, because of the Quebecois' distrust of the bigotry of the American Protestants. Americans had attacked the Quebec Act of 1774 because it afforded tolerance to Quebec's French Catholics. Information on this ill-fated parley and the anti-Catholic prejudice in New England that caused it to fail comes from Bruce Lancaster's book The American Heritage Book of The Revolution (pages 142-143), and from Thomas Fleming's book Liberty! The American Revolution (pages 166-167).

6. The French had previously tried to build a canal across the isthmus of Panama (which was then part of Colombia) in the late 1800s. But the effort ended in failure, the deaths of more than 20,000 workers and engineers, and a huge financial and bribery scandal that involved many of France's politicians.

During the Spanish-American War, the crew of the Oregon, an American battleship, had to take it around the bottom of South America to join the American fleet in the Caribbean Sea. The ship's journey was widely publicized, and navalists like Theodore Roosevelt thundered for an American canal. When he became president in 1901, one of his first orders of business was to overturn an American-British agreement to jointly control a canal. Roosevelt got the British to back out, and he determined America would build a canal in Central America and guard it with military force.

A French engineer named Bunau-Varilla, who wanted to retrieve something for the French company involved, and the company's American fixer William Cromwell convinced Congress in 1902 to vote to continue the canal project in Panama (the Americans were leaning toward putting the canal in Nicaragua) and pay the French company $40 million in exchange for getting American title to the canal route and the survey work, the engineering documents, machinery, and other Panama assets the French company had.

The Colombians heard about the $40 million offer, and demanded a share of the money earmarked for the French firm. Their diplomats reached a tentative deal with the American government to get $10 million for 100 years of use of a six-mile wide swath of the Panama isthmus that contained the canal route and another $250,000 a year as part of the profit for the tolls the canal authorities would charge. However, the dictator of Colombia vetoed the deal, and demanded all of the $40 million.

The French agreement with the Colombian government was due to end in late 1904. Then the Colombians could cut the failed French out entirely and make their own deal with the Americans. Roosevelt was at first agreeable to the Colombian offer, but then he got itchy to start work on the canal. He didn't want to wait until late 1904.

Bunau-Varilla convinced American officials they could engineer a "revolution" in Panama against the Colombian government. Locals in Panama rebelled roughly once a year; Roosevelt had been helping Colombian officials keep a lid on the rebels so the local railroad across the isthmus (which Americans built and had used for decades) could keep running.

Without committing formally to the scheme, Roosevelt in essence assisted the "revolt" to make the deal happen. An American warship showed up off of Panama, and Panamanian and American railroaders, some other locals, and some Colombian soldiers who were bought off carried out the revolt. The American warship's officers and crew, by forcibly protecting Americans in the area and by negotiation, persuaded the Colombian soldiers who wanted to quell the rebellion to back off and go home.

The locals set up a government. Bunau-Varilla, who funded the rebellion, got himself appointed as Panama's envoy. He said the new government would accept $10 million and $250,000 a year in exchange for American ownership, not lease, of a 10-mile swath through Panama for the canal. And by the way, the French company would still get the $40 million. Congress and Teddy Roosevelt accepted these more generous terms very quickly. The Panamanian leaders were outraged over the Frenchman's sellout in giving the land away, but agreed to abide by it.

Roosevelt got the canal started. U.S. Army doctors beat the yellow-fever that had killed so many men working for the French two decades earlier. U.S. Army engineers led the assault on the hills, swamps, and other terrain features that had blocked the French. By 1914, the Panama Canal was ready for ship traffic.

The Panama Canal was an impressive achievement, but like the winning of the West, there was something wrong about it. The sordid deal between Bunau-Varilla and Theodore Roosevelt basically cheated the Colombians out of a fair share of the money the canal has earned over the last century.

Roosevelt should have bought the canal zone in Panama from Colombia, left the eastern half of Panama in Colombian hands, and let the western half of Panama merge with Costa Rica or become a smaller independent state. Or he should have paid Colombia the $40 million and secured title to the Canal Zone. (In the 1920s, Americans did pay the Colombians $25 million for the takeover.)

Instead, we got a tainted land deal from the new Panamanian government that cut the little made-up country in half. In Teddy Roosevelt's time, this didn't matter. No tinpot dictator from Panama would get a hearing from our government if he tried to evict the Americans from the Canal Zone. Instead, he would find himself dead or in exile, and his subjects would find American soldiers and marines occupying the land.

But times had changed by our nation's bicentennial. (The author, a military veteran, was in Jungle School in the Canal Zone on July 4, 1976.) Prominent American leftists in the 1960s and 1970s bemoaned the "injustice" of "American occupiers" "splitting a sovereign state in two." They forgot to mention the locals could never have built the canal whose tolls propped up their country; America did it for them. They also forgot to mention Panamanians owed their independence to America. Lyndon Johnson, a president whose regime was riddled with corruption and incompetence, suggested giving up the canal.

In early 1977, the author took leave, visited his congressman in Washington, and urged him not to give away the Panama Canal. Any American who has seen the Canal like the author has can only stand in awe of the genius and courage of the men of this land who conquered the jungle, the terrain, and yellow fever to build it. However, the stupidity and/or corruption of globalists like Jimmy Carter and Henry Kissinger led American officials to give the Canal Zone to the *bandidos* who ran Panama.

In 1997, while Bill Clinton was president, the Red Chinese government firm Hutchison Whampoa Ltd. won contracts from the Panamanian government to operate the port facilities on both ends of the Panama Canal. In a national emergency, the Chinese could sabotage the canal, which still allows the quick transoceanic passage of a large amount of America's commerce. Clinton did nothing to stop the Chinese grab of these ports.

Clinton had personally assisted COSCO (China Ocean Shipping Company), a shipping firm owned by the Chinese military, in its attempt to lease a former U.S. Navy base at the port of Long Beach, California. Members of Congress in 1998 killed Clinton's bid to let the Chinese in by amending a defense spending bill to forbid port officials from granting the lease and not allowing the president the power to waive restrictions on the Chinese.

The Chinese Army used a COSCO ship in an attempt to smuggle 2000 AK-47 assault rifles into California for sale to street gangs in 1996 via two other Chinese government owned firms. U.S. Customs agents boarded the ship while it was in Los Angeles' harbor. They had to do so because a Clinton minion tipped off the Chinese about the agency's impending bust, according to U.S. Customs officials. Janet Reno or one of her people at the Justice Department had the perpetrators released, and they fled to China. The Red Chinese firms also tried to smuggle in shoulder-fired anti-aircraft missiles, rockets, and rocket launchers. Guess how these weapons would have been used if they had succeeded. A year later, Janet Reno was dodging questions from Congressmen on why the Clinton administration had allowed COSCO a lease at the port of Long Beach despite this act of murderous smuggling.

In the past few decades, Colombian drug lords have repaid America's removal of Panama from their ancestors many times over. How? They have flooded our country with drugs. They have made back the money we should have paid the Colombian people many times over by supplying the many dopers in government, media, entertainment, college campuses, law offices and elsewhere in American society with the marijuana and cocaine and other little helpers these losers seem to require to get through the day.

Info on the Panama Canal comes from Nathan Miller's book Theodore Roosevelt: A Life (pages 398-409), the book U.S. Overseas (pages 120-123 123), and David McCullough's epic book The Path Between the Seas (pages 329-402).

Info on the Panama Canal surrender and Chinese control of the port facilities comes from a 12/14/1999 BBC News article. Info on Clinton and COSCO comes from World Net Daily (9/21/1998). Info on the Red Chinese gunrunning operation that had inside help from Clinton operatives comes from Charles Smith's article for Newsmax (12/9/2002). Other sources for the dealings of Clinton with the Chinese, the Chinese control of Panama Canal ports, the Chinese export of weapons to criminals and other unsavory characters in America, and the dodging of Janet Reno include Congressman Duncan Hunter's article in the 4/21/1997 issue of Insight on the News, the 5/14/1998 Congressional Review (pages S4864-S4867), an article in Human Events (3/6/2006), and Charles Smith's 6/17/2000 article for World Net Daily.

7. Information on the railroad barons' gouging comes from Irving Stone's book Men To Match My Mountains (pages

294-301, 328-329).

8. Information on the tragic drop in the American Indian population of California comes from The American Heritage Book of Indians (page 305).

9. Excellent sources of information on the wars against the American Indians are Dee Brown's book Bury My Heart at Wounded Knee, the book The Plains States, and The American Heritage Book of Indians.

10. Statistics on the of American Indians in North America and South America before 1900 are at best educated guesses. The American Heritage Book of Indians (pages 3-15, 82, and 403) lists some numbers that seem reasonable. Guenter Lewy, in a 11/22/2004 article in George Mason University's History News Network, reported various estimates, and concluded (wrongfully) the drastic drop in numbers of American Indians was not genocide, but mere tragedy.

11. Statistics and some historical information on Alaska natives and Russian settlers comes from the books The American Heritage Book of Indians (pages 283-284) and the book The Frontier States (pages 14-15, 35). Further info on Sheldon Jackson comes from an article Stephen Haycox wrote for The Pacific Historian (Spring 1984).

12. Statistics and some historical information on Hawaii comes from the book The Frontier States (pages 94-97), John Garraty and Robert McCaughey's book The American Nation (pages 630-632), the book The National Experience (pages 496-497), and George Knoles' book The New United States: A History Since 1896 (page 50).

13. Statistics for European and American populations come from Brian Mitchell's book European Historical Statistics 1750-1970, Terry Jordan's book The European Culture Area, and the U.S. Department of Commerce book set Historical Statistics of the United States (Bicentennial Edition).

14. Information on Joseph Smith, Brigham Young, and the "mainstream" Mormons comes from Men to Match My Mountains (pages 94-100, 178-185, 213-226, 266-274, 329-351, 411-423), from Lucius Beebe and from Charles Clegg's book The American West –The Pictorial Epic of a Continent (pages 351-363), and from Robert Hine's book The American West (pages 228-234). Other information on these Mormons comes from the Winter 2003 Utah Historical Quarterly (page 14), and the article "Mormon Blood Atonement: Fact or Fantasy?" by Jerald Tanner and ex-Mormon Sandra Tanner (who like many in Utah claims descent from Brigham Young through one of his more than two dozen "wives") in the April 1997 Salt Lake City Messenger.

Information on the Strangites comes from "The Man Who Shot Strang" in the 10/10/2002 Beaver Beacon, the Beaver Island Historical Society, a June 1970 American Heritage article by Robert Weeks, an excerpt of Vickie Speek's book God Has Made Us a Kingdom by Signature Books, and an article by Jenny Nolan in the 1/29/1996 Detroit News.

Information on the Mountain Meadows Massacre comes from Will Bagley's article "Rescue of the Mountain Meadows Massacre Orphans" in the February 2005 issue of Wild West Magazine, from Cecilia Rassmussen's 6/29/2003 article in the Los Angeles Times, and from Douglas Linder's article "The Mountain Meadows Massacre of 1857 and the Trial of John D. Lee" on the University of Missouri Kansas City law school website. (Linder has written a series of articles on famous trials.) Further "blood atonement" and massacre information comes from a paper Will Bagley wrote titled "Will You Love That Man or Woman Enough to Shed Their Blood?" Bagley presented it at a conference on new religion studies in Utah in June 2002. The Church of Jesus Christ of Latter Day Saints (Mormon) official website www.lds.org carried an article from the church's September 2007 Ensign magazine by Richard Turley which attempts to exonerate Young for the Mountain Meadows Massacre. I also spoke with Burr Fancher, a descendant of a victim of the Mountain Meadows Massacre. He is an officer in the Mountain Meadows Massacre Foundation, a group of descendants and collateral relatives of victims of the atrocity and students of history whose aim is not to let this atrocity remain hidden and its victims go unmemorialized.

The abortion allegation come from the American Heritage article and the testimony of Mormon woman Sarah Pratt, which was in a reprint of Wilhelm Ritter von Wymetal's muckraking book Joseph Smith: The Prophet, His Family, and His Friends (pages 60-63). The book was first published in 1886 in Salt Lake City(!)

A personal note: My Catholicism didn't prevent Brigham Young University officials from offering me a scholarship to attend their well-respected college in the early 1970s. I interviewed with Mormon officials about their offer, and they treated me cordially. However, I instead chose to attend Loyola University for that year (all you anti-Jesuit conspiracy theorists take note); I paid most of my tuition with my earnings from a job as a mechanic and laborer in a paper mill. I then received an appointment to attend the U.S. Military Academy; I graduated from USMA and served as an officer in the U.S. Army. I would later take biology classes at the University of Dayton (a Catholic school) and organic chemistry courses at Xavier University in Cincinnati in the 1990s (all you anti-Jesuit conspiracy theorists take note again) to prepare for further forensic science and toxicology studies.

15. Statistics on immigration come from the immigration tables of the Historic Research Study, Statue of Liberty – Ellis Island National Monument, by Harlan D. Unrau, National Park Service, 1984. I did some math to come up with totals.

16. Estimates on immigration from Canada comes from the Catholic Encyclopedia, Damien-Claude and Claude Belanger's 1999 article "French Canadian Emigration to the United States 1840-1930," thanks to Marionopolis College, and an article "The Eldorado to the South: French-Canadians in the U.S.," on the Duke University website. These sources note there were 1.2 million Canadians in America, according to the 1900 census, and there were 400,000 French Canadian natives in the U.S. and another 700,000 who claimed one or both parents were French Canadians (the net number of French Canadians would be 1.1 million minus the deceased ancestors). This implies about an even distribution of French Canadian and non-French Canadian immigrants. The Belangers gave a firm estimate of 900,000 French Canadian immigrants from 1840 through 1930. My estimate of an equal number of non-French Canadians comes from the rough ratio of 1:1 the 1900 census figures imply.

The website canadianconnection.com carried this quote from a 1920s Canadian politician: "Canada cannot afford to be a preparatory school for people from European countries whose ultimate destination will be with our neighbours [sic] to the south." In other words, the Canadians were aware Europeans used their land to prepare to come to America. An article by William Siener, titled "Through The Back Door: Evading the Chinese Exclusion Act Along The Niagara Frontier, 1900 to 1924," outlined Canadian complicity in the smuggling of Chinese illegals into America. Congressmen made similar note of British and Canadian perfidy in smuggling unfit immigrants in their comments in support of various immigration reform bills in the late 1800s and the early 1900s.

A 1910 article in the Review of Reviews titled "Canada's Plan of Averting the Yellow Peril" said it was the duty of Canadians as British subjects to help Britain maintain friendly relations with Asian nations. Therefore the article's author said Canadian officials used personal diplomacy with the Chinese, Japanese, and British colonial authorities in Asia to regulate immigration. The author said many Indians from India were fighting British battles as soldiers, so that was to their credit. The author mocked Theodore Roosevelt but noted Canadian authorities used similar methods in dealing with would-be Asian immigrants. The article shows the subservience of Canadians to the British lead in handling immigration (the Canadians and British routinely violated American immigration regulations to make extra money for the British Empire).

17. Statistics on ethnicities of the immigrants comes from the Unrau study. Sources of immigration statistics specific to the Spanish, Portuguese, and Italians include J. Halcro Ferguson's book The River Plate Republics (page 30), Latin America: Geographical Perspectives (pages 417-419), and Brian Mitchell's book European Historical Statistics 1750-1970 (pages 135-149). I did some math and estimation to come up with totals.

18. Sources for estimates of immigrants who returned to Europe include Mark Wyman's book Round-Trip to America: The Immigrants Return to Europe, 1880-1930, and commentary on same by Hans Storhaug in a lecture he presented in 2002, and Donna Przecha's article "Immigrants Who Returned Home." Hard figures came from the Unrau study.

19. We leave this chapter with an account of the event in Empress Zita's 1989 funeral which made many people reflect on the meaning of life and the states of their souls. (The quotes which follow are more or less what the speakers said, given translation issues and slightly conflicting reports from observers.)

Six black horses drew the century-old royal hearse carrying Empress Zita's casket in a procession through the streets of Vienna.

When the pall bearers tried to bring Zita's casket into the *Kapuchinerkirk*, a Catholic Church run by the Capuchin monks which has served as the church where many requiem Masses for Hapsburg family members have taken place, a member of the funeral procession knocked on the massive wooden doors to have them opened. A monk inside the church thundered, "Who goes there?"

The mourners replied, "Zita, her imperial, royal, and apostolic majesty, Empress of Austria and Queen of Hungary, and all her domains."

The monk shouted, "I know her not!" He would not open the doors to the church.

Someone knocked again. The monk inside the church thundered, "Who disturbs our peace?"

The mourners replied, "Zita, the Queen of Bohemia, Dalmatia, Slavonia, Galicia, Queen of Jerusalem, Grand Duchess of Tuscany and Krakow." (These were some of her many titles as empress.)

The monk shouted, "I do not know her!" He kept the doors closed.

Someone knocked a third time. Once again, the monk inside the church demanded in an unfriendly voice to know who was bothering him.

This time the mourners replied, "Zita von Hapsburg, a lowly sinner humbly begging forgiveness before the throne of God."

The monk announced in a friendlier voice, "Enter, and find rest." Then the massive doors of the church swung open wide.

What was the moral of this ritual? All people, no matter how mighty they were in their earthly lives, are still small and imperfect figures in the presence of God Almighty. He grades everyone on his or her merits against His very objective set of measurements: Did you do My will to the best of your abilities? Did you obey the Ten Commandments and the Golden Rule? Did you love Me, and did you love your neighbor as yourself? God expects people to live according to His commandments, and He gives no man or woman favorable treatment due to his or her status in earthly life come Judgment Day.

REGULATING IMMIGRATION FROM THE AMERICAN REVOLUTION TO THE EARLY 1900s

In the first century of America's free existence, virtually the only national laws concerning immigration were laws designed to aid immigrants in coming to the United States. There was virtually no federal regulation of immigration. There was no immigration station at Ellis Island. Immigrants came by ship to American seaports, debarked, and were free to go wherever they could.

In 1795, Congress enacted the first comprehensive American naturalization law. (An earlier 1790 law had one paragraph of text.) They required free white foreigners to reside in America for five years, renounce their allegiance to any foreign government, swear an oath of allegiance to America and the U.S. Constitution, and display "good moral character." They forbade anyone who fought for the British in the Revolutionary War to become citizens unless the legislature of his state was willing to vote in his favor. President George Washington signed the bill into law.

Immigrants to America came in through a handful of seaports and border stations throughout the 1800s. Some crossed in from Mexico and Canada, often illegally, like millions do today. Until the 1920s, most illegals were Europeans or Asians who sneaked in through Canada.

Until the Louisiana Purchase, all American seaports were on the Atlantic coast. America would not have a seaport on the Pacific coast until fur traders built Astoria, Oregon after the Lewis and Clark expedition of the early 1800s. Americans and Britons, wary of each other, jointly occupied the Pacific Northwest region, and Americans would start coming in large numbers to the region in the 1840s. In 1846, the British saw the light and relinquished their claim on "the Oregon Country" – the area that is now Washington, Oregon, Idaho, and parts of Montana and Wyoming. The 49th Parallel would officially be America's boundary with Canada from Minnesota to the Pacific Ocean.

America would not have any ports in California until the Mexican War, which also started in 1846, about the time President James Polk's men settled the Canadian border issue with the British. In the 1800s very few immigrants other than Mexicans or Chinese came to America via the Pacific coast seaports. Since most immigration until the 1960s was from Europe, most immigrants came in through the Atlantic coast ports.

The Erie Canal – built not long after the War of 1812 – linked the Great Lakes states by water to the Hudson River, which flows to the Atlantic Ocean by New York City. The canal gave New York City's port an advantage no other Atlantic port had – a direct water connection to the Midwest. New York City soon became the dominant American seaport because of this water link. From after the War of 1812 until the 1960s, more than half of all immigrants to the United States landed at New York City.

In 1819, Congress enacted the Steerage Act, their first attempt at making conditions reasonable for immigrants and their first attempt to figure out who was coming to America. They required sailing ships transporting passengers to America to carry adequate provisions for passengers for the journey across the ocean, they limited the number of people that could be on a sailing ship as passengers coming to or leaving any American port, and they required ships' officers to submit passenger lists to the local American customs official of the American port in which they docked. In 1847 and in 1855, Congress updated this law to make conditions better for passengers.

The first formal immigration station in New York City was at Castle Garden. In the early 1800s it was known as Castle Clinton, because it was a small fort with cannons on the southern end of Manhattan Island, in an area called "The Battery." It formed part of the harbor defense fortifications of New York City. (A "battery" is an artillery unit similar in size to an infantry company; that's why the area was called "The Battery.") After the War of 1812, New York City got the land from the U.S. Government; the demobilized fort got the name "Castle Garden." Castle Garden became a park; the great Swedish singer Jenny Lind performed there in 1850. In 1855, New York state officials put Castle Garden to use as a place to process immigrants.

During the 1820s and 1830s, more immigrants came from Ireland than any other country. Certain Protestant bigots claimed the presence of the Irish was a threat to the United States. They conveniently failed to mention that the greatest threat to American liberty was Protestant England – whose leaders waged war against America twice already – during the Revolution and the War of 1812. British law forbade the Irish to have most civil liberties the British people had; British law also denied certain civil liberties to Catholics in Britain. The American bigots also forgot a large percentage of Washington's Continental Army had been Irish.

Samuel Morse, who later invented the telegraph, made his fortune publishing anti-Catholic books. He claimed the Pope and the Austrian emperor were in league to take over America, and many yokels and bluenoses believed him. He argued for restricting immigration, banning Catholics from public office, and closing Catholic schools. Anti-Catholic mobs in Boston and

Philadelphia burned Catholic schools and churches. Catholics were galled that their tax money, along with everyone else's, supported Protestant private schools and anti-Catholic public schools. Catholics had to build their own schools with their own money so their children could go to school without hearing anti-Catholic bigotry from the teachers and principal.

During the 1840s, the first decade which saw more than a million immigrants, 781,000 of these came from Ireland. This was the decade of the Great Hunger (the Potato Famine) in Ireland. Likewise, in this decade, 435,000 came from the German states, and another 77,000 came from France. The peoples of Germany and France experienced crop failures and revolutions that failed. Almost all of the Irish immigrants were Catholics, and a large percentage of the German and French immigrants were also Catholics. **(1)**

In that decade, the United States defeated Mexico – an almost entirely Catholic country with anticlerical leaders – in the Mexican War. A quarter of the soldiers in America's small victorious army were Irish-born. Ironically, Mexico's best unit, the San Patricio (Saint Patrick) Brigade, was made up of deserters from the American army of Irish blood. Also, as a result of the successful war with Mexico, American officials granted citizenship to many Mexican and Spanish nationals who lived in California and elsewhere in the newly-won Southwest. The Gold Rush in California at the end of the Mexican War brought many thousands of people to California from other countries, as well as from the rest of America, in a search for wealth.

In the 1850s a party comprised entirely of anti-Catholic bigots – who called themselves the "American Party," while everyone else aptly called these wingnuts the "Know-Nothings" -- rose on a platform calling for restricting immigration, banning Catholics from public office, and closing Catholic schools. Know-Nothing rioters killed people in St. Louis, Cincinnati, and Louisville – all cities welcoming many German Catholic immigrants -- in the 1850s.

Naturally, the Know-Nothings seized power among the anti-Irish in Calvinist and Unitarian Massachusetts. Know-Nothings also gained elsewhere. In the 1854 congressional election, voters elected 43 Know-Nothings to Congress and five to the Senate. There were 27 others who won elections who were members of Know-Nothing lodges. Know-Nothing candidate Millard Fillmore, the nonentity who served out Zachary Taylor's term as president after some doctors committed malpractice and killed "Old Rough and Ready" while treating him for a digestive tract disorder, got almost a quarter of the popular vote in the presidential election of 1856. **(2)**

The Know-Nothings – like the Whigs – dissolved on the slavery issue, and soon disappeared as a formal party. The bigots – depending on their views on slavery – joined the Democrats or the new Republican party. (Know-nothings of a different sort dominate both parties now.)

In the Civil War, close to 150,000 natives of Ireland served in the Union Army and Union Navy. Roughly 175,000 German-born men served in the Union Army and Union Navy. Roughly 40,000 Irish natives also served in the forces of the Confederacy; but relatively few Germans did so. **(3)**

After the Civil War, prejudice and discrimination still existed against the Irish and to a lesser extent the Germans, but these groups were now organized enough to protect themselves. Open bigotry against the newly-freed black slaves and the free blacks of America was widespread in America, but at least American-born blacks were now American citizens who could vote.

American Indians suffered a century of government-sponsored genocide in the 1800s. But many of them _did_ receive American citizenship, through individual treaties their tribes signed with the American government, through marriage with whites, through military service, or through the 14th Amendment in 1868 if they lived in states or territories under effective American government control. Many tribes not under effective U.S. government control did _not_ receive citizenship under the 14th Amendment. It would take the Indian Citizenship Act of 1924 to grant all American Indians American citizenship. **(4)**

From the 1870s until the 1920s, America's leaders would enact several laws to regulate immigration for the perceived benefit of America's citizens. First they restricted Asian immigration, then they federalized immigration, then they tried to improve screening of immigrants so those who came to America would not be a burden on American society. They decided to restrict virtually all Asian immigration. After World War One, they decided to greatly restrict all immigration.

IMMIGRATION LAWS FROM THE CIVIL WAR TO 1890

In the late 1800s, Congresses, not presidents, would usually lead on the immigration question and other questions of great importance to the Republic. From the assassination of Lincoln in 1865 to the assassination of William McKinley in 1901, Congress was a more active branch of the federal government than the presidency. Congress impeached and almost removed Lincoln's successor Andrew Johnson. Ulysses S. Grant was a sturdy, basically decent man and a great general, but he was a poor president because he was a novice at civilian politics. Many in Grant's administration were crooked, and their lust for undeserved wealth undermined his work.

Rutherford Hayes owed his election to questionable Electoral College maneuvering. In exchange for the electoral votes of some Southern states, he ended Reconstruction and allowed Southerners to persecute blacks. His questionable win earned him the nickname "Rutherfraud." Of course, his Democrat opponent Samuel Tilden carried some Southern states because the Ku Klux Klan and other organized bands of white trash prevented large numbers of blacks from voting. Hayes was also known for having a priggish wife who banned alcohol from the White House and for that act of unhospitality she got the nickname "Lemonade Lucy." James Garfield was shot to death months into his term. Chester Arthur was about as charismatic and accomplished a man as Millard Fillmore.

Grover Cleveland, the one Democrat president in this era, had a term in the mid 1880s and another term in the mid 1890s. He was an honest, able, and tough man, but still not a Lincoln. Cleveland, because he was honest, admitted to fathering a bastard child (who he was paying support for) during his first campaign for president, while his opponent James Blaine was not enough of a man to silence the anti-Catholic bigots around him in his campaign. Cleveland overwhelmingly won the Irish vote and got into the White House. Later, bachelor Cleveland would marry a young beauty named Frances Folsom and become a father while President.

Benjamin Harrison, whose term sandwiched between Cleveland's two terms, was not a bad man but was not a dynamic man as president. Like Hayes in 1876 and George W. Bush in 2000, Harrison had won the electoral vote against Cleveland but lost the popular vote. (Tilden owed his popular margin in 1876 to the suppression of blacks in the South who would have voted Republican. Al Gore owed his popular margin in 2000 to the widespread illegal voting of felons, mental patients, and unnaturalized aliens, and to the suppression of the absentee votes of military people.) Harrison's administration was the first to spend a billion dollars in a year in peacetime.

In the rematch election of 1892, Cleveland handily won both the electoral vote and the popular vote.

William McKinley followed Cleveland to the White House in 1897 after he handed William Jennings Bryan the first of his three presidential defeats. McKinley as a congressman designed tariffs that protected American industries and workers from cheap imports and won the support of bosses and laborers alike. As a lawyer, McKinley had defended strikers for free, an act untypical for a Republican.

While nowhere near as firebreathing as his subordinate and eventual successor Theodore Roosevelt, McKinley also favored expansion of American power. He was president during the Spanish-American War and he was the president who annexed Hawaii. McKinley also took Puerto Rico into American control and ordered the occupation of Cuba and the Philippines after our men beat the Spanish.

The locals in the Philippines at first welcomed American help in their uprising against Spanish colonial authorities. But some of them turned against the Americans when it became evident the Americans were going to take the Philippines as a colony for themselves. It took several years for American soldiers and marines to defeat the Filipinos, and they lost roughly 5000 men in the campaign.

The Filipino insurrectionists had courage and numbers, but American control was inevitable. Why? American military people had developed, over years of conflict with American Indians, a mixture of toughness and ruthlessness against opponents who could fight in an irregular style. They also were much better armed. And unlike today, American politicians in that era didn't quit on their military people.

Besides, the Germans and Japanese also had designs on the Philippines. It would not have been possible for the Filipinos to resist the Germans or especially the nearby Japanese if either of these colonialist powers decided they wanted the islands badly enough. American colonialism was the least distasteful option they had. American leaders sent a large enough number of soldiers, sailors, marines, and ships to the Philippines to keep the Germans and the equally militaristic and greedy Japanese at bay. Teddy Roosevelt's rise to the Presidency in 1901 did much to make the Germans and the Japanese behave.

The Americans also did much to control the Moros, the Moslem savages active on Mindanao, other islands in the Philippines, and other islands in present-day Indonesia (then under Dutch colonial rule). Moros would purposely run amok with swords and knives, killing many of the Filipinos, who were Catholics and thus infidels worthy of death in the eyes of the Moslems. Moslems also kidnapped Filipino girls for use as sex slaves. American forces shot down these Moslem fanatics, burned their villages, and shelled the palace of a sultan who supported them. The Americans thus greatly diminished the Moslems' depredations.

Now that we've given a backdrop to the era, let's examine what Congress did about immigration in that time.

The first immigration law after the Civil War reflected the long-overdue realization that America's native-born and immigrant blacks deserved American citizenship. In 1870, Congress enacted and President Ulysses Grant signed into law a naturalization act that allowed people of African blood who were not born in the United States the ability to become naturalized citizens. This covered slaves brought to America illegally after 1808, and blacks from Africa and elsewhere (like the West Indies) who wished to come to America.

The second immigration law after the Civil War was aimed at would-be immigrants from China. Many Chinese had come to America during the California gold rush of 1849. Many more had come to the Western U.S. later to mine, build railroads, and perform other labor that would enable them to earn enough money to establish themselves nicely when they returned to China.

Some unscrupulous businessmen also imported women from the Far East to serve as prostitutes in the American West. Because of the general rowdiness of the West compared to "back East" (the Midwest, the South, and the Northeast), and because of the shortage of women compared to men in the West, prostitution was legal in many communities in western states and territories. Prostitution was also widely tolerated in areas where it wasn't legal.

Prostitution had been a major problem even in the Civil War. Washington and Richmond teemed with whores, and many followed the camps of the armies. Venereal diseases disabled thousands of soldiers. Officers and men chased after the shady ladies, ignoring their duties. Union general Joseph Hooker, a devotee of trashy women, gave a certain class of them his own last name as a professional nickname. Rebel general Earl Van Dorn was shot to death during the Civil War by an irate husband of a woman whose breastworks he had carried with her consent.

The Victorian Age had a lot more sexual misbehavior than the history books and novels will tell you about. Many cities around the country had red-light districts. In fact, Seattle city government for awhile existed almost entirely on licenses and fines on prostitution, alcohol, and gambling. When a women's group threw the rascals out of City Hall in the 1880s, the politicians they elected closed so

many of the whorehouses, saloons, and gambling dens that the town went broke. **(5)**

The native Hawaiians were even more openly promiscuous in the 1800s. The local girls used to swim out to the whaling ships in their harbors to consort with sailors until American missionaries convinced native Hawaiian rulers to control their females.

Many unscrupulous western businessmen brought Chinese laborers to America to undercut the local laborers in the mines, on railroad crews, and elsewhere. Chinese people would work for less than native Americans or European immigrants who knew American customs would. Sometimes the Chinese had to; many of them came as indentured servants, little more than slaves.

The Chinese were not the only people in bondage in the Land of the Free in the 1870s. Many Americans in the West essentially used American Indians as slave laborers, especially in California, Arizona, and New Mexico. And peonage and convict labor camps were essentially extensions of slave labor – predominantly for blacks but also for many whites – in the South well into the 1900s. This of course does not count the millions of people in city tenements or company towns or sharecropper shacks laboring for pittances.

Many American working people hated the Chinese because they would work for lower wages and the bosses could make native laborers work for less also if there were Chinese around. American laborers added this legitimate grievance – although they should have focused on the greedy bosses who used the Chinese to underpay everyone – to their instinctive prejudices against the Chinese. The "Chinks" were yellow-skinned and slant-eyed. The men wore pigtails, both sexes did laundry, they worshiped pagan gods, they spoke an inscrutable language, they kept to themselves, and they didn't tell the Americans what they were thinking. In an era when most Americans openly called blacks "niggers", openly called Mexicans "greasers", and openly called American Indians "red-skinned savages," the Chinese weren't alone in being the victims of racial hatred.

Congress in an 1875 law made it illegal to supply coolie (unskilled Asian) laborers to the United States on contract. The law (called the Act of March 3, 1875) also made it illegal for Americans to bring people from China or Japan to America against their wills. The congressmen aimed at protecting American laborers against Chinese and Japanese competition, and also aimed at protecting natives of China and Japan against unscrupulous lords in their own countries and against robber barons in America.

The 1875 law also made it illegal to transport females from China or Japan for immoral purposes. The law made it illegal for any convicts to immigrate to America, except for those convicted of political offenses.

Congress followed up the 1875 law with a second law in 1882. This law, known as the Chinese Exclusion Act, stopped Chinese laborers from coming to America for the next 10 years. (The law did not restrict immigration of businessmen or other non-laboring professionals from China.) The law also barred Chinese immigrants who were not already citizens from obtaining American citizenship. The law allowed Chinese already legally in the United States to leave the country and come back as long as they had the paperwork showing they were legal residents. (Chinese immigrants as a class were not formally able to become citizens until the passage of the McCarran-Walter Act in 1952. Earlier laws (such as the Magnuson Act of 1943 and war brides laws) during and after World War Two enabled some Chinese to become citizens.)

Congress amended the Chinese Exclusion Act in 1884 to extend the 10-year ban on Chinese immigration for another 10 years. Chinese immigration dropped sharply, but never stopped.

Federal officials next enacted laws against foreign undesirables, not just the Chinese. In the 1880s, immigration was roughly double what it had been in the 1870s. American laborers started feeling the competition for work. State government leaders were trying to enact immigration restriction laws to protect American workers – who were voters – but federal judges declared these state laws unconstitutional because they supposedly restricted interstate commerce illegally.

Federal officials decided to address immigration as a whole in the 1880s. Congress passed the first such general immigration law in 1882. This law, the Act of August 3, 1882, barred convicts (except those convicted of political offenses), lunatics, idiots, and people liable to become public charges. The law also required any shipping company whose ships brought such people to the United States to return them to the countries they came from at their own (the shipping company's) expense.

The law also required a tax of 50 cents per person for those who arrived by water to defray costs of inspection. The law put overall supervisory responsibility in the hands of the U.S. Treasury Department, but put responsibility and authority for doing the hands-on work of conducting immigration inspections in the hands of the governors of states.

This law had two serious loopholes. It allowed state governments to enforce immigration policy, and it didn't tax people coming into the United States by land. Many state government workers were incompetent or crooked or both. At best, state government workers enforced the law unevenly. British shipping lines continued to take advantage of the second loophole by dropping off people at Halifax, Nova Scotia, and arranging for them to come by rail into the United States, dodging inspections and taxes. From 1881 through 1890, 393,000 came to the United States from Canada, roughly the same as the 384,000 who came from Canada to the United States from 1871 through 1880.

Congress then took aim at unskilled laborers from Europe whose presence was hurting the local workers. Unscrupulous businessmen – using false advertising – had been conning Europeans for years to come over to America to seek their fortunes. The shipping companies were only too happy to ship the immigrants to America in steerage so they could cash in on the traffic of the human cargo. When the immigrants showed up, there were often no opportunities like what the advertising promised. Or the wages the businessmen promised were high for Europe, but below the prevailing wages for America. This created an excess of labor in many areas. Since the immigrants needed to work to feed, shelter, and clothe themselves, they were willing to work for less money than the prevailing wages were for the industries whose owners lured them to America. Wages fell, severely hurting American workers.

Congress in 1885 enacted the Alien Contract Labor Law as a start at dealing with this abuse. This law made it illegal to import or assist in importing immigrants to America with any labor contract made before immigration of the immigrant to America. The law exempted certain skilled workers in industries not already established in the United States, entertainers, and relatives and friends of those already in the United States.

This law had several flaws. First of all, many unscrupulous businessmen hadn't even bothered to sign immigrants to labor contracts in the first place. They had just made promises of a better life that were tempting enough to lure the foreigners to America. Forbidding contracts would not curb this abuse.

Second, the law left responsibility for enforcement in the hands of the states. And finally, the law had no provisions for inspection of immigrants, deportations of violators of the law, or penalties on shipping companies who assisted immigrants in violating the law. In short, the law was a paper tiger.

UNCLE SAM TAKES OVER IMMIGRATION

The Alien Contract Labor Law was violated so often that even congressmen finally figured out the law needed fixing. In 1888, the House of Representatives authorized investigation of immigration.

The Congressional committee members investigated, and reported what many suspected. They determined European leaders were conniving to dump their convicts and paupers in the United States. They determined state government inspectors were checking immigrants too rapidly to do a thorough job. They determined paupers and convicts from Europe were getting by the inspectors. They determined that there were many violations of the Alien Contract Labor Law, and yet there were very few prosecutions and even fewer convictions of violators. They determined the taxpayers of New York (where most of the immigrants were coming to by ship) were having to pay $20 million a year to take care of illegal immigrants.

Later in 1889, President Benjamin Harrison's Secretary of the Treasury William Windom had issued an independent report of his own department's findings. Windom's people said it was difficult to throughly examine immigrants on "vessels that arrive crowded with immigrants all eager to land."

As bad a problem as this was, they said, it paled in comparison to the wrongdoing of British shipping company officials who sneaked around American laws to dump undesirables in the United States. They noted, "But a more serious difficulty, in the satisfactory administration of the law, is found in the facility with which prohibited persons may enter the United States from the British provinces (Canada) and Mexico. From November, 1888, to April, 1889, inclusive, twenty-eight British steamships landed 1,304 immigrants at Portland, Me., but they previously touched at Halifax (in Nova Scotia), and landed more than three times that number, most of whom, it is reported, came by rail through Canada into the United States without examination or restriction, and the steamships thereby escaped the payment of the passenger tax. Such unrestricted influx of immigrants has, it is believed, resulted in a large addition to the number who require public aid, and this increased the financial burden of the States and municipalities where they chance to fall into distress."

They recommended adding lepers, sufferers of "destructive and contagious diseases," and "all persons inimical to our social and political institutions" to the list of those barred from entering the United States.

They recommended making immigrants getting "character and fitness" certificates from American consuls in their countries.

They noted the main purpose of the Alien Contract Labor Law of 1885 was to protect American workers from unfair competition from foreigners willing to work for much less money. They said foreigners were breaking the law by coming to Canada and then sneaking into the United States by rail.

They noted the U.S. Treasury Department was supposed to supervise immigration. However, the federal agency contracted the work to the states. This led to problems in enforcing immigration laws, such as they were. State immigration officials were not under federal control. To resolve local jurisdictional disputes, Windom and his subordinates recommended the U.S. Treasury Department (his department) should take over immigration supervision from state immigration commissions.

In 1890, congressional investigators again confirmed American businessmen, foreign steamship companies, and British authorities in Canada were conspiring to flood the U.S. with illegal immigrants. They said the businessmen sent agents to Europe to lure the poor to come to America by promising them unrealistically good conditions, that steamship company executives likewise sent agents through Europe stimulating interest in steerage tickets, and that British authorities in Canada allowed these immigrants into Canada so they could make their way into America without being inspected. They blamed a division of authority between the U.S. Treasury Department and the states for American failure to punish these abuses. **(6)**

In early 1890, Windom decided the U.S. government should take over inspection and admission of immigrants in New York City. Treasury Department agents had determined Castle Garden was unsuitable to handle the tide of immigrants coming into New York City each day. Windom ended the federal immigration contract with New York state officials. Since New York City was the port of entry for most immigrants, this move in effect "federalized" most of the immigration inspection workload.

Per a congressional resolution of April 11, 1890, members of the House and Senate decided to make Ellis Island in Upper New York Bay the site of the new federal immigration station. Ellis Island was handy – it is just across the Hudson River from Castle Garden. Ellis Island is also directly north of Liberty Island, where the Statue of Liberty had been built just four years earlier. Ironically, a large number of people objected to putting an immigration station on Liberty Island, whose giant copper goddess was symbolically beckoning the foreigners to come to the Land of the Free. They said all the greasy foreigners would degrade the attractiveness of the monument. So it was Ellis Island or bust.

There was a bit of housekeeping to do before the feds could have the new facility built. Ellis Island and Liberty Island – which was called Bedloe's Island before Lady Liberty called it home – had both contained harbor defense fortifications from the time of George Washington's presidency to the Civil War, just like the Battery. Starting in 1861, the first year of the Civil War, the U.S. Navy used Ellis Island as a powder magazine, a place for storing gunpowder and other explosives. Before workers could build the immigration station, Navy men had to relocate the pyrotechnics to Fort Wadsworth on nearby Staten Island.

Castle Garden's era as the main immigration station in America would be done. The tiny converted artillery post, which had been stage to Jenny Lind and spider-dancing Lola Montez, and the site of the processing of millions of immigrants, closed in 1890. New York authorities, ticked off because the feds were taking over immigration processing from them, refused to allow the T-men to use Castle Garden.

But Windom and his people shrugged off the New Yorkers' tantrum. While workers were building the inspection station on Ellis Island, Treasury agents in 1890 and 1891 processed immigrants at their Barge Office facility on the Battery, close to Castle Garden. **(7)**

Meanwhile, Treasury Department agents kept examining immigration processing in an effort to improve it. The annual report of the Treasury Department for FY 1891 noted when federal authorities took over immigration processing from New York state officials in 1890, they saved expenses and collected more money from immigrants and steamship companies.

The report also noted federal officials in New York were deporting more aliens who were violating the Alien Contract Labor Law than New York state workers had been deporting for this cause. The authors wrote, "The defense of our wage workers against unfair competition is so essential a part of the industrial protective system of the country, that nothing should be left undone in legislation or administration to make it effective."

While acknowledging, "Our country owes too much in greatness and prosperity to its naturalized citizens to wish to impede the natural movement of such valuable members of society to our shores," the authors wrote, "The noticeable feature of our immigration in recent years has been a change in the character of many of the immigrants, who do not readily assimilate with our people, and are not in sympathy with our institutions."

In 1891, Congress and President Harrison put a new immigration law into effect, which put the states out of the immigration processing business. The law, known as the Act of March 3, 1891, ordered the U.S. Treasury Department to take over this mission in all states, like

they had already done in New York City, the port taking in by far the most immigrants. The U.S. Treasury Department's Bureau of Immigration would handle processing of immigrants.

The law made it a violation for companies to encourage immigration by promising jobs in ads in foreign countries. The law also forbade foreign steamship companies from soliciting foreigners to become immigrants to America. It allowed the companies to advertise their prices, services, and schedules. (U.S. state governments got an exemption for their immigrant inducement programs.)

The law called for medical inspections of immigrants. The law also closed an earlier loophole allowing unlimited immigration of relatives and friends of people who had already gone to the United States.

Today, the U.S. government allows relatively unlimited immigration of relatives of Third World people who have already come to the United States. The practice is called "daisy chaining."

Months after the passing of the 1891 immigration law, the Bureau of Immigration had 24 inspection stations ready in seaports and at spots along the Canadian and Mexican borders. The U.S. Marine Hospital Service's doctors conducted medical inspections at these stations.

The new immigration code still had its problems. The authors of Annual Report of the Secretary of the Treasury for FY1891 noted immigration officials needed to do more to verify the criminal backgrounds of would-be immigrants. They said in so many words the worst criminals would lie about their situations.

They also noted more aliens were landing in Canada and coming to America by rail to avoid inspection and the immigration tax. The 1891 law allowed for only a few inspectors along the Canadian and Mexican borders.

They urged the process of "sifting immigrants" should at least begin in the immigrants' homelands. That way, they argued, "aliens of the prohibited classes shall not be permitted to come across the ocean to our ports, only to be sent back penniless and stranded."

They also urged a uniform inspection of rail passengers from Canada to stop illegals coming in from the north. They urged an international agreement with Britain and Canada, but said the United States should set up its own inspection process for rail passengers whether the British and Canadians liked it or not.

In the 1890s, American officials did further work on the immigration laws to protect Americans from hazards associated with allowing certain types of immigrants to come to America. In the 1890s, immigration would drop by about a million and a half people from what it had been in the 1880s.

Two laws members of Congress enacted in early 1893 started the trend for inspecting immigrants for health and suitability.

One law prevented the introduction of contagious or infectious diseases into the United States. This law allowed a countrywide ban of immigrants from places where cholera and other serious contagious and infectious diseases were epidemic, if quarantining immigrants from the country couldn't guarantee the safety of Americans.

The second law required captains of vessels to provide lists of passengers. Inspectors were required to hold immigrants not clearly entitled to enter the United States for hearings before boards of special inquiry. The law required consuls at seaports where ships were loading passengers for America to verify the lists and verify the immigrants had undergone physical exams, and that none of the passengers was as far as they knew, excludible. Steamship companies were required to post American immigration laws where they sold tickets. Twice a year, the companies had to send certifications to the U.S. Attorney General that they were doing so.

Later in 1893, U.S. Treasury Department officials put into effect a series of regulations designed to protect the rights of the American public, set standards for screening immigrants, and protect immigrants from unscrupulous steamship company officials.

The regulations deputized customs inspectors along the Canadian border to act as immigration officials to inspect those coming into America.

The regulations required ship captains bringing immigrants from ports or parts of countries where certain diseases were prevalent to present a statement certified by an American consular officer that all steerage immigrants he transported had been held for medical observation at a barracks facility at the port for five days before the voyage, and that these immigrants had had their clothes, baggage, and personal effects disinfected. They required leather shoes and boots and leather luggage cases to be disinfected with carbolic acid in water, and they required many other items to be steamed, boiled, treated with carbolic acid, or dipped in a mercury chloride solution.

The regulations ordered the steamship company which brought any immigrant who could not be admitted to the United States to pay for the feeding and lodging of the immigrant while he or she was detained for hearings if the board of special inquiry ruled to have the immigrant deported. Likewise, the regulations ordered the steamship company which brought any immigrant who couldn't gain entry to the United States to take him or her back to Europe at company expense.

A supplement to the regulations established medical exams for immigrants. The supplement also made shipping companies pay for the treatment of people who had become ill aboard ship until they were well enough to leave U.S. hospital facilities to enter the country or return to the port they came from. In some cases, at the discretion of the immigration commissioner, the American immigrant fund would cover expenses of those who were detained due to "accident or unavoidable circumstances."

The regulations and the supplement also established the practice of questioning immigrants for literacy and poverty. If an immigrant came in with $30 or less, the agents were to know about it. If an immigrant was deemed a person likely to become a public charge, he or she had the right to show proof of support from a spouse or relative to the immigration agents.

If the immigrant came illegally and became a public charge within a year of immigrating, the person or corporation or steamship company or railroad bringing the person to America in the first place would have to pay to have him or her deported. If the immigrant came legally, passed inspection, and then became a public charge (through permanent injury or ailment) within a year, the American government's immigrant fund would pay for the deportation.

The laws were designed to protect the rights of the American public to have immigration regulated and prevent infected immigrants from carrying contagious diseases to the country, to protect immigrants from unscrupulous steamship company officials, and to set an understandable standard for steamship companies and immigration officials alike. The rules were generally fair, except for the rule that specified an immigrant getting injured and disabled in the United States through the fault of another still was sent back. This was about a generation before worker compensation laws, so American workers who were disabled on the job suffered comparably in their own homeland. **(8)**

THE EARLY DAYS OF ELLIS ISLAND

Ellis Island opened for business January 1, 1892. Annie Moore, a 15-year-old girl from County Cork in Ireland, was the first immigrant to land and be processed at Ellis Island. After Annie signed the register, Colonel John Baptiste Weber, the first commissioner of the Ellis Island immigration station, presented her with a 10-dollar gold piece, the largest sum of money she had ever had. Annie and her two younger brothers who traveled with her celebrated the New Year by being admitted to the United States as legal immigrants.

Roughly 16 million people had come to America from 1820 to 1891, before inspectors at Ellis Island and other new immigration stations had even processed a single immigrant. Inspectors would admit 20 million immigrants into the United States – more than 14 million of them through the port of New York, and 12 million or so of the port of New York arrivals through Ellis Island – from 1892 through 1924, when the quota laws slowed the tide of immigrants to a trickle.

In the era when American officials were serious about regulating immigration, 70% of all immigrants would come through New York City for processing. The remainder came through smaller immigration stations in the major ports of the East Coast, the Great Lakes, the Gulf Coast, and the Pacific Coast, and similar facilities along the Mexican and Canadian borders. **(9)**

Joseph H. Senner served as Commissioner of Immigration at Ellis Island from 1893 to 1897. He was a German Austrian Jewish immigrant, born in Moravia (in what is now the Czech Republic), who left his faith and changed his last name from Samuely when he came to America, and got involved in America's German community. Senner, a newspaper man, was nominally a Republican. But he worked for the election of honest Democrat Grover Cleveland, and received the appointment a couple of weeks after Cleveland took office for his second term.

Senner had a staff of roughly 100 employees to inspect, process, detain, feed, provide medical care to, admit, or deport a couple of hundred thousand immigrants a year. Ellis Island's slowest year in Senner's term was 1897, when more than 180,000 immigrants passed through, and its busiest was 1893, when almost 450,000 immigrants passed through.

As the 1890s ran their course, more and more people from Southern and Eastern Europe immigrated to America. Some of them did not meet standards for admission as immigrants, and they started disturbances at Ellis Island. Following is an account of one of these fracases, from the New York Times on May 8, 1895:

Four Men Escape from Ellis Island

Over 100 Italians made a determined effort yesterday to break out of the detention pen at Ellis Island.

They rushed against the gates in a body, yelling and waving their arms to scare the guards. The place was in an uproar in a moment, the scared women and children huddling into corners, and the attendants running about for extra guards.

Finally, the Italian representative at Ellis Island, Prof. Aldini, mounted a desk and spoke to his angry countrymen. This had a quieting effect, and in half an hour there was again quiet in the pen.

Four men had escaped over the railing earlier in the day, and made their way to the New Jersey shore.

This was not an isolated incident. A reporter wrote the following in an article in the New York Daily Tribune for April 16, 1896:

Small riots that threatened to develop into trouble of a more serious nature are occurring daily among the many immigrants on Ellis Island, and the officials have become so apprehensive, that Dr. Senner yesterday telegraphed to the Treasury Department at Washington, asking permission to swear in a number of special constables to be used in keeping in subjection the unruly aliens. The Tribune has already told of the arrival of thousands of peasants, penniless and dirty for the most part, from the Mediterranean ports, and they are continuing to pour in daily.

On Sunday the steamship Bolivia brought into this port 1,376 of these people, and Alesia followed with over one thousand. The Werra yesterday brought in 756 and the steamships Victoria and Belgravis are now on the way here with an aggregate of 2,820 more.

Federal authorities allowed Senner to hire more help in 1896.

Senner recommended placing Ellis Island employees under civil service regulations to weed out the unfit. However, an 1896 executive order president Grover Cleveland signed doing this exempted the incumbent jobholders. They were classified as "civil servants" without having to take exams. In other words, they were grandfathered into their jobs without having to prove they were competent to hold them. From 1896 until 1900, only four new hires at Ellis Island came from the civil service list. The rest came from people who the Civil Service Commission certified on the word of politicians. This would in time lead to a corruption scandal at Ellis Island.

Private contractors provided baggage transportation service, food service, and money changing service at Ellis Island. In the first few years, the contractors won business by submitting the highest bid. (The Immigration Bureau was self-supporting; it took in more money in contracts and fees than it spent.) However, this didn't always mean the winning contractors provided the best services to the immigrants. They had the temptation to make their money by doing as little as possible for the immigrants or charging the immigrants as much as possible.

This changed in 1896, when immigration officials awarded contacts to vendors who would charge the least percentage of interest in changing money, ship baggage for the lowest amount per piece, and provide food at the lowest costs. This change in awarding contracts made services better for the immigrants. Of course there would still be individuals who overcharged for and underdelivered on food, deliberately short-changed immigrants in money exchanges, and stole baggage. However, the bidding system improved the overall level of contract services.

In June 1897, a nighttime fire burned down the wooden immigration station building and several other wooden buildings on Ellis Island. Fortunately, no one died or suffered serious injury in the fire. Federal officials decided to build brick, concrete, and steel buildings to replace them. Meanwhile, they temporarily shifted the processing of immigrants back to the Barge Office, on the Battery, close to Castle Garden. **(10)**

Senner left his position at Ellis Island in 1897, and President McKinley appointed Thomas Fitchie, a Brooklyn politician of Scottish ancestry, to replace him. Edward McSweeney, who had been the Assistant Commissioner of Immigration at Ellis Island since 1893, continued in this office under Fitchie.

During most of Fitchie's tenure as Commissioner of Immigration at New York City, construction workers were building better structures on Ellis Island. So immigrant processing in New York City continued at the Barge Office until December of 1900.

The Barge Office didn't have the space or the isolation for control purposes that Ellis Island had. Immigration officials had to rent houses near the Barge Office so they could have room for their hospital service and their detention areas. They also tied a steamboat to the wharf and used it as quarters for detained immigrants and hospital staffers.

Large-scale corruption returned to the immigration process. Unscrupulous employees charged friends and relatives of immigrants money to see them, and stole from the immigrants. Unscrupulous contractors overcharged immigrants for food and short-changed immigrants when they changed their European money into American money. (Federal authorities allowed

moneychangers to charge a small percentage for profit, like a check cashing service, but they were grossly overcharging the immigrants beyond this allowable percentage.) Baggage theft was widespread. Some employees and contractors steered pretty single immigrants to people who forced them to work as prostitutes. **(11)**

Terence Powderly, a railroad machinist who had been mayor of Scranton, Pennsylvania as well as the leader of the Knights of Labor (one of America's first labor unions) had been one of the few prominent labor figures to work for the election of William McKinley in 1896. (McKinley was pro-industry and often was pro-labor as well.) Powderly, who also had become a lawyer after his time as head of his union, applied to become the Commissioner-General of Immigration. Powderly, the son of Irish immigrants, was a good man but a controversial figure. McKinley intended to appoint him, but ran into trouble on this. Most Republican senators were not pro-labor. Some Democrat senators were; they and many labor people were upset Powderly had worked for McKinley, so they called the appointment a payoff. The Senate would not at first confirm Powderly. So McKinley appointed Powderly to the post in 1897 on a recess appointment. The next year the Senate did confirm him.

Powderly's office was in Washington, but he would have to spend quite a bit of time checking on his subordinates in New York City. Powderly launched an investigation of the Barge Office. In 1900, at the conclusion of the investigation, Powderly had 11 immigration agents fired for various offenses stemming from the investigation. Their offenses ranged from overcharging for food, misleading immigrants about distances and destinations (meaning they overpaid for train tickets), charging immigrants' friends and relatives admission fees to allow them on Ellis Island, gypping immigrants in exchanging their European money for American money, cruelty, and other forms of petty theft.

"My chief regret," Powderly said, "was that I could not send some of the culprits to the penitentiary." **(12)**

Immigration officials had In 1899 decided to post a Marine Hospital Service surgeon in Naples to observe immigrants for any physical problems they might have that would prevent them from gaining entry to America once American agents inspected them in New York City or other ports where their ships might land them. Naples at this time was one of the busiest ports of departure for immigrants and also among the dirtiest and most disease-ridden.

The surgeon only had the authority to prevent people from boarding immigrant ships if they were suffering from communicable diseases. He managed to keep many other physical defectives from boarding the ships by telling the steamship company officials that American officials would probably refuse them entry and deport them at the steamship company's costs. It would take awhile before this practice of checking would-be immigrants before they got on ships would be mandatory practice. **(13)**

The Spanish-American War came in 1898, and it would have an indirect effect on the checking of would-be immigrants at at least one other port also.

Crooked contractors sold diseased beef to the U.S. Army, and the toxic meat poisoned many soldiers. Among them was a military band leader who had emigrated from Foggia, in the Apulia region of southern Italy. He had married an immigrant girl from Trieste – a seaport of mostly Italian and Slovenian people under the control of Austria-Hungary -- and their children would be born in America. He had joined the U.S. Army as a musician, and his children grew up in the West as he and his wife and children moved from Army post to Army post in the 1880s and 1890s.

He became deathly ill after eating the poisoned meat, and the Army discharged him. He took his wife and children back to Trieste, so she and their children could live with her relatives after he died. He died in 1901, and his oldest son, now 18, was able to find work as a clerk for the American consul's office in Budapest. The son was a native of America who could speak Italian ... and he quickly learned German and Croatian. He became the consular agent in Rijeka (which in those days was also called Fiume) when he was 20. Rijeka, near Trieste, was also a port city, and many people from Austria-Hungary would get on ships bound for America in the Croatian city's harbor.

About the time the young consul reported for duty in Rijeka, Britain's Cunard Line started sending two ships a month to the port to take emigrants to America. The consul read the immigration regulations he was supposed to enforce, and noted there was nothing specifying he should have immigrants inspected at the port for certain diseases and ailments that would keep them from gaining entry to America. However, if inspectors at Ellis Island or other American ports found would-be immigrants with these problems, they would bar them from entry and make them go back to Europe. The regs said a consul had to "certify to the health of all passengers and crews and give the ship a certificate that it had cleared from a port free from contagious diseases or illnesses subject to quarantine regulations and that bedding and other household goods had been properly fumigated." The consul believed it was wrong to allow immigrants to spend money to get to America, only to be turned back, so he got permission from his superiors to hire local doctors to inspect immigrants at Rijeka.

When the first Cunard Line vessel docked at Rijeka to load immigrants for America, the consul arrived with a doctor to have the immigrants inspected. The British sea captain and steamship line officials were furious when the consul demanded to inspect the immigrants for health problems. They refused, so the consul refused to give the ship a bill of health to land in America. When they saw the young consul was serious, they allowed inspection of the immigrants under protest. The British refused to pay the doctor's fee, so the consul made the Cunard Line post a bond before he would allow any more immigrants for America to board their ships. The Cunard Line threw in the towel, at least at Rijeka.

The young consul would spend 1903 through 1906 at Rijeka, and he would ensure the passage of close to 100,000 immigrants before coming back to America and working as an interpreter at Ellis Island to pay his way through law school. This young consul, Fiorello La Guardia, would gain a reputation for decisive action as a Congressman, a military officer, and mayor of New York City. He explained his first decisive action this way: "Inspection was speedy and efficient, and we saved many hundreds of innocent people from the expense of taking a trip all the way to New York only to be found inadmissable on health grounds and sent back."

La Guardia's idea of American-supervised health inspections done at ports of embarkation did not become government policy for a number of years. Even in the 1920s, when U.S. Public Health Service doctors examined many steerage-traveling immigrants in European ports before allowing them on the ships, doctors still examined most immigrants traveling steerage when they reached Ellis Island and other American immigration stations because it wasn't universal practice to screen immigrants overseas until the era of the Great Depression.

American authorities would start fining steamship companies for each immigrant they transported to America who was too diseased or otherwise physically unadmissible. They would also force the steamship companies to take them back to the ports they brought them from on their money. This system of fines and charges would force steamship companies to have immigrants inspected for diseases in European ports, but would not be as impartial as La Guardia's method of American supervision of the physical exam screening process. **(14)**

The new brick immigration station at Ellis Island was ready for business in December 1900. Immigration workers resumed processing immigrants on Ellis Island eight days before Christmas 1900. Thomas Fitchie at this time was still Commissioner of Immigration at New York City. Edward McSweeney was still Assistant Commissioner of Immigration at New York City. And William McKinley was still President. But their days all would be numbered.

ELLIS ISLAND WHILE THEODORE ROOSEVELT WAS PRESIDENT

The first decade of the 1900s was the heyday of Ellis Island. More than double the amount of Europeans came during this decade than had come in the previous decade. Most immigrants in Roosevelt's time were people from southern Italy, people from all over Austria-Hungary, Jews from Russia, and Poles from their occupied and divided homeland. Many Irish, Germans, and Britons came also ... but many many more came from Italy, Russia, and Austria-Hungary.

It would also be a decade of change and reform for the immigration process. This happened because Theodore Roosevelt was the president through most of the decade, and he picked men who thought like him to run the nation's immigration offices.

Ironically, Teddy Roosevelt became president because of the act of a son of Polish immigrants. This man, Leo Czolgosz, was the anarchist who shot President William McKinley in the gut while he was shaking hands at a fair in Buffalo on September 6, 1901. Cabinet members came to Buffalo to be with their chief; Roosevelt – who was vice-president at the time -- rushed from a camping trip to visit McKinley.

When Roosevelt visited his wounded chief, McKinley was in good spirits and appeared on the road to recovery. Roosevelt returned to his vacation in upstate New York because he and the other Cabinet members thought McKinley would pull through. He figured this act of going back on vacation might calm the public.

However, McKinley took a turn for the worse late September 12 and early September 13. McKinley's people sent for Teddy Roosevelt. That afternoon, an outdoors guide located the vice-president coming down from hiking up a mountain to tell him his boss was dying. Roosevelt hiked back to the lodge several miles away, then he and a driver hitched horses to a wagon and rode more than 40 miles through the mountains in a thunderstorm in the darkness (and they drove so hard they had to change for fresh horses two times on the way) to get to the nearest train station. They got there, mud-covered, as dawn was breaking on September 14, 1901. A telegraph was waiting for Roosevelt, telling him McKinley had died in the wee hours of the morning and he was now the President. Roosevelt took the train to Buffalo, met with the other Cabinet members and aides there, and took the oath of office in a private home that afternoon. **(15)**

Teddy Roosevelt would serve as president from 1901 to 1909. During Roosevelt's administration, more immigrants came to America than in any other similar length of time until the 1990s, when Bill Clinton and Congress decided to ignore enforcement of immigration laws.

Roosevelt was the most politically active president since Abraham Lincoln. He was more enthusiastic about using the power of the presidency than Lincoln. Roosevelt's mindset was crucial to how the American government would run immigration during his terms of office.

Roosevelt became president because an anarchist murdered his predecessor, so he wanted anarchists kept out of the country. Roosevelt hated corruption, so he insisted on honest administration. Roosevelt believed government officials should help the people instead of sitting on their hands while the rich and powerful took advantage of the people, so he insisted on fairness. Roosevelt believed the white race was superior to other races, but he respected Japan as a nation. He also tried to allow the immigration of skilled Chinese. Roosevelt was not bigoted against non-WASP whites, and he believed certain immigrants could strengthen America.

On a personal level, Teddy Roosevelt had a number of friends and acquaintances of many races, religions, ethnicities, levels of wealth, and stations in life. Roosevelt had many more friends who were cowboys than bluebloods. He was the first president to have a black to the White House as a dinner guest – he invited black educator Booker T. Washington shortly after he became president. (Lincoln had conferred with Frederick Douglass in the White House about the recruiting of blacks for the Union Army in 1864, but it was an office appointment instead of a dinner invite.) Roosevelt could treat American Indians and Spaniards one-on-one with respect, even though he had faced off against some braves in North Dakota and had fought in battle against the Spanish.

Teddy Roosevelt had his shortcomings. Like too many men with authority, it was hard for him to admit he was wrong after he rushed to judgment. Probably his worst such act was his decision to uphold the dishonorable discharging of 167 black soldiers stationed near Brownsville, Texas because white residents of that town falsely complained they had rioted. He couldn't admit that he had rushed to judgment and endorsed the punishing of these men after his underlings had botched the investigation and falsely accused the soldiers of covering up for other soldiers of their battalion who allegedly killed a white bartender and wounded a policeman.

Daniel Mannix, a naval officer who thought the world of Teddy Roosevelt because he made the U.S. Navy so powerful, was one of the minority who disapproved of how the incident was handled. He noted:

"A number of these Negro [sic] regiments were outstanding for their skill and pluck. It was a Negro [sic]

regiment that had distinguished itself at San Juan Hill, bravely charging the Spanish position when the white troops refused to advance. When one of those black regiments was in Texas they were attacked by a white crowd for having broken a local taboo, such as entering a restaurant reserved for whites or some such thing. In my opinion, those troopers would have been perfectly justified in taking their rifles and firing a volley into that mob of crackers and tarheels." **(16)**

Teddy Roosevelt didn't overcome Jim Crow. Of course, neither did elitist leftist Democrats Woodrow Wilson or Franklin Delano Roosevelt. In fact, Wilson and FDR used segregation to their advantage, keeping Southern Democrats loyal to them.

Aside from his substandard dealings with the black soldiers, Teddy Roosevelt believed in treating people fairly and having government employees serve the public instead of lording it over the public. He also believed in doing what he felt was right to protect America's interests. The men he picked to run the immigration services were like-minded men.

A scandal at Ellis Island in the summer of 1901, during McKinley's last few months as president, showed that many employees working at Ellis Island were still either corrupt or incompetent, even after Terence Powderly had the work force investigated and eleven of them fired. Some immigration agents were found to be extorting money from immigrants, and some New York City aldermen who performed civil marriage ceremonies overcharged immigrants and kicked back money to higher-ups, allegedly including Fitchie himself. Another facet of the scandal involved the sale of as many as 10,000 fraudulent citizenship papers to immigrants. **(17)**

Shortly after Roosevelt became president in September 1901, he decided to can Thomas Fitchie, the Commissioner of Immigration at Ellis Island. He also made up his mind to get rid of Edward McSweeney, Fitchie's assistant commissioner.

A few months later, Roosevelt replaced Fitchie with William Williams, a wealthy lawyer who had a good military record in the Spanish-American War. Teddy replaced McSweeney with Joseph Murray, an old friend of his.

Williams wasn't the Commissioner-General of Immigration (Terence Powderly held that title until mid 1902, and then Frank Sargent, a former official in the Brotherhood of Locomotive Firemen, held that title until well into 1908), but he was the Commissioner of Immigration at Ellis Island, the top man at the post where immigration was heaviest. Since he oversaw the processing of roughly two-thirds of all immigrants coming to America each year, any policies he put into effect would be important. Besides having so much

local responsibility, Williams was an outspoken man, and he made sure his views were heard.

Williams was honest, direct, and decisive, the kind of man you would expect Teddy Roosevelt to ask to serve. Williams was also opinionated and somewhat prejudiced. He stepped on a lot of toes and angered everyone from dishonest contractors and scam artists posing as missionaries whom he banned from the island to immigrant aid society people who believed he was prejudiced against their countrymen to women workers who thought he was a male chauvinist.

Williams did have some prejudices against certain types of immigrants. However, he didn't let it affect his performance of his job. His personality almost sticks an index finger in your face as you read his reports and letters. Like his boss Teddy Roosevelt, Williams would be too blunt and too politically incorrect for the nation today, because too many of us are immature and are not adult enough to hear the blunt truth coming from our leaders.

Roosevelt fired Powderly in June 1902 on a trumped-up charge he had "coerced" McSweeney. The real reason was Powderly had made so many waves that many of the careerists in the Bureau of Immigration didn't like him. Powderly asked Roosevelt to have someone he trusted review the record of the investigation he (Powderly) ordered, and of his actions concerning McSweeney, and Roosevelt did so. Roosevelt learned the charges against Powderly were untrue, and Powderly had acted justly. Roosevelt would try to make it up to Powderly by appointing him as a special official of Department of Commerce and Labor in 1906 and sending him to Europe to determine the causes of immigration to America from each of the countries of Europe. In 1907, Roosevelt appointed Powderly chief of the Bureau of Immigration's Division of Information, a job Powderly would hold until 1921. Powderly would serve as a Labor Department official until his death in 1924. **(18)**

In February 1903, Congress at the request of Theodore Roosevelt, merged several federal subordinate agencies to form the Department of Commerce and Labor. One of the agencies winding up on the new cabinet-level agency was the Bureau of Immigration.

In March 1903, Congress passed another immigration bill. The 1903 law was legislation you would expect from government when Teddy Roosevelt ran things – an overhaul of previous laws that kept the good features of the old laws and removed their bad features, and added new provisions that made sense, resulting in a code that was workable and fair.

The law aimed at providing better inspection of immigrants, and excluding undesirables. An obvious result of the assassination of President McKinley by anarchist Leon Czolgosz was a provision for the exclusion of any anarchist or other person holding beliefs supporting the violent overthrow of an elected government.

McKinley, by the way, was not the only leader of a nation killed by anarchists in the years before this law went into effect. Anarchism was a force in Europe from the 1880s through World War One. European anarchists also assassinated Tsar Alexander II of Russia in 1881, French president Sadi Carnot in 1894, prime minister Antonio Canovas of Spain in 1897, Empress Elisabeth (Sissi) of Austria-Hungary in 1898, and King Umberto of Italy in 1900.

The assassination of Canovas had had disastrous results for Spain and a direct impact on the United States. Canovas was the best of the politicians who ran Spain in the late 1800s. The mediocrities who ran the country after he died blundered into war against an all-too-eager United States the next year.

Likewise, the assassination of Tsar Alexander II of Russia had an effect on America. His successors aimed policies against Jews, Poles, and other non-Russians in Russia and the lands the Russians controlled. This would translate into the immigration of millions of Jews and Poles and other non-Russians from the Russian Empire to America.

The law aka the Act of March 3, 1903, also strengthened the ban on prostitutes and pimps emigrating to America. The lawmakers put a fine of $5000 and a 1 to 5-year prison term on the books as punishment for those who imported females for prostitution.

"White slavery" (sex trafficking) was a huge evil then, as now, and unlike now, leaders in the early 1900s were more prone to do something about it. Teddy Roosevelt was the moral opposite of Bill Clinton. Inspectors of the Ellis Island era were "tough" on unaccompanied single women because they wanted to make sure these women were not prostitutes, or were not victims being trafficked as sex slaves, or were not so destitute they would feel forced to become prostitutes. Paternalism done the right way is a wonderful thing.

The 1903 law also excluded all polygamists (this was aimed at Moslems, pagans, and Mormons). Back in the day, the Mormons, before – and sometimes after – they swore off polygamy, sent proselytizers to Britain and Scandinavia to bring in women as converts to be polygamous wives for the leaders who could afford more than one wife and could put up with multiple cases of PMS under their roofs each month.

The 1903 law also excluded "persons who have been convicted of a felony or other crime or misdemeanor involving moral turpitude." ("Moral turpitude" means crimes of dishonesty, such as perjury, burglary, fraud,

theft, embezzlement, and fencing stolen goods, or sexual crimes such as rape, sodomy, sexual assault, and child molesting, or acts of malicious violence such as murder, felony assault, and robbery, and acts against public decency such as adultery, incest, bigamy, homosexuality, and child abandonment.)

However, Congress didn't have any trouble with people whose rap sheets contained only political offenses (as long as they weren't anarchists). The law said, "Nothing in the Act shall exclude persons convicted of an offense purely political, not involving moral turpitude." After all, Roosevelt and the Congressional leaders realized political malcontents had founded the United States and their malcontent successors had made it the greatest nation in the world in little more than a century.

The 1903 law banned "all idiots, insane persons, epileptics, and persons who have been insane within five years or previous; persons who have had two or more attacks of insanity at any time previously; paupers; persons likely to become a public charge; professional beggars; persons afflicted with a loathsome or with a dangerous contagious disease."

The 1903 law also denied each immigrant the right to appeal the decision of a Board of Special Inquiry if the board members had ruled the immigrant unfit to enter because of physical or mental disabilities, or because of a "loathsome" or "dangerous contagious disease."

The 1903 law excluded people coming to America on labor contracts except for certain skilled workers whose employment would not put Americans out of jobs. The legislators made it illegal to assist or encourage immigration for jobs, and to offer contracts to foreigners in most cases, and the law carried a $1000 fine for violators. It also allowed anyone harmed by importing a contract worker (including the contract worker himself!) to sue the cheap labor importer; the private citizen or illegal alien and his lawyer could collect the $1000 fine instead of the government if his attorney filed before the government attorney filed.

This law didn't apply to contracts with domestic servants (the "Fifi" or "Lizzie" or "Maria" or "Helga" exception). Nor did it apply to white-collar professionals, clergymen, nuns, or entertainers. These folks could come in legally.

Actors, circus people, musicians, and singers didn't make the money they make now, and in the days before movies and radio and TV and recorded music, people took in their entertainment live. The "entertainer" provision was designed to encourage top-flight talent to come to America. Some immigrants would try to sneak in by falsely claiming they were singers or musicians. One of Williams' successors at Ellis Island, Henry Curran, would make a woman from Hungary show her talent with a violin, and admitted her into the country when she showed she was a virtuosa.

The 1903 law continued to make it a crime to knowingly immigrate illegally. The immigrant would have to pay his own way home, or those who conspired to help him immigrate illegally would have to do so. If the rejected immigrant was without money, then the American government (or the shipping company whose ship brought him – if it was provable that company officials were derelict in failing to keep him off their ship) would pay to ship him back.

Officials had been deporting some alien (foreigners who were not citizens) felons on the common-sense grounds that they couldn't come to America with a criminal record for nonpolitical crimes, so why should they be allowed to stay in America after robbing, beating, raping, or chiseling someone here? The 1903 law made it more easy to expel aliens from America who broke American laws. An alien who was in prison technically was a public charge, and as such, could be forced to leave the country. The law ordered immigration officials to check prisons as well as charitable institutions for aliens with an eye to deporting them as public charges.

The law also increased the amount of time an immigrant could be deported for being a public charge from one year to two years. This applied to immigrants with pre-existing problems, not to immigrant workers who became injured on the job in America.

The legislators also targeted shipping company officials and others who stood to profit from trafficking in illegals. They made it a crime to smuggle illegals or excludibles into America, punishable by a fiine of $1000 per illegal, and a prison term of three months to two years. They also made it a crime to knowingly assist anarchists into America, punishable by a $5000 fine and a prison term of 1 to 5 years They made it a crime for an anarchist or other subversive of the established order, or for any other immigrant who was in America illegally to apply for citizenship, and they made it illegal for anyone else to assist such illegals. Violators of these citizenship laws could cost the offender up to $5000, and one to ten years of penitentiary time.

Ship captains who landed aliens anywhere in America except at an immigration station faced a $100 to $1000 fine and up to a year in prison.

The lawmakers closed the loophole the British and Canadians had been exploiting in railroading immigrants into America without inspection or head tax.

Aliens could still sneak in by walking or by riding horses or by riding in horse-drawn sleds or wheeled vehicles like wagons or carriages across the border. They could also sneak in on small boats or in trains or inside those newfangled automobiles. But the law stopped some illegal immigration from Canada and Mexico. (Most were coming in illegally through Canada.)

Presumably to assist themselves and the federal bureaucrats in their judgment and in their deliberations, the legislators inserted a section into the law forbidding the sale of liquor in the Capitol Building. They didn't make it illegal for anyone to <u>give</u> them a snort or several before they attended to the nation's business.

The representatives and senators also wrote into the law a provision for making ship captains note which immigrants had the equivalent of less than $50. Although they did not enact a law requiring would-be immigrants to have a minimum amount of money to avoid vagrancy or pauperism, they did want to monitor how many very poor were trying to come to America.

The lawmakers also ordered ship captains to have would-be immigrants answer essentially the same questions that American inspectors would eventually ask immigrants. They made it illegal for ship captains to fail to have valid information about any immigrant they intended to land in America, and made such a failure a $10 fine per immigrant on whom information was missing.

The law also penalized shipping companies $100 per diseased person found in inspection in America for bringing any diseased person to America if a competent doctor in Europe or elsewhere outside of America could have detected the disease. The law also allowed American officials to forbid a ship carrying the diseased permission to land at any American port until the shipping company paid the fine. **(19)**

William Williams used the $100 penalty regulation like his own "Big Stick." He had the steamship companies fined $7500 (for 75 immigrants) the steamship companies brought to the United States negligently in June 1903.

He noted, "Already very clear signs exist that the law will hereafter be obeyed, and the former alleged inability on the part of some foreign surgeons to discover cases of favus and trachoma prior to embarkation is very rapidly disappearing. The bringing of diseased aliens, with or without a law to the contrary, is a reckless thing, if only on account of the ready disseminating of disease among the healthy immigrants." **(20)**

In other words, Williams said, some chiselers running a steamship line were willing to risk sickening many immigrants aboard a ship just to shoehorn a couple of sick people into steerage so they could collect a few dollars more.

Williams cared about the other immigrants as well as the American public. Williams fined and/or fired employees when he caught them or found out about them mistreating immigrants. He had businessmen investigated whom he suspected were defrauding the immigrants. He even barred some immigrant aid groups and clergy from Ellis Island when he determined they were corrupt.

Williams had definite ideas on the kinds of immigrants he wanted Americans to welcome, and the kinds he wanted kept out. In his annual report of 1903, Williams noted, "The great bulk of the present immigration settles in four of the Eastern States (New York, New Jersey, Massachusetts, Pennsylvania), and most of it in the large cities of those States. Notwithstanding the well-known demand for agricultural labor in the Western States, thousands of foreigners (from Italy, Austria-Hungary, and Russia) keep pouring into our cities, declining to go where they might be wanted because they are neither physically nor mentally fitted to go to these undeveloped parts of our country and do as did the early settlers from northern Europe."

"No one would object to the better classes of Italians, Austrians, and Russians coming here in large numbers; but the point is that such better element does not come, and, furthermore, the immigration from such countries as Germany and the British Isles [sic] has fallen to a very low figure."

"Past immigration was good because most of it was of the right kind and went to the right place. Capital can not, and it would not if it could, employ much of the alien material that annually passes through Ellis Island, and thereafter chooses to settle in the crowded tenement districts of New York."

Williams said at least 200,000 of the 650,000 who came to the country legally in 1902 were undesirable. He said they were "unintelligent, of low vitality, of poor physique, able to perform only the cheapest kind of manual labor, desirous of locating almost exclusively in the cities, by their competition tending to reduce the standard of living of the American wageworker, and unfitted mentally or morally for good citizenship."

He said undesirables "will be of no benefit to the country, and will, on the contrary, be a detriment, because their presence will tend to lower our standards; and if these 200,000 persons could have been induced to stay at home, nobody, not even those clamoring for more labor, would have missed them. Their coming has been of benefit chiefly, if not only, to the transportation companies which brought them here."

"I state without hesitation that the vast majority of American citizens wish to see steps taken to prevent these undesirable elements from landing at our shores. Attempts to take such steps will be opposed by powerful and selfish interests, and they will insist, among other things, on the value of immigration in the past to the United States and the enormous demand for labor, neither of them relevant as applicable to the particular question whether the undesirable immigrants should be prevented from coming here."

"Europe, like every other part of the world, has millions of undesirable people whom she would be glad to part with, and that strong agencies are constantly at work to send some of them here."

"Aliens have no inherent right whatever to come here, and we may and should take means, however radical and drastic, to keep out all those below a certain physical and economic standard of fitness and all whose presence will tend to lower our standards of living and civilization." **(21)**

Williams' remarks, true in most respects but unfortunately prejudiced in other respects, reflected the viewpoint of many Americans.

Williams was constantly defending his work and his staff's work at Ellis Island. Teddy Roosevelt, in response to Williams' critics in the German community of New York City, appointed a commission to investigate Williams and his people. The commissioners found the German critics of Williams and his people were – like the *Hindenburg* as it burst into flame – full of hot gas. **(22)**

The feisty Williams quit his job in January 1905. Why? Because he believed his assistant Joseph Murray – an old friend of Roosevelt's whom Teddy had personally appointed – was unfit for the job and Roosevelt would not remove him from the post.

Teddy Roosevelt replaced Williams as Commissioner of Immigration at Ellis Island with Robert Watchorn. Watchorn, a coal miner since he was a boy, emigrated to America from England as a young man in 1880. Watchorn went to work as a miner in Pennsylvania, and saved enough to bring his parents and siblings to America. Watchorn became the first secretary and treasurer of the United Mine Workers union, and then served the chief factory inspector for the state of Pennsylvania. He had also served in the Immigration Service as an inspector at Ellis Island, then as the chief immigration officer monitoring Canadian immigration. Watchorn had trains inspected in Canada, and he went undercover in Canada to find out where most aliens were sneaking into America. As a result, he posted officials elsewhere along the Canadian border and inside Canada to guard against illegal immigration.

Theodore Roosevelt, although a Republican, did not look down on miners. Roosevelt helped settle the Coal Strike of 1902. He was the first president to intervene in a strike on the side of the public, and to give the striking workers a fair hearing, instead of paying undue respect to the demands of the robber barons. Because of this, Roosevelt had many friends in the United Mine Workers, from leader John L. Lewis to the rank-and-file miners.

While not as combative as Williams, Watchorn was as dedicated to America's people and to the fair treatment of the immigrants. Watchorn received higher marks for kindness than did the feisty Williams. A glimpse of his motivation comes from a letter he wrote to Teddy Roosevelt after receiving his appointment to succeed Williams. He wrote, "I do not know of a more important post at your disposal, Mr. President, than that for which you have thus chosen me. To dry tears, and to assuage grief, are works worthy of the noblest of our race; but to remove the cause for tears and grief, is a more laudable endeavor. Ellis Island is the one place where this can be done, in very great measure, by the one in authority there." **(23)**

Watchorn continued Powderly's and Williams' war against corruption. He designed standards for food, money changing, and baggage handling contracts to ensure quality service for fair prices. He also checked on companies which did business with immigrants after they left Ellis Island. In one case, he filed a complaint with the Interstate Commerce Commission against several railroad companies for gouging and mistreating immigrants leaving Ellis Island. Watchorn filed his case after he had one of his assistants, Philip Cowen, an American of German Jewish heritage, pose as an immigrant and travel the rails with immigrants.

In 1905 Roosevelt appointed men to examine how to manage the cases of immigrants seeking to become "naturalized" – in other words, become American citizens. On their advice, Congress in 1906 reorganized the Bureau of Immigration into the Bureau of Immigration and Naturalization. The bureau's Division of Immigration would screen immigrants, while the bureau's Division of Naturalization would maintain citizenship records and oversee local federal courts in the citizenship process. The Division of Naturalization would ensure immigrants seeking citizenship would file a standard application, pay a standard cost, and get equal justice at any federal court. Federal attorneys with the U.S. Justice Department would do case work relating to immigrants applying for citizenship.

Ellis Island was very busy when Commissioner Williams ran it. But the most immigrants per year landed at Ellis Island during Commissioner Watchorn's watch. The vast majority of immigrants during Teddy Roosevelt's presidency were Italians, Jews coming from the Russian empire, Poles from the three empires which held Poland captive, and people of many ethnicities coming from Austria-Hungary. These people were different in religion, customs, and personal habits than the British, German, and Scandinavian immigrants of previous decades. They aroused resentment in many Americans. Out on the West Coast, many Californians were angry over the large numbers of Japanese coming to the Golden State.

However, it was overstatement to say these "unwashed" aroused the same level of mindless hatred the Irish immigrants aroused when they came by the hundreds of thousands during and after the Great

Hunger more than 50 years earlier. Angry Americans didn't form a party to fight these immigrants like the Know-Nothings had done to fight the Irish. But many Americans thought the government should do more to keep out people they called "Dagos," "Kikes," "Polacks," "Hunkies," and others from Eastern and Southern Europe. Likewise, they wanted the flow of peoples they called "slant-eyed Japs and Chinks" dried up. The politicians listened.

In 1907 Watchorn's staffers processed more than a million immigrants through Ellis Island. Early in that same year Congress adjusted immigration laws a little more with another immigration bill.

The new immigration law, formally known as the Act of February 20, 1907, was an update of the 1903 immigration law. It enabled immigration inspectors to exclude more kinds of immigrants. Besides criminals, anarchists, those guilty of acts of moral turpitude, and other problem immigrants who couldn't become American residents, immigration inspectors were to exclude imbeciles, feeble-minded persons, people with physical or mental defects that would harm their abilities to earn livings, tuberculosis sufferers, unaccompanied children 15 or younger unless they were coming to be with a parent who was legally in the United States, and persons who admitted to committing non-political crimes even when they weren't convicted of these crimes.

The 1907 law also increased the amount of time an immigrant could be deported for being a public charge from two years to three years. The law retained the clauses about treating criminals like public charges to make it easier to deport them.

The law also denied each immigrant the right to appeal the decision of a Board of Special Inquiry if the board members had ruled the immigrant unfit to enter because he or she had tuberculosis. They added this disease to the existing other mental, physical, and serious disease problems they allowed no appeal from in the 1903 law.

Unfortunately, the lawmakers weakened some of the 1903 law's punishments. They removed the specific punishments for illegals wrongfully becoming citizens. They also removed the specific penalites for wrongfully assisting illegals to become citizens.

The representatives and senators also allowed aliens facing deportation hearings to be free on bond pending final ruling on their cases. This would allow some wealthier aliens to jump bond.

The members of Congress kept the 1903 law's provision making it illegal for ship captains to fail to have valid information about any immigrant they intended to land in America. However, they capped the fine for such wrongdoing at $100 per ship. The 1903 law made the fine $10 per immigrant on whom information was missing.

The senators and representatives made it legal to deport alien females for engaging in prostitution or other immoral acts (like pornography) within three years of gaining entry to the United States. Prostitutes and white slaves from abroad soon learned to say they had been in the country longer than three years when policemen took them into custody. Regrettably, the congressmen did not apply the same punishment for those who lived off the proceeds of the sex trade, like pimps, madams, sex traffickers, and pornographers.

The 1907 law excluded those having tickets paid for by any private organization or foreign government. On the surface it might seem unfair to bar an immigrant from entry if a private organization or foreign government paid for him to come to America. However, some European governments were ethnically cleansing – for example, the Russian government wanted Jews, Poles, and other minorities to leave the Russian Empire. Likewise, all European countries had residents that the authorities and the public in those countries considered undesirable. They were dumping their misfits in America, and America's lawmakers, looking out for the good of Americans, wanted this to stop.

The 1907 law required better sanitation and less crowding on ships carrying immigrants. They ordered shipping companies to alter their ships to meet American steerage standards by the first day of 1909. Some steamship company officials used this requirement as an excuse to raise ticket prices instead of curbing their large profit margins. This kept some of the very poorest of Europe from immigrating, but most immigrants still managed to save their money for the higher fares. Still, the departure of many people from Europe would make opportunities for those poorest who couldn't afford to leave the home country because there was less competition for work and land.

The lawmakers retained most of the rest of the 1903 law. (However, they did drop the ban on selling booze in the Capitol building.) They added authorization and funding for a commission to study immigration. They gave the president the authority to sign international immigration agreements subject to the advice and consent of the Senate. They also allowed immigration officials to work with state officials in steering immigrants to states whose leaders wanted immigrants for certain purposes. **(24)**

The 1907 law did have some effect on admissions but not on the numbers of those who came to America. The flow of immigrants stayed between 750,000 and 1.3 million each year from 1907 until 1914, when World War One started. Immigration from Italy, Austria-Hungary, and the Russian Empire continued to be very high.

Immigration agents at Ellis Island and all other immigration stations had been barring 3500 to 9000 would-be immigrants a year in the years 1901 through 1904. From 1905 through 1908, the immigration agents at Ellis Island and all other immigration stations would bar 10,000 to 13,000 would-be immigrants a year. Most of those denied entry to the United States the inspectors ruled as "paupers or likely to become public charges."

Williams would return as Commissioner of Immigration at Ellis Island in 1909. During 1909, the immigration agents at Ellis Island and all other immigration stations would bar 10,411 would-be immigrants, but in the next three full years of his term at Ellis Island (1910-1912), the immigration agents at Ellis Island and all other immigration stations would bar 16,000 to 24,000 would-be immigrants a year. Most of those denied entry to the United States the inspectors ruled as "paupers or likely to become public charges." Evidently, inspectors enforced the law more literally during these years, especially those at Ellis Island, who processed roughly three-quarters of all immigrants during Williams' second watch there. **(25)**

Meanwhile, Roosevelt himself handled the problems of immigration from China and Japan.

In 1900, rebels in China, who foreigners nicknamed the "Boxers," rose against the Europeans who had carved China up like rival gangsters carve up turf. They attacked foreign-owned businesses and missions. They killed thousands of Chinese who had become Christians and they killed Catholic priests and nuns who worked among them. The Boxers beheaded several Protestant missionaries and their wives. They besieged for two months about 1000 foreigners and another 3000 Chinese Christians who had holed up in a section of Peking (Beijing) where the legation district was. (A legation is like an embassy, but with less prestige. The Europeans, Japanese, and Americans considered the Chinese as subhuman, unworthy of embassies. That's why they were so exploitative to the Chinese in the first place.)

The Chinese army had not intervened in the struggle because the corrupt and decrepit Dowager Empress Tzu Hsi had encouraged the Boxers. Finally a multinational force broke into Beijing and routed the Boxers. The leaders of several European nations, Japan, and America forced the Dowager Empress' government to pay hundreds of millions of dollars in penalties and allow the hated foreigners to rule sections of some of China's biggest cities.

American officials spent their cut of the money covering losses to Americans. But since they received much more money than they needed to cover all legitimate American claims, they refunded the balance to the Chinese government. China's rulers used the money to send Chinese students to study in America.

Although American businessmen were about as greedy as their European and Japanese rivals, Teddy Roosevelt (like McKinley) and his officials were much more ethical than their opposites in the European capitals and Tokyo in other ways as well. They tried to talk the Europeans and Japanese into acting more like reasonable businessmen and less like colonial masters, but did not make much of an impact.

The American public looked down on the Chinese as being backward pagans and feared American robber barons would use them as yellow slaves to break their wage scales. The Chinese Exclusion Act, enacted in 1882 and amended in 1884, had kept most would-be Chinese immigrants out of the United States. The related Chinese Exclusion Treaty was due to expire at the end of 1904.

American labor union leaders wanted to keep the Chinese excluded because they knew business owners would use the Chinese to reduce wages even more. American businessmen who sold products to China wanted the ban on Chinese immigration lifted.

China was still a quasi-colony of Europe, Japan, and America, but many of its "best and brightest" were planning to change this. Many patriotic Chinese – like the Japanese decades earlier – welcomed Western practices that would improve their nation but not the greedy Westerners who came with the practices. China still had a few years left under the corrupt and decrepit Dowager Empress Tzu Hsi. She died in 1908 and Chinese revolutionaries overthrew her successor in 1911 and essentially ended the dynasty.

China's emerging industrialist, merchant, intellectual, and student classes wanted better treatment from America. Chinese businessmen, travelers, students, and government officials who legally came to America complained that American immigration officials abused them and detained them in unsanitary facilities in San Francisco harbor.

Congress, on Roosevelt's urging, extended the Chinese Exclusion Act in 1904. Roosevelt wanted to protect American workers, and he also wanted to pick up some votes. He was running for a second term in 1904, and anti-Chinese sentiment ran high in the Pacific states. The Chinese Exclusion Treaty expired, but no new treaty took its place right away. So the status quo continued. Chinese laborers remained excluded. Other Chinese who traveled to America continued to suffer abuses.

Finally, the Chinese struck back. People in China, aided and abetted by Chinese businessmen in America, started threatening a boycott of American products in 1905.

Roosevelt continued to oppose the immigration of unskilled coolie laborers. However, he figured treating

other Chinese nationals coming to America fairly would ease the tension. Roosevelt ordered American officials in China to start checking Chinese people applying to come to the United States. If an American official in China issued a Chinese person an entry certificate, Roosevelt ordered, then immigration officials in the United States would have to honor it instead of refusing the Chinese entry or soliciting bribes to allow them in. Roosevelt also ordered some immigration agents guilty of corruption or abusive behavior toward Chinese immigrants fired or otherwise punished. (This was already policy toward immigration agents guilty of corruption or abusive behavior toward other immigrants.)

Many people in China were not satisfied. They began the boycott in the summer of 1905. American products went unsold. Chinese servants quit working for Americans. Cynical Europeans, who essentially wouldn't even allow Chinese into their own countries, profited by selling more of their goods to the Chinese instead. The Europeans encouraged the boycott.

Many American business leaders who profited from the China trade urged Roosevelt to loosen restrictions on Chinese immigration. Instead, Roosevelt put pressure on the Dowager Empress' government to stop the boycott. Also, powerful Chinese businessmen who profited from the American trade started to lose money, and they appealed to her officials.

When persuasion didn't work, Roosevelt threatened a military strike on China. Chinese officials put an end to the boycott in 1906. Roosevelt, Congress, and American immigration officials continued to exclude coolie laborers from China, but on paper they made it easier for other Chinese to immigrate to America. Actual Chinese immigration to America stayed at about 2100 a year in the 1900s, and at about 2100 a year in the 1910s. American immigration officials would continue to enforce American laws limiting immigration from China. **(26)**

Roosevelt took a different approach to the Japanese. He respected Japan as a military power and understood the nation's need for respect. However, he was opposed to immigration of unskilled Japanese workers to the United States. Corrupt politicians in San Francisco made him take care of business with the Land of the Rising Sun.

Large commercial farm owners in California, who wanted cheap fruit pickers and farm workers, naturally opposed any move that would deprive them of Japanese labor. However, many California union people supported the limiting of Japanese immigrants. They didn't want their wages sneak-attacked.

San Francisco mayor Eugene Schmitz and his political boss Abe Ruef were in trouble for their many crimes. In 1906, the year of the San Francisco earthquake, they were facing indictment on corruption charges, so they decided to appeal to anti-Japanese bigotry to divert attention from their legal problems. Their people on the San Francisco school board late in 1906 voted to force all Oriental children into one school to segregate them from white children.

Teddy Roosevelt was not amused. The school board's action was a probable violation of a treaty America had with Japan about the treatment of its nationals.

Roosevelt's attorney general filed lawsuits against the San Francisco school board in 1907. Southern leaders lent their support to San Francisco officials. Why? Segregation of blacks was the law in their states. They didn't want this to change. Roosevelt the Republican had invited Booker T. Washington to the White House, so in the beady little minds of the segregationists, a successful attack upon segregation in San Francisco could lead Roosevelt to attack segregation of blacks in their own states.

Roosevelt had to tread with caution and wisdom. Since the San Francisco school segregation edict was only a decade or so after the Supreme Court's idiotic 1896 Plessy v. Ferguson case ruling okaying segregation, Roosevelt might have lost in court. Meanwhile, people in Japan rioted against Americans and Japanese papers in California made threats of bloodshed against Americans. (They were lucky they did it in California. In many other states in that era, they would have been lynched or at the very least their newspaper buildings would have and should have been burned to the ground.) Japanese politicians called for more military spending.

Roosevelt "invited" the school board members to come to Washington. Mayor Schmitz came with them. Roosevelt convinced them to revoke the segregation law. Roosevelt issued an executive order banning Japanese immigration via Mexico, Canada, and American-owned Hawaii.

Roosevelt – who personally helped negotiate the end of the Russo-Japanese War -- then used a little more of his diplomatic muscle later in 1907 on the Japanese. He convinced Japanese officials that the Congress was going to virtually exclude Japanese immigration like they had virtually excluded Chinese immigration. Japanese officials got the hint; in the so-called "gentlemen's agreement" with Roosevelt, they decided to restrict the immigration of their laborers to America.

In 1907, more than 30,000 Japanese immigrated to the United States; the number dropped to about 16,000 in 1908, and then varied from about 3,000 to 10,000 Japanese immigrants a year until 1925, when quotas took effect.

Roosevelt said, "The obnoxious school legislation was abandoned, and I secured an arrangement with Japan under which the Japanese themselves prevented any emigration to our country of their laboring people, it being distinctly understood that if there was such emigration the United States at once would pass an exclusion law. It was of course infinitely better that the Japanese should stop their own people from coming rather than that we should have to stop them; but it was necessary for us to hold this power in reserve."

Juries eventually found Eugene Schmitz guilty of extortion and Abe Ruef guilty of bribery. (Ruef bribed 11 of the 18 local supervisors, and he also tried to bribe jurors.) Both men did several years in jail. After Schmitz's release from prison, a forgiving and/or stupid electorate in San Francisco would vote him back into office as a local supervisor two different times. **(27)**

In the wake of the incident with Japan, Teddy Roosevelt sent a fleet of battleships and other vessels around South America and into the Pacific to perform naval training and gunnery practice. (The Panama Canal was still under construction.) Roosevelt intended that his Great White Fleet would show the Japanese – who had recently annihilated the Russian fleet in the Russo-Japanese War – some American muscle. He saw the fleet off in December 1907.

After the American fleet had made calls at the major ports of the nations of South America and was steaming toward America's West Coast ports in 1908, the Japanese government invited the fleet to Japan. Roosevelt and his admirals, wary of a Jap sneak attack plot, accepted the invite but had the ships' men on alert. They limited shore leaves in Japan, deployed ships defensively, and had men at the ready to fight any potential attacks. The Japanese were favorably impressed with the professionalism and good will of America's navy men; their visit to Japan was a diplomatic success for America. On the way home, the American fleet passed through the Suez Canal and rendered assistance to the victims of a huge earthquake in Italy. Theodore Roosevelt greeted the Great White Fleet as it returned to America in February 1909, 10 days before he left office. (Before FDR, Inauguaration Day was March 4 instead of January 20.)

Those who complain today about how bigoted and mean-spirited the immigration officials were a century ago need to remember men like Williams and Theodore Roosevelt were looking out for the nation's interests as well as the immigrants' interests. Unlike most federal-level politicians and officials today, Theodore Roosevelt and Williams put the good of the country ahead of their own political careers.

Williams was stern and somewhat bigoted. But despite his prejudices, he was an honorable man who punished those who mistreated the immigrants. Under his second watch, immigration agents kept out more people, but almost everyone from the areas of Europe he targeted still managed to gain entry to the United States. This meant Williams' personal prejudices did not extend to discrimination against non-WASP immigrants in how he had immigrants screened and treated.

Roosevelt's other Ellis Island boss Robert Watchorn was less stern and more likeable. He radiated more charm than Williams, but was just as dedicated to giving the taxpayers good service for their money. He was also deeply motivated to protect immigrants from those who would abuse them.

Roosevelt himself was forceful, but generous. Because he was forceful he was respected. Because he tried to help people he was loved by many. Like Williams, Roosevelt was somewhat bigoted as well. However, Roosevelt usually was able to do the right thing despite his prejudices. Teddy Roosevelt allowed more non-WASP immigrants into America than any other president until Bill Clinton. Clinton, of course, in the informed opinion of many, did so because he was looking to pad voter rolls in his favor as well as deliver cheaper grunt and techie labor for his corporate sponsors.

The record of history provides a yardstick to measure those who have held power. Compare Theodore Roosevelt with both George Bushes and the Clintons and Obama, who have repeatedly ignored the nation's interests and look out only for their own interests and the interests of the corporate leaders (campaign donors and friends) who want cheap labor, bailouts, and no trade regulations to interfere with their profits on Asian-made goods. It's obvious who the servant of the people was, and who the servants of their own demented egos and the pathological greed of their donors have been.

ELLIS ISLAND WHILE TAFT WAS PRESIDENT

William Howard Taft became president in 1909. As Theodore Roosevelt's vice-president, Taft benefited from Teddy's popularity like George Bush would benefit from Ronald Reagan's popularity. Taft, a tall obese man, was nowhere near as energetic as Teddy Roosevelt -- but who was? He and Roosevelt would finally have a falling-out. Their tiff split the Republican Party so badly that Democrat Woodrow Wilson would win the 1912 election while garnering only slightly more than 40% of the popular vote. Roosevelt, angry because GOP wheelhorses cheated him out of the nomination, ran as an independent and got many more popular votes and electoral votes than Taft.

History repeats itself. Eighty years later, a short big-eared billionaire named Perot who said he worried about the disruption of his daughter's wedding would draw enough voters away from the very flawed George Bush to allow the very flawed Bill Clinton to win the 1992 election with less than 45% of the popular vote.

Taft did continue many of Roosevelt's policies and rehired many of those who worked for Roosevelt. Among these was William Williams. He brought Williams back as Commissioner of Immigration at Ellis Island when Robert Watchorn resigned in 1909.

Taft in essence helped Watchorn resign. Watchorn was a kindlier man than Williams, but not as aggressive at refuting the lies his critics spread about him. Watchorn riled the corporate thieves who wanted to profit from the immigrant carrying trade, he riled the employment agencies whose owners wanted to exploit the immigrants as quasi-slave labor, and he riled the local contractors and petty thieves who wanted to cheat immigrants. All of these swindlers had friends among the crooked politicians in New York, New Jersey, and Washington. They had been pressing for Roosevelt to fire Watchorn. Of course that wouldn't happen.

But the huge number of immigrants Roosevelt's administration let into America riled the people who were Watchorn's natural allies – labor union people. Watchorn was a former labor official himself. His former comrades in the labor unions complained that allowing so many people into America was going to depress wages. And Watchorn came in for criticism from some of his own employees on Ellis Island, because the torrent of immigrants led him to work them harder. Taft decided not to reappoint Watchorn when he took office in 1909. **(28)**

Watchorn went on to other projects. He became an oil industry operator, and made quite a bit of money as a result. But the former coal miner didn't become a robber baron.

Taft didn't exactly reward the greedy for raising the uproar against Watchorn. He brought back the brass-knuckled William Williams to run Ellis Island.

Williams in his second term as commissioner almost immediately stirred up controversy by enforcing the "pauper" and "public charge" portion of the immigration law. In a memo he wrote for his agents, he acknowledged there was no legal minimum in cash an immigrant needed to enter America. However, he said, "In most cases it will be unsafe for immigrants to arrive with less than twenty-five ($25) besides railroad tickets to destination, while in many cases they should have more." He wanted inspectors to take this into consideration when deciding whether to admit immigrants.

Williams said common sense dictated setting a minimum amount of cash needed and letting would-be immigrants and shipping companies know what America expected of them. He blamed shipping companies for bringing large numbers of practically penniless people to America, where they would require charity to survive until they could eke out meager livings. As an example, Williams noted 189 of the 251 passengers a steamship offloaded at Ellis Island on the 4th of July 1909 had $10 or less.

There would be no formal requirement for an immigrant to show he or she had at least a certain amount of cash to avoid being sent back as a pauper for a few more years. But Williams instructed his inspectors to use the $25 amount as a guideline to determine if an immigrant could be excluded as being likely to become a public charge. He noted, "This notice is not, as many have claimed it to be, a rule under which inspectors must exclude immigrants with less than $25, and thus an attempt to create a property test not found in the statutes. It is merely a humane notice to intending immigrants that upon landing they will require at least some small amount of money with which to meet their wants while looking about for employment."

Many immigrants who were in their 20s in this period would say later the inspectors let them in despite not having $25 because they looked like vigorous young men and women. Others remembered it as a hindrance. **(29)**

Bringing in destitute immigrants was a big business not only for the shipping companies, but for immigration business operators. Williams in a 1910 report to Congress, noted these men would have agents operating in Europe tell immigrants to list the immigration business street address in America as a final destination address to fool the inspectors. He said a couple of the shipping companies also brought in large numbers of boys younger than 16 even though their parents were staying at home in Europe. **(30)**

Williams in his second term as boss at Ellis Island resumed his crusade against corruption. In 1910, he revoked the food service contract of the businessmen who held it because they were not feeding immigrants properly. In 1911, he ended the baggage handling contract of the contractor who had it because he and his people were cheating immigrants.

In 1910, Williams started an investigation that led to the prosecution and imprisonment of 15 officials of the Hellenic Transatlantic Steam Navigation company for smuggling diseased aliens into America. When the trials of some of the defendants were over in 1912, the federal prosecutor in Brooklyn wrote him the following letter summarizing the convictions:

Sir:

I have the honor to inform you that on Tuesday afternoon, the 25th instant, at 4:30 P.M. the officers of the S.S. Patris of the National Steam Navigation Company of Greece, who were found guilty on June 21st of conspiracy in smuggling or landing surreptitiously into the United States ineligible and diseased aliens in violation of the United States Immigration Laws, were brought before Judge Chatfield in the District Court for the Eastern District of New York and sentenced as follows:

Demetrios Bogiazides, master of the S.S. Patris, one year and one day in Atlanta Penitentiary, and to pay a fine of $1000.

Nicholas Bogiazides, Chief Officer of S.S. Patris, (son of the Master) one year and one day in Atlanta Penitentiary and to pay a fine of $1000.

Augoustis Fountes, Chief Commissary of S.S. Patris, ten months in Atlanta Penitentiary and to pay a fine of $1000.

Andreas Dambassis, Chief Steward of S.S. Patris, ten months in Atlanta Penitentiary and to pay a fine of $1000.

Nicholas Bistis, Doctor of S.S. Patris, six months in the prison at Mineola, L.I. and to pay a fine of $1000.

The Judge in imposing sentence on the defendants expressed his sorrow that he cannot reach for punishment Embyrikoe, Charalambos and Dapontes, the owners and managers of the steamship company in Greece, as the evidence proved that they were the arch-conspirators and the defendants knowingly became their conspirators and tools in effecting the a overt acts of the conspiracy here.

After the imposition of sentence the attorneys for the defence [sic] proposed that inasmuch the company itself had directed the smuggling operations and the profits accrued to the company, the burden should fall on the company, and they could arrange to pay any fine, no matter how big if the Court were disposed to decrease the imprisonment period imposed on the defendants. The Court stated that they might make an application to him before the defendants were sent to Atlanta, and he would think it over, although he did not believe in the practice or principle of imposing big fines and reducing the prison sentences. **(31)**

Williams again took aim at some of the self-styled immigrant aid groups and clergy from Ellis Island when he determined they were corrupt. He banned representatives of the Swedish Immigrant Home, St. Joseph's Home for the Protection of Polish Immigrants, and the Austrian Society of New York from coming to Ellis Island to waylay immigrants. This is what he wrote to the Austrian Society of New York when he revoked their privileges on Ellis Island in 1909:

Sir:

You have asked me to state why I withdrew from your society the privilege of being represented at Ellis Island. I proceed to comply with your request.

(1) For some time past the quarters in which your society receives immigrants have been maintained in a condition of almost indescribable filth and ordinary sanitary requirements have been disregarded. This condition of filth appears to have extended to everything in the house, including room, floors, closets, bedding and the solitary bath tub on the top floor. Foul odors have pervaded most of the quarters. These facts have at various times in 1908 and 1909 been reported to a Congressional Committee by Government agents who went to the house in order to investigate it. Further details as to what they found are on file in my office and open to inspection. The same atrocious conditions were on August 9, 1909, again witnessed and reported to me by an Inspector of this office. That all of these Government agents have been conservative in their statements is now conclusively proved by an investigation conducted a few days ago by the Health Department of the City of New York which shows the Home's quarters to be grossly unsanitary and filthy, some of them being offensive with decomposing animal and vegetable matter. As a result appropriate orders will be issued by the Health Department.

In view of what precedes I am amazed that you should have cared to write me under date of August 11, 1909, that "now the house is in a <u>clean, good condition</u>."

(2) Your home is open to men and women alike, the records showing that a large number of both, including unmarried women, have been turned over to you. Nevertheless, you employ no matron, though your manager, at a recent hearing in my office, undertook to explain that his wife, who is most of the time in the kitchen, served also as matron. I have not only been unable to learn that there are any moral safeguards thrown around girls who reach your Home, but, on the contrary, it appears that they have been frequently exposed to coarse treatment and sounds of vulgarity.

(3) One of your chief duties in connection with immigrants going to your Home is to see to it that they promptly reach their relatives or friends, or secure proper employment, and you have been reporting to this office the alleged addresses showing where such immigrants have gone. For some time past some of these addresses have been under investigation. An agent who acted for the Congressional Committee above referred to reports that in the Spring of 1908 he found a large proportion to be false or fictitious. Out of a few which I have recently caused to be investigated I find a number to be wrong or worthless for all purposes for which the immigration authorities might require them.

Any one of the foregoing reasons justifies my statement that the Home of the Austrian Society is not a fit place for immigrants to go to. I could if I wished furnish further reasons for my action, but I deem the present ones sufficient.

Respectfully,
(Signed) Wm. Williams
Commissioner

Williams reinstated the privileges of the Austrian Society of New York, and then got word they had backslid. His follow-up letter to them in 1910 indicates why they were in his doghouse once again.

Sirs:

I had occasion last summer to withdraw your privilege of representation at Ellis Island by reason of the very bad conditions found to prevail in your so-called Immigrants' Home. Later I restored these privileges upon assurances that this Home would be conducted in a proper manner. Such, however, does, not appear to have been the case. During the month of April an agent of the North American Civic League for Immigrants (an organization composed of disinterested persons bent on protecting the immigrant after landing in New York City) spent two nights there. The beds she slept in had vermin and the mattress and bed clothing were filthy in the extreme. A serious cause of complaint last summer was that you employed no matron; nevertheless the only woman connected with the management on the occasion of this agent's visit was the cook, and she took no care of the girls. On the contrary these were looked after by two foul-mouthed men, who not only did all chamber work, but waked the girls in the morning. Instead of knocking on the door they walked in yelling "Aufstehen" ("Get up") and something in Polish. The girls who did not get up were shaken by these men who again came into the dormitory while the girls were dressing and made vulgar remarks concerning them in German and Polish. Further details I omit. These two men were not the only ones about the house who were vulgarly familiar with the female inmates. Upon leaving the agent paid the usual charges for board and lodging.

Last week I sent agents during the day time to inspect your new quarters at 84 Broad Street. They reported similar conditions as to the mattresses and bed-clothing. Two of the objectionable male employees were still there, also the same manager, who did not appear to be at all disturbed when his attention was called to the filth of mattresses and blankets. There was nothing to indicate the presence of a matron and the chamber work was still being done by men. It is an abuse of language to call such a place a "Home" for girls.

An Immigrant Society which is not conducted on a high plane of efficiency and decency by managers whose own sense of duty will make them unwilling to see it conducted in any other way, is not fit to be represented at a Government Station. Repeated experiences with your management, both on the part of this office and of a Congressional Committee, tend to show that it fails (whether purposely or otherwise I do not know or care) to grasp these facts. This office has lost confidence in it, and whether this confidence can be restored or whether, if there is to be a society for Austrian immigrants here, it must be a different one from yours, is a matter not necessary to discuss now. The immediate purpose of this letter is to give you notice that no further immigrants will be turned over to you at Ellis Island.

Respectfully,
(Signed) Wm. Williams
Commissioner

Williams conceded there were many legitimate charity organizations and missionary societies whose people helped the immigrants. But he wanted help from them in rooting out the crooks who posed as immigrant aid societies. He reported, "These could add still further to their usefulness if they would band together for the purpose of assisting the Government in detecting black sheep and the missionary for revenue, whose presence should be as unpleasant to them as it is to the commissioner." **(32)**

There is nothing new under the sun. People who say legitimate Moslem organizations should be outing people who recruit murderers and suicide bombers in Moslem circles are merely using the same approach Williams used in trying to get the legitimate operators to let him know about the crooks and vermin.

There was enough dislike of Williams among some of the organized immigrant groups that Congressman William Sulzer from New York, a Democrat, called for a Congressional investigation of Ellis Island in 1911. As a result, members of the U.S. House of Representatives investigated Williams, a Republican, and his staffers for "cruelty to helpless and unprotected immigrants." Certain immigrant protection group officials, foreign-language newspaper publishers, and those who resented Williams for his bulldog attitude in upholding immigration laws as he interpreted them witnessed against Williams.

Williams, in writing, and in his verbal testimony before the congressmen, said Sulzer and the witnesses were lying about their key charges, and offered proof to back his counterattack. He noted he was not going to argue every detail with his detractors because they were caught lying on the gist of their most important accusations.

Sulzer in essence took back his complaints, and instead asked for more money for Ellis Island's administration. Williams had proven to the congressmen's satisfaction the charges Sulzer and others had lodged against him were false. **(33)**

Two years later, Sulzer – who had become governor of New York – would himself would be on trial for misconduct in office. Sulzer committed the all-too-common crime of diverting campaign money to his own wallet. New York officials tried Sulzer, found him guilty, and removed him from office.

Besides the work of trust-busting officials, and the work of conservationist officials, Taft inherited another body of reform work from Teddy Roosevelt. It was the work if the Dillingham Commission on immigration reform. This commission, authorized by the Immigration Act of 1907 and chaired by Senator William Dillingham from Vermont, worked from 1907 to 1911 on the issues of immigration. The members of the commission keyed on the need to bar undesirable immigrants, the need to assimilate immigrants, and the need to prevent a flood of foreign workers who would allow corporate officials to lower the standard of living of American workers. They and the experts they contracted compiled more than 40 volumes of statistics, investigative testimony, and analysis on the facets of immigration, and in 1911, they released their findings.

The members of the commission made the following recommendations to make immigration laws better for the people of the United States and in some cases more fair for the immigrants:

> American officials should deport aliens who, within five years of admission to America, receive a felony conviction. (This was a no-brainer.)

> American officials in Europe should make arrangements with European officials to have would-be immigrants possess official certificates showing they had not committed any crimes that would exclude them from America. (In some cases this would work, but in many cases, immigrants were refugees from oppressive regimes. The European authorities would lie about these people, or refuse them permission to leave in the first place. Likewise, many European officials refused young men permission to leave because they wanted to draft them into their armies.)

> Immigrants becoming public charges within three years of admission to America should be deportable on a case-by-case basis. (This was aimed at saving American taxpayers money so they wouldn't have to support the shiftless. Someone hurt in an industrial accident would obviously have much more standing in such a hearing than someone who refused to work and became a professional beggar.)

> Male and female American immigration officers should travel in steerage undercover to ensure shipping companies comply with American laws. (Immigration agents who traveled incognito for the commissioners verified many instances of inexcusable conditions aboard such ships.)

Members of the Boards of Special Inquiry must meet certain standards of experience and training, their hearings must be public, and there must be an assistant secretary of Commerce and Labor (this department was later separated into the Department of Commerce and the Department of Labor) appointed to review decisions of Boards of Special Inquiry. (This was a no-brainer.)

States must regulate so-called "immigrant banks." (These were not banks, but businesses run by craftier people of the same ethnicity as immigrants from Southern and Eastern Europe. These people would hold immigrants' money "for safe keeping" or arrange to invest it in the home countries for the immigrants. The commissioners wanted to keep immigrants from being swindled, and they wanted the immigrants to keep more of their money in America as long as they were working in America. The commissioners did not attack immigrant community banks that operated as real banks.)

American officials should deport aliens who persuade immigrants not to assimilate and not become American citizens. (This was a no-brainer.)

American officials should encourage immigrants to move to rural areas where their labor would do the most good. They should also encourage immigrants to buy farms. (At this time, many rural workers were leaving farms and coming to the cities for higher paying jobs. There was beginning to be a labor shortage in the countryside. Part of it was man-made; rural employers were no more generous than urban employers. The commissioners were trying to get immigrants to sink roots in America as farmers instead of depressing urban wages as unskilled laborers.)

The Secretary of Commerce and Labor should rule on the importation of skilled laborers to establish certain industries only after investigating claims of businessmen and finding them to be valid as to the absence of such technical know-how among Americans. (This was a no-brainer aimed at protecting American workers.)

The commissioners made several recommendations to reduce the oversupply of unskilled workers in cities, and in places like mining communities and mill towns, where their presence was undercutting American laborers' wages. These included:

American officials should bar entry to unskilled men who come without wives or families. (This was aimed mostly at temporary laborers who intended to work only to save enough money to better themselves in the home countries. Their willingness to live in poverty to save money undercut Americans' wages.)

Would-be immigrants who couldn't read or write in any language should be denied entry.

Immigrants should show a higher minimum amount of money to immigration officials to gain entry.

The commissioners then made some recommendations to ensure future immigrants would reinforce instead of alter, overwhelm, or undermine American institutions. These included:

American officials should continue to exclude unskilled Chinese laborers, not formally restrict such workers from Japan (or Japanese-occupied Korea) unless the Japanese started abusing the "gentlemen's agreement" reached with Teddy Roosevelt, and make an agreement with the British to effectively prevent people from the Indian subcontinent (the British controlled it) from immigrating to America. (This was aimed at keeping America a Judeo-Christian nation. Not only did unskilled Asian workers break the wage scale; they did not tend to assimilate because their belief systems were greatly different than those of most Americans. Arabs and other Moslems were not specifically mentioned, but American officials did not admit many of them. Then, too, very few Moslems tried to emigrate to America. Even most of the immigrants from the Ottoman Empire – in which the Moslem Turks ruled Arab Moslems from much of the Arabian peninsula, present-day Iraq, Syria, Jordan, Lebanon, and Israel – tended to be Greek, Armenian, Lebanese, and Assyrian Orthodox and Catholic Christians.)

There should be a quota based on the percentage of ethnic groups already in America. (Most of the people on the commission were prejudiced in favor of a Wonder Bread-bland white Anglo-Saxon Protestant America. So they wanted to restrict immigration from Italy, Eastern Europe, and Russia.)

There should be a cap on the number of immigrants. (Some would argue this was racism on the part of the commissioners. Others would argue there were too many people coming as it was, and they were hurting the wage scale of American workers.) **(34)**

Williams agreed with most of what the commissioners recommended. He was also working for improving immigration laws for the benefit of Americans. He referred to Teddy Roosevelt's worry about incoming unskilled foreigners undercutting the American laborer and giving capitalists the excuse to reduce the standard of living because the foreigner would work for less and live in squalor because that's all he knew. He urged Congress to enact legislation to deport aliens who committed crimes in America.

Williams also urged Congress to close loopholes the steamship company officials used to evade the law. He noted steamship company operators were bringing insane people to America and escaping fines. The law forbade "idiots, imbeciles, and epileptics." Unscrupulous shipping line officials and their corrupt lawyers evidently argued insane people were not "idiots, imbeciles, or epileptics." Williams wanted insanity added to the list of reasons immigration officials could exclude would-be immigrants. Williams also wanted fines against steamship companies for committing certain violations doubled.

He also noted the law only fined shipping companies and captains for providing no information about aliens on their manifests. He wanted Congress to punish steamship lines for providing false or inaccurate information as well as providing no information.

Williams noted ship captains allowed unfit aliens to escape their ships and illegally enter the country. He also noted, "The contract labor law is constantly being violated on a large scale, and, while the immigration authorities detect many of the violations in individual instances, yet the wholesale violations they are usually unable to detect, with the result that thousands of aliens continue to come here every year as a result of encouragement and solicitation." He urged lawmakers to act against these abuses. **(35)**

Much of Williams' advice and the Dillingham Commission's recommendations would become law. But not right away. Many opposed the Dillingham Commission's and Williams' views on literacy and paupers. Taft vetoed an immigration bill containing a literacy test for adult immigrants and a minimum cash amount for entry. (Wilson would veto a ban on illiterate immigrants, but Congress would override his veto.)

During Taft's term in office, American lawmakers addressed three major scandals that affected immigration. One was the tragedy and shame of the trade in immigrant girls and young women for sex. The second was the tragedy of deaths at sea due to greedy and negligent shipping companies. The third was the exploitation of immigrants and Americans alike in sweatshops, factories, and other workplaces. The muckrakers and the Mann Act dealt with the first outrage. The sinking of the *Titanic* brought the second to light. And the horrible Triangle Fire forced the authorities to do something about the third.

It was a shame immigrants had to suffer and die for Americans to fight these abuses. But their suffering did not go in vain. The American public prodded American politicians to address the abuses that led to their deaths and suffering, and to the deaths and suffering of many more Americans as well. Theodore Roosevelt had shown it was possible for a government, only if properly led and staffed and motivated, to actually help people instead of harming them.

The hope Theodore Roosevelt gave Americans about the ability of the government to do right led generations of us to depend on his successors, and many thousands of federal, state, and local officials from then until now to do right also. American officials have gained much more power in the century or so since Theodore Roosevelt left office, but very few of them have governed in his spirit. Not every politician can be a Theodore Roosevelt, but sadly, all too many of them have been (or still are) Pee Wee Herman or Benedict Arnold.

END NOTES

1. Immigration statistics throughout this chapter come from the immigration tables of the Historic Research Study, Statue of Liberty – Ellis Island National Monument, by Harlan D. Unrau, National Park Service, 1984.

2. Information on the Know-Nothings and the anti-Catholic pogroms comes from Michael Schwartz's book The Persistent Prejudice (pages 38-60) and from James McPherson's book Battle Cry of Freedom (pages 130-144).

3. Sources for the number of Irish and German soldiers in the Civil War include William Burton's book Melting Pot Soldiers, and The Civil War Times (December 2003).

4. The 14th Amendment was aimed at giving freed slaves citizenship, not babies born to illegals. In that era, a baby born to foreign parents on American soil had the status of his or her parents – foreign nationals. This is as it should be.

Even many American Indians did not get citizenship under the 14th Amendment because their tribes were not under U.S. government control. In other words, the feds considered the Sioux, the Apaches, the Nez Percé, the Comanches, and many other tribes of the Great Plains and the West to be non-citizens and hostiles. Some American Indians gained citizenship under the Dawes Act of 1887 if they left the tribal life; of course this allowed the palefaces to grab more tribal land. Other American Indians who lived in frontier territories and states gained citizenship by marrying whites or blacks, or by serving in America's armed forces. To their shame, American leaders did not grant full citizenship to all American Indians until 1924, under the Indian Citizenship Act of 1924.

Thanks to the incompetence and chicanery of Lyndon Johnson, Teddy Kennedy and others in foisting the 1965 Immigration and Nationality Act on the American people, illegals since the mid 1960s often give birth to babies on American soil to get into the country legally as the parents of "American citizens." Teddy's brother Bobby was murdered by an Arab immigrant in 1968; his brother John was murdered by a Communist in 1963.

Irresponsible bureaucrats, members of Congress, judges, and presidents have undermined the 14th Amendment by allowing illegal foreign females to drop "anchor babies" on American soil and gain legal status as a result. They have been burdening the taxpayers with these illegals and their offspring, most of whom take in more taxpayer-covered services than they return in the form of labor.

5. The source for the Seattle tax crisis is William Speidel's book Sons of the Profits (pages 286-287).

6. The source for information on Treasury Department officials and Congressional findings from 1889 through 1891 is the Unrau study (pages 20-25).

7. Information on the federal takeover of immigration in New York City and the problems involving Ellis Island, Liberty Island, Castle Garden and the Barge Office come from the Unrau study, Edward Corsi's book In the Shadow of Liberty, Thomas Pitkin's book Keepers of the Gate: A History of Ellis Island, and Barry Moreno's book Encyclopedia of Ellis Island. Corsi was a commissioner of immigration at Ellis Island. Pitkin was a federal government historian at the Statue of Liberty. Unrau and Moreno are both well-respected National Park Service historians. Moreno is a historian at Ellis Island.

8. Info about immigration laws and policies in the early 1890s comes from the Unrau study (pages 25-39), and from the text of the Act of March 3, 1891 (26 Statutes at Large 1084-1086).

9. Other immigration stations the feds opened in the 1890s were in Boston, Philadelphia, and Baltimore. The feds also had an inspection station in Montreal, Quebec. They established other smaller immigration stations along the Canadian and Mexican borders in the 1890s.

There would later be smaller immigration stations in Buffalo, Detroit, Chicago, New Orleans, El Paso, Seattle, the San Francisco area, Los Angeles, and Honolulu. There would be even smaller immigration stations in the port cities of America, in some interior cities, and along the Canadian and Mexican borders.

By the 1920s, the second largest immigration station in terms of staffers and immigrants processed was Angel Island in San Francisco Bay. From 1910 to 1940 (when a fire at the administration building, and then World War Two intervened), the inspectors on Angel Island admitted about 200,000 immigrants, mostly Asians. This compares with the roughly 15.5 million immigrants the inspectors at Ellis Island and other New York City port inspectors processed from 1892 through 1940.

Information on these stations comes from Barry Moreno's book Encyclopedia of Ellis Island (pages 110-112).

Some people claim immigration agents processed a million people, mostly Chinese, at Angel Island. These claims don't jibe with the public record.

Per the Unrau study, American officials admitted about 900,000 people from Asia from 1820 through 1931. (The 1999 Statistical Yearbook of the Immigration and Naturalization Service claims 1.07 million people came from Asia from 1820 through 1940, but only 16,000 or so of these came from 1931 through 1940. They erroneously counted about 150,000 European immigrants from lands in the Balkans the Ottoman Empire controlled before World War One as part of the Asian count.)

Of Asians who came from 1820 through 1940, 382,000 came from China, 275,000 came from Japan, 206,000 came from the Ottoman Empire (and later Turkey after World War One), 10,000 or so came from the Indian subcontinent, and 43,000 others came from elsewhere in Asia. During this time, American officials

also admitted almost 55,000 from Australia and New Zealand, and about 10,000 from the Pacific Islands not part of Asia. Most of the people from the Ottoman Empire sailed to the Atlantic ports of America.

The vast majority of Chinese (about 270,000) admitted came through Pacific Coast ports before 1882, the year the Chinese Exclusion Act became law. Most Japanese (about 150,000) admitted came before 1910. From 1910 through 1940 (the year fire shut down Angel Island as an immigration station), American officials admitted 58,000 Chinese, 122,000 Japanese, and 7000 from the Indian subcontinent total for all immigration stations across America.

The 1882 Chinese Exclusion Act, the 1907 "Gentlemen's Agreement" limiting Japanese immigration, the 1917 immigration law with the "Asian Barred Zone" provision, and the 1924 immigration law with national origin quotas were all in effect during some or all of the operating life of Angel Island as an immigration station. These all held down immigration from Asia.

Another ugly event held down immigration from China and Japan in the 1930s. The Japanese were carrying on a war of conquest and subjugation against the Chinese. The Japs controlled the coast of China and its approaches with their navy. (This was also the decade in which they captured and evidently raped Amelia Earhart repeatedly – before executing her – for scouting out their Pacific Island installations.) This cut down on immigration from both lands.

Bottom line? American officials admitted roughly 190,000 people from China, Japan, and the Indian subcontinent from 1910 through 1940 total for all immigration stations across America. American officials admitted 26,000 other Asians (not counting the mostly Christian refugees from the Ottoman Empire and the countries that succeeded its collapse in 1918) and 25,000 people from Australia, New Zealand, and the Pacific Islands from 1911 through 1940. In other words, there were about 240,000 immigrants total admitted from East Asia and South Asia and the Philippines and Oceania in these years. And not all of them were processed at Angel Island!

A more accurate estimate is that Angel Island immigration officials admitted about 200,000 immigrants. (They admitted some Latin American and a few European immigrants along with the Asians.)

Figures come from the 1999 Statistical Yearbook of the Immigration and Naturalization Service, and the Unrau study.

Some sources note American officials detained 175,000 Chinese and several thousand Japanese on Angel Island during its time in service. This is plausible, because many Chinese tried fraudulent means to come into America. A common scam for them was to claim being born in San Francisco before the devastating 1906 earthquake. They falsely claimed the earthquake destroyed their records. Many other Chinese claimed they were the sons or daughters of naturalized Chinese immigrants ... this racket was called the "paper son" and "paper daughter" racket. Former Ellis Island boss Edward Corsi, in his book In the Shadow of Liberty (pages 159-176) talked about these and other rackets he and his people had to combat. Many Japanese women came to America as "picture brides." In some cases, this was a scam to import Japanese females (often against their wills) for use as prostitutes. American officials were right to detain them and verify their alleged husbands' situations before admitting them. This saved many a Japanese woman and girl from sexual slavery.

10. Good sources on Senner and his term include the Unrau study (pages 208-215), Keepers of the Gate (Chapter II), and 3/29/1893 and 6/13/1893 New York Times articles.

11. Information on Fitchie and McSweeney and their stays in office comes from the Unrau study (pages 215-217), Keepers of the Gate (Chapter II), and the Publishing Society of New York reference Republicans of New York (page 285).

12. Information on Terence Powderly comes from his autobiography The Path I Trod (pages 298-300).

13. Information on the Naples surgeon posting comes from the Unrau study (page 40).

14. The information on Fiorello La Guardia and his family comes from his autobiography The Making of an Insurgent. La Guardia's comments on health inspections and the eventual adoption of overseas inspection of immigrants comes from his book (pages 53-57). Terence Powderly, in a 12/8/1906 letter to Theodore Roosevelt, (The Path I Trod, pages 303-304) made basically the same recommendation.

Barry Moreno, in his book Encyclopedia of Ellis Island (page 197) noted line inspections of immigrants for health problems at Ellis Island dropped drastically in the mid 1920s. Part of the reason undoubtedly was the Immigration Act of 1924, which drastically reduced the number of immigrants coming in at Ellis Island. Part of the reason was the adoption of La Guardia's practice of medically inspecting immigrants at the port of debarkation.

In 1926, the Surgeon General noted doctors in the previous 12 months intensively examined 73,000 third class (steerage) immigrants at Ellis Island, and briefly examined the other 51,000 third class (steerage) immigrants aboard ships because American doctors examined them overseas before they shipped to America (or because they had return permits). This information comes from the Unrau study (page 919).

All immigration stations had the same basic medical inspection process for immigrants. However, Ellis Island doctors saw so many more immigrants than doctors at other immigration stations that they developed more experience. Ellis Island's doctors also had a hospital, specialists, and a medical lab at their disposal.

15. Information on the assassination of McKinley and Roosevelt's race to Buffalo include Theodore Roosevelt: An Autobiography, Walter Lord's book The Good Years, and Edmund Morris' book The Rise of Theodore Roosevelt.

16. Mannix's remarks come from his book The Old Navy (page 152). Other information on the wrongful discharge of the black soldiers comes from Nathan Miller's book Theodore Roosevelt: A Life (pages 465-469), the Handbook of Texas Online's article "Brownsville Raid of 1906," and an article by Laura Tillman in the 6/18/2008 Brownsville (Texas) Herald. Richard Nixon reversed the dishonorable discharge, and ordered some separation pay to go to the surviving soldier of the 167 and to surviving widows.

17. Info on the further investigation of corruption at Ellis Island under Fitchie comes from Hans Vought's book The Bully Pulpit and the Melting Pot, an article by Henry Guzda in Monthly Labor Review, July 1986, and a 10/1/1902 New York Times article.

18. Information on the wrongful firing of Terence Powderly and

his reinstatement elsewhere in the Roosevelt administration comes from The Path I Trod (pages 301-302, and 306).

19. Information on the Act of March 3, 1903 comes from the law itself (32 Statutes at Large, pages 1213-1222).

20. Information on Williams' fining of the steamship lines comes the Unrau study (page 43).

21. Comments from Williams' Annual Report for 1903 come from the Unrau study (pages 45-47).

22. Information on the clearing of William Williams comes from the Unrau study (pages 229-231).

23. Watchorn's letter is in the Unrau study (pages 235-236).

24. Information on the Act of February 20, 1907 comes from the law itself (34 Statutes at Large, pages 898-911).

25. Immigration statistics come from the Unrau study.

26. Information on the Boxer Rebellion and Theodore Roosevelt's handling of the Chinese boycott and Chinese immigration issues comes from George Knoles' book The New United States (pages 51-52), The Good Years (pages 9-40), and Howard Beale's book Theodore Roosevelt and te Rise of America to World Power (212-252).

27. Information on the run-in with Japan over the segregation law in San Francisco comes from Carey McWilliam's article in the Oscar Handlin-edited book Immigration as a Factor in American History (pages 171-177), Theodore Roosevelt: An Autobiography (pages 392-395), and The San Francisco Earthquake by Gordon Thomas and Max Morgan Witts (pages 276-281).

28. Information on the leaving of Watchorn comes from Henry Guzda's article in the July 1986 issue of Monthly Labor Review.

29. The sources for William Williams' quotes are his Annual Report dated 8/16/1909 in his papers (New York City Public Library) and the Unrau study (pages 251-252).

30. Information on Williams' charges against shipping companies and immigration business operators comes from the Unrau study (page 254).

31. Information on the jailed Greek shipping line smugglers comes from a 6/27/1912 letter to Williams in his papers (New York City Public Library).

32. Information on Williams' war against corrupt immigrant aid societies and homes comes from his 8/16/1909 and 5/24/1910 letters to the Austrian Society in his papers (New York City Public Library) and the Unrau study (pages 251-256).

33. Information on Williams' fight against Sulzer comes from his Annual Report dated 10/10/1911 in his papers (New York City Public Library) and the Unrau study (pages 262-264).

34. These recommendations come from the conclusions and recommendations portion of the Dillingham Commission report (pages 45-48).

35. Information on Williams' comments come from the Unrau study (pages 54-59).

WHAT WAS IMMIGRANT PROCESSING LIKE?

It is easy and irresponsible to criticize the majority of immigration agents at Ellis Island and elsewhere from the safety of today. The truth is no other country welcomed immigrants like the United States did, and as a nation the United States was barely 100 years old itself when Ellis Island opened for business. In that time, the United States grew from an Atlantic Seaboard country into a country roughly as large as Europe, and had withstood a terrible Civil War.

There was no federal immigrant inspection law until 1891.Until that time, state officials had admitted immigrants to the United States. Federal authorities had federalized immigrant processing in New York City's harbor in 1890, and they federalized immigrant processing in the rest of the country in 1891.

This chapter looks at how American officials screened immigrants coming through Ellis Island. We focus on Ellis Island for a very simple reason – volume. From when the U.S. government first started screening immigrants in New York in 1890 until the end of the great waves of immigration in 1924, federal agents on Ellis Island and elsewhere in the harbor facilities of New York City processed about 70% of all immigrants seeking to gain entry into the United States.

EVENTS THAT LED TO THE ELLIS ISLAND PROCESS

Since the opening of the Erie Canal in 1825, which tied the Great Lakes to the Atlantic Ocean via the Hudson River, New York City was the dominant seaport of the United States. Therefore most immigrants came in steerage through New York City's port. They simply got off the ships when they landed, and settled in New York or went elsewhere.

The first formal immigration station in New York City was at Castle Garden on Manhattan Island. New York state officials processed immigrants at Castle Garden starting in 1855 to protect immigrants from being ripped off by New York sharpies and other vermin in Gotham. However, the ongoing corruption of New York officials and other state officials in the immigrant processing business led the Feds to take over processing immigrants in the early 1890s. Federal officials started processing immigrants at the Barge Office on Manhattan Island in 1890 until Ellis Island opened for business in 1892. (After the fire destroyed the wooden structures on Ellis Island in 1897, federal agents processed immigrants at the Barge Office again until the new brick facilities on Ellis Island were ready in 1900.)

Ellis Island and the other federal immigration stations had a more thorough mission ... screening immigrants as well as protecting them. Processing of immigrants was supposed to screen out those deemed a detriment to the United States. The immigration officials proceeded on the reasonable standard that immigration should benefit the United States instead of benefiting only the immigrants.

As immigration officials learned their jobs and learned what to look for when inspecting would-be immigrants, they adjusted the inspection process to improve it.

The advance of science brought better medical techniques and public health practices. This allowed inspectors to screen out would-be immigrants with medical problems that forbade them from coming into the United States. This also allowed immigration officials to disinfect immigrants to prevent the spread of disease and allowed the immigration service's doctors and nurses to treat and cure many sick immigrants.

The advance of science brought better communication. The "wireless" radio telegraph joined the telegraph and the telephone as a means of rapid communication. This meant immigration officials could quickly get tips on unsavory individuals trying to enter the country, so they could detain them, arrest them, and deport them.

The advance of science also advanced industry. Industrial innovations included quantifiable standards, the discipline of quality control, and time and motion studies to improve products and production. Government officials – many who came from the private sector and after a few years went back, instead of too many of the careerists of today – applied these ideas to systematically organize the processing of immigrants.

There was at least one other factor which contributed to the treatment of immigrants at Ellis Island and other immigration stations – the growing participation of reformers in public life.

Labor unions were very controversial in the 1890s. That decade saw the bloody Homestead Steel strike in Pennsylvania, several miners' strikes in the West that involved bloodshed, and the Pullman Car strike in Illinois, which escalated into a nationwide railroad workers' strike that soldiers broke with gunfire. It wouldn't be until Theodore Roosevelt that there was a president who was openly sympathetic with strikers when their strike was just. However, more and more people who were not manual laborers began to see the appalling conditions of many job sites and the abysmally low wages for the jobs many workers performed were unjust.

Likewise, the blatantly crooked people who ran city, state, and federal governments inspired the outrage of many people. Since the people of the late 1800s were much more prone to react to corruption than we are now, there were politicians, publishers, and others who realized they could harness this anger to make reforms. Some politicians and writers decided to become reformers on principle; others did so to further their political careers or sell more newspapers.

Some of the best reformers in that era were women. Women as a rule could not work as white-collar employees in the corporations of the time, and they were by and large discouraged from being doctors or lawyers as well. As a class, about the only women executives in the United States were Catholic nuns who ran hospitals and school systems. As a class, about the only women who could shape public opinion were writers. Novelists Harriet Beecher Stowe (the author of Uncle Tom's Cabin), and Helen Hunt Jackson (the author of A Century of Dishonor and Ramona) changed many people's hearts and minds on the evils of slavery and the treatment of American Indians. Print media women Nellie Bly (who uncovered abuses at a mental institution by deliberately getting committed) and Ida

Tarbell (the muckraker who wrote The History of the Standard Oil Company) had more impact than most male journalists of the late 1800s and early 1900s.

Women had the right to vote in some states, but did not win the right to vote nationwide until after World War One. However, women still had the right to act. Women like Jane Addams (the foundress of Hull House in Chicago) and Mother Cabrini (a Catholic nun – an immigrant from Italy herself – foundress of many orphanages and schools) helped the poor and inspired others to do so.

More and more women became teachers, nurses, and social workers. Many of them worked with the working poor – the many families who needed Papa's wage, Mama's wage, and some of the children's pennies to eke out a living. Some of the women in these professions agitated for government officials to ensure the working poor got more decent treatment. The work of these women aided the work of some men of the day in trying to put government power to use to ensure fairer treatment for people.

The desire of many Americans for more humanitarian use of authority aided the people who processed immigrants at Ellis Island and elsewhere in doing their jobs more efficiently and humanely.

WHO WERE THE FEDS SUPPOSED TO KEEP OUT?

Commissioner of Immigration at Ellis Island William Williams, who ran Ellis Island from 1902-1905, and again from 1909-1913, in a 1912 report titled "Ellis Island: Its Organization and Some of Its Work" said the law required his agents to bar the following types of people from the United States:

"Idiots, imbeciles, feeble-minded persons, and epileptics.

Insane persons and those who have been insane within five years.

Persons who at any time have had two or more attacks of insanity.

Persons afflicted with tuberculosis or with a loathsome or dangerous contagious disease (including trachoma, an eye disease).

Persons suffering from any mental or physical defect which may affect their ability to earn a living.

Paupers, persons likely to become a public charge, and professional beggars.

Persons who have been convicted of or admit having committed crimes or misdemeanors involving moral turpitude.

Polygamists and anarchists.

Prostitutes, procurers, and "persons who are supported by or receive in whole or in part the proceeds of prostitution."

Persons coming to perform manual labor under contract.

Persons whose ticket or passage has been paid for by any association, municipality, or foreign government.

Children under 16 unaccompanied by either parent, except in the discretion of the Secretary of Commerce and Labor." (By 1913, lawmakers split this cabinet-level department into the Department of Commerce and the Department of Labor.) **(1)**

Yet, despite all these potential legal barriers to the immigrants, federal inspectors allowed 98 out of every 100 would-be immigrants into America during the Ellis Island era (1892-1924). Were the standards too lax? Or were the immigration agents at Ellis Island basically humane people? And were most immigrants in the Ellis Island era basically decent people able and willing to contribute to America?

We will take a quick look at how immigration agents processed immigrants in New York City's port facilities to show you how the process worked and how many people were able to get through it. Admittedly, immigration officials screened immigrants at many ports and border towns besides New York City since

the start of federal control of immigration in the early 1890s, but still well over half the immigrants to the United States in the Ellis Island era (1892-1924) landed at Ellis Island.

All immigration stations had similar procedures. But since most immigrants were processed at Ellis Island, we will discuss the screening process at Ellis Island as the typical processing experience.

THE WORKERS OF ELLIS ISLAND

During the time commissioner William Williams ran Ellis Island, the day shift started at 7 a.m. and ended at 6 p.m. There was some staggering of inspectors' hours to ensure coverage during these hours. If there were many immigrants and many problems with these immigrants, the agents had to stay until about 8 p.m. inspecting immigrants. The night watch ran Ellis Island from 6 p.m. until 7 a.m. The workers of the night watch ensured immigrants staying overnight were fed, guarded, and otherwise attended to. Workers on the night watch also did a lot of cleaning and maintenance because of the hordes of immigrants passing through.

The flow of immigrants was constant. The immigration station on Ellis Island only closed Easter Sunday and four holidays in FY 1903, said Williams. Even on holidays, the place did not shut down like a typical government office building today. People being detained still had to be watched and fed, guarded, and treated. Ellis Island had dormitories for immigrants, holding areas for people being deported, a hospital to treat the sick, and a kitchen to feed everyone who had to be on the island. The power plant had to run constantly, and firemen had to be ready to put out fires and save lives. Plus, the place required constant cleaning to prevent outbreaks of diseases. So there were employees working at Ellis Island around the clock. Sometimes the Commissioner at Ellis Island lived on Ellis Island; there was a house there for his family.

The work went in shifts to provide around the clock coverage and overlap. Usually the agents didn't process immigrants at night, but hundreds of immigrants routinely had to stay overnight if there was a problem with letting them into the country. Hundreds and sometimes thousands of immigrants had to wait aboard their ships in the harbor overnight because their ships had arrived too late in the day for them to undergo processing.

Ellis Island had about 60 watchmen and gatemen to provide security during the day shifts and the night watch. Several thousand immigrants passed through Ellis Island each day during its busiest years, and it was not uncommon for the authorities to detain 2000 or so

aliens overnight on Ellis Island. Most of the immigrants needed protection; some needed watching; a few needed incarceration.

Women who assisted in physical inspections, and in security and investigation work were called matrons. Some of these women boarded ships with the male inspectors; they assisted with inspecting first and second class female passengers. Others worked at Ellis Island, helping with the medical inspection of foreign women, helping with children, and investigating women detained on suspicion of "immoral character" (prostitutes, madams, and the like).

Doctors of Ellis Island's Medical Division performed the medical inspections (and as needed, the detailed mental evaluations) of the immigrants. Doctors, nurses, and other staffers of this group also operated the hospital on Ellis Island.

Agents in Ellis Island's Boarding Division boarded ships carrying immigrants when the ships entered New York harbor. The group had inspectors, matrons, and interpreters. Their job was to inspect all first and second class passengers aboard ship. Doctors also boarded ships to inspect non-steerage immigrants and to check for people with severe contagious diseases requiring quarantining. (The medical inspection and the primary inspection for first and second class passengers were the same as these inspections for steerage passengers, but they took place aboard ship instead of at Ellis Island.) The agents also had the job of escorting to Ellis Island the steerage passengers and any first and second class passengers they decided to detain for medical or legal problems.

The inspectors of Ellis Island's Registry Division performed the primary inspections (the legal inspections) of the immigrants. Most interpreters also belonged to this group. The interpreters also received assignments to help the other groups.

The men of Ellis Island's Special Inquiry Division formed the boards of special inquiry. Three or four three-member boards, composed of qualified inspectors, heard cases every day. They had stenographers and interpreters to help them. These boards made decisions on 50 to 100 immigrant cases a day, depending on the type of case, and the difficulty of communicating with the immigrants before them. This sounds like a huge caseload, but medical exclusions were open and shut cases, and pauperism cases were also fairly routine.

The people of Ellis Island's Discharging Division held immigrants temporarily detained due to problems such as lack of funds or inability to contact family or friends. They would try to reach immigrants' families or friends by telegram, mail, or other means. (In those days, most people did not have telephones.) They would release immigrants to people calling for them if the immigrants recognized them and agreed to go with them. Or they would release immigrants to railroad company agents once they received tickets or funds and were going to their final destination by train.

Sometimes these people would release immigrants to charitable organizations with the understanding they would help the immigrants find work and housing, and not harbor them as charity cases. Since there were many fraudulent boarding house operators posing as missionaries, immigration officials had to check on anyone representing his or her outfit as a charitable organization.

The men of Ellis Island's Deportation Division held aliens being deported, and escorted them to ships for deportation. There were two day watches and a longer night watch of deportation agents to guard and account for the detained immigrants to prevent them from escaping. At the change of each watch, the agents accounted for the detained aliens in their custody.

The men of this group also escorted detained aliens to the dining room for their three daily meals, and took them to the roof of the main building or elsewhere on the island for recreation at certain times. There was a group of men within this group who escorted the aliens being deported to the ship they were being deported on. If they had to put aliens on the ship the night before the ship was to leave New York, they would check on the ship just before it sailed to ensure no alien being deported escaped from the ship. Of course there were opportunities for aliens to bribe the immigration agents and the ship's officers to spring aliens, and some escaped or were "exchanged" and falsely accounted for.

There were men who ran and maintained the power plant on Ellis Island. They ensured the island had heat, light, water, and power. The workforce included engineers and skilled tradesmen, and about two dozen firemen.

There was a large force of janitors and charwomen who kept Ellis Island's buildings, dock, and grounds as clean as could be kept, considering the waves of people who passed through the immigration station. Besides cleaning showers, toilets, waiting rooms, work areas, and offices almost constantly, they disinfected bedding in the dormitories and other quarters where detained immigrants slept, they took blankets to be washed, and they spread disinfectants and pesticides everywhere. Many immigrants coming from Europe were dirty to begin with, and those who were clean usually became dirty in steerage because there were inadequate facilities for them to wash themselves in steerage.

The workers at Ellis Island rotated on and off night duty. They kept the place cleaned and guarded at night. Watchmen made the rounds through the dormitories and holding areas to check on the detained, and they patrolled on the outsides of the buildings as well. Matrons were available to help out. Men kept the power plant running and kept a fire watch. There were doctors, nurses, and other workers at the hospital around the clock.

The commissioner at Ellis Island had a staff and clerks, lawyers, investigators, phone operators, messengers, and runners. These people worked in the Executive Division.

The people of Ellis Island's Information Division gave family and friends of the immigrants information on the immigrants' whereabouts. These workers also kept records on the Boards of Special Inquiry and on the hospital, and kept records on people released to charitable organizations (such as religious groups or immigrant aid societies). They also dealt with inquiries by immigrants' families and friends, and gave telegrams and money orders to immigrants from relatives.

The commissioner had staffers who, besides paying the workers and handling expenses, made sure money and mail sent to immigrants on Ellis Island got to the immigrants. They also billed the steamship companies for hospital expenses run up by sick immigrants and billed the steamship companies for bringing inadmissable aliens to Ellis Island.

The people of Ellis Island's Statistical Division kept the records of all aliens arriving, verified ship landings, wrote most reports, and billed the steamship companies the "head tax" they had to pay for each of their passengers admitted into the United States. They also kept the ships' manifests as records and they kept the records of those detained at Ellis Island.

There was a tugboat for use in boarding ships, and another boat for the use of the immigration agents on Ellis Island.

Contractors operated the kitchen and dining hall for the immigrants detained on Ellis Island. There was also a laundry on Ellis Island that served the needs of the hospital, the dormitories, and the detention areas. Inside the Main Building were a telegraph office, an office for railroad and coastal ship companies, and a money changing office. The commissioners of Ellis Island also provided space for some private religious societies (who they called missionaries), and private immigrant aid societies. All this activity took place on Ellis Island, a built-up sandbar only a few football fields in size. Now let's go into the work of the immigration workers in detail. **(2)**

WHEN A SHIP CAME IN

Typically, a steamship loaded with immigrants coming into New York would anchor in Lower New York Bay, between Brooklyn and Staten Island and south of where the Verrazano Narrows Bridge is today. State health inspectors and federal inspectors would come out to the ship in a cutter, board the ship, and the federal inspectors would check the ship's manifest.

The manifest was a series of lists that American officials required the ship's officers to have prepared listing information about each alien intending to get off the boat ... the manifest would be organized by first class, second class, and steerage. If the one-page form used for those in first or second class had the entries for 30 people, for example, then it would take 10 of these forms to list the data on 300 aliens in first class and second class. The form for people in steerage was a two-page form because immigration officials screened them more tightly. If the two-page form had the entries for 30 people, for example, then it would take 40 of these forms to list the data on 1200 aliens in steerage. There would also be a manifest naming all American citizens on the ship, and it would also be organized by first class, second class, and steerage.

New York state doctors would quickly conduct a quarantine examination on all passengers aboard ship. During the quarantine examination, the state doctors would look for passengers with symptoms of serious contagious diseases such as cholera, smallpox, typhus, yellow fever, and bubonic plague. Likewise, a federal medical officer from Ellis Island would briefly check the passengers traveling in first class and more thoroughly check the passengers traveling in second class (because many immigrants who knew they might not pass muster at Ellis Island bought second class tickets to evade the medical inspection there) for these contagious diseases, and for diseases like trachoma, favus, tuberculosis, measles, chicken pox, scarlet fever, and diphtheria. The federal medical officer would also check the passengers in first class and especially in second class for other infirmities or other medical or mental disorders that would bar them from gaining entry to the United States.

If the inspectors found out people aboard the ship had cholera, smallpox, typhus, yellow fever, or bubonic plague, they would make the ship and passengers undergo quarantine. The ship had to anchor off of one of the islands used for quarantine and fly the yellow flag of quarantine. Those sick with the disease had to go to the New York Quarantine Hospital on Swinburne Island in Lower New York Bay. Those not sick but exposed to the disease had to undergo quarantine at the quarantine facility on nearby Hoffman Island. These people would have to bathe and undergo disinfection. Their clothing and baggage had to be disinfected or maybe burned. The ship would undergo fumigation and disinfection while empty. Only after the passengers passed quarantine – by waiting out the presumed incubation period of the disease and emerging without symptoms of the disease – would they be allowed to undergo processing. Those who died were buried or cremated and their belongings were burned or thrown into the ocean. Shipping companies had to pay for these costs because their agents were negligent in allowing diseased people aboard their ships.

If the inspectors found immigrants aboard a ship with milder contagious diseases like measles, chicken pox, scarlet fever, or diphtheria, these immigrants would have to go to a hospital in New York City until they were cured (or died). Later, Dr. Alvah Doty, who was the Health Officer of the Port of New York, had such unfortunates treated at the New York state hospital on Hoffman Island. When the federal government's Ellis Island communicable diseases hospital opened in 1911, immigrants suffering these less dangerous communicable diseases would receive treatment on Ellis Island. (The staffers of the Hoffman Island hospital treated some of the immigrants suffering these diseases even after the opening of the Ellis Island communicable diseases hospital. They would do so for a few more years.)

Dr. Doty personally tracked epidemics around the world. He kept in touch with American agents at port cities around the world, American Army and Navy military doctors stationed abroad, U.S. Marine Hospital Service officials, and foreign medical officials to find out what infectious diseases were cropping up in large numbers in these countries. He would then single out ships coming from ports in these countries, or ships carrying would-be immigrants from countries suffering epidemics, and order the passengers to be given the medical "third degree." His trademark, in the eyes of a reporter who wrote about him in 1908, was a globe studded with tacks representing outbreaks of cholera, bubonic plague, yellow fever, and other serious contagious diseases. **(3)**

Federal inspectors from Ellis Island would conduct a legal examination on each of the first class and second class passengers aboard ship. During the legal examination, they would question the passengers to corroborate the information about them on the manifest. Any of these passengers with medical problems or legal problems would have to undergo processing (and perhaps hospitalization) at Ellis Island ... and maybe deportation if they were not fit to enter the country.

The captain of the ship had to make sure there were on the ship's manifest answers from all the first class and second class alien passengers to questions such as the following:

- Passenger number on list
- Family name and given name
- Age (years and months)
- Sex
- Married or single
- Calling or occupation
- Able to read/Able to write
- "Nationality (country of which citizen or subject)"
- "Race or people (determined by the stock from which the alien sprang and the language they speak)"
- Last permanent residence (country, then city or town)
- "The name and complete address of nearest relative or friend in country whence alien came."
- Final destination (state, then city or town)

Immigrants who could afford to travel in first or second class didn't have to go through the processing at Ellis Island. They could be cleared aboard ship. Criminals and other undesirables often tried to sneak into the country by paying for a first or second class ticket in hopes of avoiding the screening at Ellis Island. Immigration officials who boarded the steamships would check for these lowlifes among the higher-income passengers. They looked for pimps, prostitute brokers, prostitutes, and madams – undesirables who were capable of paying to stay out of steerage. Armed with tips from American law enforcement officials, American officials overseas, foreign governments, and foreign individuals in America and overseas, the inspectors also looked for swindlers, common criminals, and other shady characters who were reported coming to America to escape prosecution or to create new trouble in America. The inspectors detained those they found for investigation.

The inspectors also checked second class passengers fairly thoroughly for another reason. Quite a few would-be immigrants with some money who had earlier come steerage to save money had a disease or a legal problem that caused the inspectors on Ellis Island to have them deported. Some of these people would then buy second class tickets and try again in a couple of weeks. Inspectors often caught these people and had

them deported again. Other rejected immigrants with better sense would sail to Canada and sneak into the United States by rail or by horse or on foot.

After the on-board inspections were through, the ship would then usually dock at Manhattan Island. Immigrants got their first look at the Statue of Liberty on the way into port.

First and second class passengers who the inspectors cleared were free to leave the ship after it docked and go their way. (American citizens traveling in steerage who could prove their citizenship also got to leave the ship after it docked.) Only those first and second class passengers being isolated for a contagious disease that was not so serious, being medically inspected further, or being detained for other reasons would have to get on the ferry for Ellis Island instead of leaving freely when the ship docked.

Why was this?

In the 1800s and early 1900s, the only way to travel between Europe and America was by ship, so first and second class passengers who were not American citizens were usually tourists or businesspeople. They usually weren't trying to sneak into America.

The inspectors checked them aboard ship because usually there were not many of them. Also, since American officials presumed a person traveling in first class had enough money to live in good health, and the intelligence or the connections to have made a good living, they assumed such a person wouldn't pose a health problem to the public, be a burden to society, or risk becoming a criminal. American officials presumed a person traveling in second class – though poorer than a first class passenger – was also enough of a cut above the steerage passengers to warrant easier inspection than those in steerage. The inspectors assumed a second class passenger likewise was healthy, wealthy, and wise enough to contribute to the country instead of becoming a disease carrier, a lawbreaker, or a public charge.

So the inspectors didn't check these passengers quite as closely as they would check the immigrants in steerage. Certainly this was discrimination and profiling, but it was based on usually correct assumptions. Putting first and second class passengers through the poverty, medical, and mental capacity screening process the inspectors put steerage passengers through would usually be a waste of the Ellis Island inspectors' time ... and could put these usually healthy passengers at risk of catching a communicable disease from one of the many carriers who came in steerage.

The vast majority of our ancestors who came to America in that era came in steerage. This meant they would undergo processing at Ellis Island.

THE ELLIS ISLAND PROCESS

This section gives a "typical" picture of how Ellis Island immigration agents processed immigrants in the early 1900s. So the "typical" inspection process described here was a more stringent than it was in the late 1890s, and less stringent than it would be in the early 1920s. Of course, the processing changed a little from year to year, but we will present the overall picture instead of hanging you up on the minutiae.

Steerage passengers would get tags with their name and manifest number, they would collect their luggage, and they would get off the ship at the dock and board a ferry in groups corresponding to their places on the ship's manifest. The ferry would take them – groups at a time – across the Hudson River to Ellis Island.

Immigration agents inspected the steerage passengers on a ferryboat load by ferryboat load basis. They would try to keep these groups together (each group would consist of the people on each list of 30 people that was part of the manifest) as much as possible, except for those who the medical inspectors and legal inspectors detained for closer examination.

Sometimes the immigrants coming off of certain ships were so filthy that the immigration officials made everyone shower and have their baggage disinfected.

The inspection process, in a nutshell, went like this:

1. Brief physical and eye exam with your clothes on. If you pass, go to Step 5. If a doctor thinks you have a physical problem, go to Step 2. If a doctor thinks you have a mental problem, go to Step 3.

2. More thorough (strip to waist) medical examination, like a doctor's office physical exam. If you pass, go to Step 4. If you have a disease or handicap which excludes you, go to Step 6. If you have a less serious disease that you could recover from, you will be treated at the Ellis Island hospital (or at a nearby hospital), and if you recover and pass the medical exam, go to Step 4.

3. Up to three mental examinations. As soon as you pass a mental exam, go to Step 4. If you fail all three, go to Step 6.

4. If you pass the medical examination, go to Step 5. If you pass the mental examination, and you don't appear to have any physical or medical problems, go to Step 5. If you pass the medical exam, but a doctor thinks you have a mental problem, go to Step 3. If you pass the mental examination, but a doctor thinks you have a physical or a medical problem, go to Step 2.

5. You undergo the primary exam (the legal exam). If the inspectors decide you will be a burden on society (someone liable to be a public charge), are a contract worker who will depress American wages, or are an undesirable such as a pimp or a whore or an anarchist or someone else of anti-American beliefs or a common criminal, go to Step 6. If not, go to Step 7.

6. You go before officials of a Board of Special Inquiry for a hearing. If they decide you are inadmissable for medical, physical, mental, or legal reasons, and you don't appeal successfully, you will be deported. (If you need a hospital stay to get well enough to go home, you will get it.) If the board members decide to admit you, or you appeal their decision and win, go to Step 7.

7. You are free to enter the United States. You have the status of resident alien, and have the opportunity to become an American citizen in a few years if you support yourself, obey the laws, learn the language, and pass a citizenship test.

Recapping, the people sent to Ellis Island would undergo a brief physical exam. If they passed the physical exam, they would undergo a brief legal exam. If they passed the legal exam, they were free to enter the United States.

People who didn't pass the quickie physical exam had to undergo a more thorough medical exam. If they passed, they could continue screening. If they didn't pass, they were either sent home, or were given some medical treatment and sent home if they weren't fit, or were allowed to continue processing when they were healthy again. People who didn't pass the medical screening were deported, usually at the expense of the steamship company.

Likewise, during the screening process, inspectors looked over immigrants for signs of mental disorders. People judged to be very stupid, insane, feeble-minded, unbalanced, or senile could not gain entry. People pulled out of line for suspected mental defects had to undergo a simple mental evaluation. If they failed, they had to undergo a second evaluation. If they failed the second evaluation, they had to undergo a third evaluation. As soon as a person passed a mental evaluation, he or she was free to continue processing; he or she didn't have to undergo more mental evaluations. Aliens had to fail all three mental evaluations to be deported, and they were deported, usually at the expense of the steamship company.

The following sections will discuss the various screening processes in detail.

MEDICAL INSPECTIONS AND MENTAL EVALUATIONS

The immigrants didn't know it, but in a way, their medical inspections started as they carried their luggage from the ferry up the steps to the first floor of the Main Building where the Baggage Room was.

U.S. Public Health Service doctors watched immigrants as they climbed up the stairs. Was someone limping, or otherwise struggling to get up the stairway with his or her luggage? Was someone having trouble breathing, or was he or she coughing on the way up? Was someone rubbing his or her scalp or eyes? Did someone seem dimwitted or burdened with a mental problem? Doctors who watched the immigrants sometimes had them rushed up the stairs so they could see symptoms of heart and lung ailments and other handicaps more readily. They would mark people they saw having problems.

People would leave their luggage in the Baggage Room and get a claim ticket. They would claim their baggage upon completing inspection successfully or upon being sent for deportation back to where they came from.

Inspectors would inspect immigrants' luggage, then move them on, while luggage handlers took charge of the luggage. This verified no contraband was coming into America, but it also made it easier for thieves among the luggage handlers to steal. Occasionally crooked luggage handlers, by watching the inspections, would know what luggage had the best items; these crooks would break into the people's luggage and steal their things while they were undergoing processing.

The immigrants would next undergo medical inspection. Two doctors checked each immigrant as he or she got in line.

Dr. E. H. Mullan, a surgeon with the U.S. Public Health Service, summarized the diagnosis as follows:

"It is the function of this officer (the first doctor to check the immigrants in his line) to look for all defects, both mental and physical, in the passing immigrant. As the immigrant approaches the officer gives him a quick glance. Experience enables him, in that one glance, to take in six details, namely the scalp, face, neck, hands, gait, and general condition, both mental and physical. Should any of these details not come into view, the alien is halted and the officer satisfies himself that no suspicious sign of symptom exists regarding that particular detail. For instance, if the immigrant is wearing a high collar, the officer opens the collar or unbuttons the upper shirt button and sees whether a goiter, tumor, or other abnormality exists. A face showing harelip, partial or complete, is always stopped in order to see if a cleft palate, a certifiable condition, is present."

"It often happens that the alien's hand can not be distinctly seen: it may be covered by his hat, it may be hidden beneath his coat, or it may be deeply embedded in blankets, shawls, or other luggage. Of all the physical details in the medical inspection of immigrants it is perhaps most important to watch the hands. In many cases where the hands can not be plainly seen at a glance further searching has revealed a deformed forearm, mutilated or paralyzed hand, loss of fingers. or favus nails."

"Likewise, if the alien approaches the officer with hat on he must be halted, hat removed, and scalp observed in order to exclude the presence of favus, ringworm, or other skin diseases of this region of the body. Pompadours are always a suspicious sign. Beneath such long growth of hair are frequently seen areas of favus. The slightest bit of lameness will show itself in an unevenness of gait or a bobbing up-and-down motion. After constantly observing the passing of thousands of immigrants the experienced eye of an examiner will quickly detect the slightest irregularity in gait. Where the alien carries luggage on his shoulder or back, it may be necessary to make him drop his parcels and to walk 5 or 10 feet in order to exclude suspicious gait or spinal curvature. Immigrants at times carry large parcels in both arms and over their shoulders in order that the gait resulting from a shortened extremity or ankylosed joint may escape notice. In like manner they maneuver in attempting to conceal the gaits of Little's disease, spastic paralysis, and other nervous disorders. All children over 2 years of age are taken from their mothers' arms and are made to walk. As a matter of routine, hats and caps of all children are removed, their scalps are inspected, and in many cases palpated. If care is not exercised in this detail, ringworm and other scalp conditions are apt to escape the attention of the examiner."

"Immigrants that are thin and of uncertain physical make-up are stopped while the officer comes to a conclusion as to the advisability of detaining them for further physical examination. A correct judgment is often arrived at in these cases by the officer placing his hands against the back and chest of the alien, so as to obtain an idea of thoracic thickness, and also by feeling the alien's arm. Very often a thin and haggard face will show on palpation a thick thorax and a large, muscular arm."

"Many inattentive and stupid-looking aliens are questioned by the medical officer in the various languages as to their age, destination, and nationality. Often simple questions in addition and multiplication are propounded. Should the immigrant appear stupid and inattentive to such an extent that mental defect is suspected, an X is made with chalk on his coat at the anterior aspect of his right shoulder. Should definite signs of mental disease be observed, circle X would be used instead of the plain X. In like manner a chalk mark is placed on the anterior aspect of the right shoulder in all cases where physical deformity or disease is suspected."

The doctors would mark in chalk on the outer clothing of anyone they spotted who had problems. If an immigrant's coat had an L on it, they saw him limping and figured he was lame. A B on his coat meant the doctors noticed a back problem. An H marked on an immigrant's coat, shirt, or dress meant they suspected he or she had heart trouble.

An SC on a person's garments meant the doctors saw a scalp problem. A P meant the doctors suspected a lung problem or some other "physical" problem. A G meant the doctors saw the person had a goiter. Likewise, F for face, FT for feet, and N for neck was doctor shorthand for problems with these body parts. Often, the doctors wrote out the words "hand," "measles," "nails," "skin," "temperature," "vision," or "voice" on an immigrant's outerwear if he detected any of these problems.

A K meant the doctors thought the marked man had a hernia. A Pg on a woman's clothing meant she was pregnant, although in many cases, this was self-evident without the chalk mark.

A C, CT, or E on someone's coat, shirt, or dress wasn't a good sight. This meant the doctors thought the marked man or woman had conjunctivitis (pinkeye), trachoma, or some other eye problem. Having trachoma was grounds for being barred from entering the United States.

A person marked with an X or a circled X on his or her garment was truly branded. The X meant the doctors suspected the person had a mental problem. If the X was circled, this meant the doctors decided they observed actual signs of mental illness. Also, doctors marking S on immigrants' garments were telling the inspectors they suspected these people were senile. People marked with an X, a circled X, or S would have to be checked further; mental problems were grounds for being denied entry to the United States.

Mullan continued:

"The alien after passing the scrutiny of the first medical officer passes on to the end of the line, where he is quickly inspected again by the second examiner. The examiner is known in service parlance as the "eye man." He stands at the end of the line with his back to the window and faces the approaching alien. This position affords good light, which is so essential for eye examinations. The approaching alien is scrutinized by the eye man immediately in front of whom the alien comes to a standstill. The officer will frequently ask a question or two so as to ascertain the condition of the immigrant's mentality. He may pick up a symptom, mental or physical, that has been overlooked by the first examiner."

"He looks carefully at the eyeball in order to detect signs of defect and disease of that organ and then quickly everts the upper lids in search of conjunctivitis and trachoma. Corneal opacities, nystagmus (involuntary rapid eye movement), squint, bulging eyes, the wearing of eyeglasses, clumsiness, and other signs on the part of the alien, will be sufficient cause for him to be chalk-marked with "Vision." He will then be taken out of the line and his vision will be carefully examined. If the alien passes out of this line without receiving a chalk mark, he has successfully completed the medical inspection and off he goes to the upper hall, there to undergo another examination by officers of the Immigration Services, who take every means to see that he is not an anarchist, bigamist, pauper, criminal, or otherwise unfit." **(4)**

Matrons would then eye the female immigrants, especially the teenage girls and young women without husbands or other adult male relatives accompanying them. They were there to check for prostitutes. Prostitutes were not allowed to immigrate to America.

All immigrants processed at Ellis Island underwent the legal inspection (called the primary inspection) after being cleared medically. Most immigrants (80 percent and more) passed the medical inspection without being marked and diverted to the medical examination or mental examination line, so after the eye doctor cleared them and they passed the matron looking for prostitutes, they went immediately to the legal inspection. (Doctors marked about 15 to 20 percent of immigrants, according to Mullan.)

There were up to 15 doctors checking as many as 5000 immigrants a day for 250 to 300 days a year at Ellis Island. They gave exams to almost a million people a year in the busiest years. This works out to each doctor checking as many as 60,000 immigrants a year or 200 to 240 immigrants each a day ... or one every two minutes in an eight-hour shift. **(5)**

Those who were marked were sent into another line for further medical and/or mental examination. For a few pages, we'll talk about these people being diverted for suspected medical or mental problems. Then we'll come back to describing the legal inspection, which all immigrants processed at Ellis Island underwent after being cleared medically and mentally.

What happened to those marked for a medical defect?

A person who the doctors determined had a minor curable disease had to go to the hospital on Island 2 which was part of the Ellis Island complex. (Because of the Ellis Island fire of 1897 that burned down the hospital along with other buildings, immigration authorities had to have immigrants with medical problems sent to the Hospital of the Health Department of New York City until the new hospital was ready on Ellis Island in 1902.)

A person who the doctors diagnosed with a contagious disease had to go to a hospital. Those sick with a serious contagious disease like cholera, smallpox, typhoid fever, yellow fever, leprosy, or bubonic plague had to go to the New York Quarantine Station on Swinburne Island at the entrance to New York's harbor.

Before 1911, authorities sent aliens of all classes having milder communicable diseases such as measles, chicken pox, scarlet fever, or diphtheria to the Port of New York quarantine hospital on Hoffman Island, or to one of several New York City area hospitals for quarantining until they were cured. However, immigrants – especially those coming in steerage — frequently escaped from these hospitals still carrying the disease and still unscreened as to whether they were fit to enter America. Commissioner Williams pushed for having another hospital built on Ellis Island to isolate immigrants being quarantined for these lesser communicable diseases. Authorities had Ellis Island physically expanded with fill; this became Island 3. They then had a quarantine hospital built on the fill; it opened in 1911. This hospital was for immigrants with less serious diseases requiring isolation. The hospital's doctors and nurses treated immigrants who had pneumonia, whooping cough, measles, scarlet fever, diphtheria, mumps, chicken pox, tuberculosis, trachoma, favus, or venereal diseases.

When doctors certified a person had recovered, officials would let him or her finish screening and hopefully enter the United States.

People deemed incurable or suffering from certain severer diseases or defects could not gain entry into the country. U.S. officials had the steamship companies take these unfortunates back to the ports they sailed from in Europe, usually at the expense of the steamship company for doing negligent or dishonest screening of the would-be immigrants they chose to transport.

Likewise, people who had trachoma or favus or contagious tuberculosis or leprosy or venereal disease or another ailment or handicap that would make them unable to earn a living would have to be deported.

Trachoma is a disease of the cornea and the conjunctiva (the eyelid membrane) caused by the *Chlamydia trachomatis* bacteria. In fact, a related disease, inclusive conjunctivitis, is a venereal disease

that attacks the eyes as well as the genitalia. The *Chlamydia trachomatis* bacteria causes growths on the conjunctiva and damage to the cornea that can lead to blindness. Trachoma is a contagious disease that spreads through close contact of people (coughing, exhaling, touching, sexual contact, etc.) who are not used to washing their hands or bathing; flies also carry the disease. Trachoma was widespread in southern Europe, Russia, the Middle East, and North Africa in the late 1800s and early 1900s. (It is still common in North Africa and is widespread in much of Asia. It is also present in rural areas of the American Southwest, where dry climate and a lack of water encourage its spread.)

During the Ellis Island era, Italians, Greeks and other people from the Balkans, Turks, Jews and others from Russia, and people from the Middle East were most likely to have trachoma. Sadly, many people who boarded a ship with undiseased eyes contracted trachoma from someone else in steerage.

Doctors inspected immigrants' eyes for trachoma by turning their eyelids up with their fingers or with leather loops used to button women's high-button shoes. Assistant Surgeon General H.D. Geddings, who checked the medical inspectors and the hospital facilities at Ellis Island in 1906, said the doctors inspecting immigrants' eyes disinfected their hands before inspecting each immigrant's eyes. He did not say if the doctors washed any of the loops; he said they used them only when their fingers got tired from checking so many immigrants' eyes. It is likely, and sadly ironic that some immigrants got trachoma from medical inspectors who didn't sanitize properly before touching their eyes.

Favus is a severe skin infection, usually in the scalp; it is a type of ringworm. Fungus, not worms, causes the disease. Favus is related to athlete's foot and jock itch but is more serious; favus is also highly contagious.

Doctors ordered marked immigrants to strip to the waist. (Female doctors and nurses would check women and girls who had to strip. There were different exam rooms for female patients.) The doctors would examine the immigrants for the problem the line doctors marked on their clothes. The doctors would check the immigrants for tuberculosis and for a number of contagious diseases. The doctors would perform ear, nose, and throat exams on them. As circumstances warranted, they would check the women's breasts and would check pregnant women.

Occasionally some of the immigrants would have to strip a little more.

William Williams in 1903 ordered inspection of some unmarried male adults being processed at Ellis Island for venereal diseases. He did this to see if VD was a large health problem among arriving immigrants and if there were enough cases of VD to warrant making such inspections part of the general inspection process. The chosen few had to strip and have their genitals inspected. The doctors as normal males did not like to check other men's privates ... and among the 3400 or so foreigners they spot-checked they found only five immigrants who were visibly infected, so Ellis Island's chief medical officer put a halt to the short-arm inspections.

If a doctor found an immigrant who had a medical problem that would keep him or her from entering the United States, two other doctors would have to check the immigrant and certify the first doctor's diagnosis. The immigrant would have to appear before the Board of Special Inquiry on Ellis Island if two other doctors agreed with the first doctor. The board members would rule on whether to deport the immigrant. **(6)**

An observer, commenting on immigrant inspection in 1913, noted, "The surgeons mark about half of the immigrants with chalk marks as they file by (a high proportion compared to the norm of about 15 to 20 percent; maybe the ship was from a questionable port in Europe), and those so marked go to another pen for further examination. Families are torn asunder, and no one has the time or opportunity to explain why. Mothers are wild, thinking their children are lost to them forever; children are frantic, thinking they will see their parents no more. Husbands and wives are separated and for hours they know not why or how." **(7)**

Children who were inadmissable posed other problems. If a pre-teenage child had to be deported, the child's mother or father had to accompany the child back to where they came from. A teenager who was inadmissable could be deported by himself or herself, or a parent could accompany him or her back home. (In the early 1900s, teenagers had more responsibilities than they do now. Most were already out of school, and were working. Many were married.) Sometimes all family members went home; often they split up so the husband could find work and lodging for the other children while the mother took the rejected child home and waited until the child was well enough to pass the medical exam or tried to get relatives to take care of the child if there was no chance of getting the child into America. Since wages were much higher in America than in Europe, immigrants could send home money for a child's care.

Having a child deported was undoubtedly a cruel blow to a family, but from a coldly practical point of view, their plight wasn't America's problem. American officials understood immigration was supposed to benefit America, not burden Americans with cripples from other countries whose own people should have been helping them. Crooked officials in the homeland countries and crooked steamship company officials should have told these people they could not all gain

entry to the United States, but selfishness and greed motivated them instead of decency, so they encouraged these people to go to America anyway.

Now that we've discussed how an alien could get rejected for medical reasons, let's note the vast majority of aliens marked for further medical inspection passed. According to federal statistics from 1892 through 1924, doctors determined 129 people had tuberculosis, 42,319 had "loathsome" or dangerous contagious diseases, 25,439 had other medical problems serious enough to prevent their becoming residents of America, and 87 were chronic alcoholics. Compared to the 20,390,289 aliens who American immigration agents inspected from 1892 through 1924, and the 20,003,041 aliens who American immigration agents allowed into America from 1892 through 1924, these 67,974 immigrants rejected for medical reasons equaled a rejection rate of about 33 out of every 10,000, or 0.33% of the immigrants screened. These numbers show doctors as a rule weren't trying to exclude aliens just because they could. **(8)**

What happened to those suspected of mental illness or senility?

According to Dr. E. H. Mullan, this was the gist of the screening of immigrants suspected to have a mental disorder:

"From 50 to 100 percent of the immigrants who enter the inspection plant (the Main Building) are questioned by the medical examiner in order to elicit signs of mental disease or mental defect. The exact number that are stopped and questioned will depend upon the race, sex, and general appearance of the passengers undergoing inspection as well as upon the total number of immigrants to be inspected."

Mullan said the medical examiner would observe immigrants for abnormal behavior and ask immigrants simple questions, like, "How many are 15 and 16?" He said the medical examiners would ask children how old they were and what their names were.

Mullan said experienced line inspectors knew idiosyncrasies of various ethnic groups and did not judge immigrants by American standards of normal behavior, speech, and mannerisms.

What kinds of symptoms got a doctor's attention? Some behavior is considered eccentric in all cultures and times. Persons exhibiting compulsive drooling, abnormal staring or fidgeting, spastic and repetitive motions, disorientation, strange actions, excessive filthiness, talking to oneself, or biting or otherwise mutilating oneself, Mullan said, would get marked. Likewise, a person who exhibited a number of other behaviors, from extreme talkativeness to refusal to co-operate with the exams to extreme withdrawal, he noted, would be a person the doctors might consider to be exhibiting signs of insanity.

Mullan said persons who engaged in inappropriate laughter, crying, yelling, or other noisemaking, meddling with other people, compulsive lying, peculiar affected manner, or excessive antisocial behavior would also find themselves marked and in line for further mental evaluation. (Using these standards, many many politicians, media people, lawyers, and entertainers would be rightly certifiable on some or all of the above behaviors.)

Doctors were supposed to screen out, besides the insane, those they judged to be "feeble minded" (mentally retarded), "imbeciles" (moderately or severely mentally retarded), "idiots" (profoundly mentally retarded), or senile. Questioning of immigrants led doctors to mark others who they thought might be retarded or senile. Although epilepsy is a brain malady that is not a mental illness, doctors were supposed to screen out epileptics also.

If a medical examiner thought the immigrant was insane or had a mental illness, or was senile, he would mark the person's outer garment with an X, a circled X, or an S. The X meant the doctor suspected the person had a mental problem. If the X was circled, this meant the doctor decided he observed actual signs of mental illness. The S meant the doctor suspected the person was senile.

Those marked for mental screening went through what the inspectors called the "Weeding-Out Process." They would go to the Mental Room and one of the doctors would question them.

The doctor would ask the alien to walk up to his desk, sit down, count, do some simple addition, maybe make a simple drawing, and figure out a simple puzzle. He would also ask the alien some simple questions. If the doctor observed what he considered obvious signs of a mental disorder, he would fill out a list of symptoms he observed and have the alien sent to the mental ward of the Ellis Island hospital for observation. If the doctor observed the alien could not perform the test, but didn't display any other signs of a mental disorder, the doctor would have the alien detained overnight in a detention room for a more thorough mental examination the next day.

Most of the immigrants would pass the "Weeding-Out Process." The doctor would release them to undergo the legal inspection.

Doctors evaluated aliens sent to the mental ward of the hospital for observation. If three doctors who observed the alien in the mental ward determined he or she was insane or suffering from another mental illness that would not allow him or her to gain entry, they would certify the alien was insane or suffering from a mental illness. People who the doctors considered insane or idiots or imbeciles or senile or feeble-minded or mentally ill would be deportable. People having none of these problems, in the doctors' judgment, could be cleared for further processing or might still have to undergo mental examination.

An alien who failed the "Weeding-Out Process" but was not in bad enough shape to be easily certifiable as having a mental disorder had to undergo a second mental examination. He or she would undergo this exam with a different doctor than the one who ordered him or her detained. The doctor would spend 20 to 60 minutes with the alien and ask him or her questions about home life customs, his or her occupation, and his or her intentions if he or she could gain entry to America. The doctor would give the alien a brief psychological test. The doctor would sometimes give the alien a vision test and a neurological exam. The alien would often also have to count, do some simple addition, make a simple drawing, and figure out a simple puzzle. Many detained aliens were able to collect themselves and satisfy the second doctor they were at least dull normal. The doctor would then release such aliens to undergo the legal inspection.

If the second doctor observed what he considered obvious signs of a mental disorder, he would fill out a list of symptoms he observed and have the alien sent to the mental ward of the hospital for observation. (And if three doctors at the mental ward who observed the alien decided he or she had a mental disorder, they would certify it and the alien would be deportable.) If the second doctor deemed the alien was merely substandard or questionable, he or she would undergo yet another mental exam from a third doctor on another day.

If the third doctor decided the alien was off-center but not abnormal, or was slow but not stupid enough to warrant deportation, he would then release the alien to undergo the legal inspection. If the third doctor decided the person was "feeble-minded" or worse, then the alien would be deportable. Why? As in medical screening, it took the opinion of three different doctors to deem the would-be immigrant mentally defective in some way.

If three doctors at the Ellis Island hospital's mental ward certified an alien was mentally defective, or if three doctors doing "weeding out" exams in the main building certified an alien was feeble-minded or worse, the alien would appear before a Board of Special Inquiry on Ellis Island. The board members would rule on whether to deport the alien.

Mullan said the line doctors marked about 9 out of 100 immigrants undergoing processing for suspected mental problems. Most of these, he said, passed the mental evaluation the doctors gave them in the Mental

Room, and they could return to the line for legal examination. He said 1 or 2 of the 9 sent for mental evaluation typically showed symptoms serious enough to warrant a thorough mental exam. (9)

The medical inspectors tried hard to keep mental defectives out of the country. One of the doctors at Ellis Island said the doctors who inspected people and certified 59 people as being mental defectives (which meant these unfortunates had to be sent back) in 1905 saved taxpayers more in not having to care for immigrants with mental problems than the entire cost of the medical inspectors in that year. This was probably the case for most of the years from the early 1900s to 1924. (10)

Most of those detained for mental evaluation did pass inspection. According to federal statistics from 1892 through 1924, doctors determined 384 people were "idiots", 518 were "imbeciles", 3215 were "feeble minded", 2473 were "insane", and 550 had other mental problems serious enough to prevent them from becoming residents of America. They also kept 416 epileptics out of the country. Compared to the 20,390,289 aliens who American immigration agents inspected from 1892 through 1924, and the 20,003,041 aliens who American immigration agents allowed into America from 1892 through 1924, these 7556 immigrants rejected for mental reasons equaled a rejection rate of 4 out of every 10,000, or 0.04% of the immigrants screened. These numbers show the doctors didn't find very many mental defectives among the immigrants.

How busy was the hospital on Ellis Island?

The hospital on Ellis Island was busier than many hospitals in the United States at that time. Here's a sample of what the doctors and nurses did there:

From July 1905 through June 1906, roughly 7500 immigrants (about 1% of the more than 800,000 immigrants passing through the port of New York in those 12 months) required hospital treatment at the hospital on Ellis Island, or at the New York Quarantine Station on Swinburne Island or at one of the New York City hospitals which did contract work for Ellis Island. The average patient stayed in the hospital for 12 days. This is an average of about 250 admitted patients per day for the 12-month period. Most of these immigrants were treated at Ellis Island.

They were busier in the next 12 months. From July 1906 through June 1907, the medical people detained about 9300 immigrants for hospital treatment. This was again about 1% of the roughly 950,000 immigrants passing through the port of New York in those 12 months.

Commissioner Robert Watchorn (who was Commissioner of Immigration at Ellis Island from 1905 through 1909, between the two terms of William Williams) blamed the steamship companies for much of the hospital staffers' workloads. He noted in 1907 his people found 1506 immigrant children were suffering from measles, diphtheria, and scarlet fever, "all of which diseases are due, more or less, to overcrowding and insanitary conditions." Of these sick children, he said, 205 died. The next year, Watchorn noted, 267 immigrants who his people treated or who they had sent to hospitals in New York City died. Of these, he said, 229 were children suffering from communicable diseases like measles and scarlet fever.

Watchorn billed the steamship companies $104,000 for medical treatment rendered to immigrant children in fiscal year 1907 (July 1906 through June 1907), much of which took place at New York City hospitals. He said it cost another $30,000 to detain a parent or a teenage brother or sister of these children so these children would have relatives to protect them when they could be released. (These dollar figures seem small by today's standards, but in the early 1900s, a family could live in America on $800 a year without being below the poverty line.)

The hospital on Ellis Island also had a mental ward for observation and treatment of would-be immigrants who had or were suspected of having mental disorders. In 1907, medical officers opened the psychopathic ward a.k.a. the "insane pavilion" for isolation and treatment of aliens with mental disorders until they could be deported. Commissioner Watchorn pushed for such a facility in 1906 following the suicide of a man who strangled himself with a light fixture cord while being in a detention cell for behaving hatefully, and the suicide of a woman being detained for mental evaluation who killed herself by crawling out a window and jumping to her death. (11)

In fiscal year 1911 (July 1910 through June 1911), doctors and nurses treated more than 6000 aliens at the Ellis Island hospital – about 1% of the roughly 700,000 immigrants passing through the port of New York) They also referred 720 people suffering contagious diseases to the New York Quarantine Hospital on Swinburne Island.

In 1911, the contagious disease hospital complex opened on Ellis Island's Island 3. The hospital's 11 buildings had a capacity of 450 beds, and its medical people treated anywhere from 30 to 130 patients per month in 1911. Doctors and nurses at the contagious disease hospital on Ellis Island treated patients with pneumonia, whooping cough, measles, scarlet fever, diphtheria, mumps, chicken pox, tuberculosis, trachoma, favus, and venereal disease.

Doctors continued to treat those suffering the more serious contagious diseases like cholera, smallpox, typhus, yellow fever, leprosy, or bubonic plague at the New York Quarantine Hospital on Swinburne Island. They continued to isolate those exposed to these terrible diseases but not visibly sick from them at the facility on Hoffman Island. They also treated some of the immigrants suffering less serious contagious diseases at the hospital on Hoffman Island for a time.

In fiscal year 1928 (July 1927 through June 1928), after the quotas took effect in 1924 and only about 150,000 people processed through Ellis Island that year, the Ellis Island hospital's doctors and nurses usually were treating on average 325 patients a day. Many of these unfortunates were merchant seamen. **(12)**

LEGAL INSPECTION OR PRIMARY INSPECTION

If an immigrant passed the in-line medical exam and no doctor decided he or she was diseased, crippled, or mentally defective, and no matron decided she was a prostitute, they would route him or her to the Registry Room, a huge auditorium-sized room that occupied the center of the second floor of the Main Building of Ellis Island.

In the Registry Room, she or he would undergo the legal inspection. (People pulled out of line for closer medical or mental evaluations who passed these evaluations would also then undergo the legal inspection in the Registry Room.) Ellis Island agents also called this inspection the "primary inspection."

During this inspection, the inspectors questioned the immigrants to account for them and to verify the information about them on the ship's manifest. They also were looking for potential "problem children" that they would have to bar from entering the United States.

The ship's captain had to turn in the manifest to American immigration officers at the port of arrival. He had to list American citizens in steerage aboard his ship and his crew members also. (Many Americans and immigrants who weren't citizens yet made more than one trip across the ocean for business or family reasons.) The ship's manifest for steerage passengers contained many more questions than did the manifest for first class and second class passengers. The captain of the ship had to make sure there were answers for all of these questions from the steerage passengers.

Each inspector had a copy of the ship's manifest, so he could double-check the immigrants' verbal answers with the entries about them on the ship's manifest. This is another reason the inspectors tried to keep the immigrants who were listed on the same manifest page grouped together as much as possible.

Inspectors asked the immigrants the "29 Questions" (or whatever questions the law said steerage aliens had to answer at the time) on the two-page form, such as:

- Passenger number on list
- Family name and given name
- Age (years and months)

- Sex
- Married or single
- Calling or occupation
- Able to read/Able to write
- "Nationality (country of which citizen or subject)"
- "Race or people (determined by the stock from which the alien sprang and the language they speak)"
- Last permanent residence (country, then city or town)
- "The name and complete address of nearest relative or friend in country whence alien came."
- Final destination (state, then city or town)
- Passenger number on list (repeated because this was the first line on the second page of the form)
- "Whether having a ticket to such final destination"
- "By whom was passage paid? (Whether alien paid his own passage, whether paid for by any other person, or by any corporation, society, municipality, or government)"
- "Whether in possession of $50, and if less, how much?"
- "Whether before in the United States; and if so, when and where?"
- "Whether going to join a relative or friend; and if so, what relative or friend, and his name and complete address"
- "Ever in Prison, almshouse, or institution for care and treatment of the insane, or supported by charity? If so, which?"
- "Whether a Polygamist"
- "Whether an Anarchist"
- "Whether coming by reason of any offer, solicitation, promise or agreement, expressed or implied, to labor in the United States"
- "Condition of Health, Mental and Physical"
- "Deformed or Crippled, Nature, length of time, and cause"
- Height
- Complexion
- Color of hair/Color of eyes
- Marks of Identification
- Place of Birth (country, then city or town) **(13)**

Inspectors would ask these questions of the men, women, and teenage boys and girls.

Starting in 1917, the inspectors would ask would-be immigrants 17 and older to read a selection in their own language, because now the law required immigrants to be literate in their native language. (They made exceptions for illiterate immigrants whose literate husbands or children or grandchildren were legally admitted immigrants or American citizens who sent for them. Immigration officials would still allow these people entry even if they could not read. Officials also made an exception for the unmarried or widowed daughters of legally admitted immigrants or American citizens who were 17 or older and illiterate.) **(14)**

Interpreters fluent in almost every language in Europe and the Middle East stood by to help the immigrants understand the inspectors' questions and the inspectors understand the immigrants' answers. (At Angel's Island in San Francisco Bay and in other ports along the West Coast, interpreters fluent in Oriental languages were available to help the immigrants and the inspectors.)

Registry inspectors (the inspectors who performed legal or primary inspections) asked immigrants how they expected to support themselves, and other simple questions aimed at determining why the immigrants were coming to the United States. They were supposed to screen out contract laborers whose presence threatened the livelihoods of American workers. They were also supposed to screen out burdens on society like paupers and the unemployable. (Medical inspectors had presumably already screened out the physically and mentally defective.) And they were supposed to screen out the chancres of human society, such as common criminals and sociopaths, anarchists and other troublemakers, and perverts such as pimps, prostitutes, and polygamists.

An observer, commenting on the primary inspection in 1913, noted, "The line moves on past the female inspector looking for prostitutes, and then past the inspectors who ask the (then) twenty-two questions required by law. Here is where the lies are told. Most of the immigrants have been coached as to what answers to give. Here is an old woman who says she has three sons in America, when she has but one. The more she talks the worse she entangles herself. Here is a Russian Jewish girl who has run away to escape persecution. She claims a relative in New York at an address found not to exist; she is straightaway in trouble." **(15)**

Many immigrants, subject to human failings like all of us, would lie if they thought it would help them gain entrance to the United States. It was the job of the inspectors to sniff out those who could be a detriment to American society, and hold them up so the authorities could decide whether to deport them.

In the following paragraphs, we will discuss some of the main reasons agents rejected would-be immigrants.

CONTRACT LABOR

Some of the first federal immigration laws – the Act of March 3, 1875, the Chinese Exclusion Act of 1882, and the Alien Contract Labor Law of 1885 – aimed to keep robber barons from importing unskilled foreign laborers to break the wage scale of American workers. In fact, the first of these laws went into effect only six years after the completion of the Transcontinental Railroad. Robber baron Charlie Crocker had imported many coolies from China at dirt-cheap wages to build the railroad line from the Sacramento area through the Sierra Nevada Mountains, across Nevada, and into Utah. Most immigrants came to seek better conditions in America, but the goal of American immigration policy was not to let the robber barons import so many people willing to work for next to nothing that the standard of living of the average American would decline to European or even down to Asian standards.

This is in stark contrast to today, where immigration from Latin America and Asia – even illegal immigration – has official encouragement because government leaders and the corporate types who bankroll their campaigns evidently have no problem with breaking the wage scales in America's basic industries.

Immigrants had to convince the inspectors they had trade skills or at least the willingness to work, so they would not get classified as losers who would be deported because they were "liable to become a public charge." However, if they told inspectors they had jobs lined up, the inspectors would pull them out of line as suspected contract laborers, and the officials would likely deport them. The best thing for an immigrant to do was to tell the truth, and not lie or exaggerate in hopes of impressing an inspector who had heard it all before.

Fiorello La Guardia, an interpreter at Ellis Island from 1907 through 1910, had this to say about the dilemma of many people on the contract labor and pauper questions:

"It is a puzzling fact that one provision of the Immigration Law excludes any immigrant who has no job and classifies him as likely to become a public charge, while another provision excludes an immigrant if he has a job! Common sense suggested that any immigrant who came into the United States in those days to settle here permanently surely came here to work. However, under the law, he could not have any more than a vague hope of a job. In answering the inspectors' questions, immigrants had to be very careful, because if their expectations were too enthusiastic, they might be held as coming in violation of the contract labor provision. Yet if they were too indefinite, if they knew nobody, had no idea where they were going to get jobs, they might be excluded as likely to become public charges. Most of the inspectors were conscientious and fair. Sometimes, I felt, large batches of those held and deported as violating the contract labor provision were, perhaps, only borderline cases and had no more than the assurance from relatives or former townsmen of jobs on their arrival."

However, La Guardia said, "The history of immigrant labor in this country fully justified such a law (contract laborer exclusion). He said before the contract laborer exclusion law went on the books in the 1880s, "Our country went through a period of exploitation of labor which is one of the most sordid and blackest pictures in our entire history. The railroads and our young industries were built by exploited immigrant labor brought here under contract."

"Shipload after shipload of immigrants were brought into this country by contractors, or padrones, who had already made contracts with the railroads and other large corporations for their services. The wages, at best, were disgracefully low. In the eighteen nineties these wages averaged $1.25 to $1.50 a day. The padrone was paid by the corporation. In addition to the low wages he paid the laborers, he took a rake-off from their meager daily earnings. In addition to that, he boarded and fed the immigrants, for which he often made exorbitant charges, deducted, too, from their small pay. Often he had a company store as well, in which he sold them supplies at excessive prices. How they ever managed to save enough to send for their families is a wonder. The twelve-hour day was not unusual, and the seven-day week was common." (16)

"LIABLE TO BE A PUBLIC CHARGE"

The inspectors were also looking to keep out of the country those foreigners who would be a burden to society. Besides asking them about what their trades were or what their plans were, inspectors would ask immigrants how much money they had on them. Being virtually penniless at first was no bar to getting into the country. In the 1890s and through most of the first decade of the 1900s, inspectors let even the indigents in. After all, many people made it in America after arriving with little more than the clothes on their backs, including Robert Watchorn, the Commissioner of Immigration at Ellis Island from 1905 through 1909. Watchorn had come from England in 1880.

Williams in his second term as commissioner at Ellis Island stirred up controversy by enforcing the "pauper" and "public charge" portion of the immigration law more strictly. Williams tried to have barred some of those immigrants who came to America with less than $25 per adult. His argument was immigrants would need that much money as a minimum to pay their expenses until they could get jobs. People who showed up with almost no money, he argued, were likely going to have to receive charity in America.

In a memo he wrote for his agents, he acknowledged there was no legal minimum in cash an immigrant needed to enter America. However, he said, "In most cases it will be unsafe for immigrants to arrive with less than twenty-five ($25) besides railroad tickets to destination, while in many cases they should have more." He wanted inspectors to take this into consideration when deciding whether to admit immigrants.

There would be no formal requirement for an immigrant to show he or she had at least a certain amount of cash to avoid being sent back as a pauper during Williams' second watch. But Williams instructed his inspectors to use the $25 amount as a guideline to determine if an immigrant could be excluded as being likely to become a public charge. He noted, "This notice is not, as many have claimed it to be, a rule under which inspectors must exclude immigrants with less than $25, and thus an attempt to create a property test not found in the statutes. It is merely a humane notice to intending immigrants that upon landing they will require at least some small amount of money with which to meet their wants while looking about for employment." (17)

Williams said common sense dictated setting a minimum amount of cash needed and letting would-be immigrants and shipping companies know what America expected of them. He blamed shipping companies for bringing large numbers of practically penniless people to America, where they would require charity to survive until they could eke out meager livings. As an example, Williams noted 189 of the 251 passengers a steamship offloaded for processing at Ellis Island on the 4th of July 1909 had $10 or less.

Williams aimed his policy not so much at the poorest immigrants themselves, but at the steamship line operators who didn't care who they hauled in steerage, as long as they made money. Williams figured setting such a money requirement, even informally, would make steamship company officials stop carrying so many paupers to America. This is because every immigrant rejected by the inspectors when the steamship company's people should have known he or she couldn't be allowed into America meant a $100 fine to the steamship company. This also meant the steamship company would have to bring the immigrant back to the port at which he or she got on the ship at the steamship company's expense.

Williams' policy caused an uproar. Many people accused him of discriminating against the poor from Italy and Eastern Europe. However, his policy was a guideline rather than an absolute rule. Many immigrants who were in their 20s in this period would say later the inspectors let them in despite not having $25 because they looked like vigorous young men and women capable of finding work and making good.

Inspectors allowed another common-sense exception to the indigence guideline. Most of the time, women coming with their children and very little money were able to gain entrance to America after they telegramed their husbands or relatives and their husbands or relatives sent back word they had money and would support their wives and children or family members.

Officials of the steamship companies found a dodge that still enabled them to transport large numbers of indigents to America and make money doing so. Percy Baker, a superintendent at Ellis Island, said, "The steamship companies often advanced ten or fifteen dollars to aliens without money. And I have an idea they got most of it back." **(18)**

An observer, commenting on the primary inspection in 1913, noted, "Sometimes men (would-be immigrants) are turned back for trivial cases. Four Greeks were going to Canada, via New York. The Canadian law requires each immigrant to have twenty-five dollars. They have $24.37 each. When they found their funds short, they wanted to come into the United States, but could not. A child is taken down with a contagious disease and is carried to the hospital. The mother must wait and cannot even see her child. A man and his son have had their money stolen from them in the steerage; they lack twenty dollars and must go back. And so the sad tale goes on every day."

He noted if there were no standards, "Then sixteen thousand debarred aliens a year would lay siege to their (the inspectors') sympathies and each would regard his own as a special case, and innumerable difficulties would result. All authorities agree that the system in vogue is just about as humane and as free from hardships as any system that might be devised, and that would maintain the interests of the nation as paramount to the interests of the individual immigrant." **(19)**

The $25 "guideline" no doubt kept many would-be immigrants at home. One of these was apparently a young mechanic from the former Yugoslavia named Josip Broz. When author Louis Adamic, an American citizen and native of Slovenia, visited Yugoslavia in 1949, Broz told him the combined expenses of a train ride to Hamburg, a steerage ticket on a ship crossing the Atlantic and the $25 he thought he would need to gain entrance to America kept him from coming here in 1910. Instead, he stayed home. He eventually became famous, infamous, or notorious, depending on your point of view. For this Josip Broz would become the dictator commonly known as Tito. **(20)**

CRIMINAL SCREENING

Inspectors asked aliens if they had been convicted of and imprisoned for any crimes. Some people told the truth. Others lied about their criminal records, thinking they could get away with it.

Many people who had committed political offenses were likely to admit to what they had done, knowing that Americans admired people who fought authoritarian rule. (We need more of that in this country today!) After all, America became free by revolution against Britain. American authorities did not hold political arrests, except those for anarchism-related offenses, against would-be immigrants. The United States welcomed large numbers of Irish rebels and German dissidents throughout the 1800s.

Others told the truth because they were honest by nature. Public disorder arrests, like for drunkenness or fighting, were not uncommon among people in the 1800s and early 1900s. (Nor are they uncommon today.) Likewise, many people, especially peasants, were arrested for acts of petty misbehavior that would not be illegal in the United States. Inspectors didn't automatically flag aliens who admitted to such problems.

Note that the inspectors asked aliens if they had ever been <u>convicted</u> or <u>imprisoned</u>, not <u>arrested</u>. This reflected the American notion that a person accused of a crime was innocent until proven guilty. Being arrested for a crime didn't make a person guilty, unlike in Europe or Asia. An alien who was wise to the American way could conceal his arrest record if he hadn't actually received a prison sentence.

On the flip side of the coin, European officials did try to send some of their losers to America. And many other immigrants tried to hide their brushes with the law because they were common criminals instead of patriots, union people, poor peasants, or guys who got into scrapes after a little too much booze or after some lowlife said something uncalled-for to his wife. (Bear in mind many Americans are the descendants of English thieves and whores who were essentially dumped here by British authorities before the American Revolution.)

Most criminals probably did escape detection, but some did not. Here's why:

The Ellis Island era (1892 through 1924) did not have international police computer networking, the computer database or the Internet. Likewise, in those days there was no DNA sampling. Forensic science, first widely popularized in Arthur Conan Doyle's Sherlock Holmes books of the 1880s and 1890s, was just becoming a formal discipline. Fingerprinting, trace evidence analysis, document examination, ballistics, and blood typing and grouping would all become acceptable forensic procedures during the Ellis Island era.

Immigration officials in that era did have the telephone and the telegraph. The Atlantic Cable connected Europe to America for telegraph messages, so American diplomats and European officials could contact American immigration authorities about wanted or suspicious people who might be sailing to America.

Because of the development of the long-range radiotelegraph ("wireless") around the turn of the century, ships at sea could receive and send telegraph messages also. In fact, such a ship-to-shore message led to the 1910 capture and hanging of Dr. Hawley Crippen, an American who fled England for Canada aboard a steamship with his young lover after he reportedly killed and dismembered his unfaithful and domineering wife in their London house. Likewise, authorities in Europe or American officials stationed in Europe could use the radiotelegraph to relay messages about criminals trying to escape to America so immigration officials would be ready for them. **(21)**

American immigration officials would use these methods of quick communication to get tips on incoming bad guys. One of the most famous cases, according to Edward Corsi, the commissioner who ran Ellis Island in the early 1930s, a generation after he underwent processing at Ellis Island himself, was that of his former fellow countryman Benito Mussolini. Corsi said Mussolini, before he became dictator of Italy, was in hot water with Italian authorities. He was reportedly contemplating fleeing to America, according to a confidential source. Word of Mussolini's potential escape to America somehow reached the State Department in Washington, Corsi said, and that agency's officials immediately gave immigration officials at Ellis Island and other inspection stations the heads-up. "If he (Mussolini) had attempted to land in the United States," Corsi said, "he would have been detained and examined by a board of special inquiry."

Mussolini might not have needed an interpreter for such a hearing. Corsi, when he was a reporter, had interviewed Mussolini in the 1920s, after he took over Italy. Evidently Il Duce was confident enough in his foreign language skills that he didn't use a single word of Italian in answering fellow Italian Corsi's questions!

Corsi's own father had been a prominent Italian politician. People in Italy elected the elder Corsi to the Italian parliament while he was in exile in Switzerland. On his return to Italy in triumph, Filippo Corsi dropped dead as he was giving his victory speech. Corsi's mother eventually married an army officer, and they decided to try life in America. She became ill after three years in the tenements of New York City and returned to Italy to die. The stepfather raised young Corsi and his brother and sisters in America. **(22)**

Even though technology in that era was not as advanced as it its now, immigration agents were not

necessarily dumber than the airline screeners of today who fail to catch weapons being smuggled aboard aircraft despite having metal detectors and X-ray machines.

There were some agents – like good policemen in all eras – who were naturals at finding people who were criminals or other undesirables. Profiling, noticing behavior untypical for a situation, and figuring out when someone is lying by listening for contradictions or improbable statements are skills not dependent upon technology. American officials had the ability to interrogate suspicious aliens or those who knew them. And they did not have anywhere near the interference from professional obstructionist groups and money-sniffing attorneys as immigration officials do today. American officials also had at their disposal the oldest of criminal investigation tools – the informants. European officials and American officials overseas and in America received many tips from informants for reasons ranging from a desire to help to a desire for revenge to a desire for money.

William Williams said, "Criminals and other bad characters, usually bearing no earmarks, seek to enter the country by taking passage in the cabin (second class), and yet the intelligent work of the boarding inspectors often results in their apprehension." Williams noted the tips his agents got were usually valid, "yet some of them are lodged here through spite." He added, "The power of the immigration officials is so summary that foreign authorities desiring to have an alien apprehended often seek to accomplish through the Immigration Service what should be accomplished through extradition proceedings. This office always declines to allow itself to be used in this manner." **(23)**

Europe was authoritarian, America was democratic. Even in alleged democracies like France and England, the government had the legal power to punish dissidents that the American government did not have. (Woodrow Wilson, FDR, LBJ, Nixon, and Clinton and their minions had to break the law to punish dissidents.) British officials routinely jailed Irish patriots who spoke their minds. French officials sentenced Emile Zola to prison on a libel charge for writing "J'accuse," a tract concerning the Dreyfus case, even though what Zola wrote was true. (Zola fled to Britain to avoid prison.) American officials, aware that America became free because Americans rebelled against British rule, would never bar immigrants just because they had committed political offenses in other countries. (Anarchists, Nazis, and Communists would be about the only exceptions to this policy.) Political offenses were not crimes of murder, rape, assault, arson, robbery, theft, dishonesty, or sexual depravity. It would be un-American to turn over immigrants to the officials of another country just because the immigrants had broken some political law that wouldn't stand in The Land of the Free. Williams, by refusing to be the toady of European and Asian governments, was simply affirming America's tolerance for most malcontents.

Williams had no similar qualms about getting information on common criminals so he could have them detained and deported. He thought America's leaders weren't doing enough to ensure the steamship companies checked immigrants and weeded out common criminals instead of making money dumping them in America. He wrote, "As matters stand to-day our Government makes no effort to obtain the valuable information undoubtedly contained in foreign criminal records as to many immigrants who come here. The transportation companies should be required to satisfy the immigration authorities as to each immigrant above a certain age that the criminal records of the locality from which he comes have been searched, and they should also be required to furnish a statement as to what, if anything, has been found therein, and a civil penalty should be imposed for furnishing false information." **(24)**

Williams' idea was a good one on paper, but it would not have worked that well in the Ellis Island era.

There was not the level of co-operation between European officials and American officials that there is today. European leaders still underestimated American power (America did not take part in World War One until 1917, and Woodrow Wilson was no Theodore Roosevelt), and viewed America as a dumping ground for their riffraff. European officials were authoritarian and much more corrupt than American officials, and American officials had a natural distrust of the slimy European officials.

It is true that most immigrants had no criminal record anyway. It was also true that many European government officials wanted *some of their people to leave, especially if they were ethnic minorities or poor people who didn't seem to be able to help their national economies. They would have been only too willing to help these people emigrate, and furnish clean criminal records on these people, even if they had to doctor their records.*

European officials also figured it would be cheaper for them to allow some of their petty criminals to come to America than to jail them, if only they could be assured these criminals would come to America and not somehow hide in Europe or come back. So they might falsely give these losers clean criminal record reports to deceive American authorities.

On the other hand, European officials punished many opponents of their regimes as criminals. Likewise, they oppressed ethnic minorities within their borders. Since many immigrants were refugees from corrupt or oppressive regimes, it would have been impossible for these people to have gotten a *favorable report from police authorities in their countries. And this wasn't just countries like Russia or Germany. Officials in Britain and France jailed dissidents also, and sought to extradite those who escaped their clutches.*

One last practical difficulty with Williams' idea was that the methods of record keeping and identifications weren't as good then. Criminals themselves could get false documents to hide their true identities. They still do it today, even with supposedly better technology and supposedly better trained agents opposing them.

If an inspector determined an immigrant was a worker coming to the United States on a labor contract that put him in direct competition with American workers, the inspector could pull him or her out of line and refer his or her case to a Board of Special Inquiry on Ellis Island. Likewise, any immigrant the inspector believed was likely to become a public charge (on grounds of anything from having no money, to having subnormal intelligence, to having no definite goals, to having no normal job skills to engaging in begging on a regular basis) could wind up in front of a Board of Special Inquiry.

Any alien who was found out to be a common criminal overseas (as opposed to being a political criminal, who Americans tended to welcome) was definitely going before a Board of Special Inquiry. Any alien involved in an immoral means of making money (such as being a prostitute or a pimp or a madam) or in other immoral behavior (such as being a polygamist – profiling aimed at Moslems and Mormons) could find himself or herself in the line for a Board of Special Inquiry. Someone who was honest enough and dumb enough to admit he or she was an anarchist, a Communist, or any other crackpot who advocated the overthrow of the American form of government would get to know a Board of Special Inquiry better as a detainee trying to argue why they should not have him or her deported from the United States. And finally, people who were caught lying to the inspectors were liable for detention and a hearing in front of a Board of Special Inquiry. The board members would rule on whether to deport the immigrant based on his or her legal fitness, ability to earn a living, and character attributes.

The largest number of aliens who the immigration officials refused entrance to from 1892 through 1924 were people they figured would be drains upon society ("likely to become a public charge," they called it). They barred 196,208 aliens on these grounds. The second largest number of aliens denied entry from 1892 through 1924 were the 72,640 aliens barred from entering the United States because immigration officials determined they were physical or mental defectives. The third largest group of people the immigration officials kept out of America from 1892 through 1924 were the 38,630 aliens deemed to be contract laborers, people who the American working public figured the robber barons were importing to break the wage structure. **(25)**

Officials at Ellis Island "temporarily detained" a large number of aliens. They were presumed qualified to enter the United States, but they needed relatives or friends to contact the officials at Ellis Island and vouch for them, and make arrangements to pick them up, or send them money for train fare. When the relatives or friends did what they needed to do, then the immigrant was free to go. If there was no contact from the immigrant's professed relatives or friends for five days after the immigrant landed, he or she would have to go before the Board of Special Inquiry. Robert Watchorn said his people detained 121,737 immigrants "to be called for by relatives" from July 1906 through June 1907, roughly one out of every eight immigrants who landed in the port of New York. **(26)**

Officials at Ellis Island "medically detained" a fair percentage of immigrants because they had an ailment needing hospitalization. (This was typically about 1% of the number of immigrants processed at Ellis Island any given year.) The immigrant would have to undergo treatment in the hospital on Ellis Island, and had to stay there until a doctor discharged the immigrant from the hospital and cleared him or her medically. When the immigrant recovered, he or she was free to go.

Now that we've covered all the potential ways the agents could detain and send back would-be immigrants, let's give the big picture. Despite the immigrants' fears, and the critiques of self-appointed do-gooders and immigrant societies, the inspectors let in the vast majority of immigrants they questioned.

Philip Cowen, an American-born son of Prussian Jewish immigrants who worked at Ellis Island as an inspector, said in 1907 (the busiest year at Ellis Island, at which a million would-be immigrants landed), there were many days when the Registry Division inspectors checked 5000 or more immigrants, and since there were at most 21 inspectors available for the two shifts during the day, this meant an inspector could count on checking about 250 immigrants on his shift on such a day. **(27)**

A 1909 labor force report by special immigrant inspector Roger O'Donnell noted there were 17 inspectors in the Registry Division, where the primary inspections took place. (This does not count the 14 inspectors serving as members of Special Inquiry Boards, or the 12 inspectors who were part of the Boarding Division, or the 21 other inspectors sprinkled throughout the other divisions on Ellis Island.) Since 580,000 immigrants came through the port of New York in 1908, and the vast majority of these landed at Ellis Island, the average primary inspector in the Registry Division inspected more than 30,000 immigrants that year, an average of more than 100 per day (assuming a six-day workweek and no help from the inspectors in the other divisions). O'Donnell noted the authorities on Ellis Island only asked for four more inspectors. **(28)**

When the inspectors were satisfied immigrants passed all the requirements for gaining entry to the country, they would hand "landing cards" to the immigrants. The inspectors sent them down to the first floor of the Main Building so they could get their belongings and make arrangements to go to their destinations.

We'll pick up this aspect of the immigrants' progress after we talk about the Boards of Special Inquiry.

BOARDS OF SPECIAL INQUIRY

Slightly more than 20 million immigrants came to the United States during the busiest years of the Ellis Island era (1892 through 1924). Of these, more than 14 million immigrants gained entry through the Port of New York; the vast majority of these gained entry through Ellis Island.

Most immigrants who came through Ellis Island and other immigration stations were able to gain entrance into America. But about two percent did not. While this is a small percentage, it means the officials at Ellis Island and other American immigration facilities turned away about 400,000 people in that era.

The members of the Boards of Special Inquiry heard the cases of those who the medical and mental inspectors and/or the registry inspectors (the legal inspectors) believed should be denied entry to the United States. An inspector could pull someone out of line, but he did not have the authority to exclude him. The board members could.

The members of the Boards of Special Inquiry reviewed each inspector's reason for sending each immigrant to them, reviewed the documents pertaining to each immigrant, questioned each immigrant themselves (usually through interpreters, but often enough someone on the board could speak the immigrant's language), and made a quick decision on whether to admit or deport each immigrant detained for possible deportation.

Each immigrant had the right to appeal a board of special inquiry decision to deport him to the commissioner at the immigration station. It was also possible for an immigrant to appeal a board of inquiry decision to the Department of Commerce and Labor (and after the split of the department into two departments, the immigrant could appeal to the Department of Labor). It was also possible for an immigrant to appeal to the Secretary of the Department himself. In reality, appeals to the Department rarely happened, because most immigrants lacked the skill to argue a technical case themselves and the money to hire a lawyer to do it for them.

It was possible for an immigrant to appeal a board of inquiry decision at Ellis Island if he could provide proper evidence that the board members had overlooked when hearing his case, or if evidence turned up later that he didn't have when he landed at Ellis Island. Such evidence, for instance, could include a witness who could come to Ellis Island and vouch for an immigrant, or a telegram from a relative proving the immigrant had a place to go, or proof of other disputed issues. Williams said on his second watch as commissioner there could be from 15 to 70 appeals a day.

Williams said hearing appeals enabled him to see how good a job each of his board members were doing, and also gave him another tool to spot-check the work of his line inspectors. He said he wanted to make sure the board members put the proper questions to immigrants to get the relevant facts of the case so they could make just decisions based on the record and the law. Williams said even if he overturned a board's decision and allowed an immigrant entry to the country, this often meant he had more discretion in hearing an appeal than the board members did in reaching a decision, and not necessarily that his board members had done wrong in denying the immigrant entry in the first place.

"Good board members are not easily found," Williams said. "They must, amongst other things, be intelligent, able to exercise sound judgment and to elicit relevant facts from immigrants and witnesses who are often stupid or deceitful." **(29)**

Each of these boards at Ellis Island made decisions on 50 to 100 immigrant cases a day, Williams said in 1903, depending on the type of case, and the difficulty of communicating with the immigrants

before them. (Medical exclusions were open and shut cases; public charge cases were also fairly routine most of the time.) Williams said in 1903 three boards were at work every day, and on days when a larger number of immigrants landed at Ellis Island than usual, a fourth board would work on cases. Williams in 1912 noted that there could be as many as eight boards hearing cases on Ellis Island on given days.

The men on the Boards of Special Inquiry worked at traffic court speed on cases where much more was at stake for the accused than points on a license. Were the board members of the Boards of Special Inquiry "hanging judges?"

In fiscal 1907 (July 1906 through June 30, 1907), Robert Watchorn said his people at Ellis Island processed more than 1,100,000 aliens from 3818 ships, detained 64,510 aliens for a Board of Special Inquiry, and the board members ordered 7408 aliens (including 288 first class or second class passengers) deported. In other words, about 6 percent of the aliens who came through Ellis Island in the previous 12 months had to go before a Board of Special Inquiry, and almost 90 percent of these aliens received permission to enter the United States. **(30)**

In 1911 and again in 1912, more than 600,000 people immigrated to the port of New York, and the vast majority of them underwent processing at Ellis Island. William Williams, in his 1913 annual report, noted the Boards Of Special Inquiry heard more than 60,000 cases a year at Ellis Island. This means about one in ten would-be immigrants had to appear before a Board of Special Inquiry in those years. Dividing 60,000 cases by 300 work days per year meant the Boards of Special Inquiry heard about 200 cases a day.

In 1911, Williams' workers at Ellis Island barred close to 13,000 would-be immigrants. In 1912, they barred about 8000. This means in the two years before Williams' 1913 report, the Boards of Special Inquiry at Ellis Island apparently ruled in favor of the aliens often enough (and aliens' appeals were successful often enough) that more than 80% of the more than 120,000 aliens who appeared before a Board of Special Inquiry in those two years received permission to enter the United States. **(31)**

These numbers imply the men of the Boards of Special Inquiry were fair-minded enough in spite of any prejudices they might have held.

DETENTION AT ELLIS ISLAND

Even though most aliens inspected at Ellis Island received permission to live in America, quite a few of them had to stay at Ellis Island one or more days until immigration officials allowed them to leave.

Quite a few immigrants had to stay in the hospital while they recuperated from their illnesses. Hospitalized immigrants, especially those who were children, often had a relative stay on the island to be near them. About 1% of those who landed at Ellis Island were hospitalized, and perhaps another 1% to 2% of those who landed at Ellis Island had to stay on Ellis Island to wait for their loved ones to get well.

There were many immigrants who had to wait for friends or relatives to pick them up, or for the arrival of money for train tickets, or for instructions from friends or relatives or proof that they had some place to go and friends or relatives to help them. Immigration agents had them telegraph their relatives or friends, or send postcards if they lived in or not too far from New York City. Agents at Ellis Island also tracked down detained immigrants to deliver them telegrams concerning travel arrangements from spouses, relatives, or friends. (Depending on the year, at least 10% of those who landed at Ellis Island were detained for such reasons.)

Then there were those who were being held for cases before the Boards of Special Inquiry, and those who were awaiting evidence that might overturn a Board of Special Inquiry ruling against them. (Depending on the year, anywhere from 5% to 10% of those who landed at Ellis Island were detained for hearings before the Boards of Special Inquiry.)

There were the unfortunates being held for mental evaluation.

And there were those being deported. Some were in the hospital awaiting the end of their treatment. Others were in confinement as criminals or other undesirables. The majority were in less stringent detention; they were being sent back because they were contract workers or people who the authorities deemed would be objects of charity. (About 2% of those who came to Ellis Island and at other immigration stations were detained for deportation.)

The immigration agents on Ellis Island provided food, shelter, security, and surveillance to all of these people.

Temporarily detained immigrants awaiting friends or money or instructions stayed nights under the charge of the Discharging Division (or later, under the charge of the Information Division).

Aliens being held for a board of special inquiry were under the charge of the Deportation Division (later known as the Deporting Division).

"Deferred" aliens (those who had appeared before a board of special inquiry but whose cases were delayed while awaiting further evidence) were under the charge of the Deportation Division.

Excluded adult male aliens (those the boards of inquiry ruled ineligible to enter the United States and were therefore deportable) stayed overnight in the "excluded" room. Excluded and deferred adult female aliens and children stayed overnight in another room. These were under the charge of the Deportation Division.

Other detained aliens without medical problems stayed in the dormitories or barracks on Ellis Island.

Agents segregated aliens being deported by sex and condition (pauperism, physical problems, contract workers). They held criminals being deported separate from the aliens who were unfortunate in their physical or mental or financial condition. The quarantine stations, local hospitals, and the quarantine hospital on Ellis Island (when it opened in 1911) held aliens being deported for contagious diseases.

In Ellis Island's busiest years, it was common to detain as many as 1800 aliens at night on the island. Sometimes the agents had to detain as many as 2100 aliens a night if an especially large number of immigrants had come to Ellis Island. These people needed to be fed, sheltered, and protected. Robert Watchorn said in his 1907 annual report that his staffers <u>averaged</u> detaining 1400 people overnight each night for the entire year. **(32)**

This meant the cooks and kitchen attendants could have served immigrants about 500,000 dinners and another 500,000 or so breakfasts that year. (They also served lunch to immigrants being detained for some reason during the day.) Fines collected from the steamship companies, not taxpayers' dollars, were the main source of money to pay for the food, the equipment, the furniture, the dishes, the utensils, and the salaries of the workers who fed the immigrants being detained.

Most aliens being detained behaved themselves, but there were some being deported who were upset about it and liable to cause trouble. Some would try to escape; others would attack immigration agents. Occasionally despondent aliens would attempt suicide. Also, there were some criminals being detained, and the violent offenders were by nature dangerous to others. Others detained as thieves, beggars, or prostitutes might try to ply their criminal trades while awaiting deportation unless they were kept away from the other immigrants. Thieves in particular required watching and disciplining. Other immigrants being detained on Ellis Island usually didn't have much disposable income to give the beggars. And usually there was not enough privacy for prostitutes to consummate the transactions of their trade with other immigrants. However, they might try to bribe or blackmail immigration officers with sex.

Occasionally there were riots that needed quelling. Riots by Italians, Gypsies, and Moslems on Ellis Island were not uncommon.

There were some immigrants who were coming to America as a group to make trouble or perpetrate evil. The underworld imported a number of immigrants from Sicily and Southern Italy for criminal activities. There were prostitute brokers in Jewish communities in Russia and Eastern Europe who sold Jewish teenage girls and young women – *their own people and sometimes their own kin* – into sexual slavery in the United States. Their prey were only a couple of days from finding out about entry the hard way. Many of the Gypsies were organized thieves and con artists. And organized beggars from the Middle East were a nuisance to many cities and towns in America in the early 1900s.

There were some immigrants were used to committing acts of violence and other unsociable acts in their own countries. Some immigrants were thieves or bullies who hadn't been caught. Some of them had criminal records but were able to escape detection as criminals because employees of the steamship lines that brought them to America had not made them prove they had clean records when they bought tickets.

And immigrants had the same kinds of flaws as people in America or anywhere else, thanks to the fallen nature of humanity that none of us is exempt from. Many immigrants had trouble behaving themselves in their homelands, and local officials all across Europe convinced many of them that getting a fresh start in America was a viable alternative to a life of crime and jail at home.

Guards would have to keep these scumbag would-be immigrants under control. Many women and children were frightened and needed protection. Despite the segregation of immigrants by sex (and younger boys with mothers also), if there weren't guards and matrons present, some aliens would undoubtedly try to sexually assault women, teenage girls, or young girls or boys.

AFTER INSPECTION

After the immigrants passed inspection, most of them were free to leave Ellis Island. Families gathered, and groups of people traveling together gathered after everyone in their family or group got through inspection. Usually this would be on the first floor of the main building, where the baggage office, the railroad office and lobby, the waiting room, and the "New York Room" were.

If a family member had to wait because he or she was sick and was being medically detained, the family would make arrangements to pick up the sick family member later, or send money for the person's train fare to rejoin them.

After passing inspection, the immigrants could exchange their European money for American money at the day's official exchange rates for a small charge at the money exchange office. Those immigrants needing to send a telegram could do so at one of the telegraph offices. Telegrams coming to immigrants from relatives and friends with instructions came through one of these telegraph offices.

Those immigrants needing railroad tickets to other cities could buy them at the railroad ticket office. Some immigrants needed ship tickets if they were sailing to another port on America's eastern seaboard. They could buy these tickets at Ellis Island also. Roughly

two-thirds of the immigrants bought tickets from one of the railroad lines or one of the Atlantic Coast steamship lines.

The immigrants would get their luggage from the Baggage Room, or make arrangements to have their luggage put on the proper trains or ships.

Immigrants going directly to New York City didn't have to worry about train tickets. Once they were free to go, they would gather in the "New York Room," and then board a ferry to Manhattan.

It was a little different for the train passengers. Each railroad company had a holding area for its immigrant passengers in the railroad ticket office lobby or a nearby waiting room. The railroad company agents would ferry their westbound and southbound customers to a railroad terminal at Jersey City or Hoboken, New Jersey. Immigrants would board the proper trains here.

Immigrants going by ship to other East Coast cities would wait for their rides elsewhere. They would take a small boat to the ship that would take them to the East Coast port they wanted to reach.

Roughly one-third of the immigrants went through the door out of the New York Room marked "PUSH TO NEW YORK", and took the Ellis Island ferryboat to

Lower Manhattan. Many of these people would settle in New York City. Immigrants with train tickets to towns in New England or upstate New York would also go to the "New York Room," take the ferryboat to Manhattan and get on the proper trains in Manhattan.

Friends and relatives could meet incoming immigrants at Ellis Island and escort them out. Agents on Ellis Island would question these people closely to make sure they were the people they said they were, and that they could prove their ties of blood or friendship to the people they came for. The immigrants themselves had to verify the callers were their friends or relatives before the immigration agents would let them go in their company.

Unaccompanied men could leave Ellis Island on their own, without having to have anyone come for them or without having to have any telegram confirm they had a place to go to.

Likewise, families with men, and groups of people traveling together with men in the groups could leave Ellis Island on their own. Ellis Island agents figured they ought to be able to protect themselves.

It was different for women and children who had no men accompanying them. Immigration officials temporarily detained these women and children and insisted they contact spouses, relatives, or friends by mail or telegraph. They insisted on the spouses, relatives, or friends verifying they were coming for their women and children, or that they were sending train tickets and money, or instructions on how to get to the places they needed to get to if the women and children had enough money.

Immigration agents tagged children younger than 15 who were unaccompanied by adults with linen tags spelling out the name and address of the relative they were going to. They also telegraphed the relatives so they would be at the train station to meet the children. Only then would they release these children to the railroad company agents.

Immigration agents also temporarily detained unaccompanied women and children going to New York City or someplace nearby. They would have to wait for husband or fiancé or relative or friend to call for them at Ellis Island. **(33)**

Sometimes charitable organizations agreed to sponsor single women immigrants. Catholic nuns, Protestant ministers, Jewish groups, and others agreed to sponsor these women and ensure they found housing and work that was not illegal or immoral. (Sometimes these organizations even put up cash bonds certifying that these women would not become public charges.) These groups daily had to account for these girls and women to the authorities at Ellis Island. **(34)**

If a man coming to pick up a woman at Ellis Island said he was her husband, she had to identify him and they had to have proof of marriage. If they didn't have such proof, then the officials would have the man and woman undergo a civil marriage ceremony at Ellis Island. If a man coming to pick up a woman at Ellis Island said he was her fiancé, then the officials would have the man and woman undergo a civil marriage ceremony at Ellis Island as well. Of course, the woman would have to consent to undergo this ritual with this man!

The authors of these policies did not intend to demean women or demean religious marriages. Immigration officials feared for the safety of women, because there were many predators in organized crime able and willing to steer them into prostitution or other degrading situations against their wills. There were also many unorganized swine who would sexually abuse unaccompanied foreign women and girls if they thought they could get away with it.

A woman could refuse to go with a purported fiancé or relative and the immigration agents would be there to protect her. Many times women needed such protection.

And as for the religious issue? Fiancés and fiancées who were religious could still refrain from consummating their marriage (having sex with each other) until they married according to the laws of their religion, in front of a priest, rabbi, or minister. Immigration officers by and large were members of religions themselves. They just wanted to make sure alleged fiances were who they said they were.

Frank Martocci, an Italian immigrant who was an interpreter and an inspector at Ellis Island from the 1890s until the 1930s, said, "We could not let a woman with her children out on the streets looking for her husband. This also applied to all alien females, minors, and others who did not have money, but were otherwise eligible and merely waiting for friends or relatives." **(35)**

The immigration officials could care less about the alleged equality of the sexes. (Remember, American women didn't have the right to vote in all states until 1920.) Their job was to protect immigrants as well as screen them. They knew it was easier for the unscrupulous to victimize immigrant women than immigrant men, so they put appropriate safeguards in place to protect them.

There was an area where immigration agents questioned callers coming for immigrants to verify they were legitimate. Immigrants, usually women and children, waited in a large waiting room nearby. When the immigration officials were sure the callers were telling the truth, they would bring out the immigrants they called for. The caller, most often an immigrant husband who had come to America alone some time earlier and had worked to bring his family over, would meet his wife and children at this post when the agents brought them out of the waiting room. Engaged couples would also reunite there. As you can imagine, the overflow of joy at these reunitings brought laughter, tears, and emotional hugs and kisses. The area naturally got the nickname "Kissing Post" or "Kissing Gate."

Now you have an idea of how it was to be an immigrant going through Ellis Island. If any of these people were ancestors of yours, thank God for their willingness to come to this great land!

Now you also have an idea of how American leaders and their subordinates did their jobs in an era when American leaders were not ashamed to put America first... in an era when the public demanded such loyalty to our nation and people. Pray to God for the return of this type of public spirit, and do what you can to further it in your circles!

END NOTES

1. Statistics on immigration come from the immigration tables of the Historic Research Study, Statue of Liberty – Ellis Island National Monument, by Harlan D. Unrau. Page 490 of Unrau's study contains Williams' quoted statements.

2. Information on the workers of Ellis Island comes from William Williams' 1903 report "Organization of the U.S. Immigration Station at Ellis Island, New York," and his 1912 report "Ellis Island: Its Organization and Some of Its Work." The Unrau study reprinted the former (pages 312-383) from the General Immigration Files RG 85, and the latter (pages 489-543) from his papers (New York Public Library). Specific pages referenced included pages 21-28 and 31-33 of the 1903 report and pages 5-12, 14-21, 28-31, 37-43, and 45-53 of the 1912 report. Other sources include "Summary of Labor Force Report by Special Immigrant Inspector Roger O'Donnell" dated 4/15/1909 (pages 397-399 in the Unrau study), and Barry Moreno's book Encyclopedia of Ellis Island (pages 40-41, and 56-57).

3. Staten Island residents, tired of losing loved ones who contracted yellow fever from immigrants being isolated at a quarantine hospital in their neighborhood, burned it down in 1858. As a result, New York authorities had Swinburne Island and Hoffman Island built from landfill nearby in Lower New York Bay to handle quarantine cases. After the heyday of the Ellis Island Era, the U.S. Public Health Service took over the islands in 1924. The U.S. Maritime Service took over the islands in 1938 and used them for bases to train merchant marine sailors and to put up artillery, submarine nets and other items to bolster the Port of New York's harbor defenses during World War Two.

After the U.S. Maritime Service stopped using the islands, New York scavenger thieves broke out all the building windows and stripped out all the usable fixtures by the early 1950s. The U.S. National Park Service now controls the islands as part of Gateway National Recreation Area. Ironically, these two man-made islands are now bird refuges off-limits to the public.

Some information on Hoffman and Swinburne islands come from 5/7/198 and 8/25/1951 New Yorker articles, a May/June 1997 Ancestry Magazine article by Rafael Guber, and an article in the March 1944 Mast Magazine, courtesy of the U.S. Merchant Marine.

Other information about the facilities of Swinburne Island and Hoffman Island include a 11/27/1910 New York Times article titled "A Little Island Near New York Peopled With Babies,"

a 9/6/1879 Harper's Weekly article called "Quarantine at New York," a 3/19/1905 Washington Post article, the General Laws of New York State 1900, Article VI, Sections 80-91, and a 5/27/1934 New York Times obituary of Dr. Doty. Reprints of these articles came from Cathy Horn's website "The Forgotten of Ellis Island." It is a nostalgic and tearjerker site well worth your time to check. (Especially read her article "My Search for Apollonia Speigel," about how she located the grave of a child from Hungary who died in quarantine on Hoffman Island in 1910. Little Apollonia would have been Cathy Horn's aunt had she survived.) Cathy Horn also reprinted an article about Dr. Doty's work from the New York Times issue of 10/4/1908 titled "How Plagues are Watched the World Around."

Further details of medical inspection of immigrants aboard ships comes from the Unrau study (pages 590-593).

4. Dr. Mullan's comments are in the Unrau study (pages 853-855).

5. Statistics on medical exams come from the Unrau study (page 916).

6. Information on how immigration officials treated those with medical problems comes from the Unrau study (pages 324, 584-587, 591-593, 598, 608, 612-613, 634-635, 656, 668, and 671-672).

7. The observer's quote comes from the Unrau study (page 549).

8. Statistics on those rejected for medical reasons come from the Unrau study.

9. Dr. Mullan's comments on mental health screenings come from the Unrau study (pages 854-865).

10. Statistics on those barred for mental health reasons and the cost benefits to the United States of these examinations comes from the Unrau study (page 594).

11. Information on the suicides and Watchorn's response comes from the Unrau study (page 597).

12. Statistics on the workload of medical people comes from the Unrau study (pages 186, 239, 601, 602, 608-609, 612-613, 669, and 921). Information on the wards in the contagious disease facility comes from Encyclopedia of Ellis Island (pages 40-41)

13. The "29 Questions" come from the form "List or Manifest of Alien Passengers for the United States Immigration Officer at Port of Arrival."

14. The law in question is the Act of February 5, 1917 (39 Statutes at Large 874-898).

15. The observer's comments are in the Unrau study (pages 548-549).

16. La Guardia's comments come from his book The Making of an Insurgent (pages 66-67).

17. The sources for William Williams' quotes on his unofficial $25 per immigrant yardstick are his Annual Report dated 8/16/1909 in his papers (New York City Public Library) and the Unrau study (pages 251-252).

18. The source of Baker's comment is Edward Corsi's book In the Shadow of Liberty (pages 123-124).

19. The source of the observer's comments is Frederick Haskin's 1913 book The Immigrant: An Asset and a Liability (pages 75-81). The excerpt appeared in the Unrau study (page 551).

20. The source of Tito's claim he almost emigrated to America is Louis Adamic's book The Eagle and the Roots (pages 109-110).

21. Information on the wireless assisted arrest of Dr. Crippen comes from Crimes of the 20th Century (page 53). People in Crippen's family tree in America and some independent forensic scientists recently cast doubt on his guilt. They blamed sloppy British police work and prosecutor work for his conviction and hanging. This book doesn't speculate on his guilt or innocence, but points out the communication technology was available to have him nabbed. And the wireless was also available to authorities to check on travelers to America or receive warnings about them.

22. Corsi's accounts of Mussolini come from his book In the Shadow of Liberty (pages 28 and 229).

23. Williams' remarks about tracking European criminals and declining to short-cut the extradition process come from page 19 of his 1912 report "Ellis Island: Its Organization and Some of Its Work." The excerpt appeared in the Unrau study (page 507).

24. Williams' comments about crime come from his 1912 Annual Report. The excerpt appeared in the Unrau study (page 57).

British officials today still demand the extradition of Irish patriots who are using the same methods in Ulster as the American patriots did to fight British rule. After the jihadist London bombings of 2005, British officials reached out to Moslems in their country, including the sizeable Moslem criminal and terrorist element. British officials never made that sort of gesture to the Irish under their control.

25. Statistics on excluded aliens comes from the Unrau study. I did some math to come up with the totals.

26. Watchorn's detention statistics come from the Unrau study (page 239).

27. Cowen's comments on inspector workload are in the Unrau study (pages 247-248).

28. "Summary of Labor Force Report by Special Immigrant Inspector Roger O'Donnell" dated 4/15/1909 is the source for O'Donnell's remarks. This report is in the Unrau study (pages 397-399).

29. Williams' comments about boards of special inquiry come from pages 32, 35, and 36 of his 1912 report "Ellis Island: Its Organization and Some of Its Work." The pages appeared in the Unrau study (pages 520, 523, and 524).

30. Watchorn's statistics come from the Unrau study (page 239).

31. Other information on boards of special inquiry comes from the Unrau study (pages 270, 334, 522). Page 334 is a reprint of Page 23 of Williams' 1903 report "Organization of the U.S. Immigration Station at Ellis Island, New York."

32. Watchorn's statistics on detentions and other statistics come from the Unrau study (pages 239 and 533). Page 533 is a reprint of Page 45 of Williams' 1912 report "Ellis Island: Its Organization and Some of Its Work."

33. Information about agents detaining unaccompanied women and children for their own safety comes from Williams' 1903 report "Organization of the U.S. Immigration Station at Ellis Island, New York" (page 21). The page appeared in the Unrau study (page 332).

34. Information about the charitable organization's aid of single female immigrants comes from Williams' 1903 report "Organization of the U.S. Immigration Station at Ellis Island, New York" (page 30). The page appeared in the Unrau study (page 341). Charity works better when it is private and personal than when it is governmental and impersonal.

35. Martocci's quote comes from In the Shadow of Liberty (page 77).

THE FIGHT AGAINST "WHITE SLAVERY"

We live in such a degenerate society today we forget human nature has been fallen since the time of Adam and Eve. So it taxes our imagination to think there was a time (before the Clinton presidency, that is) when sex slave traffickers were working actively to bring innocent girls and not so innocent women into America for commercial prostitution.

The sad and ugly truth was the first two decades of the Ellis Island era was such a time. This chapter tells this repulsive story. It also tells how citizens and leaders of good will in that era fought sex trafficking effectively, as an object lesson for us today.

Crime has been with us since Cain killed Abel. And taking girls and young women as the spoils of war for use as servants and sex slaves is older than the written accounts of this hideous practice in the Bible.

Why are we talking about sex slavery and prostitution in a book immigration? Immigration provided many of the girls and young women for prostitution in America. Many of these girls and young women were kidnaped or lured into degradation because they were immigrants.

For any crime, there needs to be motive, opportunity, and cover. In the Ellis Island era, like today, the motive of the sex traffickers was greed.

The opportunity was the relative lack of restriction on people to emigrate to the United States. Cheap steamship and rail travel made mass migration to and through America possible.

Most Europeans did not share in the prosperity of the upper classes of that continent in the late 1800s and early 1900s. Even in Britain and Germany, the most industrialized nations, most people were poor. Most of the people in the other countries of Europe lived in farming, mining, or fishing communities in near poverty or actual poverty. The relatively low price of steerage tickets and the willingness of these immigrants to leave Europe led to the cascade of aliens.

The cover was immigration. Sex traffickers, working together and sometimes working with the complicity of European officials, got many thousands of girls and young women into the country for the use of their clients. Other sex traffickers targeted girls and young women once they cleared inspection at Ellis Island and other immigration stations.

Before the crush of immigrants to the cities of America, women born in America who became prostitutes tended to sell themselves without the help of pimps. This continued of course even after large scale immigration started in the 1840s. From the Gold Rush in California and the Civil War and through the 1900s, American women ran their own houses of prostitution, not only in the West, but in other parts of the country as well. The nation's most notorious whorehouse in the early 1900s was the Everleigh Club in Chicago. Minna and Ada Everleigh, two sisters from Kentucky, owned and operated this "gentlemen's club" and were brazen enough to print a brochure describing the features of their high-roller bordello.

Most women who worked as prostitutes did so voluntarily. But many girls and young women were forced or conned into doing so. A high proportion of these unfortunates were immigrant girls and young women.

The immigration of the Irish and Germans in the 1840s brought the first of many waves of poor immigrant girls and young women to America's cities. These would be the first of the females enmeshed in the so-called "white slave" trade. According to muckraker George Kibbe Turner in a 1909 exposé "The Daughters of the Poor," New York City police in 1857 estimated at least 60% of the prostitutes in the city were born in Ireland or Germany or England or elsewhere in Europe, and half of them had worked as grossly underpaid servant girls before turning to prostitution.

The immigration from Italy, Russia, and Eastern Europe in the late 1800s and early 1900s brought many many more poor girls and young women to America. Also among the immigrants were a number of prostitute brokers from the Jewish settlements of Poland and the western lands of the Russian Empire. These swine recruited younger Jewish men to seduce many poor Jewish immigrant girls into prostitution.

These vermin weren't the only organized enslavers of immigrant females. Some young Italian men would recruit peasant girls in Italy by promising to take them to America and marry them. Instead, they turned the girls over to brothel operators. Also many Italian men worked in America when the weather was good and came home to Italy for the winter. Italians who trafficked and sold women got some of these men to bring innocent girls and young women back with them when they would return to America in the spring. The Italian traffickers got a pretty female for as little as the cost of two steerage tickets. Many of the leading criminals of the Mafia were whoremongers before the idiocy of Prohibition skyrocketed their incomes. **(1)**

Frenchmen and Frenchwomen in America brought over a large number of French women and older girls for purposes of prostitution. A very large proportion of the women had worked as prostitutes in France, and were merely seeking bigger returns for selling themselves. However, French traffickers lured the girls and some of the young women with promises of good-paying jobs, and then enslaved them in whorehouses.

Some slavers, aware of the naivete of country girls from Europe, had "cadets" case passengers on trains and at train stations for pretty immigrant girls traveling alone who looked lost and vulnerable. They would lure immigrant girls off of trains or steer them wrong at the train stations and lock them into sexual bondage. Some immigrant girls got confused and got off of trains in the wrong cities and fell into the hands of the slavers. Some of the men who drove hacks or streetcars willfully steered unaccompanied immigrant girls getting off of trains into the clutches of slavers. These girls' waiting relatives never heard from them again. "These girls are nearly all from the country districts of eastern Europe and are therefore peculiarly helpless in such a situation," the Vice Commission of Chicago members commented. **(2)**

Many immigrant girls and young women from Europe (and many girls and young women from rural and small-town America) fell for the lies of young men in the pay of the brothel owners. These predators prowled not only the train stations but also the streets of the big cities looking for pretty and vulnerable prey. These men would offer the females better jobs or take them out on dates. Once under the physical control of the sex traffickers, these females' lives turned immediately for the worse. The conditions these girls and young women worked under from then on was not at all like how the movies show whorehouses in the "Wild West."

Herbert Asbury, author of Gem of the Prairie, a history of corruption in turn-of-the-century Chicago (he also wrote The Gangs of New York), had this to say about how the traffickers prepared women and girls for lives of prostitution in Chicago:

"Some of the white-slave gangs handled only foreign women, who were shipped out to them by the bands which operated in New York and other cities of the Atlantic Seaboard. One such gang, headed by French Em Duval and her husband, with headquarters in French Em's dive on Dearborn Street, ran its own brothel on Armour Avenue and maintained a stockade in the suburb of Blue Island, known as the Retreat, where the women were kept to await buyers. Some of the rooms in the stockade were equipped with iron bars, and none of the women was allowed to have any street clothing until the time to transfer her to the brothel by which she had been purchased. French Em and her fellow slavers made profits aggregating two hundred thousand dollars before the gang was finally broken up by Federal immigration inspectors in 1908."

"Another gang with Eastern and foreign connections, said by the police to have been the best-organized band that ever worked in Chicago, operated from the Dewey Hotel on Washington Boulevard, on the top floor of which were its stockades and breaking-in rooms (rooms where the pimps

and cadets gang-raped the women to impose discipline on them). This gang was composed almost entirely of Russian Jews and specialized in the sale of Russian Jewesses, who have always brought high prices in American bagnios. Once a week the slavers held a meeting to discuss the stock in hand (in other words the females), the bordellos to which girls were to be sent, and the prices to be charged, and to make arrangements for incoming shipments from the East. Occasionally, when large stocks of women had been accumulated, auctions were held at which the prostitutes were stripped, inspected by the brothel-keepers, and sold to the highest bidders. In one week in the late fall of 1906 twenty-five women were thus disposed of at from twenty-five to one hundred dollars each. But the purchase price did not represent the whole of the profit to be gained from the sale of a harlot, for the prostitute's share of her earnings was, in most instances, turned over to the gang."

"The most vicious of the white-slave gangs were those which found their victims among the underpaid domestic servants, factory girls, waitresses, and department-store salesgirls, thousands of whom were struggling to keep alive on wages from four to seven dollars a week. Starving for pleasure and amusement, and frequently for food as well, many of these girls were easy prey for the attractive women of middle age and the glib-tongued, well-dressed young men who were employed by the white-slavers as ropers. The women offered the girls better jobs, and the young men offered them romance, and took them to the theaters, the dance halls, and the wine-rooms. The end in any case was the same – the girl was enticed into an apartment or a house, and having been "broken-in" was sold to a brothel." **(3)**

What made immigrant girls and young women (and American rural and small-town girls and young women) such easy prey for these predators?

First of all there was a demand for sex for pay, which the criminals tried to supply. American cities grew exponentially during the late 1800s. Many men came to work at the steel mills, factories, slaughterhouses, and construction sites in the cities. They came to work in the metal mining towns of the West and the coal mining towns of Appalachia and Pennsylvania. Many laborers were single men from Europe working to bring loved ones over or to save enough to buy a farm or business back home. Many more single laborers were American-born men who were natives of the cities or had come to the cities from farms and small towns looking for work. Many of these men looked to buy female companionship from time to time. Likewise, there were many businessmen of all ages in the cities looking for illicit pleasure. These men could hide their wrongdoing easier in the big cities than they could in the country. These men created a demand for prostitution.

Labor unions were weak. Wages were low. For unskilled labor, and even for most skilled labor, greedy employers severely underpaid the men who worked for them. They underpaid the women who worked for them also. Since most women didn't have the strength or the inclination to do many of the industrial or construction jobs, they had fewer legitimate ways to make money. Some single women – never-married, divorced, or widowed – considered selling themselves to make ends meet. Other single women thought prostitution would get them out of the drudgery of 12-hour-day sweatshop jobs and onto Easy Street. The bosses in private industry helped create the supply of prostitutes because – by cheating women out of fair wages for their work – they created the pressure of grinding poverty and the temptation for many girls and young women to turn to prostitution as a way out. **(4)**

Teddy Roosevelt, commenting in his autobiography, blamed the wretchedness of city life for the most part for the "white slave" trade. He said, "When girls are paid wages inadequate to keep them from starvation, or to permit them to live decently, a certain proportion are forced by their economic misery into lives of vice. The employers and all others responsible for these conditions stand on a moral level not far above the white slavers themselves."

Roosevelt was no bleeding heart. He also said some women and girls would go into prostitution because they were dumb, or lazy, or immoral, or easily swayed by finery. He wrote, "Sentimentality that grows maudlin on behalf of the willful prostitute is a curse; to confound her with the entrapped or coerced girl, the real white slave, is both foolish and wicked." **(5)**

The "Pretty Woman" syndrome existed long before the movie did. (Sadly, many women from Eastern Europe and the former Soviet Union even today buy into the warped dream they'll meet men who will take care of them if they make themselves sexually available. Many of these young women wind up victims of sex trafficking rings in America and Israel and elsewhere. Many of these young women, when rounded up and interviewed by authorities, mention the movie by name as the "inspiration" for their entry into prostitution.)

Roosevelt, the descendant of Dutch and Orange (ethnic British from Ulster) ancestors, said, "There are certain races – the Irish are honorably conspicuous among them – which, no matter what the economic pressure, furnish relatively few inmates of houses of ill fame." Roosevelt, either out of prudence or out of the desire not to hurt the feelings of people in some ethnic groups, declined to cite statistics he had on the ethnicities of the women and girls in the sex trade during his time in office. (He had been New York City's police commissioner and the state's governor before becoming vice-president, and then president.)

Theodore Roosevelt in 1908 signed the "International Agreement for the Suppression of the 'White Slave Traffic' ", an accord with European officials aimed at breaking up international sex slave trafficking. The Senate had given their okay earlier. Under the agreement, port officials and railroad officials were supposed to screen ship and train passengers to find slavers and victims. They were supposed to contact their opposites in other countries with information so authorities in the countries where the slavers and victims were going could apprehend them.

Officials in these countries agreed to interview girls and young women they detained to find out who was trafficking them, and how they were induced to leave their homes. They also agreed to arrange for charity and repatriation for the victims. Leaders of Britain, France, Germany, Spain, Portugal, Italy, Belgium, the Netherlands, Switzerland, Denmark, Sweden, and Russia signed this accord also.

When Norway became independent from Sweden in 1905, that nation's leaders agreed to the treaty. Theodore Roosevelt, on issuing a proclamation agreeing to the accord in 1908, noted the governments of Austria-Hungary and Brazil were adhering to the agreement also. Ireland was still under British occupation; Finland and most of Ukraine and the Baltic peoples were under Russian occupation; Poland was under German, Russian, and Austrian occupation. Because of the occupying powers' signatures, these lands were covered by the treaty also.

The accord needed the practical support of officials of Austria-Hungary. Before this time, officials of the realm of some of the most beautiful teenage girls and young women on the planet – Polish and Ukrainian and Jewish girls from Galicia (the Austrian occupied portions of Poland and Ukraine), Czech girls, Slovak girls, Ruthenian girls, Hungarian girls, Austrian girls, Slovenian girls, Croatian girls, Serbian girls from the Hungarian-occupied portion of Serbia, Bukovinan girls, and Romanian girls from the Hungarian-occupied portion of Romania – were not committed to co-operating in suppressing the trade in girls and young women from the lands they controlled. Jewish girls and young women from Austrian and Russian controlled Galicia were some of the most exploited prey in the United States and around the world. Many Jewish victims came from Austria-Hungary or passed through Austria-Hungary from Russia on their way to brothels around the world.

Officials of Serbia, Montenegro, Greece, Bulgaria, Romania, and the Ottoman Empire did not sign the treaty, at least during Teddy Roosevelt's time in office. Therefore, the officials of these countries did not commit to formally assisting in suppressing the trade in girls and young women from their countries and the lands the Turks controlled. Before the breakup of the Ottoman Empire, the Turks ruled modern-day Turkey, Syria, Lebanon, Mesopotamia (today's Iraq), the Holy Land (today's Israel), Jordan, most of the coast of the Arabian peninsula, much of Armenia, and – until 1912

-- Macedonia, Albania, southern Serbia, southern Bulgaria, and northern Greece.

Another flaw in the accord was that it did not apply to girls and young women from Mexico and most of the rest of Latin America, the West Indies, or the Orient. The leaders of the independent nations in Latin America, China, Japan, and Thailand had apparently not been originally invited to sign the international "white slavery" agreement. However, Theodore Roosevelt noted, Brazil's leaders were adhering to the agreement.

Nor did it apply to most of Africa, the Middle East, and South Asia, which were colonies of European countries whose leaders signed the treaties, or of the Turks, who did not. Of all the colonial powers, only the Italians, Dutch, and French agreed to submit their colonies to the agreement. Russian officials likewise agreed to submit their imperial holdings (non-Russian territories) to the pact. Ominously, neither the British nor Germans would. Nor would the Danes, Spanish, or Portuguese, who also "reserved rights", or apparently the Belgians, who promised nothing.

The upshot? Beautiful vulnerable brown, black, and yellow-skinned girls and young women from these lands for practical purposes fell outside of the protection of the "white slave" accord. Ironically, so would white females from Latin America and from British-run lands such as Canada, Australia, New Zealand, and South Africa. (6)

Another flaw in the agreement was dependence upon crooked officials in Europe and America to enforce the law. European officials were so corrupt they made Tammany Hall in New York and the Chicago machine and Schmitz and Ruef in San Francisco look pure as the driven snow. Colonial officials were also hideously corrupt.

The "white slave" trade continued. Most of the trafficking problem, from the United States' perspective, happened once immigrant girls and young women came to America and fell into desperate straits or walked into traps set for them by the slavers. The Vice Commission of Chicago members said federal immigration agents determined very few women came to America to become prostitutes. "The great majority of young immigrant women who were found in resorts (whorehouses) were virtuous when they came here," they noted, "and were ruined because there was not adequate protection and assistance given after they reached the United States." (7)

Federal prosecutor Edwin Sims, who worked in Chicago, said, "Literally thousands of innocent girls from the country districts are every year entrapped into a life of hopeless slavery and degradation because parents in the country do not understand conditions as they exist and how to protect their daughters from the 'white slave' traders who have reduced the art of ruining young girls into a national and international system." (8)

In 1910, while William Howard Taft was president, Congress enacted an immigration law and an anti-trafficking law to attack the transport of girls and young women for prostitution. These were the result of the work of Teddy Roosevelt and a number of reformers who wanted to stop the exploitation of girls and young women. These were also the result of the work of the Dillingham Commission, a U.S. Senate commission headed by Senator William Dillingham of Vermont, whose members investigated the key aspects of immigration.

Roosevelt had been New York City's police commissioner in the mid-1890s. He hated pimps and especially white slavers. He wanted to jail and whip (literally, as with a cat o' nine tails, which was still a legal punishment in some states in that era) brothel owners, pimps, and "cadets" (younger politically organized criminals who conned and trapped girls and young women into working in whorehouses or who would pimp them). He said, "As regards the white slave traffic, the men engaged in it, and the women too (as slavers, not as victims), are far worse criminals than any ordinary murderers can be." (9)

The Dillingham Commission came into existence in 1907, in Teddy Roosevelt's second term, under the authority of the Immigration Act of February 20, 1907. The members of this commission worked from that time until 1911, when they presented their final reports. When they had sex trafficking investigated, they targeted New York, Chicago, other major port cities, and several boom towns in the West. They combined analysis of records with the work of investigators on the ground with the work of honest local lawmen to study the evil, draw conclusions, and make recommendations.

The commission members sent out agents to track the traffickers in females. These agents did work with federal and local lawmen in New York, Chicago, Boston, New Orleans, Buffalo, San Francisco, Seattle, Portland, Denver, Salt Lake City, Butte, Montana (a mining town), and Ogden, Utah (a railroad town) while they were conducting their own investigations into the peddling of alien females. The undercover agents the commission members sent out of course ran into thugs, pimps, and other scum from the dregs of criminal society. Pimps severely beat one of the woman agents, and she barely escaped their clutches with her life. However she moved on to investigate other pimps and madams in another area where her cover was not blown.

The federal agents the commission members sent out to investigate the sex trade found the same basic causes, criminal tactics, offenders, and victims as other law enforcement officials found. Men in Europe used flattery, promises of good-paying work, and promises of marriage to lure girls and young women to America. (A minority of these females were already prostitutes; for them the criminals simply used the lure of much better pay for their degradation.) Some poor parents in Europe trustingly allowed their girls to go with female procurers who promised them they would watch over their daughters and employ them as their maids. Women procurers sought out pretty young nurses and governesses in Europe and conned them into coming to America for some adventure and much higher pay for work in their fields.

Other traffickers, they found, sought attractive immigrant girls and young women in American cities. They would prowl the slums; they would prowl at immigrant homes, at employment agencies, at railroad stations, at dance halls, and at large department stores (where many pretty underpaid women worked) looking for prey. The lures would be the same – flattery, better pay, and the promise of marriage.

The results were the same. When they got the women and girls under their control, the traffickers turned them over to brokers who sold them like slaves to bordello owners. The girls and young women were paraded naked before the whorehouse owners. The girls and young women were forced to service anyone for whatever sexual act he demanded, were given little money, were beaten and raped if they weren't obedient, and were grossly overcharged for clothing and rent. Arrest for these foreign victims was a release .... and often they were willing to be deported to their homelands, if only the details of their humiliating and terrifying sexual slavery in America could be kept secret.

Prosecutor Sims, reporting to the committee, said the traffickers also had spotters at ports of entry in Canada looking for pretty older girls and younger women coming off of ships unaccompanied. Besides the usual blandishments, the vermin would drug females so they could enslave them. The commission members noted that second only to New York, the North American port with the highest number of prostitutes and procurers deported from the United States was Montreal, in British-run French-speaking Quebec. (Halifax, Nova Scotia, Canada's other major Atlantic port for immigrants, was where unscrupulous British shipping companies took immigrants to avoid American maritime laws and American inspectors. Smugglers got many undesirables and otherwise inadmissible people into America from Canada, thanks to these sea pigs.)

Those who trafficked females from Europe in many cases brought in the girls over as second class passengers. Females in steerage had to undergo inspection at Ellis Island or other immigrant stations. The inspectors became good at noting men and women traveling together were often traffickers and prey. The

inspectors also tended to know where the swine who ran the sex trade operated. Many immigrant women and girls told immigration officials they were going to addresses that some of the officials knew were houses of prostitution. The savvy inspectors detained these females. Other inspectors, unfortunately, weren't so sharp. They let the slavers and the intended sex slaves slip through their fingers, even when the slavers and the immigrant females listed addresses that were clearly places of ill repute. **(10)**

Because of the sex slave traffickers, Ellis Island authorities forced men and women who claimed they were engaged to undergo a civil wedding service on the island, or at New York City Hall, with immigration agents witnessing the service. This precaution gave the woman some standing in American courts in case her "fiancé" decided to dump her or force her into the sex trade. Sometimes they forced a couple who claimed they were married to do likewise if they lacked papers, if they acted unlike a married couple, and they suspected he was a slaver.

On occasion, immigration officials at Ellis Island and elsewhere would make an immigrant woman and the man accompanying her undergo a civil wedding service at the immigration station or at a nearby city hall with agents witnessing the service if she was pregnant and he claimed he was her fiancé. Sometimes they would require proof by telegraphing authorities in the home country (or America if the man had been living in America and had gone back to Europe to bring the woman over) to verify that the man himself was single and not a bigamist. These precautions gave the woman some standing in American courts in case her "fiancé" or "husband" decided to dump her or force her into the sex trade.

Immigration officials also stopped allowing unaccompanied females to leave Ellis Island. Other officials at America's other immigration stations started doing likewise. These unashamedly paternalistic moves were aimed at protecting women, not at belittling their self-esteem.

The officials of the Dillingham Commission released their report on the trafficking of immigrant women and girls for sex in December 1909. They would release the report again as part of their 42-volume report on all aspects of immigration in 1911.

One humorous incident the commission members reported in the immigration officials' war on the sex trafficking racket was a case in which an inspector on the Canadian border had the wife of a prominent American held on suspicion of attempting to enter America to work as a prostitute. The inspector's boss knew who the woman was and had her passed. The boss was also deft enough to lie to her about why she had been detained. So she never suspected at least one Fed thought she was a whore or was likely to become one. Later, the subordinate told his boss he pulled the woman out of line because of her style of dress and her manner in replying to his questions. **(11)**

Social mores change. If they had such standards now, inspectors would have to be detaining many celebrity women and a fair share of American women in general for dressing and acting like sluts.

In a raid on one "gentlemen's club" (whorehouse), the commission members noted, police turned up several hundred letters to pimps and traffickers around the country indicating how organized they were in importing and trafficking immigrant females. The letters also contained valuable information on the practices of traffickers, from how they conned girls and young women, to how they supplied them to whorehouse owners, to what they charged for delivering females.

Evidence available to the investigators indicated a trafficker could get about $500 per French woman he delivered. A trafficker in Japanese girls could get $400 per girl delivered. Traffickers sold many girls and women who came here on their own for as little as $15 apiece. These females the traffickers conned into prostitution after they came to America. Of course, the profits for the whorehouse operators began once they started selling the immigrant females to customers.

The commission members also reported, "There is a beginning, at any rate, of a traffic in boys and men for immoral purposes. The same measures employed for the restriction of the traffic in women should be applied with even greater rigidity, if possible, in the case of men." **(12)**

In the early 1900s, people would riot if the vermin who trafficked boys for sex were not jailed or deported. When judges aborted justice, citizens from time to time would resort to tarring and feathering not only the offender, but sometimes his lawyer and the crooked judge as well. Sadly, Americans today do not resort to this form of participatory justice when ACLU lawyers do things like defend sexual predator groups who teach deviates how to get away with molesting children.

Immigrant women who had been arrested for prostitution told the investigators and lawmen in touch with the commission largely the same stories as what they found out on their own. The females said they either had to work in a whorehouse or walk the streets soliciting customers under strict supervision and discipline, they had no rights, and their exploiters gave them very little of what men paid for their services. The pimps who had them working in taverns or dance halls or on the streets told them how to approach men for sex and what to do in case of arrest. Pimps and madams paid their fines, bribed policemen not to arrest them, and bribed judges and local officials to make sure the police didn't enforce laws against prostitution too vigorously.

Madams and pimps forced pregnant women and girls to undergo abortions so they could resume prostitution quickly. Occasionally they dumped pregnant females who had hidden their conditions at a charity hospital, where they gave birth and had to give their babies away for adoption. Pimps and brothel owners beat women and girls, allowed them out only under escort when they were not "working," and threatened to expose them to potential employers or the authorities if they tried to escape and get real jobs. Occasionally pimps murdered girls and young women under their thumbs. **(13)**

The commission members noted most of the convicted foreign women lied about how long they had been in the country to avoid deportation. At the time, an alien woman convicted of prostitution within three years of arrival in the United States could be deported. This wholesale lying, they noted, indicated coaching by pimps, madams, and other weasels who knew the law.

Some of the women and girls arrested for prostitution were not prostitutes. They were foreign women who simply lost their heads over American men or immigrant men who were citizens. Often these men were their bosses or landlords; they would seduce the females and use them sexually for awhile. When these vermin who targeted these foreign females for sex tired of them or found new prey, they would report them to immigration authorities as prostitutes or as girls liable to become public charges. The used girls would then be deported, and the heels would be free to pursue others. It was this reprehensible scam that turned later Ellis Island commissioner Frederic Howe against the deportation of women charged as prostitutes.

The commission members also noted the only two ethnic groups they knew of that had pimp, procurer, trafficker, and brothel owner organizations were the French and the Jews. They did not mention the traffickers of Chinese and Japanese females for prostitution having any formal organization. However, there was an underworld of sorts in America's Chinatowns and Japtowns also.

Jewish traffickers and procurers even had their own "business association" in New York, the commission members noted. They called their ring the "New York Independent Benevolent Association." They accumulated money to pay for bribes, defense lawyers, and burials of prostitutes. Their main purpose, said the commissioners, was to "assist (their) members, many of whom were keepers of disorderly houses, pimps, and procurers, in carrying on their businesses, and especially in defeating the law." They noted one of the members of this debased trade group provided them with a funeral notice for a prostitute. Evidently she had left her pimp and she was murdered. **(14)**

The commission members noted some pimps from Italy were more violent toward their prostitutes than men of other nationalities. Organized criminals from Sicily and Southern Italy first started coming to the United States in large numbers in the 1890s – not too long before the commission made their findings. Their activities were not yet as well known as they would become.

One of the cases they reported was of an Italian girl whom a madam living in Chicago conned into coming to America when she visited Italy and saw the girl. The madam sold her to another brothel owner, and then wanted to get her back. As a result, someone slashed the girl's face open several times with a straight razor, disfiguring her for life. The madam tried to send the girl out West, where the demand for prostitutes was great enough that even a girl with a razor-slashed face would have customers. An informer who said he was a "john" who heard about the Italian girl notified federal Judge Kennesaw Mountain Landis in Chicago about her impending fate.

Another Italian girl refused to witness against Italian criminals who she overheard plotting to dissect her face in the upstate New York whorehouse she worked at as an unwilling sex slave. The vermin discussing razoring her face were connected to this bordello, which was run by Italians. She escaped from the brothel, but refused to testify against one of the conspirators when he came to trial, because she said he and other men who he associated with had also slashed the faces of other Italian girls and were members of the "Black Hand." She was so afraid of them that she chose to stay in prison as a convicted prostitute. **(15)**

The commission members noted American-born and foreign-born pimps, procurers, traffickers, and brothel owners co-operated without seemingly needing much formal organization. They were in contact with each other constantly about buying and selling females, and about the status of enforcement of vice laws. Like rats, they knew when to leave a sinking ship. They would move their females from cities and towns when prosecutors and police actually started enforcing the law. Where would they send their females? To cities and towns with no real enforcement of sex trade laws, of course. And like the white trash who chased fugitive slaves before the 13th Amendment, these scum also contacted each other to track runaway girls and women.

One of the records the commission members released was a summary of the numbers of immigrant women tried for prostitution in New York City over a four-month period. They found more than a quarter of the 2100 women convicted for prostitution were foreigners. Of the 581 immigrant women, 154 were French and another 225 were "Hebrew" (Jewish women from Russia or Eastern Europe). Of the 358 people deported

for prostitution or pimping in 1908, and 1909, they noted 110 came from France. The country with the next highest total of whores and pimps was England, with 49.

Some of the tavern maids from England dabbled in prostitution, and there was a predilection for prostitution among blue-blooded women in England who were down on their luck. Like the French working girls, they headed where the money was better for their services. Immigration officials profiled tavern maids because they suspected tavern maids as a class.

There were also a disproportionately large number of Japanese females deported for prostitution relative to their numbers in America, the immigration bureau statistics revealed. This was because many of them were "mail order brides" or proxy wives who were lied to and really brought to America so they could be used as sex slaves in the West. Japanese males in the Pacific Coast states abused these females, but they sold many of their innocent countrywomen to white American pimps and white whorehouse operators in the West as well. There was some importation of Chinese girls and young women for similar evil purposes. The people who tended to buy and abuse these unfortunate females were unscrupulous Chinese men in the Chinatowns of the West, the commission members noted. **(16)**

Criminals who traded in Japanese females took advantage of a proxy marriage law in Japan. (Seattle and San Francisco were the second and third worst ports in the nation for trafficking females, after New York City.) To combat them, the inspectors at West Coast immigration stations made the alleged partners of female immigrants from the Orient undergo civil wedding services with their alleged fiancées or proxy wives. They did this to protect the Japanese females and give them standing in American courts. These officials also ran background checks on the Japanese males claiming these women and girls to verify they were law-abiding members of the communities they said they were living in. Some thought these practices of the immigration officials were slaps in the face to the people of Japan. American officials didn't care about their complaints. They said their extra precautions were for the protection of the women and girls coming from Japan. in that era it wasn't politically incorrect to protect females from abuse by showing some paternalistic common sense.

The numbers (154 convicted and 110 deported) led the commissioners to conclude the French women involved were prostitutes in France who decided to work in America for better money. *Prostitution was legal in France. In fact, when American soldiers came to France in World War One, French officials would offer to set up regulated prostitution houses in the*

American sector. American commanders had to refuse this "perk."

This was probably also true for most of the English women sent home for prostitution convictions. In London, during that period, there were an estimated 80,000 women working as prostitutes at any time. Many were women from the upper classes who had lost their money due to divorce. *American naval officer Daniel Mannix said a British officer told him he went to a whorehouse in London and wound up being offered a woman who was his relative!* **(17)**

On the other hand, they concluded the Jewish girls and young women were duped or sold into prostitution. "Apparently the activity of the Jewish procurers and pimps in seducing young girls into this life in this country is greater than that of the French, whereas the French are somewhat more willing to adopt the bolder and perhaps on the whole more profitable plan of importing women who are already familiar with the life (of prostitution)." **(18)**

Another record the commission members published was a letter from federal prosecutor Edwin Sims in Chicago. Sims said a federal functionary in Chicago had likely leaked word of the pending arrest of 10 traffickers in sex slaves, and they were able to flee before the feds could take them into custody.

Thanks to the special agents the commissioners sent to Chicago, Sims said, he was able to successfully prosecute 23 people who were harboring immigrant women and girls for the sex trade. Of these he named, eight were natives of France or had connections to France, 12 were Jews or had Jewish-sounding surnames (two of these convicted whoremongers were named Rubin, two were named Markel (one was female), and the others were named Keller (usually a German name, but sometimes a Jewish name), Ullman, Rosenblum, Stern (female), Rothstein, Baum (female), Cooperman, and Aronson), and three had surnames that were neither French nor Jewish. Joseph Keller and Louis Ullman were two criminals who the Supreme Court would free; they and "Barney" Markel (who fled the country) had been dealing in girls from Austria-Hungary. Markel was not the only Houdini. Alphonse and Eva Dufaur, two of the leading traffickers in the country, forfeited $25,000 bail when they fled to France.

Sims said the convictions also led to the closure of eight whorehouses in Chicago. Sims also noted the fines levied on the convicted sex traffickers and the bail money forfeited by the Dufaurs, Barney Markel and several other unnamed vermin who fled the country rather than risk jail for trafficking in immigrant girls raised double the money that it cost the taxpayers for the Dillingham Commission to have sex trafficking investigated in Chicago. **(19)**

The commission members noted arrests for prostitution, pimping, trafficking females, and harboring women for the sex trade were much higher than deportations. They blamed the Supreme Court judges for this. The justices had weakened the law allowing deportation of people involved in the sex trafficking trade when they ruled in the Keller case that it was unconstitutional to prosecute people for harboring alien women for immoral purposes. Joseph Keller was a member of the New York Independent Benevolent Association, the organized crime brotherhood of Jewish traffickers in females. He and Louis Ullman had been importing and harboring Jewish immigrant girls from the tenements of the Lower East Side of New York City for brothels in Chicago. Their lawyers appealed the convictions federal prosecutor Sims and his people secured against them in Chicago.

The U.S. Supreme Court ruled in the favor of the slavers. The justices ruled importing girls for prostitution was illegal under federal law but harboring them was not. (Their escaped partner "Barney" Markel was not in on the appeal. He apparently was selling girls and young women to miners in South Africa at the time.) The judges' ruling was a bit of judicial stupidity akin to allowing the prosecution of street dealers of drugs but not the prosecution of drug traffickers who supplied them. **(20)**

The Dillingham Commission members were angry over the collective "senior moment" of the senior judges of the country. In particular, they cited the case of a victim who was a young nurse from Germany to make their case against the justices. Commenting on the woman's case, they wrote, "Parts of the remainder of the testimony as to her treatment in the house (of prostitution), the demand that she submit to unnatural practices, and such matters are entirely unfit for repetition." (In those days, the term "unnatural practices" was a euphemism for unnatural practices like anal sodomy, homosexual sex acts, lesbian sex acts, bestiality, and child molesting.) They summarized the pretty fraulein's abuse by noting her enslaver gagged her, raped her, and beat her until she passed out.

They noted the existing law as the Supreme Court interpreted it allowed the deportation of the madam who conned her into coming to America – she was also a foreigner — and the deportation of the nurse herself because she admitted to performing sex acts under duress with paying customers even though others took the customers' money and she got none. The justices' interpretation of the law, they added angrily, allowed a minor prison sentence for the man who trafficked the young German nurse in America because he falsely passed off as his wife the alien madam who helped him snare the innocent girl, but ordered no punishment for him for harboring the fraulein as an unwilling prostitute. As a result, they noted, he escaped punishment for gagging, beating, and raping her. **(21)**

Trafficking continued for another sinister reason. The women and girls wore out, and the pimps and madams sought replacements. Five to ten years of sex with 20 or 40 sweating unwashed customers a day burned up their health. The venereal diseases, the abortions, the abnormally long hours, the poor living conditions, and the deliberate attempts of brothel owners to keep them in hock by hooking them on drugs and alcohol and overcharging them for clothes, room, and board took their toll and aged these females before their time. They started losing their looks and had to take less money in lower dives than those they started out in. Many died. Many others lost their attractiveness, and thus their ability to draw customers. Many suffered depression; the primes of their lives were past them, and they had learned no trades to fall back on. Many prostitutes, overwhelmed by their situations, committed suicide. The traffickers constantly looked for younger and prettier girls to replace them.

Are you surprised trafficking of girls and young women for sex would be so widespread in the early 1900s in America – back when people could be shocked? You shouldn't be, and here's why:

The ugly truth about the commercial sex trade was that organized traffickers, pimps, cadets, and brothel owners were not the only parasites who profited off of the degradation of these women and girls. Some dance hall owners, some saloon keepers, and some landlords made money from the availability of women for a fee on their premises. Many other unworthy people – politicians, lawyers, judges, and some police officials and patrolmen – also profited from the protection money and bribes and legal fees involved in keeping laws against prostitution unenforced.

And there was one other class of those who sucked these women's and girls' blood. The doctors who performed abortions on the prostitutes and treated them for venereal diseases made a bundle off of these women and girls also. **(22)**

The members of the Vice Commission of Chicago summed it up succinctly when they reported, "The girl (prostitute) is peculiarly susceptible to all forms of graft, and is persistently grafted upon by all. Nobody respects, admires, or loves her; no one wants her but for one purpose."

"Confined as in a prison, her only resource is in "blowing in her easy money" for what she can get to make the hours fly, and she is an easy victim to each and every grafter who gets the chance to prey upon her. It is the ease of her exploitation that largely accounts for the so-called commercialization of prostitution and its perpetuation." **(23)**

The Dillingham Commission members also investigated another immigrant-related businesses

where there was potential for sexual abuse – steerage passage in ships.

Immigrants coming in steerage had to tolerate filthy conditions, inadequate food, and abusive crewmen. American officials for years had been fighting steamship operators to improve the conditions aboard their ships. The Dillingham Commission sent out female investigators who posed as immigrants to see how conditions were aboard such ships.

The female investigators noted immigrants were filthy often because there were totally inadequate washing facilities aboard the ships for steerage passengers and because quarters were so crowded privacy was impossible. One lady gumshoe also noted members of crews of two of the ships she checked tried to take indecent liberties with immigrant women.

The investigator, who posed as a Czech woman for one voyage, said stewards and other crew members of the German vessel she traveled aboard would come into the women's steerage area and watch women change their clothes. Some of them hit women or fondled women. One of the stewards tried to impose himself on a Polish girl in her presence, she said, but other passengers came running in to help her.

She said it wasn't much better for young pretty women on the outdoor decks which the captain allowed steerage passengers to use. She said sailors fondled these women and girls "in broad daylight as well as after dark."

"Not one young woman in the steerage escaped attack," she reported. "The writer herself was no exception. A hard unexpected blow in the offender's face in the presence of a large crowd of men, an evident acquaintance with the stewardess, doctor, and other officers, general experience, and manner were all required to ward off further attacks."

This investigator didn't even have the right to vote but she had the smarts to know how to take care of herself in a hostile environment.

"Two more refined and very determined Polish girls fought the men with pins and teeth, but even they weakened under this continued warfare and needed some moral support about the ninth day," she noted. "The atmosphere was one of general lawlessness and total disrespect for women."

The female investigator said some male passengers also took part in the molesting and were unrestrained by crew members. She quite rightly blamed the tolerance for this kind of abuse on the chain of command of the ship.

The investigator said, "I can not say that any woman lost her virtue (a term in that era for a woman being raped or giving up sex consensually) on this passage, but in making free with the women the men of the crew went as far as possible without exposing themselves to the danger of punishment. But this limit is no doubt frequently overstepped. Several of the crew told me that many of them marry girls from the steerage. When I insinuated that they could scarcely become well enough acquainted to marry during the passage, the answer was that the acquaintance had already gone so far that marriage was imperative."

On another trip, this female gumshoe went into Austrian-occupied Galicia and posed as a Polish woman from that area. She reported widespread cheating of immigrants by the people who ran the canteens in the train stations. She also reported steamship line officials in Germany hosed immigrants by overselling steerage tickets and making those who couldn't get aboard the ships wait for days while they charged them for room and board in the port city, or by making them pay more to upgrade their tickets so they could leave on time. She paid for an upgrade to check out third class accommodations aboard the ship.

She said third class conditions were good. She said people got enough to eat and had sanitary surroundings. However, she said, immigrants who were better off scorned the rustic unfortunates who traveled with them aboard the ship in the quarters they had to pay an upgrade for. She said the poorest people felt ashamed "and hesitated to enjoy the comforts for which they had paid."

The female investigator switched tickets with a Czech girl so she could check out steerage. She said the girl was delighted to get out of steerage.

Once ensconced in steerage, the investigator had no problem seeing why the Czech girl rejoiced. Of course steerage was crowded and filthy and foul-smelling. The handful of toilets and washbasins were filthy and there was standing water around them. And often the cooks did not prepare enough food for the people in steerage. But she said the lack of privacy really galled her. She said some German girls who wanted to change their underwear had to wait until the rest of the steerage passengers were asleep, and then they formed a circle so each of them could take turns undressing and dressing without being naked before a man. She said they did so to keep the steward from seeing them naked ... or doing worse.

Sadly, some American sailors were no better than the Euro-deviates manning the foreign steamers. One female investigator reported to the commissioners that an American sailor tried to rape a Polish girl aboard an American vessel in passenger service along the Atlantic coast. She said the woman screamed out and he ran off, but the next night he tried again, and may

have succeeded in his attempt. She said the captain of the ship hushed up the matter.

However, another investigator gave good marks to the American operated Panama Railroad and Steamship Line for conditions and discipline.

The commissioners did find out that American pressure on the European shipping companies was starting to make a difference. In 1908, American lawmakers passed a law mandating shipping companies to provide reasonable steerage accommodations for immigrants or face fines, delays in leaving American ports, and imprisonment of ship officers. Steerage after 1908 would be markedly better than what existed up to that time.

The same woman investigator who was assaulted aboard the German ship later traveled in steerage on a more modern British ship. It was much better equipped in accordance with the 1908 law. She reported that food and sanitation were much better, and that most of the crew members behaved decently. She said the immigrants were generally happy after the first couple of days and did much singing and dancing and merrymaking on the decks of the ship.

Another female investigator reported that her voyage in steerage aboard an Italian vessel was much better after Italian officials made reforms along the lines of the new American law. She said a "royal commissioner" (Italy was a monarchy then) and the captain himself spot-checked to ensure the steerage passengers were getting fed properly. She said the ship's doctor and other staffers aboard the ship treated the sick well. She said the women's steerage compartment was guarded by sailors stationed outside the doors, and women and girls were otherwise well protected.

A male investigator, who had once been a merchant seaman, also told the Dillingham Commission that his proposals for the upgrade of steerage that American officials pushed was working. He said the service and conditions aboard vessels equipped with the newer steerage facilities American officials pushed for were much better than they had been in the past. The commissioners also noted, "Some of the women whose cleanliness, neat clothing, and general good behavior he praises were from the races where the women wear no hats, but do wear boots, and were thus clad." Evidently the investigator liked Slavic women. **(24)**

The Dillingham Commission also investigated a third immigrant-related business where there was potential for sexual abuse – immigrant homes.

Most immigrant homes run by immigrant aid societies were legitimate operations. They were boarding houses whose operators for little or no charge provided a bed, meals, and assistance to immigrants seeking work. But many immigrant homes were filthy pestholes run by low-grade swine. Sadly, investigators would confirm some of these facilities were run by clergymen and "missionary societies."

Many immigrants received great care from the Catholic, Orthodox, Jewish, and Protestant immigrant aid societies and missionaries who ran immigrant homes. These people ran their places as charities and asked little or nothing of the immigrants; they were truly servants of their fellow men and women. Catholic nuns in particular kept many poor girls out of the clutches of white slavers. Other operators, while in the business for money, still treated immigrants fairly and cared about them as people.

But the immigrant home business had its share of crooks, con men, and other vermin. The Dillingham Commission members noted some immigrant aid societies were little more than a cover for those bringing in contract laborers to undercut American workers. Some others, they charged, existed to get in immigrants that were plainly inadmissible; their lawyers would try – through the appeals process – to loophole into the country many undesirables the inspectors and boards of special inquiry had refused to admit.

Some immigrant home operators would send runners to Ellis Island to steer immigrant girls to their facilities before the girls' relatives arrived to claim her. The vermin would then charge the girls money for room and board, hide them from their loved ones, and sometimes claim they had labor contracts with the girls that they or their families would have to buy the girls out of. This evil scam was one of the reasons Ellis Island agents would not release single females unless someone known to an immigrant female came to call for her, or telegraphed or telephoned Ellis Island officials with verifiable travel arrangements.

The investigators also determined "some of the missionaries and representatives (of these so-called immigrant homes and immigrant aid societies) are little more than 'runners' whose business is to secure a sufficient number of immigrants to fill their respective homes." The commissioners noted, "An inspector at the head of a discharging division stated that on one occasion he discharged about 10 immigrants to a representative of a certain home. In about 20 minutes the representative returned with the immigrants and insisted on leaving them at the station, saying that he could not take them because they had no money."

The investigators, both male and female, would rent beds or rooms at immigrant homes and then observe the homes' cleanliness, adequacy of food, and measures taken to protect female immigrants from abuse. On filthy sanitation and bad treatment alone they were able to have a number of immigrant home operators banned from contacting immigrants at immigration stations.

The commissioners noted many immigrant aid societies charged their investigators enough money and gave them so little in the way of food or rooming that their operations would be making good money. And yet these same operators were passing off their places as nonprofit charities. They concluded many missionary societies were not supervising these homes properly for fraud.

But the "chief evil" the investigators found was that all too many immigrant home operators were willing to discharge immigrant girls to unsavory people. The investigators found this out by checking to see if immigrant home operators were steering girls and young women into the sex trade.

A tried-and-true tactic female investigators used was for one to rent a bed at an immigrant home, and for an older female agent to pose as an out-of-town "sporting house" (whorehouse) operator and ask the immigrant home operator if he or she could find her a girl to do domestic work at her "place," keep her mouth shut, and maybe be open to make a little money on the side (by servicing patrons sexually). In dozens of cases, the "madam" was able to get an immigrant home staffer to try to convince immigrant girls to work for them on such shameful terms. Often it was the younger pretty agent posing as an immigrant who the operator worked on to start her employment in America in a house of prostitution. But in most cases, the operators also tried to con other females – real immigrant girls and young women, in other words – into doing the same kind of work. The investigators then had to tell these girls later on that the job they were talked into wasn't available.

The female investigators reported the operators and staff of only one-sixth of the suspect immigrant homes they investigated refused to try to supply them with girls for work in whorehouses. They also said they tried this scam on 21 missionary societies that did not run homes. Seven of the societies had people (three of whom were ministers!) evil enough to actually provide them with girls. Three other male operators tried but failed to secure girls. One female staffer at first refused, but eventually tried to find a girl for the investigator when she offered a $10 donation.

The manager of one Protestant immigrant home repeatedly came into one investigator's room during the time she was there, even while she was dressing. He tried to sexually assault her. The pastor who oversaw the immigrant home provided another investigator with an immigrant girl when she asked for one to work in a whorehouse. The staffers also lied about where many of the girls who had stayed at their place had finally gone. The investigators discovered the manager of this place told one immigrant girl he "had right over her" for a year and tried to sexually assault her, saying this was the custom all over America. The girl was so terrified she returned to her homeland; she came back a year later with a friend of her mother.

Another Protestant home's managers tried to provide the investigator with a girl and tried to charge her repeatedly for girls they tried to talk into working at a whorehouse but failed to entice. These people were greedy with a capital G ... they would lay for single females and detained immigrants at Ellis Island, and hide them from families and charge them money, or hook up the families of detained immigrants with dishonest lawyers. The lawyers would then insist upon getting hundreds of dollars, claiming the detained loved ones' cases were more difficult than they thought. The immigrant home staffers also cheated immigrants in buying railroad tickets for them by lying about how they had access to low-fare tickets, and then charging the immigrants much more for the tickets than if they had bought the tickets at Ellis Island. One female supervisor at an immigrant home turned over a girl to an undercover investigator for unsavory work, and the crooked witch also gave the investigator an envelope for sending the girl's wages back to her (the boarding house runner) because she claimed she was watching the girl's money for her own good.

A priest who represented one immigrant home on Ellis Island was often drunk, according to other missionaries who came to Ellis Island. The group who ran this home – which was partially supported with funds from one of the predominantly Catholic countries of Europe – parted company with the priest and fired other staffers there who had supplied females. The investigators decided to check on the home after the turnover, and they tried soliciting for girls at this place. The new manager told her that any would-be employer required three references before they would find a woman to work for the employer, and that the law required the home's officials to know where the immigrants were going and verify what their wages would be. He would not provide the investigator with any newly-arrived immigrant girls or young women in his home's care. However, he did provide her with a woman who said she had been in America at least five years. (The alleged alien was actually another female undercover agent.)

The staffers of another home with Catholic ties would not refer girls to immoral situations. The investigator who stayed there said the male workers were harsh to her but the female workers were kind to her. The home had other problems. Its operators were pinched for running an illegal employment agency and Ellis Island authorities banned their representatives from coming to the immigration station. Previously they had ordered one of the home's staffers to sever his ties with a bank doing business with immigrants to avoid conflict of interest situations.

An immigrant girl complained to officials on Ellis Island that a staffer at an immigrant home sexually assaulted her. Commission investigators followed up on the lead, and the manager fired the offender. However, he claimed the girl was a slut, and the person who turned his staffer in was a disgruntled former employee. They tried the "sporting house" scam with him, but he told the woman investigator he didn't have any girls in the home to solicit. However, he referred her to a group that might have such girls.

At another immigrant home, an investigator witnessed a staffer grope an immigrant girl who was a little slow. She was there looking to see if the home's staffers would supply her with girls to housekeep a brothel; they supplied her with one.

Several other immigrant home operators encouraged girls in their places to take servant jobs at whorehouses. One of them, a minister, told the girl – who was entitled to his protection -- to "try to give satisfaction" at the place he was urging her to go.

Staffers of a Protestant home the investigators checked on were willing to provide girls to a woman posing as the operator of a house of ill repute. One they provided was an undercover female investigator who had been casing their home from the inside. They also tried to recruit people from one of the Protestant countries in northern Europe to serve as contract laborers when a male investigator asked if they could steer contract laborers his way. (Supplying aliens for contract labor was also a definite law violation.) The pastor's assistant who ran the home and led Bible study at the home tried to force himself sexually on the female investigator. Then he went to the "let's play doctor" card with her by claiming he was studying medicine as well as for the ministry, so he could examine her for her health. The self-anointed scumbag also fondled her roommate, a real immigrant girl, while she was trying to get dressed. The pastor of the home tried to help find a male investigator contract laborers.

At a Protestant immigrant aid society, the pastor was no credit to his calling. He cradled the comely head of a female investigator in his hands and "attempted various offensive personal familiarities." The woman had to pry her head out of his grasping hands, but he was undeterred. While she was trying to escape from the predator pastor, another female investigator came in looking for girls to work at a brothel. The pastor interrupted his lechery to talk business with the fake madam, then returned to the girl gumshoe he had been abusing and advised her to go with the other investigator. He took a 25-cent piece for his trouble.

Not all the homes had scumbags in charge like these businesses. At one Protestant home, when the investigator asked for a girl, the woman in charge said her home stood for Christianity and purity, and the investigator should remove herself from the premises and never come back. Unfortunately, one of the woman's helpers had provided a girl for this investigator earlier, and when she admitted this to the woman in charge, the boss lady was irate.

Another female missionary at a Protestant immigrant aid society refused to let a girl eager for a job with the supposed whorehouse go because it was an immoral situation. Also, she told the girl and the investigator, the girl could be sexually abused by men passing through the shady business the investigator said she ran.

Another home's female superintendent, suspicious of an investigator, phoned the city police of the city the investigator said she was from. She gave the local cops the woman's alias and phony business name, and asked them if they knew of the investigator or her business. When the police said they never heard of her, the lady boss told the investigator to hit the road. She also locked up the coat of an immigrant girl who wanted to work for the investigator, so the girl couldn't go with the female fed to a whorehouse she said she ran.

An immediate result of the investigation of immigrant homes was William Williams and his agents at Ellis Island stepped up their own efforts in this area. Williams would have immigrant homes regularly inspected, and would have immigrants escorted to immigrant homes that passed the inspections. He continued to bar unethical immigrant homes' representatives from Ellis Island, and did more checking on where immigrants who stayed at these homes finally wound up after they left. And the unethical operators of some immigrant homes would face prosecution for their crimes. **(25)**

Another result of the investigation of immigrant homes was that Archbishop Farley, leader of the Catholic Church in New York City, pledged his support and his own investigators to the cause. Clergymen of good will in other religions would also do more to protect the innocent.

*   *   *   *   *   *   *

Congress members in 1910 would address the tragic and shamefully unacceptable practice of trafficking women and girls for prostitution with better laws. Part of the impetus no doubt came from the work of the agents and members of the Dillingham Commission, much of which they made public in December 1909.

The first law, the Act of March 26, 1910, amended the basic immigration law known as the Act of February 20, 1907. One amendment added "persons who are supported by or receive in whole or in part the proceeds of prostitution" to the list of those excluded from entering the United States. This law also allowed American officials to deport any alien prostitute, pimp, "cadet", whorehouse owner, whorehouse employee, or owner or employee of a business such as a dance hall where prostitutes gathered.

The law also contained provisions allowing the punishing of harborers as well as traffickers and others who profited from the trafficking, pimping, or procuring of females (or males) for prostitution or other commercialized vice offenses with a fine of up to $5000 and a sentence of up to 10 years in federal prison. This law closed the Supreme Court's Keller case loophole. The law also allowed the deportation of alien prostitutes, pimps, brothel owners, traffickers, harborers, and any other alien who profited from prostitution at any time, regardless of how long the alien prostitute or sex trade parasite had resided in the United States. This closed the loophole the pimps and madams used when they told immigrant women and girls to lie about how long they had been in the United States.

The new immigration act also imposed a two-year prison sentence upon aliens deported for prostitution or making money off of prostitution (traffickers, harborers, pimps, madams, etc.) if they were caught in the United States after being deported. Then authorities would deport them again. This provision was for combating the "repeaters" who kept sneaking back into the country to resume the debased activities that got them expelled in the first place.

Later in the year, Congress enacted the White Slave Traffic Act, better known as the Mann Act. This law was nicknamed for James Mann, the Chicago congressman who sponsored it.

The law made it a felony to transport or assist in transporting any woman or girl across state lines or into or out of the United States for prostitution or other immoral purposes like nude live shows or pornography. The law also made it a felony to transport or assist in transporting any woman or girl across state lines or into or out of the United States for the purpose of enticing or compelling any woman or girl to become a prostitute or perform other immoral acts. If the female trafficked was younger than 18 years old, the penalty was a fine of up to $10,000 and a prison term of up to 10 years, as opposed to a fine of up to $5000 and a prison term of up to five years for trafficking adult females.

In the law, Congress deputized the Commissioner General of Immigration to keep a centralized file on all alien women caught in prostitution or other illegal immoral activities. The idea here was for American authorities to work with European authorities of countries whose leaders signed the 1904 international accord (which Theodore Roosevelt signed in 1908) aimed at breaking up international sex slave trafficking.

The law required brothel owners and pimps to report any woman working for them as a prostitute who had been in America less than three years and was an immigrant from one of the countries whose leaders signed the 1904 accord. This provision was like the IRS requiring Al Capone and other mobsters to declare their sources of income. Violators were looking at a fine of up to $2000 and a prison term of up to two years. **(26)**

The Mann Act had two major pluses for law enforcement officials. The law made it a felony to "induce, entice, or compel" women and girls for prostitution, debauchery, or for any other immoral purpose like pornography, and to transport them across state lines for said immoral purposes. Trafficking females across state lines for the sex trade was now illegal, even for a locality where prostitution was legal or protected or unpunished. Likewise, failure to report many – perhaps most – immigrant prostitutes was now also illegal. This meant federal agents could bust the pimps and the harborers and the "cadets" and the madams and the brothel owners even if they paid off local police and politicians to avoid prosecution under local laws – or even if they operated in towns where their slimy businesses were legal.

The law had a significant defect – brothel owners and pimps did not have to report any immigrant woman or girl whose native country or colonial master did not sign the 1904 agreement Roosevelt and the Senate okayed in 1908. This meant the girls and young women of the British Empire, the girls and young women of the independent countries of the Balkans, and the girls of the many ethnic groups of the Ottoman Empire were still uncovered. This meant the girls and young women of most of Latin America, the West Indies, Africa, the Middle East, the Indian subcontinent, and the Orient were also uncovered. The vermin could avoid reporting any black, brown, or yellow-skinned prostitute by saying she came from such a country or colony. They could also say their white prostitutes came from Australia or New Zealand or South Africa or Canada or Argentina or the Balkans or the Ottoman Empire to avoid reporting.

Also, since there was a time limit of three years, brothel owners and pimps would lie about how long their prostitutes and trafficked women and girls had been in America. (Most alien prostitutes themselves lied about their length of residence in America when they were arrested.) The law should have carried no time limit for alien females.

A third flaw was the law was popularly called a "white slave" law. (European diplomats were also prejudiced against females of color – they called sex trafficking *"traite des blanches"* – trade in <u>white</u> females.) The text of the law was colorblind, but congressmen evidently didn't consider the exploitation of girls and young women of colors other than white to be as pressing a problem as the protection of those who were white when they named the law. The popular title of the law, the "White Slave Traffic Act," also seemed to exclude many females who were born in America or had come from nearby. Mexican and American Indian women and girls were long regarded as prey by too many men

in the Southwest and the rest of the West. Likewise, black women and girls had suffered generations of sexual abuse in the South. Hispanic females and West Indies females were starting to emigrate in large numbers to America; some of these were destined unwillingly for the sex trade. So were many females from the Orient.

The members of the Vice Commission of Chicago, where Mann came from, understood sex slavery wasn't just about whites. In their report, "The Social Evil In Chicago" in 1911, they noted the sexual predators who entrapped girls and young women for purposes of prostitution crossed racial lines in their exploitation when they stated, "The term 'white slave', however, is a misnomer. As a matter of fact the traffic in girls includes Negroes, Chinese, and all sorts of girls."

The Vice Commission of Chicago also attacked the politicians for allowing the swine in the sex industry to target black neighborhoods. They noted, "The apparent discrimination against the colored citizens of this city in permitting vice to be set down in their very midst is unjust, and abhorrent to all fair minded people. Colored children should receive the same moral protection that white children receive."

They also criticized the employment agency operators who refused to provide white women as cleaning women in whorehouses but eagerly sent black women and black girls to do cleaning work in these moral cesspools. They wrote, "The prejudice against colored girls who are ambitious to earn an honest living is unjust." **(27)**

These observations came at a time when most whites thought blacks had easy morals. Bear in mind slavery had been outlawed fewer than 50 years earlier. Of course the practitioners of slavery, by their breaking up of black families with slave sales, their refusal to acknowledge the validity of marriages between slaves, their prohibitions against teaching slaves how to read or write, their denial of the key tenet of the Christian religion that teaches all men and women are equal before God, and the sexual abuse of pretty female slaves by white slaveowners, their sons, and the overseers, forced blacks into generations of having to live in conditions designed to keep them degraded. In the South, blacks suffered legislated segregation and lynch mob injustice. In the North, blacks encountered discrimination and less pay for more work. Blacks were under the same kind of economic pressure as the immigrants. So the whites who were so smug had no room to talk.

In San Francisco, three decades after the 1875 immigration law made it illegal to transport females from China or Japan for immoral purposes, whorehouse operators and wealthy degenerates still could go to Chinatown and buy pretty Oriental girls and young women like similar swine decades earlier bought pretty black and mulatto women at auctions throughout the South in the days of slavery. These degenerates paid off police and port officials to overlook the trade in Asian female sex slaves. **(28)**

The fourth problem the Mann Act had was the use of the terms "debauchery" and "immoral purpose." The authors of the law intended these terms to apply to immoral commercial vices like nude shows or nude films or pornography, or to immoral crimes of sexual exploitation like child molesting or statutory rape. However, some prosecutors and shysters would use the terms "debauchery" and "immoral purpose" for divorce cases, acts of adultery, and other acts of sexual immorality between two consenting adults as well.

Some officials misused the "transportation" clause of the law to punish black heavyweight boxing champion Jack Johnson. Johnson was the first black heavyweight champion, and many whites in America despised him. Johnson had a habit of taunting his opponents and bantering with spectators in hostile fight crowds, long before Cassius Clay/Muhammad Ali was a gleam in his parents' eyes. This made Johnson an "uppity nigger" in the eyes of the bigoted. Johnson also liked to consort with pretty white women, which drove the bigoted batty. So some lawmen were laying for him, waiting to arrest him when the opportunity arose.

In 1912, Johnson wired a white female prostitute who was an acquaintance of his $75 so she could get to Chicago from Pittsburgh by train and have some extra spending money. When she got to Chicago, she checked into a hotel and he had sex with her in her hotel room. Prosecutors said this coupling was a violation of the Mann Act; they had Johnson convicted in 1913. While his lawyer appealed the conviction, Johnson fled to Europe to stay out of jail. During World War One, Johnson sought out Fiorello La Guardia, who was in Spain to expedite a steel shipment to help the war effort. La Guardia, a congressman from New York City, was also an Army aviation officer stationed in Italy at the time. Johnson told La Guardia he loved America and would volunteer for combat duty in exchange for the dropping of the trumped-up charges. La Guardia could not get the feds to drop the ridiculous charge against Johnson and make use of his services. Johnson eventually came home and served time. **(29)**

Nowadays, the pendulum would swing the other way. ACLU lawyers and other shysters of ill repute would argue against the legality of the Mann Act because "debauchery" is not defined. (Back in the Teddy Roosevelt Era, people didn't need a formal definition to know what debauchery was.) These lawyers would hold prostitution, pornography, and other forms of commercial degenerate behavior (like trafficking young boys for sodomy) are not necessarily immoral purposes, because some people (like their clients and members) think these acts are okay. Or they would argue it was "selective prosecution" to charge their scumbag clients. After all, they would note, look at the government's toleration of filth in movies and on TV.

Even with its flaws, Mann's bill was an idea whose time had come to protect not only immigrant girls and young women, but native-born girls and young women, and the public decency of communities as well. Anyone who lives where prostitution is legal or tolerated and who has at least normal intelligence and awareness can tell you how losers proposition women and girls who aren't hookers, and how there is an increase in assaults and petty crime and other forms of antisocial behavior due to the presence of prostitutes and especially the human scum who seek them.

In their final report in 1911, the Dillingham Commission members recommended having American agents abroad check on trafficking. They also recommended women who claimed they were married to be required to give their maiden names and the address of their next-of-kin or closest friend in their home countries. This way, agents could see if women were prostitutes in the home country, or could contact family or friends in the home country to assist with women or teenage girls found to be sex slaves in America.

The commissioners also recommended closer work between immigration agents at ports of entry and police in the cities immigrant women said they were bound for. Often the addresses women or teenage girls gave were the addresses of brothels or known traffickers.

They also recommended making steamship companies carry back women or girls deported for prostitution to the port they sailed from for free in the same class that they came to America. The commission members made this recommendation because they knew some unscrupulous shipping company officials would deliberately entice known prostitutes into sailing second class so they could profit by shipping them home in steerage when American authorities caught them and ordered them deported.

They criticized European officials, even those who signed the international sex slave trafficking accord. They said European officials might co-operate in forbidding women from being forced or flim-flammed into emigrating to work in the sex trade, and they might co-operate in preventing the seduction of girls for the purpose of being exported to America for work as sex slaves. But since European officials permitted prostitution, they would not stop "professionals" from performing in America where the grass was greener. The commission members diplomatically refrained from pointing out the obvious about European officials – they were far more corrupt and venal than most officials in America. **(30)**

The assault on "white slavery" by Teddy Roosevelt, the Dillingham Commission, James Mann, and prosecutors like Sims, had an immediate effect on immigration enforcement. From 1892 through 1907, immigration officials kept 199 would-be immigrants from entering America on grounds they were of the "immoral classes" -- prostitutes, pimps, madams, traffickers, or others who made their living off of sex for sale. (Polygamists, adulterers, incestors, and other degenerates were labeled, debarred, and counted separately.) From 1908 (the first year of formal American participation in the "International Agreement for the Suppression of the 'White Slave Traffic' ") through 1910, immigration officials barred 1167 prostitutes, pimps, and procurers.

From 1911 through 1920, a decade of much less immigration to America, immigration officials kept 4824 would-be immigrants from entering the country for connection to the sex trade. From 1921 through 1930, a decade of even more dramatic decline in immigration to America, authorities debarred 1392 people on these grounds. By the way, in 1910 – the year the Mann Act became law – American immigration officials barred 134 aliens from America for polygamy. This was by far the largest number of polygamists kept out of America in any year from the opening of Ellis Island to the present day.

There were no statistics on deportations for cause before 1908. But in those three years, federal officials deported 784 individuals on commercial sex charges, a rate of only about half as many per year as in the years afer the Mann Act passed. American authorities deported 4324 prostitutes, pimps, madams, traffickers, or others who made their living off of sex for sale from 1911 through 1920. They would deport 4238 such degenerates from 1921 through 1930. **(31)**

The attacks upon those who exploited female immigrants were manifestations of concern of many good-hearted people. And the attacks were more than just sentiment, they were attempts to do something about this evil trade. It is easy to point out flaws in the approaches of these people, but at least they acted instead of merely wringing their hands.

Some losers who consider themselves sophisticated make fun of James Mann and the thought process behind the law that bears his name. But Mann tried to do the right thing. If it was paternal and unfeminist to put such laws on the books, so be it. The alternative was to allow human vermin to force thousands of girls and young women to develop only the job skills of a prostitute, and to submit to the daily grind of servicing sweating degenerates, usually males.

Presidents Theodore Roosevelt and William Howard Taft supported the efforts of the men and women who combated the sexual exploitation of immigrant women. By comparison, Bill and Hillary Clinton and their

administration's officials would fight against meaningful attempts to fight the new trade in sex slaves from the Orient, Latin America, and Eastern Europe and the former Soviet Union even though roughly 50,000 young women and girls from these lands were being trafficked into America for the sex trade each year.

Bill's thought process was obvious – why would he want to lower the number of females available for sex? Hillary and many other feminists opposed fighting sex slave trafficking because they feared protecting women and girls from being used for prostitution would somehow interfere with keeping abortion on demand legal. And their Attorney General Janet Reno, according to some sources, has bought female hookers from time to time herself. **(32)**

Congressman Chris Smith of New Jersey was able to get his anti-trafficking bill passed in 2000 despite Clinton Administration opposition. Why? Because normal people and even most politicians saw it was the right thing to do.

Likewise, back in the day, certain citizens' groups tried to uphold public morals and protect women and girls from lives of prostitution. The Vice Commission of Chicago put the blame on pornography posing as art and on the double standards the wealthier allowed for themselves. They noted:

"Certain theatrical managers in the city are inclined to present plays which are on the low moral plane. The advertisement of these plays, as well as of others, appear on many of the bill boards, and are offensive to the eyes of decent citizens, and suggestive to the young boys and girls."

"Unfortunately, there are two standards of morality in Chicago. One standard permits and applauds dances by women almost naked in certain public places under the guise of art, and condemns dances no worse before audiences from the less prosperous walks of life. This same hypocritical attitude drives the unfortunate and often poverty stricken prostitute from the street, and at the same time tolerates and often welcomes the silken clad prostitute in the public drinking places of several of the most pretentious hotels and restaurants of the city." **(33)**

In other words, many leading citizens in this country in the early 1900s fought filth, no matter what palatable forms it took. Today's movers and shakers patronize filth, and get the government to dole out taxpayer-earned grant money to generate more filth that would otherwise be unprofitable.

Any objective historical comparison would show the movers and shakers in the government, Hollywood, the media, and prominent community groups today are clearly grossly inferior people compared to

Congressman Mann, Theodore Roosevelt, prosecutor Sims, the female agent who suffered a life-threatening beating while she was working undercover to save immigrant girls from sexual enslavement, the female agents who had to put up with sexual abuse while investigating steerage and immigrant homes, and public-spirited people like those on the Vice Commission of Chicago.

Protection of women and girls takes place when men act as fathers or brothers instead of as lechers or enablers, and when women work _with_ men as fellow adults instead of _against_ them as harpies. Protection of a nation's girls and womenfolk succeeds when men and women serve this noble cause out of a sense of love and duty flowing from a real Judeo-Christian morality, not merely from snobbery or prudery or feminism.

Our imperfect predecessors did not apologize for trying this general approach to protect the vulnerable. The historical record shows that, because of these good peoples' concern and their willingness to inconvenience themselves to do the right thing, sexual predators would pose much less of a threat to the average woman or girl in the Ellis Island era than they do now.

END NOTES

1. Information on the white slavery trade comes from George Kibbe Turner's 1909 article "The Daughters of the Poor," Herbert Asbury's book The Gem of the Prairie: An Informal History of the Chicago Underworld in general (and pages 269-270 of this book in particular), and Howard Abadinsky's book Organized Crime in general.

Muckraker George Kibbe Turner's article "The Daughters of the Poor," is in The Muckrakers, a book edited by Arthur and Lila Weinberg that featured reprints of some of the best muckraker articles from the late 1800s and the early 1900s. This book includes articles by Lincoln Steffens, Ida Tarbell, Ray Stannard Baker, Theodore Roosevelt, David Graham Phillips, William Hard, Mark Sullivan, C.P. Connolly, Will Irwin, John Mathews, Samuel Hopkins Adams, Upton Sinclair, William Walling, Thomas Lawson, Charles Edward Russell, and Edward Markham also.

2. Information on capturing immigrant girls comes from the Vice Commission of Chicago's 1911 report The Social Evil in Chicago (pages 227-228).

3. Information on the debased treatment of female victims of the white slave trade in Chicago comes from The Gem of the Prairie (pages 269-270).

4. Information on why some women of the Ellis Island era became prostitutes comes from The Social Evil in Chicago (pages 166-232).

5. Roosevelt's comments come from his book Theodore Roosevelt: An Autobiography (pages 202-204).

6. Information on the "International Agreement for the Suppression of the 'White Slave Traffic' " comes from the text of the original 1904 agreement, the 6/15/1908 proclamation of Theodore Roosevelt on the American ratification and signing of the accord, and Historic Research Study, Statue of Liberty – Ellis Island National Monument, by Harlan D. Unrau, National Park Service, 1984 (pages 50-52).

7. The Vice Commission of Chicago's opinion on the likelihood most immigrant females didn't become prostitutes until after they came to America is in The Social Evil in Chicago (page 227).

8. Sims' quote is in Organized Crime (page 339).

9. Roosevelt's comment come from his book Theodore Roosevelt: An Autobiography (page 202).

10. Information on the conning of females in Europe and at immigration ports, deportations, and inspections comes from the United States Immigration Commission report "Importation and Harboring of Women for Immoral Purposes" (pages 57-124). This report for the rest of these footnotes is also known as the Dillingham Commission Report.

11. The sources for the wedding policy are Edward Corsi's book In the Shadow of Liberty (pages 75, 86-87), Fiorello La Guardia's book The Making of an Insurgent (page 69) and the Dillingham Commission report (pages 72-73). The account of the prominent American woman suspected of being a whore is the Dillingham Commission report (page 71).

12. The source for the evidence of organized sex trafficking rings, the prices for females, and evidence of trafficking in boys is the Dillingham Commission report (pages 82-84, 86).

13. The source for the forced abortions and murders and other abuse of sex slaves is the Dillingham Commission report (page 75).

14. The source on the Jewish organized sex traffickers is the Dillingham Commission report (pages 77-78).

15. The source on the Italian organized sex traffickers is the Dillingham Commission report (pages 117-118)

16. Statistics on foreign born women convicted of prostitution come from the Dillingham Commission report (pages 62, 68-70).

17. Daniel Mannix's anecdote about the British officer being offered his own relative is in The Old Navy (page 123).

18. The source for the analysis of Jewish immigrant girls being lured and then used as prostitutes is the Dillingham Commission report (page 65).

19. The source for the prosecutions of Chicago area sex slave traffickers is the Dillingham Commission report (pages 87 - 89).

20. Sources for the idiotic court ruling on harboring sex slaves are the Dillingham Commission report (page 61)

and George Kibbe Turner's article "The Daughters of the Poor," in The Muckrakers (page 425).

21. The account of the rape and deportation of the German nurse is in the Dillingham Commission report (pages 104-108).

22. The sources for the profiteering of abortionists and other bloodsuckers are the Dillingham Commission report (page 83), and The Social Evil in Chicago (pages 222-227, 277-278).

23. The quotes on the abuses of prostitutes are in The Social Evil in Chicago (page 105).

24. The anecdotes and reports on steerage come from the Dillingham Commission report titled "Steerage Conditions" (pages 13-42). The 1908 law's text was on pages 50 and 51 of this report.

25. The anecdotes and reports on immigrant homes come from the Dillingham Commission report titled "Immigrant Homes and Societies" (pages 129-190).

26. Information on the Act of March 26, 1910 (36 Statutes at Large 263-265) comes from the text of the law itself. Information on the Mann Act (36 Statutes at Large 825-827) comes from the text of the law itself.

27. The "white slave misnomer" quote and other observations on victims of color come from The Social Evil in Chicago (pages 38, 39, 177).

28. Information on the selling of Oriental girls at auctions in San Francisco comes from The San Francisco Earthquake by Gordon Thomas and Max Morgan Witts (pages 144-145).

29. Information sources on Jack Johnson include the book This Fabulous Century: 1900-1910 (pages 200-201), and La Guardia's autobiography The Making of an Insurgent (pages 192-193). Another source was a legal brief written by attorney John Siegal in 2004 in support of pardoning Jack Johnson posthumously for the ridiculous conviction that sent him to prison. Siegal confirmed the brief to the author in a phone interview in May 2006.

Congressman Mann's intent wasn't to punish adultery or fornication between consenting adults. His intent was to protect girls and young women from abuse in the sex trade. In ignoring Mann's intent, the federal lawmen who persecuted Jack Johnson were as guilty of perversion of justice as were the federal and state authorities who misused the Racketeering Influenced and Corrupt Organizations Act – designed to fight organized crime – to persecute pro-life citizens for protesting against abortion.

30. Recommendations come from the Dillingham Commission report (pages 92-93).

31. Statistics come from Historic Research Study, Statue of Liberty – Ellis Island National Monument, by Harlan D. Unrau, National Park Service, 1984.

32. Jack Thompson, who Janet Reno beat in the election for district attorney in Dade County (Miami), Florida, accused her of being a lesbian who on a number of occasions paid for sex with prostitutes. On one occasion, Thompson openly named a pimp, errr, escort service operator doing business with Janet, and named one of the girls he sent to her residence. Thompson said Reno was a "predatory lesbian" with a fetish for "aggressive sex." He claimed organized crime members had videotapes of Janet in action with female prostitutes. Thompson also noted a police officer in nearby Broward County apprehended Janet Reno in the back seat of a car with a naked girl (female younger than 18), and a homosexual talk show host in the Miami area twitted about it on radio. (Queer Nation reportedly outed Janet as one of their own in 1988.) Thompson said he turned the information about Reno over to the FBI, and to the Clintons' team of vetters (specifically Lanny Davis). Thompson also said he was the divorce lawyer for a 19-year-old Central American girl who was the wife of a child pornographer when Reno was district attorney. He said Reno had the woman stripped naked, and put on suicide watch in the county jail. He also accused Reno of visiting the woman 30 times alone while she was having her held in the county jail, and accused Reno of holding his client's hand when she gave a deposition in the case.

Congressman James Traficant (D-OH) accused Janet Reno of treason for failing to call for an independent counsel to investigate the Clintons' ties to China because she was a blackmail target. He also mentioned a videotape of Janet's romp with a prostitute. Reno had Traficant prosecuted on corruption charges; George W. Bush's Justice Department minions continued the case after Reno left office and had Traficant convicted in 2002. In my opinion, Traficant's offenses compared to Reno's and Bush's and the Clintons' offenses were like shoplifting compared to rape and murder.

Info on Thompson's charges come from Geoff Metcalf's 8/31/1998 article in World Net Daily, Dean Arnold's 8/12/1998 article in ConservativeNews.com, an 8/8/2000 article in NewsMax, and Kenneth Timmerman's 10/29/2001 article in Insight.

33. The Vice Commission's quotes come from The Social Evil in Chicago (pages 31, 74).

THE SMITHS ACT

This chapter covers two tragedies involving immigrants – the sinking of the *Titanic*, and the Triangle Fire. Most of the victims in both tragedies were immigrants, and in each case, a public official named Smith changed the laws to prevent the type of predatory business practices that led to each tragedy. The author holds up the actions of Michigan senator William Alden Smith in the wake of the sinking of the *Titanic* and the actions of New York assemblyman Al Smith in the aftermath of the Triangle Fire as examples of how politicians should act when the public interest is involved. Both men performed magnificently when they saw evil situations and tried to combat them. Their efforts should stand out as examples to today's politicians and bureaucrats as how a leader steps forward and solves problems and combats injustices.

THE *TITANIC* INVESTIGATION

The *Titanic*, a British luxury liner, struck an iceberg on her maiden voyage from Europe to New York late at night on Sunday, April 14, 1912. Two hours or so after midnight April 15, 1912, the "unsinkable" mammoth ship, which had been carrying about 700 steerage passengers, 600 first-class and second-class passengers, 400 crewmen, and 500 or so staffers (people such as maids, cooks, stewards, and the like), went vertical and then sank.

About 1500 people, most of them immigrants in steerage and low-ranking crew members and staffers, drowned, were crushed to death, or died of exposure in the icy waters of the North Atlantic Ocean. Only about 700 people, mostly women and children in first and second class cabins, and female ship employees, were saved. About a third of the male first class passengers, and not quite half the women and children in steerage were saved. **(1)**

Among the dead were several multimillionaires. Also among the dead was Major Archibald Butt, an aide and personal friend of President William Howard Taft. However, J. Bruce Ismay, the chairman of the White Star Line, and most of the ranking officers except the captain, chief officer Wilde, and first officer Murdoch, were among the survivors. Captain E.J. Smith drowned or died of exposure in the water while helping others. The first officer, whose blunder in trying to evade the iceberg led to the fatal collision, shot himself or died in the water. Henry Wilde drowned or died of exposure after the ship sank.

The major tragedy was like an iceberg; below the surface was an ugly scandal. The captain and crew of the *Carpathia*, a ship of Britain's Cunard Line, rescued the survivors. The *Carpathia* did not dock in New York harbor until after 9:00 at night on April 18, 1912, almost four days after the sinking of the *Titanic*.

The *Titanic* was a ship of Britain's White Star Line. The International Mercantile Marine (IMM) trust owned the White Star Line. The trust was an American and British multinational corporation. J.P. Morgan was the force behind the IMM trust. Morgan himself was supposed to sail on the *Titanic*, but changed his plans. **(2)**

During that time, IMM officials in New York lied to family members of those aboard the *Titanic* and to the public about whether the *Titanic* sunk at all. Later, they claimed the ship was being towed, but that virtually everyone was safe. Later, they had to start admitting people died.

Also, the wireless operator aboard the *Carpathia* was not responding to inquiring messages. The "wireless" – a radiotelegraph transmitter and receiver – was coming into its own as a communication device. Among the people who the operator stiffed was President Taft, who sent anxious messages about the fate of his friend and adviser Major Butt.

On April 17, 1912, the wireless operator of a U.S. Navy cruiser sent out to intercept the *Carpathia* finally got his opposite aboard the British ship to release a list of people aboard the *Titanic* known dead, and a list of steerage class survivors. That same day, Senator William Alden Smith of Michigan called for an investigation of the causes of the sinking of the *Titanic*. His motion passed, and he put together a committee of other senators to help him with the investigation.

The next day, April 18, 1912, Smith conferred with President Taft and the attorney general to get the mourning and miffed president's blessing and to verify he had the power to hold foreigners for questioning on the investigation he planned. Meanwhile, U.S. Navy wireless operators intercepted messages from the *Carpathia* to the IMM office in New York. They indicated Ismay was scheming to get himself, the officers, and the crew aboard another White Star Line ship in New York harbor and escape for Britain as soon as possible. U.S. Navy officials had Smith informed quickly. **(3)**

Smith changed his plans. He and some of the officers of the committee bolted for a train to New York. When the *Carpathia* docked in New York harbor that night, among the huge crowd of relatives and friends of the people aboard the *Carpathia* and the *Titanic* were hundreds of reporters and photographers. Policemen held back the crowd. However, Smith, his aide, a Michigan sheriff named Joe Bayliss who Smith had deputized as a federal officer, maritime inspector general George Uhler, the sergeant at arms of the Senate, and another senator from the committee whose men would investigate the tragedy presented papers to the police and went aboard in search of Ismay and officers and crewmen of the <u>Titanic</u>. Guglielmo Marconi, the inventor of the wireless and by now a wealthy man because of the wireless business, and a reporter from the New York <u>Times</u> who accompanied him also managed to get aboard. **(4)**

IMM's vice-president, an American named Phillip Franklin, tried to delay Smith, claiming Ismay was sick. Smith pushed his way into Ismay's cabin, and Uhler and Francis Newlands, the other senator, followed. They subpoenaed Ismay and told him he would have to present officers and crewmen to testify at his hearing. They also warned him not to try to flee the country.

Because of the enormity of the *Titanic* tragedy, Ellis Island commissioner William Williams (with the approval or direction of his higher-ups) sent inspectors to the *Carpathia* to inspect steerage survivors and others who needed screening so they could clear these immigrants for entry into America without forcing them to come through Ellis Island. Evidently an officer of the *Carpathia* did a great job of interviewing the surviving women and children (and the few surviving men) in steerage because Williams himself thanked the Cunard Line for the work of the *Carpathia's* crew in getting the records of the survivors who had to undergo immigration screening organized. The *Titanic's* surviving officers and Ismay had apparently stopped doing even those duties they could perform after the shipwreck.

Williams himself was there where the *Carpathia* docked on the Hudson River side of Manhattan on the night of April 18, 1912. He and his people screened the would-be immigrants and lined up train tickets for those who needed them. Some volunteers and immigrant aid society people also helped Williams and his staffers get immigrants in touch with their loved ones, or to local immigrant homes or to St. Vincent's Hospital. Williams and his people released immigrants to their friends and loved ones who showed up after they cleared immigration processing, or let them go on their own if they were capable of doing so. Williams and his people would detain some others for their own protection until friends and loved ones came for them, or they received phone calls or telegrams with instructions for the immigrants, or they received offers from legitimate charity groups to help the immigrants. About 100 immigrants (mostly steerage passengers) were in bad

enough shape to need hospitalization for a few days. An Ellis Island officer interviewed them at St. Vincent's Hospital to help clear them for entry into the United States. (The Catholic Sisters of Charity ran this hospital; nuns from this order met the *Carpathia* at the dock to offer their help.)

Smith watched as immigration agents from Ellis Island were screening some of the steerage survivors of the *Titanic* aboard the *Carpathia*. All of them were in a pitiable state, having lost what little possessions they had. Many had lost husbands or fathers. One agent asked a young Irish woman for her immigration card. "Divil a bit of a card have I," she said. "I'm lucky to have me own life!"

The poor young woman's predicament and those of others like her was not lost on Williams and his people. They waived the "liable to become a public charge" requirement temporarily for those immigrants in steerage who had lost husbands and fathers in the tragedy through no fault of their own. They did likewise for people rendered destitute or injured by the calamity. Private charities responded magnificently to help these unfortunates. One of the rich survivors, Margaret Tobin Brown, stayed with the *Carpathia* until all the survivors of the *Titanic* met loved ones in New York, or secured transportation, or shelter, or hospitalization. **(5)**

The very next morning (April 19, 1912), Smith convened a hearing in a Manhattan hotel reception room. Ismay claimed he got in the last lifeboat only because there were no more women and children to save. (More than half of the women and children in steerage died. Almost all the women and children in first in second class were saved (249 out of 284), and 20 of the 23 female employees of the doomed ship were also rescued.) Ismay also claimed there were enough lifeboats aboard the ship to comply with British law. This was an evasion; the real point was there were only enough lifeboats available to save about half the passengers and crew the aboard the ship the night of the tragedy. British law was woefully negligent about lifesaving equipment. **(6)**

Arthur Rostron, captain of the *Carpathia*, testified next. The British officer testified when he heard of the distress signals from the *Titanic*, he posted extra lookouts and headed northwest into the iceberg-littered area to come to the aid of the people. By the time the *Carpathia* arrived on the scene, he said, the first rays of sunlight were illuminating the sea and the icebergs and the lifeboats. After his crewmen hauled the survivors and the lifeboats aboard, he said, his stewards and ladies and the passengers of his ship assisted them. Meanwhile, he said, he ordered his own ship closer to where the wreck had taken place to look for other survivors still in the water, but could find none.

Captain Rostron then explained the type of lifeboat Ismay escaped on should hold 60 to 75 people, many

CROP HARVESTING IN EUROPE

"There is a season, turn, turn, turn .... a time to sow, a time to reap." Springtime was the plowing season for grain and vegetable crops. Early summer brought the wheat harvest. Other grains' harvesting came later. Late summer and early fall brought the potato harvest and the fruit harvest. Typically, cherries are harvested in early summer, then apricots, plums, grapes, and then apples. Berries ripen all through the summer.

Farming people were constantly busy. And due to drought or downpour or frost or blight or hailstorm or windstorm, or government seizure or pillaging armies, they might have little or nothing to show for their efforts. Without the many millions of those who farmed – as small farmers or laborers or serfs, there would be no food surplus to feed those who lived in the cities.

"The (Grain) Harvesters", **top left**, by French painter Henry Moret, and "Peasants", **center**, by Russian artist Z. Serebryankova, are in the public domain. "The Grape Harvest", **top right**, and "The Potato Harvest", **bottom left**, are by Mary Petros. The picture of the Polish hay raker, **below**, is courtesy of Alamy.

LIVESTOCK IN EUROPE

Europe's people lived close to the soil. Farm people milked animals to make dairy products, they sheared them for wool, and they slaughtered them for meat and hides. Farm people also used them as beasts of burden. Even poultry provided eggs, meat, and feathers. Stock work was hard, and sometimes dangerous. Rudolf Koller's painting, **center**, shows a mail coachman having trouble stopping his team from running through a cattle drive in the Alps. Public domain.

In today's societies, most people would lack the guts to do the chores their ancestors had to do daily to feed themselves. Yet they look down on those whose labors feed them. "The Dairymen," "The Shepherds," and "The Hog Slaughterer", **top left, top right, bottom left,** are all by Mary Petros. English goose girl picture, **below**, is by William Hankey; public domain.

OTHER KEY TRADES IN EUROPE

Top left: "Norwegian Fishing Village" by Mary Petros. Note the gutted fish drying on the racks. The subfreezing winter temperatures make the area a giant freezer, preventing the fish from spoiling while letting them dry.

Top right: Swedes, shown here in a 1918 photo, Finns, and other Scandinavian and Slav workers logged commercially. Public domain.

Center: The village blacksmith made iron tools and nails for the people, and shoed horses. This blacksmith was practicing his trade in New Salem, Illinois, instead of in Europe. Photo by author.

Bottom: British coal miners, 1890s. The man on his side is undercutting the coal seam so the other man can cut the coal out more readily. Low pay and miserable conditions drove many miners to migrate to America. Public domain.

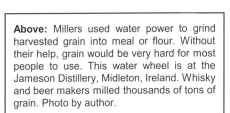

Above: Millers used water power to grind harvested grain into meal or flour. Without their help, grain would be very hard for most people to use. This water wheel is at the Jameson Distillery, Midleton, Ireland. Whisky and beer makers milled thousands of tons of grain. Photo by author.

THE INDUSTRIAL REVOLUTION made Europe a continent full of city dwellers. **Top left:** The Coalbrookdale coking coal and cast iron complex in England was a major employer in the 1700s and early 1800s. **Top right:** The British-developed steam engine liberated factories from dependence on water power. British and American inventors built machines which could make thread and cloth and remove trash from cotton cheaply; the fabric and clothing industries mechanized soon afterward. This Swedish woman is making wool thread with the aid of the machines, early 1900s. Both public domain; painting is by Philippe de Loutherbourg.

Center left: Improved techniques in mass-producing good steel and the invention of machine tools made mighty factories like the Skoda Works in the Czech lands practical. Britishers, Americans, and Germans led the way in heavy industry. Credit: Czechoslovak Legation.

Bottom: Better process control and packing practices made mass food canning and whisky production (Jameson distillery, Ireland) practical. Photo by author.

Center right: Factory owners would hire women. Some got jobs because of their dexterity and attention to detail. Others got jobs to break the pay scale for men. This young lady worked in a factory in one of the Baltic countries in the 1920s.

FAITH AND FAMILY

The Church played a huge role in the lives of the people. The clergy tended to the spiritual needs of the people and the corporal needs of the desperately poor. On the orders of Christ, the Church elevated women from slaves to partners of men with the sacrament of matrimony. The Church's priests prepared the faithful to face death with courage and a soul forgiven of sin. The family could be a very large influence for good also. The blessings of parents for marriage, and the constant prayer of the faithful for the dead were natural actions that showed love and charity. **Top left:** The Baptism" is by Hungarian artist Istvan Csok. **Top right:** "Countryside School" by Polish artist Artur Grottger, shows a priest teaching Polish youths in defiance of Prussian or Russian law. **Center:** "Children of Desze," by Austrian artist Marianne Stokes, shows girls at an Orthodox Christian worship service in Romania. **Bottom right:** "All Souls Day." Franz Skarbina sympathetically showed the devotion of German loved ones on this religious day. All four public domain. **Bottom left:** "The Parents' Blessings" by Mary Petros shows life in old Slovakia.

FESTIVALS AND HOLIDAYS

The peoples' lives were not ones of total drudgery unrelieved by happiness. Even the poorest of peasants could enjoy a festival, a religious holiday, or a celebration like a wedding.

Top left: "Irish Dancers" by Mary Petros.

Top right: Portuguese girls prepare for a procession after Mass on the festival of the Holy Spirit (Pentecost). After the procession, the parishioners would feed the poor. Portuguese took the custom with them to California; these girls were pictured on Pentecost 1942 at a Catholic church in Santa Clara. Credit: Library of Congress.

Center: "Balkan Wedding Party" by Mary Petros shows a party in Bulgaria.

Bottom left: "Shoeing the Bride." Summer festivals and harvest festivals often featured farcical rituals for young adults. Check out the women cheering on the "blacksmith" at this Ruthenian festival in Svidnik, Slovakia. Credit: "35 Rokov Muzea Ukrajinskej Kultury vo Svidniku" by Miroslav Sopoliga, a Slovak govt. museum book.

Bottom right: "Temptation of Good by Evil." Many festivals featured a pageant, like this one in Belarus, and often the theme was good vs. evil. Unwarped people wanted the former to prevail. Credit, Oleg Babinets, Belarus; www.babinets.com.

TITANIC – AVOIDABLE TRAGEDY

Left: The *Titanic's* builders and owners boasted it was unsinkable. After its captain drove it at high speed into iceberg-infested water, the ship hit one and sank. All that remained of the *Titanic* were a few lifeboats ... far too few to save the passengers and crew. About 700 were saved; about 1500 drowned or died of exposure thanks to British negligence and greed.

Right: The *Titanic's* last stop was Cobh, Ireland. This building was a terminal for the *Titanic's* shipping line. Most of the people who died when the *Titanic* sank were steerage passengers from Ireland and elsewhere in western and northern Europe. Photo by author.

Below left: Knightly British captain Arthur Rostron accepts a loving cup from Molly Brown, the outspoken spokeswoman for the survivors. He courageously led the rescue of the passengers.

Below right: Senator (and investigator) William Alden Smith.

Historical photos are from the Library of Congress.

TRIANGLE FIRE MURDER OF SEAMSTRESSES

Top left: Firemen hose the Asch Building with water, but their ladders can't reach the screaming women on the upper floors.

Top right: Ninth floor workshop after fire was out. In a matter of minutes, close to 150 people were dead. Most of the victims worked on the ninth floor. Note the wreckage, but the building did not suffer much structural damage.

Center: Many women and girls and a few men leaped out of the building. Most of them died when they hit the sidewalks or street. Most victims were Jewish and Italian immigrant girls and young women.

Bottom: Relatives look for their dead in the morgue. Harris and Blanck, the owners, escaped the fire with their relatives. Later, their shyster helped them escape manslaughter charges.

Credits: Morgue photo courtesy of Kheel Center, Cornell University. Other photos are from the Library of Congress.

OPPRESSION LED MILLIONS TO COME TO AMERICA

Top left: "Execution of the Jewess" by Alfred Dehodencq. Morrocan officials had Jewish teen Solica Hatchouel beheaded in 1834 for refusing to convert to Islam and marry a Moslem nobleman who coveted her. Public domain.

Top right: "Bulgarian Martyresses" by Konstantin Makovsky. In 1876, Turkish soldiers and police killed the young men defending the Bulgarian town of Batak, then entered the town, captured and raped the young women and teenage girls for days, killed most of the people at the village's Orthodox Christian church, then beheaded the unfortunate females they had been raping. Irish-American war correspondent Januarius MacGahan and American diplomat Eugene Schuyler saw the dead and the severed heads of the females, and exposed the atrocities the Turks and their allies the Disraeli government of Britain wanted covered up. Public domain.

Center: Pogrom victims. Russian officials from time to time incited peasants and laborers to attack Jews. The rioters killed several thousand Jews in the pogroms of 1905. Russian officials wanted Jews to convert or leave Russia. They limited where Jews could live and work. Public domain.

Bottom: Turks hang Armenians during World War One. Armin Wegner, a German officer, took this and other pictures to prove Turkish atrocities. Armenian National Institute.

Turkish officials had hundreds of thousands of Armenians, Bulgarians, Serbs, Greeks, Lebanese, and other Christian peoples in the Middle East murdered in the late 1800s. During World War One, the Turks genocidally murdered more than a million Armenians.

POVERTY AS WELL AS OPPRESSION
SENT MILLIONS TO AMERICA

British officials, police, and soldiers helped kill more than a million Irish in the late 1840s by starvation; they confiscated food the Irish grew for export, and often tried to make the Irish give up Catholicism to get a small amount of food. **Bottom left**: A newspaper artist sketched famine victim Bridget O'Donnell and her girls. They are gaunt from starving. Public domain. **Top left:** British police and soldiers evicted Irish peasants by battering their cottages to destroy them. This 1870s picture is from the National Archives of Ireland.

Poles and Lithuanians suffered poverty and oppression, thanks to the Prussians and Russians. **Top right:** Polish artist Artur Grottger's picture "Warning" shows a Lithuanian couple alerted in the dead of night. **Center:** Many Poles and Lithuanians came to America, like these Polish girls in the 1890s. Credit: Indiana Historical Society.

Bottom right: These Serbs, like many in Europe, suffered poverty. Credit: New York Public Library. Some poverty was the result of natural disaster, but most poverty was due to the greed of those who ruled the countries of Europe. The rich and the politicians and the nobility caused wars of aggression, and stole from their own people through excessive taxation and refusal to allow them to make a wage that was just for the work they did. More people came to America for economic reasons than for any other reason.

OVER A MILLION IRISH came to America in the wake of the Potato Famine in the 1840s. British authorities turned the natural disaster into genocide by seizing Irish crops for shipment to England, hamstringing relief efforts, and withholding relief unless the Irish gave up land and Catholic faith. More than a million Irish died because of the Famine and the British.

Center left: Woman and children search desperately for unspoiled potatoes. **Top:** Irish steerage passengers. Note the terrible conditions aboard the ship they were on. Many British landlords sent their Irish tenants away in leaking hulks. Many Irish died of disease or drowning at sea. **Center right:** "Defenders of the Faith," by Kevin O'Malley, for the Ancient Order of Hibernians. The Irish ran into anti-Catholic fanatics in America. They had to guard their churches from Protestant mobs who wanted to burn them down. **Bottom:** Hundreds of thousands of Irish immigrants and Irish-Americans served in the Civil War, most for the Union. After the war, Irish vets from both sides invaded Canada to force British officials to free Ireland. Some American officials wanted to take Canada because the Brits sold the South warships, so they made the Irish return to America. Photo by author.

BEFORE ELLIS ISLAND

New York officials processed immigrants at Castle Garden and state and federal officials processed immigrants at the Barge Office. Both were in the Battery district at the bottom of Manhattan Island.

Top: Castle Garden. Photo by author.

Center right: The Barge Office. This building was the first building the feds used to process immigrants. It was demolished in the early 1900s. Credit: Library of Congress.

Center left: Photo from a Manhattan building looking southwest shows Castle Garden, the Statue of Liberty, and Ellis Island, where the boats are clustered. Credit: New York Public Library.

Bottom left: Statue of Liberty (left) and Ellis Island (right), 2008. The author took this photo from Manhattan Island, on a pier a couple hundred feet south of Castle Garden.

Bottom right: Immigrants know they are in the right place when they see Lady Liberty in New York harbor. Credit: New York Public Library.

STEERAGE PASSENGERS

by the millions came to America in ships in the late 1800s and early 1900s.

Top: Passengers come on deck to breathe fresh air and pass the time. A sailing ship could take weeks to cross the Atlantic. Credit: New York Public Library.

Center left: Immigrants land at Castle Garden in New York City. Before the feds took over immigration, such landings were often disorganized messes. Criminals lined the waterfront, looking to scam immigrants and lure pretty unattached females into "white slavery." Credit: New York Public Library.

Bottom right: Steerage immigrants on a newer ship, early 1900s. These ships were not as filthy, but still crowded. Credit: Ellis Island Immigration Museum.

Bottom left: A couple find a pleasant way to while away the time aboard the S.S. *Patricia*. Credit: Museum of New York City.

Center right: Good-looking German fraulein debuts at Ellis Island, 1920s. Steerage by now was a much cleaner place to be, and her well-scrubbed look shows it. Credit: Lewis Hine, Ellis Island Immigration Museum.

ELLIS ISLAND SCRAPBOOK

Top left: Ludmilla Foxlee in her native Czech finery. She was a cheerful and kindly social worker at Ellis Island. Credit: Ellis Island Immigration Museum. **Top right:** Mother Cabrini. This immigrant from Italy founded many schools and orphanages in America. She tirelessly served the immigrants and also worked to help them assimilate. Credit: Mother Cabrini Shrine. **Bottom left:** One of the nearly 1000 Irish colleens and other European bachelorettes who came to America on the *Baltic*. A little girl and her dolly get in on the photo op. Credit: Ellis Island Immigration Museum. **Right:** "The Letter" by Slovenian artist Jozef Petkovsek. Many a wife and sweetheart waited in Europe for their menfolk to earn enough money to resettle them in America. Letters were cherished and saved. Public domain.

ELLIS ISLAND – AMERICA'S FRONT DOOR

Top left: Statue of Annie Moore, the 15-year-old Irish girl who was the first person processed at Ellis Island when it opened for business New Year's Day 1892. She was responsible enough to get herself and her young brothers to America. The author and thousands of other Ancient Order of Hibernians members paid for the statue. **Top right:** Clothing items from Eastern Europe donated to the Ellis Island Immigration Museum. The thigh boots on the right belonged to a Czech teenage girl with very slender legs. **Bottom left:** Alsatian immigrant couple Edouard Loesch and Eugenie Herter (Loesch), 1920s. They both had German last names and French first names, which summed up the mix of the region. Jeanne Loesch donated their photo to the Ellis Island Immigration Museum. **Bottom right:** "The Kissing Post" by Eileen Sherlock. Often, the husband came first to America, and then saved enough to bring his wife and children to America. Husbands would call for their loved ones at this part of the Main Building on Ellis Island. The tears and embraces and kisses as husband and wife reunited earned this post the nickname "The Kissing Post."

PRESIDENTS
AT ELLIS ISLAND

Top: This blurry picture of Theodore Roosevelt and his men, taken in September 1903, reflected the fact that they came in the midst of a hurricane with a driving rainstorm. The weather delayed Teddy (second from right, outstretched hand), but would have spelled mission scrub for virtually any other president. Ellis Island agents bet he'd show up that day, and he did. Public domain.

Center: William Howard Taft plays chief of Special Inquiry Board for a day at Ellis Island in 1910.

Bottom right: Ronald Reagan makes a speech at Ellis Island in 1987. Reagan was the driving force behind the restoration of Ellis Island, dramatically unlike his predecessors Eisenhower, JFK, LBJ, Nixon, Ford, and Carter, who allowed it to be looted and vandalized. Reagan assisted the people of captive nations of Eastern Europe in their quest for freedom, also dramatically unlike these other presidents, and unlike the Bushes, the Clintons, and Obama, who followed him. Behind Reagan's right side are the Twin Towers, which are now gone, thanks to hostile jihadist immigrants and incompetent screening of these murderers by politically correct agents on orders from our top officials. Credit: Ronald Reagan Presidential Library.

Bottom left: Loreta Asanavičiūtė, victim of Soviet Communist Gorbachev's "glastnost." Red tankers crushed her to death beneath their treads in 1991, because she and other Lithuanians dared to demonstrate for religious freedom and civil liberties like we in America take for granted. Hundreds of thousands of her countrymen and women came here in the Ellis Island era; the ancestors of Johnny Unitas, Dick Butkus, and Kimberly Bergalis were among these people.

more than were aboard the lifeboat Ismay was on. He also explained he had ordered his wireless man to send out information on the *Titanic's* survivors and dead. This was at odds with what Marconi was telling the public about the silence of the *Carpathia*. (Rostron would later send a personal letter of apology to Taft for the rebuffs the wireless man – who answered to Marconi as well as to him – gave the president.)

Like many truly great men, Rostron was decisive and heroic in an emergency, and humble when praised. He minimized his actions and praised everyone else, but the ship's log showed him alert to the big picture and to many of the details that a rescue of so many people would need. Rostron was also not afraid to show his feelings. He began to cry when he told Smith and the other investigators he held a service of thanksgiving for the living ... and a memorial service for the dead. Even Smith wept at this point.

Captain Rostron could have suffered criticism for risking his own ship and her passengers and crew to save the victims of the *Titanic*. He testified if he had known how bad the icebergs would be, he might not have attempted the rescue, but he figured he could do so safely and he took as much caution as he could once he committed to action. With his boldness and good judgment and humility and – yes, even spirituality, Captain Rostron was the kind of sea captain and true gentleman and sincere Protestant who was a credit to Britain's best naval traditions. Virtually everyone in the audience was in tears when the gallant captain finished his narrative. **(7)**

Compared to the knightly Captain Rostron, Ismay and the surviving officers of the *Titanic* would look like low-crawling weasels.

Second officer Lightoller, the highest ranking officer of the *Titanic* who survived, testified after Captain Rostron. He lied when he denied being given wireless warnings of icebergs by other ships' crews. He admitted not posting an extra lookout for icebergs, and was evasive about the speed of the ship on his watch, which was just before the watch during which the *Titanic* hit the iceberg that sunk it. He also denied the importance of testing seawater temperature, and said he didn't ask for any water temperature test results when he was on duty. The air temperature the night of the wreck was slightly below freezing. Salt water freezes at a lower temperature than fresh water, meaning salt water could remain liquid and still be cold enough to keep an iceberg frozen.

Smith, with persistent questioning, got Lightoller to admit he was sending lifeboats off only half-full. Smith got Lightoller to claim steerage passengers had no right to be on the deck. Then the officer reversed himself a little and claimed it was okay for these "unwashed" to show up on deck when the ship was being evacuated.

Lightoller then claimed the crew did not try to lock the steerage passengers into their part of the ship, or restrain them from coming to the lifeboats. Since more than half the women and children in steerage died, Smith knew Lightoller was lying. Lightoller also lied when he said no survivors he knew of tried to climb aboard lifeboats from the icy water. He refused to give straight answers to Smith about the number of people still on the deck of the tilting ship and the many who had already jumped into the water.

Smith was angered by Lightoller's evasions and lying. He wanted the relatives of the lost to be able to sue J.P. Morgan's combine for damages, and he figured American judges might dismiss the cases if Ismay, the officers, and the crew members of the *Titanic* were allowed to leave the country without testifying. So that night, he and the other officials of the hearing decided to put longer subpoenas on the officers and Ismay, and to subpoena the crew members who his sheriff buddy Joe Bayliss had listened in on who might have useful knowledge or were talking freely. Bayliss and Daniel Ransdell, the Senate's sergeant at arms, served the subpoenas early the next morning. Smith and Bayliss even had a U.S. Navy ship hold up a British ship after it left New York harbor so Bayliss could bring a couple of men back to the hearing. They also put port authorities on watch for Ismay, the officers, and the crewmen in case any should try to sneak aboard an outbound ship. **(8)**

Later that day (Saturday, April 20, 1912), Smith and the other investigators continued questioning wireless operator Cottam of the *Carpathia* and surviving wireless operator Bride of the *Titanic*. (Cottam had testified on the first day of the hearing, and would admit he sent no messages confirming who was saved form the wreck.) The operators, who were employees not of their ships but of the Marconi Company, admitted getting paid about $20 a month plus berth and board ... starvation wages. Bride testified the *Titanic* received more than one wireless warning from other ships about icebergs. Bride also testified Phillips, the other wireless operator aboard the *Titanic* (who was now dead) sent out the SOSes, and then he and Phillips told a German ship's wireless operator to keep out of the matter even while the *Titanic* was sinking. (The Germans and the British were bitter naval and merchant shipping rivals.) Bride also gave the disturbing testimony he saw many people running around on deck, that he was the last man "invited" aboard the lifeboat he got on, and that he saw dozens of people struggling in the frigid waters who the occupants of the lifeboat deliberately ignored. He said the boat had 30 people aboard it, almost all crewmen. It could have taken on 35 more people if properly deployed. **(9)**

Smith adjourned the hearing in New York, and said he would reopen the hearing in Washington on Monday morning (April 22, 1912). On Sunday (April 21, 1912), the senators, the federal officials, and the subpoenaed witnesses and IMM attorneys traveled to Washington. That day, Smith learned IMM had cut off the crewmen's pay retroactive to when the ship sank, and refused to telegraph their loved ones in Britain that they were safe. That night, Navy Secretary George von Lengerke Meyer visited Smith, arranged for him to get good maritime reference books, answered a number of nautical questions, and told Smith that Marconi Company operators often refused to respond to wireless messages sent on non-Marconi equipment. **(10)**

The hearing resumed in Washington on Monday, April 22, 1912. Joseph Boxhall, the *Titanic's* fourth officer, testified he saw another ship's lights and fired several distress rockets to signal for help. But the ship never came. At first, Smith and the other investigators weren't sure what to make of his testimony.

Frederick Fleet, the crewman in the crow's nest when the wreck took place, testified the following day (Tuesday, April 23, 1912). Fleet said neither he nor other lookouts were given binoculars to scan for icebergs, and Lightoller wouldn't give them a pair when they asked for them. The officers had taken the pair of binoculars meant for the crow's nest. (Other lookouts confirmed this.) This meant Fleet was unable to see the iceberg the ship hit until it was less than a mile away from the ship, given his estimate of the size of the iceberg. **(11)**

The *Titanic* was roughly 900 feet long, roughly a sixth of a mile long herself. The *Titanic* was traveling at about 4/10 to ½ of a mile a minute, probably too fast to stop at a safe distance from the underwater portion of the iceberg. At this point the *Titanic* had a better chance of surviving if first officer William Murdoch reversed her engines to slow the ship down and risked hitting the iceberg with her bow instead of what he actually did – try to steer around the iceberg. Only the front two compartments of the ship would have been torn open instead of the five or six compartments the iceberg ripped open when the ship skidded across its underwater mass.

Two quartermasters (petty officers who steered the ship and assisted with navigation) who were in the wheelhouse just after Fleet had sounded the warning for the iceberg testified Murdoch had given the order to try to steer around the iceberg. Smith, who had been boning up on nautical matters with the materials the Navy Secretary had given him, and maritime inspector general George Uhler, who already knew such things, realized Murdoch's order was fatal.

On Wednesday, April 24, 1912, fifth officer Harold Lowe testified. He tried to minimize the impact of his decision to lower so many lifeboats overboard when they were so underfilled. He lied in saying discipline was good and that the passengers were orderly. Smith caught Lowe lying about the number of passengers he saved whose names he had logged. Smith got out of him that the crewmen assigned to load and lower lifeboats were not at their stations when the officers were ordering the ship abandoned. Smith also got him to blurt out the officers and crew were new to the ship. In other words, they did not know the ship or the drills because they took the ship out on her maiden voyage only days after sea trials that took place April 1, 1912. (Lowe said the sea trials were about a half-hour of twists and turns.) Lowe claimed there was no class distinction against steerage passengers, but he admitted firing his pistol to scare away some passengers who he thought were going to try to jump into *his* lifeboat. Lowe called these unfortunates "Italians" and "wild beasts." **(12)**

The surviving officers of the *Titanic* thought they could take advantage of Smith's ignorance of maritime matters, so they either lied or concealed information. However, Smith was an aggressive questioner who specialized in the tried and true tactic of asking witnesses detailed questions about what they did, and when they inevitably contradicted themselves, he pounced on them. He made the officers admit the officers and crew were unfamiliar with the ship and with each other, that they had no "abandon ship" drills, that there were lifeboats available only for between 1100 and 1200 people even when there were 2300 people aboard (and the ship could have carried another 1300 people) and even these lifeboats were not well prepared for launch in case of emergency, and that they lowered many of the boats into the ocean only partially filled with people.

The surviving officers denied they were trying to run the ship at top speed. Technically this was true. However, when it hit the iceberg, the ship was going at least 21.5 knots – almost 25 miles an hour, faster than most steamships, and at the time, it was the largest ship afloat. A month later, Smith interviewed in the fireroom of the *Olympic*, the sister ship of the *Titanic*, a fireman who had been a *Titanic* fireman. In fact, he had been feeding coal to one of the doomed ship's many boilers the night it sunk. He told Smith there were more boilers operating when the *Titanic* hit the iceberg than had been fired at any other time during the voyage. If the ship was not at top speed, it was still traveling faster than normal, at night, in an area of the ocean where nearby ships' wireless operators sent the *Titanic's* wireless operator warnings of icebergs. This was either arrogant negligence or criminal negligence, take your pick. **(13)**

The surviving officers at first refused to talk about the large number of people they saw in the water who they left behind. But Smith got out of them the ugly truth that they didn't try to rescue too many people from the freezing water but thought of saving themselves and the relatively few people in their lifeboats. Many people were wearing lifejackets or were clinging to floatable deck chairs in the frigid ocean water; hundreds of them were moaning and begging for help. The officers claimed they wanted to help these unfortunates, but the women passengers objected because they feared being swamped by people trying to pull themselves into the lifeboats. Some women would claim they begged the officers to take the boats back to the wreck site to rescue people, but the officers refused. Some of the crewmen, who figured out Smith and the other senators of the hearing were trying to do some good, started opening up and telling the truth. So did some of the passengers who volunteered to testify.

The truth is most of the men commanding the lifeboats were a sorry lot, and many of the wealthier women were selfish bitches. But there were other high-society women who rowed, gave out articles of their own clothing to warm the less fortunate, and kept up the survivors' spirits.

Quartermaster Perkis and Seaman McCarthy, who were in charge of one lifeboat, decided to scout around and pick up as many people as they could. Some of the women complained, and tried to interfere with the rowers. But Mrs. Astor, whose multimillionaire husband John Jacob Astor was killed in the water by a smokestack that fell off the sinking luxury liner and crushed him flat, calmed the women. The men were then able to row back and pull eight people aboard. (Six would survive.)

Margaret (Maggie) Tobin, a big, rawboned Irish-American woman who had married an Irish-American miner named James Joseph (J.J.) Brown in Colorado when he was poor, and then shared his fortune when he discovered a huge deposit of gold for his company, rowed like a man in the lifeboat she was in and got other women to pitch in. Maggie Brown and some of the ladies aboard the lifeboat tried to get Quartermaster Robert Hichens, who was in charge of the lifeboat, to turn the lifeboat around and save some people. After all, their boat was only half-full. Hichens refused, and they sadly rowed away from the freezing moaning victims. Maggie Brown kept people rowing to stay warm and tried to keep people from fighting. Eventually Maggie Brown got tired of Hichens, and took over the boat herself. When Hichens tried to grab her, she reverted to her background and threatened to throw him overboard.

Margaret Tobin Brown was the woman better known (inaccurately) to the world as "The Unsinkable Molly Brown." She met Mark Twain, who was also from her home town of Hannibal, Missouri, when she was a girl. As J.J. Brown's wife, she did a great amount of charity work for miners and for the Catholic Church. She is credited with coming up with the idea of the juvenile court system. She hit up other surviving first-class passengers of the Titanic aboard the Carpathia to

provide for the survivors in steerage. She helped miners in the aftermath of the 1914 Ludlow Massacre, when John D. Rockefeller's goons and some Colorado guardsmen murdered several striking coal miners and their wives and children. (As a miner's wife and as the daughter of an immigrant couple from Ireland, she had empathy for the miners, many of whom were immigrants like her parents. J.J., whose money funded her projects, was also the son of an Irish immigrant couple; despite his wealth, he didn't distance himself from his roots or his working background.) During World War One, she served in France as a relief organizer. She ran for U.S. Senate in 1909 and 1911. She did a number of other works of charity and civic duty during her colorful life.

Hichens admitted hearing the screaming of victims. When prodded by Smith, Hichens made some lame excuses for why he refused to try to save any of the freezing victims in the water. Hichens, by the way, was one of the weasels who tried to flee to England. He was taken off the *Lapland* and returned to New York City at the orders of William Alden Smith. Smith called Hichens on it when he was called to testify.

Third officer Herbert Pitman was not much better. He first claimed he ordered the rowers aboard one of the two less-than-half-full boats he would later have lashed together to return to rescue people in the water. Under interrogation by Smith, he angrily tried to evade his role in leaving people behind when he was in charge of two lifeboats that had room for 60 more people. He then claimed the women complained, and then he finally admitted he was afraid of being swamped by desperate victims, admitted he heard them moaning for an hour, and broke down and cried.

Only one officer, Harold (the Italian hater) Lowe, tried to take a lifeboat back into the area around the shipwreck. According to passenger Daisy Minahan, she and the other women on his boat implored him to look for survivors in the water before he decided to do so. He dumped most of the passengers off the boat he was piloting onto other underfilled boats. Then he took aboard his own lifeboat a picked crew, and coldly waited about an hour and a half, listening as the moaning grew fainter and fainter, before venturing back to look for survivors. The moaning subsided because virtually all the people in the water by then had died of hypothermia. Lowe and his men managed to save three people. **(14)**

Smith and the other senators each interviewed several crewmen and stewards on Thursday, April 25, 1912. Several passengers would also testify before the senators. The employees and passengers also recalled what they saw to give the committee members details they could use in establishing what happened, when, where, how, and why.

While the hearing took place in Washington, another development took place that brought another IMM official unfriendly scrutiny. The spotlight fell on Stanley Lord, captain of the *Californian*, a ship of the Leyland Line, another British passenger liner outfit owned by the IMM trust. The ship had docked in Boston on April 19, 1912. On the night of April 14, Captain Lord decided to stop his ship for the night because of the icebergs. The wireless operator of the *Californian* shut off his gear not long after one of the operators aboard the *Titanic* had insulted him, and only minutes before the operator would start sending distress calls. Some crewmen on watch apparently told the press in Boston they had seen rockets coming from the south. Because of the curvature of the earth's surface, it is not possible to see too many miles at sea, even with no obstructions (like ships or icebergs). The implication was that the officers of the *Californian* saw distress signals from another ship, evidently the *Titanic*, were close enough to save the shipwreck victims, and refused to do so.

Captain Lord dismissed the talk of his crewmen. He said his ship was too far away from where the *Titanic* was after she hit the iceberg to have been able to see anything of the sort. On Wednesday, April 24, 1912, five engineers spoke to a Boston newspaper reporter. Ernest Gill, one of the engineers, swore out an affidavit saying he had seen distress rockets while on smoke break, but figured the officers on the bridge had seen them. So he turned in. He said another engineer woke him up about 6:30 a.m. on April 15 because the crew was going to go to the aid of the *Titanic*. (The *Carpathia* had reached the first of the survivors at about 4:00 a.m., about four hours after her crew received word the *Titanic* was sinking. However, it took about four hours to rescue everyone in all the lifeboats.)

Gill said other men on watch wondered why Captain Lord hadn't reacted earlier or gotten his wireless operator out of the rack to monitor for messages. He alleged Captain Lord had gotten the quartermaster who had seen the distress rockets to change his story. He ended his affidavit with the following statement: "I am actuated by the desire that no captain who refuses or neglects to give aid to a vessel in distress should be able to hush up the men." An employee of the Boston American newspaper wired the contents of Gill's declaration to Smith.

Smith had federal marshals subpoena Gill, Captain Lord, and the wireless operator of the *Californian*. They testified before Smith's committee Friday April 26, 1912. Before Gill took the stand, he told Smith privately the Boston American paid him $500 for his story and affidavit, and he took the money because he knew he would be fired and it might be awhile before another shipping company would hire him for being a whistleblower. Gill stood by his affidavit when the other senators questioned him.

Captain Lord said he saw a ship in the late evening, and had one of his men signal it with the Morse lamp (a large lamp that blinked in Morse code when keyed). He didn't get the wireless operator up to check for messages. He said the ship's people did not respond to any of the signals. He said one of his officers told him he thought he saw a rocket from the ship. A few minutes later, he said, he was asleep. He said an apprentice woke him up, telling him about "flashes or white rockets." He tried to claim what his men really saw were shooting stars.

The wireless operator aboard the *Californian* confirmed he had warned the *Titanic's* wireless operator about the icebergs. He said the *Titanic's* operator insulted him, because the wireless man aboard the soon-to-be doomed ship was sending commercial messages for wealthy passengers. He said he shut down for the night, and woke up a few hours later to learn from other ships' wireless operators that the *Titanic* had sunk. He said the crew members were talking about the rockets the captain had ignored.

Smith concluded Captain Lord had deliberately ignored distress rockets from the *Titanic*, or had negligently failed to have his wireless operator try to find out if there was a ship in distress near his vessel. As a result, hundreds of people in the water died needlessly, because the ships were about 10 miles apart. Smith also concluded there should be a wireless operator on duty at all times aboard ships.

Smith and the other investigators would also question Marconi himself. Marconi had been blaming Captain Rostron of the *Carpathia* for refusing to allow wireless operator Cottam to transmit the news about the shipwreck and the survivors. Smith believed Marconi was lying. They contacted Captain Rostron, who was now at Gibraltar, and Rostron confirmed again he had told Cottam to get the word out. It turned out the U.S. Navy ships' wireless operators intercepted two messages from the Marconi Company to Cottam telling him to keep his mouth shut because they had arranged for him to sell his story for at least $1000. Cottam was making $20 a month plus berth and board at the time, a wage out of Ebenezer Scrooge's payroll. The Marconi Company had arranged to sell the story to the New York Times as an exclusive. Smith's nephew meanwhile uncovered there had been a business relationship between the Marconi Company and the New York Times for awhile. That's how the Times reporter got aboard the *Carpathia* when it docked, by going aboard with Marconi himself.

Marconi lied repeatedly on the stand about his arrangements with the New York Times and his company's messages to Cottam. Smith basically accused Marconi of ordering the withholding of news until his company could make a profit from it. Marconi tried to weasel out of the accusation by saying his operators were allowed to take money for news stories if newspapermen offered money. The best Smith could get out of Marconi was to get him to agree to stop keeping his operators from transmitting information so he and they could benefit by selling it as an "exclusive" later. Marconi, who many accuse of stealing some of Nikola Tesla's ideas for wireless communication, was a conniver by nature. His Italian father and Irish mother raised him as a Catholic, but he became an Anglican to fit in among England's elite. Marconi would later become a leading toady of the Mussolini regime.

Frederick Sammis, one of Marconi's corporate officers, was no more helpful or truthful when Smith questioned him. Smith bit Sammis for his contradictions and evasions, much like he bit Marconi. Smith attacked Sammis for his company's cheapskate pay scale for wireless operators. **(16)**

Smith and the other senators dismissed all the *Titanic* officers and crew members on April 29, 1912. They interrogated Ismay April 30, 1912 about his plan to cut out of New York harbor, and about whether he influenced the dead captain E.J. Smith to go faster. They then released Ismay; he sailed for England to face another inquiry there. **(17)**

The day the senators released Ismay to leave, the crew of a ship sent out to retrieve bodies came back to Halifax, Nova Scotia with only about 300 corpses. The crew of the *Carpathia* saw hardly any bodies when they rescued the *Titanic's* survivors. There were about 2200 people aboard the *Titanic* when she left Cobh, Ireland. Adding the 700 or so people saved and the 300 or so whose body recoveries confirmed they were dead accounted for only about 1000 people. Roughly 1200 other people – largely male steerage passengers and male crewmen and staffers – were unaccounted for physically. They all died; some drowned or boiled to death or died of some other horrible cause trapped aboard the sunken ship. Some drowned in the water or died of exposure in the water in subfreezing weather. Many of the bodies of those unaccounted for would float across the shipping lane for weeks, to the horror of passengers on other ships.

Almost 90 percent of the men (417 of 486), most of the children (53 of 76), and more than half the women in steerage (98 of 179) died. None of the senators at first considered the steerage passengers were treated like lesser people, even though there were hints of discrimination during the hearings, especially Lowe's admission he fired a gun to keep away male steerage passengers.

These facts, and the testimony of one of the passengers who said many steerage passengers rushed on deck after all the lifeboats left, finally led Smith to consider many of the people in steerage may have died on the ship like rats in a submerged trap

because officers of the *Titanic* kept them locked in or otherwise prevented the steerage passengers from trying to come on deck for awhile.

Smith and some staffers returned to New York. He contacted several immigration societies to see if they helped anyone who survived the *Titanic* disaster and if any of these people were in New York. One steerage passenger told Smith a crew member had locked the gates from steerage to the upper portion of the ship, and steerage passengers broke the lock and rushed through the open gate. Another steerage passenger said the crewmen unlocked the gate in the area he was at to let women in steerage get through, and then later let the men in steerage through. The third steerage passenger who spoke to Smith said there were no barriers to steerage passengers leaving, so Smith dropped the matter.

Later, some of the female survivors from steerage would say the crewmen had locked gates to keep them in steerage, and the men in steerage forced these gates open for the women and children in steerage, or pushed aside crewmen whose job it was to keep the steerage passengers in their place until the wealthier passengers had left. Others would say there was little organization aboard ship, which was the reason it took so long for most of the steerage passengers to find their way to the deck.

Quite a few of the people in steerage had given up hope of rescue. Some witnesses who were able to make it to one of the last lifeboats leaving said these poor souls gathered around British Catholic priest Thomas Byles. Father Byles prayed for them, blessed them, absolved them of their sins, and stayed with them to console them. Eyewitnesses saw him giving final blessings to the steerage passengers on the deck just before the onrushing waters knocked them into the ocean.

Father Josef Peruschitz, a German from Bavaria, and Father Juozas Montvila, a Lithuanian who had been jailed and banned by Russian authorities for saying the Byzantine Rite Mass for his parishioners, were also aboard the *Titanic*. Some survivors saw Father Peruschitz assisting Father Byles. Father Montvila ministered to the Slavs in steerage. (Disturbingly, some of the nonreligious steerage passengers mocked the devout at prayer; most of the mockers would die too.) All three Catholic priests were offered spots on lifeboats; all three refused them and chose to stay with the poor steerage immigrants who had no hope of escape when the few lifeboats left. The three priests died with the other steerage victims. **(18)**

Collectively, the answers of the witnesses to the questions of Smith and the other senators showed the officers of the *Titanic* and the officials of IMM committed multiple acts of negligence, greed, and abandonment. However, the maritime regulations were so slipshod that the poor sea trials, the lack of lifeboats, the idiocy of driving a ship into iceberg-infested waters at high speed at night, and a host of other shortcomings of the officers and corporate officials in manning and operating the *Titanic* were not violations of American maritime law. (British maritime law was no better.) So this meant the survivors and families of the dead could not sue IMM or J.P. Morgan.

Senator Smith had to refocus his energy on bringing maritime laws into the 20th Century. Working with U.S. Navy men, Smith formulated a bill to regulate commercial shipping, and he had it ready by late May 1912. Among its key aims were:

Ships would have to carry enough lifeboats to rescue everyone on board.

Crews would have to have bimonthly lifeboat drills, training for crew members on how to handle lifeboats when in the water, and assigned positions for assisting people in abandoning ship. Twice a year, they would have to lower all lifeboats at the same time.

Ships would have to have a wireless operator on duty at all times, and the wireless equipment would have to have a range of at least 100 miles.

Passengers and crew members would have to have assigned places in lifeboats before sailing, and would have to be told the best way to get to their lifeboats.

Ships built after passage of the bill would have to have bulkheads running the length of the ship as well as across the width of the ship. This would limit the amount of water that could come in through a major rip in the hull of a ship.

All ships would have to have more pumps to be able to pump out inrushing seawater in case of a major gash in the hull.

Ships would have to have searchlights.

Companies would have to abide by the Sherman Antitrust Act, and also have their records made public. This was aimed at trusts like IMM.

Ships from foreign countries had to abide by these regulations or lose their privileges to enter or depart from American ports.

Smith submitted this bill and another bill calling for a maritime commission when he presented the *Titanic* committee's report to the Senate on May 28, 1912. In his speech, he said the committee blamed the tragedy on a number of people. He said they blamed the British Board of Trade for allowing the ship to go into service without adequate testing of the ship, its lifesaving equipment, or its crew training. As a result, Smith said, "When the crisis came, a state of absolute unpreparedness stupefied both passengers and crew."

Smith blamed Captain E.J. Smith for overconfidence and bad judgment in running the ship in such and unprepared state, and for running it at a fast speed through iceberg-infested water at night. In turn, he calmly critiqued the judgment of the rest of the ship's chain of command. He criticized the failure of the crew to alert the people in steerage to what was happening, and he blamed the officers for sending away lifeboats so grossly underfilled. He blasted the officers handling the lifeboats for their collective failure to save more people from dying of exposure in the water, and he called the captain of the *Californian* a liar who merited punishment for failure to aid the *Titanic's* shipwreck victims.

Smith attacked Marconi for underpaying his radiomen, for controlling them to the extent they refused to transmit vital information (like the survivors and dead) to those who had a right to the info, and for undermanning ships with radiomen and allowing slipshod radio procedures. Smith also called for the building up of a more powerful American merchant marine with better pay and better conditions for American sailors.

Smith moved to close his speech with a eulogy for the victims of the *Titanic*. People in the galleries and senators on the floor wept openly as Smith spoke. He finished with a tribute to Captain Rostron and a call for President Taft to award the gallant British captain an award for saving so many of the victims. The senators endorsed his idea by acclaim. He then submitted his bills, and asked for quick passage for them. **(19)**

Smith would not get what he wanted all at once. He and other senators got some of the provisions he wanted passed enacted in 1912. Congress and President Taft put into law the Radio Act of 1912 to regulate wireless practices. They also approved and funded participation in an international maritime conference with a resolution on June 28, 1912.

In time, American lawmakers would put in place regulations for merchant ship construction that would feature stronger hulls, watertight compartments, and other improvements that would make ships less prone to sink. American shipping companies put enough lifeboats aboard their ships so everyone would have a seat on a lifeboat, and the shippers started training crew members on lowering and manning lifeboats safely. Congressmen and federal bureaucrats began to make noises that they would exclude ships that didn't have better safety features from American ports. European shipping companies got the message. They made many of the improvements Smith was looking for in passenger ships.

A few American U.S. Navy ships and revenue cutters started patrolling the North Atlantic Ocean looking for icebergs. Smith's work resulted in an international maritime conference in late 1913 and early 1914, during which the foreign delegates fully or partially adopted many of his proposals. The delegates agreed to establish an ice watch service for the North Atlantic Ocean which American seamen would perform and American and European nations would pay for proportionate to their commercial shipping tonnages. This service would be a mission of the new U.S. Coast Guard, which Congress and President Wilson put into service in 1915. The Coast Guard Act combined the Life Saving Service and the Revenue Cutter Service to form the U.S. Coast Guard.

Some other of Smith's pet provisions would have to wait until 1915, when he added them to a bill by Senator Robert La Follette of Wisconsin establishing rights for sailors in America's merchant marine fleet. The bill also required that at least 75 percent of crew members must be able to speak English to help American sailors and to ensure sailors could understand their captains. The legislation passed and became known as the Seamen's Act of 1915. The Seamen's Act also forbade foreign vessels from leaving American ports without proper lifesaving gear as defined by the Seamen's Act. **(20)**

Smith's and La Follette's push to make foreigners comply with tougher American safety laws when in America stands in stark contrast to the unacceptable policies of the Bush, Clinton, Bush, and Obama regimes' tolerating unacceptable safety standards of foreigners such as Mexican trucks on American highways and Chinese ships and imports in American ports and stores.

The politicians, press, and ruling classes in Britain as a rule blasted William Alden Smith because he was showing the flaws of their most important industry – shipping. But merchant sailors and other union people in Britain flooded Smith's office with letters praising his regard for sailors and passengers. They told him the thorough job he did in exposing the British Board of Trade, IMM, and the chain of command of the *Titanic* would not be possible in their country because of the power of the government and the commercial shipping corporations. **(21)**

The *Titanic* investigation wasn't William Alden Smith's only good work. Smith was a leader in working for the civil rights of blacks, and even defended one wrongly accused black, a resident of his home state of Michigan, in city court in Washington, D.C. at no charge <u>while he was a senator</u>.

Before World War One, Smith defied Theodore Roosevelt and William Howard Taft in fighting against a treaty with Canada that would give more water rights on the Niagara River to a New York power company in exchange for Canada getting more water rights on the Saint Mary's River (the river that flows from Lake Superior to Lake Huron and passes by Sault Sainte Marie). Smith got the deal killed. Smith also killed a potential treaty that would have linked American naval policy with Britain's. The British ambassador in response meddled in Michigan politics in an unsuccessful attempt to get Smith defeated for re-election in 1912.

Smith opposed Wilson's pro-British tilt during World War One. He said it could only lead to our involvement in the war. Smith also blocked efforts in the U.S. Senate to restrict national women's suffrage to white women.

Smith was also the politician responsible for making Abraham Lincoln's birthday a national holiday. Smith, unlike Honest Abe, was a firebrand, but he too believed in government of the people, for the people, and by the people. **(22)**

THE TRIANGLE FIRE

There was a time when worker safety in most of America was almost nonexistent. It took an ugly tragedy -- the Triangle Fire -- to force factory owners to start making workplaces safer.

The Triangle Waist Company in New York City was a massive sweatshop for hundreds of females, mostly immigrant girls and young women who worked as seamstresses. (In this chapter, the term "seamstress" covers sewing machine operators and other females who assisted with the sewing, finishing, pressing, and packaging of garments.) Besides their seamstresses, the company also employed male fabric cutters — it took strength to cut through a stack of sheets of fabric with a knife. (One of my male collateral ancestors was a fabric cutter in Chicago in that era. He won a prize in a cutters' competition for strength, speed, and accuracy.) They also had some male tailors, maintenance people, and subcontractors on site; the latter also hired immigrant women and girls as temporary workers to sew for pittances. The company's management's callous disregard for the safety of the people who worked there would cause many of them to lose their lives when a fire swept through the premises on March 25, 1911.

The Triangle Waist Company occupied the top three floors of the 10-floor Asch Building in Greenwich Village on lower Manhattan Island. It was ironically fitting that this building was only a few miles away from Ellis Island. Most of the girls and young women who worked there came in steerage from Europe and were processed at Ellis Island.

The workers at the Triangle facility made shirtwaists – a type of fitted blouse popular with the females of that era. More than 600 people, almost all of them girls and young women of Jewish, Italian, or Eastern European ancestry, came to work at the facility.

The fire apparently started on the eighth floor – the bottom floor of the three-story Triangle Waist Company premises shortly after 4:30 p.m. on Saturday, March 25, 1911. The employees and temporary workers were there working; the businesses in the bottom seven floors of the building were closed for the day. The fire struck as the girls and young women and a few young men were waiting for the quitting bell. **(23)**

A worker who apparently lit up a smoke threw a match into some waste fabric in one of the company's huge sewing rooms on the eighth floor. This started a blaze that ignited cloth on the floor and on tables and the garments on racks and rope lines ignited quickly. The weather wasn't cold that afternoon, so many of the windows on the three floors were fully or partially open. This gave the fire plenty of oxygen and good draft. Soon the eighth floor was engulfed.

Fire is about the only thing that can move faster going up than going down. And windows on the ninth and tenth floor were open also. The flames "lapped in " from the windows of the eighth floor to the open windows on the ninth and tenth floors, and found plenty of wood and fabric to burn. The window frames and floors in the building were made of wood also. The ninth floor very quickly became a furnace, and the tenth floor was not much better. **(24)**

A reporter covering the fire had this to say:

All that those (who) escaped seemed to remember was that there was a flash of flames, leaping first among the girls in the southeast corner of the eighth floor, then suddenly over the entire room, spreading through the linens and cottons with which the girls were working. The girls on the ninth floor caught sight of the flames through the window up the stairway, and up the elevator shaft...

What burned so quickly and disastrously for the victims were shirtwaists, hanging on lines above tiers of workers, sewing machines placed so closely together that there was hardly aisle room for the girls between them, and shirtwaist trimmings and cuttings which littered the floors above the eighth and ninth stories. **(25)**

There were stairs inside the building, and two elevators. There was one inadequate fire escape in a central court of the building. The seamstresses tried to get to the stairs and the elevators, but too many would not make it.

Why? They had to fight their way out of their workrooms. There was not much space between the sewing machines and the tables. Many of the doors opened inward, which would make it harder for the panicking girls to open. But even worse, some of the workroom doors that led to the stairs and the elevators were locked. In direct violation of the fire code, managers had locked the doors that would have allowed the women and girls easy escape from the blaze in the sewing rooms. They had locked the doors because the owners wanted to prevent pilferage of cloth.

Many of the seamstresses and the men who worked on the tenth floor (and a few from the lower floors who were able to fight through the smoke and flames) got onto the roof of the Asch Building. About 200 of them, including both of the company's owners, would be saved.

At least another 200 or so seamstresses and their male co-workers were able to escape the fire by running down the stairs. Virtually all of the seamstresses on the eighth floor who made the stairway would live to tell about it. But it was a close thing. The stairs were narrow, and one seamstress fainted or fell. When she dropped, other girls fell on top of her, blocking the escape of many behind her. A policeman named Median who ran up the stairs from the street and a male "machinist" (sewing machine repairman) who worked for the Triangle Waist Company got the girl up and helped the rest of the girls on top of her and stuck behind her out to safety. **(26)**

Close to 150 people on the ninth floor were able to make the stairs. More than 100 of them managed to get down the stairs and out of the building. The others burned to death or died of asphyxiation or of shock or were crushed in the panic.

The two elevator operators kept running the tiny elevators until the elevators failed. They saved scores more people. (In those days, elevators were much less user-friendly. It took more work to make an elevator work, so buildings had men to run them.) Sadly, they were unable to get back up to rescue some women and girls choking and burning and waiting in vain for their return. A few people managed to shinny down the elevator cables to eventual rescue, but another 20 or so females jumped or fell through the elevator shafts to their deaths.

Two men escaped on the one outside fire escape; a few women and girls made it as far as the sixth floor, and managed to get back into the building through a window on that floor. A metal shutter flew open above them and blocked the fire escape. The unfortunate seamstresses coming behind them couldn't move the shutter; the would-be escapees overloaded the frail fire escape and it failed, crashing to the ground. **(27)**

Many of the seamstresses on the ninth floor had no chance of escape because they were trapped in a workroom with a locked door and a wall of fire barred their escape to an unlocked door on the other side of the huge workroom. The locked door and the flames kept them from getting onto the roof, running down the stairs, or getting to the elevators. They and those trapped on the other floors had the terrifying choice of burning to death or leaping to almost certain death from the upper floors of the building out the windows, hoping against hope they would survive the fall.

The late Saturday afternoon inferno drew a crowd of thousands. They watched the most horrible drama they would ever see. The crying and screaming of the doomed seamstresses would have broken the hearts of the dead. As horrified witnesses watched, many unfortunate young women and girls leaped from the building to escape the inferno, only to be dashed to pieces on the pavement of the street below.

Fire horses, some of the bravest animals on the planet, reared up and whinnied at the sight of the falling girls and the smell of all their blood spattered on the streets and the sidewalks.

William Shepherd, a United Press reporter who was an eyewitness to the tragedy, reported the following:

I learned a new sound – a more horrible sound than description can picture. It was the thud of a speeding, living body on a stone sidewalk.

Thud-dead, thud – dead, thud – dead, thud – dead. Sixty-two thud – deads.

The first ten thud – deads shocked me. I looked up – saw that there were scores of girls at the windows. The flames from the floor below were beating in their faces. Somehow I knew that they, too, must come down ....

There was a living picture in each window – four screaming heads of girls waving their arms.

"Call the firemen!" they screamed – scores of them. "Get a ladder!" cried others. They were all as alive and whole and sound as we were who stood on the sidewalk. I couldn't help thinking of that. We cried to them not to jump. We heard the siren of a fire engine in the distance. The other sirens sounded from several directions.

"Here they come!" we yelled. "Don't jump, stay there!"

One girl climbed onto the window sash. Those behind her tried to hold her back. Then she dropped into space. I didn't notice whether those above her watched her drop because I had turned away. Then came that first thud. I looked up, another girl was climbing onto the window sill; others were crowding behind her. She dropped. I watched her fall, and again (heard) the dreadful sound. Two windows away two girls were climbing onto the sill; they were fighting each other and crowding for air. Behind them I saw many screaming heads. They fell almost together, but I heard two distinct thuds. Then the flames burst out through the windows on the floor below them, and curled up into their faces.

The firemen began to raise a ladder. Others took out a life net and, while they were rushing to the sidewalk with it, two more girls shot down. The firemen held it under them; the bodies broke it; the grotesque simile of a dog jumping through a hoop struck me. Before they could move the net another girl's body flashed through it ....

A young man helped a girl to the window sill. Then he held her out, deliberately away from the building and let her drop. He seemed cool and calculating. He held out a second girl the same way and let her drop. Then he held out a third girl who did not resist. I noticed that. They were unresisting as if he were helping them onto a streetcar instead of into eternity. Undoubtedly he saw that a terrible death awaited them in the flames, and his was only a terrible chivalry.

Then came the love amid the flames. He brought another girl to the window. Those of us who were looking saw her put her arms around him and kiss him. Then he held her out into space and dropped her. But quick as a flash he was on the window sill himself. His coat fluttered upward – the air filled his trouser legs. I could see that he wore tan shoes and hose. His hat remained on his head.

Thud – dead, thud – dead. Together they went into eternity. I saw his face before they covered it. You could see he was a real man. He had done his best.

We found out later that, in the room in which he stood, many girls were being burned to death by the flames and were screaming in an inferno of flames and heat. He chose the easiest way and was brave enough even to help the girl he loved to a quicker death, after she had given him a goodbye kiss ....

The firemen raised the longest ladder. It reached only to the sixth floor. I saw the last girl jump at it and miss it. And then the faces disappeared from the window .... all this had occurred in less than seven minutes, the start of the fire and the thuds and the deaths.

I heard screams around the corner and hurried there. What I had seen before was not so terrible as what had followed .... girls were burning to death before our very eyes. They were jammed up in the windows. No one was lucky enough to be able to jump, it seemed. But one by one the jams broke. Down came the bodies in a shower -- burning, smoking, flaming bodies, with disheveled hair trailing upward ....

The whole, sound, unharmed girls who had jumped on the other side of the building had tried to fall feet down. But these fire torches, suffering ones, fell inertly, only intent that death should come to them on the sidewalk instead of in the furnace behind them.

On the sidewalk lay heaps of broken bodies. A policeman later went about with tags, which he fastened with wires to the wrists of the dead girls, numbering each with a lead pencil, and I saw him fasten tag no. 54 to the wrist of a girl who wore an engagement ring. A fireman who came downstairs from the building (later, after the fire was out) told me that there were at least fifty bodies in the big room ... Another fireman told me that more girls had jumped down an air shaft in the rear of the building. I went back there, into the narrow court, and saw a heap of dead girls ....

I looked upon the heap of dead bodies and I remembered these girls were the shirtwaist makers. I remembered their great strike of last year in which these same girls had demanded more sanitary conditions and more safety precautions in the shops. These dead bodies were the answer. **(28)**

Despite Shepherd's interpretation, most of the victims were not trying to commit suicide. It was sure death to stay in the inferno, but there was a slim chance they would survive if they jumped. There were many firemen and many onlookers who helped man the life nets. The life nets were made of sturdy canvas and held with many springs that would absorb shock. There were also a few brave souls holding horse blankets in a futile attempt to do what they could to break the falls of the girls jumping from the blazing building. Sadly, the force of multiple jumpers from so great a height either tore out some fire nets or knocked the would-be rescuers to the ground. A few jumpers did survive their falls.

Another reporter confirmed Shepherd's account of the young man dropping girls to the pavement. He reported: "One man ran from window to window, picked up girls bodily, and dropped them to the pavement. Either he thought the nets were there to catch them or he believed this was the easiest way. When he had dropped the last girl within reach he climbed onto the sill and jumped straight out, with a hand raised as a bridge jumper holds his arm upward to balance himself."

This reporter also noted the story of one who survived her jump for a time. He wrote:

All the girls had jumped from the Greene Street side of the building and it seemed that the ninth floor ledge on this side was clear when two girls clambered out upon it. One of them seemed self-poised; at least her movements were slow and deliberate. With her was a younger girl shrieking and twisting with fright.

The crowd yelled to the two not to jump. The older girl placed both arms around the younger and pulled her back on the ledge toward the brick wall and tried to press her close to the wall. But the younger girl twisted her head and shoulders loose from the protecting embrace, took a step or two to the right, and jumped.

After her younger companion had died, the girl who was left stood back against the wall motionless, and for a moment she held her hands rigid against her thighs, her head tilted upward and looking toward the sky. Smoke began to trickle out of the broken window a few inches to her left. She began to raise her arms then and make slow gestures as if she were addressing a crowd above her. A tongue of flame licked up along the window sill and singed her hair and then out of the smoke which was beginning to hide her from view she jumped, feet foremost, falling, without turning, to the street. It was Bertha Weintrout, whom the police found still breathing an hour later under the cataracts spilling from ledge to ledge upon the dead who lay around her.

(The "cataracts" were the rushing streams of water spilling from the building. New York City firemen were pouring thousands and thousands of gallons of water onto the fire.)

More than an hour after the last of the girls had jumped policemen who had approached the building to gather up the bodies and stretch them out on the opposite side of Greene Street found one girl, Bertha Weintrout, the last girl to leap from the ninth floor, still breathing. Two or three dead bodies were piled alongside her, and as the policemen were moving those away they heard the girl sigh. The police yelled for a doctor, and the girl, still bleeding and dripping wet was hurried to St. Vincent's Hospital. **(29)**

Shepherd also confirmed the tale of the girl, and reported the following heartrending detail: "From opposite windows spectators saw again and again pitiable companionships formed in the instance of death – girls who placed their arms around each other as they leaped. In many cases their clothing was flaming or their hair flaring as they fell."

Shepherd said the girl in question didn't jump, but fell. He wrote, "The crowds in the street ... were imploring her not to leap. She made a steady gesture, looking down as if to assure them she would remain brave. But a thin flame shot out of the window at her back and touched her hair. In an instant her head was aflame. She tore at her burning hair, lost her balance, and came shooting down upon the mounds of bodies below." **(30)**

Another unfortunate in the pile of bodies on the sidewalks survived for a time, but the overwhelmed police and firemen didn't know it. When they picked her up to remove her, she was still alive. But she died before an ambulance could take her to a hospital.

Why didn't the rescuers tend to these two girls immediately? They thought the victims had died on impact. In fact, so many girls jumped so quickly they landed on fire hoses; the firemen had to move their bodies so they could keep fighting the fire.

Another girl waved a handkerchief at the onlookers below, then jumped from a window. Her dress, which was on fire, caught on a hook or a wire dozens of feet above the pavement. One of the young women who escaped from the ninth floor evidently saw her from across the street as she was under protection of the firemen. She said the girl hung up on a hook on the outside of the sixth floor of the building. She said, "I watched a fireman try to save her. I wasn't hysterical anymore; I was just numb." Flames burned through the fabric of the hung-up girl's dress, releasing her from the wire or hook that provided temporary safety. She fell to her doom.

A tailor who worked on the eighth floor, where the fire started, said he tried to douse the burning shirtwaists, but to no avail. He said the rope they hung on broke, sending flaming garments onto his female co-workers' heads. Soon the workroom was ablaze, he said. He said he made it down a flight of stairs. Most of the other

workers on the eighth floor who survived also escaped this way.

The first girl who jumped fell through a plate glass shelter on the sidewalk below. The impact of her body on the sharp glass dismembered her.

An owner of a nearby clothing manufacturing outfit said he ran from his own business to the Asch Building and helped man a fire net that other people had dragged to the fire scene. He said he and the other men broke the falls of 15 girls, but most of them died anyway because they bounced off the net with such force they slammed into the sidewalk. "Bodies were falling all around us," he said, "and two or three of the men with me were knocked down. The girls just leaped wildly out of the windows and turned over and over before reaching the sidewalk. I only saw one man jump. All the rest were girls. They stood on the windowsills tearing their hair out in the handfuls and they jumped."

Three firemen spread a fire net just in time to catch a girl who had jumped. They hoped she would survive. But before they could help her off of the fire net, three other girls crashed into the net from nine stories above and smashed into the first girl; all four rolled out of the fire net and fell to the pavement. All lay lifeless and still. Many other women and girls would rip through fire nets because several of them hit the fire nets at the same time, or they would land on girls who survived the jump to the fire nets and kill them anyway.

An American-born seamstress who worked on the eighth floor said she tried the elevator, but it wouldn't rise to her floor. She said she got into an elevator shaft and used her hands and feet to slide down the cable. She passed out, and when she woke up she was in St. Vincent's Hospital with burns on her hands and bruises on her body. She said she tried to get another girl to slide with her, but that female ran to a window on a side of the building where Shepherd saw many girls jump to their deaths.

A male sewing machine operator who worked on the ninth floor said he tried to extinguish the fires on his female co-workers as they streaked by him, clothes ablaze. He said they ran to the windows. He said he saw an elevator crammed with workers from the tenth floor pass his floor by, and the elevator never returned. So he opened the door to the shaft and tried sliding down the cable. Several girls jumped into the shaft after him, he said, and one knocked him free from the cable. He said he fell onto a dead girl's body on top of the elevator, and firemen eventually cut their way into the shaft and rescued him and those females who had survived the drops. They also removed the bodies of the dead.

The firemen also eventually found and rescued a man hours after the fire. He was stuck *below* the elevator in the basement, neck-deep in water on top of the cable drum which drove the elevator. He had also slid down the cable and torn the flesh on his hands to the bones. His legs were virtually paralyzed from sitting in the cold water for so long. **(31)**

A black American porter named Thomas Horton risked electrocution to help the elevator operators. He manned the elevator motors in the basement until the circuit breakers failed and the electrical wiring was drenched in water. The bodies of those who tried escaping via the elevator shafts helped caused the elevators to stop working. They weighed down the cars and jammed the elevator shafts and the guide and travel hardware of the cars. **(32)**

Some students in the New York University law school building next to the Asch Building tied a couple of ladders together and lowered them from their building to the roof of the Asch Building. One of the law students, one Charles Kremer, then descended to the roof and got the frightened employees atop the building into an orderly file. He coaxed them to climb the tied-together ladders to safety. Other students in the law school building stood by to assist the females off the ladder. Scores of girls and young women and a few men owed their lives to these law school students. Kremer also went down to the tenth floor to look for other possible survivors. He found one girl, who fainted in his arms. He put out the girl's burning hair, and got her onto the roof. Another law student named Elias Kantner helped get her across the ladder to safety.

The law students also reported a very ugly scene on the roof. Evidently some Good Samaritans in an adjoining building had laid a ladder from their building to the roof of the Asch Building. It was on the other side of the building from the law school building. There was a crowd of people waiting for rescue on that side of the building. The students said some men started biting and kicking the girls and women to get them out of their way so they could escape first. Since these students did not report saving owners Isaac Harris and Max Blanck or some of their friends and relatives in management, and yet these people said they escaped from the rooftop, it is possible the owners and/or their top people were the vermin the students saw bullying the women and girls. **(33)**

Frances Perkins, a young social worker and witness to the fire, recalled: "We heard the engines and we heard the screams and rushed out and rushed over where we could see what the trouble was. We could see this building from Washington Square and the people had just begun to jump when we got there. They had been holding until that time, standing in the windowsills, being crowded by others behind them, the fire pressing closer and closer, the smoke closer and closer. Finally the men were trying to get out this thing that the firemen carry with them, a net to catch people if they do jump, they were trying to get that out and they couldn't wait any longer. They began to jump. The window was too crowded and they would jump and they hit the sidewalk. The net broke, they (fell) a terrible distance, the weight of the bodies was so great, at the speed at which they were traveling that they broke through the net ... It was a horrifying spectacle. We had our dose of it that night and felt as though we had been part of it all." **(34)**

All these accounts of the tragedy make it seem like the fire lasted for hours. Actually it went very quickly. The fire broke out at about 4:35 p.m. The fire was reported at about 4:40 pm. Firemen arrived on the scene starting at about 4:46 p.m. The last of the women and girls who jumped from the ninth floor did so at 4:57 p.m. The firemen poured many thousands of gallons of water upon the burning building from the street and from water towers and had the fire under control between 5:05 p.m. and 5:15 p.m. **(35)**

Firemen entered the Asch Building during the blaze, fighting their way up with hoses. On the sixth floor they found and rescued the girls who had been able to get down the fire escape and then through a window on that floor.

But the fire had been so fierce and conditions were so unsafe that it wasn't until after 6 p.m. that firemen were able to enter the top three floors of the Asch Building to search for survivors and recover the bodies of the dead.

Fire Chief Edward Croker, a hardened professional, was shaking with emotion himself after he saw the charred skeletons of girls still at their sewing machines, and the burned bodies of the dead piled up around doors and elevator shafts. His men found dozens of people, mostly young women and girls, burned to death or dead from asphyxiation in a room on the ninth floor. The firemen found 14 engagement rings on the floor ... this hints at the youth of the seamstresses, their ruined hopes, and the sense of loss their fiances would have. They found other bodies crowded around locked doors and in staircases. They also found about 20 women and girls who had jumped down the elevator shaft and died in the shaft. They rescued others in the elevator shaft who were still alive. **(36)**

While the firemen checked the building for survivors and the dead that evening, policemen on the fire line around the Asch Building struggled mightily to hold back the thousands of relatives and friends of Triangle workers ... and the thousands of morbidly curious who always show up at such tragedies. It took a few hours for the firemen to recover the dead and have their bodies brought to a makeshift morgue on a pier at the East River waterfront for identification and claiming.

Tens of thousands of people would stream through the morgue. Many were looking for loved ones or friends or co-workers who may have died. Some of these had the heart-rending experience of identifying their loved ones; some of these had to do it by jewelry or shoes because many of the victims' heads were burned or damaged beyond recognition ... and a couple of the girls' bodies were headless. Others were looking for a few kicks, and the nauseating sight of charred and mangled bodies made most of them regret their ghoulishness. A few especially worthless people were looking for profit. They managed to steal small items of jewelry from the corpses.

In all, at least 140 victims died at the scene of the fire. Another dozen or so died in a hospital or on their way to a hospital. They burned alive inside the building, they died of asphyxiation inside the building, they fell to their deaths inside the elevator shafts inside the building. And scores of others died jumping from the building. Several other victims died later in hospitals from the injuries they suffered when they hit the pavement or the bodies of their co-workers. Most of the victims were girls and young women 16 to 23 years old. (Only 30 or so victims were 24 or older.) Most of them were Russian or German Jewish girls and young women. Most of the remaining victims were Italian girls and young women, or girls and young women from places like Hungary or Poland or Romania. Hardly any were natives of America; few were married women. **(37)**

Thousands of people had seen the firemen's ladders were too short for rescuing victims from the Asch Building. They had also seen the life nets were far too light to save multiple people jumping from a high building. But the public sensed the heroic firemen were the only blameless men of the people involved with the Triangle Waist Company disaster. And they would soon be proved right.

The building the Triangle Waist Company was in – the Asch Building – was classified as fireproof. It was barely 10 years old. It suffered relatively little structural damage in the fire. What burned were the finished garments, the cloth for the garments, wooden benches and tables and other furniture in the company's premises, window frames and trim — and scores of females and a few young men.

It turned out the men of the New York City Fire Department knew the building all too well. The building had been the site of four previous fires. The building had only one fire escape, and it failed. Nor did the building have fire sprinklers. Triangle workers who tried to use the fire hoses to douse the blaze found out the hoses were rotted and broke when uncoiled. New York Fire Department officials had reported the building as unsafe to the city's Building Department officials because of the lack of good fire escapes. But the Building Department bureaucrats had done nothing about it.

Someone on the New York City Building Department had allowed the building's owner (Joseph Asch) and his architect (Robert Maynicke) to call for some doors that swung inward instead of outward. If they had opened outward, the crush of seamstresses' bodies against them might have forced them open. Someone on the New York City Building Department had also allowed Asch and the architect to construct the building with two narrow staircases instead of the three staircases the building code said the building should have. Was bribery involved? **(38)**

At a hastily-convened meeting of city and state officials on March 27, 1911, the Monday after the Saturday afternoon fire, New York City Fire Marshal William Beers declared the cause of the fire was cigarettes or matches igniting cloth scraps on the eighth floor of the building. When Triangle Waist Company spokesmen claimed they didn't allow smoking on their premises, Beers said his men picked up many cigarette cases near the point of origin of the fire. In other words, management didn't prevent smoking, especially in areas laden with flammable materials.

Fire Chief Croker then told the assembled officials that many of the doors of the Triangle Waist Company were locked. He said his men had to chop through them with axes to open them. If they were not locked, he said, they were still wedged so tightly that it took that sort of force to break them open. Clearly the girls would not have had the strength nor the tools that his stalwart firemen had.

Some New York City politicians tried to defend the Building Department at the meeting, and to the press. It came out that the agency's inspectors usually looked at buildings only during construction, and there were some grossly incompetent men who had inspector jobs. Officials of the state Labor Commission tried to weasel out of blame for failing to punish the owners of the Triangle Waist Company for their violations of fire safety laws.**(39)**

A week after the tragedy, the garment workers of New York City turned out to honor the memory of the dead and to push for less Hell-like conditions in their workplaces. At one such memorial rally, seamstress union organizer Rose Schneiderman said the following during her speech:

"This is not the first time girls have been burned alive in the city. Every week I must learn of the untimely death of one of my sister workers. Every year thousands of us are maimed. The life of men and women is so cheap and property is so sacred. There are so many of us for one job it matters little if 146 of us are burned to death."

"Public officials have only words of warning to us – warning that we must be intensely peaceable and they have the workhouse just back of all their warnings. The strong hand of the law beats us back, when we rise, into the conditions that make life unbearable."

"I can't talk fellowship to you who are gathered here. Too much blood has been spilled. I know from my experience it is up to the working people to save themselves. The only way we can save ourselves is by a strong working-class movement." **(40)**

On April 5, 1911, tens of thousands of workers, most of them female garment workers, marched through the streets of Manhattan in memorial for the victims. An estimated 200,000 to 300,000 spectators, many of them immigrants themselves, lined the streets in tribute.

Like Bruce Ismay and most of the top officers of the *Titanic*, Triangle Waist Company owners Isaac Harris and Max Blanck fled while roughly 150 of their workers burned to death or died of asphyxiation or jumped to their deaths. And like the management of the White Star Line, these two industrial criminals were so tight they squeaked. Harris and Blanck offered to pay survivors of the victims of their greed a week's wage – apparently to head off wrongful death lawsuits from survivors. This stunt was beneath contempt.

And even before the memorial parade, Harris and Blanck re-opened for business in another building, and advertised it. This building was not even fireproof, and Triangle's managers had already blocked the exit to the building's single fire escape with two rows of sewing machines. **(41)**

The picture of scores of girls jumping to their deaths while merchants profited inflamed the public. They made demands for reform, and finally the politicians started to listen to them more than to the businessmen who contributed to their political coffers.

The Italian consul in New York City took statements from several Italian girls who managed to escape the fire that some doors leading out of the Triangle Waist Company's premises to a stairway were locked and were never used for exit. The consul turned these statements over to the New York County (Manhattan) district attorney.

A couple of weeks after the fire, a grand jury in New York City indicted the owners of the Triangle Waist Company because there was evidence they had the seamstresses habitually locked in during working hours in violation of state law. A month after the fire, a coroner's jury in New York City comprised of engineers, architects, builders, and businessmen found the owners of the Triangle Waist Company were responsible for the deaths of at least two women trapped behind a locked door. They also decided the owners were generally responsible for the deaths of

many others because of their disregard for safety for maintaining a clothing manufacturing firm with crowed aisles, no good passages, and locked doors to prevent the seamstresses from escaping. The jurymen also recommended a strengthening of fire and safety codes to prevent similar future tragedies. **(42)**

Manhattan district attorney Charles Whitman decided to put Isaac Harris and Max Blanck on trial for manslaughter because some of the doors out of the premises of their company were locked when the fire broke out. In particular, he said, the door from a workroom on the ninth floor that led to the stairs and the elevators was locked because firemen recovered the door lock mechanism in the locked position, and some survivors made statements saying it was locked. The door locking, he said, done at the orders of the owners, led to the deaths of some of the seamstresses.

Why were the doors locked? Because Harris and Blanck, two of the most prominent businessmen in the shirtwaist trade, claimed the girls were pilfering some cloth and shirtwaists from their business. They even had the females' purses searched as they left the premises every day. **(43)**

Virtually all of the 200 or so people on the tenth floor of the Asch Building (including the owners and their family members) when the fire broke out were helped to safety. Most of the more than 200 people on the eighth floor when the fire broke out escaped. More than 250 people were on the ninth floor when the fire broke out. More than half of these, almost all girls and young women, died. The Italian seamstresses were telling the truth about the locked doors. A man was able to unlock the locked sewing shop door on the eighth floor; no one could open the locked sewing shop door on the ninth floor.

While the Manhattan district attorney prepared to prosecute Harris and Blanck, a large segment of the populace of New York City, many of whom were factory workers laboring in similar conditions, seethed in anger and demanded reform. Other public-spirited citizens bypassed the courts and approached the state government to push for reform. New York City, so full of corruption, on paper at least was subordinate to the state government in Albany. Perhaps a state government hearing on workplace safety might benefit the workers of New York.

One of the political leaders these genteel people approached was Alfred E. Smith. Smith, a coarse, raucous, and (gasp) *Catholic* politician from Manhattan's Lower East Side, was a part of the Democrat's corrupt Tammany Hall machine in New York City. On the surface, Smith didn't seem like the type of man who would be a reformer. But the do-gooders had made a great decision when they went to see him. For Smith, then the Democrats' majority leader in the state assembly, was the rare big wheel in the state legislature who had not forgotten the station of life he had come from. And Smith was a skillful enough politician to know how to spearhead an investigation and translate the results into a workable labor code.

Fundamentally, Al Smith was one of the people, despite being a politician. His father had worked himself to death as a teamster, loading and unloading horse-drawn wagons in all kinds of weather, and driving horse-drawn wagonloads of freight in the city. He died just before Al turned 13. His mother had to do piecework, assembling umbrellas at home, to piece together a living for herself and Al and his sister. When her health deteriorated, she bought a very small neighborhood store and ran it.

Al had to quit school in 1888, a month before the end of the school year, when he was 14, to help out his mother. Most of eighth grade at St. James' Parochial School, his Catholic parish school, was as much formal education as Al would get. He worked as a "truck chaser," getting orders along the waterfront and finding his company's teamsters so they could make extra deliveries during the day without having to return to the company stables. This work, which required stamina on foot, decent salesmanship, and a loud voice, all of which Al had, brought him $3 a week. Al quit this job and went to work as a night shipping clerk at an oil company for $8 a week.

After Al turned 18, he got a job at New York's Fulton Fish Market, where commercial fishermen brought in their catches each day. For a salary of $12 a week in the early 1890s – good money for a young man in those days – plus all the free fish he and his mother and sister could stand to eat, Al did the books, estimated catches on incoming ships so the buyers and sellers of his firm could set prices and make deals, and did other jobs for his firm. In the bedlam that was the dockside fish market, Al's voice developed depth, volume, and carrying power. Al's loud harsh voice would become one of his trademarks when he went into politics.

Al Smith had hundreds of friends and acquaintances who struggled in similar fashion to himself. Maybe the Triangle Fire victims' stories hit him personally because of his own experiences. He had been able to escape that cycle but many people he knew still toiled for very little. **(44)**

In his autobiography Up To Now, Smith talked about the Triangle Fire but said nothing about what _he_ did in the days after the horrible fire. Despite being a politician, he had a fair amount of humility. Frances Perkins spoke about Smith's actions as follows:

"Al Smith ... found that many many of these young people (the victims) were residents of the same district

he was a resident of and he did the most natural and humane thing. As he said: 'Why I did it just as I would if they had died of anything else, you know, you go to see the father and mother to try to help them.' He went to the places where they lived; he went to the tenement they had occupied to see their father and mother and tell them how sorry he was or their husband, as the case might be, or their wife, to tell them of his sympathy and grief. It was a human, decent, natural thing to do and it was a sight he never forgot. It burned it into his mind. He also got to the morgue, I remember, at just the time when the survivors were being allowed to sort out the dead and see who was theirs and who could be recognized. He went along with a number of others to the morgue to support and help, you know, the old father or the sorrowing sister, do her terrible picking out. " **(45)**

Smith would credit the public rather than himself with the pressure that led to the reforms he would one day guide into the state's lawbooks. He wrote, "There was an immediate conviction in the public mind that this appalling disaster resulted from neglect to enforce laws for the protection of the lives of people in factory buildings." Smith also credited some public-spirited engineers, labor officials, and social workers for bringing ideas to him and asking him to do what he could to reform the state's labor and safety codes. Smith noted, "Prior to that year (1911), a number of beneficial statutes had been enacted for the protection of industrial workers, but they were entirely ineffective because the legislature had failed to make adequate appropriation for their enforcement." (This was much like Congress passing a law ordering a border fence in 2006, and then refusing to pass an appropriation measure to fund it.) **(46)**

Smith held a meeting with prominent reformers and he said someone during the meeting suggested a commission to study worker safety laws. That jibed with Frances Perkins' recollection:

"We decided to ask the legislature to create a commission and this is where Al Smith came in. I went to see him and another woman went with me, and one man ... I went to ask his advice and he gave me the most useful piece of advice, I guess, we've ever had. It was this: 'You're going to form a commission, that's all right, that's a good idea, but let me tell you. Don't get started asking the governor to appoint a commission, or anybody else to appoint a commission of citizens. Citizens is all right,' he said, 'but they have got to be where they belong. If you want to get anything done, you got to have this, a legislative commission. If the legislature does it, the legislature will be proud of it, the legislature will listen to their report and the legislature will do something about it. But if the governor appoints the commission, they will just give it the cold shoulder; they won't pay any attention to it.' "

"Well I thought that was absurd at the time. But I learned by long experience that it is not absurd; it's the way to do it. This is the way that the legislatures are persuaded to act." **(47)**

Smith introduced a bill in the assembly for creating this legislative commission, and state senator Robert Wagner, the majority leader in the state senate, carried the bill in the state senate. The state legislature – assemblymen and senators together – enacted a law creating the commission, and the state's governor signed it into law within weeks. The commission law went into effect at the end of June 1911, three months after the Triangle Fire. Wagner and Smith would be the chairman and vice-chairman of the commission. Labor union titan Samuel Gompers, head of the American Federation of Labor, and Miss Mary Dreier, a prominent child welfare social worker and labor activist, among others, were also appointed to the commission, which would be known to posterity as the New York Factory Investigating Commission. Frances Perkins would help the commission as well. (She would become FDR's Secretary of Labor, the first female Cabinet member.) Two very talented Jewish lawyers, Abram Elkus and Bernard Shientag, who provided their services for free, did most of the legal work and interrogation of witnesses.

Smith noted that fires, although spectacularly tragic, actually killed far fewer workers than bad workplace conditions routinely did. So he said he and the other commission members decided not to limit themselves to changing fire codes, but to studying workplace conditions so the commissioners could devote themselves "to a consideration of measures that had for their purpose the conservation of human life." He ensured the law he sponsored and got enacted would give the commissioners the leeway they needed to tackle the health and safety problems of industries, not just fire safety concerns. **(48)**

The commissioners hired investigators, and started personally checking factories around the state to see what they could see. They would have their work cut out for them.

Smith recalled, "So lax had the state been prior to 1911, that the commission hardly began its labors when it was discovered then there was no way for the state even to know when a factory was started. A man could hire a floor in a loft building, put in his machinery, and start his factory. There was no law requiring him to notify the state that he was engaging in a business which came under the supervision of a department of the state government."

"Factory inspection forces were so small that the inspections in some cities were made only once in two years and in others once a year. Factory managers know just about when to expect an inspection, and

consequently, during the day of the inspector's visit everything was in ship shape. The rest of the year it was allowed to run haphazard, there being no fear of detection by the authorities in charge of the Department of Labor. Once an inspector arrived at a factory a day ahead of time. There were children under the legal age employed in that particular factory and they were hastily put into the elevators, the cars were run between the floors and kept there until the inspector left." **(49)**

While Smith and the other commissioners were checking and judging factory conditions across New York, Triangle owners Isaac Harris and Max Blanck were awaiting a different kind of judgment in court. The two robber barons would stand trial on manslaughter charges for the deaths of some of their employees. This trial ran during most of December of 1911.

Most of the people in a workroom on the ninth floor burned to death, asphyxiated to death, or leaped to their deaths. The workroom had two doors out to the stairs and the elevators – one door was locked, and a wall of fire separated the seamstresses from the door that was unlocked. The prosecutor, to make his case, believed he had to prove the door not enveloped in flames was locked.

More than 100 people testified for the prosecution. Most of them were seamstresses who escaped the blaze or firemen who fought it. Seamstresses testified some workroom doors were locked, and someone had to unlock or break down these doors so they could escape.

There were some defense witnesses, many of whom were relatives or friends of Harris and Blanck who had the better positions at the company. They tended to testify that the doors were unlocked but the fierceness of the fire prevented the escape of many victims on the ninth floor to the stairs or the elevators. Some of them apparently lied on the stand, because in previous sworn statements to the district attorney, they averred a door on a ninth floor workroom was locked.

Harris, when questioned, claimed he had a male employee check women's handbags for cloth and garments because of pilferage. He also said he sent private detectives to girls' tenements and had them prosecuted for theft if they found cloth scraps or shirtwaists. He said he stopped having girls arrested because some sued him; so he would fire suspected thieves instead. He admitted the total value of the girls' thefts amounted to only a few dollars a year.

Firemen had recovered the door knob and lock from the door in question in the rubble. The door lock bar was extended, meaning it was locked at the time of the fire. The prosecutor, over the objections of defense attorney Max Steuer, presented the locked door lock as evidence at the trial. Naturally the oily defense lawyer claimed the lock was tampered with after the fire.

The prosecutor, to make his case, also believed he would have to present at least one witness who escaped who saw another person die because of that locked door. Kate Alterman was one survivor who could do so. She testified at the trial that she and a co-worker named Margaret Schwartz could not get the locked door opened, and she tried to get Margaret to run through the fire with her to possible safety. She said smoke rushed over them, and when she called to Margaret, she didn't reply. Kate said she finally caught sight of Margaret on her knees, her dress and hair aflame. Kate said she covered her head with her coat and some shirtwaists, ran through the wall of flames to the open door on the other side of the floor, and escaped up the stairs to the roof of the building, with the people from the tenth floor. She was one of the many girls the law school students rescued.

Kate's testimony should have been the dagger in the heart of the defense case. But Steuer, a very talented but essentially conscienceless lawyer, was defending Harris and Blanck and their company. He had a different fate in mind for Kate Alterman, or at least her testimony. He got her to repeat it again and again, which helped numb the jurymen to her story. He also picked at her story subtly, by having her repeat herself, to get the jurors to think she was repeating a story she had memorized at the prompting of the prosecutor instead of testifying truthfully.

Harris and Blanck had another advantage – the trial judge. Judge Thomas Crain had been the New York City Tenement House Commissioner before he became a judge. No thanks to Crain's evident negligence on the job, a tenement house fire killed 20 people. Crain should not have been allowed to judge the trial because of this; he would be too prone to sympathize with the defendants. But Crain did not recuse himself from presiding over the trial.

Judge Crain, in his instructions to the jury, told the jurors even if they determined the ninth floor workroom door Margaret Schwartz burned to death near was locked, in order to convict Harris and Blanck of a felony, they would have to determine that the two personally knew that door was locked _at that time on that day_. He told them the owners wouldn't have to know the door was locked to be guilty of a misdemeanor, but he worded his instructions in such a way that most of the jurymen concluded he wanted them to decide only whether to convict or acquit Harris and Blanck of felony manslaughter in connection with the death of Margaret Schwartz. **(50)**

This was a Hanukkah present from the judge that Harris and Blanck did not deserve. Two days after Christmas 1911, the jurors, mostly German-American and Jewish-American middle class men, acquitted the robber barons. One juror, trying to justify his vote, said he and the others voted the way they did because of the judge's instructions. He also claimed, "They (the surviving seamstresses) told their stories like parrots, and I could not believe them." **(51)**

It might not have occurred to this putz that the girls were mostly foreigners who didn't know much English. They probably had to memorize their testimony in English to give it so they could be understood in court by mental midgets like himself. The talkative juror said he didn't know for sure if the locked door was the fault of the owners or of the seamstresses fumbling with the skeleton key supposedly tied to the door trying to get the door open. Of course, this would have been proof the door was locked by design, if someone had to fumble with a key to get it open.

Judge Crain knew the verdict would be an unpopular abortion of justice. So he allowed the jurors to sneak through his chambers and out of the courthouse by a back entrance. Blanck and Harris left the courthouse through the judge's chambers, surrounded by many policemen. Angry relatives and friends of the fire victims chased the robber barons from the courthouse to the subway station and reviled them. **(52)**

The Triangle Fire was the worst in a string of abuses that Isaac Harris and Max Blanck committed. Harris and Blanck had at least four other fires on their premises in the previous decade. These other blazes usually started in the early morning hours at the end of the peak periods of the year for shirtwaist production. Since Harris and Blanck carried fire insurance, the fires (on paper, anyway) got rid of unused cloth and unsold shirtwaists, and the insurance companies paid them for their "losses." The insurance companies never investigated Harris and Blanck for arson. Fire science wasn't advanced enough in that era for investigators to prove forensically whether some kinds of fires were deliberately set.

After Harris and Blanck fired 150 or so females for supposed union sympathy, girls and young women struck against the Triangle Waist Company and many other garment businesses in 1909. Harris and Blanck hired hoods, prostitutes, and pimps to attack girls on the picket lines, and they got the strikers arrested. One of the striking girls' sympathizers arrested outside of the Asch Building was Mary Dreier, who would, as a member of Al Smith's commission, help reform industries of the abuses committed by criminals like Harris and Blanck. When the strike ended, Harris and Blanck, who operated possibly the largest shirtwaist company in the country, settled things on their own terms, which were much more favorable what than the lesser operators settled for. For example, they didn't have to recognize the lady garment workers' unions, while lesser manufacturers did. And yet Harris and Blanck still welshed on portions of their agreement.

After the Triangle Fire, Harris and Blanck filed fire insurance claims for much more than their losses. Steuer extorted $60,000 to $200,000 more from the fire insurance companies over and above the crooked couple's documented losses by threatening nuisance litigation. In 1914, Joseph Asch, who owned the building, offered a settlement of $75 apiece for each of the dead, and the pitiable family members of 23 of the victims accepted these pittances. Harris and Blanck reportedly paid out a victim's week's salary to the survivors of each of the dead ... in most cases less than $10 per victim, and in some cases as little as $3 per girl victim. Harris and Blanck netted roughly $400 to $1300 per dead seamstress or male employee.

Blanck got over again in 1913. He was caught locking exit doors at his facility during work hours. A corrupt judge apologetically fined Blanck $20, the minimum amount prescribed by law for the criminal offense.

The best that could be said about Harris and Blanck is was that it was not racial or religious prejudice against their workers that caused them to do what they did. Most of their victims shared their background. Harris and Blanck were Russian Jews who emigrated to the United States in the late 1800s and worked in the garment trade themselves before they connived their way to the top. They were cunning, greedy, predatory, and amoral; at the time of the fire they were both millionaires. Their lawyer Steuer was a Jew who emigrated from Austria with his family when he was a boy. His main clients were mobsters and crooked politicians (sorry for the redundancy). He was one of the most skillful and avaricious lawyers in the country in his heyday. **(53)**

If there is a proper eternal flame for the memories of the Triangle Fire dead, it may well be among the fires of Hell tormenting Harris, Blanck, and Steuer.

By the time Harris and Blanck escaped the punishment they richly deserved, Smith and the other commission members and especially their investigators and inspectors had done a great amount of spadework. Through much of he second half of 1911, the commissioners had been concentrating on investigating fire hazards, sanitation of factories, hazards to women at work, conditions of bakeries, lead and arsenic poisoning, and child labor in tenements. They and their inspectors and investigators had covered more than 1800 factories and 500 bakeries across the state. They heard testimony from state inspectors, union inspectors, victims, fire officials, undercover agents, managers, workers, and public health officials.

A detailed analysis of the Factory Investigating Commission is beyond the scope of this book. But a few bits of testimony can give a sense of what conditions were like for many unfortunates. They also give a sense of the greed and callous indifference of the owners of some of these places. It also gives a sense of the stupidity, indifference, and dishonesty of some of the officials whose job it was to enforce labor, health, and fire codes.

One inspector testified a large factory he inspected had no fire escapes, but only some flammable wooden stairs and bridges for the workers to try to escape on. He said he found one man who made lead items eating lunch with his hands covered in lead because the managers would not give him enough time to clean his hands. There was no vent hood over the lead melting pot; he and other workers had lead poisoning.

Another large factory the inspector checked was filthy and dusty and unventilated. Ironically, the factory's workers made vent fans and ducts for other businesses, and yet the cheapskates who ran the company wouldn't provide their factory workers with the benefit of the ventilation systems they made for other factories. Of course, the factory's office complex was ventilated.

Another witness told the commissioners some owners put stoves in factories for heating without bothering to install vent pipes to exhaust the carbon monoxide and other gases. Smith asked the man what it cost to install vent pipes, and the man said they were relatively cheap. Smith then asked him, "If men didn't get dizzy, (aren't they) apt to do better work?" Smith figured not cutting corners so workers wouldn't get sick or poisoned on the job due to owner-caused health hazards was not only just, but cost-effective. The witness said the factory managers ignored him, so he (the witness) got a factory inspector (a state labor department employee) with a sense of duty to make them have the vent pipes installed. **(54)**

Smith, when he entered a factory, invariably would demand the operators to have all the elevator cars brought down for inspection. He would not be fooled by a factory owner's bland assurance no underage children were working for him, while such children were being hidden in an elevator during the commission's visit.

In one city, the commissioners discovered the owners of a business whose workers made pants for boys had help in exploiting them – negligent government health and labor agents.

One worker, Frank, a boy whose parents came from Germany, evidently lied about his age on the prompting of his mother to get a job at the clothing making firm. He was so puny and soft-spoken, the commissioners asked him repeatedly why he was lying about his age. Frank said he didn't know what year he was born in, and the town had no birth certificate or proof of age for him, but the city's health official issued him a work certificate just the same. On questioning,

Frank admitted he left school three months earlier, after finishing fifth grade. When they asked the boy how much he weighed, he replied, "83 pounds, in the city hall."

Frank's father made $10.50 a week in a meat business, and his mother made $6 a week mopping floors in an office building six nights a week six hours a night. The boy made $3.50 for a 48-hour week of doing cutting work on trousers, and another 25 cents each week for mopping shop floors and bathroom floors after closing on Saturday evenings. Frank had five sisters and a brother, all in school; he said his 15 year-old sister kept house when his mother was at work The boy's family – father, mother, and seven children – were existing on a gross income of about $1050 a year – well below the poverty level for a non-farm family of that size.

Another young worker of German parentage, Josephine, age 15, told the commissioners she had gotten through seventh grade. She told Al Smith in response to his questions about her family life and religious development that she had made her First Communion a couple of years earlier, and might be able to make Confirmation in a year or so.

Smith, himself the father of five children, asked children questions about their religion as well as their schooling to get a sense for their home lives. Parents all too often lacked the time and energy to raise their children like they should because they were worn out working so hard for so little money. Josephine's answer told Smith her parents were taking the time to see to her religious development, despite their poverty. Her parish priest would not allow her to take these sacraments unless she was schooled enough in her religion to do so. In Smith's day, public leaders and the public practiced their religion more openly. School teachers were expected to develop children's sense of Judeo-Christian morality and patriotism. The good American was a Christian – Catholic, Orthodox, or Protestant -- or an observant Jew, and a patriot.

Today, of course, many school officials, public officials, and other elites would try to discredit a child who talked about her or his religious training ... and the politician who asked the child such questions sympathetically.

Josephine was making $4 a week for helping make boy's pants 48 hours a week. She said it took her 45 minutes to an hour to walk to work in the morning and a little more time in the evening to walk home. She walked when the weather was good instead of taking the streetcar because to do so daily would cost her 60 cents a week – about a day's pay for her. Josephine sais she had never been through a fire drill or used the fire escape ... she worked on the fifth floor of the building the business was in.

Josephine's father made $10 to $12 a week as a helper at a foundry, and her 18-year-old sister made $6 to $8 a week assembling typewriters. Besides Josephine and her sister, there were five younger children at home.

Josephine's family – father, mother, herself, her older sister and five younger children – were existing on a gross income of about $1050 to $1150 a year – again, well below the poverty level for a non-farm family of that size.

One of the clothing company's owners, one Abraham Rubenstein, when subpoenaed to testify, tried to give the impression he paid his workers well. But under questioning, Mr. Rubenstein started to admit the truth about what a tightwad he and the other owners were.

Rubenstein said 20 men and more than 100 women and girls worked for the company. When asked what his company pay scale was, Rubenstein said men made from $9 to $30 a week working for him and the other owners of A. S. Shapiro Co. Under further questioning, Rubenstein admitted the foreman made $30, a clerk made $20, and every other male made far less for working a 60-hour week.

Rubenstein was similarly evasive on the women's pay scale. He said women made $9 to $14 a week for working a 60-hour week for him, Under further examination, he admitted paying girls as little as $3.50 a week for a 48-hour week. He also admitted many of the women at his business were doing piecework and were making only $6 a week.

A tightwad owner shorts his workers on more than their pay. Rubenstein, when asked about sanitary conditions in his business, said someone cleaned the toilets once a week. He said he wasn't sure if soap and water were used in the cleaning. When questioned on why the cleaning was done so seldom, in a crowded facility where almost 150 people worked, he said once a week was sufficient.

Rubenstein admitted his company didn't perform fire drills. He said there were some water pails present for fires, but the water kept evaporating. When he said a boy swept up around the seamstresses in the late afternoon, the committee members taunted him about how the sweeping would let the girls "get the benefit of all that dust." With a straight face, Rubenstein said his cloth and lint-laden facility had no dust.

Rubenstein, when asked, claimed he didn't know if his seamstresses were unionized. He was lying, because if they were, there would have been collective bargaining and a contract ... and wages wouldn't be so abysmal. **(55)**

Abetting Rubenstein and his partners was a state labor department inspector named Bernard Wilbur. Wilbur apparently was a plodding stooge who was more concerned about his paycheck and procedures than in doing his job well.

Wilbur was well acquainted with the A. S. Shapiro facility but had done nothing substantial to prod its owners into complying with the law. He said Rubenstein did not have his business' toilets or other shop messes cleaned, but only the floors of the bathrooms mopped. Wilbur said in so many words taking action on unsanitary conditions wasn't part of his job, so he didn't report the filthy toilets or other messes to public health officials in town. He said his only concern was to report problems to his superiors in Albany ... and under questioning he said he may or may not have reported the filthy facilities to his bosses.

Wilbur proved he was a dunce in other ways. He said he ignored unsigned or verbal complaints from workers as untrustworthy. Under questioning, he admitted it never occurred to him that if they signed their names to complaints, they could get fired and sued.

The commissioners tried to pin Wilbur down on about how many citations a year he wrote. He finally came up with 1000 as a guess. When they asked him how many citations were serious enough to go to court, he said four against two companies were.

Wilbur said he would not consider investigating the age of Frank, the underage boy. He said even though Frank was puny, he would take the city health office's word on his age, even though evidence suggested the city's agent had screwed up in issuing the boy a work certificate.

Wilbur said he would hesitate making a business install reasonable ventilation. He said he was not sure if state labor officials considered it a violation. When Smith asked Wilbur why he didn't have an air tester for checking air quality in factory premises, he had no valid response.

When asked why he didn't cite a business for having a substandard fire escape, Wilbur said there was enough space for women in the place to crawl through a window and use it. Wilbur admitted women would find it hard to use many fire escapes. He just didn't see it as his job to order better fire escapes.

Wilbur, like many government employees, was consistent in his obtuseness. When he was asked what he did about the hazardous handling of white phosphorus at a match plant, he said he made no report or citation, because he figured it was a medical issue. Smith questioned Wilbur a little, then said there was little purpose talking to him about health because Wilbur wouldn't know anything. (56)

The commissioners heard from a city official who said immigrant kids who couldn't learn English well and slow students should be allowed to get work permits. When Smith and Miss Dreier asked him what was wrong with giving them remedial schooling, he said they could be put in the schools for incorrigibles. The commissioners and their attorney implied they thought the city official was a little slow himself. (57)

The commissioners often found officials who should have been citing, fining, and closing unsafe workplaces didn't want to do the jobs they were paid for. A particularly bad example was one Calvin Nichols, the health officer of the city of Troy. He was a lying hairsplitting excuse maker.

Nichols had essentially stopped his medical practice to get this cushy government job, so he couldn't have been too good as a doctor in the first place. Nichols didn't have sanitary conditions in factories inspected like he should have been doing. He said it was a fire inspector or a plumbing inspector or a factory investigator job, not his job. Under pressure, he then said he didn't go to factories to inspect health conditions but sent his men.

Then Nichols said he didn't have authority to enforce health codes. The commission's attorney, in the process of examining him, read Nichols the law and said Nichols was wrong.

When the commissioners asked Nichols why he didn't show initiative, he said, "I have too much work at hand to do it."

Nichols was a lying, niggling, quibbling witness. He contradicted himself often and was called on it. He claimed lack of memory. He claimed he had people arrested for violating the health code, but he couldn't recall details, he admitted none involved factories, and he provided no records to cover his stories. When he said health hazards were reduced on his watch, he didn't have records to back his claim.

Nichols hanged himself with his own tongue. He said he knew of underage children in factories, then he didn't, then he said employers were getting underage children to get fraudulent work certificates. When Smith asked Nichols if it his department that was issuing these certificates, he lamely admitted it was. Then he tried to claim he wasn't issuing underage kids work certificates.

Smith and the other commissioners slammed Nichols for his act. They told him he was violating sanitation laws himself to allow health nuisances to exist. When he said other cities were as bad as Troy, they made his time on the stand miserable. (58)

Following Nichols, the commissioners and their attorney interviewed a local doctor who was working to fight tuberculosis. Nichols had claimed 161 people had died of TB in Troy the previous 10 months, and of these victims, 16 were collar makers. (Troy had several collar manufacturers whose products fed the garment trade.) This doctor said Troy had about the highest rate of TB in the state. But he seemed ignorant about some of the causes of transmission of the disease. Smith asked the doctor if he was aware that many collar makers took work home, and moistened the collars with their own spit to make them more pliable. The doctor said he was unaware of this. Of course, unsanitized collars on garments could readily spread TB germs.

Smith asked the doctor if it wasn't possible that the conditions of the workers was also leading to more of them falling victim to tuberculosis. In other words, he elaborated, wouldn't the workers working long hours in unsanitary facilities for low wages, and going home to work in overcrowded tenements to make a little more money be weakened and exposed to more germs and thus be more prone to suffer illnesses and spread more germs?

The doctor allowed that was possible, but in so many words he hadn't taken the conditions of many of the working poor into account. He admitted he thought many collar makers made $25 a week, and was legitimately startled when the commissioners said one of their female investigators had found out some collar makers were making as little as $2.50 a week. The commissioners and their attorney were trying to limit TB by ensuring sanitary work practices and reasonable pay for workers so they could live in healthier conditions. The good doctor, who sincerely wanted to help people, was still mired in a way of thinking that would not solve the problem he hoped to solve. Like many of his type, he was unaware how bad things were for many people, and he hadn't really viewed public health as being related to working conditions and wages. He admitted this to the commissioners, and they treated him with respect. (59)

The commissioners also looked at bakeries and confectionaries, where much of the public's food and treats were prepared.

The conditions discovered in many cellar bakeries in New York City might make most people swear off bread, cake, pie, and donuts. Investigators found people with communicable diseases coughing into and putting their hands into dough. They saw drain pipes dripping into dough. They found street drainage leaking into pails of pie filling. They found many poor people bought cheap bread sitting on the dirty steps and sidewalks in front of some of these bakeries. An investigator routinely found employees sleeping on the tables and machinery they used to make bread. She also said she saw a cat giving birth to kittens on a bread tray in a cellar bakery. (60)

It would have been no surprise if a female investigator assigned to scope out a New York City chocolate maker didn't touch sweets for the next decade after her gig there. She said the bathrooms were filthy, and people with filthy hands went back to work and dipped their germ-laden paws in the chocolate. She said buzzing flies also added germs to the product going out of the facility. (61)

In the transcripts of the Commission's first year on the job, Al Smith stuck out as the commissioner who seemed to ask the most down-to-earth and person-to-person questions of the victims and the toughest questions of the corporate offenders and the negligent labor and health officials. His line of questioning also displayed quite a bit of human understanding that the average politician of today lacks.

Smith, having been poor himself, understood why many of the poor would buy discount bread from dirtbag businessmen who employed tubercular employees, whose facilities were filthy, and who displayed their wares on filthy steps and sidewalks of buildings.

Smith also understood why many thousands of people, like his mother a generation earlier, did piecework at home. He said he tried to regulate the types of piecework people could do in their homes to promote good sanitation. Assembly of some consumer goods might not pose a health risk. Making clothes in a tenement full of germs without disinfecting those garments before sale was another matter. (62)

Al Smith did not demagogue the issue and call business owners as a class corrupt. He said many of the facilities he inspected were clean and the workers there made good money. Smith said he believed many legitimate businessmen would welcome fair regulations. Some, he thought, would do so out of a sense of personal integrity, others would do so out of a regard for their reputations, and still others would do so to remove some of their competitors whose blatantly substandard practices were undercutting their prices. If nothing else, he reasoned, reasonable health and safety laws would put pressure on the chiselers to put them out of business if they got arrested, shut down, fined, or jailed often enough.

Smith and the other members of the commission did not target factory owners by party either. However, Smith's work did lead to the exposure of one of his Progressive opponents in his own party.

Thomas Mott Osborne, a leader of the "Progressive Democrat" faction, was bitterly opposed to Smith's Tammany Hall Democrat organization. Osborne, like the top Progressive, one Woodrow Wilson, was good at spouting pious platitudes about reform and good government. However, like most political do-gooders, he could be a hypocrite. The Factory Investigating Commission found in Osborne's Auburn, New York factory "the vilest and most uncivilized conditions of labor in the state." **(63)**

Smith was not a Progressive, even though many historians place him in their ranks. Progressives tended to be from the genteel classes, they tended to be anti-black and anti-Catholic (and some tended to be agnostic), and they tended to have a "we know what is best for the masses" mentality. They looked down on and talked down to most people. They opposed the established machine politicians. This was because they wanted to establish their own machines to run things.

Smith was a machine politician himself, but a remarkably honest one. He favored some reforms the Progressives favored, but opposed Progressives on other issues. Many of the Progressives, their opponents charged, cared more about wildlife than they cared about people. **(64)**

Even though Smith opposed giving voting rights to women, he was likely the first prominent politician to pay any attention to female social workers. This wasn't due to any sympathy for Progressives on his part; it was due to his basic charity and his desire to help people help themselves.

As the Democrats' leader in the New York state assembly, Smith personally spoke for passage of a number of bills he and the commissioners favored that would reform fire, safety, and labor conditions in factories. Smith was no longer majority leader because the Republicans won the 1911 fall elections and were the majority party in the assembly. (The Democrats still held the majority in the state senate in 1912.)

Cannery operators opposed a law Smith and the commissioners proposed to the legislature in 1912 limiting workers to a six-day week. The cannery bosses managed to find some Protestant ministers to shill for the seven-day week. Smith, in refuting their argument for an exception to a six-day week, rose on the floor of the assembly, and made a very short speech. Smith said something like, "I have read carefully the commandment, 'Remember the Sabbath Day, to keep it holy,' but I am unable to find any language in it that says 'except for the canneries.' " He then sat down. There was a long and uncomfortable silence.

Smith had made his point. The state assemblymen, now mostly Republicans, passed a six-day work week bill that did not exempt cannery operators. **(65)**

During the 1912 session of the state legislature, Smith and Wagner got bills enacted mandating the following:

- Physical exams of children before issuing them work certificates.
- Registration of factories.
- Fire drills and automatic sprinklers.
- Fire prevention measures.
- Prohibition of eating in toxic substance areas.
- Adequate hot and cold washing facilities.
- Forbidding women working for four weeks after childbirth.
- The ability of the state labor commissioner to shut down unsanitary facilities.

Smith also pushed for a worker compensation law in 1912. One opponent of Smith's, a Republican assemblyman from a remote county in upstate New York, tried to needle Smith on his proposal. "Mr. Tammany Leader," he sneered, "what good is the Workmen's Compensation Act to the 350,000 men who are out of work in this state?" (Of course, the measure would greatly help the millions of men and women who were working, but the GOP gomer overlooked that.)

Smith ignored his critic and addressed the speaker of the assembly. "As I was walking down Park Row one morning," Smith said, "a friend of mine tapped me on the shoulder and said, 'Al, which would you rather be, a cellar full of stepladders, a basketful of doorknobs, or a piece of cracked ice?' and I replied I would rather be a fish because you can always break a pane of plate glass with a hammer."

Smith's needler said, "Mr. Speaker, I certainly do not get the point to the Tammany Leader's answer."

"You don't get the point to my answer?" Smith shouted. "There is just as much point to my answer as there is to your question. The bill is a meritorious measure, and its passage should not be impeded by unnecessary delay, due to the propounding of silly questions and foolish answers."

Smith did get most of the other assemblymen to support a resolution supporting a worker compensation amendment to the state constitution in that 1912 session. The worker compensation proposal would become part of the state constitution in 1913. **(66)**

In 1912, Smith and the other commissioners continued their checks on sanitation in places of business and on fire safety. They also widened the scope of their investigation on manufacturing in tenements and on women in factory trades. They concentrated on child labor, canneries, mercantile businesses, the tobacco industry, the printing industry, factories using hazardous procedures in the making of chemicals, foundries, and on some diseases and accident hazards in some of the more risky trades. They and their inspectors and investigators covered more than 1300 factories across the state that year.

Frances Perkins would recall she took Smith "to see the women, thousands of them, coming off the ten-hour night shift on the rope walks in Auburn. We made sure that Robert Wagner (the chairman of the commission) personally crawled through the tiny hole in the wall that gave egress to a steep iron ladder covered with ice and ending twelve feet from the ground, which was euphemistically labeled 'Fire Escape' in so many factories. We saw to it that the austere legislative members of the Commission got up at dawn and drove with us for an unannounced visit to a Cattaraugus County cannery and that they saw with their own eyes the little children, not adolescents, but five-, six- and seven-year-olds, snipping beans and shelling peas ... We made sure that they saw the machinery that would scalp a girl or cut off a man's arm." **(67)**

The commissioners also trained their sights on the cannery operators. Cannery owners had more power then than they do now because canneries were more important then to the well-being of the public than they are now. In that era, very few people had access to refrigeration. The iceman brought ice to families who could afford an ice box. Women did a lot of their own canning and sauerkraut making. Farmers and even many townspeople with just enough of a parcel to fatten a hog or a couple of sheep or goats would slaughter animals and smoke or salt the meat. Many many townspeople raised chickens in their yards for eggs and meat. Canneries provided – at reasonable prices – preserved vegetables, fruits, meats, and fish to the public.

Canning of produce could only take place in the short time fruits and vegetables were ripe and unspoiled after farm workers harvested them. Canning of meat and fish had to take place right after the animals were slaughtered and cooked or netted and cooked. So the canneries needed a lot of helpers working long hours for a short period of time to get the foods processed and canned. Canning involved preparing raw food, processing as needed (like, say, cooking beans and molasses and salt pork for pork and beans), then packing the food into cans, adding water or syrup or broth or gravy or brine or vegetable oil as needed, sealing the cans, cooking the cans in boiling water to kill germs, and then labeling and packing the cans.

Besides despising hypocritical Progressives, Smith tended to despise operators in the cannery trade. He noted: "Probably nowhere were there more shocking revelations than in the factory commission's investigation of the canneries, where women and small children worked as many as 16 hours a day. It is a surprising fact that the owners of the canneries of this state for a great many years wielded powerful political influence. Their establishments were entirely free from state regulations of any kind."

"At one of the sessions of the commission ... the superintendent of a well-known cannery denied the testimony brought out by counsel. The commission immediately confronted him with Mary Chamberlain, a young girl whom he recognized at once and admitted had been employed in his cannery. She was a student at Vassar College who had been sent to the cannery by the commission to work on the same basis and under the same conditions as the others. In the face of such overwhelming testimony he broke down and admitted the charges were true." **(68)**

Mary Chamberlain and the other investigators the commissioners used to get the skinny on the cannery industry in New York found a number of revolting and wrong conditions during 1912. She and the other investigators found large numbers of underage children (many 8 years old or younger) working at canneries, husking corn and snipping beans outside of the processing plants in sheds. These children worked 40 or more hours a week; most of them were less than 14 years old. An inspector who came at 5:30 a.m. to one cannery watched as the managers ran off about 200 underage children -- mostly Italian and Polish immigrants – into the nearby fields to avoid being caught having so many children working on the premises of the cannery. Ironically, the state attorney general in 1905 had allowed working children in cannery sheds as long as they were detached from the cannery's other buildings and had no machinery. Then the children, according to the attorney general, would be engaged in essentially unregulated agricultural work instead of somewhat regulated factory work.

The problem was that canneries were factories like other places. Certainly some food processing, like corn husking, pea shelling, bean snipping, and other preparation work took place in sheds outside ... which could be wet and cold on rainy days and during the harvest of fall crops. The grading, canning, cooking, and labeling of food took place in cannery buildings under factory conditions. The cannery machinery was noisy and often unsafe to workers. The sorting machinery ran so fast that many women suffered eye strain and nausea trying to ensure produce was going to the canning lines properly and there was no dirt or debris mixed in with the raw foods. Other hazards for female workers were handling cans, which often cut their hands, or doing extra processing jobs, like peeling scalding hot tomatoes. Some women lost fingers to cutting equipment. Other women and children could lose limbs or scalps to some cannery equipment.

Many women worked 80 or more hours a week during the canning season, which ran from June through October. Some days would be 16-hour days, and others would be short days because there was little produce coming from the fields or orchards those days. Women received as little as seven cents an hour to can food, and children received even less to prepare beans and shuck corn. Children of immigrants often worked 50 or more hours a week in canning sheds, more than the operators would work American children. Children often wrapped their hands in rags because shucking corn and snipping beans wore their flesh. The owners paid their mothers pittances, and the mothers beat their children to stay on the job because they needed the extra dollar or two a week a child could make at such a facility.

Many women and children fell asleep from exhaustion in the canneries. The commissioners decided the conditions they were working under ruined their health and rendered young women in particular unable to bear healthy children to build up the next generation of New Yorkers. **(69)**

An ethical cannery supervisor gave Smith and the other commissioners a way to stop the overwork. He said, "In my opinion, the only way that the State can govern canning evils is to make the factories adhere to the rule of supply and capacity. Many factories contract for an acreage which the capacity of the factory could not turn out, making extra work and harrowing conditions for their employees inevitable. This is the root of the evil, to my mind." **(70)**

Cannery operators had the habit of buying as much produce as possible to keep their canneries working at as close to full capacity as possible for as many hours of the day as they could. This made their operations more profitable.

The commissioners noted the following:

Certain canners contract year after year for an acreage which they must know from repeated experience foredooms their employees to work overtime and, if the crop is a good one, extreme overtime. 'The Lord ripens the crop' truly, but every canner determines, to a certain extent, how much of a crop the Lord is to ripen for him. The relation between the acreage contracted for and the capacity of the plant, more than any other thing, determines how much overtime will have to be worked. Some canners, when asked on what basis they determined the size of the acreage they would carry, frankly testified that they contracted for all the acreage they could get the farmers to grow. Canners usually sell from 50 to 100 percent of their goods the winter before they are packed.

The time records of canning factories show that the situation is not beyond the canners' control. A few factories have kept reasonable hours although others packing the same products have worked extremely long hours. Factories which keep more reasonable hours have done so year after year, and on the other hand those which require extreme hours persist in that habitual practice. Two companies operated 6 of the 13 factories which worked women over 18 hours on their longest day, and 5 of the 12 factories which worked women over 90 hours in their longest week. One of these companies,

which operated factories from one end of the cannery region to the other, worked women extreme hours in all of them, regardless of local conditions.

Canners stated that one cause of overtime work was the difficulty they experienced in getting sufficient help. In spite of this difficulty the wages of both men and women in the industry are very low. One factory pays women as little as seven cents an hour. The supply of labor depends upon the wages paid. In cannery towns as elsewhere a high wage attracts many workers, a low wage attracts few. The wages of women in the canning industry is lower than in other industries in which large numbers of women are employed. Until women are paid more than seven or ten cents an hour for seasonable and intermittent work, no canner can claim to have exhausted his labor supply.

The average weekly earnings of cannery women are $4.53. No woman could maintain a decent standard of living, even were she able to have steady work the year round on such a wage. Room and board may be secured in the cannery towns for $3 to $5 a week. One of the 'working investigators' secured them at $3 and reported that the food was so scant and poorly prepared that she could hardly live on it. But even if room and board are secured for that amount, it is obvious that there is little left for clothing, to say nothing of other necessary expenses. Clearly the industry may be considered parasitic in the sense that a woman working in it cannot make a living wage, but must find other means of support. True, many of the workers have fathers, husbands, and brothers able to help them, but the unmarried girl trying to make a living out of this work finds it hard. This fact does not pass unnoticed. The report follows of a young woman investigator who worked in the factories:

"There are several very 'fresh' bosses at the factory and the youth who keeps time and has charge of the sorting tables has a good deal of influence over the girls he puts at the tables. The situation is much like that in a department store where the floor-walker has a lot of girls under him receiving low wages and all more or less at his mercy. Only up here night work makes the situation even more dangerous."

A few days later she reported again:

"I find that the time-keeper who was objectionable to me the other day has been insulting several girls. He said to me, 'You can't make enough to pay (your bills), but I will give you a chance to make 2 or 3 dollars on the side any time. If you come up here to work at night, we can go for a stroll.' I feel that this ought to be repeated to you by me to show what the effect of an 8-cent wage is in the canning industry."

The time-keeper of this factory was the superintendent's cousin, using the low wage as an inducement to immorality.

Nor is this the only effect of the low wage. We have seen that in some cases children are routed out of bed at 4 A. M. and forced to work until late at night, not by the canners, but by their parents. The canners supply the materials to work on, the parents do the driving. Clearly this is not alone due to the hard-heartedness of the parent. It is the necessary and logical outcome of a wage of $4.53 a week for women workers, and a correspondingly low wage for men. Yet certain canners argue that children should be allowed to work because of the poverty of the parents.

The willingness of the women to work long hours is also the logical outcome of so low a wage. One woman in 90 hours' work was able to make only $6.75. A canner argues against restricting women's hours by saying, 'The longer the day the better, because then the more money can be made.' Of course the women want to work long hours. They must do so to make anywhere near a living wage.

That is not saying, however, that a restriction of hours will lower their wages. One working investigator reported :

"I believe that were the 54-hour law enforced here the wage would have to be increased from 8 cents because the girls would leave rather than work for 72 cents in a 9-hour day. I have talked with many girls about the new 54-hour law and they all say, 'Believe me, if I've got to work here for 72 cents a day I ain't staying long.' "

Were the hours restricted, the canners, to keep their help, would have to raise the wages.

The commissioners found the following of many cannery operators:

"(The operators) have made no intelligent effort to prevent women from working overtime by equalizing daily working hours for each employee, since one woman may be employed long hours on consecutive days while other women in the same plant work short hours or not at all."

"Although women are rarely compelled to work overtime, their compensation is, as a rule, so low that there is every incentive to work long hours."

"Long hours of labor are often not related to the alleged perishable nature of the crops, since such work as the labeling of cans is done at night."

They concluded:

"The state cannot regard with indifference any system permitting women to work excessively long hours of labor. Even if this extreme overtime lasts only a few weeks, we believe it to be injurious to the health of women engaged therein."

"Few people will claim that a woman can recover from the fatigue of working fifteen hours a day for several weeks in succession by thereafter working only five hours a day. Average hours do not measure the strain on the worker. We recommend therefore that during the canning season, between the 15th day of June and the 15th day of October, the hours of labor of women should be limited to 10 hours a day and 60 hours a week. (They then recommended a maximum 66-hour week during pea season because of the extreme perishability of the crop.)

"We believe that these limitations on the hours of labor of women in the canning industry are entirely fair to the industry and are calculated to protect the health and safety of the women employed therein. This restriction on the hours of labor of women will stimulate the canners to more scientific management so that the necessity for overtime may be largely eliminated."

"It has been urged that if the hours of labor were reduced the women employed in the canneries would be deprived of a livelihood. But we do not believe this to be so. No woman works 10, 12, 15, or 20 hours a day for pleasure. She does it for money. The lower the wages the greater is the incentive to long hours of labor. The very low wages paid in the canning industry largely explain the desire of the women to work long hours. It has been the experience all over the world that low wages and long hours go together hand in hand; that the lowest paid industries are the industries in which the longest hours of labor prevail. A reduction in the hours of labor in this industry will soon result in a compensating increase in the wages of the women workers, which we believe the industry can well afford.

The interests of the state demand that extreme overtime by women be prohibited and that women workers be surrounded with every protection and safeguard to enable them to perpetuate a race of strong, sturdy citizens. **(71)**

The commissioners in 1912 also checked on the bad effects of tenement work more closely. They noted businessmen who made women and children do piecework in tenements were in effect frustrating the intent of the hour restrictions on women workers and were also subverting the laws against child labor. They noted the owners were freeloading the cost of utilities and workspace from the tenement workers by making them work at home after normal hours, and they were subjecting the public to unsanitary conditions.

The commissioners found out that many of the people who made garments or intimate use items like sanitary belts (which many menstruating women and girls used with washable napkins or pads in the days before inexpensive disposable sanitary napkins) in tenements were suffering from tuberculosis, typhoid fever, diphtheria, scarlet fever, measles, or polio, or someone in their quarters was suffering from similar serious contagious ailments. A little more than a decade earlier, tenement-made uniforms had sickened a large number of servicemen during the Spanish-American War. Therefore, federal purchasers would not buy military gear that was not made in real factories with adequate sanitation. Lawmakers and local health officials and doctors knew allowing the making of clothing and food items in tenements was wrong. Yet they still allowed tenement manufacture of clothing and preparation of food, among other things.

A candy manufacturer testified to the commissioners he hired tenement workers to crack nuts for his firm. He admitted he didn't provide them with tools for doing the job sanitarily, and he did not deny some tenement food preparers were applying saliva and many other breathing and hand-transmitted germs to the food they were preparing. He also admitted he wasn't sure if his tenement workers were cracking nuts with their teeth.

The commissioners heard evidence of the relation of the early toil of children to dropping out of school and to teenage delinquency. They also heard evidence of more serious problems than mere delinquency. Miss Maud E. Miner, secretary of the Probation Association, told them:

"I have seen girls from these homes (homes where children had to perform many hours of take-home hand labor), who have been leading lives of immorality and lives of prostitution. I have known of girls who have told me that they have become tired of work long before it was time for them to go to work; in other words, before they could go out into the factory, simply because they had to work in the home day after day, night after night, and on Sunday." **(72)**

They also heard evidence that 20% of all the saleswomen in the cities (those females working in department stores and other stores) earned less than $5 per week, 51% of all the saleswomen earned less than $7 a week, and 62% of saleswomen earned less than $8 a week. They noted the following:

In New York City, where living expenses are highest, the proportion of those earning less than $7 was 44%. These wages, though higher than those paid in five and ten cent stores, are also clearly beneath the level of subsistence. Yet, in some way, the difference must be met between the earnings of the women and their expenses of living. For women who are wholly dependent on their own earnings the difference is made up in one of three ways. They may live in subsidized boarding houses or homes for working girls, where charity pays a part of their maintenance. Secondly they may live with such excessive economy and upon such short rations that health is shattered and future earning capacity is permanently undermined. Thus the worker herself is made to pay unfairly in strength and vitality, instead of receiving a living wage from the industry that employs her. Lastly, in some cases, the impossibility of living upon the pittance which they are paid undoubtedly leads some women to supplement these earnings by leading an immoral life. In this connection, as the Massachusetts Commission on Minimum Wage Board says significantly:

'It is remarkable that more saleswomen do not turn to vice. It is impossible to say how many do. No estimate whatever can be made of the extent to which the workers are subsidized because of illicit relations with one or two men. Only a few of the women had the appearance of prostitutes. Women who were making a brave fight against tremendous odds were many times more often in evidence.' **(73)**

Because of testimony such as this, and because of the investigative work done by garment union official Rose Schneiderman (the same Rose who had made the Triangle Fire speech cited earlier this chapter) and many others for the commissioners, Smith and his colleagues would recommend the banning of such practices as overworking women and children. They would recommend the immediate banning of tenement food processing and tenement manufacture of children's toys and children's garments. They agreed to allow some tenement work to continue for a few more years under much stricter health codes, with an eye to its eventual banning. **(74)**

In 1912, there was a massive split between William Howard Taft and Theodore Roosevelt in the Republican Party. Taft supporters controlled the party machinery even though Roosevelt won more primaries and convention delegates. The chicanery of the Taft people led Teddy Roosevelt to run as an independent; this split ensured Woodrow Wilson and the Democrats would win the White House, Congress, and control of many state legislatures in the November elections that year. New York was one of many states where the state trend mirrored the national trend. Because of the split of the GOP in New York, the Democrats won the vast majority of seats in the state legislature despite winning fewer votes than Taft's people and Roosevelt's people combined. When 1913 opened, Al Smith would become speaker of the New York state assembly. This gave him quite a bit more leverage to enact laws than he had earlier.

During the 1913 session of the state legislature, Smith and Wagner got bills enacted mandating the following:

- More fire prevention measures.
- Prohibition of children younger than 14 working in canneries or tenements.
- Regulation of manufacturing in tenements.
- Regulation of hours and working conditions of women in canneries.
- Labor camp housing standards.
- Physical exams of children in factories.
- Improvements in foundry work conditions.
- Improvement of lighting, ventilation, sanitation, washing and toilet facilities, and other conditions in factories.
- Restrictions on employing women and children in certain hazardous jobs.

Smith considered 1913 as a key year for the Factory Investigating Commission's work. He said he and the others pushed these bills hard, for to put them on the law books would be to complete most of the commission's work for factory safety.

But 1913 did not mark an end to the Commission's investigations. Smith and the other commissioners investigated wage levels in several trades in New York City. They also investigated fire hazards in department stores and other businesses open to the public. They also worked to draft and propose more labor and safety laws in New York.

Since Smith was the speaker of the New York state assembly in 1913, he said 1913 was a busy year for him. Besides being the main driver of the Factory Investigating Commission's proposed bills, Smith pushed through a number of other important measures. These included a law for a direct primary (having the voters choose parties' candidates during primary elections instead of letting bosses do it at party conventions), and the ratification of the Sixteenth Amendment, which called for the direct election of U.S. senators by the public, not the legislature.

Smith also played a leading role in impeaching and removing from office the state's governor, William Sulzer, on corruption grounds in 1913. Sulzer, also a Democrat, was a progressive and a self-professed do-gooder; he was the same man who William Williams exposed as a posturing liar earlier.

In that 1913 session, the legislature also passed a resolution calling for voting rights for women. Smith said he opposed female suffrage, and said he pushed for the resolution to grant women the right to vote only after the Democratic Party as a whole in New York came out in its favor. (New York's male voters gave females the right to vote in the 1917 fall elections.) Smith, as governor, would later crack, "I believe in equality, but I cannot nurse a baby."

Smith accused certain suffragettes of fraud in sending him a petition signed by people purported to be residents in his district to try to sway his vote. He noted, "I was greatly amused by the petition. Half of the people on it had no existence at all and some of the addresses indicated numbers that would require the city to build out into the East River." **(75)**

Women in politics are no more moral than men. White suffragettes appealed to racial bigotry against blacks to secure the vote for themselves. In our era, Hillary Clinton and Janet Reno have taken a back seat to almost nobody in terms of the willful abuse of government power.

The Republicans won a majority in the New York state assembly for 1914, so Smith reverted to being the minority leader in the assembly. The Democrats still held the majority in the New York state senate in 1914.

In 1914, Smith and the other commissioners completed their investigation of wages in the industries they were monitoring. They studied what wages were in relation to the cost of living. They studied the impact of starvation wages on the decision of females to commit acts of prostitution and males to commit other crimes. And they completed their work on drafting and proposing various labor and safety laws for New York for the legislature and governor to consider.

During the 1914 session of the state legislature, Smith and Wagner got bills enacted mandating the following:

- Improvement of lighting, ventilation, sanitation, washing and toilet facilities, and other conditions in department stores and other stores open to the public for the women who worked at these places.

- Dropping the number of hours per week bosses could work women in mercantile establishments to 54.

- Dropping the number of hours bosses could work children per week from 54 to 48 ... and also forbidding bosses from working children at night or for more than eight hours a day.

Democrat Martin Glynn served out the deposed Sulzer's term as governor. In the 1914 fall elections, Republican Charles Whitman, the district attorney whose deputies prosecuted the criminal case against Triangle Waist Company owners Isaac Harris and Max Blanck, beat Glynn and became governor in 1915. The Republicans also gained control of the state senate for 1915, and held their majority in the state assembly for 1915.

The Factory Investigating Commission members issued their fourth and final report in 1915. Most of the reforms Smith and the other commissioners pushed since 1911 would hold. After all, they were reasonable measures that a majority of Democrats and Republicans in the New York legislature had voted for over the previous few years. They also recommended minimum wage laws, but the legislature would not enact such laws in 1915.

Republicans and some Democrats would gut the worker compensation law in 1915 by taking away state supervision of worker injury settlements between companies and workers. Smith and Wagner fought this bill tooth and nail, but they failed. The change Smith and Wagner fought against allowed companies to drag out settlement cases using their obstructionist attorneys, often until after the injured workers died.

When Smith became governor of New York in 1919, he got the legislature that same year to repeal this unfair provision and restore state supervision of worker injury settlements. In doing so, he restored the guts to the worker compensation law. **(76)**

Smith had better success with a widowed mothers' pension bill in 1915. While he was assembly speaker in 1913, Smith started the groundwork to write into law a measure that would grant poorer widows pensions that would allow them to raise their children at home instead of surrendering them to state authorities to be placed in orphanages.

Smith saw the idea as the decent thing to do. Smith, whose own mother had been a widow with children, believed a decent mother was a much better person to take care of her own children than state employees or charity workers. Smith also argued the pension made sense financially. After all, the support of children taken from a destitute mother had to be paid for by state taxpayers or donors to charity anyway. Smith also knew undisciplined children or resentful children could turn into criminals who would victimize others and cost the taxpayers money in court and incarceration costs.

The poor widow's pension idea faced the opposition of those who objected to giving tax money to near-destitute women, and also faced the opposition of many charitable organizations whose people ran orphanages. So Smith took part in naming a commission to study the matter, and naturally the commissioners saw things his way. On their recommendations, Smith would push a child welfare bill providing poorer widows with small pensions in 1914. The bill passed the state assembly but failed in the state senate.

The supporters of the poor widows' pension idea got another child welfare measure through the state senate in 1915, but this time the state assemblymen balked at passing the bill. Smith, who was more in the habit of sarcasm than exhortation as a speaker, said he tried to take a more personal tone for his support of the bill. Excerpts of Smith's speech to his colleagues for the Widowed Mothers' Pension bill follow:

"What happens when death takes from the family the provider? The widowed mother goes to the police court or to the charity organization and her children are committed to an institution, and from the moment the judge signs the commitment, the people of ... New York are bound to their support."

"The mother stands in the police court. She witnesses the separation of herself and her children. They are torn away from her and given to the custody of an institution, and nothing is left for her to do but to go out into the world and make her own living. What must be her feelings? What must be her idea of the state's policy when she sees these children separated from her by due process of law, particularly when she must remember that for every one of them she went down

into the valley of death that a new pair of eyes might look out upon the world? What can be the feelings in the hearts of the children themselves separated from their mother by what they must learn in after years was due process of law?"

"We have been in a great hurry to legislate for the interests. We have been in a great hurry to conserve that which means to the state dollars and cents. We have been slow to legislate along the direction that means thanksgiving to the poorest man recorded in history -- to Him who was born in the stable at Bethlehem."

"We have been especially blessed by Divine Providence in this state .... by the adoption of this policy we are sending up to Him a prayer of thanksgiving for the innumerable blessings that He has showered upon us, particularly in the light of the words of the Savior Himself, who said: 'Suffer little children to come unto Me, and forbid them not, for of such is the kingdom of Heaven.' "

Smith, in discussing the poor widow's pension and child welfare legislation he pushed as an assemblyman and enforced as a governor, credited several women with the concepts instead of himself. His attitude was he was happy to be in a position to help the bills along. **(77)**

In 1915, the state's politicians held a constitutional convention to consider amending the New York state constitution. At this gathering, Smith tried to convince the other delegates to enact a law establishing a minimum wage board whose members could fix minimum wages for women and children. Smith argued men had unions to fight for them, but most women and children who worked were not in union-organized jobs and needed this extra protection. He argued his point in the following speech:

"What is the effect of it {a minimum wage law) upon the employer? The effect is that he gets better work... A railroad costs the same per mile to complete whether you pay a man two cents a day or two dollars a day, and it is predicated on the reasonable and unquestionable theory that you get what you pay for; no more and no less."

"There is another side to this, too, which deserves something of our consideration. We have spoken of what must be the natural effect upon health. The girl who is insufficiently paid and improperly clothed will in time become a charge upon the state. About that there can be no question, and if she is to be the mother of future citizens, look straight and deep down into your heart for a moment, and see what we are looking forward to if the state refuses to bring them up in health and decent comfort."

"There is another side worthy of consideration, I will quote from a part of the testimony of one of the investigators (of the Factory Investigating Commission). There is the moral side. It is an awful weight! It is an awful temptation!"

"One of the investigators went out among the employees of the mercantile establishments and in the course of her testimony she said: "I do not think the problem ever presents itself to a girl, 'Shall I sell myself in order to make more than six dollars a week?' But the absence of amusement, the barrenness and the ugliness of life, the whole thing combined with unemployment, does tend powerfully in that direction. Low wages put too severe strain on the moral strength of the individual."

Smith's argument didn't carry enough of the other delegates. His proposal failed. Years later, of course, the legislatures of New York and other states would enact such legislation for all workers. **(78)**

Smith's legislature career ended at the end of 1915, because he did not run for re-election to the assembly. Instead he won election as sheriff of New York County (Manhattan) for 1916 and 1917, and he won election as president of the New York City Board of Aldermen for 1918. He ran successfully for the New York governor's office in 1918. He served a term in 1919 and 1920, lost in the national Republican landslide of 1920, then won re-election as governor three more times and served as governor from 1923 through 1928. Smith would make Frances Perkins a member of the state Industrial Commission when he was governor. Smith would run for president of the United States, but lose to Herbert Hoover in the 1928 election, and then get stabbed in the back (figuratively) by Franklin Delano Roosevelt in the 1932 Democrat presidential nomination struggle.

For the record, while Al Smith was pushing real reforms, FDR was a young Democrat lawmaker who was in the Progressive camp. FDR gravy-trained on cousin Theodore's name, lived well on money that derived from his grandfather Warren Delano selling opium to the Chinese, and married his own cousin Eleanor. FDR posed as an opponent of Tammany Hall, like Thomas Mott Osborne, his supposed mentor. Despite being Democrats, FDR and "Progressives" like him opposed a lot of what Al Smith was trying to do. FDR and Woodrow Wilson and men of their ilk essentially saw Americans as subjects to be herded, not citizens to be served. Years later, FDR would take credit for many of Al Smith's initiatives and incorporate them into the New Deal. FDR did introduce one innovation into national politics – he was the first national politician to drastically raise spending, and then buy people's votes with their own tax money.

Smith was not a political theorist, but a practical man. He was willing to examine the various sides of an issue, and once he understood it himself, could explain it to the public in plain language as well as anyone since Abraham Lincoln. For example, is explanation of the then-new idea of worker compensation — which he gave in a speech in 1915 -- is still to the point today. He said, "Workmen's compensation is an indirect tax upon the industry of the state for the purpose of relieving the shoulders of all the people from carrying the burden of the men injured or destroyed in the upbuilding of an industry." **(79)**

In his autobiography, Smith did not take much credit for his work on behalf of workers. He gave credit to the public for demanding reform in the wake of the Triangle Fire. He credited the investigators and social workers who exposed the terrible conditions many people labored under. Naturally Smith credited Tammany Hall leaders and Robert Wagner for their roles in getting the proposals of the Factory Investigating Commission into law. Smith was not too partisan to credit Edward Merritt, the Republican state assembly speaker in 1912. Merritt could have wrecked many of the proposals for reform, and a number of Republicans in business wanted him to do so. But Smith credited Merritt for assisting in the passage of many of the reforms the Commission members proposed.

Frances Perkins again had the last word on the issue and it was this:

"Al Smith had never heard the words 'New Deal', he was governor of the State of New York, he had been in the legislature before. As a member of the legislature he was the majority leader. He could have appointed anybody he wanted to the factory investigating commission, but he had himself appointed to the factory investigating commission so that he could see with his own eyes what was going on. As he said, "This is too raw, we can't have any mistakes here, we can't make any blunders and I am going to sit there myself, I am not going to turn this over to somebody else." **(80)**

Miss Perkins also said in so many words the good work of the New Deal (and there was a lot of good as well as a lot of bad that came from FDR's administrations) didn't begin with FDR, but with Al Smith. She said, "We had in the election of Franklin Roosevelt the beginning of what was come to be called a New Deal for the United States.

"But it was based really upon the experiences that we had had in New York State and upon the sacrifices of those who, we faithfully remember with affection and respect, died in that terrible fire on March 25, 1911. They did not die in vain and we will never forget them." **(81)**

CONCLUSION

The story of the *Titanic* investigation belongs in this book about immigration for two reasons. The first was that many hundreds of poor immigrants died in the disaster, thanks to British incompetence and condescension. Captain Rostron and the people aboard the *Carpathia* and American immigration officials and some immigrant aid societies and some private charities were about the only people who lent them a hand.

The second reason was the object lesson that William Alden Smith could teach today's politicians and the public in his handling of the investigation of the tragedy. He acted boldly, decisively, imaginatively, diligently, accurately, and justly. We need to know such work is possible if we elect good men and women to office and demand excellence from them.

Will there ever be another investigation so quick and so potent as the one William Alden Smith led on the *Titanic* disaster? How many senators are energetic enough to raid foreign ships and lay down the law to powerful foreigners? Smith acted like he was the people's servant and protector, not big business' or big government's servant and mouthpiece. By comparison, too many senators today (and presidents like the Bushes and the Clinton couple and Obama too) vie to see how much money they can get from multinational corporations.

The story of the Triangle Fire and the New York Factory Investigating Commission is in here for a similar reason. It took the gruesome deaths of scores of immigrant girls in plain view of thousands of people to light a fire under the politicians' behinds to reform the unjust laws that allowed corporate pirates like Isaac Harris and Max Blanck to operate the way they did. But the end result was a real tribute to the deaths of these girls – that their deaths led to reasonable conditions in the workplaces of New York and eventually America as a whole.

Al Smith's work and the work of the other Factory Investigating Commission members was not a quick hitter like the work of William Alden Smith. Theirs was a painstaking years-long effort on a series of labor issues. But Al Smith's thought process was the same: Let's reform the laws to protect people – to reflect the Ten Commandments and the Golden Rule instead of social Darwinism and the law of the jungle.

Al Smith and his colleagues recommended a number of measures aimed at improving fire safety, ventilation, sanitation, prevention of accidents, and prevention of exposure to chemical and biological hazards. They also recommended reforms of the child labor laws and women's labor laws. Many of these recommendations became law. The work Smith and the other heavyweights of the commission did helped make New York's worker safety laws a model for the nation and led to further reforms across America. Al Smith's work is part of the foundation virtually every worker safety law in this country is built on.

Unlike many of their colleagues, William Alden Smith and Al Smith were true to their wives and were real fathers to their children. They never used the excuse "many great leaders were lechers," because many many poor leaders (like many in government today) are also lechers. They were men of great political integrity because they were men of great personal integrity.

William Alden Smith's work and Alfred E. Smith's work are marks any politician of good will can aspire to, and are standards we the people should consider when we elect people to office. Are they honest? Energetic? Courageous? Hard-working? God-fearing? Do they have good judgment? Can they lead others? Can they handle success and failure properly? Are they intelligent in affairs other than manipulating the law and other people for their own gain and their backers' gain? Are they willing to act in the best interests of the American people? We the people need leaders who can pass the Smith test.

END NOTES

1. Statistics come from the U.S. Senate Inquiry (Causes of the Sinking of the *Titanic*), Wyn Craig Wade's book The Titanic: End of A Dream (pages 22-24, 63) and Walter Lord's book A Night to Remember (page 176).

2. The source for J.P. Morgan's absence from the cruise of the *Titanic* is The Titanic: End of A Dream (pages 12-16, 329).

3. Info on Smith's meeting with Taft and the intercepts comes from The Titanic: End of A Dream (pages 43-44, 99-100).

4. Info on Smith's boarding of the *Titanic* is in The Titanic: End of A Dream (pages 50-51, 101-103).

5. Information on immigration officials' treatment of *Titanic's* steerage passengers comes from The Titanic: End of A Dream (pages 50, 104), and from the U.S. Citizenship and Immigration Services website article "This Month in Immigration History: April 1912." The professionals of St. Vincent's Hospital treated victims of the Triangle Fire and the 9/11 attack as well.

6. Statistics on those saved comes from A Night to Remember (page 104) and the report of the U.S. Senate Inquiry. Ismay's testimony comes from the transcript of the U.S. Senate Inquiry. Independent researchers from the Titanic Inquiry Project (www.titanicinquiry.org) made the

transcript of the testimony of those who William Alden Smith and the other senators questioned available electronically.

7. Captain Rostron's testimony comes from the transcript of the U.S. Senate Inquiry. Information on Captain Rostron's testimony comes from The Titanic: End of A Dream (pages 113-119).

8. Lightoller's testimony comes from the transcript of the U.S. Senate Inquiry. Information on Lightoller's testimony, and Smith's attacks on his cover-up, and Smith's subpoenas against the British because of their evasions, lying, and desires to flee America come from The Titanic: End of A Dream (pages 121-137, 141-142) and A Night to Remember (page 114).

9. Cottam's and Bride's testimony comes from the transcript of the U.S. Senate Inquiry. Information on Bride's testimony comes from The Titanic: End of A Dream (pages 137-142).

10. Information on these issues comes from The Titanic: End of A Dream (pages 145, 153).

11. Fleet's testimony comes from the transcript of the U.S. Senate Inquiry. Information on Boxhall's and Fleet's testimony comes from The Titanic: End of A Dream (pages 158-159, 162-167).

12. Lowe's testimony comes from the transcript of the U.S. Senate Inquiry. Information on Lowe's testimony comes from The Titanic: End of A Dream (pages 181, 195-216).

13. Information on the speed of the *Titanic* comes from Pitman's testimony and from fireman Frederick Barrett's testimony (from the transcript of the U.S. Senate Inquiry) and from The Titanic: End of A Dream (page 278).

14. Perkis' testimony comes from the transcript of the U.S. Senate Inquiry. Info on his testimony comes from The Titanic: End of A Dream (page 236).

Hichens', Pitman's, and Lowe's testimony comes from the transcript of the U.S. Senate Inquiry. Information on the actions of Margaret Brown and Mrs. Astor, and the testimony and actions of Pitman and Lowe comes from The Titanic: End of A Dream (pages 232-241) and A Night to Remember (pages 123-124, 128-130). Hichens would attempt murder and suicide two decades later over a debt he owed, and would fail in both attempts.

Daisy Minahan's affidavit in the U.S. Senate Inquiry records lists her charges against Lowe.

The "unsinkable" Margaret Brown's maiden name was Tobin.

15. Information about the *Californian* comes from The Titanic: End of A Dream (pages 243-255).

16. Marconi's testimony comes from the transcript of the U.S. Senate Inquiry. Information about Marconi and his wireless operators comes from The Titanic: End of A Dream (pages 262-267).

17. Information on Ismay comes from The Titanic: End of A Dream (pages 270-272).

18. Information on the plight of steerage passengers and the devotion to God and service to fellow human beings of

Father Byles comes from The Titanic: End of A Dream (pages 272-276), A Night to Remember (pages 64-68, 104-107), the 4/22/1912 New York Telegram (courtesy of the www.fatherbyles.com website, and the Encyclopedia Titanica website.

19. Information on Smith's findings, proposals, and speech comes from The Titanic: End of A Dream (pages 283-293).

20. Information on Smith's proposals comes from The Titanic: End of A Dream (pages 300-306). Other info comes from the acts themselves, to include actions such as the Radio Act of 1912 (aka 37 Statutes at Large 302-308), the Joint Resolution for the maritime conference (6/28/1912) aka 37 Statutes at Large 637-638), the Coast Guard Act (aka 38 Statutes at Large 800-802), and the Seamen's Act of 1915 (aka 38 Statutes at Large 1164-1185). The Seamen's Act was enacted 3/4/1915.

21. Information on British reaction to Smith comes from The Titanic: End of A Dream (pages 297, 310).

22. Other facts about the life of William Alden Smith come from The Titanic: End of A Dream (pages 77-87, 150-152, 169).

23. Quitting time was 4:45 p.m on Saturdays, according to trial testimony. The owners broke many labor laws, and were considered not to be above having the time clock turned back to get some extra time out of the girls and young women who worked for them. However, independent time records indicate the fire started before 4:45 p.m., regardless of what the Triangle time clock read. Cheating girls out of time, as reprehensible as it was, wasn't the cause of their deaths, because the fire started while they were still supposed to be on the job by even a legitimate time reading. The truth about the factory's other hazardous conditions would prove to be bad enough.

24. The explanation of how the fire spread comes from an article by Tom Brooks (a former official of the International Ladies' Garment Workers Union) for American Heritage, August 1957, and from an article by John Hoenig in the April/May 2005 History Magazine.

25. These quotes come from a 3/26/1911 New York Times article titled "141 Men and Girls Die in Waist Factory Fire..."

26. The account of the policeman hero comes from the August 1957 American Heritage article.

27. The account of the fire escape failure comes from the August 1957 American Heritage article and the April/May 2005 History Magazine article.

28. United Press released Shepherd's account nationwide; it first made the papers on March 27, 1911. He reportedly dictated it by phone to another writer, who transcribed it.

29. The story confirming Shepherd's tragic account and adding the dramatic account of the girl who singularly drew the attention and the pity of the onlookers was in the 3/26/1911 Chicago Sunday Tribune.

30. Shepherd's confirmation of the Chicago Tribune reporter's heartrending account was in the 3/26/1911 New York World.

According to issues of the New York Times, which historians of Cornell University's Kheel Center cited in their naming of the dead, a girl named Bertha Wondross suffered a broken leg and internal injuries; she was taken to St. Vincent's Hospital, where she died that evening. Another girl, Sally Weintraub, 17, was also listed as a fire victim, but nothing else about her injuries or demise was listed.

Tom Brooks said "Sallie Weintraub" was the girl in question. Shepherd didn't name the girl who caught the pity and the imagination of so many. The survivors, witnesses, and reporters didn't agree on some key details, besides the name of the girl whose dramatic courage and ultimate fall to her doom captured the emotions of so many. There is a very simple explanation for this. A tragedy like a fire scrambles the perceptions of those involved. This author has covered fires and crimes as a reporter. Try to keep your cool in a similar situation of stress, where you could lose your own life, or where you could watch people dying horribly before your eyes.

31. The accounts of the girl who died before ambulance men could get her to a hospital, the dismembered girl, the girl who hung above the street before falling to her death, and the women who hit the fire net and killed the women who the firemen saved came from a 3/26/1911 New York Times article titled "141 Men and Girls Die in Waist Factory Fire..." Leon Stein's book The Triangle Fire (page 54) contained a slightly different version of the story of the girl on the wire.

The accounts of the tailor, the girl found alive who died at the scene, the garment shop owner, the seamstress who escaped down the elevator cable, and the male sewing machine operator who did so came from a 3/26/1911 New York Times article titled "Stories of Survivors."

The account of the man found under the elevator came from a 3/26/1911 New York Times article titled "Lived Amid Flames, But Nearly Drowns."

32. The account of hero Thomas Horton comes from the August 1957 American Heritage article.

33. The account of the law students' heroism and the ratlike behavior of the men on the roof of the Asch Building comes from the 3/26/1911 Chicago Sunday Tribune.

34. Frances Perkins' account comes from a lecture she gave at Cornell University 9/30/1964. The excerpt from her lecture is courtesy of the Kheel Center at Cornell University.

35. The "timetable" of the fire comes from a 3/26/1911 New York Times article titled "141 Men and Girls Die in Waist Factory Fire ..." and from the chronology on the University of Missouri Kansas City "Famous Trials" website.

36. The accounts of the firemen in the building rescuing girls and finding the dead comes from the August 1957 American Heritage article and from Shepherd's article in the 3/26/1911 New York World.

37. There is a dispute of how many victims died. The official death toll is 146, according to New York City authorities and garment union officials. Other sources say 148 died, 141 at the scene, and 7 in hospitals. The Kheel Center at Cornell University maintains a list based on New York Times articles and the work of Leon Stein, an author and expert on the Triangle Fire, listing 145 victims who died at the scene and

another 11 who died in hospitals from their injuries. This list contains names, ages, and some marital status and ethnic background and other personal data.

38. Information on the Asch Building's unsafeness comes from the 3/26/1911 New York Times article titled "141 Men and Girls Die in Waist Factory Fire..." An account of the building's design flaws and the owner's finagling to get the unsafe building permitted comes from a New York City government website for the Landmarks Preservation Commission. It gave the history of the Asch Building, which is now the Brown Building and is still in use as an academic building for New York University. Other information on the illegal design flaws of the Asch Building comes from Leon Stein's book The Triangle Fire (page 23).

39. Information on the post-fire meeting comes from a 3/28/1911 New York Times article.

40. Information on Rose Schneiderman's speech comes from Leon Stein's book Out of the Sweatshop (pages 196-197).

41. Martha Bensley Bruere, writing for the May 1911 issue of Life and Labor, reported Harris and Blanck's offer, the move of the Triangle operation, and the blocking of the fire escape. Leon Stein excerpted her article in his book Out of the Sweatshop (pages 194-195).

42. Information on the grand jury, the Italian consul, and the coroner's jury in the Triangle Waist Company case comes from 4/22/1911 and 4/29/1911 articles in The Outlook.

43. Harris' claims of employee theft and his admissions about searching females was in the 12/23/1911 New York Times.

44. Background on Al Smith comes from Up To Now (Smith's autobiography), Emily Smith Warner's book The Happy Warrior: A Biography of My Father, Henry Moskowitz and Norman Hapgood's book Up From the City Streets, Frank Graham's book Al Smith, American, and Richard O'Connor's book The First Hurrah: A Biography of Alfred E. Smith.

45. Miss Perkins' comments about Al Smith's helping the families of the victims comes from the lecture she gave at Cornell University 9/30/1964.

46. Smith's comments come from his book Up To Now (pages 90-92).

47. Miss Perkins' comments about Al Smith's advice on how to handle the investigations comes from the lecture she gave at Cornell University 9/30/1964.

48. Smith's comments come from his book Up To Now (pages 90-92).

49. Smith's comments come from his book Up To Now (pages 92-94).

50. Historians of Cornell University's Kheel Center researched witnesses by checking the trial transcripts. (Sadly, according to John Hoenig, New York City bureaucrats "lost" the public record set, and then the goofs of a law library lost one of the three volumes of the transcripts Steuer or one of his people donated to them. Or maybe a "researcher" stole it.) Leon Stein also named witnesses through his own

research. Harris' claims of employee theft and his admissions about searching females was in the 12/23/1911 New York Times. The 12/28/1911 New York Times contained information on defense witnesses' contradictions. The trial transcript was courtesy of the Kheel Center at Cornell University. Other info on the trial came from Doug Lindner's article on the University of Missouri Kansas City "Famous Trials" website. David Von Drehle, who wrote Triangle: The Fire that Changed America, provided background on Judge Crain for the Cornell website.

Steuer explained to a bar association meeting in Missouri in 1928 that he got jurors to forget one girl's testimony. He said, "What can you do when the jury is weeping, and the little girl witness is weeping too? (Laughter by the lawyers in attendance.) Do not attack the witness. Suavely, politely, genially, toy with the story."

He then said how he painstakingly cross-examined Kate Alterman until she stopped crying, and then had her repeat everything she told the prosecutor. He said he had her do it again. He pointed out to the lawyers the girl repeated her story almost verbatim two more times. By now, the jurors, no longer in the first state of shock, had recovered their own composure, he said. It also made it possible for him to argue the girl wasn't really telling the truth but had simply been coached by the prosecutor to memorize a story and repeat it by memory.

No doubt many of these attendees would have the required lack of conscience to foreclose on widows and orphans during the Great Depression. Law school text books, websites, and New York Times reporters and editors who favor criminals still recount Steuer's despicable act as a work of legal genius, and discuss using such an approach when cross-examining children and the mildly retarded who are crime victims also.

Information on Max Steuer's talk comes from Leon Stein's book Out of the Sweatshop (pages 197-198). A reporter's story about defending the rapists of a retarded girl referred to Steuer's crooked ploy as legal brilliance, and ran in the New York Times 12/9/1992.

51. The names and addresses of the jurors appeared in the 12/28/1911 New York Times. The names of the jurors were Leo Abrahams, Anton Scheuerman, Harry Roder, Charles Vetter, Abraham Wechsler, William Ryan, Joseph Jacobson, William Akerstrom, Arlington Boyce, Victor Steinman, Huerston Hiers, and Morris Baum, according to the Times. An article in the 1/6/1912 Literary Digest quoted a reporter in the New York Evening Mail who named Steinman as the goofball blabbermouth juror.)

52. Information about the protection given Harris and Blanck and the jurors and the outbursts of the victims' loved ones comes from the 12/28/1911 New York Times, and from Douglas Linder's article on the UMKC "Famous Trials" website.

53. Information on the background and crimes of Harris and Blanck comes from the April/May 2005 History Magazine article, from the UMKC "Famous Trials" website, and from the New York City government website for the Landmarks Preservation Commission on the Asch Building. Further info comes from an article in the May 1911 issue of Life and Labor by Martha Bensley Bruere that was in Out of the Sweatshop (pages 194-195). More info on Steuer comes from a 9/2/1940 Time article.

54. The record of the inspector's testimony is the Preliminary Report of the Factory Investigating Commission 1912 (3/1/1912) (pages 780-794, Volume 2). The source for Smith's comments about unvented fires is the same report (pages 1208-1210, Volume 3)

55. The record of the testimony of the boy, the girl, and owner Rubenstein is the Preliminary Report of the Factory Investigating Commission 1912 (3/1/1912) (pages 1048-1065, Volume 3).

56. The record of the testimony of inspector Wilbur is the Preliminary Report of the Factory Investigating Commission 1912 (3/1/1912) (pages 1144-1160, Volume 3).

57. The record of the testimony of the knotheaded city official is the Preliminary Report of the Factory Investigating Commission 1912 (3/1/1912) (pages 1215-1217, Volume 3).

58. The record of the testimony of Calvin Nichols is the Preliminary Report of the Factory Investigating Commission 1912 (3/1/1912) (pages 1403-1424, Volume 3).

59. The record of the testimony of the doctor is the Preliminary Report of the Factory Investigating Commission 1912 (3/1/1912) (pages 1424-1433, Volume 3).

60. The record of the testimony of Frances Perkins (who also testified about inspections she made before the Factory Investigation Commission started their work) is the Preliminary Report of the Factory Investigating Commission 1912 (3/1/1912) (pages 309-333, Volume 2).

61. The record of the testimony of the female inspector at the chocolate factory is the Preliminary Report of the Factory Investigating Commission 1912 (3/1/1912) (pages 722-728, Volume 2).

62. Smith's comments on how far to go with regulating home work come from his book Up To Now (pages 94-95).

63. Information on Osborne comes from Oscar Handlin's book Al Smith and His America (page 59) and from Richard O'Connor's book The First Hurrah: A Biography of Alfred E. Smith (pages 71-72).

Osborne has been cited as a mentor to Franklin Delano Roosevelt. Osborne would eventually run Ossining State Prison ("Sing Sing") as its warden. His overtly friendly approach to convicts would get him set up on sodomy charges. All charges against him would eventually be dismissed.

64. When a wealthy citizens' group who wanted Smith to kill a park project to keep the public (these people termed them "the rabble" when they were talking to Smith) away from their exclusive retreats, he roared at them, "I'm the rabble!"

65. The source of Al Smith's barb about canneries comes from Up To Now (page 96) and from Emily Smith Warner's book The Happy Warrior (page 67).

66. A source for Smith's crackback on the opponent of the worker compensation law he was pushing is Richard O'Connor's book The First Hurrah: A Biography of Alfred E. Smith (pages 72-73). Information on his work for worker compensation comes from Up to Now (page 122).

67. A source for Frances Perkins' remarks was Richard O'Connor's book The First Hurrah (page 71).

68. Smith's anecdote about Mary Chamberlain comes from Up To Now (pages 95-96).

69. Background information on the cannery industry comes from the Second Report of the Factory Investigating Commission 1913 (1/15/1913) (pages 124-175).

70. The cannery supervisor's remarks come from the Second Report of the Factory Investigating Commission 1913 (1/15/1913) (page 163).

71. The commissioners' findings, and the anecdotes about exploited workers and sexual abuse of pretty young women come from the Second Report of the Factory Investigating Commission 1913 (1/15/1913) (pages 163-175).

72. Miss Miner's remarks come from the Second Report of the Factory Investigating Commission 1913 (1/15/1913) (page 107).

73. The data on salesgirls comes from the Second Report of the Factory Investigating Commission 1913 (1/15/1913) (page 283).

74. The commissioners' findings on tenement worker abuses are in the Second Report of the Factory Investigating Commission 1913 (1/15/1913) (pages 90-123).

75. Smith's humorous remarks about the equality of the sexes and his slam of the corrupt feminists come from Let's Look at the Record (quote 31) and from Up To Now (page 126).

76. Information on Smith's fight for worker compensation comes from Up To Now (pages 134-135), Smith's book The Citizen and His Government (pages 146-148 and 158-161), and Moskowitz and Hapgood's book Up from the City Streets (pages 83-87).

77. Smith's speech excerpts and his thoughts on the Widowed Mothers' Pension law come from Up To Now (pages 127-130, and Progressive Democracy (pages 159-161). The latter book was a collection of Smith's speeches and state papers chosen by Henry and Belle Moskowitz. Belle was an aide to Smith; her husband Henry was also a friend of Smith.

78. Smith's speech excerpts and his thoughts on minimum wage legislation come from Up To Now (pages 142-143), and Progressive Democracy (pages 165-168).

79. Smith's speech excerpt come from Progressive Democracy (page 163).

80. Miss Perkins' comments about Al Smith's role in the Factory Investigating Commission comes from the lecture she gave at Cornell University 9/30/1964.

81. Miss Perkins' comments on the New Deal and the Triangle Fire were at a memorial on the 50th anniversary of the tragedy in 1961. Excerpts of her comments come from Leon Stein's book Out of the Sweatshop (pages 200-201).

Finally, some thanks are in order. I am not a *Titanic* buff, but Wyn Craig Wade's book The Titanic: End of A Dream was a compelling book on the disaster and especially on the investigation. Wade rightly made William Alden Smith the protagonist of the book. Thanks to Wade, I learned a great deal about Smith, and about the right way to conduct an investigation. Smith was the kind of senator We The People need to put into office more often. In so doing, we will have to push aside the corporate candidates and the pressure group candidates and the vanity candidates and the party hacks.

Likewise, the people of the Titanic Inquiry Project helped make my research easier by providing the transcripts of William Alden Smith's inquiry electronically. We benefit from the work of people who, out of personal interest in an event or period of history, dedicate their efforts to making as much information as possible accessible to the public.

A special thanks goes out to the historians and staffers of the Kheel Center at Cornell University in Ithaca, New York. They hold many of the records of the Triangle Fire and of the New York State Factory Investigating Commission. They also maintain a sad but extremely informative website on the Triangle Fire. Cornell University's historians also maintain a great website on the work of the New York State Factory Investigating Commission. I used the Kheel Center's archives and the websites for information in preparing this chapter. Patrizia Sione of the Kheel Center, herself an immigrant from Italy, in particular helped produce the Triangle Fire website and assisted me in my research at Cornell. Thanks also goes out to the staffers of the Museum of the City of New York for their help in my research on Al Smith.

AMERICA AND IMMIGRATION
IN THE WORLD WAR ONE ERA

World War One and the fallout from that incredible tragedy would drastically change immigration and how America's leaders would regulate it. America's people went through some major and sometimes disturbing changes themselves during the World War One era.

This chapter covers immigration to America during World War One. It also covers the Red Scare, Prohibition, women's suffrage, and the race riots and violent bigotry of the nation in these years. Woodrow

Wilson, the president from early 1913 through early 1921, deserves much of the blame for the injustices and tragedies of this time. This chapter covers these facets of American history in those troubled years to give you an idea of what America was like back then, and why the people of our nation would undergo the suffering and turmoil they endured. It will also give you an idea of why America's leaders regulated immigration the way they did in during this time.

IMMIGRATION AND ELLIS ISLAND DURING WILSON'S FIRST TERM

Woodrow Wilson became president on a fluke in the 1912 election, much like Bill Clinton did in the 1992 election. The Republican Party leaders cheated themselves out of a united party when party wheelhorses who supported William Taft cheated Theodore Roosevelt out of the Republican nomination even though the dynamic Teddy was much more of a vote-getter in the primary elections than the plodding Taft. Roosevelt ran as a third-party candidate and garnered 28% of the vote. Taft got only 23% of the vote. Socialist Eugene Debs got 6% of the vote, and a Prohibition candidate got 1% of the vote. Wilson only got 42% of the vote, but the split in the Republican Party, whose two candidates combined won a majority of the popular vote, was enough to guarantee Democrat Wilson an Electoral College victory.

Woodrow Wilson would be the second president in the 20th Century to use the power of the presidency enthusiastically. Wilson, unlike Theodore Roosevelt – who had been a rancher, the police commissioner of New York City, the assistant Navy secretary, an Army officer, and the governor of New York before becoming vice-president and then president – was an educator. Wilson held a law degree, but could not make it as a lawyer and left the profession after a year. Wilson got a doctor's degree in "political science," then became a professor, then a college president, and then the governor of New Jersey for two years before he became president.

Wilson was a fuzzy idealist except for when it came to his own career moves. Like many leftists, he loved humanity but couldn't stand people. He had the heart of a teacher, not a leader of men. (Some of you teachers out there are heroic exceptions to this rule, but you know too many of your colleagues fit my broad-brush description that follows.)

Coming from the closed-minded world of academia, where Teacher is always right unless Principal has

other ideas, where snitching on others doesn't bring you punishment, and where you can profess theories without needing to test them in the real world, Wilson was very intolerant of ideas not his own.

Wilson brought Jim Crow to the White House. He ordered facilities in federal buildings segregated against blacks, or allowed his subordinates to do so. He replaced black Republican civil servants with white "deserving Democrats." He supported segregation and on at least one occasion tried to get a Boston newspaper to write positive things about segregation.

There were some segregation policies in place in the federal government (most notoriously in the Armed Services) when Wilson took office in 1913. Of course, segregation was rampant, especially in the states of the Old Confederacy. But Wilson as a tolerant Progressive academician expanded segregation to the entire federal government. It was "good politics" up until the 1970s to race-bait, and sensitive progressives like Wilson and Franklin Delano Roosevelt were among the most skillful of the race baiters.

Most Southerners who voted in the two elections FDR's cousin Theodore Roosevelt ran for president voted against him because he was a "black Republican" and was soft on race relations. In their eyes, Teddy had also committed the unpardonable sin of inviting black educator Booker T. Washington to the White House for dinner. White Southerners overwhelmingly supported segregationist Wilson and would later do the same for cynical opportunist FDR.

FDR would receive much undeserved credit for being the friend of blacks. Yet black track and field superstar Jesse Owens worked for Republican candidate Alf Landon against FDR because FDR wouldn't invite him to the White House or even congratulate him after he won four medals at the "Hitler Olympics." FDR needed the votes of Southern bigots (especially the bigots who were leaders in his own party) to beat Catholic Al Smith for the presidential nomination, and he needed the votes of Southern bigots in Congress to enact his legislation. It was Eisenhower, not FDR, who first used troops to ensure equal access to schools for black children in the South. Neither FDR, nor leftist Southern Democrats LBJ, Carter, or Clinton ever pushed for an anti-lynching law. Nor, as this book goes to press, has Obama. Nor did any Republican president. Democrat and World War One veteran Harry Truman tried, but his own party wheelhorses worked against him. (1)

Wilson showed his "educator" self most clearly in pushing the passage of the Espionage Act and the Sedition Act during World War One. Wilson and his flunkies acted as if these laws made it illegal to criticize his government. (Criticizing the government is as American as apple pie. In the author's opinion, failure to criticize the government could be a sign of anti-American behavior or at least mental disorder.) Wilson and his henchmen violated the rights of thousands of people in enforcing these laws. In Wilson's ivory tower world view, Teacher is always right, and can be as intolerant as he/she wants to be.

Wilson wasn't all bad. He did have some charitable inclinations. Legislation making the eight-hour work day the standard for railroad workers and laws regulating child labor went on the books with his approval during his administration. (However, there was some politics behind Wilson's stance on child labor. Wilson had opposed child labor laws but voters made him see the light.) For humanitarian reasons, he vetoed some bills aimed at tightening immigration. However, with his intolerance of dissent, with his institutionalizing of racism against blacks, and his bungling of World War One and the peace treaties that followed, Wilson did much more harm than good as president.

In 1913, Congress split the Department of Commerce and Labor into the Department of Commerce and the Department of Labor. The Bureau of Immigration and Naturalization went with the Department of Labor. The legislation also divided the Bureau of Immigration and Naturalization into the Bureau of Immigration and the Bureau of Naturalization. Agents of the former bureau would inspect immigrants; agents of the latter bureau would handle naturalizing resident aliens who became eligible for citizenship. There was no Border Patrol (lawmakers would not form this group until the 1920s). There were only a few score mounted agents patrolling the borders from the presidency of Theodore Roosevelt until the Mexicans' raids of 1915 and 1916.

In his first term, Wilson had large Democrat majorities in the Senate and the House of Representatives. However, his party was not united on how to regulate immigration. Big city Democrat leaders in the Northeast and Midwest didn't mind immigrants as long as they could get them citizenship and get them to vote the Democrat ticket. Democrat leaders from the South and other rural areas tended to oppose immigration due to bigotry. So Wilson didn't have any definite approach to the immigration question.

Shortly after Wilson became president, William Williams resigned again. Wilson replaced him with long-time Ellis Island employee Byron Uhl. Uhl ran Ellis Island until the fall of 1914, pretty much as a caretaker, until Wilson could find a man more to his liking. Wilson replaced Uhl with Frederic C. Howe in September 1914. Howe, a one-time student of Wilson's in college, would last until late 1919, when he resigned because he disapproved of Wilson's quasi-fascist policies toward suspected radicals and he feared prosecution by federal authorities for being too easygoing on suspected radicals.

Howe was one of Wilson's better appointments. Howe was a bleeding heart do-gooder liberal in the good sense of the term. He had compassion for the immigrants and tried to improve their lot, especially the lot of those who had to be detained at Ellis Island.

Howe brought skilled women to Ellis Island to teach detained women and girls how to make clothes. He put some of the detained men to work making doormats. Howe started a kindergarten for the children. He brought teachers to the island to offer classes in English language, civics, hygiene, and child rearing for the adults. He had the island landscaped and the great hall and the detention areas decorated with artwork.

Howe allowed detained immigrants to exercise and use the lawns of the island like a park. He brought in silent movies for people to watch three times a week and he had band concerts for the immigrants on Sundays. Because of Howe, Italian-Americans in New York City arranged for Enrico Caruso to sing for the detainees.

Howe allowed husbands and wives to keep company. And scandal of scandals, Howe did not have his guards discourage the young single men and young single women from mingling during daylight hours.

Howe also had staffers round up some of the bums and other homeless along New York City's waterfronts and let them use one of the detention buildings for shelter during the winter. He would let them buy a cheap breakfast and had immigrant groups find them work and serve them free lunches.

This was more doable in Howe's day. Many homeless people today are drug addicts or people who in Howe's day would have been in jail or in a mental institution. In the early 1900s, and especially during the Great Depression, there were many working hobos and homeless families down on their luck who were seeking work. Many hobos did legitimate hard labor, like logging, harvesting crops, and railroad maintenance. Hobos were often sympathetic figures, and many Americans in the cities, including my grandparents and my wife's grandparents, gave them money and fed them if they came by asking for help and offered to do some work for them. During the Depression, many families had to live in their cars by the sides of the roads at night as they sought day work somewhere. If the elites' and corporate lords' economic treason of sending American manufacturing overseas continues, unfortunately the vast majority of the homeless will once again be families down on their luck living in their cars, assuming they have money for gas.

Howe ordered the missionary groups to work together instead of trying to poach converts and bad-mouth each other. Most of his effort in this vein was aimed at his fellow Protestants. Howe also continued the work of William Williams and Robert Watchorn in sifting out the charlatans among the immigration aid societies and the missionary groups.

Howe's honeymoon on the job lasted about a year. Then he ran into trouble. Howe ticked off steamship company owners when he had the rates they had to pay the taxpayers for putting up sick immigrants adjusted well upward. Howe, like Williams and Watchorn, was looking out for the American taxpayers. He wanted steamship operators to reimburse the government for medical treatment given to immigrants crossing the ocean in their ships to reflect the real cost of treating the sick who the steamship operators so willfully and negligently transported to America.

Howe also wanted the railroad companies busted for fraud for overcharging immigrants and routing them out of their way to pick up extra fare money. He likewise wanted New York City area bankers punished for making off with millions of dollars of immigrants' money each year.

Howe angered a number of local businessmen in 1915 when he urged all second-class passengers to New York be routed through Ellis Island. At the time the "Ellis Island experience" was confined to steerage or third-class passengers, or to passengers in higher classes with diseases or legal problems. (Those inspected at Ellis Island were still more than half of all immigrants to America.) Howe's reason was to keep the second-class passengers from being rooked or enslaved by railroad operators and owners of local hotels, taverns, baggage services, and whorehouses in New York City and New Jersey. These businessmen raised enough of a stink with their politicians that Howe could not get this done.

Howe came under fire in 1916 when he decided not to renew the food service contract of a local company for feeding the immigrants on Ellis Island. He wanted the government to operate the island's food services. New York City Congressman William Bennet, the one-time lawyer for the company which was due to lose the food service contract, attached a rider to an appropriations bit that forbade Howe from having the feds feed the immigrants on Ellis Island. Howe could not get this rider overturned, but he got the terms of the government contract changed to limit the food service contractor to a 10 percent profit.

Bennet falsely claimed Howe brought prostitutes to Ellis Island. He also called Howe a socialist for wanting to elbow out his former clients. Bennet even criticized Howe for allowing the sexes to mingle. He slurred Howe as a "half-baked radical, with free-love ideas." **(2)**

Howe did not let Bennet's false criticism of his work slide. Howe challenged Bennet to a debate. Howe tore into the Republican congressman in the affair, which took place in the streets of upper Manhattan. He dared Bennet to repeat his lies in public, because he could then be sued for slander or libel. (Representatives or senators who lie on the floor of the House or Senate are protected from slander and libel prosecution by a loophole they put into the law.) He also exposed Bennet as having a conflict of interest for being a lawyer for a firm seeking a fat contract with the U.S. Government. Bennet lost his bid for re-election.

Howe did deserve harsh criticism for making light of the trafficking of women. He was upset he had to deport several immigrant women who were essentially used sexually by their bosses or "lovers," and were then turned in to the authorities as being immoral women when the immoral men who used them found new females to use. But Howe used his justifiable anger over the misuse of the immigration codes to slur Congressman Mann (author of the Mann Act) and the dedicated male and female investigators and advocates for girls and young women who fought the "white slavery" trade. Howe did not see anywhere near as many immigrants being trafficked as his predecessors Williams and Watchorn did, because he ran Ellis Island from 1914 through 1919, the slowest years for immigration in the 20th Century before the 1930s, because of World War One. Also, the Mann Act made it harder to import girls for lives of sexual slavery.

Fiorello La Guardia, the one-time interpreter at Ellis Island, attributed the drop in trafficking in women to good enforcement. In particular, he credited Andrew Tedesco, an inspector who for years ran the White Slave Division of the Immigration Service and relentlessly attacked female trafficking. La Guardia said, "He (Tedesco) faced the opposition of hotels, resorts (euphemism for whorehouses), and politicians. To all in those trades, the white slave traffic was potentially profitable." La Guardia also credited Felix Frankfurter for his work against the white slavers as a federal prosecutor in New York. Frankfurter later became a Supreme Court justice.

Howe came at the white slavery issue as a liberal attacking moral codes. Coincidentally, many big city politicians in his party (the Democrats) got payoffs from pimps and whorehouse operators, who depended on fresh supplies of pretty impressionable young girls. **(3)**

Foreign events would drive immigration issues during Wilson's presidency. World War One started in 1914. Britain's navy could control non-American shipping traffic in the Atlantic Ocean. This essentially cut off German shipping and immigration from Germany, the portion of Poland Germany controlled, and other lands in Eastern Europe. (Before World War One, German ships carried many immigrants from Germany, Russia, and Eastern Europe.) British naval supremacy in the Atlantic Ocean also essentially cut off Austria-Hungary's shipping. This virtually shut off immigration from southern Poland, Polish and Ukrainian Galicia, the Czech and Slovak homelands, Ruthenia, Bukovina, Transylvania, Croatia, Slovenia, Bosnia, Vojvodina, and from Austria and Hungary also. Germany and the Ottoman Empire controlled the Baltic Sea and the passage from the Black Sea to the Mediterranean Sea; this cut off almost all Russian shipping and immigration from Russia, Ukraine, Belarusia, Finland, Armenia, eastern and central Poland, and the Baltic lands. (Theoretically, one could travel overland from Russia via Finland to neutral Norway or Sweden, or risk taking a ship from Murmansk or Archangel to Britain or Norway and then sail across the Atlantic. Difficulties within Russia prevented most such travel. Some subjects of the Tsar took the Trans-Siberian Railway to the port of Vladivostok on the Sea of Japan, and sailed around Japan and across the Pacific; most of these people underwent immigration processing at Angel Island in San Francisco Bay.)

German submarines also prowled the Atlantic Ocean. They added great risk for people wishing to come to America in British, French, or Italian ships, and later on, in Allied Portuguese or Greek ships. Dutch, Danish, Norwegian, Swedish, and Spanish ships were not safe from submarine attack either, once the Germans resorted to unrestricted submarine warfare against neutrals in 1917.

During the war, the Germans overran Belgium, northeastern France, and Russian-ruled Poland and Lithuania. The Germans and men from their Central Powers allies Austria-Hungary and Bulgaria also occupied Serbia, Montenegro, Macedonia, and most of Romania. The Turks, meanwhile, murdered at least a million Armenians in a formal genocide campaign. This meant there would be fewer people who could leave, even if they wanted to. Besides, all the nations at war started drafting young men – the people most likely to come to America. Immigration dropped dramatically, from 1.22 million in 1914 to 327,000 in 1915, to 299,000 in 1916, and to 296,000 in 1917, the year America entered the war. Immigration bottomed at 111,000 in 1918, the final year of the war. **(4)**

Immigration officials' duties changed during World War One. They checked more closely for saboteurs and spies entering the United States. However, they did not have to check many immigrants total because of the drastic drop of immigration during the war.

Meanwhile, the people of Mexico suffered a decade-long series of wars between rival politicians, military leaders, and bandit chiefs in the wake of the overthrow of dictator Porfirio Diaz. Mexico lost about a million people dead -- killed on various battlefields, murdered for reasons ranging from terror to revenge to removing future opposition to sport, or as victims of disease or starvation due to the warring between factions. One of the main characters in the tragedy of Mexico, Pancho Villa, would play a role not too much different than future ally turned enemy of America Osama bin Laden.

Villa was a mix of government official, military leader, and bandit chieftain. Woodrow Wilson favored the side Villa was fighting on. During the wars in Mexico, Villa was able to buy weapons, horses, and supplies in America. Later there was a falling out between Villa and his erstwhile allies. Wilson chose to side with Carranza, one of the other Mexican leaders, and not Villa. Wilson allowed Carranza's men to use American railroads to bypass Villa's positions in northern Mexico and attack his men from the United States. So Villa took a page out of the book of many prominent Latin American criminals. He decided to blame his country's problems on his former *gringo* benefactors.

Villa's men pulled about 20 Texas mining engineers off a train in northern Mexico in January 1916 during a train robbery and murdered them. Wilson and/or his officials responded in an idiotic or cowardly fashion by declaring martial law in the El Paso area, presumably to stop enraged Texans from crossing into Mexico to seek vengeance.

Villa then led several hundred of his mounted soldiers, mercenaries, and bandits in a pre-dawn raid on tiny Columbus, New Mexico and on a nearby U.S. Army camp, where about 300 men, largely cavalrymen, were stationed. Villa's varmints were looking to steal horses, firearms, ammunition, food, and money. During the March 9, 1916 raid, which lasted for several hours, Villa's villains burned much of the little town to the ground, looted stores, stole money, and murdered 10 American civilians and eight soldiers.

How did they get away with it? Wilson's War Department goofuses and/or the chain of command, much like the cowardly Defense Department functionaries of today, ordered the men to lock their rifles and machine guns in rifle racks instead of having them at the ready. So only a few sentries were armed, and Villa's villains overwhelmed them. Likewise, the colonel of the soldiers had ignored the signs of an impending raid, including a warning report of a Mexican ranch foreman who saw Villa's men assembling, and the fleeing from the area of many civilians of Mexican blood.

However, thanks to the courage of some soldiers and armed civilians, the raid cost Villa much more than he gained. During the raid, 30 to 40 junior officers and enlisted men were able to get machine guns and rifles from the locked rifle racks, and start blasting the *bandidos*. These men drove the raiders out of camp and out of town. Armed citizens in town grabbed their rifles and handguns and shot at Villa's invaders. Some of the cavalrymen pursued Villa's vermin across the border into Mexico and killed more of them before they ran out of ammunition and had to return to camp. Our soldiers and armed civilians killed at least 100 of Villa's men and wounded another 300 or so. Villa had planned to steal the cavalrymen's horses, but our soldiers and armed citizens killed many of Villa's own horses. **(5)**

The Columbus, New Mexico raid was the most spectacular of the raids Mexican outlaws and/or government hoodlums perpetrated against Americans in 1915 and 1916. Villa's raid on the little border town and the outcry against him in America finally prompted Woodrow Wilson to order the U.S. Army and the National Guard to do something about his former pal. General John Pershing led a punitive expedition of about 7000 men (eventually reinforced to about 10,000 men) several hundred miles into Mexico against Villa.

Again, Wilson put an intolerable leash on Americans. He would not allow Pershing to attack Carranza's men, because he viewed Carranza as the rightful leader of Mexico for now. Carranza's *federales* often attacked Pershing's men instead of helping them round up Villa like Carranza promised. Wilson put tens of thousands of National Guard men on the border with Mexico, but forbade them to aid Pershing's men. Meanwhile, traitorous arms dealers in the El Paso area sold Villa more guns and ammo. Pershing had to withdraw to a base camp much closer to the American border. Pershing's men at least hurt Villa's abilities to make attacks by keeping him on the run and killing many of his followers. Villa was still at large in February 1917, when Wilson recalled Pershing's punitive expedition to prepare for entering America into World War One.

Villa would not quite live out the series of upheavals in Mexico which cost the unhappy people of that country a million dead in the 1910s and early 1920s. Several of Villa's many enemies would gun him down in his car in 1923, much like American lawmen would ventilate Bonnie and Clyde in 1934.

America was officially neutral until April 1917, but Wilson and most of his people were incredibly pro-British. Powerful corporate people stood to make a great deal of money selling weapons, war materiel, oil, food, cotton, wool, and other goods to the Allies, so they spread their money and influence throughout the

federal government to ensure American commerce policy would favor their business goals. There were many German nationals in the country, so it was not unrealistic to expect they might try to hinder the flow of weapons and military supplies to the enemies of their homeland.

American officials expelled German military attaché Franz von Papen in December 1915 for "improper activities." American officials discovered the German code book in his secretary's desk, which enabled them to decode and read the infamous Zimmerman note of 1917. British officials seized von Papen's luggage off the ship he was on coming back to Germany and found his checkbooks which allegedly detailed his payments to German agents in America. However, there didn't seem to be a large number of arrests that came from these records. Was this due to Wilson's officials' incompetence, or British officials' lying?

Von Papen was a certifiable nogoodnik. He was Germany's chancellor in 1932 and he helped put Hitler in power in 1933, thinking he could control him. Hitler showed otherwise. His goons killed Von Papen's aides during the Blood Purge of June 1934; Von Papen barely escaped with his life. Von Papen would wind up in the defendants' dock in the Nuremberg trials after World War Two. He was acquitted, but German authorities imprisoned him for a few years on other charges. **(6)**

The people of Ellis Island got a foretaste of World War One in 1916. About 2 a.m. on July 30, explosions rocked 14 barges loaded with gunpowder and shells. These barges were set to be towed out from the pier at the Black Tom portion of the Jersey City waterfront to a Russian ship waiting in Lower New York Bay. The ship's crewmen were planning to load the ordnance onto the ship and bring the explosive cargo to Russia for use against the German and Austro-Hungarian armies.

A German saboteur or saboteurs evidently made sure this particular shipment was going up in smoke. He (or they) caused the explosions. He (or they) started a string of fires on the pier where the explosives were being loaded shortly after midnight. Facility guards tried to fight the fires for about two hours, but then finally called the Jersey City fire department for help. The firemen would get there too late to prevent the explosions that followed.

The first string of explosions wrecked the warehouses, railroad tracks, rolling stock, and pier of the Black Tom facility. The blasts broke thousands of windows in New York City and in New Jersey, and damaged a number of buildings and subway tunnels. It also shook the Brooklyn Bridge. Nocturnal human jackals took advantage of the shattered plate glass on storefronts to loot stores. The fire burned through the ropes tying the barges to the pier, setting the barges adrift toward Ellis Island, less than a mile east of Black Tom.

Sparks from the blaze soon ignited the cargos of the barges. Exploding shells from the barges arced spectacularly over Ellis Island, causing some of the immigrants to believe Americans were putting on a late night fireworks show for their benefit. They applauded the explosions until it became clear to them the display was something much more dangerous. They then began to panic.

Immigration officials evacuated 350 or so would-be immigrants being detained aboard a ferryboat to the Battery on the bottom of nearby Manhattan Island. Staffers evacuated the sick and the insane being detained (another 130 or so people) from the hospital to the east side of Ellis Island behind the cover of the main building and the hospital buildings.

For more than three hours, shells, shrapnel, and debris rained down on Ellis Island from the flaming barges and the burning hellhole which was once the warehouse complex and rail yard in the Black Tom area. Some of the burning barges grounded off of Ellis Island and ignited the wood cribbing of the island's western seawall. The hospital's roof caved in, other buildings' roofs collapsed, and the main building's roof suffered extensive damage. The dining room on Ellis Island was reduced to rubble, and the buildings suffered extensive masonry damage as well as losing their windows and some doors. Shrapnel from the blast damaged the skirt, arm and torch of the nearby Statue of Liberty. This would forever close the torch to visitors.

Incredibly, the explosion killed only a few people at Black Tom. A few staffers and immigrants on Ellis Island suffered superficial wounds. The 125 or so immigration agents, guards, workers, and medical people on duty that night did great work in rescuing immigrants from harm and keeping order.

Ellis Island officials credited the tugboat sailors of the Lehigh Valley Railroad (which owned the Black Tom facility) with courage in towing some flaming explosives-laden barges out to sea to save the lives of the people of Ellis Island and Jersey City. Firemen and maintenance men on Ellis Island and fireboat crews and tugboat men also poured water on the exploding

barges and the burning cribwork. New York City firemen also landed on Ellis Island to help out. Even the doctors at the hospital pitched in to help put out the fires on the blazing barges. Crews from several New York naval militia vessels aided in the firefighting, the guarding of immigrants, and the running off of various pyromaniac knuckleheads who sailed into the water around Ellis Island to sightsee.

It took about half a million dollars in 1916-1917 money (six to ten million dollars today) to repair the damage the blasts caused to Ellis Island. The New York City and New Jersey area reportedly suffered more than $20 million in damages from the blasts and subsequent artillery shell detonations ... equal to about $300 million to $400 million in damages in today's money. Two million pounds (1000 tons) of ammunition and 100,000 pounds (50 tons) of dynamite, TNT, and other explosives detonated due to the fire.

Local prosecutors went after railroad officials for allowing railcars full of explosives to stay at the now-destroyed Black Tom port facility without their cargos being quickly unloaded onto barges for loading onto ships. Railroad personnel also violated a time limit to get dynamite and other explosives out of the warehouses and onto the barges, and they had tied up a barge loaded with explosives at a Black Tom pier to avoid a lousy $25 towing charge.

A Slovak immigrant who would later become an American soldier admitted doing some work for the Germans. He claimed some of the guards at the Black Tom facility were in the pay of the Germans. An investigation determined saboteurs caused the Black Tom explosions, but no one was convicted for this very successful act of sabotage.

In the late 1930s, a German and American arbitration board decided the German government owed the railroad money. In the 1950s, they awarded $50 million to the Lehigh Valley Railroad, and the German government finished paying the reparation in 1979. New Jersey officials turned the site of the Black Tom facility into a state park. Visitors to Ellis Island and the Statue of Liberty from the New Jersey side of the Hudson River use the ferryboat that docks at this park today to go to Ellis Island and Liberty Island. **(7)**

THE *LUSITANIA* TRAGEDY

During World War One, the British and the Germans tried to starve each other into submission with naval weapons. At the time, the British had the best navy and the best merchant fleet. The Germans had a very good navy and merchant fleet, but the British were so much better in this regard that they were able to keep German vessels from bringing supplies from America, and they were able to bring many supplies from America themselves.

The British declared a blockade of Germany and Austria-Hungary and the Ottoman Empire, and they had the navy to back it up. However, the British got too arrogant. They set limits of imports to Denmark and the Netherlands, two neutral seafaring countries which bordered on Germany. The British didn't want these nations' shippers to transfer food and raw materials brought in from around the world to the Germans. The British soon took to forcing neutral ships into British and French ports and seizing the cargos. Often the British did not repay the shippers for the goods they took from the ships. So essentially the British resorted to hijacking and piracy, long-time tactics of theirs since the days of Queen Elizabeth. Some of the ships they seized were American ships.

When the British combined piracy with impressment (kidnaping and forcing American sailors to serve in the British navy) in the early 1800s, Americans went to war against them in 1812. Wilson was nowhere near the man that the Americans of the early 1800s were. He did nothing to punish the British for their piracy.

The British hoped for an American alliance, but desperately needed at least America's friendly neutrality. Edward Grey, the British official whose duties were like those of an American Secretary of State, would admit, "The ill-will of the United States meant certain defeat. The object of diplomacy, therefore, was to secure the maximum of blockade that could be enforced without a rupture with the United States." In other words, the British were going to push America as much as they thought they could get away with. Since Wilson was very willing to be their punk, they succeeded. **(8)**

America had a good navy, but our fleet would not overtake Britain's until after World War One. Still, the U.S. Navy was good enough to defeat the British off of the American coast and in the Caribbean Sea. Our Navy could have also interfered with the flow of food and raw materials from British-owned Canada to Britain. The British would not have been able to maintain the blockade in Europe, keep a lid on the German navy, protect their merchant fleet from German commerce raiders and submarines, and tangle with the U.S. Navy in the Western Hemisphere at the same time.

Also, a simple American embargo on exporting goods to Europe would have crushed the British. Why? Even though British-owned Canada and Australia provided meat, grain, wool, wood, and other raw materials to Britain, they didn't provide <u>enough</u> to the "mother country." So the British imported much of their meat and grain from America and a high percentage of raw materials as well. America was the leading oil exporter in the world at the time, and also one of the leaders in the export of cotton. The British were among America's best customers for oil and cotton. **(9)**

The French were largely self-sufficient in food, but not in oil or cotton. The French needed huge amounts of these raw materials from America also. Many of France's mines and factories were in German hands because of the Germans' 1914 offensive. Many of France's peasants – the men who kept the French fed – were in the army or were already dead. So the French had more of a need for food, manufactured goods, and iron ore than they normally would. Also, British and French factories could not keep up with the demands for weapons and equipment their armies and navies needed. So the British and French had to turn to American manufacturers for many of these items, plus many of the consumer goods their people needed. America was the most productive manufacturing nation in the world; America's workers could readily make these products.

The interests of the merchants and moneylenders, therefore, conflicted with the right of Americans to enjoy peace and security.

If American leaders decided to prevent trade with Europe, it would have hurt America's economy somewhat, but it would have crushed the economies of Britain and France (and Italy, whose economy the French and British in turn had to prop up). This would have the same effect as a successful German blockade, and unlike any such German action, it was possible.

Why didn't Wilson declare an embargo if he wanted America to be neutral? Wilson's love of Britain and British institutions went beyond Anglophilism; it was almost like a submissive sexual obsession on Wilson's part. Wilson's four grandparents were born British subjects; his mother was born in England. Also many key American magnates, including Wilson's financial backers, were making big money as war profiteers. Weapons manufacturers, other manufacturers, food brokers and speculators, and similar sharpies in oil and other commodity markets stood to make a killing by supplying the Allies, no matter what the cost might be to American pride and rights. So they lobbied Wilson and other government officials to do nothing about the British violations of American shippers' rights.

Wilson would allow American bankers and other speculators to make billions of dollars of loans to the British and French governments, over Secretary of State William Jennings Bryan's protests. In order to collect their money, the moneylenders needed the Allies to win. When Congress did declare war in April 1917, bankers were requiring the British to post gold or other collateral. In other words, the British government's credit was no good. The Wilson administration would solve the Allies' credit problems by advancing the British, French, and Italians billions of dollars of loans.

Eventually the moneylenders would make big profits even though the Europeans all defaulted on their loans from the U.S. government. The American taxpayers picked up the tab for the U.S. government loans to the freeloading and ungrateful British, French, and Italians. The tab was not cheap, either. It was more than $10 billion in 1920 money, which would be maybe $150 billion to $200 billion in today's deflated money. The descendants in crime of these moneylenders likewise don't care if Third World dictators default on loans. They know American politicians will use taxpayer money to cover their losses.

The Germans had one naval weapon that frightened the British – the submarine. German U-boat captains started sinking British warships and cargo ships. In early 1915, the Germans declared the waters around Britain and Ireland (Ireland was still under British oppression) to be a war zone. The Germans announced they would sink without warning Allied merchant vessels as well as Allied warships in these waters.

The German policy was ruthless, but no less so than British piracy policy. And it was about as despicable as the British practice of putting war materiél from the United States in the holds of British passenger ships, using the passengers aboard these vessels as human shields. By promoting this practice, British navy boss Winston Churchill and other unscrupulous British officials stooped to endangering the lives of many thousands of innocent people.

Wilson chose to be offended only by the Germans. He made unspecified threats against the Germans over their declared policy. Secretary of State Bryan opposed his boss. The "Cross of Gold" Nebraskan said truthfully, "A ship carrying contraband should not rely upon passengers to protect her from attack – it would be like putting women and children in front of an army." Bryan, true to his principles, resigned his post in protest over Wilson's lax treatment of the British for their violations of American neutrality in comparison with his reaction to German submarine warfare. Wilson replaced Bryan with Anglophile Robert Lansing.(10)

William Alden Smith, the Michigan senator who spearheaded the *Titanic* investigation, also slammed

Wilson for his pro-British tilt. (Smith in 1912 prevented the boss of the White Star Line, the surviving officers, and the surviving crewmen of the doomed ship from fleeing the country when the *Carpathia* docked in New York with them and the rescued passengers aboard. Smith personally served the key figures, and had the men of the *Titanic* held on subpoena and forced them to answer his inquiry. Smith was able to show the *Titanic's* officers negligently sailed the ship into an iceberg-strewn area at high speed. He also proved the corporate bosses deliberately launched the ship with far too few lifeboats. And he exposed the poor leadership and slipshod operation of the vessel that helped cause 1500 or so people, mostly steerage passengers, to drown or die of exposure at sea.) Smith said the Germans would eventually retaliate; this would force Americans to fight in the holocaust in Europe.

Smith and Bryan were not alone. Many political leaders and most of the public wanted to heed George Washington's advice and avoid entangling alliances.

Many Americans wanted Wilson to build up the United States Army and Navy. Men ranging from the warlike Teddy Roosevelt to many calmer men who also loved their country were disgusted with Wilson when he refused to do so. One of them was Wilson's own Secretary of War Lindley Garrison, who resigned in 1916 when Wilson refused to commit to military preparedness. **(11)**

The British and German leaders thus realized they were dealing with an American president who lacked the will to back up his hot air. Therefore, British naval officers kept on stopping American ships and seizing American cargos, and German U-boat captains kept on sinking Allied merchant vessels without warning.

Wilson allowed the British to get away with violating American shippers' rights in their fight to keep American ships out of German and neutral northern European ports. He continued to pressure the Germans when they sunk Allied merchant vessels. America's trade with the Germans shriveled, while America's trade with the Allies mushroomed. In the long run, the low opinion of the courage of Americans that the German leaders had because of Wilson, and their own desperation, led them to decide to sink American ships as well as Allied ships. This move on the Germans' part, along with the pull of Britain and the war profiteers, would cause Wilson to take America into the war on the side of the Allies.

A key event on the way to America's entry into World War One was the sinking of the *Lusitania*. German submariners sunk the *Lusitania* off the coast of Ireland on May 7, 1915. The huge British ship sank in just 18 minutes; 1200 or so passengers and crew members lost their lives. Of the dead, 128 were Americans.

The sinking of the *Lusitania* was one of the most horrifying events of World War One in the minds of people of America. In an age before TV and radio, government officials and war correspondents could cover up the slaughter taking place in the trenches on the Western Front. And of course, since Slavs barely counted as people in the eyes of the elites in Britain, France, and America, these elites said very little about the massive loss of life, starvation, pestilence, and destruction of homes and farms taking place in Poland, Belarusia, Ukraine, Ruthenia, Lithuania, and Serbia.

But the images of screaming passengers trying frantically to leave the listing ship as explosions ripped through its hull, and the images of frightened women and children drowning or dying of hypothermia in the cold waters of the Atlantic were too terrible to cover up. Remember, the *Titanic* sunk only three years earlier.

In fact, British officials ghoulishly played up the tragedy. They were trying to bring America into the war on their side. They knew Americans would be outraged about a German atrocity that killed more than a hundred of their men, women, and children.

They didn't have to try too hard. The story on the surface was ugly enough. Germans had torpedoed a defenseless passenger ship, and sent 1200 men, women, and children to their deaths. Woodrow Wilson was a crawling Anglophile almost to the point of being a submissive. America's ruling classes were Anglophiles. So naturally the Germans took a beating in the American press. Public opinion of the Germans, already tagged as monsters for atrocities some of their troops committed in Belgium and France, sank to a new low. Many in America clamored for war against the hated "Huns."

The truth under the surface was even uglier. The British were using the *Lusitania* and other of their passenger vessels to carry ammunition from America, and they would continue to use the other ships to do so. British Navy boss Winston Churchill and other British leaders figured the Germans wouldn't be cold-blooded enough to torpedo passenger ships, so they were cold-bloodedly using the innocent passengers as human shields, much like criminals use hostages to try to escape police gunfire.

German intelligence agents knew about the British treachery. Their bosses in Berlin decided to order German submariners to sink certain passenger ships like the *Lusitania* to keep the munitions from getting to the British, who would use them to kill German soldiers. *Lusitania* was one of the three fastest large ships afloat. British naval leaders subsidized these ships so they could convert them as needed to British armed merchant cruisers. *Lusitania* and her sister ships could be armed with a dozen 6-inch guns. British authorities listed the ships as auxiliary cruisers in their navy.

German officials accused the British of smuggling war materiél aboard passenger ships. They even took out ads in the New York papers a week before the *Lusitania* left New York for Britain to warn travelers they were in danger of being aboard a ship targeted for torpedoing because of the British gunrunning. Theodore Roosevelt, on hearing about the ads before the *Lusitania* sailed, said he would order the German ambassador deported aboard the *Lusitania* if he was president. **(12)**

British officials and their apologists among the upper crust in America denied the Germans' accusations. Many Americans, aware of German acts of barbarism in the war, concluded the Germans didn't have any room to talk about the British acts of treachery.

However, some newspapermen put the facts together and raised questions about the British role in the tragedy. Two powerful explosions had rocked the *Lusitania* and she had sunk quickly. British authorities naturally claimed the German U-boat captain ordered the crew to fire a second torpedo into the sinking ship. However, since British authorities were known liars (and their attempted *Titanic* coverup happened only three years earlier), some journalists concluded the U-boat's torpedo hit explosives concealed in the ship.

Even though the New York *Times* was pro-British, one of its reporters noted a German spokesman charged the manifest of the Lusitania showed it was carrying 189 cases of "military goods," 1271 cases of ammunition, 4200 cases of cartridges, 260,000 pounds of brass, and 60,000 pounds of copper. (These metals see use in rifle cartridges and artillery shells.) **(13)**

Although British officials and their American collaborators like Port of New York official Dudley Field Malone denied everything, these journalists rightly pointed out to the American people the British government might have had a hand in causing the tragedy. An assistant manager of the British steamship line which owned the *Lusitania* admitted a few days later the ship had at least 4200 cases of rifle cartridges in the hold. Therefore, the sinking of the huge passenger vessel (with a double life as an auxiliary British cruiser and ammo carrier) did not lead to America's immediate entry into the war.

However, most Americans were not happy the Germans sank a passenger ship, which led to the deaths of all those women and children. The Germans tried to avoid sinking passenger ships for almost two years to keep America out of the war. When they decided to retaliate against the British blockade by declaring unrestricted submarine warfare and sinking American ships supplying the British in early 1917 (and also decided to try to get Mexicans to attack the United States by promising them Texas, New Mexico, and Arizona), Congress soon declared war.

In 1993, famed oceanographer Robert Ballard and a crack team probed the wreck of the *Lusitania* to determine the truth behind its sinking. They concluded the torpedo's explosion did not touch off explosives in the ship's hold but instead probably triggered a coal dust explosion in a bunker that was low on coal. However, Ballard noted, the *Lusitania* was definitely carrying munitions for Britain. "The manifest for her last voyage reads like a contraband shopping list," he wrote. "She was carrying 4200 cases of rifle ammunition, 1250 cases of shrapnel, and 18 boxes of percussion fuses. In 1982 salvagers recovered several boxes of the fuses, which bore the initials of the Bethlehem Steel Corporation."

Neither the British nor the Germans ever apologized to the people who lost loved ones in the *Lusitania* sinking. To my knowledge, of the guilty, only the German U-boat captain whose men sunk the *Lusitania* expressed sadness over the terrible deaths of the innocent people. He saw the wounded and dying people swimming for their lives, the overloaded lifeboats, and the corpses on the surface of the ocean, and he said they formed the most terrible vision he had ever seen. He also said it would be impossible to shoot a second torpedo into the doomed ship because of all the people around it struggling to save their lives.

But this ugly tragedy still had facets of heroism and kindness. Magnate Alfred Vanderbilt, one of the wealthy passengers aboard the ship, had his servant round up terrified children on the tilting deck of the sinking ship and bring them to him so he could put lifejackets on them. Vanderbilt saved many children's lives by this simple act of charity; he died in the shipwreck.

Alice Lines, an 18-year-old English nanny, tied an infant girl named Audrey Pearl she was caring for to herself with her shawl when she felt the boat quiver from the explosions. She took Audrey's brother, a toddler named Stuart, by the hand and got him safely aboard a lifeboat. The sailor manning the lifeboat told Alice there was no room for her aboard the little craft, so she held the little girl around her neck, jumped into the water, and tried to keep up with the lifeboat as best she could. Alice was wearing no lifejacket, so she tried to swim next to the lifeboat and did her best to keep the infant's head above water. A woman in the lifeboat had pity on Alice and little Audrey, so she grabbed the bedraggled teenager by her hair and pulled her and the baby aboard.

Young Alice and little Audrey both lived to be elderly ladies and remained close friends through the years. Ballard interviewed them for the article and book he wrote on the *Lusitania* project. **(14)**

And the Irish did their part, too. Irish fishermen rescued survivors and retrieved the bodies of the dead. The people of Cobh, where the fishermen brought the survivors, sheltered and fed them until they could be safely taken to England. (Ironically, Cobh – which in those days the British called Queenstown – was also the last port of call of the doomed *Titanic*.)

The Irish fishermen came out to rescue the victims because the British navy refused to. The British cruiser *Juno*, which was near Cobh harbor, at first went to aid survivors . But officials in the British Admiralty (the navy headquarters which Churchill ran) ordered the warship's captain to abandon the rescue and hide out in the port to avoid the German submarine. As a result, several hundred people who could have been saved drowned or died of exposure. **(15)**

What are we to learn from this terrible tragedy? First, power corrupts, and absolute power corrupts absolutely. None of the British or German officials really cared about the fates of the people in the *Lusitania*. Their own silly prestige in that silly war was all that mattered to them. World War One was the result of the sins of greed and pride of all the leading rulers of Europe. They did not hesitate to sacrifice young soldiers, old people, young women, or helpless children to the pagan gods of their egos. And they didn't hesitate to lie and hurl accusations against each other to whip their own people and people of neutral countries like America into a frenzy of bloodlust.

Second, it is the right and the duty of a nation's people and especially its journalists and scientists to keep its rulers accountable. America's journalists did our nation a favor by trying to investigate the underlying causes of the *Lusitania* tragedy. They kept young Americans out of the senseless carnage of places like Gallipoli, Verdun, and the Somme for another two years. And the dedicated scientists of the National Geographic project used their intelligence -- a gift from God, who is Lord and Creator of all science -- to determine the truth forensically.

And finally, there is something in the human spirit that has the capability to soar even in times of tragedy. It exists in almost all of us, regardless of sex or position in life. The good-hearted Irish of Cobh rescued the survivors and showed a hospitality toward the victims, regardless of their money or their blood. They took seriously the lesson Christ tried to teach when He told the parable of the Good Samaritan. Alfred Vanderbilt and his servant, and Alice Lines and the unnamed woman who pulled her to safety showed the courage and the care for others that most of us have within us, if only we would dare to call upon it!

IMMIGRATION AND ELLIS ISLAND DURING WORLD WAR ONE

Woodrow Wilson narrowly won re-election in 1916 while running on a peace platform. His campaign slogan was, "He Kept Us Out Of War." This wasn't totally true; Wilson had been carrying on an undeclared war against Mexico for years because he disapproved of the men who were trying to run that country.

Wilson's Republican opponent Charles Evans Hughes was too honest to make a claim that he could guarantee peace for America if elected President. Both the British and the Germans were violating the rights of neutral nations, and the leaders and ruling classes of both nations were evil and corrupt.

Wilson narrowly won re-election in 1916 with a minority of the popular vote, much like Bill Clinton in 1996. Wilson got 49% of the votes, Hughes got 46% of the votes, and Socialist and Prohibition candidates got the other 5% of votes. The Electoral College vote was close also.

To Wilson's chagrin, the Republicans won more House of Representatives elections than his Democrats did in the 1916 elections. (Three Progressives, a Socialist, a Prohibitionist, and an independent kept the Republicans from gaining a majority.) In the 1918 end-of-World War One elections, Wilson's party would lose the House and the Senate to the Republicans. This meant there would be much more Republican input into what happened in Wilson's second term.

The major immigration bill that became law during Wilson's presidency was the Immigration Act of February 5, 1917. This new immigration law would be one of the basic immigration laws for the next 35 years.

The 1917 law added exclusions against unskilled laborers from most of Asia (besides unskilled Chinese laborers, who were already banned). The law established a "barred zone," which was "west of the 110th meridian of longitude east from Greenwich and east of the 50th meridian of longitude east from Greenwich and south of the 50th parallel of latitude north ...., " from which they would allow no immigrant laborers. In essence, they barred non-white-collar immigration from India (which at that time also included present-day Pakistan and Bangladesh), Ceylon (Sri Lanka), the small Himalayan countries, the interior of China, Mongolia, Burma, Thailand (then known as Siam), Indochina (Laos, Cambodia, and Vietnam), the Malay States (Malaysia and Singapore), Afghanistan, the eastern part of the Arabian Peninsula, and what we have known as "Soviet Central Asia" – Kazakhstan, Uzbekistan, and the other khanistans collectively called "Turkestan" in geography books and atlases.

Ironically, the congressmen did not forbid immigration from the lands the Turks controlled – present-day Iraq and Kuwait, much of the Arabian peninsula, present-day Israel, Jordan, Lebanon, Syria, Turkey, and some of Armenia. Most of these areas were full of Moslems, but there was not much immigration from these lands, except for the Greeks and Armenians and Christians from Lebanon and Syria and Assyria (today's northern Iraq), who the Turks were running out. By cutting a rectangle into the globe bounded by the 50th and 64th meridians in the west and east, and the 24th and 38th parallels in the south and north and exempting the people of this area from the Asian Barred Zone, the congressmen allowed immigration from present-day Iran – almost totally a Moslem land -- to continue. (Immigration from the land, then known as Persia, was also a trickle in those days.)

The congressmen considered the Turks and Arabs and Iranians bloodthirsty and backward, but did not bar most of them; they apparently figured these Moslems wouldn't come to America, or would be deterred by laws forbidding polygamy and entry of those who had beliefs inimical to American institutions (such as belief in sharia law and jihad). Unlike China and the Indian subcontinent, these lands were not exporting coolie labor all over the globe. Possibly because these lands were the lands of the Bible, the congressmen relented a little and did not formally bar immigration from them.

The law also forbade non-white-collar immigration from the many East Indian Islands (present-day Indonesia, New Guinea, and Timor) and Pacific islands west of the 160th meridian and between the 20th parallel above the Equator and the 10th parallel below the Equator not under United States control. The law allowed immigration from Australia and New Zealand, two countries south of this area whose people were predominantly of British or Irish blood.

Laborers from the British-controlled Indian subcontinent had been coming to Canada, which at the time was under much more British control than it would be after World War One. British leaders were upset Australian, New Zealand, and South African politicians in the British Empire banned immigration from the Indian subcontinent. They wanted to prevent nationalists in the Indian subcontinent from having another reason to act against British colonial rule. So they leaned on the Canadian government to allow immigration from the Indian subcontinent. The "Hindoos" (and Sikhs and Moslems) from the Indian subcontinent undercut Canadian workers. Finally the Canadian government restricted their immigration to Canada in the early 1900s. Some of these people then started filtering across the Canadian border into America. American officials and the American people didn't want these people from the Indian subcontinent undercutting Americans either.

Since the Japanese had seized Korea, Korea wasn't mentioned in the law, but Theodore Roosevelt's "gentlemen's agreement" with Japan kept out most Koreans as well as most Japanese anyway. The same applied to Taiwan, which the Japanese took from the Chinese after a war between the two countries in the 1890s.

Engineers, chemists, scientists and other technical professionals, doctors, merchants, lawyers, teachers, missionaries, and clergymen from these Asian and Pacific lands where immigration was excluded could still immigrate to America. Asians of Oriental, South Asian, and Middle Eastern blood could still come to the United States to study and work. However, in those days, there were not many such professionals from Asia compared to today.

America operated the Philippines and some other islands in the western Pacific Ocean like Guam, so this law didn't apply to Filipinos or the natives of the other American-run islands. Filipinos and other such native islanders were able to emigrate to the United States. Most of the people of the Philippines and Guam were Catholics; Spanish missionaries had evangelized the people of these islands.

The law also kept or expanded the bans against immigrants for certain types of immoral or antisocial behavior, for the probability of needing public assistance, for certain types of diseases, and for certain mental problems. The law continued to bar from entry all those who were idiots, imbeciles, feeble-minded, epileptics, insane, those who had had one or more attacks of insanity, "persons of constitutional psychopathic inferiority", chronic alcoholics, paupers, professional beggars, vagrants, the tubercular, and persons with a loathsome or dangerous contagious disease. The law barred from entry anyone with a physical or mental defect which would affect his or her ability to make a living.

The law also continued to bar from entry those who committed crimes of moral turpitude (crimes of dishonesty, such as perjury, burglary, fraud, theft, embezzlement, and fencing stolen goods, or sexual crimes such as rape, sodomy, sexual assault, or child molesting, or acts against public decency such as adultery or cohabitation (aka "shacking up") or homosexuality), polygamists, subversives, anarchists, those who believed in or advocated (unlawful) overthrow of the government, those who believed in assassination of public officials, those who advocated unlawful destruction of property, those affiliated with any organization teaching the foregoing views, prostitutes or anyone else coming for any immoral sexual purpose, procurers, pimps, and sex traffickers.

The law also continued to bar skilled or unskilled contract laborers, laborers coming in response to advertisement for laborers published abroad, persons likely to become a public charge for any reason, and persons whose passages were paid for by a foreign government, or by any corporation or society. The law also excluded stowaways and previously deported persons seeking admission again unless the U.S. Secretary of Labor was willing to approve their entry. Further, the law excluded unaccompanied children younger than 16 unless they were coming to live with a parent, unless the U.S. Secretary of Labor was willing to approve their entry.

The law retained the $1000 fine for contract labor importers, and added prison time of six months to two years. The lawmakers took away the blanket right of anyone harmed by contract worker importation to sue the cheap labor importer and collect the fine. They substituted a reward program for informants, covered by the take in fines from busted cheap labor importers. They did allow some lawsuits under the new law.

The law specifically allowed the president to expel aliens on evidence foreign governments had allowed them to emigrate to another country for the purpose of sneaking from that country into the United States and worsening labor conditions in the United States.

The law still allowed those convicted of political offenses to gain admission to America, as long as they were not anarchists or subversives.

The law allowed foreign nurses, professors, clergymen, nuns, other persons belonging to any recognized "learned profession", entertainers, and domestic servants into America even if they held contracts. The law also allowed the admission of some skilled laborers if the U.S. Secretary of Labor decided people of their profession were in short supply.

The law increased the time in which American officials could expel most aliens from three years after arrival in America to five years after arrival in America. The law allowed expelling aliens who had committed felonies in America or who had committed crimes of moral turpitude elsewhere before coming to America at any time without any time limit. The law allowed expelling those immigrants who committed misdemeanor crimes of moral turpitude within five years after arrival in America. The law also allowed expelling any alien who lawmen caught within three years of their illegal entry of America.

However, the law did allow judges to make recommendations to the Secretary of Labor not to deport the aliens they sentenced for crimes of moral turpitude or illegal entry.

The law also allowed American officials to deport any immigrant who had become a public charge because of a disability unless the immigrant could prove he or she was in good health when entering through an immigration station and had suffered the accident or injury after landing in America.

The law also made most persons 17 or older pass a simple literacy test or they could not enter the United States. However, any U.S. citizen or legally admitted immigrant could later send for his illiterate wife, illiterate parents, illiterate grandparents over 55 years old, or illiterate single or widowed daughter, and immigration officials would allow these people entry even if they could not read, as long as they were otherwise admissible.

The law also strengthened the ban on "white slavery." The lawmakers put a fine of up to $5000 and a prison term of up to 10 years on the books as punishment for those who imported females (or males) for prostitution or other sexually immoral purposes. They also imposed a two-year prison term on any alien previously deported for such crimes who lawmen caught in America later. They also forbade alien females found guilty of morals offenses to avoid deportation by marrying American citizens.

The law still did not allow any immigrant the right to appeal the decision of a Board of Special Inquiry if the board members had ruled the immigrant unfit to enter because of physical or mental disabilities, or because of a "loathsome or dangerous contagious disease." However, in some cases, a relative or friend could put up bond for an alien if officials thought he or she might become a public charge for less serious physical reasons. If the alien became a public charge, he or she would be deported, and the expenses for deportation and public charity would come from the bond, so the taxpayers wouldn't be hurt.

The legislators also targeted shipping company officials and others who stood to profit from trafficking in illegals. They raised the penalties on the crime of smuggling illegals or excludibles into America to a fine of up to $2000 per alien, and a prison term of up to five years. For ship officers falsely reporting aliens as crew members so they could smuggle them in, they provided a penalty of up to $5000 per alien and allowed seizure of the vessel. (Some Chinese sneaked into America by posing as crewmen, going ashore, then failing to return to the ship when it left the port.)

They also altered the punishment for knowingly assisting anarchists and subversive into America to a maximum prison term of five years with no minimum term. They kept the $5000 fine in the law. The new law did not overturn the previous immigration law that made it a crime for an anarchist or other subversive of the established order, or for any other immigrant who was in America illegally to apply for citizenship, and it was still illegal for anyone else to assist such illegals. They added a $1000 fine and a six-month prison term for those convicted of aiding aliens who advocated the destruction of property.

Ship captains who landed aliens anywhere in America except at an immigration station faced a $200 to $1000 fine and up to a year in prison. Shipping companies also faced a lien on any of their vessels caught landing aliens at places other than immigration stations.

The lawmakers continued to order ship captains to have would-be immigrants answer essentially the same questions that American inspectors would eventually ask immigrants. They kept it illegal for ship captains to fail to have valid information about any immigrant they intended to land in America, and made such a failure a $10 fine per immigrant on whom information was missing. They also extended the $10 fine to shipping companies for immigrants on whom the information was false. The law also allowed port authorities to deny clearance to land to any vessel whose officers they suspected were violating this proviso, but they allowed shipping companies to post bond for their ships equal to the proposed fines pending the outcome of the checking of the aliens.

The representatives and senators also kept in the law a provision for making ship captains note which immigrants had the equivalent of less than $50. They still did not enact a law requiring would-be immigrants to have a minimum amount of money to avoid vagrancy or pauperism.

The law called for fining shipping companies $400 per alien they encouraged or solicited to come to the United States. In other words, shipping lines could advertise their schedules, but could not drum up immigration business by advertising extremely cheap one-way tickets or rebates. The law also allowed port authorities to deny clearance to land to any vessel of the shipping company suspected of violating the law unless the shipping company posted bond equal to the potential fine while the case against the company was proceeding. The Secretary of Labor got the power to ban port calls of ships whose companies were persistent offenders.

The Congressmen raised the penalty on shipping companies to $200 per seriously diseased or disabled person found in inspection in America for bringing such persons to America if a competent doctor in Europe or elsewhere outside of America could have detected the disease or disability. They also applied this fine to shipping companies for negligence or indifference in screening out the mentally defective from the would-be immigrants. The lawmakers added a $25 fine per mentally or physically defective person as an extra fine to the $200 already being assessed. The law also called for fining shippers who negligently or indifferently brought in aliens from the Asian Barred Zone or inadmissible illiterates from anywhere $200 per inadmissible Asian or illiterate. The lawmakers ordered the custom collectors at American ports to take enough money from the shippers to pay for the return of the inadmissible aliens in the same class to the same port as they came from.

The law required shipping companies to pay for detention and medical treatment (and burial, if applicable) of any aliens detained pending decision to allow them to enter the country or require them to leave. Shipping companies faced a $300 fine for each alien whose detention and medical expenses or return trip they refused to pay for. The law also allowed port authorities to deny clearance to land to any vessel whose officers they suspected of violating this proviso, but they allowed shipping companies to post bond equal to the proposed fines pending the outcome of the cases against them.

The senators and representatives, in the law, called for placing American immigration officials and matrons aboard ships in the immigration trade. These agents were to stay in steerage or other parts of the ships where most of the would-be immigrants were staying. Their jobs were to report to American officials about the admissibility of aliens aboard the ships.

The law set minimum standards for doctors who conducted physical and mental evaluations of immigrants. It gave immigrants the right to have medical experts testify for them at their own expense to contest a finding of mental unfitness. It also specified procedures for boards of special inquiry and allowed immigrants before such boards to have a friend or relative present, in addition to any witnesses he could present. The law also allowed aliens to post bond to stay out of jail pending deportation if prosecutors needed their testimony in criminal or civil cases, and they promised to appear for their own deportations.

The law, aka the Immigration Act of 1917, made it a crime to interfere with immigration officers in their duties. Violators faced penalties ranging from up to a year in jail and/or a $2000 fine for minor offenses, to a prison term of up to 10 years for using a "deadly or dangerous weapon" in resisting an immigration officer doing his duties. **(16)**

Woodrow Wilson vetoed the bill meant to put these changes into law because the bill contained a literacy test provision. But Congress, despite the Democrats' majority in the Senate and their rough parity with Republicans in the House (there were more Republicans than Democrats in the House, but several representatives voted with the Democrats to elect Democrat Champ Clark as Speaker of the House, and he controlled committee assignments), overrode Wilson's veto, and they made the Immigration Act of February 5, 1917 law.

The literacy test wasn't hard. All the prospective immigrant had to do to pass it was to read 30 to 40 simple words in his or her own language.

Some parents today might complain about the severity of such a test for their children. Some teachers today might complain they wouldn't have a chance to teach the test so their underachieving kids would pass. In opposing such a test in 1917, Wilson may have been an educator who was ahead of his time. His anti-test stance was like that of many teachers today.

Also in early 1917, the U.S. Congress voted to make all citizens of Puerto Rico citizens of the United States. America had taken Puerto Rico from Spain as a result of the Spanish American War in 1898.

Events in Europe would affect American immigration policy in a more practical way. Woodrow Wilson and the U.S. Congress entered America into World War One in April 1917.

Wilson's 1916 campaign slogan ("he kept us out of war") and his falsely implied promises of peace sent the wrong message to the Germans. Because of Wilson's campaign and narrow victory in the fall of 1916, the German high command figured Americans would be too cowardly to attack them if they decided to sink American ships bringing goods to Britain.

The British navy was blockading Germany and Austria-Hungary, and hundreds of thousands of the people in the lands the German and Austrian and Hungarian governments controlled were dying of starvation while they commandeered food for their soldiers. Germany didn't have a navy capable of beating Britain's surface fleet. But Britain too would be vulnerable to starvation if German submarines could sink enough ships bringing to Britain the food its people needed. German leaders decided to sink neutral ships supplying the Allies on the gamble they could make the British and French sue for peace before America's leaders would declare war, or send large numbers of troops and naval units into combat against the Germans.

The Germans started unrestricted submarine warfare in February 1917. Soon German U-boats were sinking American ships and other neutral ships in the waters around Britain, as well as sinking British, French, Italian, Russian, Australian, Canadian, and Portuguese ships. The shipping losses reduced the amount of food in Britain to an estimated six weeks supply of food for the people. In the short term, this looked like a good move for the Germans. However, the Germans were killing Americans as they were sinking American ships.

German leaders and diplomats were about as hamfisted as a guy who wants to date a woman threatening to rape her if she won't go out with him, so sooner or later they were bound to blunder. And blunder hugely they would. Some *scheisskopfs* in the German government tried to talk Mexico into attacking the United States. In March 1917, just before his

OPEN FOR BUSINESS

Top: Ellis Island in its heyday. **Right:** Immigrants land at Ellis Island. Immigrants (mostly the steerage folks) left the ships that brought them across the ocean and boarded ferryboats that were small enough to dock at Ellis Island. **Below:** "Ticket in Her Teeth." Imagine bringing what little you could pack to come to a new land, and keep alert so your children wouldn't stray. **Bottom right:** Italian immigrants ready to land at Ellis Island.

Credits: Bottom right picture by Lewis Hine, and other three pictures from New York Public Library.

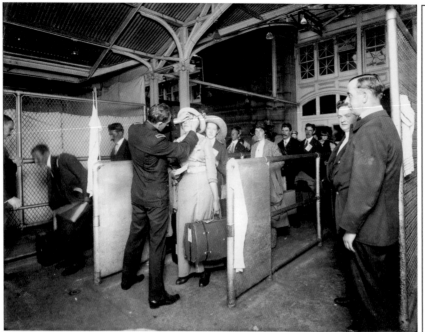

SCREENING IMMIGRANTS

Just showing up at Ellis Island didn't give you an automatic pass into America. You had to pass physical and mental evaluations.

Top: Medical inspector examines immigrant's eyes. They were looking for evidence of trachoma, a very infectious eye disease. Credit: Brown Brothers.

Center: Mental exam of woman. Corrupt European officials tried to dump people with mental problems on America. American doctors tested people suspected to have such problems. Credit: Brown Brothers.

Bottom right: Jewish teenage girl undergoes exam. Many European women were embarrassed by such exams and by semi-public showers and delousing. It was not common practice to be seminaked or naked in front of anyone but a spouse. Credit: Ellis Island Immigration Museum.

Bottom left: This nurse is checking an immigrant girl's hair for lice. Many immigrants practiced very poor hygiene. Credit: U.S. Public Health Service.

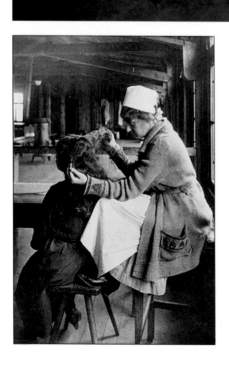

DETENTION AT ELLIS ISLAND

Officials detained hundreds of thousands of would-be immigrants at Ellis Island. About 400,000 had to return to Europe from America from 1892 through 1924; most gained admission.

Top: Stoic mother and her well-cared-for children look out at New York harbor from behind a chain link fence. Is Father a little late getting to Ellis Island to claim them? Is another child sick and recovering in the hospital on Ellis Island?

Bottom: A meal at Ellis Island. Americans fed the immigrants they detained three square meals a day. Most detained immigrants ate better at Ellis Island than they did in their homelands.

Right: Detained youngbloods find a good way to pass the time – meeting and dancing with detained ladies. An accordion player gives this couple some melodies of home.

Credits: New York Public Library.

PRIMARY INSPECTION

at Ellis Island.

Top: Inspectors checked immigrants to make sure they were legally able to become U.S. residents. They asked questions and profiled immigrants who were questionable.

Center right: Ellis Island commissioner Robert Watchorn (sitting, second from left) and Special Board of Inquiry members hear a case to decide if they will deport or admit a questionable alien. Watchorn was himself an immigrant from Britain.

Center left: William Williams, legendary Ellis Island commissioner.

Bottom: Inspector prepares German family for a railroad trip. He is tagging them so railroad employees will help them get to their destination safely.

Credits: Wiliams photo in public domain. Watchorn picture courtesy of Ellis Island Immigration Museum. Other pictures courtesy of New York Public Library.

HEALTH CARE AT ELLIS ISLAND

Many thousands of immigrants became sick on their voyage to America, no thanks to steerage conditions, or other less sanitary immigrants traveling with them. American doctors and nurses treated thousands upon thousands of sick aliens at the hospital on Ellis Island and in other hospitals and quarantine facilities.

Top: Nurses and doctors of the Ellis Island hospital. Credit: Ellis Island Immigration Museum.

Center: Nurse checks baby at Ellis Island. Many infants came through Ellis Island with their mothers. Doctors on Ellis Island also delivered 500 babies on Ellis Island. They were counted as aliens, not anchor babies. In the Ellis Island Era, a baby born in America to alien parents had the national status of his alien parents. Credit: U.S. Public Health Service.

Bottom: Ellis Island officials allowed detained women and children to get milk and crackers during the day besides getting their three meals. The Ellis Island "milkman" is taking care of these eager detainees. Bottom line? Ellis Island's staffers by and large treated immigrants kindly, even the ones they had to deport. Credit: New York Public Library.

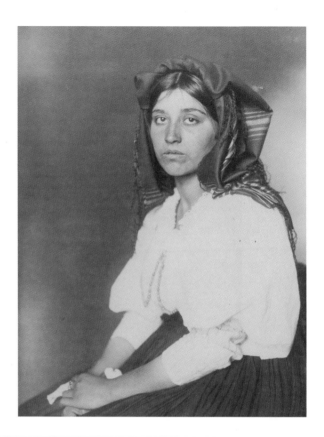

IMMIGRANT WOMEN AND GIRLS faced double jeopardy. They could be exploited in a sweatshop or in a factory or as a maid or as a store clerk or in some other business. They could also be lured or forced into prostitution.

Top left: Clara Lemlich, a Jewish immigrant from the Russian Empire and a garment maker, triggered a general strike against the shirtwaist makers in 1909 by calling for a general strike vote after her employer Louis Leiserson had goons beat her while she was leading a strike against him. She is wearing a shirtwaist with her skirt. Most of the victims of the Triangle

Fire were immigrant girls and very young women. The owners underpaid them and locked them in their work areas. Credit: Kheel Center, Cornell University.

Top right: Italian girl. **Bottom left:** Romanian woman. **Bottom right:** Jewish girl. Jewish females and those from Italy and Eastern Europe were among the most victimized of those enslaved in prostitution. Immigration agents worked hard to prevent women and girls like these from becoming sexual prey. Credit: All photos by Augustus Sherman, New York Public Library.

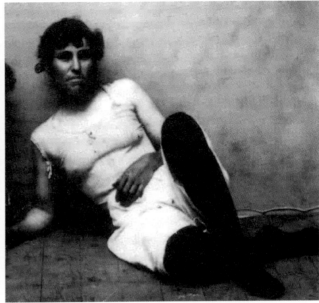

WHITE SLAVERY was a euphemism for one of the vilest kinds of crimes – kidnaping and rape for cash. **Top left:** Ada Everleigh shows off some of her charms. Ada and her sister Minna Everleigh ran the Everleigh club in Chicago, a high-dollar whorehouse. A large percent of their profits went to paying off Chicago authorities. **Top right:** The sad truth of the trade ... a prostitute on her way down, in a squalid crib. Night after night of sex with dozens of sweating strangers led many prostitutes to depression and alcohol and drug use as they realized they were losing their looks and had not saved enough to get out of the whore's life. Suicides of prostitutes were common. Credit: Bill Manns, Old West author, photographer, and collector.

Below left: Mona Marshall, the girl who sent word she was being held as a prostitute against her will in a Chicago whorehouse. Her plight helped lead to the Mann Act. Credit: Chicago Daily News, Chicago Historical Society. **Below right:** The silent movie "Traffic in Souls" was somewhat of an exposé of sex trafficking in the 1910s. Immigrant women and their American sisters, paid serf wages by sweatshop owners, store owners, and other employers, were often starving and were often easy prey for the handsome smooth talking hustlers who conned them into forced prostitution.

TRAFFIC IN SOULS

PHOTO-DRAMA TODAY OR WHILE NEW YORK SLEEPS

UNIVERSAL FILM MFG. CO.

ANGEL ISLAND

in San Francisco Bay was where American agents processed 200,000 immigrants (mostly Asians) from 1910 through 1940. It is now a state park.

Top: Buildings for immigrants. These buildings at Angel Island were undergoing renovation when the author took this photo in 2006.

Bottom right: Angel Island commanded the Golden Gate. The Golden Gate Bridge was built during the Depression. Before then, artillery batteries pointed west to blast any unfriendly foreign naval vessel. The island was big enough to handle being an immigration station and a harbor defense fort. It would later host women soldiers and Army missile men. Photo by author.

Bottom left: Asian immigrants arrive at Angel Island to undergo processing. Photo courtesy of Angel Island State Park.

Center: Katherine Maurer, in black with pompomed hat, teaches detained Asian female immigrants English. Miss Maurer, a Protestant deaconess, ministered to the immigrants from 1912 through 1940. She was remembered for her kindness; she put the "Angel" in Angel Island. Photo courtesy of Angel Island State Park.

IMMIGRATION SCRAPBOOK

Top: Jewish immigrants from Russia. Roughly 2 million Jews came to America in the Ellis Island Era. Credit: New York Public Library.

Center: Immigrants from Galicia (either Polish or Ukrainian) land in Montreal. Many immigrants to America came to Canada, and then took the train to America. Many immigrants from Ukraine and Russia settled in the Prairie provinces of Canada. Credit: New York Public Library.

Bottom left: Mum and seven children, immigrants from England, at Ellis Island. Credit: Augustus Sherman, Ellis Island Immigration Museum.

Bottom right: Before the Clintons' and the Bushes' presidencies, most Arab immigrants to America were Catholics or Orthodox Christians from Lebanon and the Holy Land. These Christians were escaping Ottoman Moslem oppression. This contrasts with the Moslems and the large numbers of sleepers and overt jihadists in their midst who come to America today with the assistance of the State Department. This attractive young Lebanese woman is Arab and Christian also. Credit: Alamy. Many Catholic, Coptic, and Orthodox Christian women like her face kidnaping, rape, forced conversion, and forced marriage in too many Moslem lands today. Christians in these lands today also face similar indications of Moslem intolerance, like robbery and murder. Ironically, the safest overwhelmingly Moslem country for Christians today is probably Turkey.

WOMEN AT ELLIS ISLAND

Top left: Ruthenian woman. **Top right:** Albanian woman from Italy. The Turks ruled Albania until 1912; most Albanians were and are Moslems. Many Catholic and Orthodox Christian Albanians lived in safety in nearby Italy. **Bottom left:** Lapp woman from Norway. Did her headgear inspire pilots' helmets? **Bottom right:** Greek woman. She was no stranger to the needle, judging from the embroidery on her clothes. Credits: Augustus Sherman, Ellis Island Immigration Museum and New York Public Library.

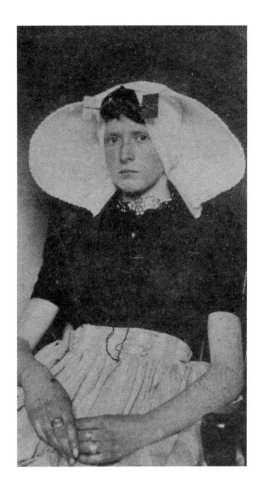

PAGEANT OF ELLIS ISLAND

Many Europeans displayed the picturesque clothes of their homelands when they came through Ellis Island for processing. **Top left**: Cossacks from Russia or Ukraine. They look somewhat prepared to fight street crime in New York. **Top right**: Dutch girl in native dress. She doesn't look too happy about being photographed by Augustus Sherman, long-time Ellis Island civil servant and shutterbug. **Bottom left:** French girl. She was probably from Alsace, because she is wearing the huge black ribbon headdress of that region. **Bottom right:** German man from Bavaria. Was he slyly eyeing the frauleins at Ellis Island? Credits: Augustus Sherman, Ellis Island Immigration Museum and New York Public Library.

MOTHERS AND CHILDREN AT ELLIS ISLAND

Top left: Italian mama and bambina. This well-loved photo got the nickname "Madonna of Ellis Island." **Top right:** Hungarian mother takes her baby for an airing in front of the Main Building of Ellis Island. **Bottom left:** Little Swedish girl wins hearts at Ellis Island. **Bottom right:** Scottish boys. They undoubtedly didn't show up for school in America like this, or if they did, they would have had to be good with their fists. Credits: Augustus Sherman, Ellis Island Immigration Museum and New York Public Library.

NEW WORLD FASHION vs. OLD WORLD FASHION AT ELLIS ISLAND

Top: This trio of pretty women from Guadeloupe in the West Indies make a fashion statement at Ellis Island. Their dresses were not much different than what American women were wearing at the time. The tallest lady of the three will soon be adding a child to America to help build it.

Bottom left: This girl, the sister of Danish painter Vilhelm Hammershoi, displays garb typical of many young Western European women of the middle class in the late 1800s – dark and simple, yet thoroughly feminine. She didn't come to America, but many who dressed like her did.

Bottom right: These Slovak sweeties are wearing peasant dresses and boots long before this look was "in." Boots were a must as women's footwear in snowy and muddy Eastern Europe, as were skirts that were relatively short for that era, compared with Western and Southern Europe. Who needed to spend time washing a long skirt that got muddied so easily?

ASSIMILATION BEGAN AT ELLIS ISLAND

Left: School at Ellis Island. Many families were detained for awhile at Ellis Island. The commissioners brought in teachers to teach the children the American language, American ways, and basic hygiene. Credit: Brown Brothers.

Right: Christmas at Ellis Island. Ellis Island officials tried to help the detained make the best of their situation. They had festivities for the immigrants. They arranged for Catholic Mass, Orthodox Divine Liturgy, and Protestant worship service for the detained. (They also arranged for rabbis to minister to Jewish detainees on their holy days.) Christians and Jews alike got presents from the aid societies. Pro-American schooling and celebrating Our Lord's birth were natural to officials who had patriotism and Christian charity. In today's poisoned world of political correctness, celebrating American culture and Our Lord's birth would cost some official his or her career. Credit: Ellis Island Immigration Museum.

SCHOOL AND STREET helped immigrant children become real Americans. Back in the day teachers taught patriotism along with readin', 'ritin', and 'rithmetic.

Top: Gary, Indiana school children. Top row standing; left to right, American black, Romanian, Lithuanian, Italian, Polish, Croatian, Hungarian. Middle row; Greek (white dress), American white (with book), Austrian, German, Bulgarian.

Front row, all seated, Scotch, Russian, Irish, Assyrian, "Slavic," Jewish and Spanish. Gary was a steel mill town with a very high immigrant population. Credit: New York Public Library.

Bottom: Kids play ball in a tenement neighborhood in New York City. Being with American kids helped alien kids learn the language and some of the customs of their new homeland. Credit: Lewis Hine.

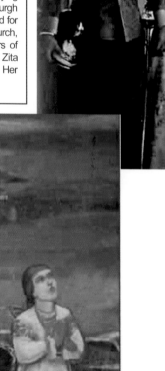

IMMIGRANTS CAME HERE FOR MANY REASONS

Top left: Many young men in Europe came to America to avoid being used as cannon fodder in a war. The great-uncle of the author's wife wasn't so lucky. He had to serve in the army of Austria-Hungary. Later, he and the author's wife's great-aunt lived in their village in Slovakia. **Top right:** Some cowardly European guys left pregnant girlfriends behind. Some single moms left Europe to avoid the merciless people in their villages. Women who weren't virgins often had to marry in a color other than white. One pair of the author's great-grandparents were Germans. She wore a purple dress to her wedding because they married during Lent. One of the author's Czech ancestresses was already a single mom (by her eventual husband) who presumably had to wear black at her wedding. **Bottom:** Croatian artist Maxo Vanka painted this mural of peasants praying the Angelus (the noon prayer) in St. Nicholas Croatian Catholic Church in the Pittsburgh area. Eastern Europeans made good Americans, but understandably they longed for their loved ones in the old country. Credit: St. Nicholas Croatian Catholic Church, Diocese of Pittsburgh. **Center:** Emperor Karl and Empress Zita, the last rulers of Austria-Hungary. They were exiled after World War One, and he died in 1922. Zita would flee to America during World War Two when Hitler sought to execute her. Her sons served in the U.S. armed forces and U.S. government during the war.

inauguration and before the seating of the new Congress, Wilson made public an intercepted telegram known as the "Zimmerman Note." The telegram promised the Germans would have Texas, New Mexico, and Arizona returned to Mexico in case of German victory. Mexicans had no chance of invading the United States and winning. Besides, the Mexican warlords were busy butchering hundreds of thousands of their own unfortunate people during the Mexican Revolution in the 1910s. The Germans had no way of aiding the Mexicans in such a war, except for providing them money to buy small arms from neutral countries. (Some Germans had been smuggling weapons to Pancho Villa in coffins.) The German move, besides being a pipe dream of major proportions, was a HUGE blunder that infuriated many Americans!

Because of the arrogance, cold-bloodedness, and stupidity of Germany's leaders, America's Congress declared war on Germany in April of 1917, a month into Wilson's second term. Wilson asked for Congress to declare war on April 2, 1917. The Senate obliged him with an 82 to 6 vote for war on April 4. Robert La Follette of Wisconsin was the key opponent of the declaration of war in the Senate; Wilson would scheme unsuccessfully to have La Follette removed from office and jailed.

In the wee hours of the night, April 6, 1917, which happened to be the first hours of Good Friday, the U.S. House of Representatives voted to declare war on Germany. After all the speechmaking was done on Holy Thursday and past midnight into Good Friday, the House members voted on whether or not to declare war on Germany with a yes or no roll call vote only. Jeannette Rankin, a young Montana Republican who was the only woman in Congress, didn't follow the format. Miss Rankin, who was new to the House (it was only her fifth day on the House floor), said in a quavering voice, "I want to stand by my country but I cannot vote for war." She then broke down and sobbed in her seat in the House. Fiorello La Guardia, then a freshman Republican congressman from New York City, said he couldn't see Congresswoman Rankin crying because of the tears in his own eyes.

The House vote was 373 for war, 50 opposed. La Guardia could be accused of voting for war because he favored the Italy of his parents against the emperor of Austria-Hungary who still ruled some Italians. At least La Guardia would serve in combat as an aviator during the war. La Guardia was more kind in his words toward the lady pacifist Jeannette Rankin than he was about the judgment of most of the congressmen who voted along with him to declare war. He said most of his colleagues believed the United States would only have to do a little more Navy work and supply more war materiél to the Allies, and would not have to send troops to Europe. He said they had no idea that so many Americans (two million by the end of the war) would wind up in the trenches of France. **(17)**

Ellis Island itself, besides serving as an immigration station, would see use as a military hospital and as a detention facility for interned German sailors and other German nationals during the war as well. In fact, the Registry Room (the great hall that you see in most historical pictures of Ellis Island) became the nation's largest hospital ward. U.S. Army and Navy medical people essentially took over most of Ellis Island's facilities. Immigrants who had to be detained for any length of time from early 1918 through early 1919 were held at the immigration station in Philadelphia. Immigration officials farmed out sick immigrants to other hospitals in New York City and New Jersey. Only a relative few immigrants would stay on Ellis Island – these included those being held for boards of Special Inquiry, and those awaiting pickup by relatives. **(18)**

Most of the Germans interned at Ellis Island were merchant seamen whose ships were in American ports when Congress declared war on Germany in April 1917. They received reasonable treatment at Ellis Island, but they complained about being poorly fed, and mistreated. Howe was about the last federal official in the country who would have tolerated such abuses, and an investigation by neutral Swiss officials quickly showed the Germans were exaggerating. Howe and military officials arranged to have the great majority of these men interned in internment camps in the South.

Howe also had to serve as temporary jailer for a couple of thousand Hungarian, Austrian, and German nationals living in America who in many cases had married American women or naturalized women from Europe. He received criticism for trying to treat these men humanely. He said he met many a crying wife on the doorstep of his house when he got home each night beseeching him for information on her missing husband, who often was at Ellis Island as a prisoner, or would soon be there. **(19)**

In 1918, Howe had to be temporary jailer for about 2600 neutral Dutch seamen because officials in the Wilson administration decided to seize Dutch ships in American harbors for use in the war. There was no justification for this, as the Dutch were neutral. But Wilson, an admirer of all things British, copied the British in pirating ships.

The British had stolen or destroyed most of Denmark's ships during the Napoleonic Wars even though the Danes were neutral at the time. And one of the key reasons the Turks fought alongside the Germans in World War One was the British theft of two battleships they had finished building for the Turkish navy on contract in 1914. The British didn't even refund the Turks' money! Since the Turkish people made direct contributions to raise the money for these ships, there was widespread anger among them toward the pirates in the British government. Turks killed many thousands of British, Australian, New Zealander, and Indian subcontinent soldiers, and raped many of their British and Commonwealth captives – including Britisher Lawrence of Arabia – in reprisal.

Howe arranged to have most of the Dutchmen sent home. Some he allowed to go to islands the Dutch owned in the West Indies, some men he allowed to go to the Dutch East Indies (present-day Indonesia, which was a Dutch colony at the time), some he allowed to join other countries' merchant ship crews, and some he allowed to enter America as immigrants. **(20)**

The Communists seized power in Russia in November 1917. Even though they dropped Russia out of World War One in early 1918, the new Communist masters were not eager to let people leave their Red paradise. The leaders of Germany, Austria-Hungary, Bulgaria, and the Ottoman Empire finally decided to stop fighting in the fall of 1918. But German submarines had sunk enough ships to decrease the available carrying capacity for the immigrant trade. Besides, the war cost the lives of millions of young men – the people most likely to come to America. Immigration plummeted to 110,618 in 1918, and to 141,132 in 1919. **(21)**

The U.S. Congress passed the Joint Resolution of October 19, 1918 for some aliens fighting in the war. This law, aka 40 Statutes at Large 1014, allowed readmission of aliens who had served with America's armed forces or those of America's allies, or if they had served with Czech, Slovak, or Polish units on the Allied side. Poland was under German, Russian, and Austrian control from the 1790s until after World War One, so some Polish freedom fighters were fighting against the Russians while others were fighting against the Germans. The Czechs and Slovaks, under Austrian and/or Hungarian rule for hundreds of years, had an easier time of picking sides. Many Czechs and Slovaks deserted the army of Austria-Hungary and fought on the Allied side.

During World War One, roughly four million men served in America's armed forces. Since the country was half rural, this meant there were a lot of able-bodied men away from the farms and in uniform. U.S. Labor Department officials allowed many Mexican laborers to enter America on temporary visas to work on fruit, sugar beet, and cotton farms, to mine lignite coal, and to maintain railroad rights-of-way. Later on, U.S. officials allowed Mexican laborers to work in mining and on government construction projects in

Texas and in the Southeast. This program ended in 1921, and government officials asked employers to send the Mexicans back to Mexico. But they didn't really check to ensure the employers did so.

In 1918, the U.S. Congress enacted a law expanding the power of federal officials to expel Communists, anarchists, and similar people who advocated violent overthrow of legitimate government. Per the terms of this law (Act of October 16, 1918 aka 40 Statutes at Large 1012-1013), grounds for deportation of aliens would include membership in organizations advocating violent overthrow, or belief in such actions.

In 1920, the U.S. Congress enacted a law to deport aliens involved in trading with the enemy, or in interfering with American neutrality or foreign policy or interfering with American commerce after the start of World War One, aliens who destroyed war materials or damaged military facilities, aliens involved in making or possessing explosives, aliens involved in conspiracies related to such actions, and aliens making threats against the United States or the president. Congressmen and Wilson aimed this law (the Act of May 10, 1920 aka 41 Statutes at Large 593) at German and Austro-Hungarian agents, and also at Communists and other militants. **(22)**

The law was good on paper but it was not evenly aimed. If it was, then American officials would have to deport hundreds of British agents who interfered with America's neutrality and foreign policy and commerce. And they would have to have barred virtually everyone from Britain's government and shipping industries from entry into this country.

Why? Because the British essentially wiped their boots on the American flag in the years running up to America's entry into World War One. The British spent millions of dollars on propaganda, bribes, and other devices aimed at getting America into the war.

The British interfered with American shipping. The British confiscated cargos from American ships. The British smuggled armaments aboard passenger ships, using American passengers like human shields. Men like Winston Churchill, who devised the evil scheme of munitions running aboard passenger liners and authorized the stopping of American ships and seizures of cargos, rightly should have been barred from ever coming to the United States. **(23)**

PRELUDE TO THE RED SCARE

The regime of Woodrow Wilson ended in incompetence and turmoil. Wilson himself ended his stay in the White House as a drooling meglomaniac. Meanwhile, America convulsed as his minions violated civil liberties, furthered the oppression of blacks, outlawed alcohol, and dithered over whether to give women the right to vote. Ironically, the de facto president during Woodrow Wilson's post-World War One meltdown was his hateful lying second wife, who didn't even have the right to vote until the last few months of her reign. (Wilson, an adulterer, outlived his first wife Ellen Axson. He married businesswoman and adulteress Edith Galt. She knew how to keep an eye on wayward Woodrow.) This section and the ones following it cover these troubles, because they all happened together, and to an extent they impacted each other.

The runup to the Red Scare started about the time Wilson asked for a declaration of war against Germany. The Red Scare would climax in 1919, then go limp when Wilson's second term ended ignominiously in early 1921.

Wilson hated a number of people and he deviously aimed government force against them in the name of patriotism and supporting the war effort. Wilson and his minions ignored the Constitution and tried to run an elected dictatorship to the best of their ability. Thankfully, some Democrats and many Republicans would oppose him enough to keep him from doing more harm than he did. But Wilson and his boys did plenty of harm anyway.

The first group of people Wilson targeted were Germans and Americans of German descent. Most of them opposed declaring war on Germany, and many of them correctly noted Wilson had steered American foreign policy in support of the British. Wilson did have a legitimate reason to crack down on some of the Germans because of the acts of espionage and sabotage against America's war effort. The memory of the Black Tom blasts in New Jersey, where Wilson taught in college and was briefly governor before he became president, could not have been easy for him to forget. People of German ancestry became convenient targets of Wilson and his regime.

In Russia, the Communists in November 1917 overthrew Kerensky and the democrats who overthrew the Tsar in March 1917. Because the Reds openly desired to instigate world revolution, the followers of the criminals Lenin, Trotsky, Stalin, and their ilk became persons of interest to the American government. Wilson was also jealous of Lenin in a way, because Lenin had also argued for peace. (Lenin did so even as he was having his opponents killed, while Wilson was only having his opponents jailed or allowing lynch mobs

to kill a few of them without fear of federal prosecution). Lenin had also released the details of the secret treaties divvying up the spoils in Europe and the Middle East that Tsar Nicholas II had signed with the British and French. This made Wilson look like a liar and a stooge because it contradicted Wilson's public stand against secret treaties and showed his allies to be grasping pirates. However, Wilson was not wrong to have Lenin's people targeted, because if Communism prevailed, there could be no liberty in the United States.

There were also anarchist vermin who had come in to the United States during the Ellis Island era. Anarchists had murdered President McKinley, Empress Elisabeth (Sissi) of Austria-Hungary, and a number of European leaders in the 1890s and the early 1900s. They were not above an occasional bombing to make their presence known. Agitator Emma Goldman, who emigrated to America with her family in 1886 to escape the anti-Jewish pogroms in Russia, was the most visible of the anarchists. McKinley's assassin Leon Czolgosz attributed his desire to shoot the president to her inflammatory speeches and articles. Wilson was not wrong to have these people targeted either.

Sadly, there were many decent people in America who Wilson attacked out of mindless bigotry or out of political chicanery.

Woodrow Wilson was a bigot who despised Catholics and especially the Irish and Americans of Irish ancestry. These sorts of hatreds came naturally to the prune-faced Calvinist whose mother was a native of England and whose four grandparents were born in Scotland or in British settlements in Ulster. Wilson's father was essentially a Copperhead preacher. Wilson's father moved to Virginia from Ohio, owned slaves, and helped split the Presbyterians by helping form a proslavery splinter church organization.

Wilson's inbred prejudices went hand in hand with Wilson's submissive devotion to all things British, including their colonialism. The British hypocritically claimed they were fighting so small nations might be free, but they had just bloodily suppressed the Easter Rebellion against their colonial rule in Ireland in 1916. Many Americans of Irish blood (including my own grandfather Charlie Sherlock, who came through Ellis Island in the first decade of the 1900s) opposed war on the side of Britain, or favored it only on grounds that the British leave Ireland. Even though Irish Americans were traditionally among the most reliable Democrat voters, Wilson scorned them, belittled them, and told them they were disloyal troublemakers when they asked him to work for freedom for Ireland.

Grandpa Charlie, like many Americans of Irish blood, served in uniform during the war despite his reservations about the honesty and decisionmaking ability of Woodrow Wilson. So did my other grandpa, second-generation Irish-American Leo Hurley. Many Americans of Irish blood would turn on Wilson and make his party the minority party in both houses of Congress in the 1918 election.

Wilson also derided Americans of Italian ancestry as "hyphenated Americans." He considered Italian Americans backward and criminal. Wilson was also jealous of Pope Benedict XV, an Italian, who had nearly gotten the warring parties during World War One to negotiate an end to the apocalypse that was tearing Europe apart. Before he pushed the United States into war on the side of the British, Wilson falsely viewed himself as the only man capable of arbitrating a just peace for the Europeans.

Wilson also despised people who didn't agree with him. Like most leftists, especially those who are teachers, he was intolerant of opinions other than his own, and he longed to crush dissent. Wilson, who had never served in the military but was a sheltered student and professor, wrapped himself in the Flag and made self-serving pronouncements about the purity of his purpose. Meanwhile he and his henchmen schemed to punish those who stood in his way of waging "the war to end all wars."

At Wilson's urging, Congress considered passing the Espionage Act in 1917, which was on the whole a good bill aimed at punishing saboteurs, spies, and traitors. It had a section which made it a crime to "wilfully obstruct the recruiting or enlistment service of the United States," which should be invoked today to punish anti-American college administrators and city politicians who try to ban military recruitment. However, the proposed law also had a section which allowed the prosecution of anyone who the government deemed was criticizing "national defense." This meant Wilson could jail not only his antiwar critics, but also those who would criticize him for running the war incompetently.

Fiorello La Guardia was one of the congressmen to oppose this bill, because he believed Wilson's men would use it to stifle legitimate criticism of his regime. He also opposed it because he believed Americans should be allowed to donate money to freedom movements in Europe. The Irish were being oppressed by the British, and the Poles had been oppressed by the Russians, who were allies of the Americans, as well as by the Germans and the Hapsburgs. (Germans replaced Russians as the oppressors when they pushed the Russian Army back into Ukraine and Belarusia.) Many American citizens were supporting the freedom fighters in these lands. The House dropped one of the sections concerning prosecution of those criticizing "national defense," and then enacted the Espionage Act in June 1917. La Guardia and some other congressmen (and congresswoman Jeannette Rankin) voted against the

final bill because they thought it still gave government officials powers they should not have. **(24)**

Wilson's prosecutors and Cabinet officials misused the Espionage Act to abuse and convict many Americans who were loyal to America but were not followers of Wilson. Among the first victims was moviemaker Robert Goldstein, who made an epic called "The Spirit of '76" about America's original Patriots. The film, which he released in the summer of 1917, depicted vividly the most gruesome atrocity of the Revolutionary War, the Wyoming Valley Massacre of July 1778. The British, Tories (pro-British American traitors) and their Iroquois allies butchered the people of this Pennsylvania valley after killing or scattering the local militiamen. They raped some women, and sadistically tortured many of their victims before killing them. They took 225 scalps and burned roughly 1000 American settlers' homes. (The British, Tories, and some Iroquois repeated this outrage on the women and children of Cherry Valley, New York in November 1778.) Wilson's prosecutors argued this truthful portrayal of the British would cause Americans to question the good faith of ally Great Britain, and that it would cause dissension within the military, in essence interfering with America's war effort. The judge gave Goldstein a 10-year term in a federal prison. **(25)**

Americans still ran their own local affairs in that era to a much greater extent than they do today, and they were much tougher people than we are now. The country was just one generation removed from the Indian wars of the Great Plains and the Far West, and the end of the frontier era. The Alaska gold rushes happened only two decades or so earlier. Most people were farmers, miners, laborers, or tradesmen who worked with their hands and their backs for a living. Roughly half of the people were farmers, which meant roughly half of the people in the country slaughtered live animals for meat on their own property. So did many city dwellers up from the farm or over from the old country. Hunters were a much larger proportion of the population in that era than they are now. More people made their own wine, beer, and liquor than we do now, and there was a greater amount of alcohol consumption per person than there is now, even though many states were "dry." (The foolish Prohibition law would soon trigger massive public disobedience, and cause the exponential growth of organized crime.) There were fewer restrictions on pyrotechnics. A typical small town Fourth of July celebration featured many youths and young men detonating explosives powerful enough to damage small buildings or blow the foliage off of an acre of trees. Because the government was corrupt (but nowhere near as bad as it is now) and people were independent (at least half the men in the country were self-employed as farmers or small businessmen), the people often had to enforce the laws themselves. This led to vigilante activity and to a certain amount of lynchings, shootings, and beatings of undesirables. (In the South, racists aimed this violence at blacks. Elsewhere, people were more evenhanded in whom they killed.)

In the opinion of the author, certain vigilante activity, especially if it is aimed at murderers, child molesters, corrupt businessmen who steal people's farms and livelihoods, or corrupt government officials, is perfectly within the right of the people for reasons of self-government and self-defense. If government officials do not protect the people, and actively thwart the licit and just will of the people, the people have the right to rise up and protect themselves.

What Wilson's administration and many other Democrats cynically did was manipulate the vigilante tendency in many Americans of that era to suit their own evil purposes. They put out vicious and often blatantly untrue attacks on those who opposed them, in essence calling them cowards or agents of the Kaiser. This enraged some Americans enough to commit vigilante style violence against fellow Americans who weren't sufficiently vociferous against the Germans. And many Republicans made similar intemperate remarks for political advantage against those who weren't ready to embrace the cause of "making the world safe for democracy" and "punishing the Hun."

Wilson and his subordinates tolerated hysterical mobs who lynched, murdered, or beat leftist critics of his administration by failing to prosecute them for their acts of violence. Nor did he have marshals or troops try to stem the violence. State and local leaders likewise restrained their prosecutors and policemen from punishing mobs when they sensed doing so would gain them political advantage by posing as American patriots.

One nationally prominent Democrat – New York governor Al Smith (the same Al Smith who fought for America's working people in the aftermath of the Triangle Fire) – opposed Wilson. Smith was willing to support Wilson's war leadership and diplomacy as a loyal Democrat, but he vetoed all the laws the New York legislature passed that smacked of Wilsonian Red Scare oppression. **(26)**

Woodrow Wilson had a group of other victims in mind. He wanted to imprison and suppress many labor union leaders and Socialists, especially Bill Haywood of the Industrial Workers of the World (IWW) and Eugene Debs, former leader of the American Railway Union and Socialist candidate for president in 1912.

What made Haywood and Debs so dangerous to Wilson? They and men like them opposed the war because the working men would have to fight it while the rich would profit from it. They were right, because American men were essentially sent to fight and die in World War One to make the world safe for British and French imperialism, thanks to the greed of war profiteering bankers, brokers, and manufacturers, the utter lack of principle of the Allied leaders, and Wilson's own inherent baseness and delusional self-worship. **(27)**

As Americans geared up for the war in 1917, Haywood and Debs and others of like mind spoke out against the military draft. The IWW did more than just talk against the draft. Some IWW men struck at mines and at factories making gear for the war. And the IWW, from its leader down to many in its rank and file, had a Red tinge. These factors gave Wilson the excuse he needed to move against Haywood and the Wobblies.

Wilson's federal agents raided IWW offices across the country in September 1917 on false charges the IWW was in the pay of the Germans. Federal prosecutors soon indicted Haywood and 166 other IWW leaders and members for various offenses against the Espionage Act of 1917 and for various related offenses against the Selective Service Act (the draft) and against government contractors. The biggest trial of the accused was the mass trial of Haywood and 100 other Wobblies in federal court in Chicago before Judge Kenesaw Mountain Landis.

Prosecutors claimed the IWW men were unpatriotic tools of the Kaiser. The IWW men pointed out in rebuttal that there were no acts of sabotage in any factory their men worked, or against any ship their men loaded, or aboard any ship aboard which any of their men were crew members.

Judge Landis in 1907 had heard one of several cases Theodore Roosevelt's prosecutors were bringing against oil refinery monopolist John Rockefeller. Judge Landis ordered Standard Oil smashed into several pieces and had fined Rockefeller's corporation $29.2 million for multiple violations of the Elkins Act. This law forbade railway rebates; Standard Oil executives forced railroads to give them rebates due to volume, which gave them an advantage on their competitors. Landis fined the oil trust $20,000 per illegally rebated tank car load of oil; this was where the fine total came from. A judge who evidently had ties to Rockefeller overturned Landis' decision. Theodore Roosevelt was furious with this judge over the judge's sabotaging of his war on illegal trusts. The appellate judge, whose name was Grosscup, soon quit the bench. (Rockefeller's son-in-law invited the judge to his estate after he overturned Landis' ruling. Could he have been bribed into overturning and retirement?)

Eventually, other prosecutors won a conviction against Standard Oil on grounds the refinery giant violated the Sherman Anti-Trust Act by being a "combination in restraint of interstate commerce." The conviction withstood crooked appellate judges and even withstood the Supreme Court. The high court judges allowed the breakup punishment Landis had pioneered to stand.

(Some conclude Rockefeller profited anyway because the justices didn't limit the amount of interest any one man or corporate entity could have in the various parts of the broken-up oil refinery monopoly.) **(28)**

Later as baseball commissioner, Judge Landis would often rule for the players against the owners in matters of player contracts and discipline. So Landis was not an automatic out for the IWW. During the trial, he made comments against some of the prosecution's stupider statements, and he allowed many of the defendants to be out on bail. But Judge Landis was a patriot in his own harsh way, and he saw the IWW men as a cancer for their activities and their antiwar stance. When the jury members rendered a guilty verdict against all of the defendants at the end of the trial four months later, Judge Landis sentenced Haywood to 20 years in the pen. He sentenced the others to equal or lesser sentences. He allowed Haywood and many of the others to remain free on bail while they appealed their sentences.

Haywood skipped the country when the U.S. Supreme Court ruled against him in 1921. Haywood died seven years later in the Soviet Union. The IWW would be broken.

Republican Warren Harding would release most IWW defendants after he became president in 1921. Franklin Delano Roosevelt, who as Wilson's assistant Navy Secretary, had a hand in whipping up hatred against these union people for political gain, would quietly issue most IWW men full pardons in 1933 and 1934. **(29)**

While the Wobblies' trial was ongoing, Congress in May 1918 expanded the Espionage Act of 1917 to make it illegal to interfere with the selling of war bonds or to write or speak "profane" or "abusive" criticism of "the form of government of the United States." In the amendment, they also authorized the U.S. Postmaster General to censor the mail accordingly. These amendments went by the name "Sedition Act of 1918."

Woodrow Wilson and his minions acted like this meant criticizing his administration was illegal. However, they didn't have the firepower to silence their most effective critics – Theodore Roosevelt, General Leonard Wood, Henry Cabot Lodge, and other powerful Republicans. The GOP men effectively criticized Wilson because Wilson was an inept commander in chief and would prove to be an even worse peace negotiator. Wilson, while angling to get the United States into World War One, had refused to prepare for it. As a result, the American army had no tanks, no combat-ready airplanes, and very little heavy artillery.

Incompetence and fraud were the hallmarks of the Wilson administration's civilians' work during the war. For example, American taxpayers shelled out almost a

billion dollars for aircraft, and yet virtually none were fit for combat use. As a result, American pilots had to use second-rate French, British, and Italian flying machines. Teddy Roosevelt's son Quentin lost his life as an aviator in part due to the lousy French biplane he was flying when a German pilot shot him down. (The French dishonestly sold Nieuport biplanes to the Americans when they started building Spads, which were much better aircraft.) Fiorello La Guardia, who took a leave from Congress to serve as an aviator with an American unit on the Italian front, got Wilson's bean-counters to cancel a contract to buy Italian-made SIA aircraft because they were unreliable and dangerous; the crooked Italian manufacturers hoped to dump them on the Americans. La Guardia insisted on getting better Italian aircraft, and government officials took his advice. La Guardia noted American planes with Liberty motors were "flying coffins." **(30)**

Likewise, American tankers had to use French tanks and American gunners had to use French artillery pieces until our factories could gear up for war production. The War Department was so incompetent that Teddy Roosevelt paid for and shipped 200 pairs of boots to his son Archie's unit in France in the winter of 1917-1918. Supply channels were so abysmal that his son and the other men in his outfit could not get boots to replace those they had worn out. **(31)**

Wilson took out his ire on Roosevelt by refusing to let Teddy raise a division of volunteers for duty in the war. Wilson also underhandedly demeaned Roosevelt's old commander in the Rough Riders, General Leonard Wood, by exiling him to duty in the western United States instead of letting this skilled general command American troops in France. Wood now joined Teddy Roosevelt as an effective and vociferous critic of Wilson's ineptness and chicanery. American soldiers and sailors and airmen and marines would win World War One for the Allies in spite of Wilson's bungling and the bungling of his subordinates.

Wilson's prosecutors targeted the Socialists when they couldn't take down men of stature like Theodore Roosevelt. Using the Espionage Act of 1917 and the Sedition Act of 1918, they got an Ohio federal judge to sentence Eugene Debs to 10 years in federal prison for obstructing recruiting, committing offenses related to trying to damage military discipline, and obstructing the draft. The Supreme Court upheld his conviction.

Wilson would also single out former Milwaukee Socialist congressman Victor Berger for prosecution under the Espionage Act in 1917, after noting Berger was no friend of the government. (Berger, a German Jewish immigrant from Austria-Hungary, opposed the war.) Wilson's prosecutors indicted Berger, and tried him in Judge Landis' district court in Chicago. Judge Landis sentenced Berger to a 20-year stay in a federal pen, and meanly told him he regretted he couldn't have him shot. Voters in Berger's district sent him to Congress twice despite his conviction because they were largely Germans and German Americans who tilted to the left, but other congressmen voted to exclude Berger from his seat. The U.S. Supreme Court in 1921 overturned Berger's conviction. Berger won another Congressional election in 1922, so instead of reporting to Kansas to serve a term with other convicts in Leavenworth, he reported to Washington to serve his term with other unindicted criminals in Congress. **(32)**

Wilson also had Irish American opponent Jeremiah O'Leary, the editor of the anti-British newspaper "Bull" prosecuted in 1918 and 1919. By the time O'Leary came to trial, many Americans were starting to see the greed of Britain's leaders. O'Leary won acquittal on all charges. **(33)**

Much of the Espionage Act and the Sedition Act were repealed in 1921, the year Warren Harding replaced Wilson in the White House. However, enough of the Espionage Act has remained on the federal lawbooks that federal prosecutors cited it as one of the laws Lewis "Scooter" Libby allegedly broke while working as

Vice-President Dick Cheney's henchman. **(34)**

In the November 1918 elections, the Republicans crushed Woodrow Wilson's Democrats in elections across the country. Republicans would now hold majorities in both houses of Congress.

World War One ended with an armistice a few days later on November 11, 1918. The war was over, but Europe remained in turmoil. The Communists had taken power in Russia, they were taking over Hungary, and it was looking like they would take over in Germany. The British maintained the naval blockade of Germany and the countries that used to comprise Austria-Hungary until after the Germans and their former allies signed the peace treaties in mid 1919. They expanded the blockade to Communist Russia. Hundreds of thousands of people died while the British interfered with the food importing of most of Europe. Every sort of disorder, from strikes, to rebellions against occupiers, to civil war, to open warfare between nations, was taking place in Europe in 1919 and the early 1920s. So much for the big lie that World War One was the war to end all wars.

PROHIBITION – WET DREAM OF THE WACKY

The end of World War One did not end turmoil on the American home front. In fact, social unrest escalated. American servicemen came home to find they had no jobs. Those who did have jobs found their paychecks shrinking as the price of living had skyrocketed, thanks to Wilson's policies. Meanwhile, roughly 120,000 families were mourning dead servicemen. War profiteers raked in huge profits, and did not share their ill-gotten gains with their workers. The attitude of corporate bosses was responsible for roughly 2600 strikes across America in 1919. These strikes involved about four million workers.

The soldiers, sailors, and strikers couldn't even drown their sorrows legally. Why? Because the War Time Prohibition Act banning alcohol sales came into effect on July 1, 1919, and then the 18th Amendment, commonly known as Prohibition, came into effect six months later.

How could something as stupid as Prohibition come to pass? Congress was dominated by pro-Prohibition members. Feminists and fundamentalists favored outlawing alcohol. Many women thought they could control the menfolk by restricting their access to booze. John Rockefeller, Henry Ford, and many other magnates wanted to limit alcohol consumption, so they could squeeze more productivity out of their workers without increasing their pay. Nativists slurred Americans with heritage from Catholic lands in Europe and immigrants from these lands, most notably the Irish, as presumed alcoholics. They also slurred the

Italians and to a lesser extent, the South Germans and Slavs, for their supposed weakness for strong drink.

Millions of the manliest men were away in the Service during World War One. Most of these young men and middle aged men would have voted against Dry candidates if there was a choice. But virtually none of them got to vote.

When America entered World War One, Wilson wanted a drastic cutback in alcohol production. So he argued conservation of grain for the war effort was involved. (Wilson was a preachy hypocrite; the solemn Calvinist was an occasional adulterer. His second wife Edith Galt was an occasional adulteress. They deserved each other.) Wilson got this authority from Congress via the Lever Act (40 Statutes at Large 276-287) in August 1917. Prohibitionist lobbyists started slandering brewery owners, especially the German-American ones, by accusing them of undermining the war effort and for being tools the Kaiser for brewing beer. Wilson used the power the Lever Act gave him to prohibit the making of most alcoholic beverages stronger than 2.75% alcohol in December 1917.

The politicians of most Protestant countries of northern Europe enacted some form of silly prohibition during this era. British officials limited pubs' hours, ordered the supply of beer and ale reduced and the potency cut while taxing it highly, and for awhile forbade the distilling of spirits like whisky and gin. Lloyd George, the shifty little liar and serial adulterer who ran Britain as its prime minister, was a holier-than-thou temperance freak who didn't practice what he preached. However, enough Britons of good sense and good cheer (there were many of these blokes and birds, thankfully) kept him from imposing completely on their right to drink. The leaders of neutral Norway and Sweden – whose grain supplies were low thanks to British naval domination of their shipping trade – also imposed prohibition on their subjects. So did the leaders of the Finns when the Finns won their independence in 1919. Danish leaders made the people of their colony Iceland go without, but wisely refrained from drying up their home turf.

Russian leaders tried to limit alcohol use during the war, but wealthier people seemed to have booze, wine, and beer when they needed it. The Communists tried limited prohibition (but not for their leaders) for a few years, then dropped it in the mid 1920s. British-dominated Canada and New Zealand enacted some sort of silly prohibition at this time also. New Zealand's soldiers returning from World War One provided the thrust people needed to overturn prohibition in Kiwi country. Aussie men and their sheilas were much less prone to listen to nanny state prattle from their leaders than other Commonwealth subjects, so Australians didn't suffer prohibition but remained cheerfully wet.

Wilson asked for and signed into law 10 days *AFTER* Armistice Day in November 1918 a bill called the War Time Prohibition Act. This law (aka 40 Statutes at Large 1045-1049) would outlaw the production and sale of any beverage the president considered intoxicating. The Progressive liars in Congress and the White House wrote into the law that it was "for the purpose of conserving the man power of the Nation, and to increase efficiency in the production of arms, munitions, ships, food, and clothing for the Army and Navy." In February 1919, Wilson's Internal Revenue Service commissioner decided any beverage with an alcohol content of 0.5% or more was intoxicating. The War Time Prohibition Act, which Wilson let go into effect July 1, 1919, effectively banned alcohol on the false ground America was still at war even though the Germans had quit and Austria-Hungary was no more as an empire.

Meanwhile, Congress members had enacted a proposed Prohibition amendment in December 1917. Enough state legislatures ratified it by January 1919 that it would go into effect as the 18th Amendment by January 1920. But typical of many politicians today, the congressmen did not pass an enforcement act to ensure the dumb law they had enacted would be enforced. (This was similar to what members of Congress would do in 2006 in voting for a border fence without voting the funds to pay for it. George W. Bush and others in his administration were complicit in this deception.)

The congressmen fixed this oversight somewhat in October 1919 by passing the Volstead Act aka the National Prohibition Act (41 Statutes at Large 305-323). The Volstead Act ordered federal and state officials to enforce the Prohibition law. Wilson, by now a virtual invalid because of his stroke, vetoed the bill for technical reasons. Wilson wasn't opposed to Prohibition, but supposedly vetoed the bill because of the "wartime" prohibition tie-in of the bill. Or maybe he had a moment of clarity after his emotional and physical breakdown. Or maybe he was just thirsty. It didn't matter. Congress overrode his veto. **(35)**

However, Prohibition was essentially an unfunded federal mandate. The Volstead Act did not provide money for enforcement of the prohibition law because the knotheads who passed this law either did so for political reasons only or they reckoned without the ingenuity of the Mob or of average citizens in violating it. A relatively small number of federal agents were assigned to enforce Prohibition, and many of them were bribable. So were many local cops.

Vermin in organized crime branched out from prostitution and protection rackets to supplying illegal, substandard, and often poisonous alcohol to a thirsty public. They soon made hundreds of millions of dollars from the sale of illegal hooch, much more than enough to keep many policemen, prosecutors, judges, and politicians in their pockets. Al Capone, whose thugs murdered scores of people in Chicago as he paid off all kinds of local authorities, would be the posterboy of Prohibition nonenforcement.

SUFFRAGETTES, RACISM, AND RACE RIOTS

The year 1919 was also the year Congress would redress a longstanding wrong and enact a Constitutional amendment granting to women citizens the right to vote. Unfortunately, this result came from a lot of bigotry also.

For roughly 70 years, suffragettes had been working to gain the right of women to vote. In many of the Western states, women won the right to vote long before the 19th

Amendment would enter the lawbooks. Men greatly outnumbered women out West for many years, so women who were willing to live in the rougher society of the mining town or the lumber camp or the isolated ranch or homestead had more choices for mates and got more consideration from men as a result. Some say women got the right to vote because of the contributions pioneer women made in "winning the West." The less charitable say women got the right to vote because their husbands and fathers wanted their votes to counter the votes of the itinerant single miners, cowboys, and laborers who might vote into office men who might break their power. In Utah, women, including the multiple "wives" of the polygamous, got the right to vote because the Mormon elders saw it as a domestic way to stuff the ballot boxes against "Gentiles" (non-Mormons). Regardless of their motivation, the men out West did the right thing in giving the womenfolk the vote.

The frustration and militancy of some of the suffragettes in other parts of the country picked up by the 1910s. They organized parades and rallies. Some of the more militant suffragettes (the predecessors of the distaff floozies of the 1960s who burned their bras and then complained they felt like sex objects when the more buxom of them bounced without support) started disturbing the peace, trespassing, and doing other things that led them to being housed for short stays in local jails and being force-fed with feeding tubes down their throats or nostrils if they decided to go on hunger strikes.

This was not overly gallant of the authorities, but it was very mild treatment compared to the violence company goons and police and troops were inflicting on striking workers. And force-feeding the feminists with tubes down their throats was almost foreplay when compared to the hundreds of murders lawmen and lynch mobs were committing each year against law-abiding black men, even black men who were wearing their country's uniform as soldiers or sailors. American men laughed at the suffragettes, but they would not tolerate them being beaten in an organized way. In fact, the sinking of the *Titanic* in 1912 hurt the feminist cause somewhat because all their talk of equality sank temporarily when people realized most of the men aboard the doomed luxury liner died because they allowed women and children to board lifeboats first so they could be rescued. This was a grim reminder women were the weaker sex.

Neither party's politicians in most of the country wanted to antagonize women, because women who had the vote might vote against their party. Wilson opposed women's suffrage when he was governor of New Jersey. Militant suffragette Alice Paul and her buddies upstaged Wilson's first inaugural parade in 1913 with a big parade in Washington of their own, to remind him they were holding him accountable.

Wilson opposed giving women the vote during his first term as president. Then he told suffragettes he didn't know how he felt about women's suffrage. Then he did something worse. Wilson, with practice as a cheater, became a false friend of the feminists. He claimed he traveled to New Jersey in 1915 to vote for women's voting in the state election. (The measure lost.) But he did nothing to further their cause with the power of his office. Some feminists urged women in the Western

states to vote against Wilson and all Democrats in the 1916 elections.

Wilson won re-election (barely, without a majority of the popular vote) in 1916. So he kissed off the suffragettes; he refused to meet with suffragette leaders. Besides his first wife, Wilson lied to and stiffed many people during his life; the feminists chose to take it personally. Some spurned suffragettes started demonstrating outside the White House. They also staged protests at and near the White House designed to embarrass Wilson and humiliate him.

They succeeded. By 1918, Wilson was whipped enough to publicly call for enactment of an amendment giving women the right to vote. Wilson made a speech to the Senate in September 1918 pleading that they pass an amendment giving women the right to vote; he claimed (like he did with banning alcohol) that it would somehow help the war effort. (Wilson never made that argument for easing segregation; he favored more segregation to "keep Negroes in their place.") Wilson's fellow Southern Democrats sneered the nation's menfolk had never seemed to need women having voting rights to fight wars effectively before. So they voted down women's suffrage in the Senate in October 1918, and the Germans sued for peace within weeks.

Enraged feminists retaliated by spanking Woodrow a little harder. They started burning Wilson in effigy and calling him "Kaiser Wilson." They also tried to undermine his self-styled mission of civilization at the Paris Peace Conference by pointing out he was an undemocratic hypocrite who kept women in his own land disenfranchised. They started a "fire watch" vigil complete with a burning fire in a trash can outside the White House over the winter of early 1919. *Any American of normal beliefs and normal sexuality trying that stunt now would be shot or beaten and jailed by assorted federales.* In one respect the ladies were wasting their time because Woodrow had already run away from their discipline and had shipped off to the Paris Peace Conference with his own battle-ax of a second wife to tolerate another form of private and public punishment and humiliation at the hands of the leaders of the French and the British. The lame duck Democrat Senate voted down suffrage a second time in February 1919 before the members of the new Republican-dominated Congress took their seats in March 1919.

Southern politicians – almost all Democrats – were the most disposed to keep the vote from their womenfolk. Some did so on grounds letting women vote would somehow help blacks. Their fears were unfounded. Suffragettes were as bigoted as their menfolk.

Many earlier white suffragettes had turned their backs on abolitionist and suffragette Sojourner Truth while she was alive. (Sojourner Truth was a New York slave who escaped before New York leaders ended slavery in that state.) Susan B. Anthony and Elizabeth Cady Stanton, the two most prominent feminist leaders of the 1800s, opposed the 15th Amendment giving black men the right to vote, supposedly because it didn't include giving women the right to vote.

The anti-black pattern of most white feminists continued through the decades. The National American Women Suffrage Association – the largest feminist group, held a convention in Atlanta in 1895 and asked Frederick Douglass, the legendary black abolitionist and U.S. ambassador, to stay away from the convention even though he was a long time supporter of giving women the vote. Black suffragettes had to form their own organizations like the National Association of Colored Women because they were not welcome in the white women's feminist groups. However, women of the Women's Ku Klux Klan, who also spewed hatred against Catholic women and Jewish women, were welcome in the ranks of the white suffragettes, or were at least tolerated because they could sway Southern legislators in a way Northern feminists could not.

With the conspicuous and honorable exception of the legendary social worker Jane Addams of Hull House fame, most WASP feminists also claimed giving them the vote would allow them to help WASP men counteract the "machine politics" voting of the naturalized non-WASP immigrants and their "all-too-numerous offspring." All too many Progressives believed in eugenics and social Darwinism, which supposedly made WASPs the most superior group of people in the world. Starting at the top with Wilson, who damned "hyphenated Americans" (Americans of non-British ancestry), the Progressives made it politically correct for these suffragettes to exploit the biases of many American men and for these suffragettes to vent their own prejudices in claiming the "native stock" Americans of WASP blood were biologically superior to all those "Micks, kikes, dagos, Polacks, hunkies, and greasers" with roots in Ireland, Jewish communities, Italy, Eastern Europe or Latin America who were filling up America's cities, mines, mills, and ranches.

White suffragettes, while playing the fairness card, did nothing to protest the denial of voting rights to black men in the South in the decade before they got the 19th Amendment passed. In fact, black activist W.E.B. Du Bois denounced the National American Women Suffrage Association on this very issue in 1912. **(36)**

Carrie Chapman Catt, head of the National American Women Suffrage Association from 1900 to 1904 and from 1915 to 1920, told her minions to keep black suffragettes out of her organization. She told them to tell the black women "you (white NAWSA suffragettes) will be able to get the vote for women more easily if they (black suffragettes) do not embarrass you by asking for membership." Militant Alice Paul allowed black suffragettes in the 1913 Washington, D. C.

parade, but they had to march in the back.

One of the white feminists' key arguments to sway the Rebel representatives was the underhanded one that giving white women the vote would counteract the voting of black men, because these white women claimed they were smarter and more virtuous than blacks. And since there were more white women than black men and black women combined, they argued, their sheer numbers would blot out the blacks.

The white suffragette leaders tangled the sheets with the Klan, and they also got into bed with the bigoted crackpots of the Woman's Christian Temperance Union. The WCTU was a long-time wanna-be girlfriend of the National American Women Suffrage Association, because its leaders and members wanted to ban alcohol and they figured women would be more prone than men to vote for Prohibition if they got the vote. In 1918, 1919, and 1920, the Prohibition movement was peaking, and the *liaison* between the female prohibitionists and the suffragettes would assist the suffragettes in achieving their goal of getting the vote for women. The suffragettes also helped the prohibitionists achieve their goal of making booze illegal, so the dalliance was as good for the prohibitionists as it was for the suffragettes.

The Republican-controlled Congress in June 1919 passed the women's voting amendment and sent it to the states for ratification without waiting for Woodrow Wilson to return from further humiliation in Paris.

In early 1920, the leaders of the National American Women Suffrage Association, anticipating victory, changed their group's name to the League of Women Voters. They forgot to add the word "White" to their title. Ms. Catt and her white sisters had done nothing to help black female or black male voters in the South. But the white suffragette leaders were not a bit ashamed of themselves. In a mood of what some might call "spoiled bitch entitlement," they still lobbied the NAACP and black male voters to urge them to petition state legislators to vote for the 19th Amendment. **(37)**

In fairness to Carrie Chapman Catt, she ate her own, too. Ms. Catt and most other suffragettes tended to be anti-war, but they pussyfooted around in 1917 because they saw the best way to advance women's suffrage was to act like golddiggers, suck up to men, and support a declaration of war to show "patriotism" and "toughness." This meant Ms. Catt and many other leading suffragettes would backstab Congresswoman Jeannette Rankin, the only elected federal female officeholder, because Miss Jeannette had the courage of her convictions to vote against American entry into a war to make the world safe for British and French imperialists and American war profiteers.

Despite Jeannette's service to women by helping get them the vote in Washington, Oregon, California, Arizona, Kansas and her own Montana (where this rancher's daughter rode on horseback around the state to round up votes), C. C. Catt and NAWSA wouldn't help her win her seat in Congress in 1916. Because Democrats in Montana gerrymandered Jeannette Rankin out of her House seat in 1918, she ran for Senate in the November 1918 elections. While most men in public life with an opinion assaulted Jeannette as an example of unreasonable feminine softness, "a crying schoolgirl," for her dramatic vote against U.S. entry into World War One, Sister Carrie and her followers delivered the unkindest cut of all. They supported a Democrat male over Miss Rankin. He won. Carrie Chapman Catt was proving women in politics could be as conscienceless as men.

By August 1920, enough state legislatures had ratified the act to make it the 19th Amendment. It came in time for many women to vote for Republican Warren Harding over Democrat James Cox for president on the grounds they found him more handsome. Columnist H.L. Mencken grumbled that giving women the right to vote merely doubled the number of ignorant voters.

After World War One came to an end, and women's suffrage was in the bag, it became chic for women to become peace activists. Carrie Chapman Catt and many other leading feminists decided to fight for peace when it was safe and fashionable to do so. Jeannette Rankin, who – when it counted – voted against sending American men into a war America had no business being in even though she sensed it would end her political career, faded from view for years. Sister Carrie's League of Women Voters did nothing to help black men or black women fight those in the South who kept them from voting in the Klan-dominated 1920s.

The real short-term winners of the ratification of the 18th and 19th Amendments were organized criminals. These vermin would use Prohibition and women voting in favor of dry candidates to profit greatly by making and selling alcohol. They would use the increased profits to expand the organized sexual sales of willing and unwilling females, to lay siege to Chicago and many other cities and towns, and to undermine the respect for law Americans had. The women's vote was overdue, but they wasted their first use of power on the stupidity of Prohibition. There are always unintended consequences to every government action taken.

And there was one other set of disturbances that first caught the nation's attention in 1919 – race riots. The suffragettes had left America's blacks behind. The upheaval of World War One would give America's blacks further eye-openers as to who their friends and enemies were.

The gallant service of many blacks in World War One and the migration of many blacks from the South to work in the factories of the Northeast and Midwest led to changes of attitudes among many blacks. They had fought for democracy in Europe, and had made weapons for the fight for democracy in Europe. Why should blacks endure mob violence, formal discrimination and other trappings of slavery in their own land, supposedly the land of the free? Race riots in Chicago and Washington and about 20 other cities, mostly triggered by whites who were angry about the new so-called "uppityness" of blacks, erupted over the summer of 1919. Rioters, mostly whites, killed scores of people, wounded hundreds, and left hundreds homeless. **(38)**

Many good authors have chronicled the rise of America's blacks to get themselves their due in America's society in much greater detail than this book has the space or the scope to do. At the end of the 1910s, heavyweight boxer and former champ Jack Johnson wasn't the only black fighter who was willing to stand up to white America. By the end of the decade, blacks were starting to exercise their First Amendment and Second Amendment rights much more than they had ever done in previous decades. (I don't really count Reconstruction, because it took U.S. Army troops to protect the blacks who held public office in the states of the occupied Confederacy.) Blacks saw that they were going to have to fight and work for what was rightfully theirs.

THE RED SCARE

During all the race riots and labor unrest and the exponential growth of organized crime, where was Woodrow? Wilson was busy wasting the last weeks of 1918 and much of 1919 giving in to the unscrupulous leaders of Britain, France, Italy, and Japan at the Paris peace talks in order to get them to approve his pipe dream League of Nations. Meanwhile, his fellow Allied leaders concentrated on stealing land, enslaving people, and double-crossing each other. Instead of addressing the problems besetting America, Wilson would travel the country by train to try to sell the poisoned fruit of his incompetent and dishonest labor in Paris to the American people. In September 1919, Wilson would break down physically and emotionally during his snake-oil tour and have to cut it short. He was kept in seclusion in the White House, but suffered a stroke in October 1919. Wilson would spend the rest of his time in office as a drooling meglomaniac under the control of his bossy frumpy second wife Edith Galt.

Wilson was such an insecure individual that most of the people he appointed for his cabinet were at best second-rate men. Attorney General A. Mitchell Palmer was one of the most prominent nobodies in the Wilson administration's legion of mediocrities. Palmer, a failed Democratic candidate for senator from Pennsylvania, got Wilson to appoint him "Alien Property Custodian" in late 1917. Palmer and his subordinates would have time to check for leads on foreign and domestic subversives by going through the seized property and records of aliens in custody.

Wilson would appoint Mitchell as his Attorney General in March 1919. Mitchell didn't blame the strikes, race riots, or mob violence on Wilson and his subordinates, who had unleashed mob hatred, made the war safe for profiteers, enabled organized crime to start flourishing because of Prohibition, persecuted union people, jumped the cost of living, and stomped on the rights of black Americans and allowed others to do likewise. Either out of stupidity or deceit, and perhaps because he saw a path to a higher office, Palmer decided to attribute the riots, the strikes, and the lawlessness to foreign intrigues involving people like the Socialists, the anarchists, and the Communists.

Within days of taking office, Palmer ordered raids on suspected Socialist, anarchist, Communist, and leftist union people, using the Espionage Act of 1917 and the Sedition Act of 1918 as the authorities for these actions. Many leads he got for these raids came from the 1917 raid on the office of "Mother Earth," the anarchist journal of Emma Goldman. While they were on the premises, they raided the office of "The Blast," the anarchist publication of Ms. Goldman's fellow anarchist and on-and-off sex partner Alexander Berkman. *(Nice name for a paper appealing to bomb throwers, Alex.)*

Berkman, by the way, had already had to go without Emma's lovin' for more than a decade. Berkman failed in his attempt in 1892 to shoot and stab to death Henry Frick, the greedy white-collar criminal who ran the Homestead Steel mill for Andrew Carnegie. Frick was to blame for the Homestead Steel Strike, which caused the deaths of several workers and several Pinkerton men, brought in as goons to help break the strike. Berkman went to prison for the assault on Frick.

The raids took place because Emma and Alex preached resistance to the draft. The seized subscription lists in particular led to 10,000 suspected members of the lunatic fringe. These records, along with records taken in other raids Palmer's predecessor as Attorney General authorized in 1917 and 1918 on IWW members, Socialists, and other suspected subversives, gave Palmer a good data base on these people to work with.

Palmer's eagerness on the job led persons unknown to mail him a dynamite bomb at his fashionable Washington digs in April 1919. These individuals

mailed similar tokens of esteem to Judge Kenesaw Mountain Landis (who was trying the IWW men), Supreme Court Justice Oliver Wendell Holmes (who wrote the briefs in some cases which favored Wilson's prosecutors over dissidents), the Secretary of Labor, the Commissioner of Immigration (one Anthony Caminetti, who Frederic Howe railed against), and some senators and congressmen involved in probes against radical causes. They also mailed these "care packages" to the mayors of New York City and Seattle. (The latter, Ole Hanson, was an accomplished anti-union demagogue who broke a general strike of tens of thousands of workers by bringing thousands of federal troops and policemen into the city and threatening to fire the strikers or shoot them.) Certain well-known robber barons also made the bombers' gift list.

One bomb blew the hands off of a maid of a senator; two others failed to go off when their targets or their clerks opened them. Postal officials managed to intercept most of the others; in one case a New York City postal worker held up delivery of 16 of the packages because they didn't have enough postage on them for mailing with red sealing tape. Other less fussy clerks had let other bomb packages through.

Palmer next heard from those who didn't wish him well in June 1919. One evening an individual put a bomb on the front steps of his upscale house and detonated it. The blast blew off the front of Palmer's house, damaged FDR's house across the street, and blew out windows and doors up and down the block. It also blew the bomber, later determined to be an Italian immigrant with anarchist tendencies, into chunks and fragments of meat and bone that scattered through the neighborhood. Like-minded individuals that night bombed the houses of the mayor of Cleveland, a judge and a legislator in Massachusetts, an immigration official in Pittsburgh, a judge in New York, and a New Jersey silk manufacturer (this industry was the target of a failed IWW strike in 1913). Someone on that night also bombed a Catholic church in Philadelphia; this sacrilege was linked with the other bombings. An elderly woman servant of the New York judge died in the blast at his home. **(39)**

Palmer soon announced he intended to enforce the War Time Prohibition Act when it was to go into effect July 1, 1919. His excuse was as weasely as the tactics used to enact the law in the first place. Drys in Congress and Wilson had put in place anti-alcohol statutes ostensibly aimed at taking wheat, corn, and other grains away from brewers and distillers so there would be more food for men in uniform and for the Allies, and cheaper grain for the public. Of course, what actually happened was that the Wilson administration and Congress hiked the price of wheat and corn to encourage more grain growing during the war. They gave away much of the grain to worthless allies Britain, France, and Italy. The American public paid more taxes for the government to buy the grain, and they also paid more for bread, meat, and milk despite the glut of grain.

Prohibition was supposed to stay in effect only as long as the United States was at war. Even though the Germans had stopped fighting, signed an armistice, turned their ships over to the British (and scuttled them in a British naval base), and turned over most of their artillery and machine guns to the French, and had gone home, and even though Germany, Hungary, and Austria were imploding as nations, since the Congress hadn't ratified the peace treaties with Germany, Austria, Hungary, Bulgaria, and Turkey, then the United States was still technically at war. And, by golly, said Palmer, a Quaker, the ban on alcohol would have to continue.

Meanwhile, Palmer's neighbor Franklin Delano Roosevelt – whose family's fortune had come from selling opium to the Chinese -- was telling women's groups with a straight face that America joining Wilson's League of Nations was the best defense against the alleged Communist doctrine of "free love."

If practicing "free love" made one a Red, then FDR was a Stalinist. FDR was sexually involved with his wife Eleanor's secretary Lucy Mercer at the time. He had a large number of adulterous affairs before and after the blast at the Palmers' house, and even his eventual crippling evidently did not affect the one organ he needed most to continue to commit adultery.

FDR reportedly enjoyed the sexual favors of his secretary Missy Le Hand [sic], his cousin Margaret Suckley [sic], Crown Princess Martha of Norway (who lived at the White House and at FDR's Hyde Park digs for periods during World War Two while Norway was under Nazi occupation), and the wife (Dorothy Schiff) of at least one of the men who were his followers. The husband of Dorothy Schiff, for example, even bragged about her being hot enough to capture the attention of their President. Lucy Mercer, by the way, and not Eleanor, was with FDR when he suffered the stroke that ended his life. **(40)**

On Ellis Island, Commissioner Frederic Howe tried to get Palmer and others who were running the Red Scare to obey the laws regarding due process before deporting people. He said judges who had tried cases involving people he was supposed to deport told him there was no evidence supporting the deportation of many of these people. So he released hundreds of these unfortunates. Howe blamed the Red Scare on certain big businessmen who wanted to depress wages and break the militant IWW and other less militant unions. So, he stated, they colluded with the Justice Department to go after many union people and fed effective propaganda to the press about the alleged revolutionary and/or anarchist tendencies of union members. Howe also said many people were being railroaded unfairly due to vengeful neighbors and associates, and due to civilian detectives and others

deputized to be on the lookout for anti-government subversives. These men, he said, in many cases were looking for money and a free vacation to New York and possibly to Europe to ensure the people they accused made it back to their homelands after being deported.

Howe was away from Ellis Island for a few months after the end of World War One. Woodrow Wilson had summoned him to work with the American delegation to the Paris Peace Talks. On returning to Ellis Island from the confab, Howe threw up his hands in despair. He said he gave his word to many would-be immigrants and other detained aliens they would receive fair representation to argue why they should not be expelled, then when he was away on official business, his boss Anthony Caminetti or some other government functionary had arranged to deport the aliens. Howe finally quit as commissioner in September 1919. Fearing investigation and criminal prosecution for his leniency, Howe burned his private records and notes before leaving Ellis Island for good. **(41)**

Many members of the Republican-dominated Congress decided to vie with Democrat Palmer on who could be a better anti-Red. So in November 1919 they investigated Howe for deporting only 60 aliens for deportable offenses related to subversion when officials had issued 697 arrest warrants for such individuals as of November 1, 1919.

These figures were padded. The cases of 94 men of the 697 were still open, and lawmen had not served the warrants yet on another 52 suspects. In another 162 cases, judges had ruled the defendants were not guilty, or were American citizens, or were undeportable as aliens at the time for other reasons. (Of these, seven were dead, seven couldn't be found, seven left the country on their own, and two were insane.) Another 88 were awaiting deportation, but there was not yet suitable transportation available to ship them back to their homelands. Of these 88, six were fugitives and one left the country on his own.

In the cases of 47 suspects, they had received warrants, but they hadn't had hearings. Most of them were already in prison on other charges. Hearing decisions had not yet come in from field officers for 23 suspects. Judges dismissed cases against five aliens on habeas corpus (unlawful detention) motions.

There were 166 aliens out on bond or out on their own recognizance. So their cases were still open pending final appeal rulings. They should have been in custody so they wouldn't escape before the judges resolved their cases, because they were potential flight risks. Howe or the judges who granted bail or own recognizance releases were in the wrong.

Howe didn't deserve the false charges leveled against him that he allowed gambling and loose women for detainees, or that he let a Bolshevik propaganda bureau operate on Ellis Island, or that he was trying to get dangerous subversives off the hook. A newspaper writer in Cleveland, where Howe first made his mark as a reformer, wrote Howe ran Ellis Island as "a government institution turned into a Socialist hall, a spouting ground for Red revolutionists, a Monte Carlo for foreigners only, a club where Europe's offscourings are entertained at American expense." When Howe demanded the right to defend himself, cross-examine hostile witnesses, and present his witnesses, the congressmen expelled him from the hearings. Neither the congressmen nor Palmer punished Howe formally for being a do-gooder, but they were wrong in preventing him from defending himself. **(42)**

Howe said many government employees interfered with good government. "In a generation's time," he said, "largely through the Civil Service reform movement, America has created an official bureaucracy moved largely by fear, hating initiative, and organized as a solid block to protect itself and its petty unimaginative, salary-hunting instincts. America has paid a heavy price for its permanent classified service."

"When I asked for an assistant woman commissioner to look after the cases of women and children and had finally induced Miss Grace Abbott, of Hull House, Chicago (Jane Addams' organization), to accept," Howe said, " I found the position filled one morning by a woman dependent on a job-hunting congressman; she was utterly ignorant of immigration and had a New England morality that made her a nuisance to everybody, and a telltale tongue that carried her to Washington with every conceivable mare's nest that she could uncover."

Howe defended Andrew Jackson's "spoils system," admitting its evils, but noting a president could staff agencies with employees that reflected his will instead of letting the inertia and petty grubbing and power seeking of the career bureaucrats hinder him. "Even Presidents came and went, but the permanent official, protected by the Civil Service regulations, was there for life," he noted. **(43)**

In October 1919, coal miners went on strike for pay increases. The coal mine operators were profiting from the rise in the price of coal, but the workers were suffering because the dramatic rise in the cost of living had shrunk the buying power of their paychecks, which had stayed more or less static in the previous few years.

A coal strike in the face of an oncoming winter was a serious thing in 1919. Very little machinery, relatively speaking, was oil-fired; nuclear power was a thing of the future. So were massive hydroelectric power projects. Coal propelled trains and ships, heated buildings, and ran power plants to a much larger extent percentagewise then than coal does today. Palmer

said a law forbidding strikes in wartime was still in force, and most of Woodrow Wilson's other cabinet members and key advisers went along with him. Palmer also arranged for troops to descend upon coal mining towns. Palmer took action against the coal miners in court, and various judges ruled for the government and against the coal miners.

United Mine Workers president John L. Lewis, sensing Palmer and Woodrow Wilson's other henchmen were fixing to do to them what they did to the IWW, called off the strike. But many coal miners refused to go back to work, which kept the pressure on. Some of Wilson's top men said the miners deserved nothing, and Wilson (or his wife acting in his place) agreed. Some of Wilson's other cabinet men said the miners deserved no more than a 14% increase. The miners were holding out for more, and Wilson's labor secretary said they deserved much more than a crummy 14% increase. Wilson (or his second wife Edith Galt) changed his (her) mind and okayed a 14% pay increase offer. The mine operators agreed to it, and the miners reluctantly went back to the mines. **(44)**

Palmer meanwhile found time to organize raids against various radicals on November 7, 1919, the second anniversary of Lenin's putsch against the democratic government of Russia. Any foreign-born among those arrested and found guilty of offenses in this wave of raids Palmer ordered deported. He also wanted aliens previously found guilty of offenses against the war effort to join them in exile.

Emma Goldman and Alexander Berkman and about 250 other foreign-born radicals were deported from Ellis Island aboard the steamer *S.S. Buford* in December 1919. The press called the ship "the Red Ark" or "the Soviet Ark." The captain and crew of the ship dropped off Emma, Alex, and their fellow undesirables at a port in Finland, because the British were blockading Russian ports. They made it into the Soviet Union, where they claimed they were received like heroes.

Later Emma Goldman and Alexander Berkman became disillusioned with the workers' paradise because Lenin and his cronies were much more barbaric than the crooked men who ran American commerce and American government. Emma was intellectually honest enough to denounce the Communists, which caused many of her former supporters to denounce her. She longed to come back to the United States. Despite all the agitating she had done against the institutions of this country, she still missed it, and discovered to her sorrow there was no better nation on earth. American officials would let her return once for a few-months-long book tour to peddle her autobiography, but she would spend the rest of her days in France, England, and Canada. Berkman, who would live elsewhere in Europe, would commit suicide in 1936. Emma Goldman died in Canada in 1940. **(45)**

In January 1920, Palmer ordered the largest of the series of raids against suspected Reds and other suspected troublemakers. Federal agents made about 5000 arrests in 33 cities. The suspects faced charges of attempting to overthrow the government by force and similar offenses. The charges were spurious enough that judges found most of these individuals innocent of wrongdoing and had them released. However, some guilty vermin and some wrongfully accused men found themselves clapped aboard trains and literally railroaded to Ellis Island. In January 1920, there were about 500 detainees at Ellis Island awaiting possible deportation. However, the officials who reviewed the cases of these people in most cases decided they had not broken any laws, and ordered them released on bail. **(46)**

Palmer was not a one-trick pony when it came to repression. Besides the radicals, Palmer had targeted union people and drinkers. The energetic Attorney General also found time in early 1920 to scheme with Woodrow Wilson on how to get enough senators' seats declared vacated so Wilson's treaty and League of Nations could win ratification in the Senate. **(47)**

What finally burst Palmer's bubble was his own foolish prediction that the Communists would launch a bombing campaign on May Day of 1920. When this didn't happen, Palmer stood discredited. He would be out of office along with his boss in early 1921.

Why did Palmer foment all the hysteria?

Part of it had to be self-preservation. Two times some anarchist or other enemy of the social order had tried to kill him with a bomb, and it was only natural for him to want to wipe these nutcases out. And he had the power to do so.

Part of Palmer's motivation was no doubt the orders he received from Woodrow (and possibly Edith) Wilson. Wilson, like many self-styled idealists who gain power, was essentially authoritarian. He could not tolerate dissent, and he falsely demonized people who sincerely disagreed with him. He and his minions tried to enact and enforce laws they thought would allow them to jail people critical of the government.

Part of it was political. Palmer, who must have known Wilson and Wilsonism were headed for the junkpile of history, hoped to become president himself even though worn-out Woodrow delusionally thought he could win a third term. Palmer wanted a record to run on. With the Red Scare, liberal Democrat Palmer got a record, all right, that of a wholesale violator of civil liberties in the mode of Woodrow Wilson. Palmer still ran for the Democratic Party's presidential nomination later that year but his campaign balloon went limp. (So did the campaign attempt of William McAdoo, Wilson's Secretary of the Treasury and Wilson's own son-in-law.) Wilson never forgave either "traitor."

The dumbest part of Palmer's move against aliens was the fact that he ignored many immigrants who richly deserved to be deported because they were truly evil criminals who already were or soon would become organized crime big shots. Such men included Chicago whoremongers and mobsters Big Jim Colosimo, Johnny Torrio, and Al Capone, not to mention the Terrible Gennas, or Frank Nitti. They also included New York mobsters Lucky Luciano, Francesco Castiglia aka Frank Costello, and Vito Genovese. These men had criminal records and should have been deported to Italy. Non-Italian organized crime figures like Meyer Lansky in New York and Chicago brothel owner, white slaver, and Capone financial officer Jake Guzik should likewise have been deported to Russia, from whence their families fled the anti-Jewish pogroms. Crooked Chicago politician Anton Cermak could have been sent back to the newly independent Czechoslovakia. My own Grandpa Charlie would have wanted to deport an immigrant criminal he collared named Vicenzo De Mora aka Vicenzo Gebardi. Charlie Sherlock was the first copper to arrest De Mora; he was better known to the world as Jack McGurn, Al Capone's enforcer and mastermind of the Valentine's Day Massacre.

Despite the claims of some nativists, many other leading Jewish organized crime figures such as Lepke Buchalter, Bugsy Siegel, and Arthur Flegenheimer aka Dutch Schultz, were <u>not</u> immigrants. They were born not long after their immigrant parents settled in New York City. The biggest of the Jewish organized crime figures, Arthur Rothstein, who fixed the 1919 "Black Sox" World Series, was a third-generation American. These vermin could not be deported. However, they could all die violently, and did. Other mobsters took out Schultz, Siegel, and Rothstein; New York authorities put Buchalter in the hot seat and electrocuted him for murder.

Top organized crime figures had powerful protectors in local and state governments. Possibly Palmer knew enough about the power structure not to buck it.

Palmer wound up on the ash heap of history, but he was still very fortunate he was living in America, which had no established church. Throughout the centuries, Jews and Christians alike considered the fitting fate for a false prophet who wrongfully stirred up the people to be execution.

END NOTES

1. Congressman John Conyers (D-Michigan), during a 1998 hearing on "hate crimes" legislation, said there was essentially no federal anti-lynch law and specifically blamed FDR. Charles Schumer (D-NY) then talked much more about homosexuals than he did about the rights of blacks in this hearing, which seemed to minimize the violence aimed at blacks in this country throughout the centuries. (HR 3081 hearing, 7/22/1998)

Although federal "hate crimes" legislation might be in the neighborhood, there is still no federal anti-lynching law on the books as this book goes to print. Senators George Allen of Virginia and Mary Landrieu of Louisiana co-sponsored a "Senate apology" for the refusal of U.S. senators to enact anti-lynching legislation in 2005, but offered no anti-lynching legislation. When I asked Ms. Landrieu's aide (he identified himself as Brian Appel) in April 2008 what his boss did to put an anti-lynch law on the books in the wake of her apology, he said he had no idea. He limply suggested I call my senators. I told him I called her office for comment because it was his boss who raised the issue. He told me didn't know if such a law was in force. So much for informed and helpful staff.

Most Democrat and Republican action on these issues is, in my opinion, worthless posturing. Likewise, federal and state prosecutors are not seeking "hate crime" specifications for the jihadists who have committed murder, run down people with cars, and plotted murder of Americans because they hate non-Moslems.

2. Much information about Howe's term as commissioner at Ellis Island comes from his book The Confessions of A Reformer (pages 252-282 and 326-328). Information on the criticism Bennet and others aimed at Howe comes from Historic Research Study, Statue of Liberty – Ellis Island National Monument, by Harlan D. Unrau, National Park Service, 1984 (pages 752-766), and The Confessions of a Reformer (pages 259-265).

3. Herbert Asbury, in his epics The Gangs of New York, Gem of the Prairie, and The Barbary Coast, chronicled the corruption of the politicians who took money from brothel operators and other organized criminals in New York, Chicago, and San Francisco, respectively. Henry Curran, in his book Pillar to Post (pages 163-171) detailed some of the whorehouse graft in New York City while he was an alderman. Howard Abadansky wrote extensively about the payoffs of brothel operators to politicians in several big cities in his book Organized Crime.

4. Immigration statistics come from Historic Research Study, Statue of Liberty – Ellis Island National Monument, by Harlan D. Unrau.

5. Here are some other facts on the Villa raid:

An armed citizen saved a teenage boy by shooting two bandidos who had stripped him to his underwear. Mexicans who lived in Columbus saved many of the American women and children in town.

A soldier who couldn't get his rifle killed and wounded Villa varmints with a baseball bat. The camp's cooks, who were out of the rack early fixing breakfast, attacked the bandidos with shotguns, axes, mess utensils, and scalding water.

Riding into Columbus against her will with Villa's villains was a pretty young American woman rancher. She was a captive of Villa's; his men had killed her husband after taking them from their ranch on the Mexican side of the border days earlier. Villa was probably reserving her for rape. However, one of Villa's men cut her loose and let her go when she begged for her freedom. She came across another rancher woman whose husband Villa's men stripped and stabbed to death before her eyes. American soldiers rescued the women and had them medically treated.

The soldiers turned over the Villistos they captured to federal and New Mexico authorities. New Mexico lawmen executed several of these raiders after trials. Republican governor Octaviano Larrazolo pardoned Villa's men and boys who General Pershing's men captured in Mexico weeks and months after the raid on Columbus. Although this was probably the right thing to do, because there was little or no proof they participated in the murder of American civilians in the Columbus raid, and because some of them may have been coerced to join Villa's ranks, Larrazolo's pardons cost him any chance he had at re-election. Later in the 1920s, a more forgiving New Mexico electorate sent Larrazolo to the U.S. Senate.

Sources include Joe Griffith's article "In Pursuit of Pancho Villa 1916-1917" (written for the Historical Society of the Georgia National Guard), Leon Wolff's article in the April 1962 issue of American Heritage, Jessie Thompson's article "My Brush With History" in the December 1996 issue of American Heritage (Villa's people burned her grandfather's hotel and killed him during the raid; she came for his funeral in Columbus), Don Bullis' 12/15/2005 article in the Rio Rancho, New Mexico Observer, Bill Rakocy's book Villa Raids Columbus, N.Mex., and the Railroad Depot Museum in Columbus, New Mexico. I also interviewed New Mexico historian Richard Dean (a grandson of one of the Villa raid victims) in 2009 for help in resolving source conflicts. Dean is a nationally-known expert on the Villa raid.

6. Information on Franz von Papen comes from John Gunther's book Inside Europe (pages 50-51, 94-95), and William Shirer's book The Rise and Fall of the Third Reich (pages 184-185, 222-223).

7. Information on the Black Tom explosion comes from the Unrau study (pages 767-773), Edward Corsi's book In The Shadow of Liberty (pages 117-120), and the New Jersey City University website "Jersey City Past and Present."

8. Grey's quote was in John Garraty's and Robert McCaughey's book The American Nation (page 696), and in Robert Massie's book Castles of Steel (page 509).

Edwin Clapp, in his 1915 book Economic Aspects of the War, (Chapters VII and VIII) noted British seizures of American cotton cargos from American and neutral European ships did depress the price of cotton severely, and British merchants and government agents then snapped up the cotton at ridiculously low prices. This British piracy exasperated William Jennings Bryan, Wilson's Secretary of State. In a 12/26/1914 letter to Anglophile American ambassador to Britain Walter Page, Bryan ordered Page to impress upon the British that their seizure of American ships and American cargos on neutral European ships was unjustified, and was possibly an attempt by the British to deliberately hurt the American economy by depressing the price of American exports.

The British paid Bryan little heed, because he was virtually the only American patriot in the top echelons of a State Department loaded with American lackeys of Britain. The British in January 1915 seized the S.S. *Wilhelmina*, an American ship carrying grain and other foodstuffs to an American businessman based in Germany. They did so after stating publicly they would not seize shipments of food unless the German government had ordered them. (Sources: New York Times, 2/11/1915 and May 1915 (per its Current History: The European War April-September 1915), and Clapp, Chapter IV)

Clapp (Chapters VII and VIII) noted there was some agitation among Americans to build a nationalized merchant marine, and then take goods to Germany in spite of the British, but Wilson wouldn't allow it. Clapp noted in 1915 the British agreed to pay for the cotton cargos they seized from 60 ships. He noted the British agreed to allow some American and neutral European vessels to bring cargos to Germany. However, the British in February 1915 instigated the French navy to seize the S.S. *Dacia*, an American ship loaded with cotton headed for the neutral Netherlands. (The *Dacia* had been a German ship; an American shipper bought it when it was docked in Port Arthur, Texas in 1914. The New York Times reported 3/1/1915 that FDR's former law firm was representing the American owner in French prize court over the seizure.) Clapp also noted the British seized the S.S. *Kina* in April 1915 after telling U.S. State Department officials they would not interfere with this ship's voyage to the Netherlands, Sweden, and Denmark.

The British rulers in a 3/11/1915 Order in Council arrogated for themselves the "right" to seize all cargos from neutral ships in British ports. This was piracy pure and simple.

The British seized an American sailing ship *Pass of Balmaha* in 1915. The cargo was cotton destined for Britain's ally Russia, but that didn't seem to matter. While they were taking the ship to a British port, Germans took over the vessel and took it to a German port. They fitted the sailing ship with guns, an engine, and a wireless set, and the newly refitted *Seeadler* (Sea Eagle) had a successful career as a German commerce raider. The German captain of this motorized sailing ship and his career as a commerce raider was the subject of the book The Cruise of the Sea Eagle by Blaine Pardoe.

In Chapter XVII of his 1917 book My Four Years in Germany, James Gerard, the American ambassador to Germany, noted he sailed for America aboard a Danish ship in 1916. He said the British made the ship stop in the Orkney Islands north of Scotland, and they searched the vessel. He said the crew of a British cruiser stopped the Danish vessel he was aboard on the return trip to Europe and made the ship stop again in the Orkney Islands for another search. He had no complaints with the British actions and claimed they arrested a Swede aboard the ship for allegedly making sketches of the port for espionage purposes. Gerard was a thorough Anglophile like Wilson, Secretary of State Lansing (who replaced the pacifist patriot Bryan), Edward House, and other top traitors in the control of American foreign policy.

Eventually Wilson allowed the British to become middlemen in the American cotton trade. We were to ship cotton to Britain and get only a fraction of what it was worth on the European market, and the British would resell it. The British in effect made themselves piratical middlemen by taking American cotton at a fixed price and then deciding who in Europe the cotton should go to and for what price they should pay. Even if Wilson didn't want to declare war on the British, he could have withheld American food, ammunition, and oil from the British in protest, but he did not. On this trade issue alone, Wilson proved himself a traitor to American interests and a whore to British interests.

9. Information on American exports comes from the 1917 book New Geographies, by Ralph Tarr and Frank McMurry (page 411).

10. Information on the *Lusitania* tragedy comes from The American Nation (pages 697-698), Thomas Fleming's book Illusion of Victory (page 70), and Castles of Steel (pages 528-541). Massie noted Edward House, Wilson's foreign affairs adviser, had been aboard the *Lusitania* in February 1915, and reported without protest crew members ran up the American flag when the ship approached Ireland to deceive German submariners. Hiding behind an American flag was a common and illegal trick of British merchant vessel mariners which Wilson never protested. Massie noted the *Lusitania* was carrying roughly 5000 artillery shells, and close to five million rounds of rifle ammunition when the Germans sank her.

11. Information on Lindley Garrison's resignation comes from The American Nation (page 698).

12. Theodore Roosevelt's quote is in William Thayer's 1919 book Theodore Roosevelt: An Intimate Biography (Chapter XXIV).

13. The German official's comments were reported in the 5/11/1915 issue of the New York Times.

14. Information on the *Lusitania* comes from an article titled "Riddle of the *Lusitania*" in the April 1994 issue of National Geographic by famous oceanographer and shipwreck investigator Robert Ballard, and from his book Exploring the Lusitania.

15. Information on the British navy brass refusal to let the crew of the *Juno* rescue *Lusitania* victims is in Castles of Steel (pages 532, 534).

16. Information on the Immigration Act of February 5, 1917 comes from the act itself (39 Statutes at Large 871-898) and the Unrau study (pages 59-65).

17. La Guardia's account of the congressional vote for war against Germany is in his book The Making of an Insurgent (pages 140-141).

Miss Rankin, by the way, would be the only representative voting against declaring war on Japan in the wake of the Japs' treacherous sneak attack on Pearl Harbor. Most believed her to be a peacenik ninny. She charged FDR was working in cahoots with Winston Churchill to protect British Empire colonies in Asia, and deliberately provoked the Japs to strike. Many historians and declassified documents have belatedly supported much of her reasoning.

FDR did have such an unconstitutional deal in place with Churchill by 1941. Churchill had closed the Burma Road to

China for awhile in 1940 at the demand of the Japanese, who were butchering millions of Chinese in their war of aggression. Churchill cut the supply line to the Chinese to appease the Japs so maybe they wouldn't attack British colonies. FDR threatened the Japs with bombers based in the Philippines, although there was not a strong enough American presence there to deter the Japs. He also cut off oil sales to the Japanese, which prompted them to seize the oil-rich Dutch East Indies (present-day Indonesia). This would make the Philippines even more vulnerable. The commanders in Hawaii did not receive intelligence that FDR's top people had on the Japanese task force heading for Pearl Harbor. General Douglas MacArthur, commanding in the Philippines, knew about the Jap sneak attack on Pearl Harbor but did not strike the Japs' Philippine invasion force on Taiwan. Pearl Harbor expert John Costello in his epic Days of Infamy noted MacArthur took a $500,000 payoff from the Filipino commonwealth government. Costello speculated this was a bribe for MacArthur not to strike the Japs first; local Filipino officials hoped to avoid the war. Instead, the Japs would catch MacArthur unprepared, invade and ravage the Philippines, murder many Filipinos, rape the females, and plunder the land. Americans who could not escape the Philippines wound up suffering savage murder or bestial treatment as prisoners of the Japanese.

However, I believe the Japanese would have probably taken the Philippines even without the treachery of FDR and Churchill and the gross incompetence and possible treason of MacArthur. (As a cadet, I was an extra in the movie on MacArthur starring Gregory Peck, in the scene when he gave the "Duty, Honor, Country" speech, so it is not with glee but with a sense of justice I attack the general.) So I have to disagree with Miss Rankin about the need for that war. I also believe Americans had every right to nuke Japan. The Japs murdered millions of people, they treated the people of East Asia like cattle; they raped Asian, Pacific Islander, European, Australian, and American women; they deserved it. The A-bombings finally made those bestial fanatics understand we could wipe them out if they didn't quit. The atomic bombs saved hundreds of thousands of American lives, including those of my father and my uncles Chuck and Rusty, who were in uniform against the Japs.

18. Information on the use of Ellis Island during World War One comes from the Unrau study (pages 790-799).

19. Howe's account of meeting the loved ones of the detained comes from The Confessions of a Reformer (pages 272-273).

20. Information on the seizure of Dutch ships comes from the Unrau study (page 780). U.S. Customs agents seized roughly 90 Dutch ships in American harbors after Congress declared war on the Germans, according to the U.S. Navy's Naval Historical Center. The U.S. Navy used about 30 of these ships. The seafaring Dutch were neutral but they traded with the Germans; they had a common border and Rhine River connections with the Kaiser's realm.

21. Immigration figures come from the Unrau study.

22. Information on the law allowing readmission of aliens who fought for America or the Allied side, the Mexican laborer program, the law for deporting aliens who called for the violent overthrow of the government, and the law for deporting those who interfered with America's neutrality come from the laws themselves (the Joint Resolution of

October 19, 1918, the Act of October 16, 1918, and the Act of May 10, 1920) and from the Unrau study (pages 66-69).

23. Winston Churchill's own mother was a high-strung hottie named Jennie Jerome, from an extremely wealthy American family. She married Churchill's father, a future member of Parliament named Randolph Churchill. He gave her venereal disease from one of his many romps, so in revenge she tried to set some sort of record in female blueblood infidelity (not counting Blood Countess Elizabeth Bathory, who evidently sexually abused hundreds of peasant girls before murdering them) by copulating with reportedly more than 200 different men from England's flaky upper crust, including the eventual King Edward VII. Randy and Jennie (who was also randy) left young Winston in the charge of a nanny and caroused like drunken lechers. They and other adult relations turned away the old nanny into the cold when Winston and his brother went off to school. Randolph Churchill died insane in his forties. Jennie Churchill lost her looks and grew fat; Churchill would eventually treat her like his sister instead of his mother. These sleazy details of Churchill's parents are courtesy of Robert Massie's book Dreadnought (pages 750-767).

24. La Guardia's account of his opposition to Wilson's laws is in his book The Making of an Insurgent (pages 148-154).

25. Information on the film maker jailed for truthfully portraying British atrocities in the Revolutionary War comes from The Illusion of Victory (pages 189-190), and from the American Revolution Round Table's article "The United States vs. The Spirit of 1776," as reported in a Kean University website.

26. Information on Al Smith's vetoes of Red Scare legislation comes from the book Progressive Democracy (pages 270-284). The book is a collection of Al Smith's speeches and writings as an assemblyman and a governor. Henry Moskowitz, the husband of Smith aide Belle Moskowitz aka Belle Israels, put this book together to illustrate Al Smith's record as a political leader and help him in the presidential election of 1928.

27. Debs was associated in the public mind with the disastrous Pullman strike of 1894. The Pullman strike happened because railroad car manufacturer and robber baron George Pullman laid off many of his workers, and slashed the wages of his remaining workers, while keeping rents in the company town they had to live in at the same level. Debs, as leader of the American Railway Union, organized the Pullman workers, and got railroad workers in half the states to refuse to hook Pullman cars onto trains. The railway hub of much of the country was Chicago, and it was in Chicago that a number of more radical union men and some out-and-out criminals started holding up trains and fouling up freight traffic. Of course, the railroad bosses who already had their hired killers and goons in strikebreaker mode lied about the extent of the disorders and screamed the rioters were trying to overthrow American society.

President Grover Cleveland sent thousands of federal troops to Chicago to ensure trains could pass through the city safely. Mail and most interstate travelers and freight traveled by rail then. Rioters – very few of whom were union men -- burned railroad cars and smashed tracks when the troops arrived. Federal troops and hired corporate goons responded with violence of their own. The authorities unfairly pinned blame for the violence on Debs and other union leaders. Prosecutors misused the new Sherman Anti-Trust Act against the union people. Debs and some other union men served prison terms for ignoring an injunction not to strike. Cleveland, by nature an honest and moderate man, looked like a corporate puppet for using federal force and federal law to break a strike for Pullman and the other railroad robber barons. Debs' union was broken, and other union organizers moved in like evangelical hucksters to con his rank and file away from him. Debs became a Socialist and ran for president on that party's ticket more than once. However, he urged nonviolent acts, such as voting and striking, for workers to win their rights.

Bill Haywood was another character altogether. He advocated a certain level of violence, and had very nearly been hanged because of his union's use of violence to achieve its aims. Haywood, a native of Utah, had been a miner who turned to homesteading. The U.S. government took away his homestead in Nevada in 1893 because they intended to use the desolate area as a reservation for American Indians. He got nothing for all the work he had done to make 160 acres of the high desert a real ranch.

Haywood returned to mining, and then to union activism. Haywood led the Western Federation of Miners during Teddy Roosevelt's presidency. Since mine operators used shootings, beatings, and jailing against miners, Haywood's miners retaliated with bombings and shootings. Haywood and two of his associates went on trial in 1907 for reportedly ordering the murder of former Idaho governor Frank Steunenberg in December 1905. Steunenberg in 1899 had used federal troops to break a miners' strike after some of the miners blew up an ore concentrator at a lead and silver mine and effectively took over the area. The troops arrested all the men in the area, including non-miners, and trashed many of their shacks and cabins. This show of force cost Steunenberg, a Democrat, his political career.

Harry Orchard, who worked for the union, wired a bomb to Steunenberg's yard gate, which exploded as he opened it. Police caught Orchard in town, and found bomb gear that connected him to the blast. Orchard, under the constant pressure of the notorious anti-union Pinkerton detective and fink James McParland, said he had done the job on orders from Haywood and others.

In what could best be described as a kidnaping, McParland and other Pinkerton goons and some Colorado lawmen, aided and abetted by politicians in Idaho and Colorado, arrested Haywood and the two other Western Federation of Miners officials in Denver to bring them to Idaho for trial. The Pinkerton men lacked the grounds to seek extradition so they falsely claimed the union leaders had been in Idaho when Orchard murdered Steunenberg to get permission for the lawmen to make the arrests. Deputies arrested Haywood while he was in a cheap hotel having sex with his wife's sister. Haywood and his associates were frog-marched onto a special train for the trip back to Idaho.

However, the dicks' multiple acts of lawbreaking went for nought. The prosecutors could not produce a corroborating witness to pin the union bosses to the murder, possibly because the key defense counsel Clarence Darrow (who during his lifetime of shysterism was as unscrupulous in his own way as the Pinkerton men were) bribed or threatened a man who said he had planted bombs on Haywood's orders to retract his confession. (Haywood's supporters claimed the man's confession was coerced.) Others claimed Darrow had agents bribe jurors or threaten their families. The judge, who

thought Haywood was guilty, nonetheless instructed the jurors to take the lack of a corroborating witness seriously in their deliberations. The jurymen acquitted Haywood. Other jurymen acquitted one of the other kidnaped men in a separate trial. Charles Moyer, the third kidnaped man, was not tried; prosecutors dropped charges against him.

Moyer wrested control of the Western Federation of Miners away from Haywood in 1908. But Haywood had bigger plans with a larger union he had helped found in 1905. This union was the Industrial Workers of the World. His intent was to organize miners, industrial laborers, farm workers, and other workers into a large union. Then, working with other unions, the IWW could, by leading a general strike, paralyze industry and commerce until the union men won their demands.

Union leaders like Samuel Gompers of the American Federation of Labor and John L. Lewis of the United Mine Workers Union opposed Haywood and the IWW because they were already representing many workers effectively. John L. Lewis had gotten Teddy Roosevelt's help in ending a coal miners' strike in 1902 to the benefit of the miners.

But many workers like loggers, crop harvesters, longshoremen, and unskilled factory laborers did not yet have effective unions. Many of these men, especially in the Western states, followed Haywood. So would many black laborers, because Haywood didn't discriminate against blacks in offering union membership. The IWW, nicknamed the "Wobblies" by its foes, had about 150,000 members at any one time, but it had about three million different members from its start in 1905 to its decline in the 1920s.

The IWW helped textile mill workers in Massachusetts win a bitter strike in 1912. The national union provided aid for the workers who were cold and starving in the winter. IWW leaders were able to hold up starving, cold, and beaten women and children victims of the companies' men and their goons to the public for sympathy. Haywood backed a strike of New Jersey silk mill workers in 1913, but this strike failed.

Haywood was a Socialist Party member for a time, but other Socialists took away his power in the party for advocating Socialists and union men commit sabotage and other aggressive illegal acts to further their goals. He became a nominal Communist, but not a politically correct one, because he believed that workers and not the state should own the means of production.

The account of the Idaho trial of Big Bill Haywood and the other IWW men, and other info on Haywood is in J. Anthony Lukas' book Big Trouble (pages 66-72, 92-97, 206-208, 224-225, 248-249, 255-260, 291-299, 310-311, 330-339, 439-440, 544-546, 722-726, 748).

28. Information of Judge Landis and Standard Oil comes from New York Times articles dated 8/10/1907, 7/23/1908, 7/26/1908, 9/11/1908, and 10/22/1908, from a 6/11/1923 Time article, from a March 1970 article titled "The Gentlewoman and the Robber Baron" by Virginia Van Der Veer Hamilton in American Heritage magazine, and the 1911 Supreme Court ruling on the 1910 case Standard Oil Company of New Jersey et. al v. U.S. (221 U.S. 1, Case No. No. 398).

29. Information on the pardons of the IWW men comes from an article by William Seraile in Pennsylvania History (3rd quarter, 1979, pages 228-229).

A brief monograph on the attacks on the IWW and other opponents of the Wilson regime that has some decent information from a point of view other than mine is Deportation and the Red Scare of 1919-1920, by Jeffrey Dosik. Dosik is now a National Park Service historian who works on the staff of the Ellis Island National Monument. He has forgotten more about Ellis Island than I'll ever know.

30. Information on the poor-quality and unsafe aircraft comes from The Illusion of Victory (pages 202-204, 235, 240) and from The Making of an Insurgent (pages 157-160, 174-175, 182-183).

31. The account of Theodore Roosevelt paying for the boots of the men in his son's unit comes from Nathan Miller's book Theodore Roosevelt: A Life (page 558).

32. The source for Judge Landis' opinion of Berger is In the Shadow of Liberty (page 194)

33. Information on Jeremiah O'Leary is The Illusion of Victory (pages 63-66, 404-405).

34. The case is United States v. Libby, U.S. District Court, District of Columbia, 2003.

35. The sources of information on Prohibition include the texts of the Lever Act, the War Time Prohibition Act, the Joint Resolution proposing the Prohibition amendment (40 Statutes at Lange 1050), and the Volstead Act themselves. Also included is the case Jacob Ruppert, Inc. v. Caffey, U.S., 251 U.S. 264 (1920). Ruppert owned a brewery and the New York Yankees; he sued to prevent enforcement of Prohibition and lost. The case gave the background of enforcement decisions. Info on the attempts of lying Lloyd George to impose Prohibition in Britain come from a 3/9/2005 review by Omer Belsky of John Grigg's books on Lloyd George, and from C.T. Baker's website "The History of Whisky." Britain's 1914 Defence of the Realm Act, which Parliament passed days after they declared war on Germany, gave Lloyd George and other hypocrites like him undue power over the British people. Lloyd George, besides being a serial adulterer, was also a grasping bribe taker, a pathological liar, and a corrupt politician in so many other ways who wound up repudiating virtually all his core values to remain in power.

36. W.E.B. Du Bois' attack on the white suffragettes' racism appeared in the journal The Crisis in June 1912. The summary for the Public Broadcasting System's program "One Woman, One Vote" done with the help of Marjorie Spruill Wheeler noted the exclusion of Douglass and the ties between the WCTU and the NAWSA. Information on suffragettes in the Ku Klux Klan comes from Kathleen Blee's book Women of the Klan: Racism and Gender in the 1920s and a resulting interview she did with Dinitia Smith for the 1/26/2002 issue of the New York Times.

37. Another info source for the racism of America's white suffragettes is the book One Woman, One Vote (pages 61-79, 109, 134-155, 268-290, 325, and 344-345). Marjorie Spruill Wheeler edited this book, and almost a score of feminist scholars wrote chapters for it. It was a companion book to the PBS show of the same name. One chapter of the book had the title "White Women's Rights, Black Mens' Wrongs."

Information on the suffragettes' affair with the Woman's Christian Temperance Union comes from One Woman, One

Vote (pages 255-256, 298, 320-323, 327-328, 341-342, 345, 358, 368-369).

Info on Jane Addams' stand against pandering to the nativists (what many feminists were doing) comes from One Woman, One Vote (pages 192-194).

38. Information on the race riots of 1919 comes from The Illusion of Victory (pages 397-399), and William Klingaman's book 1919 (pages 442-446, 451-453, 558-560, 580).

39. Information on the bombings of 1919 comes from 1919 (pages 279-281, 352-354) and The Illusion of Victory (pages 399-401).

40. Info on FDR's pinheaded claim the League of Nations was a bulwark against alleged Soviet-endorsed promiscuity comes from The Illusion of Victory (page 401).

Eleanor Roosevelt was a tall woman who was homely. Her uncle Theodore Roosevelt was fond of her, however, and encouraged her. He also "gave her away" when she and FDR wed during his (Teddy's) presidency because her father was dead. Theodore chafed his own high-spirited and gossipy daughter Alice for not being more serious and dutiful like Eleanor. Alice turned on Eleanor and evidently helped FDR cheat on her. FDR's own daughter Anna also helped him cheat on her.

Some of Teddy's other children turned against Cousin Eleanor for a more valid reason. When Democrat Al Smith sought a third term as New York governor, Theodore Roosevelt Jr. ran against him. Eleanor and Franklin as Democrats supported the popular and capable Smith and not their cousin. Fair enough; Al Smith was a great man. But Eleanor crossed the line when she took part in an unjustified smear campaign against Theodore Jr. without Al Smith's approval. Theodore Jr. (who would be the only general to land at Normandy with the first wave of troops on D-Day, and who would earn every medal for heroism the U.S. Army gave), and his sister Ethel Roosevelt Derby (whose service as a nurse in World War One, and whose 60 years of service in the Red Cross dwarfed Eleanor's public service) were cool toward Franklin and Eleanor. But unlike Alice, neither of them tried to help Cousin Franklin cheat on her.

Eleanor evidently developed a somewhat unpleasant private personality. Her children reportedly greatly preferred their domineering grandmother to her, their own mother. Many observers have compared her to the PTA mom who is Miss Charity outside her home and is a shrew and a nag inside it. How much of this was due to her unhappy marriage is open to speculation.

Like some victims of serial adultery, Eleanor allegedly sought love or at least release through liaisons with other women. Lorena Hickok, a journalist, was Eleanor's confidant and the most likely suspect. Eleanor also reportedly had flings with at least two men during the last 25 years of her marriage to FDR. One was reportedly her bodyguard Earl Miller. FDR had her hotel room bugged, and reportedly listened to a tape of her having sex with Joseph Lash, a younger leftist, in 1943. FDR, in a rage, sent Lash off to Europe to take part in the war, and reportedly ordered the tapers sent to fight in the Pacific Theater until they were killed in combat. (Lash wrote a biography of Eleanor and FDR in the 1970s.) FDR routinely spied upon others, like LBJ spied on Martin Luther King and his pretty daughters' boyfriends. LBJ trusted Lady Bird more than FDR trusted Eleanor.

The passage of time has softened the nation's memory of Eleanor, because in public she seemed the very embodiment of compassion. Her marriage to FDR would be one of convenience, much like the Clintons' marriage, although Eleanor was a much more sympathetic figure and high-minded person than Hillary. Eleanor did a lot of good that Hillary never deigned to do.

Info on FDR's affairs and info on Eleanor's own dalliances come from Bill Hutchison's article in the 2/2/2000 New York Daily News, Ellen Feldman's article "FDR and His Women" in the January 2003 issue of American Heritage, the PBS show transcript for "Eleanor Roosevelt – Part Two," Charles Peters' 2004 article for Washington Monthly titled "Tilting at Windmills," an article on socialite Dorothy Schiff in the 6/7/1976 issue of Time, and the book Encyclopedia of American Scandal (pages 287-288).

41. Details about Howe's fight against Palmer and his eventual resignation as commissioner at Ellis Island come from his book The Confessions of a Reformer (pages 274, 326-328).

Howe's heart seemed to be in the right place most of the time. He did deserve criticism for trashing the efforts of those who were protecting girls and young women from sex trafficking. Similar lapses happen today, on a massive scale. Many government officials criticize parental consent laws for teenage girls getting abortions or birth control or venereal disease treatment. These laws are on the books to protect girls from unscrupulous medical people. Many of them also oppose mandatory reporting laws which are on the books to protect underage girls from incest, rape, and sexual use by adult males.

42. Information of the attacks of Congress and Palmer on Howe come from his book The Confessions of a Reformer (pages 273-277), and from the Unrau study (pages 809-812).

43. Howe's comments on civil service reform come from his book The Confessions of a Reformer (pages 255-256).

Howe was right about the bureaucrats. Unfortunately the Clintons took Howe's advice too well when they had Janet Reno fire all chief federal prosecutors and replace them with loyalists and pliable stooges. This enabled the Clintons' people to gain illegal access to 900 FBI files on politicians, judges, media people, and others of importance, in turn subjecting the people being spied on to blackmail. Many whose files were not grabbed still thought they were among the 900, so this action had a chilling effect upon them too. (Most politicians, judges, and media people have something to hide.)

No prosecutor ever troubled the Clintons for this crime, which essentially allowed them to criminally abuse power without fear of criminal prosecution. The nation tittered when Bill had to give DNA to match the sperm stain on Monica Lewinsky's blue dress, but neither he nor Hillary were ever queried about the death of Vince Foster, the death of Ron Brown, the transfer of nuclear technology and missile technology to China in exchange for campaign contributions, or the many other felony-weight law violations of the presidential couple.

44. Information on the coal strike of 1919 comes from The Illusion of Victory (page 424).

45. Information on Emma Goldman and Berkman comes from In The Shadow of Liberty (pages 190-201), The Illusion of Victory (page 425), 1919 (pages 597-599), and from the PBS show transcript for a show on Emma Goldman.

46. Information on the raids on the radicals comes from the Unrau study (pages 816-821), In The Shadow of Liberty (pages 186-190), The Illusion of Victory (page 439), and 1919 (pages 612-613).

47. Information on Palmer's and Wilson's plotting to remove senators from the Senate comes from The Illusion of Victory (page 435).

Map 16. Europe in the 1920s, after the Peace Treaties, Revolutions, and Boundary Wars

AMERICA AND IMMIGRATION AFTER WORLD WAR ONE TO THE GREAT DEPRESSION

Immigration to America would slow drastically in the 1920s, due to American restrictions, and then because of the Great Depression. America's leaders and people for a number of reasons wanted to keep a flood of post-World War One immigrants out of the country. Also, economic problems in America and Europe kept many people home who would have wanted to come to America. The Great Depression also caused many foreign nationals to return home.

This chapter covers immigration to America in that era. It also gives a quick "aftermath" report on immigration during World War Two, and the demise of Ellis Island as an immigration station.

EUROPE AFTER WORLD WAR ONE

World War One left Europe in a mess. Many innocent people were left in poverty, and millions faced starvation after the war.

In the era of World War One, a high percentage of people were farmers or farm workers, and European agriculture was not very mechanized. Nor were the city people, to the extent they are today. This meant horses and other draft animals pulled plows and farm machinery, pulled wagons, and carried people. The armies needed large numbers of horses to pull artillery pieces and wagons, and carry cavalrymen, so the military men took horses from the farmers. The horses needed large amounts of feed. With fewer able-bodied men and animals working the farms and estates, there would naturally be less food raised in Europe for the people and for the animals they worked and ate.

Agriculture had to be a factor in war planning. The peasants and other farm workers who raised and harvested the crops were also most of the soldiers for most of the nations. The peasants harvested their potatoes and cabbage in the late summer and into the fall, but the basic crops in most of Europe were grain crops. These would be harvested in the summer. Hay for the animals would be harvested in the early summer. (In the Mediterranean countries, wine, olive oil, citrus fruit, and other warm-weather crops were largely cash export products. In Denmark and the Low Countries, dairy products were also cash export products.)

World War One started not long after the grain harvests, in August 1914. Bulgaria's leaders entered their country into the war in September 1915 after most of the farm work of their nation was done for the year. Romania's leaders likewise committed to the war in late August 1916 after most of the farm work of their nation was done for the year.

Wine grapes and apples would not need harvesting until September and October; peasant women and children could do these jobs. Butchering of livestock took place all the time, but most often in the fall, so the peasants wouldn't have to feed so many animals in the winter, when they wouldn't gain weight. Field corn for the animals, so vital a crop in America, was a minor crop in Europe. Hay and grain, harvested in the summer, and turnips and mangels, harvested in the fall, fed the livestock of Europe over the winter.

We who are so far from the soil now are unaware of these basic facts, and the basic rhythms of the seasons. Those who raise crops and livestock, and those who fish commercially, are the only people who are keeping us from starvation. Now because of the war, many of these workers lay dead or were crippled for life, many of their work horses lay dead, their cattle and hogs were long gone – requisitioned as rations for soldiers, and many farms lay in ruins thanks to the soldiers who plundered them, dug trenches in them, and fought in them as they pushed back and forth across northern France and Belgium, across Lithuania, Belarusia, Poland, Ukraine, and the Carpathians, across northeast Italy and Slovenia, and throughout the Balkans.

Before we talk about American immigration policies in the 1920s, let's summarize how screwed up Europe was in the years following World War One.

When the Germans threw in the towel and marched home in 1918, Belgium and especially northern France were in shambles. The Germans deliberately committed large-scale vandalism in those areas out of spite.

The Allies could play that game too. The British, French, and Italian blockade of Germany and Central Europe continued well into 1919 to weaken Germany, Austria, Hungary, and Bulgaria even further, and force their leaders to sign the peace treaties. British navy units even prevented Germany's herring fishermen from fishing in the North Sea or the Baltic Sea.

The British, French, and Italians, besides blockading the Germans, Austrians, Hungarians, and Bulgarians (all defeated enemies) also blockaded Poland,

Czechoslovakia, and Romania (all allies of France!). They lifted the blockade of former enemies Austria and Bulgaria and on friends (who they treated like enemies) Poland, Czechoslovakia, and Romania in April 1919, five months after the end of World War One. In July 1919, they lifted the blockade of Germany and Hungary.

Italian navy units occasionally blockaded the Adriatic ports of Yugoslavia in 1919. Italian troops seized the cosmopolitan Austria-Hungary port city Trieste after Austria-Hungary's government formally quit. (The city was mostly Italian, but the surrounding countryside was Slovenian.) The Italians would eventually take the port cities Rijeka (Fiume) and Zadar to limit the flow of food to the people of Yugoslavia as well as to those of Austria and Hungary. They also occupied some islands which belonged to Yugoslavia. The Italian troops mistreated the locals of Slovenia and Croatia (parts of the new Yugoslavia). They committed these cruel acts to wring concessions out of the new Yugoslavian government.

Meanwhile, the Allies blockaded Russia and Ukraine because of the ongoing war between the Communists and their opponents. The blockade affected the newly free nations of Lithuania, Latvia, and Estonia also. Romanian soldiers invaded Hungary with the okay of the Allies after Communist Bela Kun took over Hungary and sent troops into Slovakia. The Romanians overthrew his regime, and then systematically looted the country. Herbert Hoover, America's humanitarian relief chief who was running food relief to Europe, had to order a stop of food shipments to Hungary so the Romanians wouldn't steal them.

Tens of thousands of children in all these countries died of starvation and malnutrition and diseases that their weakened bodies couldn't overcome because of the avarice of the leaders of Britain, France, and Italy – and the collaboration of Woodrow Wilson. Many thousands of old people also died of these causes.

American and British troops occupying the Rhineland felt sorry for the starving people. These warriors showed more pity than their crooked civilian leaders who had to lie to their constituents to keep their jobs. The French soldiers were less charitable, but their standoffishness toward the Germans was understandable. After all, German soldiers had devastated much of France and had shot and shelled thousands of French civilians.

The ongoing blockade made it tough for humanitarian aid to reach the suffering, and Herbert Hoover, who was the key American humanitarian aid official, said so. He was angry at the way the greedy and deceitful Allied politicians dallied in putting together the peace treaties, and he was angry at the vengeful nature of the treaties. Hoover predicted uprisings would follow in the wake of the suffering. He was right; there were uprisings and coups in Germany and in virtually every other state in

Eastern and Central Europe after World War One. Hoover also predicted correctly the peace treaties eventually foisted on the defeated countries would lead to further economic hardships for many innocent people, and would lead to another war. (1)

Hoover, a Quaker, was also a pacifist but not a coward. Want proof? He did relief work in occupied Belgium during the war. He did relief work in Eastern Europe and Russia after the war. Hoover was a mining engineer and business executive by trade, so he brought businesslike practices to the projects of relief. Despite being somewhat anti-Catholic, and quite a bit of a prig (he favored Prohibition), Hoover was a good citizen with charitable instincts who had the savvy to get things done for the suffering. Sadly for the people of America, he would be unable to solve the Great Depression when he was president later.

The German army was weak and in disarray since the armistice. What ships were left of the German navy were interned at Scapa Flow, a British naval base in the Orkney Islands north of Scotland, for divvying up between the French, British, and Italians. The interned German sailors deliberately scuttled these ships in late June 1919 to keep their enemies from using them against Germany. Under threat of invasion, the Germans agreed to sign the Versailles treaty two days after their sailors sunk their own ships. American, French, and British troops were on the Rhine already, preparing to attack.

The Germans had to give back to France the parts of Alsace and Lorraine they had taken in the Franco-Prussian War. They also had to give up some area to Belgium. The Germans had to give up some territory to Denmark they had taken in the 1864 war Bismarck started. (The Danes got over, because they stayed out of World War One.) And the Germans had to give up much territory in Poland they had held wrongfully since the late 1700s. A series of plebiscites in East Prussia and in Silesia set some of the boundaries between Germany and the resurrected Poland. The Allies limited the size of Germany's military forces; when Hitler came to power he would defy the Allies.

After the war, Austria-Hungary was no more, but Woodrow Wilson and the Allied leaders tried to bleed the Austrians and the Hungarians for more than they could ever have given.

Some of the almost unknown outrages of the European treaties after World War One were the "Liberation Payments." The British, French, Italians and Woodrow Wilson charged the people of Czechoslovakia, Poland, Yugoslavia, and Romania roughly 300 million dollars in gold coins collectively for the privilege of being "liberated" by the Allies. Since the Czech lands were not the scene of any fighting, while the war ravaged Poland, Romania, and Serbia, and since the Czech lands held most of Austria-Hungary's factories, the people of the new Czechoslovakia were ordered to pay about half of the total amount. (2)

Let's recap: The leaders of Britain, France and Italy had suckered the goofs who ran Romania into coming into the war, and then had reneged on promises to help Romania. It was largely the fault of the Allies that the Germans and their allies had conquered and occupied Romania. The Allies had sold out the people of Yugoslavia – they sold out the Serbs by trying to make them give up territory to Bulgaria, and they sold out the Croatians and Slovenes by promising much of their land to the Italians for entry into the war. As for Poland, an Allied power – Russia – had oppressed more Poles than the Austrians and Germans combined. Allied soldiers did not come to Poland's aid. Nor did Allied soldiers come to the aid of the Czechs or Slovaks. The reverse was true. Certainly the peoples of these countries benefited from an Allied victory in tandem with a defeat of Tsarist Russia, but the armies of France and Italy and Britain together had fought not many more German divisions than the Russian army had done. Likewise, as Russia was dropping out of the war, the British would not have survived the submarine war without American naval and maritime help, the French would not have held out against the Germans without American help, and the Italians would have quit without the help of their allies. The greed of the French, British, and Italians in collecting "Liberation Payments" was akin to crooked local prosecutors demanding money from kidnap victims who the FBI rescued.

In addition, Woodrow Wilson and the greedy swine who ran Britain, France, and Italy demanded the people of these countries – who had been subject peoples – to assume shares of the national debt of Austria-Hungary. They called these acts of extortion "Liquidation Payments." Herbert Hoover, who had criticized the postwar treaties as hateful, harmful to Europe as a whole, and damaging to the interests of the United States, finally put an end to these money grabs when he was president during the Great Depression. (3)

Germany had been plunged into near-anarchy since the Kaiser fled to the Netherlands. The new democratic leaders had a hard time trying to gain control of the country. Communists, Socialists, militarists, and other anti-democratic factions fought the government and each other. They stole and they raped and they murdered, treating their own people and womenfolk like the conquered Belgians and Serbs.

German authorities used troops to crush the Communists and Socialists. Then hyperinflation, which German government officials caused so they could pay off their war debt in deflated money, wiped out millions of people's life savings. Then as the people were recovering from this disaster, the Great Depression struck in the late 1920s and early 1930s. The German

people were weak and ripe for abuse by any set of politicians who would promise them relief. Hitler and the Nazis would eventually win enough votes to form a government. They would use their authority to seize control of the police, the military, and the courts, and then use this power to pervert or overthrow all democratic institutions and crush their opponents. The rest is terrible history. Compared to Hitler and his demonic psychopaths, the Kaiser's Prussian militarists behaved like sensitive gentlemen.

Finland became free in the fallout of the Communist revolution. The Baltic countries would become free after the German armistice. But not easily. Fighting between rogue German army units and national patriots, and between Communist and anti-Communist forces would bedevil the fledgling countries for many more months.

After the war, people from the parts of Poland stolen by the Germans, Austrians, and Russians merged into one state. The Poles fought Russia's Communists until late 1920. The Communists tried to conquer Poland, but the Poles drove them off. The Poles then helped themselves to some land in Belarusia and Ukraine populated by Belarusians and Ukrainians. The Poles also took Vilnius from Lithuania; the city itself was largely a Polish city, but the surrounding countryside was mostly Lithuanian.

Austria-Hungary was no more. The Czechs, Slovaks, and Ruthenians merged to form Czechoslovakia. The Croatians, Slovenes, Montenegrins, Bosniaks, Hercegovinans, and some Macedonians merged with the Serbs to form Yugoslavia. Hungary lost Serb-populated Vojvodina to Yugoslavia and Romanian-populated Transylvania to Romania. Romania also gained Bukovina. Austria and Hungary started anew as two small countries. All of the countries except for Czechoslovakia would be poor. (Czechoslovakia had a good mix of manufacturing, agriculture, and mining.) Austria and Hungary became poor because they lost the subject lands they had ruled like colonies.

Hungary dissolved into internal fighting between factions. The Communists seized power in 1919 and tried to take land from Slovakia and Romania. The Czechs and Slovaks fought back. The British and French deputized the Romanians to send their army into Hungary and crush the Reds. The Romanians did so, and returned to Romania afterwards with as much plunder as they, their trucks, and their freight trains could carry.

After the Romanians left, a former Hungarian admiral named Horthy established a military dictatorship. Austria would become a civilian authoritarian state until after Hitler's men murdered Engelbert Dollfus, the patriotic clerical anti-Nazi ruler in 1934. Hitler eventually forced the Austrians to join the Third Reich by ordering the invasion of his homeland in 1938.

Yugoslavia would become a royal dictatorship under King Alexander. This lasted until a Macedonian hitman named Vlada Georgiev shot him dead while he was on a state visit to France in 1934. King Alexander would die in an open car like Franz Ferdinand, who people in Alexander's father's government had connived to murder 20 years earlier. His killer was also a zealot like Gavrilo Princip. Alexander's cousin Prince Paul tried to run Yugoslavia as regent until World War Two.

The Bulgarians, losers in World War One, had to give up their Aegean Sea coast and some of their Black Sea coast, and let Serbia keep most of Macedonia. King Ferdinand of Bulgaria had to abdicate, and his son Boris became king. Macedonian immigrants and the Communists attacked the people; Macedonian terrorists literally cut prime minister Stambuliski into squirming pieces for signing their land over to the Serbs at Allied gunpoint. Communists killed many with bombs. Finally King Boris would take over as a royal dictator and crush the Macedonian terrorists and the Communists.

After World War One, the Italians grabbed territory in the Alps from Austria. Most of the land was populated by Italians. They also grabbed Trieste, the Istrian Peninsula, and Fiume (Rijeka) and other territory on the Dalmatian coast from the new Yugoslavia, lands which were populated mostly by Slavs. Benito Mussolini, an above-average actor with a personality that was half-bully and half-Bozo, would make himself Italy's dictator.

All these tragic events were sideshows compared to the Russian Civil War. (The continent-wide butchery of the Nazis would climax some years later. Russia's massive bloodletting started right away, and continued without interruption through the Cold War.) The Communists had seized control of the Russian Revolution, and had started to make life miserable for other Russians. The Communists did not have the support of much more of the populace than the Tsar did, but they were smarter, better organized, and far more ruthless.

British and French leaders stuck their noses into the mess vicariously with the troops they sent to northern Russia, Ukraine, and the Caucasus region. Woodrow Wilson abused American soldiers in a similar manner by sending them to far northern Russia (near the Arctic Sea ports of Murmansk and Archangel) and Siberia. The predatory Japanese sent many thousands of soldiers into Siberia. Other American officials, who wanted no part of the greed and the power politics, finally convinced Wilson to bring the American troops home.

The Communists, fighting from the heart of Russia, eventually beat monarchists, militarists, and ethnic opponents operating from Siberia, Estonia, Ukraine, and other areas in the massive country. The Communists were united; their opponents were divided

and often fought each other. By the early 1920s, the Communists had wiped out their opponents, the British and French deserted the non-Communist forces, and Soviet and American pressure made the Japanese leave Siberia.

The people of Ukraine, Armenia, Georgia, and Azerbaijan, all briefly free in those years, had to submit to Communist rule from Moscow.

The war between the Communists and their enemies in Russia had an unknown number of dead. But an estimate of 10 million to 12 million who died from disease and famine and enemy bullets and murder of civilian populations from 1918 through 1923 is not unrealistic. Some estimate 20 million died in this period in what was becoming the Soviet Union. At least another million or so fled the Red Paradise in these years; most settled in Eastern Europe or in France. This compares with the roughly 10 million soldiers who died on the battlefield or of other causes in World War One, and roughly 10 million more civilians who died due to the war, from starvation and diseases which starvation made more deadly, from the influenza pandemic in Europe, from murder, and from dying of various causes while fleeing the fighting.

Most of the dead in the new Soviet Union were victims of famine and disease. Millions of non-peasants – former white-collar workers, members of titled families, non-Communist intelligentsia, and Orthodox priests and nuns – starved to death because Communist authorities withheld ration cards from them. The famine which Lenin and the Communists caused in Russia in the early 1920s by their war upon the peasants cost several million people their lives. This estimate does not count the peasants the Communists murdered. The death toll in the Soviet Union was so high that Lenin eventually admitted some of his policies were wrong and allowed some private enterprise.

Lenin asked for foreign aid. Herbert Hoover and the American Relief Administration fed 10 million starving Russians a day when the relief effort was at its peak in 1922, according to scholars at the Herbert Hoover Presidential Library and Museum. They estimated Hoover and his people gave humanitarian assistance to more than 80 million people in the Soviet Union and 20 other European countries from 1914 through 1923.

The Communists would deliberately starve to death, execute, and drive to suicide roughly five million to seven million Ukrainians in the early 1930s. These poor people, the uncounted millions of other poor souls who were murder victims of the Communists or their enemies during the Russian Revolution and Russian Civil War, and the many thousands of victims of the Stalinist purges of the 1930s are largely forgotten or unheard-of by the people of the United States and Europe today. **(4)**

Because the Turks were losers in World War One, the sultan had to give up all land that ethnic Turks did not form a majority in (except for the Armenian land they got from the Soviet Union when the Communists surrendered to the Germans in 1918). The lands of Mesopotamia -- ancient Babylon and Assyria – which Turkey lost became the new country of Iraq, which the British grabbed for oil for awhile. The British and French also grabbed Israel, Jordan, Syria, and Lebanon. Although the unhappy people of these lands exchanged one master for two others, at least the British and French were nowhere near as bloodthirsty as the Turks. The British and French allowed most of the Arabs of the Arabian Peninsula to become subjects of the Arabian king. They did not yet know Arabia was loaded with oil.

The British and French occupied the Ottoman capital of Constantinople, and in secret treaties, they decided to help themselves to the Straits of Constantinople and southern Turkey. Italy's leaders – who sold their people's peace to the British and French during World War One and entered that terrible war for the chance to take land from their neighbors -- also felt they should also help themselves to some Turkey.

The British also conned the leaders of Greece to "police" (invade) southwestern Turkey in 1919 after World War One. At least there was somewhat of a reason for the Greek action – there were many Greeks who lived in this part of Turkey; they were descendants of the Byzantine Greeks who the Turks conquered centuries earlier. But the British and French wanted the Greeks to squeeze out the Italians, whom they suddenly now viewed as pushy golddiggers. (It takes one to know one.) The Sultan abjectly agreed to these land grabs in 1920. It was now Turkey's turn to bend over and suffer national rape.

This sort of buggery didn't sit well with Turkey's World War One veterans. Kemal Ataturk, who was known as Mustafa Kemal before he changed his name and took over the country, rallied the Turks against the Allies. Ataturk, an officer with a good war record in the Ottoman army in World War One, led a rebellion against the Sultan, and eventually deposed him. Meanwhile, he organized the Turks into armies that could invade Armenian and Georgian territory, slaughter more Armenians, and now some Georgians also, beat the Greeks, and menace the land-grabbing expeditionary forces of the three bigger nations. He also got critical military supplies from the Soviet Union in exchange for giving up the Georgian land Turkey had gotten in the Treaty of Brest-Litovsk.

The Allies paid lip service to the cause of the Armenians. The Allied leaders in the postwar treaties ordered the Turks to give up the land that had been populated by the Armenians before the genocide during World War One so the remaining Armenians could form a nation of their own. The Allied leaders proposed to join to it to the briefly independent state Armenians set up after freeing themselves from Russian rule during the Russian Civil War after World War One.

The set-aside was on paper; no state can exist if its people are helpless or dead. Turkish forces in 1920 again seized Armenian territory they once held, and invaded newly-independent Armenia. The Allies did nothing as the Turks swept into Armenian lands, killing and raping, and brutally committing infanticide against the new Armenian state. Instead, the leaders of France and Italy agreed to pull their troops out of Turkey after the carnage. Although British troops stayed in Turkey around Constantinople, they didn't want to get involved. Meanwhile, the Communists with a Soviet army pressured the Armenians in the remaining independent Armenian land into submitting to the new Soviet Union. Armenian leaders saw the Communists as the lesser evil, and threw the lot of what was left of Armenia in with the Soviets.

Turkish soldiers beat the Greeks in 1921 and 1922. They raped, burned, and slaughtered the Greek residents of Smyrna and the other Greek communities of Turkey so remorselessly that the Greek leaders sued for peace and offered homes in Greece to the surviving Greeks in Turkey if only the Turks would stop killing them. Again, the British, who had suckered the Greeks into sending soldiers into Turkey in the first place, did nothing to prevent the killings that their actions led to. Turks in Greece moved to Turkey as the Greeks in Turkey evacuated to Greece.

When the Turks made moves to clear the British from the Straits of Constantinople, the British decided to run like cowards. British politicians didn't want to send enough soldiers to withstand the Turks, and the British officers and men on the ground didn't want to undergo the bloodlust of a second Gallipoli or the prison rape that was an especially unwelcome feature of being a captive of the Turks. The leaders of Britain, France, and Italy, humbled by the lowly but brave and unrepentant Turks, formally recognized Ataturk's victories in a revised peace treaty in 1923. The Turks got to keep the Straits of Constantinople and the rest of what is now Turkey.

Ataturk, by now the dictator of Turkey, moved Turkey's capital from Constantinople (which was renamed Istanbul) to his base of Ankara. He also changed the name of the once Greek city of Smyrna to Izmir. While he was at it, he dragged Turkey several centuries into the 20th Century. He ended most of the laws that discriminated against women. He essentially locked scholars in a building until they ditched the Arabic-Turkish alphabet and came up with a readable language written in a European (Latin) style alphabet.

Ataturk was bigoted against all religions, and thought largely of amassing power and dictating to people.

Even well-intentioned laws are oppressive to people who are streamrolled into living under them. However, to his credit, Ataturk tried to strengthen and modernize his nation so his people would not be the victims of the colonialist intriguers of Britain, France, Russia, Italy, or Germany again.

Over in Western Europe and Northern Europe, the Spanish, Swiss, Dutch, Danes, Norwegians, and Swedes had been smart enough and/or lucky enough to stay out of World War One. They made money selling goods to both sides.

Britain's leaders had suckered Portugal's leftist leaders into the war and into sending troops to the Western Front for questionable reasons. Many Portuguese died for nothing. Some of Portugal's rightist officers overthrew the leftists (who had overthrown the king and each other) and Portugal would be under a relatively mild dictator named Antonio Salazar. Salazar was an economics professor before he took over Portugal.

The Spanish would suffer leftist and Communist butchery in the 1930s. The leftist government's followers and Communist and anarchist allies murdered many thousands of their opponents, and targeted the Catholic clergy for annihilation. They murdered almost 8000 priests and monks, murdered 500 or so nuns (after raping the prettiest young nuns and novices), and destroyed or heavily damaged roughly 5000 churches. The regime's Catholic, military, and civilian opponents rebelled in 1936, and fought a civil war to drive the leftist government from power. The fighting cost Spain 500,000 military and civilian dead before the forces of rebel leader Francisco Franco won the war in 1939. The Spanish would then endure decades of General Franco's paternalistic dictatorship.

The British and French, victorious due to the Americans, showed their selflessness and commitment to democracy by grabbing all the German colonies and all the land north of Arabia the Turks had controlled that had Arab or Jewish populations, and allowing their Italian allies to help themselves to Slavic-populated land in Yugoslavia. The British leaders managed to double-cross both Arabs and Jews who supported them. They promised the Holy Land to Arabs who fought the Turks. They also promised the Holy Land to Zionist Jews in exchange for political and financial support of Jews. (Many Jews favored the Germans in World War One because of the brutal pogroms of Tsarist Russia, an ally of Britain and France.) In the end, the British took the Holy Land for themselves, refused to let many Jews immigrate to the Holy Land, and held it until after World War Two, when it got too hot for them to handle.

The British leaders hypocritically claimed they were fighting for the rights of small nations in World War One. One small nation they "overlooked" and continued to oppress was Ireland. The Irish people rebelled against the British during and after World War One. Ireland's rebels were able to free most of Ireland and secure independence for 26 of the 32 counties of Ireland in 1921. Meanwhile, bigots of British blood still clung to the Union Jack in the six counties of northeastern Ireland.

The British and French people were exhausted by the war and angered by their own politicians' false promises. This resulted in a number of strikes and civil unrest in both countries. In the long run, their exhaustion and anger would lead to their leaders' aversion to use force to back up the Versailles Treaty that British and French leaders had imposed upon Germany with the help of their dupe Woodrow Wilson.

WILSON'S FOLLIES – THE LEAGUE OF NATIONS AND THE PEACE TREATY

The victors of World War One formed a group called the League of Nations. Like the United Nations, the international body was a farce that was contrary to America's interests. The League was one of Woodrow Wilson's most hallucinogenic pipe dreams. The American politicians who held power after World War One at least had the sense to keep America out of the League.

After World War One, Americans started to learn the truth behind how America came to enter the war and how its politicians ignored George Washington's advice against foreign entanglements.

The truth was a chain of money winched by profiteers and ingrate European imperialists pulled Americans into World War One.

The strongest multinational corporations and similar business arrangements involving American robber barons and their opposites in Britain helped bring about American entry into the war. British and French purchasers bought American weapons during the war, then started borrowing from American financiers to finance their purchases. They also bought huge amounts of grain and cotton and oil from American brokers and speculators, and usually did so on credit. If the Allies lost the war, the British and French and Italians would repudiate their debts. So the bankers and the corporate profiteers in this country worked hand in hand with Woodrow Wilson and the other Anglophiles in his administration to maneuver America into the war to make the world safe for their profits.

Woodrow Wilson and his government minions lent the British, French, and Italians more than 10 billion dollars (a sum worth $100 billion to $200 billion dollars in the early 2000s) of taxpayer money. Americans won the war for the British and French and Italians and yet the parasitical Allies still ungratefully refused to repay the loans the American taxpayers made them.

The British even had the gall to offer to forgive their loans to their other allies if the Americans would forgive their massive loans to the British. Since the British had loaned less money to other European governments than they had borrowed from the American people, this of course would be a money maker for the British, a form of bloodless piracy or massive white-collar crime.

Like deadbeats everywhere, the British, French, and Italians made excuses. They claimed they were waiting on repayment from the Germans before they could repay the Americans. American leaders in the 1920s rightly pointed out there was no connection. The Allies were liable for the loans whether they won or lost the war, or whether the Germans paid war reparations or not. Eventually American leaders let the Euro-ingrates off the hook. So guess who wound up paying for the war loans? That's right, the American taxpayers. **(5)**

The sad truth is if Woodrow Wilson and his government had kept American munitions makers, brokers, financiers, and other profiteers from aiding the Allies on credit the American taxpayers would eventually have to pay for, the Allies would have had to negotiate a peace with the Germans and the Hapsburgs. Millions fewer people would have died, and Europe would not have been as ripe for Communist and Nazi takeovers.

Frederic Howe sparred with Wilson about the rights of Americans critical of Wilson during the war. Howe, a sincere liberal, believed Wilson was becoming a spiteful power-hungry leftist who was allowing arrests of dissidents simply because they didn't kowtow to him.

After World War One was over, Howe overcame his mounting suspicions about his boss and joined Wilson's entourage at the Paris Peace Conference. Howe traveled through Europe and the Middle East as a fact-finder for Wilson. He also had the eye-opening experience of dealing with the British and French. The young guns in Britain's foreign service condescended to him as an American.

Howe finally snapped. He said to these British functionaries, "It looks to me as if America is to be asked to carry the bag, to police Europe and remove from England and France the burden of protecting imperialistic ventures. You are asking us to assume the biggest, most dangerous, and costliest job of all."

"The young men admitted the danger," Howe noted. "They felt, as all Englishmen who I met seemed to feel, that America owed a debt to England, much as did Canada, Australia, and other colonies. We ought to be proud to pay our debt to the Empire. That America was a colonial dependence [sic], not yet a sovereign nation, seemed to be their fixed idea."

Howe, in his gentleman's vocabulary, dissected Wilson also. He noted Wilson pretended he didn't know about the secret treaties between the Allies for dividing the spoils after the war. He said Wilson's Fourteen Points, which helped persuade the Germans to stop fighting and ask for an armistice, were nothing more than propaganda to the leaders of the British, French, and Italians.

(Wilson's Fourteen Points included an open peace treaty and open diplomacy, freedom of the seas, removal of trade barriers, reduction of armaments, fair adjustment of colonial claims, evacuation of Russia by the Germans and their allies, the restoration of Belgium, the return of Alsace-Lorraine to France, giving Austrian land with Italian majorities to Italy, autonomy for the subject peoples of Austria-Hungary, evacuation of Romania and Serbia and Montenegro and access to the sea for Serbia, autonomy for the subject peoples of the Turks, an independent Poland with access to the sea, and a League of Nations.)

The British and French leaders granted an armistice to the Germans, but maintained the blockade on Germany to aid in the destabilization of Germany. They kept the pressure on until German society and military discipline broke down so they could force the Germans to accept a humiliating peace treaty. Wilson, Howe said, went along with them.

Wilson's Fourteen Points had no point for the freedom of Ireland, because as an Anglophile with an English-born mother, he hated the Irish. The craftier European leaders whose countries American soldiers had saved easily outmaneuvered Wilson, who had little in the way of hard negotiating ability.

"President Wilson's sense of insecurity, when outside of his study, made him vulnerable. He was unwilling to face defeat," Howe wrote. "He would not face failure. To escape failure he sacrificed principles."

"When he (Wilson) began to barter, he lost all," Howe continued. "A man less idealistic would have been betrayed as he (Wilson) was betrayed, but he would have made a better bargainer."

"When President Wilson returned to America," Howe wrote, "people were ready to accept his failures and understand the cause (his naivete, his refusal to bring capable American negotiators who might outshine him, and his allies' criminal greed, author's note). "It was his assertion that he had brought back the peace he had promised that turned the tide. The people did not believe what he said. They heckled him in his meetings. They forced him to see himself. It was then that his strength gave way, his health broke. He lost his vision of himself when he discovered that it was no longer held by others." (6)

Wilson was such a pathetic toady to the British that he allowed the British Empire to get six votes in the League of Nations to America's one. Canada, Australia, New Zealand, South Africa, and India, the latter two still colonies of Britain, were to have votes in the League of Nations along with Britain. Franklin Delano Roosevelt told lies to try to sell this sell-out of the American people when he campaigned for the vice-presidency in 1920. *Stalin would get a similar deal out of an addled and dying FDR at Yalta 25 years later. Even though the Red Army occupied Ukraine and Belarusia against the wishes of the Ukrainian and Belarusian people, the Soviets would get votes for these lands in the General Assembly of the United Nations.*

Wilson, while traveling the country in September of 1919 trying to sell the League of Nations to the American people like a traveling snake-oil vendor, suffered a breakdown. Then he suffered a stroke in October 1919. His second wife Edith Galt and his doctor covered up his drooling debilitation for many months. She essentially ran the country during this time, three generations before Hillary Clinton shared presidential power with her panting partner. Edith maintained the charade by keeping her hubby out of the public eye, screening out his visitors, and propping him up at his desk when she wanted to show him at work. Leading Democrats complained impotently; leading Republicans were glad. The Democrats were like a ship without a rudder; Ms. Galt and the nonentities in Wilson's cabinet couldn't run the country effectively. The Republicans controlled Congress; they figured they would let Edith and the stooges in Hubby's cabinet make a mess of things and then they could elect anybody as president in the 1920 election.

The Republicans' strategy worked. They elected a virtual nobody named Warren Harding, because of Wilson's failed policies, Wilson's failings as a man, and Wilson's second wife's domineering dishonesty. (If the legendary Theodore Roosevelt hadn't died in early 1919, he instead of Harding would have been the Republican candidate.) In the election of 1920, Harding beat Democratic nominee (and League of Nations supporter) James Cox and his running mate sidekick FDR by 16 million votes to 9 million votes. Cox carried only 10 of the 11 states of the former Confederacy (minus Tennessee) and Kentucky. Socialist Eugene Debs got about one million votes despite being still in prison, jailed by the Wilson regime.

Americans rightly punished the Democrats to impress on them the need to keep out of any more deals with the murderers, pimps, and con artists who ran Europe. The British and French-driven League of Nations would do nothing to prevent the Japanese from tromping on the Koreans or seizing Manchuria or invading China and massacring millions of people with barbarism so great that even one of Hitler's Nazi envoys would protest in disgust. Nor would they do anything to stop Mussolini from murdering and colonizing the independent people of Ethiopia. Nor would they do anything to stop Hitler from invading Austria or Czechoslovakia. Nor would they try to stop Stalin from starving millions of Ukrainians to death. Nor would they try to stop British and French colonialists from oppressing hundreds of millions in Africa and Asia.

THE ROARING TWENTIES

The 1920s featured three of America's lesser presidents, all of whom were Republicans. Warren Harding, who succeeded Calvinist pruneface Woodrow Wilson in the White House on March 4, 1921, was a prototype of Bill Clinton. Harding was an affable boozer (despite the stupid Prohibition laws he was supposed to enforce) and an enthusiastic lecher with a domineering wife. One of his mistresses, Nan Britton, wrote a book titled The President's Daughter when Harding's family wouldn't pay her child support for the girl who was the result of one of their many liaisons. (Some say the Clintons avoided this sort of book by paying for a number of abortions and/or having goons threaten the women in question similar to what evidently happened to Kathleen Willey.)

Like Clinton, Harding's presidency featured massive corruption which even involved members of his Cabinet. Harding, though untrue to his battle-ax wife Flossie, was not a crook nor a seller of missile and nuclear technology to America's enemies like Clinton was. Nor did Flossie loot the White House on moving out like Hillary did. Harding set himself up for problems because he rewarded unworthy friends with high office. Harding ultimately avoided indictment because he died in office in August 1923. Many people suspect Flossie had him poisoned after learning the extent of his infidelities. (She did evidently retain a detective to spy on his suspected honeys.) She died in November 1924; there was no investigation done on her role, if any, in her husband's death.

Harding was flawed but at least he wasn't a preening busybody like Wilson. Harding had many of Wilson's political prisoners freed, including socialist leader Eugene Debs. Harding, after freeing Debs, invited the old Socialist to the White House. Harding, presumably too busy with booze and broads, but actually because he was a believer in smaller government, deliberately let a recession in 1921-1922 take its course instead of jumping in with massive government programs and huge deficit spending. When the economy roared into overdrive in 1923, Harding was publicly happy with the recovery but was too humble and astute to take credit for the recovery. This was a lesson that FDR and Obama should have taken.

Calvin Coolidge replaced Harding when the former died in office in August 1923. Coolidge won re-election in 1924 and served one full term as president. The Democrats were divided between Prohibitionists, Ku Klux Klan members, Southerners, and Westerners who supported Wilson's son-in-law William McAdoo and Midwesterners, Easterners, Catholics, and opponents of Prohibition who supported New York governor Al Smith. Neither man could gain the nomination, so John Davis, a compromise candidate, got the Democrats' nod after two weeks of convention balloting. Davis got eight million votes and carried the 11 states of the former Confederacy plus Oklahoma. Coolidge got 16 million votes and carried every other state except Wisconsin. Honest Wisconsin dissident Republican Robert La Follette ran as an independent, got five million votes, and carried his home state.

Coolidge was best known for breaking the Boston police strike in 1919 when he was governor of Massachusetts. As president, he said little and did less. At least he had the leading criminals of the Harding administration prosecuted and jailed.

The 1920s became known as the "Roaring Twenties" because of the party atmosphere of the decade compared to earlier ones in American history. Despite Prohibition, most of the men in the country and a large minority of the women found alcohol to slake their thirst. Unfortunately, organized criminals wrapped their tentacles around much of the nation because of the economic power they developed selling illegal alcohol.

Radio stations and talking motion pictures made their debuts in the 1920s. Babe Ruth and Lou Gehrig and their Yankees dominated baseball, Notre Dame and Army dominated football, and Jack Dempsey and Gene Tunney were the giants of the boxing ring.

Women really started to strut their stuff openly in this decade. They now had the right to vote, and they had greater purchasing power. The cutesy short-skirted short-haired "flapper" was the trendy female of the 1920s; she replaced the elegant pompadour-haired shirtwaisted "Gibson Girl" of the "Gay Nineties" and pre-World War One America. Many of the celebrities of the 1920s were women or men whose fans were women.

In 1926, Romania's Queen Marie – the veddy English granddaughter of Queen Victoria -- made a famous and notorious tour of the United States. Queen Marie reportedly had affairs with a young Romanian cavalry officer (setting a bad example for Princess Diana, who would have her own romp with a mounted British

officer), American financier Waldorf Astor, and Romanian nobleman Barbu Stirbey (who reportedly fathered her daughter Princess Ileana), among others. Apparently her favorite forbidden stud was Canadian mining and timber businessman and sports promoter Joe Boyle. Klondike Joe won the queen's favor when he daringly rescued her gold, her crown jewels, and some of her noblemen and noblewomen from the Bolsheviks during the Russian Civil War. (Because German, Austro-Hungarian, and Bulgarian armies overran and occupied most of her realm, she had to move her valuables to the bordering Russian Empire. Many of her noblemen and noblewomen sought refuge there also. When the Reds overthrew the democrats who overthrew the Tsar, Queen Marie's gold, jewels, and courtiers were at risk.) The dashing Canadian also brought the heart and the libido of the queen to a boil; she was disconsolate when he died a few years later.

Queen Marie, to her credit, had done her duty during the war as a nurse. (So did Queen Elisabeth of Belgium, and Tsaritsa Alexandra and her daughters Olga, Tatiana, Maria, and Anastasia. Both Elisabeth and Alexandra were born in Germany and had German fathers. Alexandra, like Marie, was a granddaughter of Queen Victoria. Elisabeth was named for her aunt Elisabeth, who was known to the world as the notorious Empress Sissi of Austria-Hungary. Elisabeth's cousin Zita would be the last empress of Austria-Hungary.) Queen Marie used her charms in a ladylike and professional way when she attended the peace treaty conferences after the war in Paris. She did an excellent job at promoting Romania's interests. Romania doubled in size when the Allies allowed the Romanians to annex Transylvania from Hungary and keep Bessarabia (present-day Moldova, which the Germans had allowed to join what was left of Romania during their occupation) away from the Soviets largely due to her engaging and businesslike personal diplomacy. In all fairness, Romanian-speaking people were in the majority in both regions she lobbied to get. But without Queen Marie's work for her adopted nation, the criminals of Versailles might not have given the Romanians these areas. After all, they were very unfair to a great number of people.

Queen Marie spiced up the 1920s with her pen as well. She wrote advice features and sob sister prose for magazines. She also wrote several books. As an Englishwoman, she was perfectly capable of expressing herself in terms most celebrity-worshiping British and American women would understand.

Queen Marie got to America barely too late to appraise the virility of Rudolf Valentino in person. The ladykilling Latin lover of the silent screen, himself an immigrant from Italy who was processed at Ellis Island, died suddenly earlier that year. However, she shared gossip column ink in 1926 with two other high-bracket hotties, film star Clara Bow and woman evangelist Aimee Semple McPherson.

Miss Bow, the "It" Girl, (or more snidely, the "Those" Girl ... because of "Those" she had "It") reportedly got to know many men around Hollywood and reportedly some members of the USC football team in the Biblical sense. The former rumors were definitely true; the rumors about Ms. Bow huddling *au naturel* with the Southern Cal football players – whose squad included Marion Morrison, who would ride to fame as the great John Wayne – were false. This was back before USC started specializing in NCAA violations in their football program. Clara Bow did pay the young Trojans a lot of attention, however.

Sister Aimee, the lady evangelist whose huge church was in Los Angeles, chose that year to apparently have a month-long road trip and fling with her radioman (who was married) and then claim she was kidnaped by white slavers. At least that's what prosecutors claimed when they charged the pretty preacher turned paramour (allegedly) with obstruction of justice. (Sister Aimee made emotional religious broadcasts also. That's why she had a radioman in her service.) Her guy fell on his sword for her, claiming the woman who checked in with him at motels all over California who motel clerks thought was Sister Aimee was just a playmate who <u>looked</u> like the notorious woman of the cloth, but was <u>not</u> her. Sister Aimee went on trial, claiming white slavers had set her up because she was leading too many prostitutes out of the cathouses and into the chapels. The prosecutor dropped charges in mid-trial.

Some said Los Angeles' movers, shakers, and fixers wanted Sister Aimee jailed and discredited because they did not favor her brand of exuberant Protestantism and they believed the feminine fundamentalist and her many thousands of hayseed followers were bad for the city's image.

The City of Angels now has the public image of sunshine over a smoggy cesspool crawling with druggies, sexual deviates, illegals, gang-bangers, and the narcissistic dopers, sexual misfits, and pond scum of the entertainment industry. Well done, movers, shakers, and fixers.

Sister Aimee fell from grace, but during the Great Depression she would regain the substance of her calling. She and her followers fed many hungry people and she performed many other corporal works of mercy for the poor of all races. The author talked with a good number of older Americans in the Los Angeles area who she and her donors fed when they were down on their luck during the Depression; they had nothing but kind words for Sister Aimee. **(7)**

Unfortunately, not all ministers were as charitable to people from all walks of life as Sister Aimee. The 1920s was a decade of virulent anti-Catholicism, because of the rise of the Ku Klux Klan, and the stirring of other bigots because of the rise of Catholic Americans in industry and politics. To some extent this was linked with many Americans' views on immigration, because more immigrants came from Catholic countries in Europe (and from next-door Mexico) than from countries where other religions (or state atheism) were predominant. The 1924 election, for example, ended disastrously for the Democrats because of the hatred many of their own showed for Al Smith because of his Catholicism. The 1928 election would also go to the Republicans because of this bigotry of many Democrats against their most able national candidate (Smith) because of his religion.

Another string of anti-Catholic incidents aimed at the best-known Catholic university in America in 1924 went against the bigots as the students of that school shook down the thunder on them.

In May 1924, Ku Klux Klan members decided to hold a rally in South Bend, Indiana. They chose this town because it was the home of the University of Notre Dame. The Catholic college was rising to national prominence because of the play of their football team under immigrant coach Knute Rockne, a native of Norway who would convert to Catholicism.

When a gang of Klansmen paraded through the streets of South Bend, students from Notre Dame beat them down, stripped off their robes and hoods, and paraded in them themselves to mock the Klansmen. Meanwhile, Notre Dame students vandalized Klan offices in South Bend and students and other anti-Klan residents beat up Klan reinforcements as they got off the trains coming into the city.

The city's police chief did not restrain the Notre Dame men, so the Klansmen were in a pickle. The students said they would not interfere with the Klansmen's right to assemble if they put away their guns and kept their hoods off. The Klansmen agreed to this, and they had a small rally at a park, then left.

Two days later, local Klansmen tried another show of strength, and about 500 Notre Dame students attacked them again. This time the police tried to break up the melee, which the Notre Dame students were winning. The president of Notre Dame came to the scene and convinced the students to return to campus. This the students did; but they formed ranks and *marched* back like a military unit instead of slinking back like the average stoop-shouldered college kid today.

The mayor of South Bend persuaded the Klan members to cancel further demonstrations in South Bend. He also got the co-operation of Notre Dame authorities to call off their students. Rockne himself talked the students into staying on campus to aid in restoring calm to the city.

The Indiana Klan paper "The Fiery Cross" screamed falsely **"STUDENTS TRAMPLE U.S. FLAG"** and **"NOTRE DAME MOB BEATS MEN AND WOMEN."** (The students trampled no flags, and beat up no females.) In their impotent fury the sheetheads blamed the Catholic Church for their beatdown because the Notre Damers used their fists and improvised weapons like men as was their right to beat down those who hated them and threatened them.

Klan officials plotted another parade in South Bend for October 1924, but called it off, after allegedly receiving threats about Catholic "gunmen." More likely, they were afraid Catholic Americans would kick their asses, for these Klansmen were essentially cowards. **(8)**

The Fighting Irish home victory over the Klan didn't translate nationally four years later. Quaker Protestant Herbert Hoover beat Catholic Al Smith in the 1928 presidential election. The power of the Ku Klux Klan and the traditional anti-Catholic bias of many Americans helped keep Smith out of the White House. The economy seemed in good shape, and the Republicans got credit for this.

But, like many house flippers and financial paper hucksters in the late 1990s and the first decade of the 2000s, many people in the 1920s were doing their investing and stock buying by financially unsound means. Likewise, the productivity of farmers and industrial workers had been rising without a comparable increase in their earning power. So many farmers and workers couldn't afford to buy what they and their countrymen were making and growing.

Nor could the people of Europe. They and their governments were broke. (You can't do business with people who have no money.) The European governments slapped tariffs and quotas on American exports. These problems together would soon lead to the Great Depression.

Hoover's accomplishments as a mining executive and humanitarian to the starving people of the world were stellar. But Smith was a very good man also, despite being a politician, especially one who came out of the filthy Democrat stronghold of Tammany Hall. In the wake of the Triangle Shirt Waist Factory tragedy, Smith had spearheaded the move to reform labor and workplace safety laws in factories in New York. Thanks to Smith's work, the state would have labor and workplace safety laws that would serve as models to the nation. In other words, Smith was a humanitarian to the working people of *this* country. Smith, as governor of New York, appointed almost as many Republicans as Democrats to high positions in the state. Smith actively sought the advice of Theodore Roosevelt despite their party differences. And Smith gave no special favors toward those of his own faith.

This didn't matter to many. Bigoted ministers and politicians in the South and elsewhere furiously spread incredible lies about Smith being a pawn of the Vatican who would somehow bring the Pope to America to rule the country as a king. Smith defended his faith and his patriotism, and the faith and patriotism of all the Catholics who had fought for America in the nation's wars. (Catholics have traditionally been at least as prone – and sometimes more prone – to serve in the American military as people of other faiths). Smith also called his detractors bigots.

Hoover pulled 21 million votes to 15 million for Smith. Smith won many more votes than Cox in 1920 or Davis in 1924, but he carried only Massachusetts, Rhode Island, and six states in the Deep South. Hoover beat him closely or widely in the other 40 states. One trend that Smith started for Democrats was carrying the big city vote. Smith outpolled Hoover in the 12 largest cities in the country and most of the other cities of any size. No Democrat had ever done this before. But Hoover, thanks to a well-oiled campaign of virulent anti-Catholic bigotry waged by Klansmen, Masons, preachers, Prohibitionists, militant feminists like Margaret Sanger, and other hate-mongering white trash, walloped Smith in the rural areas to counter Smith's gains in the cities.

AMERICAN IMMIGRATION POLICIES IN THE 1920s

Americans were tired of bailing out Europe's grasping politicians and having their servicemen sacrifice for a continent full of ungrateful foreigners. World War One and the attendant problems the leaders of Europe caused the people of America were leading causes of a desire among most Americans to limit immigration.

A desire to limit immigration was not necessarily the result of bigotry on the part of most Americans. Most of the desire was based on practical self-interest. There were also a public health dimension and an economic dimension to this desire.

In 1918 and 1919, a worldwide outbreak of influenza debilitated many people in the United States. Roughly 105 million people lived in America during those years; close to 30 million of them came down with influenza and 500,000 to 700,000 Americans died of the disease. Public health officials and local officials in the United States banned or cut down on mass meetings, got people to wear gauze masks to protect themselves and others, and urged a number of other measures, such as staggering of factory and store hours to minimize the risk of mass contamination.

In Britain, 200,000 people died from the disease during the pandemic; in France another 400,000 people died from the disease, and similar or greater numbers of people no doubt died in Germany, Italy, Austria-Hungary, and Russia. Japanese officials reported 250,000 deaths from influenza in their country during 1918 and 1919. In India, roughly 17 million people – including many colonial soldiers in Britain's army – died from influenza in these years.

It is unclear whether World War One caused the worldwide outbreak, but the movement of infected troops, sailors, medical people, merchants, and politicians through and out of Europe carried the disease far and wide. Woodrow Wilson's Secret Service protectors had influenza when he was in Europe for the postwar peace treaty talks in 1919. Franklin Delano Roosevelt, who at the time was the assistant Navy Secretary, came home from France with influenza and had to be carried off his ship because he was so weak. In the United States, the first reported outbreak was at a military post.

Many people attributed the influenza to the "dirty foreigners" Americans came in contact with. British crews had been calling at American ports to pick up food, oil and military supplies for years. British vessels regularly hauled people to and from India, including all those soldiers in their Indian regiments. And the pandemic started in Europe before it did in the United States. The disease got the popular nickname "Spanish flu" because Spanish officials were probably about the only European leaders not lying about the extent of the disease in their country. So many people thought the Spanish were the source of the pandemic.

The economic dimension that led Americans to want to limit immigration was the postwar slowdown of the economy. American manufacturers, mine and oilfield operators, and food and cotton and lumber brokers made lots of money selling factory goods, fuel, food, and other commodities to the British and French ... and also to the American government once the United States entered the war. But the boom ended when the war did. Many soldiers found their jobs taken by other people. Congress stopped the issue of temporary visas to Mexican laborers and urged employers to send them home. There were many calls to keep European and Asian aliens from taking Americans' jobs also.

World War One had drastically dropped immigration to America. There were 327,000 immigrants admitted in 1915, 299,000 in 1916, 295,000 in 1917, the year America entered the war, and 111,000 in 1918, the final year of the war. In 1916, 1917, and 1918, fewer than half the immigrants came from Europe.

The same would hold true for 1919. In that year, there were 141,000 immigrants to the United States, (and only 25,000 from Europe) largely because American ships were busy transporting American soldiers home from Europe and many British and French ships were taking colonial troops home, because many British and French and Italian merchant ships were sunk in World War One, because the German merchant fleet was due to be delivered to the Allies, because the former subject peoples of Austria-Hungary were now independent, and because Soviet authorities forbade emigration.

But immigration started to return to prewar levels in 1920. In 1920, there were 430,000 immigrants to the United States. About 250,000 of these came directly from Europe, 90,000 came from or through Canada (many of whom were European nationals), and about 50,000 came from Mexico.

In 1921, more than 800,000 immigrants flooded into the United States. About 650,000 of these came directly from Europe, and of these, more than 220,000 came from Italy. Poland was in second place with 95,000 immigrants, and Britain, Czechoslovakia, Spain, Greece, Ireland, and Yugoslavia followed with between 20,000 and 30,000 immigrants each. The British were recovering from World War One, and all of the other countries were experiencing warfare or internal unrest. More than 70,000 came from or through Canada (many of whom were European nationals), and about 30,000 came from Mexico. **(9)**

There were hard feelings among many in the United States about the influx of Italians. Enough of them were in organized crime that many Americans started to stereotype them as criminals.

The Sacco-Vanzetti trial took place in 1921, a year after a gang of thieves shot to death a payroll guard and a paymaster outside a shoe factory in South Braintree, Massachusetts and stole from them $16,000 of workers' wages before getting away in a car. (The murdered guard in the fatal April 1920 robbery – committed during the "Red Scare" years – was also an Italian-American.) Jurors convicted Sacco and Vanzetti of the murders.

The Red Scare eventually died down thanks largely to Warren Harding's easygoing attitude toward dissenters. Lawyers for Sacco and Vanzetti appealed the convictions, and many prominent liberals and leftists tried to pressure the governor of Massachusetts into saving the two from the electric chair and setting them free.

However, forensic evidence indicated a pistol in Sacco's possession fired the shot that killed the payroll guard, and Vanzetti was caught with what appeared to be the pistol of the murdered payroll guard. The governor had the trial reviewed in 1927. One of the best ballistics experts in the country volunteered his services for free to get to the truth of the matter, and his careful examination tied the fatal bullet to Sacco's gun. As a result, Sacco and Vanzetti went to the chair later in 1927. **(10)**

Thanks to know-nothings among the fundamentalists and feminists who saddled the country with Prohibition laws, the Italian immigrants who were organized criminals branched out from the white slavery, prostitution, and protection rackets into the much more lucrative and socially acceptable offenses of distilling and distributing alcoholic beverages. The warfare between Italian gangsters and other gangsters, and their bribery of key politicians, judges, and police officials led to unprecedented lawlessness in the streets of New York, Chicago, and other big cities of the nation.

Many leaders predicted the devastation of World War One would lead to immigration of the lowest classes of Europe in numbers much greater than in any year before the war. So they were busy devising ways to limit immigration.

After Warren Harding won the 1920 election, members of the House of Representatives and the Senate, in the "lame duck" session before Inauguration Day, passed a one-year quota bill that would limit maximum immigration of each nationality to 3% of foreign-born members of that nationality who were living in the United States in 1910.

In practice, this bill, if signed into law, meant Americans would allow about 200,000 to come from western and northern Europe, and about 155,000 to come from southern and eastern Europe. This was aimed at lowering the percentages of Italians, Poles, and Jews coming into the country. The overall limit of 355,000 immigrants per year from Europe was lower than the number of legal immigrants who entered the country from Europe in every year between 1900 and 1914.

This bill counted nationality not by citizenship or residence of most recent country, but by land of birth. However, a European willing to live in Canada, Mexico, or another country in the Western Hemisphere for at least one year could come in as an immigrant from the Western Hemisphere. There was no quota on people from the Western Hemisphere in this measure.

Members of Congress presented the bill to Woodrow Wilson on February 26, 1921. (Wilson had to leave the White House for good on March 4, 1921. Before 1937, Inauguration Day was March 4.) Wilson was now incapacitated in everything but his own selfish ego. He was bitter because of the public's repudiation of his dream of the League of Nations, and he was angry because the Democrats would not renominate him for a shot at a third term in 1920. He vetoed the bill with a pocket veto.

But the congressmen were not overly perturbed. They passed the bill again and Warren Harding signed it into law anyway three months later, on May 19, 1921. It went into effect June 3, 1921 as an addition to existing American immigration laws. This bill would become known as the Quota Act of 1921 (aka 42 Statutes at Large 5-7).

What made the Quota Act of 1921 a practical hardship to many was a proviso limiting the maximum number of immigrant from any nationality to 20 percent of the annual total maximum in any month. This led to ship captains jockeying their mammoth vessels like boat racers to try to get their immigrants offloaded in ports before rival ship captains could do likewise. Losers in this bizarre rush were immigrants who were in line when monthly quotas for their nationalities filled. They would have to go back to where they came from.

The quota law worked well at limiting immigration. From July 1, 1921 through June 30, 1922, immigration officials admitted only 244,000 immigrants from the Eastern Hemisphere. Immigrants from lands like Italy, Poland, and those of the old Hapsburg Empire and the Balkans used up their homelands' quotas quickly. Countries like Britain, Germany, France, the Low Countries, and the Scandinavian countries did not send enough immigrants to the United States to fill their national quotas. Nor did the Soviet Union's immigrants fill the regime's quota, because the Communists' ban on emigration was still in effect. Close to 30,000 people born in Russia and Ukraine and other lands of the Soviet Union still came to America. Most of these no doubt were Slav exiles and Russian Jews who were unwelcome elsewhere.

Members of Congress evidently liked the results well enough, so they extended the Quota Act in May 1922 to run for two more years through June 30, 1924. They stiffened the law (the extension was also called 42 Statutes at Large 540) to allow Old World nationals who had resided in Canada or any other Western Hemisphere country for five years to be exempt from nationality quotas. They also tweaked the law to levy a fine on steamship companies of $200 a person for each immigrant brought in excess of quota. They also ordered steamship companies to refund all money they charged aliens for passage and related expenses if American officials had to turn these aliens away for being in excess of quota. **(11)**

However, all was not sweetness and light. Because the congressmen hadn't written the quota bill properly, there was still a seaborne replay of the Oklahoma Land Rush at Ellis Island and other immigration stations in port cities. Ship captains still jockeyed their vessels unsafely in New York Harbor and in other harbors so they could offload their human cargoes before rival ship captains could do likewise. Why? Because consuls in the various countries handed out many more immigrant visas than the number of authorized immigrants from the countries under their quotas. This meant the first alien nationals from the countries in question to get to America would win out.

The rest would have to go home, at the shipping companies' expense.

Headlines like "Twelve Ships Make a Midnight Dash with 10,000 Aliens" and "2000 Emigrants Wait at Windsor or Are En Route to Enter Today" appeared in the New York papers. A typical story read:

"Swarms of motor launches were cruising around the ships with friends of aliens who shouted greetings in every language from Arabic to Zulu. The small boats became so numerous that the police boats Manhattan and Blue Boy were sent from Pier A to keep them clear of the channel where the steamships had to pass through."

Here's another:

"Deputy Commissioner of Immigration Byron H. Uhl said that the Greek steamships would probably have enough aliens on board to exhaust the July quotas of two continents, Asia and Africa, and of five countries, Albania, Greece, Turkey, "other Asia," and Syria." There are about 10,000 aliens on the incoming vessels due today ..."

Henry Curran, the commissioner of Ellis Island from 1923 to 1926, said, "It was dangerous to human life to have twenty great ships crowding through the (Verrazano) Narrows at the stroke of midnight. It was tragedy to the immigrants who pulled up stakes, left home behind, and (had) come hopefully here only to be turned back at the gate, through no fault of their own, as "excess quota." They had no place to go – the old home gone, the new home forbidden – it was tragedy that tore the heartstrings of those of us who understood."

Curran said Congress should have ordered U.S. consuls around the globe to hand out only enough immigrant visas to meet the quotas for the countries they were stationed in. Instead they handed out immigrant visas to any would-be immigrant who looked like he could qualify to enter the United States, and then it was a race to see who could get to America first before the nation's quota was used up.

Curran blamed the steamship companies for the mess also. During his first month on the job, Curran said, "Sooner or later the (U.S.) Government will have to regulate what the steamship companies have failed to control – their own savage cut-throat competition for immigration business." **(12)**

Curran did what he could to shoehorn some of the immigrants coming to Ellis Island in on other countries' unused quotas. Eventually what Curran proposed (U.S. consuls overseas could only hand out enough immigrant visas to meet the quotas for the countries they were stationed in) became the law, and the "boat race" aspect of landing at Ellis Island stopped.

Meanwhile, back at the realm, the ungrateful leaders of Britain, disgruntled that more British immigrants moved to America than to Canada or Australia or other parts of the British Empire, and peeved that American officials didn't show favoritism to their nationals, started complaining openly about Ellis Island's conditions in 1921 and 1922. They demanded that British immigrants be segregated from the "lesser races" coming in from elsewhere in Europe.

James Davis, Harding's Labor Secretary, was the Cabinet member responsible for immigration stations. Davis was himself an immigrant from Wales and was much too worried about what politicians in his homeland thought. He invited British ambassador Auckland Geddes to inspect Ellis Island. Geddes did so in December 1922.

Davis said he would try to segregate races (he may have meant nationalities when he said races) at Ellis Island. Instead of saying he agreed with the British diplomat (his former countryman) that non-WASPs were dirty and uncivilized, he reportedly said he favored segregation, claiming Jews being held at Ellis Island objected to performing some of their religious practices while Gentiles were about. Davis also said he wanted most inspecting of immigrants done overseas (instead of at American immigration stations.)

In a report made public in August 1923, Geddes complained about the detention cells, inspectors, the boards of special inquiry, medical services, and sanitation of the Ellis Island facility. Geddes wanted segregation of immigrants by nationality, but realized such a discriminatory policy could not happen at Ellis Island. So he argued for multiple facilities in New York City area. The British diplomat placed most of the blame for conditions he criticized on non-British immigrants, and the rest on the way America's leaders made laws. Geddes said American authorities should have immigrants to America inspected in their homelands instead of at Ellis Island or at other American immigration stations.

This of course would degrade America's security and public health, because foreign government agents were more corrupt than American agents. A foreigner who meant America harm who received a cursory inspection overseas could evade a thorough inspection at Ellis Island or another American immigration station, and come into America and cause harm. Also, corruption or coercion of European officials or consulate personnel could allow many inadmissible immigrants to get visas and crooked inspections giving them approval to come to America.

Former Ellis Island commissioner Frederick Wallis (a Wilson appointee) agreed with Geddes' complaints. He claimed, "I have seen a thousand people sleeping on the cold floors in winter without clothing." He then called Ellis Island "a vale of tears" and "the saddest place in the world."

Curran, who had been on the job only since July 1, 1923, a few weeks before Geddes' uncomplimentary report was made public, called the Geddes report pure propaganda. He added, "This report is grossly misleading and out of date." Curran blamed foreign governments for ignoring the Quota Act of 1921. He also blamed foreign shipping companies for making no effort to regulate the flow of immigrants, many of whom would be inadmissible. (The more people the shipping companies shipped, the more money they made. Even if they had to pay some fines, they gambled most would-be immigrants would be admitted.)

Curran also blasted Wallis and defended his workers. Curran said if Wallis was telling the truth about people sleeping on the floors, then it was a result of Wallis' incompetence in failing to provide bedding. Curran also charged Wallis with making Ellis Island employees work for free after hours to help his campaign for mayor of New York City and allowing graft to run rampant among the inspectors. (Wallis, to his credit, did start moving against crooked employees later in his short term at Ellis Island. However, if what Curran said about Wallis taking advantage of employees was true, Wallis had still done wrong.) Curran said it took Robert Tod (a native of Scotland who Harding appointed, who succeeded Wallis and preceded Curran as the Ellis Island Commissioner) a year to clean up after Wallis left. Tod was well-known for his philanthropy; he spent a lot of his own money trying to improve Ellis Island.

Curran took aim at the British press also. His agents had barred an Englishman named E. C. Mordaunt and sent him and roughly 60 other Englishmen back to England during his (Curran's) first month on the job. Mordaunt complained about his treatment, and the British press made an issue of it. Curran revealed Mordaunt had worked as a clerk for the American consulate in London in 1921, and lost his job when he was caught stealing money from the consulate.

"We are not welcoming embezzlers into this country – either English or any other kind – nor are we concerned about their complaints," Curran said. **(13)**

At the same time, Curran's boss aired a gripe with the way his own agency was handling the expense of running Ellis Island and other immigration stations. W. W. Husband, Commissioner General of Immigration, noted various immigration laws mandated shipping companies had to pay for the "maintenance" of immigrants while authorities decided if they were admissible. There was a system of fines and immigrant fees in place, but a large portion of money for the cost of running Ellis Island and other immigration stations came from Congressional appropriations (taxpayer subsidies) since 1909, President Taft's first year in office. Husband said it cost American taxpayers more

than a million dollars a year above and beyond what the feds collected in fines and fees to operate Ellis Island and other immigration stations. He claimed the feds were not charging shipping companies what they really owed, but merely were charging shipping companies for food fed to detained and sick immigrants. He said this was in effect a subsidy of more than a million dollars a year to foreign shipping companies.

If what Husband said was true, then the bureaucrats in his own Labor Department were incompetent. Or maybe the Anglophiles who infested the State Department were applying pressure illegally for them to circumvent the enforcement of the law. If true, this was a scandal.

In 1925, what Husband and other high government officials had in mind leaked out. They intended to reduce the role of Ellis Island, or maybe lease it out to foreign shipping lines. (This leasing option was implied by the writer of a 1923 New York *Times* article.) This would be even a worse scandal. They intended for European immigrants to undergo inspection in their homelands and then be free to leave the ships when they docked in American harbors. Under the guise of efficiency, they intended to close Ellis Island and other immigration stations and let hundreds of thousands of aliens come to America without proper screening.

They started their plan by allowing British immigrants to undergo some screening in Britain, sail, undergo a brief medical exam aboard ship, and leave when the ship docked instead of going to Ellis Island or to another immigration station for inspection and processing. Husband said, "We want to bring about a condition that will enable the immigrant coming into our ports to walk right off ship and go about his business."

Henry Curran attacked the policy publicly. He said the minimal screening for the British "would discriminate in favor of the British." Curran said a person who got an inspection in Britain could get sick enough after getting a visa to become inadmissible. Such a passenger, he added, could spread disease to other passengers, and spread disease once he or she was let into America.

Curran added, "Of course the British are still kicking about Ellis Island, and they always will, no matter how good a place we have. They are the only people who keep up the whining."

The minimum screening proposal couldn't protect the national security concerns of America. Nor could it prevent corruption. A foreigner who meant America harm who received a cursory inspection overseas could still evade a thorough inspection at Ellis Island or another American immigration station, and come into America and cause harm. Also, corruption or coercion of local officials or consulate personnel (like E.C. Mordaunt in England) could still allow many inadmissible immigrants to get visas and crooked inspections giving them approval to come to America. And if corrupt foreign shippers were allowed to lease and run Ellis Island, all sorts of undesirables would be able to get into America easily.

Curran also charged high government officials were conspiring to do away with Ellis Island and proper screening of immigrants. He accused Husband, who had just been promoted to become the Assistant Secretary of Labor. James Davis, the pro-British native of Wales, was the Secretary of Labor. Curran had already trashed the Geddes report, which Davis agreed with, for advocating most inspections for immigrants to America be done in Europe.

Curran said there was a humanitarian need for immigration stations as well as a national security need for them. "A more sinister phase of this agitation (to close Ellis Island) is the throwing of aliens open to being fleeced, swindled, and worse, if they are to be turned loose at a hundred different points on the waterfront at any hour of the day and night, by being examined on the ships, or on shore, instead of coming to Ellis Island," he said.

Ellis Island officials checked immigrants, especially young unaccompanied women, to ensure they got to where they needed to go without being swindled or forced into white slavery. Curran said, "Immigrants are not all of them able-bodied young men who speak English. There are thousands of unaccompanied young girls who must be cared for, and who will be, if Ellis Island is continued, instead of scrapped."

Bottom line? Curran said immigrants needed final screening in America by Americans at Ellis Island and other immigration stations, and there should be no favoritism to the British. In other words, Curran was trying to be fair and was trying to put American interests first. In the 1920s, this was not politically incorrect.

Labor Department officials seethed. President Coolidge was not happy about Curran attacking his own hierarchy publicly. Curran noted Coolidge sent word to him "to stop talking about the English. He said he had a State Department to handle foreign affairs."

Labor Department officials and other bureaucrats and politicians demanded Curran's firing. Curran said he had to account for his actions at Ellis Island. He was considered insubordinate for his attack on the government's lax inspection policy.

This wasn't the first time Curran crossed swords with his superiors. Earlier, Curran had refused to allow a political appointee to handle the money changing at Ellis Island. Labor Secretary Davis had summoned Curran to Washington and ordered him to put the appointee to work. Curran told Davis to his face he would not employ the man because he suspected he

was corrupt, and added, "What is more, I won't even let him get on the ferryboat at the Battery in New York, to come over to Ellis Island, for any reason at all. The guards have their orders. Is that clear?" Curran proved right about this also, because the political hack would later get caught smuggling immigrants into America and would have to go to prison for a year.

So Curran wrote a report defending himself. Coolidge told Curran's friend, Senator James Wadsworth of New York, "He (Curran) wrote a brief about it. He wrote 10,000 words. I read 'em all, every word, and he didn't say once that he was sorry. They say he's a nice feller, and he's a good commissioner. But Jim, ain't he a little peppery?" Coolidge retained Curran for awhile after this incident. **(14)**

Ironically, a case involving a big-mouthed blueblood British bimbo would be the last straw for Curran.

Vera, Countess of Cathcart, came aboard a ship that arrived in New York February 11, 1926. She had come to America to peddle a play called "Ashes of Love," which she had written about her life as an adulteress. Evidently she also had an epic of a book to share with the American public also. Its working title? "The Truth About My Love Affairs."

An inspector who evidently was aware of Vera the Vixen's trashy play script and book manuscript and her not-so-prim-and-proper past had her detained and sent to Ellis Island. Authorities at Ellis Island detained her on a charge of moral turpitude.

Immigration laws forbade people from coming into America for sexually immoral purposes. Under these laws, Vera was inadmissible for trying to peddle a play and a book that could be considered smut.

But the inspector didn't use that common-sense approach. Instead, he chose to rule the catty countess was a moral turpitude case based on her admission she was divorced on grounds of her adultery. In some states adultery was still a crime, and theoretically, she was excludible for this reason.

Countess Vera's past in England was not unknown. While she was married to the Earl of Cathcart, she committed adultery with the Earl of Craven. She evidently spent thousands of dollars on stylish dresses in preparation for sneaking off to a French resort with Craven, who was also married. The adulterous pair fled to South Africa and he holed up with her in that British colony. The Earl of Cathcart divorced Vera on grounds of adultery. He accused the Earl of Craven of being the "other man" she was cheating with. Later the Earl of Craven tired of his countess playmate, and returned to his wife. Vera hooked up with a playwright in England, but hadn't yet married him when she came to America to sell her salacious literary properties.

The vivacious Vera appeared before a board of special inquiry at Ellis Island attired in a black silk and wool frock. The board members were not impressed. They ruled the countess was not admissible. Immigration officials had banned 261 people on adultery charges in 1925, so the easy Englishwoman wasn't going to get special treatment just because she was a noblewoman, if not a noble woman.

Curran confirmed his board members excluded the countess because she admitted to adultery. He said she could appeal her case, but she would be staying in a private holding cell on Ellis Island until there was a final decision to admit her or expel her.

While immigration authorities made plans to deport her, Countess Vera hired a lawyer to appeal her case to Labor Secretary James Davis. One of her traveling companions, another blueblood named Lady Huntington, ditched her and sailed back to England. Meanwhile, her other traveling buddy, a Mrs. Carr, stood by her. Mrs. Carr told the press her countess companion needed to sell her works to pay her bills. She said Vera had written another novel titled "Woman Tempted," that was selling in England. The countess, for her part, blamed an enemy for allegedly tipping off immigration authorities to her background.

What enemy? The father of the Earl of Craven's wife – the father of the woman he cheated on when he ran off with Vera – also lived in New York City.

In a note of coincidental buffoonery, the Earl of Craven chose exactly this time to show up in New York with his wife. He was smart enough not to admit he was an adulterer. And in a note of serendipitous buffoonery, helpful New York officials chose this very moment to release from a state insane asylum a man who had been claiming he was the Earl of Craven's brother. The father of the Earl of Craven's wife had the knucklehead slapped into the loony bin some months earlier because the guy kept pestering him by phoning him repeatedly and by trying to visit him at his apartment and his office.

This was the Roaring Twenties, and it was the same year that would feature the frolics of Queen Marie, Clara Bow, and Aimee Semple McPherson. (Two of these three were natives of the British Empire.) Naturally the Countess of Cathcart case became fodder for the gossip columns and editorial pages immediately.

The countess played her role as wronged victim perfectly. From her detention cell at Ellis Island, she posed as the victim of a cruel double standard. A writer noted, "She ejaculated before reporters: 'Thank God this isn't British justice ... Thank God they couldn't put me in the electric chair. I daresay Mr. Davis would like to if he could. Poor little me, why did they consider me a dangerous woman?' "

In a bit of class snobbery, the captive countess said adultery was not a crime in England, and if it was, most of the noblemen and noblewomen of her country would be criminals. *Great argument, countess. Ask Anne Boleyn and Katherine Howard if they used that argument before Henry VIII had them beheaded. And we overthrew the rule of your nobility in this country.*

Then Vera turned vexatious. The little foreign minx demanded the Earl of Craven be excluded also because he participated in her adultery against her ex-husband by cohabiting with her and copulating with her continually. Feminist group leaders across the country started bitching about the double standard involving Craven and his ex-maven. Commissioner Curran, a believer in equality, swore out a warrant for the sleazy earl's arrest, but the Craven one played "Duck of Earl's" when he ducked into the Dominion of Canada a step ahead of American lawmen. Meanwhile his wife remained in New York for medical treatment. Vera called the Earl of Craven a craven coward.

Feminists played their part in the farce well. A bevy of broad-beamed buttinskys from various women's groups descended upon Ellis Island. They met with Curran to seek the countess' release. Doris Stevens, wife of Dudley Field Malone, the New York port official who let the *Lusitania* sail with ammunition and other war materiél on her fatal final voyage, did most of the hectoring. She demanded Curran protest the countess' detention or resign his office.

Another feminist leader falsely claimed immigration officials tried to trap women by getting them to admit they were divorced. Of course the inspectors asked the marital status of immigrants and visitors, because it might impact on other immigrants claiming to be their admissible relatives. Also, immigration agents at Ellis Island consciously tried to protect single girls and women from being exploited and abused.

Henry needed the hot air from this herd of harpies like he needed a hole in his head. He told them he wasn't resigning. He told them what the procedures were for admitting immigrants and visitors, he let them bitch a few minutes more, and then, according to a reporter, he "seemed to breathe an audible sigh of relief when the committee left his office."

Curran allowed the feminists to console the Countess Vera. They pledged solidarity, sisterhood, and all that jazz to the exposed Englishwoman. One of the ladies suggested she write a scene about her ordeal at Ellis Island into her play to ridicule immigration officials. Vera thanked the women and admitted Curran was treating her very well.

Many newspaper men and Society people in America and Britain attacked Curran. But some people backed Curran for treating the silken slut with no more favor than the average European skank.

While Lady Vera was in detention at Ellis Island, she hooked up with another sleazy earl. This one wasn't a titled Brit but an American Earl – Earl Carroll. Carroll, well-known for his "Vanities" burlesque show and his theater in New York City, was the brooding genius who invented pasties to skirt the obscenity law regarding topless dancers. He was known among chorines for making them audition naked. New York City police raided and interrupted a 1924 show of his that featured a starlet swinging nude. Carroll was arrested on obscenity charges the next day. New York City movers and shakers who were in Carroll's audience when the cops raided the joint helped him beat the rap.

Earl Carroll offered to buy Countess Vera's play and put her in the leading role. Countess Vera, no stranger to stripping for earls, okayed the deal. However, the script didn't call for her to show her 40-something intimate assets to the theater-going public.

On February 21, 1926, 10 days after officials first detained Countess Vera, Secretary Davis ordered her released for 10 days on her bond of $500. The next night, Washington's Birthday and into the wee hours of February 23, Carroll hosted an after-hours party for the Countess of Cathcart at his Manhattan theater. The party's main attraction was a bathtub on wheels full of champagne. At Carroll's orders, a 17-year-old chorus girl named Joyce Hawley stripped nude before the crowd, stepped into the tub, and immersed herself in the bubbly. As men lined up to dip glasses into the tub she occupied, the girl started crying in shame. Word of the gathering leaked out. Compared to the noise they made over her detention, the countess' female defenders (and the easy Englishwoman herself) were AWOL in regard to condemning the exploitation and abuse of the underage girl.

Despite the complication of attending a party in her honor that violated Prohibition, obscenity, and child sexual abuse laws, the Countess of Cathcart was able to roam free for awhile, thanks to Secretary Davis and her creative lawyer. On her instructions, her lawyer asked for a second hearing because she claimed the "moral turpitude" clause didn't apply to her. He also got a judge to rule to free her from the control of the Commissioner of Immigration, and the judge granted Vera a stay of up to six months in America. Davis made an appeal in federal court, more to clarify how to interpret the moral turpitude clause of the Immigration Act of 1917 than to try to get Countess Vera deported. A federal judge denied the appeal.

Carroll opened "Ashes of Love" in the nation's capital in March 1926, and it went down like an anchor. The quality of the play, Carroll's production, and the Countess' acting in the drama of her adultery and abandonment wasn't as compelling as the real-life media circus she had helped create. Dame Vera was a little too old for public nudity or even pasties, about the only wardrobe effects Carroll understood well.

The Countess bought her way out of the deal she made with Carroll, and she put on her adultery saga herself in New York City later in the month. She still acted in the play, and she was still clothed on stage. The reception in the Big Apple was no kinder. People laughed at parts that were supposed to be serious, much to Vera's discouragement. A critic wrote, "The engagement at the National Theatre is for a week only – just about the right length of time to take care of the curious." The show did not draw well enough to last longer. Conspicuously absent were the hundreds of thousands of women who supposedly stood in solidarity with the countess about her adultery but didn't want to see her actually re-enacting her adultery – or at least pay for this dubious artistic privilege. So vanquished Vera returned to England March 31, 1926, a scant seven weeks after she sailed into New York.

Lady Vera evidently didn't marry the playwright, or if so, it was for the very short haul. She would marry a rich old coot named Sir Rowland Hodge in 1930. "Lord" Hodge, a shipbuilding magnate, bought his title with the help of Lloyd George, the crooked little hypocrite who ran Britain during and after World War One. Lloyd George claimed selling titles was "the cleanest way of raising money for a political party."

There is nothing new under the sun. Lloyd George anticipated the Clintons' sale of nights in the Lincoln Bedroom for political contributions by three generations. Like Clinton, the doper who didn't inhale, Lloyd George was a prohibitionist who drank like a fish; both were serial adulterers.

Vera ran up bills on Hodge, then tried to divorce him in 1934. She alleged he was guilty of "misconduct." The British judge denied her suit on grounds of "insufficient evidence."

In 1928, a film based on Vera the Vamp's opus "Woman Tempted" hit the movie houses. The plot was straightforward: Girl marries for money, becomes promiscuous with men she meets in Society, destroys the life of one swain, and is about to ruin another lecher when the first guy's discarded fiancee kills her.

Earl Carroll was temporarily unavailable to pimp Vera's silver screen soap opera. His party for the countess got him into trouble with federal authorities, who were a little less tolerant of blatant vice than the political hacks on the benches in the state courts of New York City. Carroll had also shafted the girl he had undress and sit in the tub; Joyce Hawley said Carroll had never paid her for the stunt. Prosecutors charged Carroll not with sexual exploitation of an underage girl or with violation of Prohibition, but with lying about what liquid was in the tub, and with lying about whether the girl in the tub was naked. The girl and the drinkers said it was champagne and she was nude; Carroll claimed it was ginger ale and she was covered. John Marshall Harlan, who would later serve on the U.S. Supreme

Court and often cancel out Hugo Black's vote, helped prosecute Carroll and helped get him convicted of perjury and sentenced to a year and a day in the federal pen in Atlanta. Carroll fought the conviction, but had to report. He suffered a nervous breakdown while on the train to Atlanta, and spent two months recuperating. A fed with a sense of humor leaked that Carroll would have to become a bath house orderly while in the pen. Carroll, after his time in the can, resumed his career as a female body merchant until he died in a plane crash with his mistress in 1948.

Joyce Hawley made a little money from her shame, then left show business altogether. Under her real name, she evidently decided to go to college and learn a profession. She managed to avoid the harsh glare of publicity thereafter.

And what about Davis and Curran? Davis kept his job as Secretary of Labor. Curran didn't keep his as commissioner at Ellis Island.

While the Countess of Cathcart fiasco was at its peak, a New York civic group offered Curran a job at better money and better hours than the thankless job he had been doing on Ellis Island, so he took it. Curran stayed on at Ellis Island until March 31, 1926, the same day the countess got on the ship to return to England. He refused to comment on whether her case was the last straw, but he told reporters he had asked Congress to enact a law giving him authority to rule on certain cases. He noted, "I am not going to be held responsible for something I had no more to do with than the cop on the corner or the king of the Fiji Isles."

Curran would not mention the Countess of Cathcart case in his autobiography. He did say the immigration laws which allowed the Secretary of Labor but not the commissioner of any immigration station to review boards of special inquiry rulings led him to decide to leave. He said, "Although the immigrants and I were there on the island together, where I could meet them, talk with them, size them up from actual contact and rich experience, and so decide the cases capably and well, the law left me out ... The public, not understanding this vicious centralization of power at the top, was prone to hold me responsible for the decisions, although in fact I had no part in them .... It was this aspect of the job that led me to drop it like a hot cake when an offer of another job came along three years later." Curran called Ellis Island a place of concentrated sadness for the detained and the excluded. **(15)**

Curran jumped from the frying pan of Ellis Island into the fire after the end of his service with the civic group two years later. He helped spearhead the fight to repeal Prohibition (and in 1930 came close to going to jail on a contempt of Senate charge for cheerfully and sarcastically baiting the Prohibitionist hypocrites in that body who subpoenaed him). He then served as a magistrate in New York City, as the deputy mayor of

New York City, then as the chief magistrate of New York City.

During Curran's watch at Ellis Island, the number of immigrants took a sharp drop, largely due to a major immigration law Congress passed and Coolidge signed in 1924. Curran said, "Even Coolidge was moved to say, 'America must be kept American.'" **(16)**

The tighter quota bill for immigration Congress passed was known formally as the Immigration Act of May 26, 1924, and was more commonly known as the Immigration Act of 1924. This law proposed to limit maximum immigration of each nationality to 2% of foreign-born members of that nationality who were living in the United States in 1890. This would be at first much more discriminatory toward the Italians, Jews, Poles, and others from Eastern Europe and Southern Europe than the 1921 quota bill had been. It limited total immigration from around the world (except for the independent countries of the Western Hemisphere) to about 165,000 per year.

This proportion was to last for three years, and then starting in July 1927, the total number of quota immigrants could only be 150,000. However, starting in July 1927, maximum immigration of each nationality would be 2% of foreign-born members of that nationality who were living in the United States in 1920. This would be much more fair to Italians, Jews, Poles, and other would-be immigrants from southern Europe and eastern Europe.

They exempted most people from the Middle East and Iran as not being Asians from the "barred zone" spelled out in the Immigration Act of 1917. (The 1882 Chinese Exclusion Act and the 1907 "Gentlemen's Agreement" with Japan put a lid on immigration from China, Taiwan, Korea, and Japan.) However, the quotas limited the number of Turkish immigrants to under 200 a year, the number of "Syrians" (essentially Lebanese and some Syrians – the French ran both lands as a colony under one government) to fewer than 600 a year, the number of people from "Palestine" (essentially Israel and Jordan, run by the British as colonies) to 100 a year, and the number of people from "Hedjaz" (the Arabian Peninsula), "Mesopotamia" (Iraq) and "Persia" (Iran) to 100 a year.

Commissioner General of Immigration W.W. Husband noted he understood the 1924 law (aka 43 Statutes at Large 153-169) allowed his people at Ellis Island and elsewhere to admit only whites and blacks. In his annual report for 1924 he noted, "Included in the category of persons ineligible to citizenship are the Chinese, Japanese, East Indians, and other peoples indigenous to Asiatic countries and adjacent islands."

This law also aimed at diminishing Canada's business of laundering Europeans for export to America. The law closed the loophole allowing a European to evade the quota on his or her homeland by living in the Western Hemisphere for five years. People born in Europe would count against the quotas for their homelands regardless of where they were living when they decided to come to America.

In 1922, 310,000 immigrants had gained entry to America; 210,000 of them had done so through the port of New York and 100,000 had done so at other stations. Of the immigrants, 47,000 listed Canada as their place of last permanent residence. In 1923, 523,000 immigrants had gained entry to America; 295,000 of them had done so through the port of New York and 228,000 had done so at other immigration stations. Of the immigrants, 117,000 listed Canada as their place of last permanent residence. In 1924, 707,000 immigrants had gained entry to America; 316,000 of them had done so through the port of New York and 391,000 had done so at other immigration stations. Of the immigrants, 201,000 listed Canada as their place of last permanent residence.

Was the drop in immigrants coming to Ellis Island as a percentage of the national total a coincidence? Was the rise in immigrants at other immigration stations and the rise in declared Canadian residents due to less-thorough screening of those who claimed Canadian residency at other immigration stations?

In 1925, the first full year the Immigration Act of 1924 would be in place, 294,000 immigrants would gain entry to America; 137,000 of them would do so through the port of New York and 157,000 would do so at other immigration stations. Of the immigrants, 103,000 would list Canada as their place of last permanent residence. The Canada trend reversed.

Congress did not discriminate against immigration from Canada, Mexico, Latin America, or natives of free countries of the West Indies. Congressmen realized men and women from Quebec or Ontario or Mexico or Cuba or Brazil or Argentina were more desirable immigrants because of similarities in religion and culture. There was no quota on people from these places (other than the total number of immigrants American officials were going to allow into the country in any given year), and they only had to show they were admissible when processed.

One very reasonable provision of this law was a proviso that would place the burden of proving admissibility on immigrants. Before this time, the U.S. government had the burden of proving a would-be immigrant was inadmissible.

Another very good provision of this law made each would-be immigrant get an American consular official in their country of origin grant him or her an entry visa. This meant immigrants would receive proper legal vetting and proper medical inspection to verify they were eligible to enter the United States – pending immigration station inspection – when they arrived. This also meant very few immigrants would be sent home because they failed some legal or medical test for admission to the United States. Fiorello La Guardia's foresight and Theodore Roosevelt's basic sense of fair play were thus encoded into the national immigration law.

The law also had a provision enabling the limiting of the number of visas American officials could hand out to would-be immigrants. This was a nod to the thinking of people like Henry Curran, who argued Congress should allow U.S. consuls around the globe to hand out only enough immigrant visas to meet the quotas for the countries they were stationed in.

The lawmakers put a fine of up to $10,000 and a prison term of up to five years into the law as punishment for those who forged immigration visas or permits. They ordered the same penalties for aliens using other aliens' visas to get into the United States, aliens who sold or gave their visas to others to allow them to sneak into America, and aliens who lied to American officials to gain entry into America.

In the law, the congressmen and senators prescribed a $1000 fine per alien for ship companies whose ships brought in aliens without unexpired visas or with falsified nonquota visas. A nonquota visa usually applied to Latin American, Caribbean island, and Canadian natives. (Some nonquota immigrants were wives or minor unmarried children of immigrants of citizens. Others were clergy members, college professors, and college students.) It was usually fairly easy for shipping company officers to determine if someone carrying a nonquota visa deserved to have one.

The lawmakers also put into the law a provision fining shipping companies $1000 for each excludible alien seaman an officer of one of their ships allowed to go ashore or failed to detain aboard ship or failed to prevent from escaping due to lax ship security. (This didn't count if the sailor in question required medical treatment unavailable aboard ship.)

The Congressmen raised the penalty on shipping companies to $1000 per seriously diseased or disabled person found in inspection in America for bringing such persons to America if a competent doctor in Europe or elsewhere outside of America could have detected the disease or disability. They also applied this fine to shipping companies for negligence or indifference in screening out the mentally defective from the would-be immigrants. The lawmakers added a $250 fine per mentally or physically defective person as an extra fine to the $1000 already being assessed. The law also called for jumping the fines on shippers who negligently or indifferently brought in aliens from the Asian Barred Zone or inadmissible illiterates from anywhere to $1000 per inadmissible Asian or illiterate. The lawmakers ordered the custom collectors at American ports to take enough money from the shippers to pay for the return of the inadmissible aliens in the same class to the same port as they came from.

Among quota immigrants, the Immigration Act of 1924 gave preference to immigrants "skilled in agriculture" and their families. Although this law did supersede the Quota Act of 1921, the authors of the law intended it to add to rather than replace the Immigration Act of 1917 and other immigration laws still on the books. **(17)**

Some controversy surrounded the law. The bill's authors aimed at dropping the numbers of all immigrants. Since the law favored immigration from the WASP nations of Europe, people of Italian, Jewish, Polish, Greek and other ethnic ancestries from southern and eastern Europe felt demeaned. Many immigrant societies and some ethnic groups complained about the numbers of immigrants to be allowed entry to the United States.

On the inherent fitness of WASP immigrants compared to other European immigrants, the immigrant pressure groups had a point. Based on the behavior of the leading people of their homelands, it was naive to think British and German and Scandinavian and Low Country immigrants would be the most prone to be democratic. Britain's leaders were ruthless colonialists and liars, and naval militarists besides. The practice of piracy was ingrained in too many Britons. Too many Germans believed in authoritarian rule because they were natural followers, and they took back seat to nobody in terms of militarism. The Scandinavians and Low Country people submitted to rule by kings and queens also. Conversely, most Italian, Slavic, and Jewish immigrants were Christians (though not Protestants) or Jews. They were not at odds with the Judeo-Christian ethical underpinning of American society.

The quota system's unracist proponents argued America had a certain ethnic mix, and should keep it. They argued quite rationally that people from Asia and the Moslem countries did not agree with most Americans on religion or customs, and would be very hard to assimilate. They did not make this same argument against people from Canada, Latin America or the West Indies because most people from these areas adhered to one of the Christian religions, and most had some exposure to American ideas. Other backers of the law believed Americans had taken in a huge amount of foreigners over the previous three decades, and Americans would need time to assimilate these newcomers into the American way of life.

Millions of honest men and women felt threatened by the rise of organized crime in the 1920s. Mafiosi from Italy, Jewish gangsters in New York whose roots were in Russia or eastern Europe, and Chinese tong wars did nothing to allay their fears. The lawlessness of these individuals gave their countrymen a black eye in the mind of the American public and made many an unbigoted person support severe limits on immigration.

Of course there were those who supported immigration limits and quotas for reasons of racism. The Ku Klux Klan, endorsed by Woodrow Wilson, peaked at roughly four to six million members in the 1920s, including many suffragettes. **(18)**

The Klansmen were white Anglo-Saxon Protestants. Since the nation in the early 1920s had about 110 million people, this meant possibly as many as one household in six across the country had a bedsheet-wearing Kluxer in it. (Assuming some wives of Kluxers were in the Women's Ku Klux Klan, the actual percentage was still probably above one household in seven nationwide.) The Klan was almost as strong in certain parts of the Midwest as it was in the South. The Klan was powerful in other states like Oregon, where they tried to destroy the Catholic school system in that state by pushing into the books a law that required children to attend only public schools. (The Supreme Court threw out the unconstitutional law in 1925 with their ruling on the Pierce vs. Society of Sisters of the Holy Names of Jesus and Mary case.)

The Klan had friends in places even higher than the state governments of the South and other states like Indiana and Oregon. Woodrow Wilson, the sensitive Progressive, watched the pro-Ku Klux Klan film "Birth of A Nation" at a private screening in the White House in 1915. He said of the hate flick, "It is like writing history with lightning, and my only regret is that it is all so terribly true." Wilson despised blacks and pushed segregation. He supposedly loved humanity but despised many people.

Hugo Black, a white trash lawyer who defended an Alabama priest-killer in 1921, was also a Klansman. The murderer was a Methodist minister, a Klansman, and a barbershop owner named Edwin Stephenson. Black argued Stephenson was temporarily insane because Father James Coyle, a native of Ireland, dared to convert the Klansman's daughter to Catholicism and marry her to a Puerto Rican who had some black blood. Black got the peckerwood acquitted. Black was later one of our most leftist and pro-criminal Supreme Court judges, thanks to his undeserved appointment to that court by FDR. **(19)**

The service of many blacks in World War One and the factory jobs that were opening up in the Northeast and the Midwest caused many blacks to leave the South. This led to anti-black race riots in a number of cities up North, and to a rise in Klan membership north of the Ohio River and the Mason-Dixon line. The Klan's leaders expanded their anti-black message of hatred to Catholics and Jews also. This gave many Midwestern and Western bigots who couldn't hate blacks in person some targets to attack in their towns. Immigrants were mostly Catholic or Jewish, so they were instant targets to Klan members.

There were millions of more racists who didn't become Klan members simply because they were not joiners.

Beyond these garden-variety knuckleheads and products of incest were those who were truly evil sociopaths – the eugenicists. Eugenicism was a social disease too many American elitists caught from interfacing with their infected British and German counterparts. Of course, racism was institutionalized in America's laws against blacks and American Indians, and in practice against Hispanics. But eugenicism – the belief in breeding of human beings from "the fittest" parents and the sterilization of the "least fit" – was an even worse doctrine that came from the imperialistic circles of the British Empire, and in the cities of defeated imperial Germany, because it justified the "birth control" and enslavement of perceived weaker people and in many cases the extermination of these people once they were deemed incapable of being useful to the elites. This pathological viewpoint would lead to continued British oppression of black and yellow people around the globe, and to Hitler's wars upon Slavs and Jews and the handicapped.

As Americans wised up, the Klan would plummet into becoming the moth-eaten relic it is now. The Klan would also decline in large part because one of its leaders D.C. Stephenson was convicted of second-degree murder for kidnaping and repeatedly raping an Indiana woman and biting her breasts and other body parts severely enough that he drove her to attempt suicide, and because other Klan leaders were caught stealing the sheetheads' dues. So the ethnic and race-baiting demagogue with the most long-term influence on America would be the bisexual pro-abortion eugenicist Margaret Sanger.

Margaret Sanger tried to be a teacher, then quit. She later tried to be a nurse, but quit without getting a nurse's license. She married William Sanger, a young architect. Because Sanger decided to try being an artist for awhile, Margaret decided to find work. She said she did nursing work in New York City's Lower East Side, which teemed with Jewish, Italian, and Eastern European immigrants. Maybe her employer was easy to please; Margaret still was not a licensed nurse. Nor was she particularly sensitive. "I hated the wretchedness and hopelessness of the poor," she said in her autobiography, "and never experienced the satisfaction in working among them that so many noble women have found." She noted, "The wives of small shopkeepers were my most frequent cases," so evidently she didn't spend most of her time helping the poor people in that tenement district.

Margaret's snobbishness was at odds with her professed politics at the time. She became a socialist, and she and her husband opened their New York City digs to some of the leading radicals of the day. Emma Goldman, Alexander Berkman, Bill Haywood, and Eugene Debs were among the people who the Sangers tried to hobnob with; radicalism was chic in their circles at the time. Margaret also started dabbling in serial adultery. The Sangers went to France with their children in 1913. Bill studied art, while Margaret "researched contraception" and left Bill.

Ms. Sanger came back to New York City and ran afoul of the law in 1914 with her writings on sex and birth control. She fled to Europe under an assumed name without a passport and without even tipping off her estranged husband or family. She left them and her friends to look after her three children, including her daughter, who she said was suffering from a swollen leg when she ditched her and her two brothers. (The ailment evidently turned out to be polio.) Margaret spent a year in Europe collecting birth control devices and engaging in sex with other debauched "sex researchers." Back in New York City, Bill took a fall for Margaret; he drew a 30-day jail sentence for handing out her printed screeds. Margaret came back late in 1915 to face charges, and her young daughter died of pneumonia. If Margaret hadn't run off, maybe she could have used what nursing training she allegedly had to help her girl get well. Margaret gravy-trained the sympathy many people had for her over the death of her little girl she had abandoned; prosecutors dismissed charges against her.

After her escape from charges, Margaret spent much of 1916 touring the country speaking about birth control. She evidently had a fling with Portland abortionist Marie Equi during the time she spoke (and got arrested with the Equi woman) in the Oregon city. After returning to New York City, Ms. Sanger set up a birth control facility in a Brooklyn neighborhood teeming with Jewish and Italian immigrants. Whether she was trying to help the poor, as she claimed, or target them for birth control or sterilization, which is more likely, is subject to debate. Her foray into birth control and practicing medicine without a license cost her and her sister Ethel (who unlike Margaret allegedly was a real nurse and not a quack) some jail time.

Margaret Sanger claimed she was a pacificist. She was like the suffragettes who opposed war but failed to oppose World War One in order to further their agenda. She did not protest the war, and essentially abandoned her radical friends so she could appear to be a loyal American. She pursued her only love, birth control. She went back to Europe in 1920, collected still more birth control devices, and presumably tried out at least some of them in her second round of romps with male birth control advocates in England. (She didn't need them for her cunnilingual trysts with European females in the movement.) Margaret got a divorce from Bill in 1921; she had sought it since 1914.

Margaret's sheet-tangling with the flaky in the upper crust of Europe led her to conclude being a gold-digger paid better than being a radical. The elites would always have money for her. So for money she married J.N.H. Slee, the elderly British South African multi-millionaire who owned the Three-in-One Oil Company, in London after wangling an open marriage prenuptial agreement out of him. She used Slee's money to romp around the globe with like-minded men and women, and pimp recreational birth control for the rich and pimp mandatory birth control and sterilization for the poor. Slee eventually got into trouble for tax evasion for claiming his subsidies of Margaret's birth control activities were charitable donations.

Margaret Sanger also solicited donations from many wealthy Americans, especially society dames, who agreed with her on the desirability of easy birth control for themselves and their daughters, and on how birth control and sterilization could reduce the numbers of the less desirable. Ms. Sanger had the business acumen and morality of a prostitute who became a madam. She comfortably shilled to robber barons, socialites, and rich Republican clubwomen while she ignored her old leftist comrades. It was like white suffragettes ignoring black suffragettes all over again.

In her 1938 autobiography, Ms. Sanger bragged she addressed the Women's Ku Klux Klan in Silver Lake, New Jersey in the 1920s. To reassure her genteel readers aghast at her slumming, she noted, "My address that night had to be in the most elementary terms, as though I were trying to make children understand." She said the Klanswomen and their guests dug her well enough to make a dozen offers to her to speak in front of like-minded groups. Possibly to reassure her racist followers, Margaret admitted to her rendezvous with the Klanswomen after seeing FDR appoint Klansman Hugo Black to the Supreme Court a few months earlier in 1937, and suffer very little negative fallout from it.

In 1939, the year after she publicly acknowledged her *liaison* with Klanswomen in the 1920s, Ms. Sanger set up a birth control project aimed at American blacks which she called "The Negro Project." She duped a few prominent blacks into supporting her. In a letter to her accomplice Clarence Gamble, she wrote, "We do not want word to go out that we want to exterminate the Negro population and the (black) minister is the man who can straighten out that idea if it ever occurs to any of their more rebellious members." Gamble claimed in the proposal he wrote that won funding for the project, "The mass of Negroes, particularly in the South, still breed carelessly and disastrously, with the result that the increase among Negroes, even more than among whites, is from that portion of the population least intelligent and fit, and least able to rear children properly." He continued, "Public health statistics merely hint at the primitive state of civilization in which most Negroes in the South live."

Margaret Sanger clearly meant blacks no good. In her autobiography, any black she quoted she quoted the black talking like Mammy or Stepin Fetchit. She used a "feeble-minded" black woman who had 16 children who got into various scrapes with the law as her poster child for the "need" to control the breeding of the "defective."

In her 1920 book Woman and the New Race, the genteel bigot Sanger noted, "Among our more than 100,000,000 population are Negroes, (American) Indians, Chinese, and other colored people to the number of 11,000,000. There are also 14,500,000 persons of foreign birth. Besides these there are 14,000,000 children of foreign-born parents and 6,500,000 persons whose fathers or mothers were born on foreign soil, making a total of 46,000,000 people of foreign stock. Fifty percent of our population is of the native white strain. ... So it is more than likely that when the next census is taken, it will be found that following 1910 there was an even greater flow from Spain, Italy, Hungary, Austria, Russia, Finland, and other countries where the iron hand of economic and political tyrannies have crushed great populations into ignorance and want. The census of 1920 will in all probability tell a story of a greater and more serious problem than did the last."

Mad Margaret, the fake nurse, considered blacks and American Indians to be "foreign stock." By her own twisted definition, she had to consider Hispanics with black or American Indian blood (virtually all Puerto Ricans, Cubans, and Mexicans, and most Latin Americans) "foreign stock" also. She didn't have much love for the non-WASP immigrants of Europe either. Maybe it was because nearly all of them were Catholics or Jews.

In her fellacious 1922 manifesto Pivot of Civilization, Ms. Sanger falsely claimed 75 percent of America's schoolchildren were physically or mentally defective. She claimed hysterically 10% of the American public were mental defectives or morons who were encouraged to reproduce. And she claimed deliriously 2/3 of men of military age in America were "physically too unfit to shoulder a rifle." This book was Margaret's Mein Kampf.

Although she publicly bemoaned the lives of the poor, and claimed she was pushing population reduction on them for their own good, Margaret Sanger did little or nothing to help them gain better wages and working conditions once she started pushing birth control. In fact, she said charity was useless for the poor because they kept overbreeding, which negated the good done for them. She made fun of the Vice Commission, of Chicago, whose members had done much to rescue girls and young women from sex trafficking, something she never attempted. She criticized the Communists and her former fellow Socialists for blaming capitalism for the woes of the working class; she said overbreeding of the working class was to blame for their problems. She condemned American government programs for assisting poor mothers with prenatal and postnatal care, because, she said, "Instead of decreasing and aiming to eliminate the stocks that are most detrimental to the future of the race and the world, it tends to render them to a menacing degree dominant."

Like her fellow New Yorker FDR, Margaret Sanger was AWOL when Al Smith was pushing labor reforms through the New York legislature in the 1910s. She worked against Smith when he ran for president in 1928 because she despised practicing Catholics.

During the time of the debate over immigration quotas, Ms. Sanger argued, "The most urgent problem to-day is how to limit and discourage the over-fertility of the mentally and physically defective. Possibly drastic and Spartan methods may be forced upon American society if it continues complacently to encourage the chance and chaotic breeding that has resulted from our stupid, cruel sentimentalism."

What sort of Spartan methods, Margaret? She noted, "Every feeble-minded girl or woman of the hereditary type, especially of the moron class, should be segregated (from men) during the reproductive period. Otherwise, she is almost certain to bear imbecile children, who in turn are just as certain to breed other defectives ...We prefer the policy of immediate sterilization, of making sure that parenthood is absolutely prohibited to the feeble-minded."

Bear in mind Ms. Sanger claimed most military age men were physically defective, most American children were mentally or physically defective, and at least 10% of the American populace was mentally defective. Like Hitler, she used the Big Lie approach to dramatize her demands. If she had gotten her way, her sterilization gulags for Americans would have been Nazi or Soviet in size. Money from robber barons and crooked financiers like the Rockefellers, Carnegie, Paul Warburg, and Henry Morgenthau, and money from millionaire lawyers and socialites supported Ms. Sanger's programs, so many of the elites put their money where their hard hearts were on their desire to cut down on the numbers of the masses who were not useful to them.

So what was Margaret Sanger's long-term effect upon America? Planned Parenthood is the result of a merger of two groups which Margaret Sanger founded in the years between World War One and World War Two. Planned Parenthood people are proud of their common-law mother and have named several of their abortion facilities after her.

Like Hitler and many Nazis, Margaret Sanger and many of her like-minded spirits were bisexuals. However, Ms. Sanger differed with Hitler and his ilk on one important issue. She believed WASP women could be conscientious objectors in the war to birth genetically superior supermen and superwomen if they didn't want to bear any children. This mindset would eventually lead to Planned Parenthood's lucrative birth control and abortion trades, largely financed by American taxpayers.

Ms. Sanger supported ethnic quotas on immigration. In a speech she gave in Oakland, California in 1929, she remarked, "Up to 1914 Uncle Sam was rather negligent about the kind of folk who emigrated [sic] here; he was like the parents who, although they scarcely know what they will do if their family is increased, yet do nothing to prevent it ... Not until 1924 was it necessary to recognize that there was a population problem and that SOMETHING must be done for the future of the country. So bars were put up at the entrance of the United States ... If it is necessary to keep such types out of the country, why is it not just as important to stop their breeding?" **(20)**

Harry Laughlin, one of Margaret Sanger's many associates who shared her eugenicist views and her bigotry, designed a model compulsive sterilization law that 18 states' lawmakers passed. The Nazis would later use Laughlin's model sterilization law for their own war against those they deemed inferior. In 1936, Nazi Germany's Heidelberg University would award Laughlin with an honorary doctorate for "services on behalf of racial hygiene."

Ironically, Laughlin developed epilepsy after he had argued epileptics should be sterilized. But he didn't volunteer his own gonads to the knife. Like most elitists, Laughlin didn't practice what he preached.

Tragically, Laughlin, a high school teacher, had another claim to infamy – that of a quack statistician pimping ethnic restrictions based on the false science of eugenics. (This was like Margaret Sanger's false claim she was a real nurse.) Money that robber barons Andrew Carnegie and E. H. Harriman stole from their workers and the public funded the Eugenics Record Office, which Laughlin directed. Laughlin used this post to worm his way into the fight for the Immigration Act of 1924. Using false and flawed statistics, Laughlin testified extensively to congressmen on the "need" to restrict immigration of non-WASP countries. Sadly, this lying crackpot had an impact on the law the lawmakers enacted. **(21)**

Because of the twisted input of moral defectives and mental cases like Laughlin, and the supporting sentiment of like-minded moral defectives and racist sociopaths like Margaret Sanger and the elites of industry and finance, and because of the agitation of their ideological bedfellows in the Ku Klux Klan, the Immigration Act of 1924 would be a flawed product.

The specific bias the Immigration Act of 1924 had against Latin Europe and Eastern Europe made it a flawed law. However, it had many good provisions. Just because many racists and sexual deviates supported the Immigration Act of 1924 because of their own demons doesn't mean the law was totally worthless.

The intent of many nonracists who backed the passage of the Immigration Act of 1924 was to lower the total number of immigrants per year to assist Americans in assimilating immigrants without being overwhelmed by them. According to the censuses of 1890, 1900, 1910, and 1920, the percent of foreign-born in America was 15% in 1890, 14% in 1900, 15% in 1910, and 13% in 1920. In 1930, the percentage of foreign-born would drop to 12%. By 1940, the percentage of foreign-born would drop to 9%; this would lead to better assimilation and national cultural cohesion. Americans could keep their ethnic identities and still be loyal Americans, as the military service of the many with roots only a generation old in America would prove during World War Two. **(22)**

Henry Curran, the commissioner of Ellis Island in 1924, said, "The foreign groups fought it (the bill) tooth and nail. They behaved more like foreign colonies than American citizens, and they were powerful."

"My own estimate of the situation, in a nutshell, was that our country needed a rest from the task of assimilating so many millions of foreigners piling in here from every part of the world to become voting Americans in five years from the day they came ashore at Ellis Island," Curran said. "The art of self-government is not acquired so easily. It is a long, hard road. There must be a habit of it, a strong element of matured experience in it, if the composite sum of our American population is to succeed at it. We have done pretty well so far, but we are still an experiment, with only a hundred and fifty years of national life behind us – a tick of the clock, against the ages! And most of the immigrants were coming in from countries where for centuries they had lived under the heel of dictators, knowing nothing of the obligations of self-government that must go hand in hand with its blessings – if self-government is to survive." **(23)**

Curran proved right. As the experience of the last few decades have shown, immigrants from places like China, India, and the Middle East are not as assimilable as the Europeans or Latin Americans. Their cultural and religious norms are very different from those of America. So is their sense of practical patriotism. People of East Asian and South Asian descent (except for people with Filipino or Guam roots, who are overwhelmingly Catholic) tend to serve in our Armed Forces at rates much lower than whites, blacks, or Hispanics. This also holds true for people of Middle Eastern descent. Most service members of Arab descent have roots in the Catholic and Orthodox

communities of Lebanon, Syria, and Iraq. The majority of Moslems in uniform are American blacks. (24)

Hispanic immigrants and immigrants from the Caribbean islands have traditionally assimilated into American society while retaining their customs and religion, like most European immigrants. This has changed considerably only in recent years because politicians of both parties, in a selfish and shortsighted drive for more votes, cheap labor, and Social Security contributions, have deliberately allowed millions of illegal immigrants from Mexico and Central America to come to and stay in this country.

Curran was also prophetic about the need for jobs for Americans. In 1941, while Americans were still digging out of the Great Depression, he said, "Incidentally, it would be good to have enough jobs to go around among ourselves – if we ever get near that millennium again – without letting in more impecunious millions to compete with us for relief and for such jobs as we have."

The Immigration Act of 1924 was a needed fix because the steamship companies and shifty Europeans were still using the loophole of unregulated immigration from Canada and elsewhere in the Western Hemisphere to evade the intent of the 1921 law. In 1922, there were 310,000 immigrants to America. The number jumped to 523,000 in 1923, and to 707,000 in 1924. Roughly 200,000 of the total came in through Canada, and another 90,000 came in through Mexico. In 1924, another 75,000 came directly from Germany, 56,000 came directly from Italy, 36,000 Poles and Jews came directly from Poland, 33,000 came directly from Scotland, 26,000 came directly from England and Wales, 18,000 came directly from Sweden, and 17,000 came directly from Ireland. In all, more than 360,000 immigrants came directly from Europe and at least another 100,000 Europeans came in by way of Canada.

The 1924 law caused a large drop in immigration. In 1925, there were 294,000 immigrants admitted to America. In 1926, 1927, 1928, 1929, and 1930, the numbers were 304,000, then 335,000, then 307,000, then 280,000, then 242,000, respectively. **(25)**

Harry Hull, the Commissioner-General of Immigration, noted the following about Ellis Island in 1928:

"Ellis Island was the great outpost of the new and vigorous Republic. Ellis Island stood guard over the wide-flung portal. Ellis Island resounded for years to the tramp of an endless invading army. Its million or more immigrants a year taxed its resources to the utmost. It was the target of the demagogue, the sob-story writer, the notoriety seeker, and the occasional fault-finding busybody puffed up with conceit, who meekly submitted to every form of official surveillance in his own country, accepting the same as a matter of course, but felt it unbefitting his dignity on entering free America to conform without protest and criticism to reasonable and necessary immigration regulations. Ellis Island is freed of this inundating horde and largely freed of carping critics, but Ellis Island has lost its proud place in the grand immigration scheme. Its million or more immigrants yearly have shrunk to several hundred thousand." **(26)**

During the 1920s, Congress and the presidents and the courts addressed several other immigration and citizenship issues. Their most overdue action was in enacting the Indian Citizenship Act of 1924. Many American Indians had received American citizenship, through individual treaties their tribes signed with the American government, through marriage with whites, through military service, or through the 14th Amendment in 1868 if they lived in states or territories under effective American government control. But many tribes not under effective U.S. government control in 1868 had *not* received citizenship under the 14th Amendment. American politicians did not give citizenship to American Indians after the soldiers, settlers, and speculators forced them into reservations. The Dawes Act of 1887 promised American Indians *might* become citizens only if they left tribal life and adopted white man's ways. The Dawes Act allowed the theft of most of the reservation lands. The nation's leaders put the Indian Citizenship Act of 1924 on the books only after the valiant service of many American Indians in World War One. This long-overdue law granted all American Indians American citizenship automatically. **(27)**

Indians from India took a hit in the 1920s. But then, many of the Indians from India had sneaked into America. And unlike the American Indians, none of the Indians from India was the target of a genocidal policy of the American government in the 1800s. In the U.S. vs. Bhagat Singh Thind Supreme Court case of 1923, the justices upheld the Act of February 5, 1917. They decided under its authority Singh and other immigrants from India were not whites or blacks or American Indians, and were therefore not eligible for citizenship. They noted, "It is not likely Congress would be willing to accept as citizens a class of persons whom it rejects as immigrants." The high court judges were referring to the Asiatic Barred Zone, and the Chinese Exclusion Act, both which were still valid parts of American immigration law in 1923. (Congress ended these restrictions during World War Two and into the early 1950s.)

Thind should have merited an exception. Thind, a college student at UC Berkeley legally, enlisted in the U.S. Army in July 1918. He didn't see combat and received his discharge in December 1918, a month after Germany's and Austria-Hungary's leaders quit. However, he still put himself in harm's way for America by enlisting, and he should have received citizenship on those grounds. Ironically, Thind, a victim of injustice in America, would have been the beneficiary of injustice

as well as a victim of injustice had he stayed in India. The British ruled the Indian subcontinent as grasping colonial masters. Thind, as a high caste Sikh, still could have lorded it over people in lesser stations of life in his homeland.

Thind had the last laugh. Authorities still let him live in America even after he lost his case. He married a WASP American woman. He lived the American dream in another way. He was able to make a good living like some televangelists and "gurus" by selling his books on philosophy and spirituality and becoming a "spiritual guide" to those who believed in what he was peddling.

What happened to Thind also happened to would-be immigrants from the Orient. Takao Ozawa, an immigrant from Japan, sued to gain American citizenship. The Supreme Court in 1922 ruled against him because at the time citizenship was limited to white and black people (and by status, to the American Indians, before the Indian Citizenship Act of 1924).

On the precedent of this ruling, officials revoked the citizenship of Hidemitsu Toyota, an immigrant from Japan who served in the U.S. Coast Guard on and off for several years, and was in uniform during World War One. His loss of citizenship was a greater injustice than Thind's because he spent more time in military service. Toyota appealed, and the Supreme Court in 1925 decided against him also. In their ruling, the justices did affirm Filipinos and Puerto Ricans had naturalization rights because they swore allegiance to America after the Spanish-American War.

In 1935, Congress enacted a law specifically granting eligibility for citizenship to veterans like Thind and Toyota who were from countries from which immigration was now barred, or were from countries whose nationals could not gain American citizenship. (This was the Naturalization of Certain Resident Alien World War Veterans Act of June 24, 1935.) Thind applied for citizenship again in 1936 and this time the feds allowed him to keep his citizenship. **(28)**

In the 1920s, while mobsters were smuggling alcohol into America, Chinese "entrepreneurs" were doing a thriving business smuggling their own countrymen and countrywomen into America. The law allowed certain white-collar Chinese and their wives and children to come to America. To exploit this loophole, the smugglers, errr, nontraditional travel agents had been for years giving illegal immigrants crib sheets to memorize about Chinese who were already legally in America, or about the Chinese man or woman who were traveling with the illegal and posing as the illegal's parent. (The older Chinese man or woman would be one who was admissible under immigration laws.) The illegal would then pose as the "paper son" or "paper daughter" of the legal resident or admissible alien.

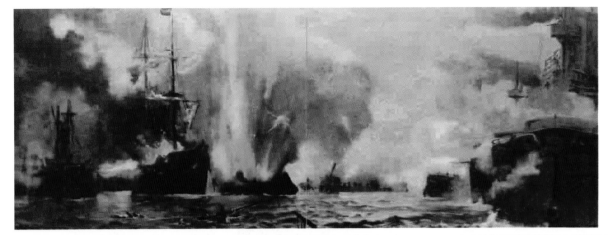

AMERICANS FLEX THEIR MUSCLES

In the Spanish-American War, American sailors, soldiers, and marines showed their stuff. **Above:** Admiral Dewey's fleet KO's the Spanish fleet in the Philippines. Another American fleet does likewise in Cuba. **Left:** Col. Teddy Roosevelt (on horse) rallies the Rough Riders in combat against the tenacious Spanish infantry in Cuba. Teddy Roosevelt would become president three years later. He would start the building of the U.S. Navy into the world's best. Pictures courtesy of the U.S. Navy and U.S. Army.

"Speak softly and carry a big stick" was Teddy Roosevelt's motto. He sent the Great White Fleet on a round-the-world voyage to remind other countries' politicians of America's growing might. **Right:** American and Japanese officers pose aboard the USS *Missouri* in Japan. The battleship's guns were covered to keep water out. Credit: U.S. Navy. **Below:** The Great White Fleet's 16 battleships anchor in San Diego harbor ... a breathtaking sight! Credit: San Diego Historical Society.

THE PANAMA CANAL

became a reality thanks to Teddy Roosevelt and many other worthy Americans. American doctors beat yellow fever and malaria, and American engineers and men beat the jungle and the mountains to build the canal. It would be ready for ship traffic in 1914.

Top and center: "Gatun Dam" and "Installing a Lock Gate", both by W. B. Van Ingen. American men and machinery went to work in incredible heat and humidity to dig the canal and channel the rivers and bolster unstable land that the canal went through. Jamaicans and other men from the Caribbean Basin joined the Americans in building the canal. Courtesy of the Panama Canal Society.

Bottom right: "The Conquerors" by Jonas Lie, 1913. The Panama Canal was not an easy sea level canal over desert terrain like Suez, but one that had to crack a barrier of mountains and jungle. The mountains dwarf the steam shovels and locomotives used to cut earth and rock out of the area and haul it away. Credit: U.S. Army.

Bottom left: The USS *Minnesota* passes through the Panama Canal. The canal was a geopolitical triumph of the first magnitude. It enabled American naval officials to shift warships between the Atlantic and the Pacific. It also saved merchant sailors the expense and the danger of going around Cape Horn at the bottom of South America. Credit: U.S. Navy.

By 1976 (when the author was undergoing military training in the Canal Zone), incompetents like Gerald Ford, Jimmy Carter, and alien Henry Kissinger were planning to give it away. The author visited his congressman and tried to talk him out of supporting this idiocy. The Bushes and the Clintons completed this abortion of American policy. The Chinese now have working control of the ports at both ends of the American-built canal.

TEDDY ROOSEVELT was a man of action, courage, justice, and vision. He pushed to protect the public from corporate abuses. He built the U.S. Navy and the Panama Canal. **Top left:** TR is being TR ... animated and forceful. **Top right:** TR checks out a steam shovel on the Panama Canal project. **Left:** TR's pretty and spirited daughter Alice – America's best known bachelorette of that era – captured the hearts of the American public. Her sister Ethel did not come of age until TR was back in private life. Ethel served with honor as a nurse in World War One. **Bottom:** Left to right, TR's sons Archie, Theodore Jr., Kermit, and Quentin all were wounded in World War One; Quentin died when a German pilot shot down his biplane. Their cousin FDR held a cushy government job during the war. Credits: Alice is courtesy of the Library of Congress. The other photos are courtesy of the National Park Service.

TR Jr. was the only general who landed in the first wave at D-Day in World War Two. He got his tankers and infantry men inland. He died weeks later of a heart attack. Archie would see combat against the Japs in that war, and get wounded again. Kermit raided the Nazis in Norway and had coastal defense duty in Alaska. Kermit saved TR's life in the Amazon but would take his own during the war due to depression. Alice said it was unfair that her gallant brothers always were measured against their father.

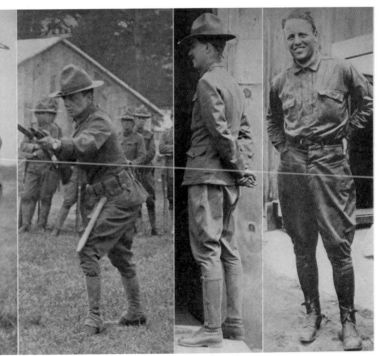

Conditions were bad in many industries, especially the coal industry. The needle trades were not as dangerous, but girls working as seamstresses received serf wages and often received unwanted advances from the men who worked them. Many immigrants worked in these trades.

Top left: Boy mine workers at a Pennsylvania mine. Credit: Library of Congress.

Top right: Slavic coal miner. Credit: Lewis Hine, New York Public Library.

Center: Slavic woman washes clothes in a coal camp. Credit: Lewis Hine, New York Public Library.

Bottom right: These girls worked for a clothing manufacturer. They seem startled; perhaps because the business was being inspected. Credit: Chicago Daily News, Chicago Historical Society.

Bottom left: Muckrakers like Lizzy Cochran (aka Nellie Bly) exposed evil conditions, and pushed for reform.

AMERICANS vs. CRIMINALS HIDING BEHIND RELIGION

Top: "Decatur Boarding Tripolitanian Gunboat" by Dennis Malone Carter. America's first war after independence was the war against the Barbary pirates during Jefferson's presidency in the early 1800s. These Moslem pirates operated out of Morocco, Algeria, Tunisia, and Libya thanks to local Islamic officials. They seized American ships for ransom, and enslaved crewmen. They also raided European countries for women to rape and enslave. American sailors and Marines beat these vermin. Stephen Decatur, in the blue coat, was one of the naval heroes of this war. Credit: U.S. Navy.

Center: Moros, Moslem fanatics from Philippine and Indonesian islands, raided Catholic settlements of the Philippines for centuries and attacked Americans in the early 1900s. The Moros hopped up on intoxicants, which made them hard to drop with revolvers. Americans started carrying 45 caliber pistols to kill them at close range. Americans shelled a palace of a sultan who aided the Moros. The Moros decided to behave. Credit: U.S. Army.

Bottom left: Mormons in Utah butchered pioneers on their way to California on 9/11/1857, a gross of years before other jihadists acted in 2001. The Mormons, polygamous separatists, escaped punishment for many years while the feds handled the Civil War and smashed American Indians. A bad Supreme Court ruling also delayed their punishment. Public domain. **Bottom right:** Nancy Huff was only 4 when Mormons butchered her family and kidnaped her after the massacre. U.S. Army captain James Lynch and his men rescued her and 16 other children from Mormons in 1859. Her sad stark account of the murder of her family, the murder of females who begged for mercy, her own kidnaping, and her seeing her mother's clothing and goods in the home of her kidnapers would make a statue cry. Nancy's photo appears with the permission of her descendant Sue Staton. Film maker Brian Patrick restored this photo of Nancy as a beautiful young woman.

TELEGRAM RECEIVED.

FROM 2nd from London # 5747.

"We intend to begin on the first of February unrestricted submarine warfare. We shall endeavor in spite of this to keep the United States of America neutral. In the event of this not succeed-ing, we make Mexico a proposal of alliance on the following basis: make war together, make peace together, generous financial support and an under-standing on our part that Mexico is to reconquer the lost territory in Texas, New Mexico, and Arizona. The settlement in detail is left to you. You will inform the President of the above most secretly as soon as the outbreak of war with the United States of America is certain and add the suggestion that he should, on his own initiative, invite Japan to immediate adherence and at the same time mediate between Japan and ourselves. Please call the President's attention to the fact that the ruthless employment of our submarines now offers the prospect of compelling England in a few months to make peace." Signed, ZIMMERMANN.

THE WAR IN EUROPE drastically dropped immigration to America. **Top:** A key reason was that it was unsafe to cross the ocean due to British warships and German submarines, like the one whose crew has just torpedoed a cargo ship. Public domain. **Above:** A German sub crew torpedoed the *Lusitania* off the coast of Ireland in 1915 because it was carrying weapons to Britain. This monument in Cobh, Ireland, is to the Irish fishermen who saved hundreds of survivors and brought them to this port city. More than 1000 died. Photo by author.

Center right: The Zimmerman Telegram, as purportedly intercepted by the British. German officials tried to sucker the Mexicans into attacking America. Congress declared war on Germany soon after this act of idiocy; the Germans didn't disavow the telegram! **Right:** Texas Rangers provided border security against Mexican "bandidos." These bit the dust during the 1915 Las Norias raid. Photo by Robert Runyon, Library of Congress and University of Texas. Pancho Villa's rabble raided Columbus, New Mexico in 1916 and killed a number of townspeople and ranchers. Mexican raiders made other forays into America; we responded with a formal but small-scale military invasion of Mexico. Armed American citizens protected themselves and their loved ones during that crisis. We need a lot more of that today.

AMERICANS ENTER WORLD WAR ONE

Top: Americans land in France. They bolstered the sagging British and French. Scheming British and French generals wanted Americans put in their units to serve as cannon fodder. General John Pershing, America's highest ranking officer, told them to pound sand in almost all instances. Americans served under American officers.

Top mid: Americans train a machine gun with a caliber of more than an inch on German lines. Rounds this big would shred enemy soldiers and most vehicles.

Bottom mid: American soldiers wear gas masks against a German gas attack. In World War One, the author's grandfather Leo Hurley and great-uncle Emil Nebgen suffered serious injuries due to German use of phosgene and mustard gas.

Bottom left: Pershing let some outfits, usually black outfits, serve under French or British command. Our black GIs, shown here in action wearing French helmets, added courage and physical prowess to buck up the overwhelmed Euros.

Bottom right: Jack Johnson, shown beating Jim Jeffries. He was the first black heavyweight champion. He offered to fight as a front line infantryman if Wilson administration officials would drop the Mann Act conviction he was unfairly railroaded on in 1913. They wouldn't, so Jack sat out the war and returned to America to do his time.

All pictures public domain, most courtesy of U.S. Army Signal Corps.

AMERICANS LEAD THE WAY TO VICTORY

The "can do" sprit of American soldiers and their physical prowess and courage helped them beat the Germans and help the British and French do likewise. American entry in the war saved France from defeat and Britain from cross-channel retreat.

Top: American infantrymen advance behind a smoke screen. One way to avoid the withering fire of soldiers in good defensive positions was to put up a smoke barrage to conceal your own men in the assault. They couldn't see the enemy either, but artillery shells would find the enemy as ground troops advanced to be close enough to see them, surprise them, and shoot them or bayonet them.

Upper mid: American men drink German beer out of captured German beer steins.

Lower mid: Americans march into Germany to help occupy Germany west of the Rhine after the Germans quit the war on November 11, 1918. American soldiers were much easier on German civilians than the British and French soldiers who they bailed out.

Bottom left: Roughly 80,000 Americans dd not come home from Europe. Their fellow soldiers buried them in the fields of France. Among the dead was one of Teddy Roosevelt's sons. Another 40,000 died in American training camps of disease, thanks to the ineptness of the Wilson administration.

Bottom right: Crippled black soldier comes home. He still manages a smile as he visits with a lady among the home folks who have come out to welcome his unit home.

All pictures public domain, most courtesy of U.S. Army Signal Corps.

AMERICAN SAILORS, MARINES, AND NURSES HELPED WIN THE WAR

Top left and right: Many American women served as Red Cross nurses during the war, or entered the Army or the Navy, as this nurse did, shown with two of her Marine patients. Teddy Roosevelt's resolute daughter Ethel served as a nurse in France. She was also active in the Red Cross for at least 60 years.

Center: U.S. Navy men lay antisubmarine mines in the North Sea. This crippled German submarine operations against British shipping and against ships bringing Americans to the war. **Bottom:** U.S. Navy warships enter a British port. Churchill and other British officials schemed to get America into the war. They needed American naval strength as well as ground troops to avoid disaster.

American warships protected convoys of supplies and soldiers from submarine attack. After the war, the Brits downplayed the U.S. Navy effort. British officials also tried to pressure America's leaders into not expanding the U.S. Navy. We did surpass their navy, and we would bail the Brits out of a second world war they helped cause.

All pictures public domain, most courtesy of the U.S. Navy.

FEMINISTS AND PROHIBITIONISTS allied to get votes for women and take away alcohol from men. The results? Organized crime skyrocketed due to the ignorance of many of these ninnies.

Top left and right: Feminists put their best feet forward with white booted lady lawyer Inez Milholland in the 1913 parade they put on to upstage Woodrow Wilson. But the feminists gave blacks little more of a role than the man who held Inez's horse. Black suffragettes had to march in the back of the parade. Later, suffragettes took to picketing Wilson at the White House. **Center:** Western women had the vote because they helped build up the West. Jeannette Rankin, a Montana Republican, was the first woman elected to the U.S. Congress. She is addressing other women in March 1917. A month later she would tearfully and dramatically vote against war with Germany. She was right, but it helped cost her her seat. A generation later, she returned to Congress; she was the only member to vote against war with Japan. She was wrong, but her accusation that FDR and the British and the moneyed interests helped lead to Pearl Harbor turned out to be right. Irate voters turned her out again. **Bottom left:** A collection of stoogettes tries blackmail for Prohibition. From the looks of them, some would get lucky only if men had been drinking hard. **Bottom right:** This congenial woman helps introduce the term "bootlegging" to the American vocabulary. Note the swastika on the floor was a good-luck sign in America until Hitler turned it into the mark of Satan. All photos public domain; most are courtesy of the Library of Congress.

VIOLENCE MUSHROOMED after

World War One. **Above left:** The Ku Klux Klan had several million members in the 1920s. Many were women, like these two at a cross burning. Credit: Library of Congress and Colorado Historical Society.

Center: A mob of thousands in Omaha shot, lynched, and burned William Brown in 1919 on the unproven charge he raped a white woman. They burned the courthouse and jail, looted stores for guns and ammo, and nearly murdered the mayor of Omaha in the process. Lynchings with crazed celebrators on souvenir postcards were all too common in this era. Credit: University of Washington.

Bottom: Valentine's Day Massacre, Chicago 1929. Capone's thugs, masquerading as policemen, raided rival mobster Bugs Moran's headquarters and shot six of his men to death. Vicenzo De Mora aka Jack McGurn, Capone's enforcer, masterminded the hits. Charlie Sherlock, grandfather of the author, arrested McGurn years earlier. Grandpa Charlie also advised Moran to behave himself. De Mora was shot to death; Moran died in prison.

Top right: Margaret Sanger slinks into Chicago to spew hatred against blacks, immigrants, and the poor. She addressed Klansmen, wealthy WASPs, and others known for hatred and greed on the "need" to wipe out the "unfit." She railed against non-WASP immigrants, especially Hispanics and other Catholics. Some of Ms. Sanger's associates advised Hitler's people on "racial hygiene." She was a virulent racist who advocated birth control, abortion, and sterilization, all of which the Nazis would use on Jews and Slavs. She supported mandatory sterilization for a very large proportion of Americans. She was a serial adulteress and a bisexual, an advocate of abortion and birth control for sluts like herself, and was the common-law mother of Planned Parenthood, which won her the support of many of the abnormal and degenerate in America. Preppy Prescott Bush helped her raise money for Planned Parenthood.

Credit for Chicago photos: Chicago Daily News, Chicago Historical Society.

THE ROARING TWENTIES

was the first decade of the open soap opera in America. Romania's English Queen Marie, **right**, and Canadian preacher Aimee Semple McPherson, **far right**, were two foreigners whose peccadilloes shook America's cocktail shaker in the 1920s. Mixed drinks became vogue in that decade because Mob-run rotgut was much harsher (and very toxic) compared to alcohol made by legitimate distilleries (which were shut). Photos are public domain.

Meanwhile, Europe seethed with wars and murders and hatreds. **Below:** Poles kept Soviets from extending their empire in 1920. Pilsudski, with notepad, was the rare general who listened and took notes. Poster shows Polish cavalrymen attacking Red infantry. These images came from Polish sources.

Lower mid: Father Miguel Pro faces firing squad of Mexican dictator Plutarco Calles in 1927. Padre Pro died bravely. Fervent Catholics and Calles' other enemies, called Cristeros, waged guerrilla war against his corrupt regime. Many thousands of Mexicans escaped the warfare by fleeing to America. In 1929, Calles' successor ended the harshest anti-Catholic policies, and the Cristeros ended the war. Calles regime photo. **Bottom right:** Americans tried to save Armenians, Greeks, Syrians, Lebanese, and Iranians from murder and starvation, regardless of religion. Many Moslems and America's internal enemies seem not to remember our charity. Public domain. **Lower left:** "Baptism in Kentucky" by Marion Post (Wolcott). USFSA photog Miss Marion took this photo in the late 1930s. Her picture accurately reflected the good faith of these Baptists and many other Protestants who tried to follow the word of God in the 1920s and in other decades. The snotty chattering classes started to mock religion openly in the 1920s, especially the Protestantism of America's country people, and the Catholicism of America's city blue-collar people. Public domain.

THEY SHALL NOT PERISH
CAMPAIGN for $30,000,000
AMERICAN COMMITTEE
FOR RELIEF IN THE NEAR EAST
ARMENIA · GREECE · SYRIA · PERSIA

DEPRESSION & OPPRESSION

hit around the world in the 1930s. Bad weather, greedy landlords and middlemen, and poor government policies drove many from the land. Many hardworking people lost their farms and their savings in this decade. Fewer jobs meant pressure to keep immigration low. **Top left:** Dust storm, Elkhart, Kansas, 1937. Credit: Library of Congress. **Upper mid left:** Eviction of sharecroppers, Arkansas 1936. Credit: Library of Congress. **Bottom left:** Emaciated children and "headless" mom in Ukraine, 1932-1933 Holodomor (Death by Forced Starvation). Stalin had crops of Ukrainian peasants who did not want to have their land stolen by the state seized. He had 5 to 7 million Ukrainian peasants starved to death or executed in 1932-1933. **Lower mids:** Criminals of Munich Hitler and Chamberlain, Nazi-Soviet Pact criminals Stalin and Ribbentrop. Cowardly sell-out of Czechs by British and French leaders and Stalin's backstab of Poles led to the carve-up of Czechoslovakia and Poland.

They also led to World War Two, the Nazis' murder of 6 million Jews and 20 million Slavs (the holocaust you never hear about), and Red domination of Eastern Europe. Nazi German govt. archives. **Right:** "Anichka the Hired Girl" by Yarka Burés, in "Happy Times in Czechoslovakia." Brit Chamberlain labeled Slavs "faraway people" not worthy of help against aggression. Libushka Bartusek wrote the book after the Munich sell-out to win sympathy for the Czech people.

Above: Polish sisters 1939. One dead, one wounded and heartbroken, thanks to a Nazi divebomber. Public domain.

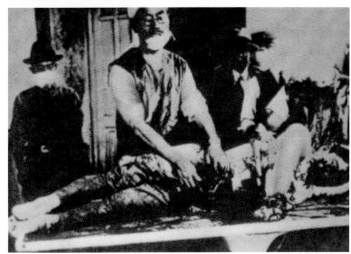

AGGRESSION AND OPPRESSION led to the deaths of tens of millions of people in the 1930s and 1940s. **Top left:** Rape of Nanking. 1936. Jap soldiers murdered at least 300,000 people and raped tens of thousands of females in this orgy of blood. **Center right:** Jap sadists in Unit 731 gassed, infected, and dissected Chinese, Russian, European, Aussie, and American victims. Here, a Jap criminal is preparing to dissect a Chinese man without anesthetic. Japs murdered 20 million Chinese, several million natives of Indochina and Indonesia, and a million Filipinos. Imperial Japanese photos credit Nationalist Chinese government.

Top right: Day of Infamy. Japs sneak-attacked Pearl Harbor on December 7, 1941, the 9/11 of our parents' generation. Rescuers speed to the USS *West Virginia*, one of eight battleships hit that day. US National Archives photo. **Bottom left:** German soldiers force Jewish captives out of Warsaw ghetto, 1943. Sadistic Nazi scum would murder most of them in concentration camps. Nazis would murder six million Jews and 20 million Slavs. Nazi photo, released by Polish govt. **Center:** Katyn Memorial, Baltimore. Soviet scum murdered captive Polish officers (including Janina Lewandowska, the female pilot whose head is shown) at Katyn in 1940 and elsewhere during World War Two. Stalin deliberately stopped his army east of Warsaw when the Polish Home Army rose against the Nazis in 1944. Stalin wanted all non-Communist Polish leaders dead. Photo courtesy National Katyn Memorial Committee.

VENGEANCE, RED OPPRESSION

Top: Americans hit the beach at Normandy on D-Day (June 6, 1944) to liberate the people of Western Europe. It was the second time in the century Americans would spill their own blood to help Europeans, who would ultimately be ungrateful. US Army photo. **Center left:** Booted Nazi bitches of Belsen (under British guard) bury their victims in a mass grave. Some female guards would be hanged as war criminals. British government photo. **Center right:** Justifiable Homicide. Americans dropped nuclear weapons on Hiroshima and Nagasaki. Truman knew it would take this kind of force to show the suicidal and homicidal maniacs who ran Japan that further resistance was futile. US Army photo. **Bottom left:** Czech girl Maria Dolezalova, who survived the Lidice massacre, testifies in Nuremberg Trials. Nazi vermin shot the men of her town and sent the women and children to concentration camps, where most died. Photo from US Holocaust Memorial Museum. **Bottom right:** Hungarian girl during 1956 uprising against Soviet Union. Reds crushed the rebellion in blood. *Thank God your ancestors came here. You missed incredible amounts of genocide and oppression.*

Other Chinese posed as crewmen aboard ships, walked off of ships in ports, and failed to return when the ships sailed. Some claimed they were born in San Francisco before the 1906 earthquake. They claimed the quake and the resulting fire which destroyed public records in that city caused their proof of American nativity to go up in smoke. And still others came in illegally by crossing the border from Canada or Mexico illegally or with the help of a ship's crew who dropped them ashore on a deserted American beach.

Chinese "entrepreneurs" had three other weapon in their arsenal – forgery, perjury, and bribery. Chinese businessmen in America and in China made false documents for illegal immigrants. They provided Chinese citizens and legal residents who could make false business partnerships to get men in on the businessman loophole. They also provided "witnesses" who could lie about the would-be immigrant's relatives and place of birth.

Immigration officials came to believe most Chinese immigrants they allowed into America had lied convincingly enough about their place of birth or their occupation or their family relationship that immigration agents believed they qualified for entry.

In 1915, federal investigators, responding to a tip written in Chinese, raided the American steamship *Mongolia* in San Francisco Bay. They found 86 Chinese stowaways who were aboard ship with the connivance of the crew. The haul of so many illegals made it look like immigration agents at Angel Island and in the San Francisco area were in cahoots with smugglers.

In 1916, federal investigators uncovered an illegal Chinese immigration ring in the San Francisco area. The ring members placed Chinese workers on Angel Island or bribed existing Chinese staffers to steal records and run messages to detained Chinese aliens on the island. They bribed Chinese and American workers on Angel Island to obtain immigration records and photos. They also bribed immigration officials.

The Chinese scams were old news to the inspectors at the West Coast ports, because most Chinese sailed to San Francisco, Seattle, and other ports in the Pacific Coast states and tried to gain entry at these ports. There had been a "Chinese Division" in the American immigration bureaucracy since the 1890s.

But the illegal practices the Chinese tried evidently mushroomed in the early 1920s. So did the overall numbers of Chinese attempting to become legal residents and the number of Chinese the immigration agents rejected. More and more illegals from China started coming to New York City after World War One.

To thwart the illegals, Bureau of Immigration officials put Chinese Division agents on Ellis Island in the early 1920s. They checked for fraud among incoming Chinese aliens, and assisted in roundups of Chinese illegals in New York City. **(29)**

As the Immigration Act of 1924 became law, President Coolidge and Congress started the U.S. Border Patrol. They did it by enacting an appropriations bill (43 Statues at Large 205-242) for the Labor Department and some other federal agencies. One of the provisions of the law ordered the starting of a "land-border patrol." And unlike Congress and Senate members in 2006 who voted for a border fence but didn't appropriate the money to build it, Congress members in 1924 actually funded the Border Patrol This appropriation took effect the day the bill became law, May 28, 1924.

Congress and President Coolidge put two more significant immigration laws into effect during the "lame duck" session in early 1929. The first law, approved on March 2, 1929, updated a number of existing immigration and naturalization laws. This law also allowed any alien without a record of admission for permanent residence who had been in the country before the Quota Act of 1921 became law to register as a permanent resident. The alien had to have resided in America since before the enactment of the Quota Act of 1921, show "good moral character," and not be subject to deportation according to current immigration laws. Some might claim this was possibly the first bill that had an "amnesty" provision. Others would claim otherwise. If the alien could not have gotten into the country legally in the first place because he or she was liable to be a public charge, sick with a "loathsome" disease, an illegal contract worker, an illegal entrant, one of the immoral classes, a person convicted of a crime of moral turpitude, or an anarchist, Communist, proponent of violent overthrow, or someone else with views inimical to the United States, he or she would have been deportable when he or she first came to America, and would not be eligible for registering as a permanent resident.

The second law, approved on March 4, 1929, made it a felony for an alien to try to enter America illegally after being deported. Instead of merely deporting these individuals again so they could try again, federal officials would have to imprison illegals for up to two years. The law permanently banned any illegal alien who the feds had deported earlier. **(30)**

The two 1929 laws in a way tied together American fairness with the American desire that people do things the right way. Congress and the president gave immigrants a chance to clear up their status to avoid being rounded up and deported for not having proper proof of legal resident status. They also banned illegals who tried to enter after already being caught and deported after a fair hearing.

AFTERMATH: THE DECLINE AND FALL OF ELLIS ISLAND

In the years 1931 through 1939, there were 457,000 immigrants total admitted to the United States. Many thousands of immigrants left America for their homelands during this decade, hoping they could do better. In 1940, immigration picked up some, as 71,000 immigrants came to the United States; 50,000 of these came from Europe, and of these, 22,000 came from Germany. This was the year of the Nazi blitzkrieg over Denmark, Norway, the Low Countries, and France, and the air battle over Britain.

From 1931 through 1940, American officials would deport 117,000 aliens. Roughly 50,000 of these they caught trying to enter the country illegally without inspection, or illegally with forged, false, or faulty documents. Another 15,000 had to leave because they violated laws pertaining to their permission to be in the country, and 10,000 or so joined them on a boat ride back to Europe or a train ride back to Canada or Mexico for being caught after previously being barred or deported. The feds sent home another 17,000 convicts, 5000 members of "immoral classes" (mostly pimps and prostitutes), 1000 drugrunners, and 253 subversives. They also expelled 8000 illiterate adults, 6000 physical or mental defectives, and 2000 public charges. They deported about 3000 for miscellaneous causes. American officials "required to depart" another 93,000 aliens for various reasons. These people had to get back to their homelands on their own.

From 1941 through 1945, 171,000 immigrants came to the United States. Of these, only 53,000 came from Europe. This was because of World War Two. **(31)**

Hitler was the main cause helping FDR limit immigration. Hitler's secret police were very effective at limiting the escape of people from the countries of Europe his forces controlled. And his submariners sunk many more ships. The Netherlands, Denmark, and Norway, which had great merchant fleets and were neutral nations during World War One, were under German occupation during World War Two. Sweden, another World War One neutral with a decent merchant fleet, was surrounded by German-occupied Norway and Denmark, and by German ally Finland. (The Finns were fighting a revenge war against the Soviets, who had attacked them and stolen some of their land in the winter war of 1939-1940.) The Germans also occupied Greece, another country with a good merchant fleet.

There was some movement of refugees, but not many of them came to America. The Turks were neutral during the war, so Pope Pius XII's envoys operating out of Constantinople (Istanbul) smuggled many thousands of Jews out of Eastern Europe with fake baptismal certificates. The Pope's men helped many Jews relocate to neutral Portugal and neutral Ireland, and even helped many hide out in Italy, which was an Axis country but whose people were not enthusiastic in helping Hitler murder the Jews. Even the Spanish took in some Jews and helped others make it to Portugal despite Franco's "official" attitude against receiving refugees. Some Jews sneaked into the Holy Land, braving Arab attacks and the British blockade. Pope Pius XII paid ransoms to free Jews. He also hid 3000 Italian Jews in his own summer palace near Rome from the Germans who essentially were occupying Italy after the overthrow of Mussolini. Pope Pius XII also had hundreds of other Jews hidden from the Nazis in the Vatican itself. **(32)**

Spanish and Portuguese authorities allowed refugees from elsewhere in Europe to escape to America and other places. Spanish dictator Francisco Franco despised Hitler, but used him to help win the Spanish Civil War. Franco refused to help Hitler against the British and Americans, which helped the British and Americans in the North African Campaign. But Franco still allowed a division of Spanish volunteers to fight against the Soviets in World War Two for two years as revenge for Stalin's aid to the Communist-dominated government Franco overthrew, and as revenge for Stalin's agents looting several hundred million dollars worth of gold ingots from the Spanish national treasury during the Spanish Civil War. In 1943, under American and Catholic Church pressure, Franco ordered the volunteers to return to Spain. Portugal's government was neutral but would tilt pro-Ally. They had allowed German U-boats to refuel in the Azore Islands, but eventually they allowed the Americans and British to use bases in the Azores. This chased away the U-boats.

As Hitler rose to power, rearmed Germany, and started persecuting the Jews, many Jews in Germany sought to emigrate to America. Many Jewish leaders in the United States pleaded with FDR to allow more Jews fleeing Hitler to come to America. FDR was worried about how Southerners and union members would react to the importation of roughly a million Jews from Germany, Austria, and the Czech lands (which Hitler's army controlled before the outbreak of World War Two). They would compete for jobs and would not be Christians. Since Southerners and union members formed a large percentage of FDR's voting base, he did nothing.

In one notorious case, FDR in 1939 turned away the *St. Louis*, a German ship carrying 930 Jews who were fleeing Hitler. American officials tried to cajole Cuban officials and other Latin American officials into taking them in, but failed. The captain had to return the ship to Europe. Many of these Jews perished during the Holocaust when German armies overran western Europe. The plight of these Jews was memorialized in a book and later a movie called "Voyage of the Damned."

It is easy to criticize FDR now for not helping Jewish refugees. But in FDR's defense, his job was to be president of the United States, not runner of a refugee camp for Europe. In America, many patriot groups and labor unions opposed more immigration during the Great Depression because of the competition immigrants would offer for scarce jobs. In FDR's first eight years in charge -- 1933, 1934, 1935, 1936, 1937, 1938, 1939, and 1940, unemployment stood at 25%, 22%, 20%, 17%, 14%, 19%, 17%, and 15%, respectively. (In Hoover's four years of 1929, 1930, 1931, and 1932, unemployment percentages were 3%, 9%, 16%, and 24%, respectively.) The unemployment figure for 1940 would have been higher if FDR and Congress hadn't started a peacetime military draft. The unemployment figures for 1939 and 1940 would have been higher if FDR hadn't allowed businesses to sell implements of war and related supplies to the British and French. They would also have been higher in the 1930s if Hoover's men hadn't deported or forced to leave on their own hundreds of thousands of illegals from Mexico to lessen competition for jobs in America. Some of FDR's policies were worthwhile, but some of his and his underlings' policies prolonged the Depression and drove many thousands of small farmers from their land. **(33)**

The Jews weren't the only victims of genocidal oppression, as the Chinese and the Slavs could point out. The patriot groups and labor unions noted if America had to take in Jewish refugees because no other country would, then they would be obligated by a sense of equality to take in millions of other non-Jewish victims of Nazi, Soviet, and Japanese genocidal aggression. And they understandably viewed these mass murders and oppressions as evils the people of Europe and Asia should deal with, not the people of America. Americans were still paying for World War One, a quarrel between rival groups of European imperialists. They didn't want to have to shoulder the burden for a second such war. However, FDR was essentially a political schemer, so his decision to do nothing essentially looks like a calculated move on his part to protect his political power.

The United States' population during the war rose from about 135 million to about 140 million. About 16.3 million able-bodied people were in uniform. Roughly 11.2 million served in the U.S. Army and Army Air Force, 4.2 million served in the U.S. Navy, 700,000 served in the Marines, and 200,000 served in the Coast Guard. Others served in the merchant marine during the war; due to submarine attacks, this was essentially a combat branch also. The vast majority of these were young men, including all the men of my family who were of service age. During the war, my Dad, my uncles Chuck and Rusty (Uncle Don was too young for the war; he fought in the Korean War), and my wife's father all served in the Navy or the Army. So did virtually every man who was a friend of my father's that was roughly his age. So did virtually every father of every friend of mine. My aunt Wilma served as an Army nurse. (That's how she met Uncle Chuck.) Roughly 200,000 other women who were not Armed Services nurses also served in uniform during World War Two. My Dad's Uncle Joe, who was too young for World War One, tried to enlist in World War Two, but Uncle Sam kept him at his job as a foreman in a shipyard. Grandpa Charlie, who had served in the U.S. Navy in World War One, did training films for the Armed Services in World War Two. Grandpa Leo, who served in combat in the U.S. Army in World War One, was an armed guard at a defense plant during World War Two. Both my grandpas had been Chicago police officers crippled in the line of duty.

Also, many women worked in industrial jobs the men had to leave behind to join the Armed Forces. And since there was a greater demand for manufactured items such as ships, tanks, planes, artillery pieces, explosives, rifles, trucks, and uniforms, many men and women worked at these jobs, which paid better than farm work or semiskilled manual labor.

This meant the largest group of aliens in the United States legally during World War Two would be braceros (manual laborers) from Mexico. These people replaced refugees from Oklahoma and other Dust Bowl states as the people who picked crops in California. (Most of the young men who were "Okies" were serving in uniform in World War Two.) The braceros soon started doing farm labor across the country. They also did railroad maintenance work and other work requiring raw muscle throughout the war. Roughly 220,000 Mexicans signed bracero contracts and worked in America during the war. The Bracero Program would last until 1964. There were roughly 4.5 million bracero contracts signed by Mexican nationals during this two-decade period. But since the average bracero signed many contracts while working in the United States after World War Two, the actual number of braceros was much lower – about 400,000 braceros. **(34)**

In the final four years of the 1940s, the Cold War replaced the war against Germany and Japan as the main concern of American foreign policy. American taxpayers spent billions of dollars to rebuild an ultimately ungrateful Europe, Japan, and China. During these years, at least 610,000 people immigrated legally to the United States. Of these, roughly 370,000 people came directly from Europe; most came from Britain (105,000), defeated enemy Germany (91,000), and defeated reluctant enemy Italy (44,000).

Formal immigration from Eastern Europe was much lower because the Red Army occupied most of these countries and Stalin essentially forbade emigration.

However, the great majority of the roughly 215,000 refugees and asylees American officials admitted from 1946 through 1950 came from Eastern Europe. Of these, almost 80,000 came from Poland, more than 20,000 came from Latvia, almost 20,000 came from Lithuania, roughly 10,000 came from Yugoslavia, more than 8000 came from Czechoslovakia, 7000 came from Estonia, 6000 came from Hungary, 4000 came from Romania, and 14,000 or so (most probably from Ukraine or Belarusia) came from the Soviet Union. We also admitted more than 35,000 refugees and asylees from Germany and about 5000 from Austria.

Throughout the decade, far more legal immigrants came to America via Canada than via Mexico. However, some of the braceros did not return to Mexico when they stopped doing farm labor under the terms of their contracts. Instead, they stayed illegally in the United States.

From 1941 through 1950, American officials would deport 111,000 aliens. Roughly 65,000 of these they caught trying to enter the country illegally without inspection, or illegally with forged, false, or faulty documents. Another 14,000 had to leave because they violated laws pertaining to their permission to be in the country, and 18,000 or so joined them on a boat ride back to Europe or a train ride back to Canada or Mexico for being caught after previously being barred or deported. The feds sent home another 9000 convicts, 759 members of "immoral classes" (mostly pimps and prostitutes), 822 drugrunners, and 17 subversives. They also expelled roughly 2000 illiterate adults, 1600 physical or mental defectives, and 143 on public assistance. They deported 812 for miscellaneous causes. American officials "required to depart" another 1,471,000 aliens for various reasons. These people had to get back to their homelands on their own. Most of these people were illegal immigrants from Mexico. **(35)**

Dwight Eisenhower and his underlings would close down Ellis Island as an immigration station in November 1954, after moving the last of the detainees off the island. Meanwhile, rival government agencies scavenged the facilities at Ellis Island for goods like grave robbers.

Eisenhower tried to sell Ellis Island to private businessmen from 1956 through 1960. The prices they offered were so shamefully low the feds had to pull Ellis Island off the real estate market. **(36)**

Ellis Island lay barely guarded or largely unguarded through the 1960s and 1970s. The buildings deteriorated because of bad weather, salt fog, and lack of preventive maintenance. Vandals broke windows; thieves stole electrical wire, plumbing fixtures, and anything else of any conceivable resale value. Millions of pigeons and sea birds lived in the derelict buildings, and defecated heavily inside all of them. The degradation and violation of Ellis Island mirrored a similar breakdown in American government and society in those years.

John Kennedy's underlings offered Ellis Island to the United Nations, but the racketeers of the world organization turned it down. Lyndon Johnson pulled the guards off of Ellis Island in 1965, only to be chagrined when professional criminals not in government service looted the island for scrap metal and other items. The old ferry boat that offloaded so many immigrants from passenger ships to the island was allowed to deteriorate and sink in 1968. This incident paralleled LBJ's pathetic underachievement in doing nothing when the North Koreans captured the USS *Pueblo*, killed an American seaman, and abused the rest of the crew of that ill-fated vessel in 1968.

Ellis Island became so devastated and ignored that American Indian militants tried unsuccessfully to squat on it, and later black activists tried unsuccessfully to get the feds to allow them to set up a trade school and other services on the island.

This devastation of a place many Americans viewed as hallowed ground because of the sacrifices their ancestors made to leave Europe behind was to be expected from a string of self-serving politicians and bureaucrats without an appreciation for history or the practical worth of a facility designed and maintained with such care as the facility on Ellis Island. It wouldn't be until Ronald Reagan's presidency, and several years of work in the 1980s after Reagan pushed for the renovation of Ellis Island, that dedicated people would finish renovating Ellis Island and reopen it as a living monument of Americana – an immigration museum.

1. Sources of information for the Allied atrocities of imposing further blockades to starve the people of central Europe after the Armistice include Herbert Hoover's and Hugh Gibson's book The Problems of Lasting Peace (pages 86, 110, and 206), Thomas Fleming's book The Illusion of Victory (pages 322-326, 332, 356-357, and 375-376), and William Klingaman's book 1919 (pages 5-6, 88-90, 101-102, 140-142, 157-165, 331-332, 467-468).

2. Information sources for the piratical "Liberation Payments" include Leslie Tihany's book A History of Middle Europe (page 211), C.E. Black's and E.C. Helmreich's book Twentieth Century Europe (page 339), and a U.S. Commerce Department memo of Herbert Hoover's dated 5/22/1924.

3. Information sources for the despicable "Liquidation Payments" include Twentieth Century Europe (pages 339-340) and the multi-author book History of Yugoslavia (pages 516-519); Vladimir Dedijer wrote the chapter in question.

Vladimir Dedijer, who would rise to prominence, then fall from it in Tito's Red Yugoslavia because he backed criticism of the greed of Communist leaders, noted tersely, "The country's (Yugoslavia's) position in this respect was extremely difficult as it had inherited the public debts of Serbia and Montenegro, and some of the debts of the Ottoman Empire in proportion to the territory allocated to Serbia and Montenegro." In other words, the international financiers, backed by the governments of Britain, France, and Italy, were squeezing Yugoslavia for money supposedly owed by the Turks. The Serbs and Montenegrins had liberated land their people lived on from the Turks in the First Balkan War of 1912-1913; the men of finance and government in Britain, France, and Italy felt a sense of entitlement to rob the Slavs. Although Dedijer didn't mention the situations of the Greeks, Bulgars, and Albanians, it is safe to assume the men of finance and government in Britain, France, and Italy committed similar acts of extortion against them after World War One because their peoples had also liberated their countrymen from the Turks in the First Balkan War.

4. In 1908, six years before the start of World War One, the Russian Empire had 155 million people. After World War One, Poland was independent and some Belarusian and Ukrainian borderlands were under Polish rule, Moldova was under Romanian rule, Finland was independent, and so were Lithuania, Latvia, and Estonia. However, the population of the reduced-size Soviet Union in 1926, according to Sidney Harcave in his book Russia: A History (page 524), still should have been about 175 million, given the advances in medicine and public health, and the natural increase in population due to the virility of their young men and the robustness of their young women. Instead, Stalin's headcounters reported finding only 147 million people to count, a "population deficit" of almost 30 million people. Russia lost maybe two million war dead to World War One. The hardships the war imposed on the civilian population probably cost another two million to three million civilians in Russia, Ukraine, Belarusia, and the Baltic lands their lives. (This doesn't count the deaths of those in the paths of the German, Austro-Hungarian, or Russian armies. Unlike World War Two, the Germans weren't out to exterminate the Slavs in World War One, but civilians inevitably die when they are unfortunate enough to

be in the path of an invading or even a friendly army.) The war between the Communists and their enemies in Russia had an unknown number of dead. Estimates of 10 million to 12 million who died from disease and famine and enemy bullets and murder of civilian populations is not unrealistic.

These figures are educated guesses. So are the estimates of historians like Nicholas Riasanovsky, who reported about 20 million died from starvation, disease, combat, murder and execution, and the general breakdown of Russia's society and economy from the Communist putsch of November 1917 through the end of the Russian Civil War and the famines of 1921 through 1923 in his book A History of Russia (page 488). To quote Spector in his book An Introduction to Russian History and Culture (page 299), "Since the rise of Stalin, and especially during the Cold War that followed World War Two, there has been wilful and wholesale falsification and distortion of the history of this period (the Russian Civil War) in the Soviet press, in Soviet historical publications, and even in Soviet fiction."

Ivar Spector, in the same book (pages 300-301) reported Hoover and his people and the Red Cross cared for about 10 million people in Russia. He mentioned 40 percent of the money Americans contributed voluntarily to help the starving people of the Soviet Union came from Jewish groups. Sidney Harcave, in Russia: A History (page 532), reported 33 million people were starving in the Soviet Union and five million died of the effects of starvation and disease in 1921 and 1922. W. Cleon Skousen, in his book The Naked Communist (page 120) reported similar figures.

Also, at least a million people left Russia because the Communists took power.

The prewar population estimate of the Russian Empire comes from Ralph Tarr and Frank McMurry's book New Geographies.

Figures do not count Stalin's wars against the peasants and various ethnic minority groups from 1924 when he took power to the start of World War Two. Maybe another 15 million people perished due to the bloodthirstiness of Stalin and his goons.

In the early 1930s – primarily 1932-1933 – Stalin waged war on the peasants of Ukraine. Roughly five million to seven million Ukrainians died from starvation, disease, or other effects of starvation. The Communists also executed many thousands of Ukrainians for resisting collectivization of their small farms.

Several million other peasants died in similar fashion in European Russia, the Caucasus region, and Kazakhstan because the Communists declared war on peasants in these lands also. Miron Dolot and Adam Ulam provided this information in Execution by Hunger: The Hidden Holocaust (pages vii-xvi). New York Times liar, errr, reporter Walter Duranty helped Stalin cover up the extent of these mass murders, and received a Pulitzer Prize for his crooked efforts. He viciously attacked those who were telling the truth about the mass murders. Neither the New York Times nor the association that awards the Pulitzer Prize have stripped Duranty of it posthumously, even though many urged them to do so in the early 2000s.

During the 1920s and 1930s, the Soviet Union's Communist masters exported grain – just like the British exported grain and meat from Ireland during the Great Hunger of the late 1840s. In each case the rulers deliberately starved people to death to make money.

What about the Stalinist purges of the 1930s? Estimates vary from several hundred thousand executions to several million executions and deaths of family members made destitute by the execution of the family breadwinner(s). For a truly breathtaking recap of the scope of the purges, read Aleksandr Solzhenitsyn's amazing classic The Gulag Archipelago (pages 24-143). For insider information on the purges, read The Secret History of Stalin's Crimes by Alexander Orlov. Orlov, a former Soviet intelligence agent and diplomat on duty as part of the Communist effort against the Spanish people in the Spanish Civil War, fled Europe with his wife and daughter in 1938 because Stalin wanted his life too. Orlov said Stalin executed so many competent police and intelligence agents that the replacements "Uncle Joe" sent to entrap him were not cunning enough to get the job done.

5. The sources of information on the inter-Allied loan and reparations fiasco are F. Lee Benns' book European History Since 1914 (pages 169-170), George Knoles' book The New United States: A History Since 1896 (pages 311-312) Twentieth Century Europe (pages 223-224, 300-301), and The Illusion of Victory (pages 473-475).

Benns argued that the British would come out ahead if American leaders cancelled Britain's war loan debt to America in exchange for Britain's leaders cancelling war loan debts of Britain's allies to Britain. Fleming and Knoles reported the British owed America $4 billion and they had lent their other allies $10 billion. Fleming was skeptical enough to say the British were "supposedly" due this sum.

Given the policy of piracy of the British leaders, I have to agree with Benns and Fleming. I believe the amount due the British from their allies was much less than the amount the British owed the American people. The British wouldn't have made such an offer unless they stood to gain. (However, even if the British were telling the truth about what they were supposedly owed, they would still welsh on the $4 billion they borrowed from the American taxpayers. If they figured they couldn't be repaid, they might as well take advantage of Americans.) The British cooked their books routinely. They had lied about transporting weapons in passenger ships, they had tried to whitewash the criminal negligence and actions of the officers of the *Titanic* and their own maritime regulations for business reasons. They lied about their ability to transport American soldiers to Europe for World War One because they wanted American soldiers to serve under the Union Jack as subservient cannon fodder. They had lied about the extent of the murders they committed in their attempt to subdue the Irish. They had blatantly stolen two ships from the Turks at the start of World War One, which helped throw the Turks into the arms of the Germans and lead to the collapse of Russia. (The Turks blocked ship traffic to Russia's Black Sea ports. The Germans were choking off ship traffic to Russia's Baltic Sea ports. This led to a constant shortage of military supplies for the Russians; their remaining ports of Vladivostok and Archangel and Murmansk could not take in enough supplies.) After the overthrow of the Tsar, British authorities were busy cleaning out Russian assets deposited in British banks. Lloyd George and other British officials had routinely lied openly at the Paris Peace Conference. They were also exploiting hundreds of millions of Asians and Africans in their colonies. In summary, the word of British officials on matters concerning their own selfish interests was worthless.

As a final note on this issue, Fiorello La Guardia wrote he had argued for the loans to the Allies to help win the war. But he said he warned his colleagues in Congress the Allies might not be able to repay the loans in full, and they should level with the American people on this issue. At least La Guardia was one politician who voted to throw away money honestly. The source of his remarks is his book The Making of an Insurgent (pages 146-148).

6. The source of Frederic Howe's comments is his book The Confessions of a Reformer (pages 296, 309-316, 326-328). Howe was a sincere liberal who tried to help the less fortunate in his public service, not a phony liberal who used people for votes, then gained power and then cut back their liberties.

7. Information on Queen Marie comes from the chapter "Scandal at the Quiet Nest" in Leslie Gardiner's book Curtain Calls: Travels in Albania, Romania, and Bulgaria, the book Lest the Ages Forget – Kansas City's Liberty Memorial (which Queen Marie visited) by Derek Donovan, and the Canadian Encyclopedia article "Joe Boyle: King of the Klondike." Marie's daughter Princess Ileana, who was a sultry dark-haired beauty in her own right, came to America with her six children in 1950 as a refugee from the Communists. (The princess had accompanied her mother to America in 1926.) Her husband had left her, and she raised her children without his help. When they grew up, Ileana became an Orthodox nun and founded an abbey in western Pennsylvania. She also ministered to people and gave religious talks across America. She was able to return to Romania for a brief visit in 1990 after the overthrow and execution of the Communist reptile Ceausescu and his vile wife on Christmas Day 1989. Ilieana died after a severe fall in her abbey in 1991 at the age of 82. The article "The Princess Abbess" in the 1/2/1990 Philadelphia Inquirer and her obituary in the 1/22/1991 New York Times, and the other non-Canadian articles were on the www.tkinter.smig.net website about Romania.

Information on Aimee Semple McPherson comes from Paul Sann's book The Lawless Decade (pages 149-152), a 5/25/1959 article in Time, the transcript to the PBS show "Sister Aimee," and on discussions I have had with old-timers who were members of her church or beneficiaries of her charity while she was alive.

Information on Clara Bow comes from The Lawless Decade (pages 133-137).

8. Accounts of the Notre Dame home victory over the visiting Indiana Klan come from the 5/18/1924 Chicago Examiner, the 5/21/1924 South Bend News Times, the 5/18/1924 and 5/20/1924 South Bend Tribune, the 5/23/1924 The Fiery Cross, the 10/ 24/1924 The Fiery Cross, a 1974 article by Mary Ellen McAndrews, and a 1996 article by John Haigh. These all are courtesy of the University of Notre Dame Archives.

In 1924, most Southern colleges likely had some Klan activity, as did many colleges in the Midwest, Texas, and the Plains States. Knute Rockne openly wondered if Fielding Yost, the football coach of the University of Michigan, was a

Kluxer because of Yost's open anti-Catholic bigotry. The Ivy League schools were anti-Catholic out of ethnic prejudice and also out of disdain for Catholic teaching on sex and morals. So the students of Notre Dame made a unique collegiate statement against bigotry when they shook down the thunder on the Klan.

9. Immigration statistics come from the Historic Research Study, Statue of Liberty – Ellis Island National Monument, by Harlan D. Unrau, National Park Service, 1984.

10. Nicola Sacco and Bartolomeo Vanzetti, two Italian immigrants who were anarchists and had ties to anarchist bombers (including Carlo Valdioci, the bomber who blew himself up while trying to blow up the home of A. Mitchell Palmer), were tried for the murders. They had accompanied two other suspects to an auto repair shop. The shop owner's wife had contacted the police on suspicion the car had been used in the crime. Police captured Sacco and Vanzetti; the other two men escaped. One of them (Mario Buda aka Mike Boda) would be blamed for detonating a bomb in a horse-drawn wagon on Wall Street in New York City in September 1920 that killed more than 30 and wounded about 300 others. (Buda fled to Italy and died there.) The police noted Vanzetti had what looked like the dead guard's pistol, and Sacco had a pistol of his own when they were caught.

The judge who presided at the Sacco-Vanzetti trial, an old WASP crank named Webster Thayer, hated the defendants for their background and their politics. Thayer was smart enough not to reveal his biases in court, but he said a lot to other people which made them realize he was a full-blown bigot. Radical defense attorney Fred Moore made the trial a political case, basing his defense of the two on class politics instead of on guilt or innocence. Moore also came up with a string of perjurers to give his clients alibis.

Forensic evidence offered by the prosecutor did show a handgun owned by Sacco fired at least one of the fatal bullets. (This still didn't prove beyond the shadow of a doubt Sacco actually was the one who pulled the trigger, but it was devastating circumstantial evidence.) This nicely matched the fact that the pistol of the dead guard had work done on it that matched work done on the pistol in Vanzetti's possession when police arrested him. It was also the same model as the handgun taken from the murdered guard. The jurors convicted Sacco and Vanzetti.

Moore appealed the convictions and turned up more perjurers to cast doubt on the case. His alleged ballistics expert Albert Hamilton tried to destroy evidence against Sacco by taking the barrel of Sacco's pistol off of the frame of the pistol, swapping the barrel with the barrel of one of two pistols he (Hamilton) brought into court, and trying to walk out of court with his two pistols, one of which had Sacco's weapon's barrel on it. The judge ordered Hamilton to stop and hand over his two weapons. Later, the prosecution ballistics expert noticed the barrel swap; Sacco's weapon, which had a rusty barrel, now had a shiny new barrel. Hamilton accused prosecutor personnel of switching the gun barrels. Another profound ethical failure of Hamilton's was his self-awarded doctor degree.

Another lawyer took over the case in 1924 when Moore resigned at Sacco's demand. Meanwhile, the Red Scare was dead, and liberals and leftists in America and elsewhere felt safe to make Sacco and Vanzetti their cause. Due to the national and international uproar in the anarchists' favor by

these prominent pinks, the governor of Massachusetts had the case reviewed. A forensic expert armed with the newly developed comparison microscope offered his services free to both sides to determine whether the shot that killed guard Alessandro Berardelli was fired from Sacco's pistol. The replacement defense attorney disapproved, but didn't try to stop the test. Calvin Goddard, the forensics expert, determined the fatal bullet did come from Sacco's weapon. Two months later, in August 1927, Sacco and Vanzetti went to the hot seat.

In 1961, firearms forensic examiners examined the handgun and the bullets and also concluded the prosecution's firearms expert was correct.

Information on the Sacco and Vanzetti trial comes from Francis Russell's article "Sacco Guilty, Vanzetti Innocent?" in the April 1962 issue of American Heritage, Douglas Linder's article about the trial on the University of Missouri Kansas City "Famous Trials" website, and James Hamby and James Thorpe's paper "The History of Firearm and Toolmark Identification" in the Summer 1999 issue of the Association of Firearm and Tool Mark Examiners Journal. Russell had long claimed Sacco and Vanzetti were innocent, and he pushed for the re-examination of the forensic evidence. Because of his efforts, forensic experts conducted the 1961 tests, and Russell was man enough to admit he was wrong about Sacco.

11. Information on the Quota Act of 1921 comes from the act itself and from the Unrau study (pages 113-119). Information on the 1922 extension of the Quota Act of 1921 (42 Statutes at Large 540) comes from the extension act itself.

12. Two such articles came out of the New York Times 7/1/1923 issue; they were typical of many I have read. Curran's comments come from his book Pillar to Post (pages 289-290). Curran's blaming the shipping companies was in the 7/31/1923 New York Times.

13. Info on the Geddes flap and American officials' response to it comes from the 12/7/1922, 12/8/1922, 7/31/1923, 8/15/1923, 8/16/1923, and 8/18/1923 issues of the New York Times, and from the Unrau study (pages 277-279).

14. Information on overseas inspections, the possible leasing of immigration stations, the alleged scheme to close Ellis Island, and Curran's head-butting with his superiors over these issues comes from Pillar to Post (pages 308-310), the 8/24/1925 issue of Time, and the 8/17/1923 and 8/12/1925 issues of the New York Times.

15. Information on the Countess of Cathcart fiasco comes from articles in the 2/12/1926, 2/17/1926, 3/13/1926, 3/23/1926, and 1/14/1931 issues of the New York Times, articles in the 3/1/1926, 5/31/1926, 6/20/1927, 10/6/1930, and 12/10/1934 issues of Time, an article about Earl Carroll's show "Vanities" in the July 2007 Showbiz Time Magazine, a 2/12/2006 Los Angeles Times article, the federal case U.S.A. vs. Gribben and Maldonado (which quoted the history of the perjury case against Carroll),and two articles about Jodie Kidd in the 4/13/2008 Sunday Sun and the 9/6/2008 Daily Mail, both papers in England. Edward Corsi, in the book In the Shadow of Liberty (pages 202-211) discussed the fiasco, and so did Paul Sann in The Lawless Decade (page 153).

"Sir" Rowland, one of the countess' hubbies, had done an unnoble thing during World War One. He was a large-scale food hoarder, which was illegal under Britain's Defence of the Realm Act. Acting on tips, police raided Rowland's mansion in 1918 and busted him and his then-wife Mabel. They confiscated most of the food, and the Hodges had to pay about $3000.

The Countess of Cathcart was in a sense the godmother of reality TV. She got to re-enact her sluthood before live audiences, she had the moral failings of a celebrity, and her life was suitable fodder for gossip columns. In a bizarre replay, the great-granddaughter of her husband Hodge – Jodie Kidd, herself a model and an exposed drug seller – found out what a dirtbag her esteemed ancestor was in a British reality show in 2008.

16. The Coolidge quote is on page 306 of Pillar to Post.

17. Info on the Immigration Act of May 26, 1924, and Husband's interpretation of it as a guide for who from Asia to bar, comes from the act itself and from the Unrau study (pages 124-125). Immigration figures come from the Unrau study; I did some math to come up with totals.

18. Info on suffragettes in the Ku Klux Klan comes from Kathleen Blee's book Women of the Klan: Racism and Gender in the 1920s and an interview she did with Dinitia Smith for the 1/26/2002 issue of the New York Times. Info on Wilson's approval of "Birth of a Nation" comes from a PBS website on the film, and from Illusion of Victory (page 189).

19. Information on Hugo Black comes from an article in the 8/20/2006 Birmingham, Alabama News, a memorial website to Father Coyle hosted by the Diocese of Birmingham, and an article about Black by Alabama judge Robert Propst in the September/October 1998 issue of Liberty. Info about the Oregon government attack on Catholic schools comes from an article titled "Catholic Patriotism on Trial: Oregon's 'Compulsory School Law' " on the Catholic University of America's website. Info about D.C. Stephenson comes from a 10/18/1926 article in Time. Michael Schwartz's book The Persistent Prejudice (pages 91-101) covers all of the above incidents.

20. Key info sources on Margaret Sanger (including her quotes) are her own books. Info came from Margaret Sanger: An Autobiography, (pages 40-41, 57, 68-87, 94-96, 104-105, 119-162, 176-190, 192-250, 268-291, 312-313, 315, 355, 366-367, 370-371, 388-391, 395, 409-410, 433-459, 490), her book Pivot of Civilization (Chapters I, II, IV, V, VI, VII, VIII), and her book Woman and the New Race (Chapter III).

Only a thorough racist who viewed people like breeding stock like Ms. Sanger did could offhandledly drop a ridiculous observation like the following in her much more cautious autobiography (page 490): "Not only the features of the cultured types of the Island (Hong Kong), but even those of the coolies, the longshoremen, struck me as growing less Oriental and more Anglo-Saxon, the foreheads fuller, the eyes less slanting."

The Speaking of Margaret Sanger in the Birth Control Movement from 1916 to 1937, by William Morehouse (pages 184-185) is the reference for her 1929 Oakland speech.

New York University maintains the Margaret Sanger Papers Project. The school has copies of many of her writings (speeches, letters, pamphlets, etc.) and researchers dedicated to preserving her twisted legacy. Info sources include their articles "Biographical Sketch," "Birth Control or Race Control? Sanger and the Negro Project," "American Birth Control League," "Birth Control Clinical Research Bureau," "Birth Control Federation of America," and "The Town Hall Raid."

Harry Laughlin's ties to Margaret Sanger are noted in the papers he donated to Truman State College in Missouri. More information on Harry Laughlin comes from the University of Virginia's article collection "Eugenics" on the school's Claude Moore Health Sciences Library website.

An article in the 3/18/1929 issue of Time discussed Slee's tax evasion problems. He was in hot water for calling the money he shoveled into the birth control movement a charitable donation. The authorities noted Sanger's organization was neither charitable, scientific, or educational. Slee had to cough up $40,000 to settle his tax problems with Uncle Sam.

Kitty Kelly's book The Family about the Bushes (pages 17-20, 114-116) is the source for the info on Prescott Bush. A website Random House has maintained to promote the book had a copy of Margaret Sanger's money appeal with Prescott Bush listed as treasurer.

Info on Ms. Sanger's genteel genocide "Negro Project" comes from the book Woman's Body, Woman's Right by Linda Gordon (pages 332-334).

Other info on Ms. Sanger comes from the book Woman of Valor: Margaret Sanger and the Birth Control Movement in America by Ellen Chesler (pages 45-51, 88-98, 102-143, 150-169, 172-176, 180-198, 250-268, 316-317, 348-351, 384, 388, 417, 429-434, 438-447, 454-468). Ms. Chesler, who was a big fan of La Sanger, admitted Margaret lied repeatedly and invented stories to make herself look good and make others look bad.

Ms. Sanger claimed she was active in IWW labor activity when she was married to Bill Sanger. This might have been true, but it was due to Bill's brand of socialism. When she left Bill and started pimping birth control in 1914, any labor activity to help workers she might have engaged in stopped.

Info on Marie Equi and Margaret Sanger comes from the Oregon Historical Society's "Oregon History Project," and from Volume 1, Nos. 3 and 4, Northwest Gay and Lesbian Historian (1997).

Margaret Sanger had two board members for her birth control group that neither she nor her devotees have apologized for. One was Lothrop Stoddard, a virulent racist who wrote a well-selling book titled The Rising Tide of Color Against White World Supremacy. Another was C. C. Little, the former University of Michigan president who would later spend his time as a whore for the tobacco industry. As late as 1969, he was claiming smoking didn't cause cancer or any other disease.

La Sanger befriended German eugenicists before Hitler took power. She spoke approvingly of a female German doctor she met who persuaded insurance carriers to pay for sterilizations if doctors recommended them. She of course got a kickback for her doctor's orders. Margaret said she saw the distaff Deutsche doc write up 75 such orders in a 2-1/2 hour stretch, one every two minutes. Shortly, Adolf Hitler would come to power and order the sterilization of the "unfit." Sanger's associate Laughlin provided Hitler with the model his goose-steppers used for the Nazi law.

Margaret Sanger virtually worshiped her mentor Havelock Ellis, the English sexologist under whose spell she came in 1914. She wrote a whole chapter of her autobiography about him (pages 133-141), and worshipfully enthused, "Ellis has been called the greatest living English gentleman. But England alone cannot claim him; he belongs to all mankind. I define him as one who radiates truth, energy, and beauty ... This Olympian seems to be aloof from the pain of the world, yet he has penetrated profoundly into the persistent problems of the race." And so on; you get the picture.

But not everyone else would have seen Havelock in that way, especially if they knew the sexual secrets of the sexologist who rocked Margaret's world. For Ellis, a rival of Sigmund Freud, needed someone like Freud to give him shock therapy. Ellis had a urine fetish, which he claimed he got from his mother.

Along with enjoying his urine fetish, Ellis enjoyed watching his wife engage in lesbian sex with their female visitors. (This sentence summed up his sexual preferences, according to the biography Arthur Colder-Marshall wrote about him called The Sage of Sex. This book was reviewed in the 1/25/1960 issue of Time, not long after the uproar over the twisted sexologist Kinsey.)

Many report Margaret and Havelock had a long-running affair. But Ellis was impotent most of his adult life. Was Margaret guilty only of trying to cheat with him repeatedly, because she could never get her "Olympian" to rise to the occasion? Or did Havelock have Margaret lock her body parts with his wife or some other woman while he kibitzed?

Another associate of Margaret Sanger's (pages 354-355, 376 of her autobiography) was English economist John Maynard Keynes. Besides championing deficit spending, Keynes advocated sex with young boys in Moslem countries, and he practiced what he preached in this regard, noted Zygmund Dobbs in his book Keynes at Harvard (Chapter IX).

Ms. Sanger made a trip to the Soviet Union in 1934, but failed to convert the Reds to her birth control cause. The Communists allowed abortions, but they also encouraged large numbers of children. Why? Because the Communists denied God and religion, they accepted abortion as one of the most blatant affronts to God and religion available. And besides, a pregnant woman or a nursing mother might not work as hard at fulfilling a Five Year Plan as a non-pregnant female comrade. But because Stalin and his minions desired soldiers and workers to "build Socialism," they still needed people. They rewarded mothers who bore large numbers of children. They also gave Russian women the "right" to be cannon fodder and slave laborers.

Ms. Sanger still managed to ignore or deny the holocaust of the peasants Stalin was carrying on during her trip. She also found time to indulge her libido. She said she spent some happy moments skinny-dipping at a Black Sea resort with fellow traveling American women, most notably some New England schoolteachers whose actions and physiques gained her favorable attention. Margaret, by now a sagging 54-year-old, said she, the schoolmarms, and other American feminists became naked capitalists – they stripped in full view of thousands of Russians who dotted the beach. Presumably

most of the audience consisted of privileged Communists on break from their labors of "building Socialism." Margaret said their Russian guide woman was much more modest; she swam in her bra and panties before her male comrades. Margaret "forgot" to explain that since the pretty Russian woman was not a Communist, the leering Reds would view raping her as a party membership perk.

Margaret Sanger's criticism of the Vice Commission of Chicago was another bad example for Planned Parenthood personnel to follow. Planned Parenthood officials openly oppose mandatory reporting laws which are on the books to protect underage girls from incest, rape, and other forms of sexual abuse by adult males. They oppose these laws because enforcement of such laws would cost them millions of dollars of business every year. Why? Because sexual abuse would drop dramatically due to imprisoning the molesters, and Planned Parenthood staffers would see fewer underage girls as "customers." Planned Parenthood provides birth control, abortions, and VD treatment to about 50,000 to 60,000 girls 15 or younger each year nationwide. Most of this is paid for by taxpayers.

When Margaret Sanger made the first formal nationwide funding appeal for Planned Parenthood Federation of America in 1947, her treasurer was Prescott Bush. He was George H. W. Bush's father and George W. Bush's grandfather. Prescott Bush bragged about desecrating American Indian chief Geronimo's grave and stealing his skull. Actually, Prescott the preppy pinhead desecrated the grave of another American Indian. At last report, the punks of the Skull and Bones fraternity at Yale still had the skull. Prescott also was a director of a bank the feds seized in 1942 because of its ties to Nazi Germany.

Many Republicans would finance Planned Parenthood with taxpayers' money to cut down on the number of blacks and Hispanics ... and because of their silent practice of debauchery. Many Democrats would fund Planned Parenthood with taxpayers' money because of their philosophical belief in debauchery ... and because of their silent support of limiting poverty by limiting the number of nonwhites. Many abortion providers and advocates are racists who view abortion as a way to control the numbers of blacks and Hispanics.

Margaret Sanger incited anti-Catholic bigotry, anti-immigrant racism, and anti-black genocide. She solicited and got the support of Democrat and fellow bisexual Eleanor Roosevelt. She campaigned against Democrat candidates Al Smith and John Kennedy because they were Catholics. Supporters of the victorious JFK mockingly offered to give Margaret a one-way ticket out of America after she declared she would leave if he won. Ms. Sanger, by this time an elderly booze and drug addict, stayed put.

Margaret claimed her daughter's death seared her soul. So was she helping Jonas Salk find a vaccine for polio in the 1950s? Nope. In the 1950s, she was involved in developing the birth control pill. Katharine McCormick, the society dame who Margaret Sanger talked into funding most of the research, wrote Ms. Sanger in 1955, complaining, "How can we get a 'cage' of ovulating females to experiment with?" (Was rich bitch Kate the model for Cruella de Vil? Or do the Bitches of Belsen and Buchenwald ring a bell?) The researchers tried the Pill out on female patients in a Massachusetts mental hospital (evidently coercively or at least without their informed consent). They also tried it out on other women without telling them what they were getting. Later, they used poor women in Puerto Rico as guinea pigs before they and the drug companies would dare sell the Pill to affluent white women. (PBS' website "The Pill" added some info on the testing.)

Margaret got a little payback for abandoning her children, and later putting them in boarding schools. Her two sons dumped her in a nursing home in Arizona, where she died in 1966.

Like Margaret, many Planned Parenthood staffers have been caught doing jobs they were medically unqualified to do. There are hundreds of malpractice lawsuits, hundreds of health code violations, and many many other cases against Planned Parenthood doctors and staffers for wrongful death, malpractice, cruelty, incompetence, unsanitary and negligent medical practice, and related wrongful acts.

Critics ranging from Hispanic women (who have charged Planned Parenthood staffers have tried to coerce them into abortion, sterilization, or artificial birth control) to black ministers and activists, to other citizens' groups have accused Planned Parenthood of racism. These critics say Planned Parenthood has routinely targeted blacks, Hispanics, and other minorities for population control.

Planned Parenthood people haven't refuted these charges. In fact, they *brag* about how they are reducing the population growth of these people!

A report I obtained from an official of a Planned Parenthood affiliate titled "The Role of Planned Parenthood-World Population" mentions "a growing number of uneducated people who can become neither worthwhile employees nor customers." The report noted Planned Parenthood has taken on itself the role of reducing population growth in the U.S. and in the African, Latin American, and Asian countries whose numbers, they claim, pose "inevitable serious consequences" to the U.S.

21. Virginia state officials used their Laughlin law and Laughlin's shysterish testimony to forcibly sterilize Carrie Buck. Laughlin the liar didn't even meet Miss Buck, much less examine her clinically (because he didn't have the skill set or the formal training to do so). He claimed Carrie and her kin were part of the "shiftless, ignorant, and worthless class of anti-social whites of the South."

Carrie Buck, placed with a foster family after her mother was committed to an institution, dropped out of school after sixth grade to help her foster parents. The foster parents' nephew raped Carrie when she was 17, and she became pregnant as a result. The white-trash foster parents (their name was Dobbs) covered up the rape, falsely claimed Carrie was stupid, incorrigible, and promiscuous, and put her in a state facility for the feeble-minded.

When state officials tried to sterilize Carrie, her court-appointed appealed. Carrie's lawyer was in cahoots with the state's lawyer; the shyster was in on the fix to make Carrie's case a test case to support the Virginia sterilization law. The state's lawyer falsely claimed Carrie's infant daughter was mentally defective also, and Carrie's lawyer didn't challenge this. (Nor did he attribute the child's supposed backwardness to the genetic defectiveness of the white-trash vermin who raped Carrie.) The case (Buck vs. Bell) went to the Supreme Court in 1927. Justice Oliver Wendell Holmes, in ruling with most of the other justices it was okay to sterilize Carrie against her will, made the idiotic statement, "Three generations of imbeciles are enough." Medical hacks sterilized Carrie and her sister Doris. Doris didn't even know about it; they sterilized her without her consent when she was having her appendix taken out. Carrie's child by the rapist nephew had average grades, but died before she could enter third grade; the white trash foster parents had taken her from Carrie and let her die of an intestinal disease. Carrie eventually was released; she married and always regretted she could have no more children. News reporters and scholars visited Carrie over the years and determined she was of normal intelligence, something a slew of pinhead judges, including Holmes, who was no Sherlock, failed to do. Carrie's forced sterilization was a crime against her on several levels. And hers was the first of 60,000 or so sterilizations the quasi-Nazi doctors in Virginia government pay would commit in the Old Dominion.

Information on Harry Laughlin and Carrie Buck comes from the University of Virginia's series of articles "Eugenics" on the school's Claude Moore Health Sciences Library website, and from Stephen Jay Gould's article in the July/August 2002 issue of Natural History. Both acknowledged Paul Lombardo, a lawyer and ethicist who befriended Carrie Buck, and became her advocate.

22. Census statistics for foreign-born residents of America come from the U.S. Commerce Dept. book Historical Statistics of the United States: Colonial Times to 1970 (Bicentennial Edition). I did some math to come up with percentages.

23. Henry Curran's observations come from Pillar to Post (pages 304-305).

24. There are about 7 million Moslems in America. About 2.1 million of them are American blacks, about 1.8 million have roots in Arab countries, and about 2.3 million have roots in the Indian subcontinent. Most of the remainder have roots in places like Iran, Turkey, Bosnia, Albania, Somalia, Nigeria, Indonesia, Malaysia, and Mindanao.

A 12/27/2006 article in The Christian Science Monitor titled "Uncle Sam Wants US Muslims to Serve" noted the armed forces had roughly 3400 Moslems out of a total of 1,370,000 men and women in uniform, according to Defense Department figures. This is about 0.25 percent of the population; Moslems make up 2.3% of America's population. The vast majority of Moslems in American uniform are American blacks, not people with roots in Moslem countries.

A 2/16/2007 article in Voice of America News by Mohamed Elshinnawi said there were 3500 Arab-Americans in uniform. This is about 0.25% of the total in the Armed Services. There are about 3.5 million Arab-Americans, about 1.2% of the population. Bear in mind not all Arabs are Moslems, nor are all Moslems Arabs.

A 1/26/2007 Democrat Party release titled "Democrats Advancing the State of Our Union for Asian Americans and Pacific Islanders" noted 59,000 of the 1.37 million Americans in uniform were Asian-Americans, about 4% of the total. On the surface, this about proportional with the percentage of Asian-Americans in the country They did not break the number down by country to show the high number of Filipinos relative to other Asian-Americans.

Before the Japs overran the Philippines in 1941-1942, the American government drafted 200,000 Filipinos, and perhaps another 50,000 volunteered for duty in the Armed Forces. These included men like the legendary leader and patriot Ramón Magsaysay, who fought Japs, Reds, and corruption in the Philippines. (Source: U.S. Marine Corps Master Sergeant James North's 8/6/2005 article in Veterans Today.) This doesn't count the thousands of non-U.S. Armed Forces Filipinos who also joined the guerilla effort against the Japs during World War Two.

Arthur Hu, columnist for Asian Week, noted in his "Index of Diversity" people with roots in the Philippines and Guam are much more likely to serve in the Armed Forces than other Asian-Americans. He noted Asian-Americans were less prone than other Americans to join the Armed Forces and were more prone to go to college.

Another source of information includes the July 2007 Congressional Budget Office report "The All Volunteer Military: Issues and Performance."

25. Immigration statistics come from the Unrau study.

26. Hull's quote was in the Unrau study (page 127).

27. The Dawes Act of 1887 aimed at destroying the tribal system. On paper, the bill allowed Indians who left tribal life to get portions of the reservation land and the possibility of becoming citizens. However, dividing all the acres of reservation by the number of acres each Indian could own under the Dawes Act left plenty of land. White speculators got their hands on this land. They also bought up land cheaply from American Indians who left their tribes and sold land that was due to them under the Dawes Act. Under the Burke Act of 1906, which amended the Dawes Act, the federal government could seize land from American Indians who they deemed incompetent.

By 1934, American Indians would lose 86 million acres out of the 138 million acres in the reservation system in 1887. To this day, federal bureaucrats mismanage land that belongs to the American Indians, and steal money that rightfully belongs to the various tribes and individuals in these tribes. At the rate our government expands and arrogates authority and steals from the public, some argue we are all becoming American Indians.

Information on the Indian Citizenship Act comes from the act itself (43 U.S. Statutes at Large 253), Nebraska State Historical Society articles on the Dawes Act and on the Indian Citizenship Act, the Dawes Act itself (24 Statutes at Large 388-391), the Burke Act itself (34 Statutes at Large 182-183), and an article by Gary Mitchell about the theft of the land of American Indians in Kansas in the 5/18/1995 Topeka Capital Journal,

Evon Peter, an Alaskan Native American, in a 10/3/2008 article, noted Congress in 1971 put the Alaska Native Claims Settlement Act onto the books. This law, he said, invalidated all Alaska Native American land claims and took away hunting and fishing rights, much like the Dawes Act did more than 80 years earlier. There is nothing new under the sun.

As this book goes to press, a lawsuit based on the Dawes Act is in federal court. Eloise Cobell, an American Indian woman from Montana, sued the government for mismanagement and theft of trust funds. She asked for roughly $50 billion, to be divided among roughly 500,000 American Indians. This works out to about $100,000 per American Indian plaintiff. Given the fact that the feds got their hooks on land owned by American Indians that contained oil and gas wells and mines and forests and grazing land and water sources all over the American West and Plains states, and then essentially stole or wasted the money these resources brought and gave the American Indians a pittance, the figure is not excessive. America's politicians routinely waste more each year on the Middle East.

Ms. Cobell sued the Department of the Interior in 1996 after Janet Reno gave her the brush-off. Clinton and Bush administration minions lied repeatedly to try to defeat the lawsuit. Judge Royce Lamberth, the Reagan appointee who was about the only federal judge willing to discipline the Clintons for their and their underlings' felonies, drew the case. Lamberth knew perjury, falsification, fraud, and theft when he saw it. He consistently ruled against the Clinton administration and the Bush administration and ruled officials of both administrations to be in contempt of court. So George W. Bush's henchmen got him removed from the case in 2006.

James Robertson, the sock puppet Clinton appointee who dismissed or monkey-wrenched several cases against the Clintons and/or their underlings, replaced the indomitable Lamberth. Robertson ruled in 2008 the plaintiffs deserved only $456 million for the theft of almost 90 million acres and more than a century of oil, gas, and mineral royalties, and more than a century of grazing, timbering, and water rights. The plaintiffs appealed. So did the feds; they thought the insult to the Indians was still too much money.

Obama's minions have continued the foot-dragging. Instead of offering a reasonable settlement, they have dug in their heels fighting the case. Meanwhile, Obama and his people have offered $1 billion to the Palestinians, and several trillion dollars to crooked bankers and brokers and other assorted gypsies, tramps, and thieves and paper hangers in the upper echelons of banking and finance. (Bush started the bailout, with bipartisan help from the gypsies, tramps, and thieves and check bouncers in the House and Senate.) Sources for the Cobell case include a 3/23/2009 article in Indian Country Today, an article in the September/October 2005 issue of Mother Jones, a column in the 10/13/2008 High Country News, and a 9/1/2005 article on the motherjones.com website.

28. Information on the Thind case comes from an article on the PBS website on Thind, the U.S. Supreme Court case United States vs. Bhagat Singh Thind (261 U.S. 204, 1923), a 4/25/2007 article by Inder Singh on the www.sikhpioneers.org website, an article by Rashmi Sharma Singh titled "The Adventurous Road to Finding Historical Records of the Thind History," and the law itself (aka 49 Statutes At Large 397-398, June 24, 1935) granting Singh and Toyota and those like them citizenship.

Information on the Ozawa case comes from the Supreme Court case Ozawa vs. United States (260 U.S. 178, 1922). Info on the Toyota case comes from the Supreme Court case Toyota vs. United States (268 U.S. 402, 1925).

It is interesting U.S. officials even allowed Toyota to join the Coast Guard. The Japanese had started wars against China and Russia with sneak attacks. Naval tension between America and Japan had decreased due to Theodore

Roosevelt's Great White Fleet ploy, but the Japanese remained a cunning and formidable potential foe to America in the Pacific Ocean in 1913, when Toyota came to America.

Daniel Mannix, in The Old Navy (pages 145-146), said the U.S. Navy sent him as an admiral's aide by Canadian passenger ship to link up with an American vessel in Yokohama harbor in Japan in 1907. He said Japanese customs officials knew he was an admiral's aide, so they tore apart his cabin looking for classified documents. Mannix was carrying the plans for the defense of the Philippines with him, something the Japanese would love to find. He outwitted the Japanese by hiding them in a lifeboat. He retrieved them after the inspectors left the ship. He didn't say what naval knucklehead sent him by Canadian passenger ship to save money put him and our defense secrets into that kind of jeopardy.

In 1920, a young Japanese named Isoroku Yamamoto was a student at Harvard. In his free time, he "quietly surveyed U.S. oil fields and refineries," wrote Nathan Miller, on page 303 of his book The U.S. Navy: An Illustrated History. Yamamoto was also a junior officer in the Japanese navy; two decades later, he would be the evil genius behind the sneak attack on Pearl Harbor. Our airmen shot his plane out of the sky and killed him in 1943.

Moslem fanatics have a track record similar to Japan's of spying and sneak-attacking this nation. And their piracy against American ships goes back to the beginnings of our nation. (Moslem piracy against the fleets and towns of the English, Spanish, and French who built America goes back far beyond 1776.) Some of those from Moslem lands in our nation's uniform and our nation's civilian government service in recent years have become spies against us. This means we must screen every service member and government employee from these lands with great caution. Profiling is a great crime-stopper.

Japanese Americans served honorably during World War Two. Some Moslems have served honorably also in our recent wars in the Middle East. However, the American Moslem communities, with the exception of American blacks of the Moslem faith, have not yet made a gesture in recent years similar in magnitude to the one which the Japanese Americans made in World War Two.

29. Information on the Chinese sneaking into America from the Ellis Island point of view comes from In the Shadow of Liberty (pages 159-176) by Edward Corsi, a commissioner at Ellis Island from 1931 to 1934. Barry Moreno's book Encyclopedia of Ellis Island (pages 34-35) also contains information on the feds' activities concerning Chinese immigrants in New York.

Information on the Chinese sneaking into America from the Angel Island point of view comes from the 2004 article "The Scandalous Ship Mongolia" by Robert Barde, an article titled "An Alleged Wife: One Immigrant in the Chinese Exclusion Era" by Robert Barde in the Spring 2004 issue of Prologue, and the article "Angel Island: Guardian of the Western Gate" by Valerie Natale (which appeared in a University of Illinois website). Other sources include the article "Ritualization of

Regulation: The Enforcement of Chinese Exclusion in the United States" by Adam McKeown, which was in the April 2003 American Historical Review, and the 2009 article "Minor Daughter of a Merchant" by William Warrior (which appeared on the Angel Island Immigration Station Foundation website).

30. Information on the Acts of March 2, 1929 and March 4, 1929 were the acts themselves (aka 45 Statutes at large 1512-1516, and 45 Statutes at Large 1551-1552).

31. Immigration statistics come from the Unrau study, and from the U.S. Commerce Dept. book Historical Statistics of the United States: Colonial Times to 1970 (Bicentennial Edition).

32. Father Pierre Blet, in Pius XII and the Second World War (pages 229 and 230), noted the Churchill government refused to lift the blockade of Greece for a number of months so the Vatican could send food to starving Greeks. The British rationale was the food would help the German war effort. The British had hampered Herbert Hoover from getting food to the Belgians during World War One on the same grounds. Churchill, who ran the British Navy until he was canned in the wake of the Gallipoli fiasco, was consistent in both wars. Churchill reportedly called Hoover a "son of a bitch" for trying to feed the Belgians instead of letting the effects of the British blockade starve many of them to death. The source for this unoriginal Churchill utterance was Thomas Fleming's book The Illusion of Victory (page 323).

33. Unemployment statistics come from the U.S. Commerce Dept. book Historical Statistics of the United States: Colonial Times to 1970 (Bicentennial Edition).

34. Statistics on the braceros comes from a 1/14/2004 Associated Press article by Juliana Barbassa, a Smithsonian Institute website article titled "Opportunity or Exploitation: The Bracero Program," a University of San Diego website article titled "Bracero Program," and an Associated Press article that appeared in the 1/8/2007 Madera, California Tribune. Madera is in the heart of California's San Joaquin Valley, as great an agricultural area as our great nation is privileged to have.

35. Immigration and refugee/asylee statistics come from the Unrau study, from the U.S. Commerce Dept. book Historical Statistics of the United States: Colonial Times to 1970 (Bicentennial Edition), and from the 1999 Statistical Yearbook of the Immigration and Naturalization Service.

36. Something similar happened in 1995. Bill Clinton and his administration closed the San Francisco Presidio military base. Congress made it a national park but also allowed commercial development of the picturesque military base on the north coast of the city. The feds allowed "Star Wars" movie tycoon George Lucas to put a megamillion dollar commercial development inside the Presidio in 1999. Other big-money deals followed. Because of the shortsightedness of the feds, the Presidio is now basically unavailable in case of another major earthquake in the San Francisco area (like those in 1906 or in 1989) as a place to muster emergency workers or to shelter large numbers of victims.

THE TRUTH ABOUT ELLIS ISLAND

Over the years, many people have made many comments and complaints about immigration to America during the Ellis Island era. Since there are public histories and public records on the facts, we'll discuss how many of these were true and how many were lies that got good PR.

TRUTH, LIE, OR URBAN LEGEND?

"We came to America packed in like sardines, in filthy quarters, with little food and with many sick people."

That all too often was true until into the 1900s.

Steerage passengers were almost pure profit for steamship companies. Officers and employees of these companies sold cheap tickets to people, and fed them very little and provided them with very little in the way of sanitary facilities. They advertised all over Europe to lure poor people to buy tickets, and they were greedy enough to transport people who were sick, handicapped, or otherwise unfit to gain entry to America. They figured enough of these unfit people would somehow get by the inspectors and get into America.

American officials put laws with teeth in them into effect, and this pressure forced the steamship companies to do better. American officials started fining steamship companies for bringing in undesirables. They made steamship companies pay to feed, shelter, and provide medical treatment for aliens detained at Ellis Island or elsewhere in America, and they made steamship companies take rejected people back to Europe for free. They also quarantined ships in harbors and made steamship companies pay for related medical, feeding, lodging, and sanitation costs.

The more astute steamship company officials got the point. In the ports of Britain and Germany, the two greatest European maritime powers, there were fairly well-organized facilities for immigrants to clean themselves and undergo some medical screening. In some of the other countries, officials likewise upgraded their standards when they figured out America meant business.

American immigration officials wanted to save American taxpayers from having to bear the burden of caring for and sending back people they didn't want to admit to America. They also wanted to save would-be immigrants the expense and shattering experience of being turned back from America. So they made the standards known and prompted the steamship companies to follow them or lose money.

"Immigration officials and agents were corrupt."

Before Ellis Island opened in 1892, this was very true. In fact, the reason Congress federalized the immigration process was to cut down on the rampant corruption of state and local officials who had been processing immigrants.

Some corrupt employees continued in office. But when the incorruptible and cantankerous William Williams and his successors found them out, they became former employees and often became inmates of prisons.

Williams ordered railroad ticket agents to stop selling unsuspecting immigrants railroad tickets that would take them way out of their way to their destinations or face punishment. His successor Robert Watchorn had employees check on the levels of service railroad companies were giving immigrants. Based on what they found, Watchorn concluded the railroad company officials were cheating immigrants. Watchorn, himself an immigrant from Britain, filed a complaint against the railroad companies with the Interstate Commerce Commission to make them give immigrants better services or reduce their ticket prices. **(1)**

Unscrupulous vendors and agents could take advantage of immigrants who paid for services such as telegrams or train tickets or food for travel or baggage handling, and immigrants who exchanged their foreign money for American money. Williams and his successors tried to stomp down hard on this sort of corruption.

In one such case, Williams had a telegraph office employee jailed for short-changing a Czech immigrant by five dollars. In another case, Williams noted a money-changing contractor was turned out of Ellis Island because of his crookedness. Williams cancelled a vendor's baggage handling contract in 1911 when his people discovered the vendor was cheating immigrants. Williams canned a food contractor who was not feeding immigrants properly. Williams punished or assisted in jailing many others who broke immigration laws for financial gain. Williams' toughness and integrity set the standard for the men who followed him at Ellis Island. **(2)**

"They fed us swill at Ellis Island."

This was probably true before William Williams took over.

Frank Martocci, the interpreter at Ellis Island, was probably the agent who admitted immigration commissioner-to-be Edward Corsi and his mother, stepfather, brother, and sisters when his family passed through Ellis Island to New York from Italy in 1907.

Close to a quarter-century later, when Italian immigrant Corsi became the head man at Ellis Island in 1931, Martocci was still on the job. Corsi asked the old interpreter to reminisce about the early days of his service.

One of the things Martocci said he remembered was food service workers slopping ladles of stewed prunes onto rye bread to dole out to the immigrants for several meals in a row. He said the quality and quantity of food served changed for the better when Williams became commissioner. **(3)**

Williams cancelled the contract of the food vendor in 1902, his first year at Ellis Island. He cancelled the contract of another food vendor not long after he returned to Ellis Island in 1909, the first year of his second term as commissioner. He determined the vendor was not feeding immigrants properly. **(4)**

The 1902 food service bid requests from the U.S. Immigration Service was the first dealing done for food by Williams. Williams noted the previous food service vendor collected $65,000 from the steamship companies for a year at 10 cents a meal for breakfast and "supper" (the evening meal), and 15 cents for "dinner" (the midday meal, which typically was the big meal for rural people). This meant the vendor served at least 433,000 meals to as many as 650,000 meals to detained immigrants during the previous year.

Since it was often the fault of shipping companies that many would-be immigrants were detained at Ellis Island for sickness and unfitness, American officials decided it was only right to fine the shipping companies and use the money they collected from these outfits to pay for the food and shelter they gave to aliens they detained. Shipping companies did not directly have to pay for meals served for those being detained until family, fiancé, or friends could come for them or send them money for transportation to their new homes.

Williams specified the winning food service vendor would have to provide immigrants bread for breakfast, beef or fish, soup, and potatoes for "dinner," and bread and stewed prunes for "supper." (The prune ladles still found use, even after Williams took over.) Coffee and tea, and milk and sugar were to be available.

Williams also allowed the food service vendor to sell bread, ham, cheese, bologna, smoked fish, bread, pies, donuts, fruit, milk, soft drinks, and beer to people leaving Ellis Island so they would have something to eat while they were taking train rides to their final destinations. (Later, puritanical feds would ban alcohol sales at immigration stations.) Williams allowed the vendor a 20 percent profit margin on food to go.

Henry Curran, the Commissioner of Immigration at Ellis Island from 1923 through 1926, said he tried to have the immigrants served some ethnic foods, but immigrants whose native dishes were not on the menu would complain. He said with a twinkle in his eye, "If I added spaghetti, the detained Italians sent me an engrossed testimonial and everyone else objected. If I put pierogi and Mazovian noodles on the table, the Poles were happy and the rest were disconsolate. Irish stew was no good for the English, and English marmalade was gunpowder to the Irish. The Scotch mistrusted both. The Welsh took what they could get. There was no pleasing anybody. I tried everything, then went back to United States fodder for all. They might as well get used now to the baked beans, assorted pies, and anonymous hash that would overwhelm them later on." **(5)**

If the immigrants weren't getting food their way, a 1908 food contract request for bid and four immigrant dining room menus from 1917 indicate they sure weren't getting starvation fare.

The 1908 food service bid requests from the U.S. Immigration Service (made when Robert Watchorn was the chief at Ellis Island) specified the winning food service vendor would have to provide immigrants hot cereal and milk, hash or pork and beans, and bread and butter for breakfast. For "dinner" (the midday meal), the vendor would have to provide immigrants meat or fish, potatoes, vegetables, bread and butter, and soup. For "supper" (the evening meal), the vendor would have to provide stew, pork and beans, or hash, a fruit dessert or pie or pudding, and bread and butter. Coffee and tea, and milk and sugar were to be available. Kosher substitutes for pork were to be made available. This was a step up from the fare Williams was allowed to offer immigrants in 1902. On Williams' recommendation, fines against steamship companies for violations increased, and this undoubtedly led to better food for detained immigrants.

The 1917 dining room menus (made when Frederic Howe was the chief at Ellis Island) showed for breakfast, immigrants got hot cereal, milk, bread and butter, and fruit. For "dinner," immigrants got meat, vegetables, potatoes, bread and butter, and soup. For "supper," immigrants got a one-pot entree such as stew or hash or meat and beans, bread and butter, and fruit. Coffee and tea, and milk and sugar were to be available. Food service people served milk and crackers to children between meals. Okay, so maybe the onset of World War One led to the cutoff of the breakfast ration of pork and beans. (Or was it complaints of gas?)

So what's not to like? Do you and your children eat as heartily today? **(6)**

"Ellis Island was a filthy zoo where sadistic officials mistreated immigrants."

After Theodore Roosevelt became president, this was basically untrue.

Imagine having to undergo processing with 5000 other people on a very hot or very cold day. Underpaid and overworked immigration officials and employees – many working 6 or 7 days a week -- would be sorely tempted to lose their tempers, especially if crying children puked on them, or if greasy immigrants coming out of a two-week stretch in steerage tugged on their coats trying to get their attention, or if lice and other vermin hopped off of dirty foreigners and onto them.

Children's shrieks, women's crying, men's arguing, and the constant pushing and pulling and ordering going on would make an unpleasant mark on anyone's memory. So would being detained while waiting for loved ones to pick you up. *Ellis Island was not a hotel, but a gateway.*

By the early 1900s, immigrant groups in the cities made reasonably powerful blocs of voters. If they complained, there would be some vote-chasing politicians with no more morals than an ambulance-chasing lawyer looking to attack the workers at Ellis Island to endear themselves to these ethnic communities.

Journalists of a German-language paper in New York City started criticizing William Williams and his people for allegedly mistreating immigrants and deporting and excluding people cruelly. Theodore Roosevelt in 1903 appointed a commission to investigate the charges the Germanic newspeople made. The commissioners cleared Williams and his people and praised Williams for the job he did. **(7)**

Among immigrants, the British were the biggest complainers. A typical British bitcher was a minister named Sydney Bass who whined that he had to wait with other immigrants. This alleged disciple of Christ bitched because American immigration officials made him and other Englishmen and Englishwomen stay in the same area with unwashed immigrants from presumably less genteel lands.

Bear in mind the British were colonial masters of the Indian subcontinent, much of Africa, portions of Southeast Asia, many places in the West Indies, and Ireland when Bass tried to come to America. The British also were among the leading commercial plunderers of China at this time. They also had a lot to say about the running of Australia, Canada, and New Zealand. In short, their tentacles stretched around the globe, which gave many of them a dangerous sense of ethnic and racial superiority, every bit as objectionable as the "love myself, hate my neighbor" attitude many of the Germans had.

"I objected to being placed there in such close proximity with the filthiest people of all nations, covered with dirt and vermin," he complained in 1911. Besides showing a high amount of bigotry and persnicketyness for someone who was allegedly a follower of Jesus, Bass demonstrated a flair for dramatic exaggeration as well. He moaned, "I was peremptorily ordered back into the common room. There were 600 people in that little room, crowded together. It seemed to me the most like the black hole of Calcutta of anything that I have seen."

The short but large-mouthed Bass complained about taller Italians in the room. "They were eating garlic, and you can imagine how offensive it was," he whined. "It was very unpleasant. It made it difficult for me to breathe." Were his delicate sensitivities to blame, or was it anti-Catholic bias – against the people in whose land the Pope lived and usually was a native of – on the part of this alleged man of God?

Maybe Bass was miffed at being labeled an undesirable. Bass had to stay overnight on Ellis Island, and a board of special inquiry declared he should be deported as being liable to be a public charge. Bass admitted complaining about the filthy foreigners he as an Englishman was cooped up with when he appeared before the board members. The immigration officials might have considered his attitude unworthy of a real minister of the Lord. Maybe they considered him a charlatan akin to many of today's televangelists.

Evidently someone higher up than the agents at Ellis Island gave Bass a break, because six months later he was preaching in Pennsylvania. Maybe it was a catch and release situation for Bass.

Corrupt New York congressman William Sulzer fished Bass out of Pennsylvania and put the crabber in front of Congress in 1911 to make the above charges. Bass also complained the British gave him a clean bill of health before he emigrated. Because of his stay at Ellis Island, Bass carped, he couldn't get such a clearance anytime soon. Bass produced a note from a local doctor saying he (Bass) couldn't perform many of his functions as a minister for some time after he came to Pennsylvania because "I found him in a state of collapse." (In other words, the Ellis Island people evidently got it right about Bass' problems.) Bass also made the spurious charge that some young women being detained at Ellis Island were being denied religious services. This was a ridiculous lie, because priests, ministers, and rabbis routinely held religious services for the detained.

Williams wrote his boss a letter that refuted Bass' fish story. He said Bass was a liar on all his charges and cited facts to support his charge. He said a Protestant minister on Ellis Island had checked on Bass at Ellis Island and Bass said he had received good treatment. He said Bass thanked his deputy Byron Uhl for his treatment. Williams also noted his agents detained Bass for physical deformities affecting his ability to earn an honest living. So, Williams concluded, Bass turned to earning money dishonestly by making up stories about Ellis Island so he could hit the lecture circuit. (Before radio and TV, traveling lecturers made good money as entertainers.) He noted Bass claimed he was not only a minister, but also a journalist, lecturer, and salesman. (All four occupations unfortunately hide many charlatans.) Williams closed his blast with, "I do not know what part of the Scriptures he read; but he failed to read, or reading it failed to heed, the commandment – "Thou shalt not bear false witness against thy neighbor." **(8)**

Sulzer, a Democrat, was likely angling for the ethnic vote in his 1912 campaign to become governor of New York when he made charges against Williams in 1911. Members of the U.S. House of Representatives investigated Williams, a Republican, for "atrocities, cruelties, and inhumanities" that were allegedly taking place on Ellis Island under his watch. Certain immigrant protection group officials, foreign-language newspaper publishers, and those who resented Williams for his bulldog attitude in upholding immigration laws as he interpreted them witnessed against Williams. One of the fishy witnesses Sulzer produced was Brother Bass.

Williams, in writing, and in his verbal testimony before the congressmen, said Sulzer and the witnesses were lying about their key charges, and offered proof to back his counterattack. He noted he was not going to argue every detail with his detractors because they were caught lying on the gist of their most important accusations.

Sulzer in essence took back his complaints, and instead asked for more money for Ellis Island's administration. Williams had proven to the congressmen's satisfaction the charges Sulzer and others had lodged against him were false.

Sulzer would win the governor election later that year because the Republicans split into pro-William Howard Taft and pro-Theodore Roosevelt factions, each of whom ran candidates, splitting the anti-Sulzer vote. (His election as governor occurred in the same way as the election of Woodrow Wilson to the presidency that same year.) New York state assembly speaker Al Smith and other Democrats in Sulzer's own party – with the help of Republican legislators – would impeach

Sulzer in 1913 for violating the state's Corrupt Practices Act. Sulzer had broken this law by diverting money donated to his campaign into his own pockets. A court made up of state senators and state judges tried Sulzer for the charge and removed him from office later in the year. **(9)**

There were many complaints from British immigrants about Ellis Island that were publicized. Every one of the complaints I reviewed revealed the Britishers' bigotry and classism at having to share the facility with other nationalities. I used Sydney Bass' complaint as an example of the tone of condescension typical of the British who complained.

Frederic Howe, the Commissioner of Immigration at Ellis Island during the World War One era, said, "The British gave the most trouble. When a British subject was detained, he rushed to the telephone to communicate with the consul-general in New York or the ambassador in Washington, protesting against the outrage. When ordered deported, he sizzled in his wrath over the indignities he was subjected to. All this was in effect a resentment that any nation should have the arrogance to interfere with a British subject in his movements. All Englishmen seemed to assume that they had the right to go anywhere they liked, and that any interference with this right was an affront to the whole British Empire."

In 1922, politicians in Britain criticized the treatment of British immigrants at Ellis Island, and sniped at the sanitation and the food service as well. They were shocked – *shocked!* – that migrating Britons didn't have separate eating, bathroom, and sleeping facilities and actually had to mingle with other foreigners while awaiting processing, admission, or deportation in America. **(10)**

The British had no right to talk. Dr. Alvah Doty, for many years the epidemic-tracking Health Officer of the Port of New York, blamed the British (and Moslems and peoples of the Indian subcontinent) for the spread of many epidemics. Doty said the British didn't regulate sanitation in their colonial ports well enough, and didn't do enough for public health in the Indian subcontinent (which they ruled as a colony). Moslems coming from British colonies in Asia and Africa (and from elsewhere) on pilgrimages to Arabia didn't use proper sanitation. Many of them passed through the British-run Suez Canal or came to and from British colonial ports aboard filthy ships. These wandering Moslems, Doty said, carried the germs of epidemics far and wide. (11)

These British blowhards overlooked the fact their own countrymen and countrywomen had chosen to leave their country for ours.

Ohio congressman John Cable expressed the thoughts of many when he shot back, "I cannot understand how these particular people (British aliens) can travel from seven to 14 days in steerage accommodations on the steamships (British ships, by the way) and do so willingly, and then suddenly develop the most acute culture and sensibilities as soon as the Statue of Liberty comes into view."

Congressman Cable said British officials should investigate the immigrant quarters at their own ports before critiquing American immigration stations. He added the admission of immigrants to America should be "for the benefit of America and not for Europe." In the 1920s, it was not politically incorrect for American politicians to be proud of America and put America's interests ahead of those of other nations.

James Davis, President Warren Harding's Labor Secretary, was the Cabinet member responsible for immigration stations during this flap. Davis was himself an immigrant from Wales. He seemed much too worried about what politicians in his homeland thought. He leaned toward segregating British immigrants from other immigrants.

Ironically, William Williams had favored a kind of segregation of immigrants at Ellis Island ... a segregation of immigrants by class. He noted the relatively few second class passengers detained for reasons other than disease might be held apart from the mass of steerage passengers so they might avoid exposure to the germs and vermin the poorer passengers were carrying. Even though Williams was a WASP of the bluest type, he would never have allowed the British such privileges as native Britisher Davis was contemplating granting them.

Davis invited British ambassador Auckland Geddes to inspect Ellis Island. Geddes did so late in 1922. Geddes saw that isolation of British immigrants from others could not happen at the small Ellis Island facility. So he said Americans should spread out the work of Ellis Island at several facilities. Geddes made this kibitz (which if carried out would cost Americans millions of dollars but the deadbeat British nothing) in a report made public in August 1923. **(12)**

Henry Curran, who Harding had just appointed as the Commissioner of Immigration at Ellis Island before he died in office in August 1923, blasted the British and those American officials who sucked up to them. Curran, during his three years as boss of Ellis Island, scuttled other attempts to show favoritism toward British immigrants and make it easier for aliens to avoid proper screening. Thanks to Curran's vociferous efforts, segregation of nationalities on Ellis Island for the satisfaction of the British would not take place. **(13)**

Curran, a reform politician in New York City, an Army officer in World War One, and a man of letters, was more known for his puckish sense of humor than for bombast. When a noblewoman emigré from Russia made fantastic and well-publicized charges against Ellis Island in 1923, Curran used this gentler touch to debunk her complaints publicly.

Baroness Mara de Lillier Steinheil said she was imprisoned by the Communists during the Russian Civil War, and the Reds murdered her husband and brothers. But instead of being grateful for the chance of coming to America, she claimed conditions at the immigration station were in many ways worse than a Bolshevik prison.

Even though she said she had titled relatives all over Europe, Madame Mara chose to come to democratic America. (Maybe her blueblood kin didn't like her act either.) Agents at Ellis Island detained her for three days and made her go before a board of special inquiry. The board members allowed her entry to America. Then she complained to the press.

Curran deflated the balloon of the boorish baroness by producing a letter from a Russian Orthodox priest who edited a Russian ethnic paper in Newark thanking him for helping the Russian refugees who underwent processing at Ellis Island. Curran added, with the tongue-in-cheek humor that was his style, "It is to be regretted that we can't provide a kaiser's suite for each immigrant." **(14)**

Curran said the immigrants who complained the most while he was commissioner were the English. "They talked a good deal about their rights as British subjects. To many of them Americans were still "colonials" while the other nationalities were always "foreigners." The English refused to sleep in the same room with "foreigners." They sent delegations to me about it. One batch of detained English immigrants even objected to living in the same room with another batch of English, who had come in on a later ship. 'They are English but they are newcomers,' said the leader of the delegation. 'We are the same as old inhabitants. We have been here for a whole week. Why do we have to associate with them?' "**(15)**

Curran did improve the sleeping arrangements for detained immigrants. He said, "In several small rooms for the detention of special cases there were beds, but in the large rooms that served as dormitories there were no beds at all. There were bedbugs, but no beds. It took me two months to exterminate the bedbugs. It took me two years to exterminate the wire cages that served as beds and replace them with real beds. To do that I had to have an appropriation by Congress, and the argument and red tape that had to be gone through with in Washington were such that it seemed to me sometimes as though Washington were the one place in the world that was completely motionless. Finally I got a couple of congressmen to come up to Ellis Island and stretch out in the cages for a few minutes. Those congressmen were flaming missionaries for beds instead of cages." **(16)**

What Curran referred to as cages were essentially wire grids held together with steel frames and steel rails and steel posts, stacked three high. Since the mechanics on Ellis Island tied these together head to foot, the end result looked like a series of giant rabbit hutches (minus the sides) instead of a series of three-bunk bunkbeds. Sleeping on a wire grid with only a blanket instead of a mattress would be uncomfortable, like sleeping directly on the lateral springs and wires of a military bed frame.

Several well-heeled immigrants singled out black workers at Ellis Island as being too forward. In this they shared the prejudice of most American whites of the time. Most Europeans had never seen a black person, and those who did had seen them in colonial servitude. (The prostitutes of France were exceptions. They cheerfully serviced black American servicemen during World War One.) They were surprised to see blacks in government service in the United States. They were surprised the black workers they ran into at Ellis Island could be as blunt and as unapologetic as white workers.

Without question, some employees at Ellis Island and other immigration stations were jerks or crooks or both. That's true with all organizations. Individuals will remember injustices done to them. However, the archives of Ellis Island bristle with personnel paperwork proving Williams, Watchorn, and other commissioners in the 1900s suspended, fined, fired, and/or had jailed employees who were abusive, dishonest, or criminal. This means they cared about how their people were doing their jobs and treating immigrants.

Will researchers a hundred years from now checking on the discipline of civil servants today find as many disciplinary cases proportionately on the many government employees who loaf, lie, cheat, steal, commit negligent acts, are inefficient on their jobs, seize property wrongfully, commit sexual abuse, or shoot or burn people alive without cause or due process? Given the strength of government employee unions today and the poor quality of government officials in general today, I doubt it.

Ellis Island was not a hotel. It was a station designed for the protection of America as much as it was designed for the temporary quartering of immigrants until they could leave or be deported.

The conditions I described at Ellis Island were Spartan by our standards of today, but not by the standards of the late 1800s or early 1900s. People were harder back then. Almost all immigrants were peasants who lived in small cottages or city laborers who lived in slums. Most lived without electricity or indoor plumbing. Most raised their own food, and made their own wine or beer. Most slaughtered their own livestock.

Many European immigrants slept in fields, haystacks, and wagons on their way to the ports of departure. They then tolerated days to weeks in steerage, packed closely in the poorly-ventilated filthy holds of ships with less-than-outstanding food. Many immigrants were beaten and/or stolen from on their way to the immigrant ships, and many were mistreated by the ships' crews or other steerage passengers on the way to America.

By comparison, the immigrants were fed and housed for free at Ellis Island, and they were guarded for their protection. They had access to shower and toilet facilities that were being cleaned constantly. Accommodations at Ellis Island were better than what a poorer person would have to endure while traveling in Europe, or traveling in steerage.

The immigrants would not dare to complain about their treatment at home. But since they were free in America, and moved on to a higher standard of living and political freedom than they knew at home, they could vent about Ellis Island without fear of jail.

"They changed my name at Ellis Island."

This was an "urban legend" long before there was such a term. I have heard people make that excuse to me for their ancestors many times, and I have read this charge many other times. On the whole it is not true.

Some immigrants did walk out of Ellis Island with different legal names than they had when they left their villages in Europe because of clerks' errors, clerks' rudeness, clerks' laziness, and clerks' obtuseness ... not only Ellis Island clerks, but clerks for the steamship companies and clerks at the ports where immigrants boarded ships for America.

However, these immigrants were not the norm. Starting with Theodore Roosevelt's administration, there were enough interpreters at Ellis Island to get immigrants' names straight. Many interpreters were themselves immigrants or children of immigrants. These agents would be naturally sympathetic to the immigrants and would be conscientious enough to record their names correctly.

Some immigrants undoubtedly got "name changes" because of ignorance ... their own and the ignorance of local officials in their homelands. Before World War One, there was no literacy requirement for adult immigrants. Many people came here not knowing how to spell their own names. Civil servants in Europe were not as a whole known for their honesty or efficiency. So any papers from home an immigrant carried (except, perhaps, a baptism certificate or a marriage record from his or her parish) might have his or her name misspelled. So how were the agents at Ellis Island going to make sure every immigrant's name was spelled correctly? They likely copied the immigrants' names off the ships' manifests and the tags they were wearing when they got off their ships. In other words, they were relying on papers the shipping companies' clerks prepared and maybe they relied on papers some people carried with them.

But these two reasons only account for some of the immigrants. The sad truth about most immigrants whose "names were changed at Ellis Island" is that they did it themselves.

Some immigrants changed their names when they left their villages to avoid problems on their trips to the ports where they would board the ships. Europeans and Turks were much more brazen in their mistreatment of minorities in their own countries and nationals from other countries passing through their countries than they are now.

Some immigrants changed their names for other rational, if less honorable, forms of deceit. These were criminals and other undesirables leaving their homelands. They needed to change their names to avoid detection.

Then there were the cowardly young men running from young women they impregnated. And there were the shamed young women who had to leave their villages because they conceived without the benefit of husbands. No doubt many of them felt they needed new names in their new country.

But most of the immigrants who left Ellis Island with names different than names they had at home simply wanted to fit in and avoid discrimination. They had heard enough about America and knew enough about human nature to figure out they would fit in better with Anglo-Saxon sounding names than with names ending in "ello" or "iani" or "vich" or "wicz" or ""witz" or "ski" or "sky" or "stein" or "berg" or "olsen" or "enko" or "poulos" or "anian."

In the Ellis Island era, it was a common sight for heaps of peasant clothing from Europe to lie discarded at or near the immigration stations. Why? Many people who were already established in America met their relatives at the immigration station bearing changes of clothes so the newcomers could throw away their Old World garments on the spot. They didn't want their loved ones being marked as foreign bumpkins because of their clothes. And they didn't want the embarrassment of being seen in public with their "greenhorn" relatives.

It was also not too unusual for some immigrants to change religion to fit in. For example, many Scandinavians, going from countries where Lutheranism was the state-established religion, heard from their pastors the advice that they should become Episcopalians in America because the pastors thought that was the dominant or established religion in America, even though America as an independent nation has never had an established religion. Lutheranism in Europe was a religion whose leaders and adherents tended to submit to civil authorities. **(17)**

That sort of thing still happens today. In the wake of the American hostage crisis in Iran during the Carter administration – and the resulting anger toward Iranians by the American public – many natives of Iran who were living in the U.S. in the late 1970s and early 1980s petitioned the courts to Americanize their names. And even today, Hollywood is full of actors and actresses who Gentilicized their Jewish names for business purposes. So the mindset of wanting to sound "mainstream" to the American public on the part of these immigrants was understandable, if regrettable.

Years later, many of these people, ashamed of denying their heritage in order to get off to a good start in America, did what many people do. They blamed others for their own weakness. It's easier to claim you were a victim of the authorities than to admit to being cowardly enough to want to fit in or avaricious enough to want to make it big that you willingly turned your back on your heritage.

If there was a scheme by Ellis Island officials to neuter immigrants of their ethnic names, there would be far fewer ethnic names in America today.

If these allegedly renamed foreigners didn't like their new moniker, then why didn't they file in court to have their names officially restored, properly used, and properly spelled? Under American law, they had that right! Ethnic societies could have helped them do so if they really wanted the help to right such an injustice, if it actually took place.

Bottom line? The people who processed immigrants at Ellis Island did much finer jobs than they were ever given credit for. Millions of people and their descendants owe these people gratitude for their basic decency and devotion to duty.

INSPECTION'S BOTTOM LINE

How tough on immigrants were the inspectors at Ellis Island and other American immigration stations?

U.S. immigration officials admitted 3,127,245 immigrants into the United States from 1892 through 1900, and excluded 22,515 aliens from entering the country. Of these, they kept out 15,070 on grounds they were "likely to become public charges," 5792 manual laborers claiming they had contracts, 1309 mental or physical defectives, 89 "immoral classes" (prostitutes, pimps, and the like), 65 criminals, and 190 people for other reasons. They allowed 99.3% of all would-be immigrants into the country.

U.S. immigration officials admitted 8,795,386 immigrants into the United States from 1901 through 1910, and excluded 108,211 aliens from entering the country. Of these, they kept out 63,311 on grounds they were "likely to become public charges," 12,991 manual laborers claiming they had contracts, 24,425 mental or physical defectives, 1277 "immoral classes" (prostitutes, pimps, and the like), 1681 criminals, 10 "anarchists or subversives," and 4516 people for other reasons. They allowed 98.8% of all would-be immigrants into the country.

U.S. immigration officials admitted 5,735,811 immigrants into the United States from 1911 through 1920, and excluded 178,109 aliens from entering the country. Of these, they kept out 90,045 on grounds they were "likely to become public charges," 15,417 manual laborers claiming they had contracts, 42,129 mental or physical defectives, 4824 "immoral classes" (prostitutes, pimps, and the like), 4353 criminals, 27 "anarchists or subversives," 1904 stowaways, 5083 people 17 or older who were illiterate, and 14,327 people for other reasons. They allowed 97.0% of all would-be immigrants into the country.

From 1921 through 1924, the year of the big quota law, U.S. immigration officials admitted 2,344,599 immigrants and turned away 78,413 would-be immigrants. In other words, they allowed 96.8% of all would-be immigrants in those four years into the country.

Overall, immigration inspectors at Ellis Island and elsewhere barred 387,248 would-be immigrants for medical, mental, or legal reasons from 1892 through 1924. When compared to the 20,390,289 aliens the inspectors inspected, and the 20,003,041 immigrants the inspectors allowed to enter in these years, this means the inspectors kept only 1.9% of all would-be immigrants out of America. *In other words, 98% of all would-be immigrants to America in that era got in.*

These numbers show doctors and inspectors as a rule weren't out to exclude people maliciously or obtusely. A majority of Americans would have been happier if they had rejected more people for medical, mental, or legal reasons. It appears the doctors and inspectors erred more on the side of leniency than on the side of firmness in deciding whether to allow immigrants into the country.

Paradoxically, Ellis Island inspectors were known for their firmness but barred a slightly lower percentage of immigrants than inspectors at other stations. Probably a lot of the questionable immigrants tried to avoid Ellis Island and sneak past inspectors elsewhere. But they were caught anyway.

Who did they keep out?

According to federal statistics from 1892 through 1924, inspectors at Ellis Island and elsewhere barred 196,208 would-be immigrants as paupers or people likely to become public charges. They refused entry to 38,630 people on grounds they were contract laborers. They barred 6 people as "coming in consequence of advertisement."

They refused entry to 3690 people who were "assisted" in coming to America with money from foreign governments or private organizations. They did so to combat European governments who were dumping their misfits and unwanted on America. They sent back 10,043 people who "assisted" themselves in getting to America as stowaways.

They barred 6037 children younger than 16 coming in without a parent if no parent would call for them at Ellis Island or send them money for train tickets from New York to join them. (Before 1908, there was no restriction against taking in unaccompanied teenagers.)

They refused entry to 11,585 people 17 and older who could not read in their native language. (Before 1917, people who were illiterate could gain entry.) The literacy requirement took effect in 1917; but there were several exceptions. The biggest loophole allowed admission of illiterates if they were females immigrating with a husband or immediate family member who could read.

They barred 384 "idiots," 518 "imbeciles," 3215 "feeble-minded," 2473 "insane persons," 292 people diagnosed as "constitutional psychopathic inferiority," and 258 people branded with a surgeon's certificate there was something else wrong with them mentally that could keep them from earning a living. They also barred 416 epileptics. In all, they excluded 7556 aliens with a mental problem severe enough to make them threats to others or make them unable to earn livings.

They refused entry to 129 people with tuberculosis, 42,319 people with a "loathsome" or dangerous contagious disease, and 25,439 people marked with a surgeon's certificate there was something else wrong with them physically that could keep them from earning a living. They also turned away 87 people for "chronic alcoholism." In all, they excluded 67,974 aliens with a severe disease or a medical problem severe enough to make them threats to others or make them unable to earn livings.

They barred 44 anarchists. From 1917 through 1921, they barred 101 aliens from enemy nations. (America entered World War One in 1917, and Germany signed the armistice ending the war on November 11, 1918, but America was technically at a state of war against the Central Powers (Germany, Austria, Hungary, Bulgaria, and Turkey) until 1921. The U.S. Senate refused to ratify the peace treaties Woodrow Wilson signed because they favored Britain and France over America, and they would allow globalist Woodrow Wilson to subject America's sovereignty to the League of Nations, a pipe-dream multinational group he wanted to form that the rulers of the British Empire and France intended to dominate. The senators declared the end of the state of war with the Central Powers in 1921, after Wilson had to leave office.)

They barred 7363 criminals. They barred 4350 aliens (almost all females) coming to America to be prostitutes or for "immoral purposes," 2771 procurers and pimps of females for "immoral purposes", and 70 people "supported by the proceeds of prostitution."

They excluded 1210 people for passport violations. They excluded another 2562 people from 1921 through 1924 for not having proper passports.

They excluded 6139 Chinese under the Chinese Exclusion Act. They excluded 140 people coming from other Asian countries America didn't allow immigration from in the "Asiatic Barred Zone." They barred 399 polygamists.

They barred 298 people as professional beggars, and barred 10 as vagrants. They barred 220 aliens trying to come back into America because they had been already deported within a year or less earlier.

They sent back, from 1921 through 1924, 14,457 people who "exceeded quota." In other words, American officials decided there were enough people from these countries coming in as it was, and their "crime" was getting to America after officials had let in all of their countrymen and countrywomen they were going to let in for that month.

They barred 4992 people for "accompanying aliens." These were usually aliens who were the guardians or protectors of rejected aliens, like infirm children. They had to go back with the rejected aliens because the rejected aliens needed their help. Also, such aliens and their charges had to go back even if the dependents were admissible but the guardian aliens were not.

They barred 689 people on "last proviso" of Section 23 of the 1917 immigration law or Section 17 of the 1924 immigration law. These were aliens who claimed residence in Canada or Mexico but hadn't lived in one of those countries for at least two years before applying for admission to America. After the passage of the Immigration Act of 1924, such aliens would be subject to quotas applying to the land of their birth anyway. **(18)**

*   *   *   *   *   *   *

An incredible fact about the Ellis Island process is that most people passed the medical and legal inspections and cleared the island in three to five hours.

Clerks at motor vehicle license bureaus, smog check stations, unemployment offices and other government agencies seem to need almost that much time to issue you a license, check your car, or do whatever else they have to do for your case!

On average, about 80% of the immigrants got through the screening process on Ellis Island in three to five hours. Officials detained perhaps as many as 20% of the immigrants for medical or legal reasons. Of this 20 percent, nine-tenths of them (or 18% of the overall total of immigrants coming through) were eventually able to enter the U.S. after their sicknesses cleared up or after immigration officials decided they wouldn't pose any threat or be any burden to the citizens of the United States. Officials only had 2% of the sea of humanity flooding through Ellis Island and other U.S. immigration stations sent back to Europe or the Near East or elsewhere as undesirables.

Two percent was still close to 400,000 mostly decent people (well, not the criminals, subversives, pimps, or other sociopaths), heartbroken and abandoned, who had to go back to a way of life they were hoping to escape. Their personal hardships were no doubt overwhelming.

However, the vast majority of would-be immigrants got in. The agents at Ellis Island and other American immigration stations by and large tried to treat immigrants fairly, but tried to serve the interests of the American public first. In other words, they tried to keep out criminals, people liable to be objects of charity, those who carried dread diseases, and those whose contract-labor presence would undercut the wage structure of the American worker.

Despite their prejudices against immigrants of other ethnic groups and religions (or maybe because there were so many former immigrants working at Ellis Island and other immigration stations), the immigration agents still let in almost all of those seeking to come to America.

Most commissioners at Ellis Island were kindly men, and most of them were honorable men. Some of them were immigrants themselves. Many took huge cuts in salary to be Commissioner at Ellis Island. Many were disillusioned by their higher-ups. Most of these men were worthy commissioners because they were asked to do the job ... most of them didn't seek it. There was nowhere near the careerist mindset among major government officials then that there is now. Back then, many worthy men served as government leaders for a time then went back to the private sector.

In summary, the large majority of immigration agents and officials tried to protect the American public. And while they were at it, they tempered justice with mercy. And they did it on unexorbitant salaries. The aliens they processed by and large got a square deal like Teddy Roosevelt and other leaders of good will expected. Can the same be said of the attitude and the dedication and the competence of all too many government employees today?

END NOTES

1. Information on Watchorn's actions against railroad companies comes from the Historic Research Study, Statue of Liberty – Ellis Island National Monument, by Harlan D. Unrau, National Park Service, 1984 (pages 245-246).

2. Information on Williams having crooked employees punished and cancelling contracts comes from the Unrau study (pages 224, 257, 535).

3. Martocci's comment about the prunes comes from Edward Corsi's book In the Shadow of Liberty (pages 78-79).

4. Information on Williams firing the food vendors comes from the Unrau study (pages 257, 535).

5. Curran's comedic comments on chow came from his book Pillar to Post (pages 291-292).

6. Information on the food service at Ellis Island comes from the Unrau study (pages 386, 866-869).

7. Information on the 1903 charges against Williams comes form the Unrau study (pages 229-230).

8. The complaints of Sydney Bass, the peewee preacher, come from pages 130-135 of the Hearings on House Resolution No. 166 Authorizing the Committee on Immigration and Naturalization to Investigate the Office of Immigration Commissioner at the Port of New York and Other Places. (This was the Congressional investigation of William Williams.) The investigation record started May 29, 1911. William's comments were in a letter he wrote to Commissioner-General of Immigration Daniel Keefe dated 3/9/1911. This letter, like his other letters and many reports he wrote, are part of the collection of papers he donated to the New York Public Library.

9. Information on Williams' fight against Sulzer comes from his Annual Report dated 10/10/1911 in his papers (New York City Public Library) and the Unrau study (pages 262-264). Information on Sulzer's rise and fall comes from the Unrau study (pages 417-419), Al Smith's book Up to Now (pages 123, 130-132) and Richard O'Connor's book – a biography of Smith – The First Hurrah (page 76).

10. Frederic Howe's quote comes from his book The Confessions of a Reformer (pages 257-258).

11. Information on the blowhard British politicians comes from the 12/7/1922 and 12/8/1922 issues of the New York Times. The source of Dr. Doty's comments on the disease-carrying Moslems and the British who negligently allowed them to spread diseases around the globe comes from the New York Times issue of 10/4/1908 titled "How Plagues are Watched the World Around." A reprint of this article came from Cathy Horn's website "The Forgotten of Ellis Island."

12. Cable's quotes come from the 12/9/1922 New York Times. Information on the Geddes report and the flap between the British and Americans over Ellis Island in the 1920s comes from the Unrau study (pages 284-285, 563-570) and the 8/16/1923 New York Times. Davis' comments come from the 12/17/1922 New York Times.

13. Sources of information on Curran's attacks on the British when they complained about Ellis Island include New York Times articles of 7/31/1923, 8/18/1923, and 8/12/1925, an 8/18/1923 London Times article (reprinted on Sue Swiggum's and Marj Kohli's TheShipsList.com website), 8/27/1923 and 8/24/1925 Time Magazine articles, and Pillar to Post (pages 309-310).

14. Information on Curran's handling of the Russian noblewoman comes from the 7/9/1923 and 7/10/1923 issues of the New York Times.

15. Curran's comments on the English come from his book Pillar to Post (page 309).

16. Curran's account of the "cages" comes from his book Pillar to Post (page 293).

17. Information on Scandinavian Lutherans whose pastors told them to convert to Episcopalianism in America comes from Oscar Handlin's book The Uprooted (page 139).

18. Statistics on immigration come from the immigration tables of the Unrau study. I did some math to come up with totals.

ELLIS ISLAND, NOT GILLIGAN'S ISLAND

Our current immigration mess did not happen overnight. Like many societal ailments this nation has today, its germs came from the 1960s. In the mid 1960s there was a dumb but harmless sitcom called "Gilligan's Island." It was about a group of people who survived a tourist boat wreck and landed on an uninhabited island. It had some nice eye candy in Dawn Wells and Tina Louise, but the focus of the show was on Bob Denver's character Gilligan, the poor stooge who was the butt of everyone else's jokes because of his dumb ideas which he expressed dumbly.

Gilligan's bumbling would be an apt metaphor for the nation's immigration policy from that time forward to today. What is considered the "modern era" of immigration began during the administration of Lyndon Johnson in the mid 1960s, while "Gilligan's Island" was a popular show. Johnson and his Congress produced the Immigration and Nationality Act of 1965, which introduced daisy-chaining of families of aliens into this country as federal immigration policy. The law was so poorly or deviously written that aliens were able to exploit it to give birth on American soil and get residency status because of their "anchor babies." In a way it is fitting, because Johnson owed his seat in the Senate (and his subsequent career which put him in the White House when Communist Party member Lee Harvey Oswald murdered John Kennedy) to illegal votes attributed to Mexican nationals in South Texas.

There are roughly 12 million to 25 million illegal immigrants in this country. There are another 20 million or so immigrants who came here legally or got amnesty in the last 20 years (1989-2008, the regimes of the Bushes and the Clintons). This doesn't count the 1.01 million refugees and asylees from 1981 through 1990, the 1.11 million refugees and asylees from 1991 through 2000, or the 525,000 refugees and asylees from 2001 through 2008, according to the U.S. Department of Homeland Security, and records of the now-defunct Immigration and Naturalization Service.

Most of these immigrants don't have too much in the way of education or job skills. A very large proportion of them cost the rest of us more in government benefits than they contribute in taxes. Thanks to their presence, we taxpayers may be looking at coming up with a trillion or so dollars in the next decade just to put back into the social services sectors what these immigrants take out.

There are about four million people and dependents here legally on work visas. They are undermining the pay scale of American technical people and they are providing substandard work to the firms that hire them. Some of the sharper ones are spying for China or stealing for India. Legal and illegal immigrants are getting hired by cheapskate employers who refuse to pay Americans a living wage. The net job loss to American natives is in the millions; this has equaled the increase in hiring of aliens in America. **(1)**

Unlike the Ellis Island Era immigrants, today's immigrants are a net drain on the taxpayers. The authors of a Congressional Budget Office report in 2006, which they did as a financial impact statement for the proposed immigration bills in the House and Senate that year, determined granting 11 million illegals amnesty and allowing 800,000 legal immigrants a year for 10 years by enacting the so-called "Comprehensive Immigration Reform Act of 2006" would cost the nation's taxpayers $26 billion to possibly more than $50 billion from 2007 through 2016. They estimated spending on food stamps, Medicaid, Medicare, and other social welfare programs (including aid for "undocumented students") would cost $54 billion more for 11 million amnestied illegals and 8 million new immigrants over the 10-year period. Reimbursements to state governments for some of these programs would add another $13 billion to the federal budget, they reported. They estimated the added immigrants and legalized illegals would pay $66 billion in taxes and fees from 2007 through 2016. They figured discretionary spending on immigrants by federal agencies would rise another $25 billion in the first five years after enactment of the Senate bill, and an unspecified amount more in the five years after that. Summing these numbers yielded the $26 billion figure, but that did not include discretionary spending for the last five years of the 10-year period. (Adding $25 billion for five more years of discretionary spending would raise the total to $51 billion.) Since the 2006 Senate immigration and amnesty bill didn't pass, the taxpayers saved some money. **(2)**

This government estimate of the cost of immigrants to American taxpayers was chump change compared to the estimate of a key researcher of the Heritage Foundation, a conservative think tank, for the Senate in May 2007. Robert Rector, the Heritage Foundation staffer, testified the Senate's 2007 immigration and amnesty bill, if passed, would cost American taxpayers hundreds of billions of dollars in the coming decade.

Rector noted federal, state and local spending on welfare programs such as Medicaid, food stamps, and public housing in FY 2004 was $564 billion. He noted federal, state and local spending on schools in FY 2004 was $590 billion. He noted spending on direct benefits such as Social Security, Medicare, and worker compensation in FY 2004 was $840 billion. He noted federal, state and local spending on population based services such as police, fire and emergency services, roads, highways, courts, parks, and public health inspectors in FY 2004 was $662 billion. He said allowing more unskilled immigrants into the country would impose more taxes on the American public. He also said the crush of immigrants would degrade the nation's social services and population based services because of the loads they would place on them.

Rector noted most immigrants were very uneducated and unskilled compared to the average American, and as such would consume more public benefits. (In the Ellis Island era, many immigrants were unskilled, but there were no welfare programs for them to abuse (public charges were deported). They became productive workers and taxpayers.) He estimated the average "low skill" immigrant household received more than $30,000 in welfare, education, and population based services in FY2004, and paid taxes of less than $11,000 that year on earnings of about $29,000. In other words, he argued, in FY2004 the average low skill immigrant household took in almost $20,000 more in government benefits than they paid in taxes to support. He said there were roughly 4.54 million such households in the country accounting for 15.9 million people in FY2004, so if his figuring was correct, these legal and illegal immigrants cost the American public almost $90 billion in taxes in that year, or more than $5500 per "low skill" immigrant and each member of his household.

Where did these numbers come from? Rector figured government spending on the average household headed by immigrants without high school diplomas took in $10,428 in welfare benefits, $4891 in cash transfers like Social Security and Medicare, $8462 for schooling for children, $2746 for police and public safety, $809 for transportation, and $2724 for other government services. This tallied $30,060 per such household.

Rector figured the average household headed by immigrants without high school diplomas paid $2878 in FICA taxes, $1815 in state and local sales and use taxes, $1171 in federal income taxes, $1618 in state and local property taxes (part of someone's rent covers the landlord's property tax), $873 in purchases to cover corporate taxes, $714 in state lottery ticket purchases, $504 in unemployment insurance and worker compensation taxes, $431 in state income taxes, $264 in federal excise taxes, $192 in federal highway taxes through gas purchases, and $113 in other taxes. This tallied $10,573 per such households. Subtract $10,573 in taxes paid from $30,060 in benefits received to get a deficit per household of $19,487. Multiply this by 4.54 million such households to get $88.5 billion.

Rector noted giving amnesty to illegal immigrants would allow them to collect Social Security and Medicare and Supplemental Security and Medicaid benefits legally. Assuming the average legalized illegal might, after retiring, get 18 years of benefits costing taxpayers a net of $17,000 a year, the cost to the taxpayers of paying for benefits for 7.9 million amnestied illegal retirees who presumably live long enough to get them would be $2.4 trillion in 2004 dollars. This is a tax of more than $9200 in 2004 dollars on every man, woman, and child in the United States (260 million or so of us) who is a native of this country. (3)

The truth is probably somewhere between the $26 billion figure of the Congressional Budget Office and the nearly $90 billion figure Rector of the Heritage Foundation estimated in costs of "new immigrants" per year (not counting illegal retirees). Given the propensity for government people to soft-pedal a problem unless they want to scare the public into coming up with more money to throw at it, the latter number may be high but may very well be closer to the truth.

Adding another million or so legal and illegal immigrants to the country per year, most of who would be unskilled and would also include many elderly parents of immigrants who could daisy-chain them into the country, would take more taxes out of your wallet or purse.

At least another two million to five million aliens have come here legally by plane, then have overstayed their visas and are living here illegally. And there are another 800,000 or so foreign students and family members in our universities or here accompanying them. Some of them have gone jihad on us. Most of the 9/11 hijackers got in on tourist visas. Three hijackers had student visas. Some of them overstayed their visas; one of the student visa holders didn't report to school. (4)

And there are the common criminals among these ungrateful aliens. A 2005 federal report noted about 265,000 of our two million local, state, and federal prison inmates are aliens. This doesn't count those being deported as illegals; it only counts those convicted as murderers, rapists, robbers, thieves, muggers, and the like. Nor does it count the tens of thousands of alien criminals the feds and state authorities released instead of deporting. Aliens murder almost 4400 Americans per year – by comparison, the jihadists in Iraq and Afghanistan have killed roughly 800 American servicemen per year since the start of 2002. Drunk-driving or drugged-driving aliens and other homicidally negligent aliens also kill more than 4700 Americans per year. And there are scores of thousands of sex offenders among those aliens who have come here legally or otherwise. (5)

There are many jihadists and spies and separatists among the millions of aliens in America. May Day 2006 brought out many Mexican illegals who favor forcing California, Arizona, New Mexico, and Texas back into the paws of the corrupt men who run Mexico. For every Chinese government-recruited vermin caught stealing secrets when they never should have had a security clearance in the first place, there are many others ransacking the restricted databases of the military installations and the defense contractors stupid or greedy enough to hire them. And almost daily there seems to be some sort of incident of Moslems shooting Americans or working on their bomb techniques or running over Americans with cars or getting into the country and linking up with jihadist countrymen or scoping out military facilities or stalking girls or probing airline security or raping their servant girls or honor-killing their daughters or raising money for Islamist terrorist groups.

There are public health issues involving the new immigrants. Here's a sampler of public health statistics, courtesy of the Centers for Disease Control:

Two-thirds of all cholera cases came into the country with people who contracted it abroad.

Four of every five cases of measles reported in the United States in 2003 came from people who were immigrants or were traveling abroad and served as carriers from measles-infested areas overseas.

In 2004, more than half of the tuberculosis sufferers (about 8000 out of 15,000) were foreign nationals; Asians had a much higher rate of this disease than others in the United States. Foreign-born people in the United States have nine times the TB rate of native-born Americans.

Typhoid fever and travel by Asian nationals visiting relatives in the Indian subcontinent in the 2000s were related effect and cause.

The problem is likely much worse than what is being reported. Officials with Centers for Disease Control don't tell the truth too often about health care issues when political concerns are involved. In reporting on SARS (severe acute respiratory syndrome), they forgot to mention SARS was an unknown disease in America until recently. It came here from China, from Chinese nationals and from businessmen and tourists who caught it while visiting that nation.(6)

Despite the problems they pose to the people of America, the "new immigration" has support from both major political parties. They and the special interests who own them have agendas at odds with the good of the nation. They view the immigrants as cheap labor. Some view the illegals as workers whose Social Security taxes can be used to prop up the Social Security system. Many Democrats and some Republicans see immigrants as welfare clients who can be steered to vote for the party that gives them more benefits. They don't care that these people drive down the standard of living of the average American by burdening the social services of this country, driving down the wage scale, and committing many crimes.

Red China's Communist dictators aren't only trying to put American factories out of work with the shoddy products their toiling serfs make for the shelves of Wal-Mart, K-Mart, and other emporiums of low-value merchandise and inferior imported hardware. They are actively spying on America's defense installations, defense contractors, computer industries, and other industrial concerns with a mind toward stealing military and industrial secrets, undermining our military and industrial concerns, and eventually overpowering us.

The leaders of India doesn't intend to confront America militarily. However, they aren't above spying and weapon-running and dumping cheap goods in America. Nor are their crooked entrepreneurs above undermining the computer programming industry in this country with their by and large lesser skilled techies.

Jihadists intend to use our dependence on oil and our political correctness against us also. They are aided and abetted by multinational oil executives in this country who make billions of dollars dealing with the assorted pirates who run Saudi Arabia, Iran, Libya, and oil-rich sheikdoms. They make much more profit on Middle Eastern oil because they can charge the same amount per barrel on Middle Eastern oil as they can on American oil even though it costs less to drill. It is easier to drill for oil in the Middle East, there are hardly any environmental restrictions, and the average Arab working in an oilfield or a refinery can be paid little. Drilling and refining oil in America means these oil executives would have to pay a living wage to American oilfield workers and refinery workers, and abide by environmental regulations.

The jihadists and oil executives are aided and abetted by politicians, school officials, media types, and others who give Islam a privileged status the jihadists would never consider giving Christianity. The jihadists are also aided by fifth-columnists and useful idiots in the environmental movement who oppose drilling for and refining oil, mining and burning coal, or using nuclear power. How much Arab money is being pumped into these environmentalist groups to lobby against American energy independence? The Bushes and the Clintons and many other politicians are up to their necks in Arab oil money or other oil interests. Their financial disclosure records say so. So do their actions. No matter which party holds the White House or majorities in Congress, the oil companies and the Arab rulers never get punished for gouging the American people. Nor does either party push for making energy cheaper or more plentiful.

The corporate leaders, and the globalists in colleges, organizations, and government agencies treat us as if we were retarded children. These people view us as suckers, and we have yet to prove them wrong.

THE RED HERRING ARGUMENTS

The corporate and ideological and political shills for immigration know most of the people they want to flood into this country can't meet reasonable standards for admittance. So they use arguments, none any more honest than those of the average politician or ACLU lawyer, to sway us. Here are their top red herrings:

They say, "We need more engineers and scientists."

We can hire our own engineers, and maybe only the elite of the elite from other countries. The average foreign engineer is not better than the average American engineer, otherwise their countries would be technologically more advanced than our nation. The greatest impact foreign engineers as a group have on our nation is depressing the engineer's wage.

Many Asian engineers work hard. But they don't invent and create like Americans do. If they could, they'd be ahead of us in technology. But they aren't. They are really good at stealing and reverse-engineering, errr, perfecting our ideas.

Besides, manufacturing jobs are pouring out of this country, thanks to the corporate lords. They are reducing the work of American engineers. So the only reason they really want foreign engineers is to further depress the American engineers' wage scale.

Any engineering shortage we have in this country now is being created artificially by the corporate leaders who cheat engineers of their due. This widespread cheating of American engineers is reducing the motivation of many good American college students to study to become engineers. Instead, too many of them go into essentially non-productive but personally lucrative fields like marketing or law or public administration.

The same applies to scientists. America's door should be open to the brilliant scientists who want to become real Americans and improve this nation, like those who fled from Hitler and helped us develop atomic weapons. But the average foreign scientist is no better compared to an American scientist than foreign engineers are compared to American engineers.

They say, "We need more laborers."

No, we don't. As previously noted, there is more competition for blue-collar jobs now, because of the presence of 12 to 25 million illegal aliens in America. This drives down the wage scale and forces many able-bodied Americans out of work. Besides, until manufacturing increases in America to the stage it was at in the 1950s and 1960s – American international dominance – there are fewer such jobs for more people to fight over as it is. Like with the engineers and scientists, employers are lobbying for more foreigners

to further bust the American wage scale. The American man who served his country as a serviceman or who still could be drafted in time of national emergency does not need the problem of an alien who did nothing for America competing for his job at a lower wage than what is fair.

They say, "We need more doctors and nurses."

Our experience with foreign doctors who hospital administrators have tried to pawn off on us has been entirely bad. Too many of them are rude as well as underskilled. In many developing countries, there is a more formal social order than in America, and doctors in those countries usually come from among the higher-caste people of their lands, or they become high-caste people because they are doctors. This leads many of them to act like arrogant jerks. They bring their snotty attitudes here.

Foreign nurses may be more kind than foreign doctors, but they aren't any more qualified than our own nurses. Some nurses from Islamic countries refuse to sanitize themselves properly on grounds it is un-Islamic to bare more flesh than their hands. Thus they pose health risks to American patients.

Greedy HMOs and others who want a cheaper but not better health care system in America are behind the push to admit these lesser-talented foreigners. If we ease the artificial shortage of American doctors by expanding the capacity of medical schools, we'll produce all the doctors we need. We had to do so to provide enough military doctors for World War Two, and we can do it again. Taxpayers of states whose rural areas are underserved with medical professionals could subsidize medical students in college in exchange for making these students work in underserved rural areas for a length of time after becoming doctors.

Reducing the number of foreign doctors and nurses in America is also an act of charity for the sick around the world. Foreign doctors, especially those from places like India, China, and Iran, need to serve the people in their own lands. Then there wouldn't be so many suffering people in those lands.

They say, "America is rich. Why can't you be less callous and give these people a home? Why are you such racists?"

The charge of racism is a red herring dishonest people throw when they can't back up their argument logically and they sense people aren't buying their lies.

Those people should practice what they preach and bring some of the aliens in the big cities to their houses to live. They should also quit their jobs and take jobs flipping hamburgers or scrubbing toilets so aliens can take their higher-paying jobs. Then when they bring home grossly reduced paychecks, and when foreign bums pilfer their possessions and foul their homes, they will get an understanding of what so many aliens are doing to the people of this country now.

China may have a robust economy (thanks to corporate traitors who export our jobs there) but you don't see poor people breaking into China to participate in their economy. Why? Because there is nothing to participate in that would reward them (except if they came from North Korea, where the alternative is starvation). Illegal immigrants would be punished severely by the Red Chinese.

Mexican authorities do not allow illegal immigration, even though they encourage their own to come to America illegally. Combating illegal immigration is within our rights as a nation, just like it is within Mexico's right.

The average American understands the immigration crisis is not about Mexico vs. America; it's about a sucker country with more opportunity whose politicians are unwilling to enforce its laws. Most Mexicans are not vermin. I have some Spanish blood, and I dated and partied with women from Mexico, Puerto Rico, and elsewhere in Latin America before I married a woman of predominant Slavic ancestry. Those who have come here legally from Mexico and elsewhere in Latin America have made wonderful citizens. Up to a generation ago, even the illegals tended to serve in our Armed Forces in high numbers.

Latin Americans should have a priority equal to that of Europeans in immigration policy, but we need a much lower ceiling for how many legal immigrants we let in. We need to prevent illegals from coming here and we need to send those who are here home.

Many of those who would emigrate here from Asia and the Middle East pose other problems. They are more prone to steal military and corporate secrets than Latin Americans, they are much more at odds with our way of life than Latin Americans, and they come from societies that are at war with America due to Communism or trade considerations or religious extremism.

Aliens have homes ... in their homelands. Family reunifications can always take place in the homelands of the family. These people don't have to come here to have a family circle. What they want is a daisy chain.

They say, "It is charitable to give illegals sanctuary."

Charitable to whom? Not to those who have to pay the tab or endure being the victims of illegals who commit crimes, or suffer poorer health care and basic

government service because of the presence of so many illegals competing with them for these services!

Politicians who maintain "sanctuary" cities and other such illegal jurisdictions are phonies who are not spending any of their own money to feed illegals or cover their other social costs. They rob the taxpayers to do so.

Nor are these politicians endangering their own health or personal safety by harboring these fugitives. They are putting illegals among the poorer people of their communities, to catch the illegals' diseases and suffer as the illegals' crime victims. They are also impoverishing many in their communities by letting crooked businessmen hire illegals to take the locals' jobs. They are also in effect depriving many Americans of health care as hospital caregivers have to deal with illegals flooding their emergency rooms ... and in some instances close these facilities altogether because the illegals have descended on them for routine health care they know they won't have to pay for.

These politicians aren't ensuring local labor exploiters and traffickers in the sex trade aren't abusing the illegals. It's no coincidence that the most victimization of illegals, as well as the highest rates of crime by illegals, and the largest payments in social services, and the largest number of hospital closures, are taking place in communities and states whose officials are not enforcing the law against illegals.

Engaging in behavior that spreads disease, crime, and joblessness is many things, but it sure isn't charitable!

Those in the sanctuary movement who are part of organized religions need to cease and desist. They need to concentrate on pulling the logs out of their own eyes – these denominations need to purge the sex offenders and sexual deviates out of the ranks of their clergy and youth ministers. They need to concentrate on helping the poor here in America and giving charity to their legitimate missionaries and aid workers in other countries. They need to work to defend human life against atrocities like abortion and euthanasia and sexual abuse. They need to behave according the tenets of their professed faiths. They do not need to be aiding and abetting illegals, and hiding them from the law, so they can lie, cheat, and steal, commit sex offenses, and commit homicide.

Those in the sanctuary movement who are secularists likewise need to cease and desist. They are all too often frontists for labor exploiters and sex traffickers. Many of them are also sexual predators, and the trafficked daughters of the illegal immigrant poor (and sometimes the sons as well) they view as naked meat. After all, these illegals are victims who are in a position where they can't really report their victimization.

Public school teachers and politicians, two classes of people who are very prominent in the secularist sanctuary movement, are much more prone to molest children and commit other sex offenses than normal people, and are more prone to molest children and commit other sex offenses than even members of the clergy and youth ministers in religious groups. Their behavior must be unspeakable, because their friends in the media rarely mention it, even though crime statistics scream it. Lawyers and social workers, two other classes of people in the secularist sanctuary movement, can be very good at making excuses for sexual predators; many of them also prey upon women and children. These groups also need to purge the predators from their midst and concentrate upon serving the American people, not aiding and abetting illegals. They need to become public servants instead of merely government employees.

They say, "Today's immigrants are just as good a group of citizens as your ancestors were."

The experience of the last few decades have shown, immigrants from places like China, India, and the Middle East are nowhere near as assimilable as the Europeans, or even Latin Americans. The fact that they work hard is nothing special in their favor. They would have to work hard if they stayed in their homelands. European immigrants engaged in nowhere near the industrial espionage or military espionage that the Asians have committed in the last few decades. No immigrant group from Europe systematically waged war upon the American people like Moslem immigrants from Middle Eastern countries have done.

People of East Asian and South Asian descent (except for people with Filipino or Guam roots) tend to serve in our Armed Forces at rates much lower than whites, blacks, or Hispanics. This also holds true for people of Middle Eastern descent. The majority of Moslems in uniform (about 3400 or so as of 2006, out of a total of 1.37 million) are American-born blacks, not people with roots in Moslem regions of the world.

Hispanic immigrants and immigrants from the Caribbean islands have traditionally assimilated into American society while retaining their customs and religion, like most European immigrants. Legal immigrants from Mexico and elsewhere in Latin America and the Caribbean islands usually still make assimilable citizens. Many of their sons are still willing to serve in our Armed Forces.

They say, "You are picking on Moslems."

The reverse is true. Moslem extremists from the Middle East and elsewhere are picking on us. They have declared war on us. They are raising money even in this country to fund jihad. And some of their brightest young people are making bombs and attacking people in America who mean them no harm.

These people come from societies where trafficking of females for sexual servitude is the norm, where slavery is legal or is tolerated, and where foreigners are severely mistreated if they are poor.

Many Moslems have also declared war upon their own females. Read about "honor killings" of females, and read about how Moslem women who are rape victims get flogged. Those of you who want unchecked immigration who are attractive females should go over to those lands and live like their females live. Then give us a full report on how much you love these people when you get back ... assuming you haven't been forced into sexual slavery, or assuming you haven't been beheaded for refusing to give it up or for being promiscuous before coming to their lands.

Too many Moslems hide behind their religion to commit crimes. They are not the first group in this country to do so. And thanks to the historical record, we were able to talk elsewhere in this book about another group who claimed their religion gave them permission to practice polygamy, theft, and murder of outsiders. They were a WASPy bunch known as the Mormons.

The Mormons rebelled against the social order of this country and violated our laws. They continued to do so until our nation's leaders in the late 1800s punished them enough so their leaders got the "revelation" their predatory and immoral behavior needed to change.

Even today, Protestant and Catholic and Jewish clergymen and youth ministers who commit sex offenses face criminal charges. *And they should!* A crime is a crime, no matter what the religious status is of the swine who commits it.

By comparison, our prosecutors have been cowardly about prosecuting Moslems for inciting murder and funding it, and abusing and molesting their daughters and other females among them. They never invoke hate crime laws in what few cases they do bring against Moslems who target Americans. This must change, and quickly.

They say, "We need more diversity."

What is wrong with America's heritage and culture the way it is? If you don't love America, you are free to leave. Be prepared to have foreign officials reject you for the diversity you represent to their societies.

It was the amalgamation of European, Native American Indian and Polynesian, American Hispanic, and African cultures under a common belief in God and a sense of the rights and responsibilities of the people that made America the greatest and most vibrant nation on Earth.

Virtually no other country has leaders who favor diluting their culture or ethnicity or identity out of a misguided sense of inclusion or political correctness. Preserving the essential ethnic cultural makeup of this nation is the birthright of Americans. We the people of America, as do the people of every nation, have the right to try to preserve our culture.

We don't need the cultural diversity of the harem, female circumcision, hara-kiri, suicide bombing, the Cultural Revolution, servant abuse, government-sponsored slave labor, selling girls and boys for sex, organ harvesting, harvesting dogs for food, dowry murder, and human sacrifice. We need controlled immigration, fewer immigrants, and immigrants from lands whose people have natural cultural ties to America and are historically are prone to assimilate into the American way.

They say, "Immigration is a net benefit to this country."

At one time it was. But it hasn't been for decades.

Your taxes and hidden taxes you pay for the costs of goods and services pays for the burdens that immigrants place upon schools, health care, other social services. The extras you have to pay for health insurance and car insurance and the like covers somewhat the costs of allowing aliens to get free care at hospitals and allowing uninsured underskilled aliens to drive cars. The extra taxes you pay allows companies like Wal-Mart to allegedly use government programs as their worker benefits package for their underpaid workers. They reportedly coach their employees on how to freeload benefits instead of paying them better wages. What you save at Wal-Mart or at a foreign car dealer you make up in higher costs elsewhere (and a lower paycheck due to downward pressure on your salary) to support this ruinous spending due to all too many of the "new immigrants."

When illegal immigrants compete for blue-collar jobs, and when underskilled people from India compete for techie jobs and when underskilled people from China compete for engineering jobs, and when medical people from overseas compete for health care jobs, your kids lose out to them in hiring. Big companies are putting the difference between your paycheck and the immigrant's or illegal's paycheck in their pocket.

Many Asians and Middle Easterners are daisy-chaining their older relatives into America. They get access to our social services and our health care system, to which they have not contributed. You, I, and the next generations of Americans have to pay for this.

Aliens murder roughly 4400 Americans each year and kill more than 4700 more Americans each year by driving drunk or driving recklessly or committing other acts of negligent homicide. They also commit tens of thousands of rapes and other sexual assaults a year. Since many of their victims are their own females, the numbers of such unconscionable offenses they commit is grossly underreported.

By breaking into the country, aliens steal benefits and degrade security and clog the courts. Even assuming the crime rate of aliens isn't quite as high as the crime rate of natives of America, which is an apparently false assumption because aliens reportedly commit violent crimes like homicide and rape at rates above those of natives of America, why do we need to welcome more criminals?

None of the immigration pushers' arguments hold any water when analyzed. The bottom line is this: It's our country, so immigration policy should benefit We The People. What we must do is force our public officials and those who run our other public and private institutions to respond to our will, or drive them from their offices if they won't do so.

THE ELLIS ISLAND TEST

Ronald Reagan used to say if he brought up a problem, he would propose a solution to that problem. The Gipper was right. Pointing out problems without trying to solve them is little more than whining or nagging.

The Ellis Island Era immigrants became real Americans. Very few of them wound up being supported by the public. Instead, they literally built this country – they built roads, railroads, canals, dams, bridges, buildings, and port facilities. Their children fought in America's armed forces in World War One or in World War Two ... this even includes the Japanese-American kids who fought in the famed "Go For Broke" outfit in World War Two while their families were being interned by leftist civil liberties proponent FDR and his leftist henchman Earl Warren.

After reading the history of our immigration laws, you now have some understanding of what we used to do in terms of regulating immigration. It is never a bad start to use tried-and-true methods and update them as circumstances require.

The politicians, the corporate elite, those who run the schools, and those who run the various media excoriate you for wanting to defend your country and your children's birthright from these people and from the millions of others who come here illegally. They call you racist and throw into your faces the fact your ancestors immigrated here too at some time in our nation's history.

What we need to do is return the favor. If the "New Immigration" people are supposedly the moral equivalent of the "Ellis Island Era" immigrants, then wouldn't it be fair to subject them to the same kinds of screening the earlier immigrants had to undergo?

Using the Ellis Island set of standards, the following would apply today:

Any immigrant unwilling or unable to earn a living would be barred or deported. Also, immigrants would not be able to daisy-chain in old relatives and ask the American taxpayers to give them Social Security benefits ... benefits they never did a day's worth of work in this country to earn. Enforcing this standard would send millions of legal and illegal aliens home.

The ban on immigrants with labor contracts and visas (with a few exceptions) would drastically drop the number of immigrants looking to displace Americans in the technical fields. There are roughly 800,000 Asian low-skilled techies and similar types here on H-1B and L-1 visas. (This doesn't count their millions of dependents they brought with them.) These are not "elite" professionals; only 36,000 aliens received O-1 (extraordinary ability or achievement) visas (even with resume inflation) in 2007. Enforcement of the ban on labor contracts would restore hundreds of thousands of jobs to their rightful owners – skilled Americans. **(7)**

Due to legal immigration, there are about three million more foreigners working legally in this country now than there were in 2000. (This doesn't count their millions of dependents they brought with them.) During this decade, the number of younger American men and women working declined by about three million. There are roughly 250,000 seasonal labor workers in America on H2 and H3 visas. (This doesn't count their dependents they brought with them.) Americans could do these jobs also. **(8)**

Excluding those with criminal convictions for violent crimes, property crimes, drug crimes, and other serious offenses would drop the number of people allowed into this country. Likewise, enforcing the punishment and deportation of criminal aliens would send home hundreds of thousands of immigrants, legal and illegal. (Executions of alien murderers would also stop their killings.) Not only street crime, but white collar crime, industrial espionage and regular espionage convictions would send alien criminals home after their punishment in our prisons.

This would take a serious bite out of crime. Each year it would save thousands of American lives, prevent scores of thousands of rapes and other sex offenses, and cut down on other violent crimes, drug crimes, property crimes, and crimes against the social order. It would also free up jail space because there would be far fewer alien repeat offenders. At last count, there were more than 250,000 alien criminals in federal and state prisons and county jails. This doesn't count the hundreds of thousands of aliens released by the feds who failed to show for their court dates or deportation, and are running around loose in this country. **(9)**

Trying to enter illegally would earn an illegal a trip home. Shutting down the government benefits gravy train would decrease the attraction for them to come here. So would the drop in employers willing to hire illegals if we were to force our leaders to arrest more corporate criminals who hire them and send them to prison instead of plea-bargaining lesser sentences with their oily defense lawyers.

Our officials need to enforce the "loathsome disease" provisions of the immigration laws also. In the Ellis Island Era, our inspectors were intolerant toward serious communicable diseases. Our overseas visa granters are much less insensitive to pathogens now. We the people are entitled to public health. Alien disease carriers and their germs have no inalienable right to come here.

The ban on polygamy would ban Moslems and others who practice this relic of barbarism. Likewise, the ban on immigrants guilty of moral turpitude – crimes of dishonesty, violence, sex offenses, and sexually immoral lifestyle – would keep out many undesirables. We have far too many liars, thieves, vicious thugs, molesters, and degenerates as it is.

The ban on "moral turpitude" aliens would do deep damage to the sex slavers who import 50,000 or more older girls and younger women for the sex trade. It would also keep out or force the deportation of scores of thousands of alien gypsies, tramps, and thieves. A few Euro and South African and Aussie actresses, actors, and singers with questionable morals would have to ply their trades at home, but last time I checked, we have plenty of native-born deviates, sluts, and sleazes in the entertainment industry without needing to import any degenerates.

"Inimical attitude" and unwillingness to adjust to American institutions would ban very many people from the Middle East and a large proportion of other Asians. It would also ban Mexican separatists who believe Texas, New Mexico, Arizona, and California should be governed from Mexico City.

Enforcing "inimical attitude" laws would mean there would be many fewer jihadists and sleepers from the Middle East, industrial spies from China, and chiselers from the Indian subcontinent in this country as a result. You wouldn't be reading about honor killings of young women or female circumcisions of young girls in your daily paper. Nor would you hear about thefts of dogs for use as meat in Asian eateries.

Ellis Island Era officials made sponsors and others put up bonds for hundreds and often thousands of dollars apiece for questionable immigrants whose causes they advocated. Applying that law to today and adjusting for inflation to about $50,000 per bonded alien could bankrupt many immigrant advocacy groups and individuals who front for criminals, sleepers, and other alien undesirables. This would help slow the flow of questionable immigrants further.

Ellis Island Era officials and other lawmen knew a baby born here to foreign parents didn't automatically get American citizenship. The babe took the citizenship status of his or her alien parents, which is as it still should be. Returning to this common-sense interpretation of the law, as it was before LBJ's failed presidency, would end the anchor baby scam.

And finally, Ellis Island and other immigration stations served as place of physical inspection and detention of would-be immigrants. Even after our State Department people started issuing immigrant visas overseas, our immigrant inspectors still took a good look at would-be immigrants at Ellis Island and other immigration stations when they got here.

Nowadays, those who come here legally get inspected and approved overseas, with no real backup inspection on American soil. For an alien to immigrate to America legally, he or she does need a visa. American officials stationed throughout the world can help foreigners apply for visas in the countries they are living. American immigration officials stationed throughout the world can screen visa applicants for eligibility to come to America. They can screen people for health and likelihood of becoming a public charge and keep would-be immigrants from coming. They can also screen would-be immigrants or temporary visitors for criminals, but if foreign governments want to get rid of their trash, or want to send agents into America to foment trouble, odds are these applicants will come up clean. Then the immigration official will have to use his or her intelligence to sort out the scammers, and compare their paperwork with the profile of a problem immigrant or problem temporary visitor.

When an immigrant arrives at an airport or another port of entry, like a harbor or a border crossing, he or she has to report to an officer of the U.S. Customs and Border Protection agency. That officer has the immigrant's baggage checked. The officer checks the immigrant's documents issued abroad to verify the immigrant is who he or she says he or she is, and that the individual has the authorization to enter America. The officer has the discretion to detain someone he or she suspects has bogus documents, but in almost all cases he or she does not detain immigrants. In almost all cases, the officer does not do any background inspection on the immigrant or examine the immigrant for conditions that could bar him or her from entering America. The immigrant who clears this inspection retrieves his or her luggage and is free to move about the country.

There are about 20,000 U.S. Bureau of Customs and Border Protection (CBP) employees available to check immigrants and alien travelers at the airports and other ports of entry into America. (There are fewer than 20,000 Border Patrol agents. Border Patrol agents monitor border zones instead of looking at those who present themselves at ports of entry.) These 20,000 have to screen roughly 400 million entries (mostly border crossings, but also close to 100 million air travelers from abroad). Assuming 2000 hours yearly per inspector, this gives each CBP screener an average of 10 aliens per hour to check for entry into America, assuming all 20,000 are checking aliens. (10)

This minimal screening can't protect the national security concerns of America. Nor can it prevent corruption. An alien who means America harm could still come to America and cause harm. Also, corruption or coercion of local officials or American consulate personnel overseas could still allow many inadmissible immigrants to get crooked inspections giving them visas and approval to come to America. Backup screening at immigration stations on American soil, like an Ellis Island or an Angel Island, is needed and must be done again to protect the American people.

This won't necessarily stop those on travel visas from overstaying their visit. But proper detection and arrests of those who overstay their welcome using existing federal databases to check on travelers and students, and even local and state police checking aliens pulled over for traffic stops or minor arrests using the DHS' Law Enforcement Support Center can locate wayward foreigners and have them detained pending expelling or jailing them.

Henry Curran said immigrants needed final screening in America by Americans at Ellis Island and other immigration stations. Curran was trying to put American interests first. In the 1920s, this was not politically incorrect. Nor should it be today.

At the end of the Ellis Island Era, the nation's leaders imposed ethnic quotas on immigration, except from Latin America. These quotas remained in effect until the corrupt and incompetent rule of Lyndon Johnson. Many in the leftist camp claim the quota system was racist, and to a great extent racists supported it. However, so did millions of reasonable people who wanted their America to retain a certain cultural identity. We the People have the right to maintain American culture and American heritage. We the People also have the right to expect that immigrants will try to assimilate and become real Americans, instead of aliens standing aloof from American society and American values. Europeans, Latin Americans, and sub-Saharan Africans are more like Americans and more likely to adopt American values than are Middle Easterners and most other Asians. Social engineering can't change that self-evident truth.

Even without a quota, the statistics are brutally clear. None of the illegal immigrants and far fewer than half of the million or so people our government officials allow in as the legal immigrants of today could pass the Ellis Island test our ancestors had to pass. Using laws that are proven to work is the best solution to the immigration problem.

Tens of millions of European and Western Hemisphere immigrants had to play by these Ellis Island Era rules I just outlined. What makes the immigrants of today any more special than those who came in steerage to this nation and helped _build_ this nation instead of bombing it, or spying on it, or leeching off its taxpayers?

WHO SHOULD WE ADMIT, AND HOW MANY?

A country as populated as ours doesn't need too many newcomers. Some have suggested a limit of 400,000 immigrants a year; others have suggested a ceiling of fewer immigrants, like 200,000 to 300,000 tops.

Before admitting anyone in any year, we should ask questions like these:

Is there a need for immigrants?
Is it wise to let them in?
Will they support themselves and not freeload?
Will it cost more to give them benefits than what they will pay in taxes?
How can they help the people of this nation?
Will their values clash with American values?
Will they take on American values?
Will they try to assimilate besides economically?
How patriotic will they become?

It will help America to admit aliens of exceptional scientific, engineering, medical, or other talents who want to build America and want to become real Americans. Immigration statistics show the vast majority of those here on work visas are not exceptional talents, but people who do not have quite the abilities that Americans in these fields have.

Favoring the admitting of people from countries whose people have an affinity for American values, and whose blood is most similar to the ethnic makeup of America is rational.

Natives of Mexico should probably have the most slots of any nation. Before 1976, there was a quota of about 120,000 immigrants who could come from the Western Hemisphere. The worldwide immigrant quota was about 290,000. Fewer than 70,000 legal immigrants a year came from Mexico from 1965 to 1976. Then in 1976, American politicians enacted Public Law 94-571, which adjusted Mexico's limit down to about 20,000 immigrants a year. Illegal immigration from Mexico skyrocketed. Dialing the worldwide quota back to 300,000 immigrants a year tops (1/10 of 1% of the 300 million or so people in America now) and giving Mexicans a large percentage of the immigrant visas – along with enforcing laws against employing and housing illegals – will diminish the illegal immigrant problem from Mexico.

Natives of Canada, a European, American Indian, and African roots country, should also get preference. These people also have quite a bit in common with we Americans, especially compared with people from the Eastern Hemisphere. And after the Canadians should come the other Latin American, Native American, and Euro-American and African-American natives of the Western Hemisphere. These peoples usually have an understanding of American values and could assimilate better than the peoples of the Eastern Hemisphere.

Of the Eastern Hemisphere, we should favor immigrants from the countries of Europe and Sub-Saharan Africa, in rough proportions to the number of people of those continents' ancestry already here. Our basic cultural heritage is from Europe. Nowadays, the peoples of Eastern Europe seem the most grateful for our help in bringing down the Iron Curtain, and I believe they, as well as the Irish (who have always served in our Armed Forces at high rates), will tend to make the most loyal Americans.

The millions of African slaves forced to come here have also left their mark on the cultural heritage of America, and for the better. They and their descendants have also contributed to the America we know and love. The Orthodox Christian peoples of Ethiopia and Sudan and Egypt, and the few Catholics of these countries, while not here in great numbers, also have the tie of common faith with us. The most prominent member of the Orthodox Christian faith in Africa, Haile Selassie, was a constant friend of America. (The emperor of Ethiopia also welcomed Armenian refugees from the Turks.)

Of the peoples of Asia and the Middle East, those who have traditionally shown the most aptitude for assimilation have been Filipinos (about 90% of whom have Catholic roots) and the people of Guam and other islands whose names first became household words in World War Two. The Christians of Armenia and Lebanon and Syria and Israel, and the Christian Assyrians and Chaldeans of present-day Iraq, and Jews from Israel have also tried to fit in. We involved ourselves in wars in the Philippines, Korea (about 40% of the people in South Korea are now Christians of the Catholic faith or various Protestant denominations), Vietnam (which used to be about 30% Catholic until the Communists drove most of the Catholics out or killed them), Lebanon, and Iraq, and the Christians of these lands have shown us loyalty and the willingness to assimilate, so they should have priority also among Asians. The Australians, New Zealanders, and Pacific Islanders have traditionally been our friends; they should have similar consideration.

Who should we worry about letting in?

China's rulers are essentially at war with us in Cold War Two. Since those who emigrate from China do so with the approval of the Red government, we should regard them as potential spies. Why do we need more spies?

In World War Two, many Americans lost their lives and their countrymen spent a fortune aiding to the Chinese who were fighting sociopath Jap invaders. But the Chinese have been in the grip of militant Communism for more than two generations since the end of World War Two. They fought us directly in Korea, and they fought us indirectly in Southeast Asia. They are of a non-Judeo-Christian tradition poisoned by decades of Communist thought control.

The Chinese immigrants of today are nothing like the Chinese refugees of the World War Two and early Cold War era who were very pro-American in orientation and wanted to become real Americans when they came here, and who have made great citizens. I have done business with the Cold War immigrants and consider them honorable people.

However, I have met Chinese students in graduate school in the last two decades who are arrogant and xenophobic and committed to their regime. So have millions of other Americans studying in the colleges across our nation. These Chinese and many like them who China's dictatorial government allows to come here are not here to become Americans; they are here to get rich and/or help China. They should be kept out.

Governments of many Islamic countries and many wealthy Islamists like Osama bin Ladin are at war with us. The Saudi Arabian government subsidizes jihadist groups and subsidizes mosques in this country whose imams spew hatred and recruit potential killers of our own people. The Iranians haven't been noticeably better. Pakistan also has some troubles in this regard. Why do we need more sleepers who will kill Americans ... or who will fundraise and provide cover for their countrymen who will do so?

The government of India has agents in this country doing industrial and military spying and illegal arms buying. India also has many corporate pirates who are systematically undermining our computer programming industry. The face of real India is very likely the rude and ignorant call center employee you get on the phone when you are looking for help. So what if they speak English? How will they help America when their government and business tycoons have been spying on America and waging economic war on an important part of our technical base?

The Japanese are a more complex case. They are worthy adversaries in business, and they proved their toughness fighting against us in World War Two. They have a standard of living that is not much below our standard of living; they have a diligent and educated society. I have done business with Japanese-American people of high caliber.

However, the social norms of the people of Japan in many ways clash with ours to a much greater extent than do those of the Europeans or the Latin Americans, or even many Africans. Japanese militarists were even worse than the Nazis in murdering, raping, and conducting experiments on people under their control during World War Two. There has been no Japanese apology or indemnification of victims of their aggression in the World War Two era. The dominant social culture in

Japan still allows for predatory business practices in the name of nationalism. There is still an undercurrent of sadism and embrace of the culture of death in Japan that manifests itself in the sexual abuse of less advanced Asian women and in the high rate of suicide.

The Japanese are more open to American ideas than most Asians and in many ways they have embraced our culture, but there is still a nationalism that is frankly racist and colonialist in many of their people. Can Americans benefit from the pluses of the people of Japan without importing their minuses?

Who should we let in, and how many? No matter what decision is made, someone is going to whine. The yardsticks for how many should be the needs of this country. The yardsticks for who should be ethnic makeup of our country, cultural similarities of immigrants to Americans, and relative friendliness or unfriendliness of the countries of the world to America. Again, we should welcome people like us, not people different enough from us that they want to come here only to earn money or plot against us. Gratitude and assimilation are two minimum requirements. Basic cultural, political, and religious antagonisms should be, in the minds of most Americans, disqualifiers. The line has to be drawn somewhere; that's where we should choose to draw it. The "who" and "how many" questions will need plenty of reflection, by leaders of good will, who will put the American people's interests above all other considerations. We the people need to lead our leaders to make the right decisions.

END NOTES

1. The sources are the 2007 Yearbook of Immigration Statistics by the U.S. Department of Homeland Security, and the report "The Impact of New Immigrants on Young Native-Born Workers, 2000-2005," by Andrew Sum, Paul Harrington, and Ishwar Khatiwada of Northeastern University.

2. The Congressional Budget Office report was called "Cost Estimate S. 2611 Comprehensive Immigration Reform Act of 2006," dated 5/16/2006.

3. The source is "The Fiscal Cost of Low-Skill Immigrants to State and Local Taxpayers," by Robert Rector, which he released at a 5/17/2007 Congressional hearing.

4. Sources include a U.S. General Accounting Office report GAO-04-82, "Overstay Tracking", dated May 2004, the 2007 Yearbook of Immigration Statistics, a 5/20/2006 Boston Globe article, and a 9/11 Commission staff report titled "Entry of the 9/11 Hijackers into the United States." The GAO report contained the admission that it was possible as many as 6.5 million people overstayed their visas in FY 2001.

5. The source for the number of criminal aliens in American custody is a U.S. General Accounting Office report GAO-05-337R titled "Information on Criminal Aliens Incarcerated in Federal and State Prisons and Local Jails" dated 4/7/2005. Figures were for the end of 2004. The source for the number of deaths of Americans due to foreigners committing murder or negligent homicide (driving while intoxicated, driving recklessly while sober, firearms "mishaps", etc.) is a 11/28/2006 World Net Daily article featuring homicide statistics released by Iowa congressman Steve King. King also noted illegal aliens sexually abused close to 3000 American children per year.

King forgot to count American women and foreign females, according to Deborah Schurman-Kauflin of the Violent Crimes Institute. She noted 2% of all illegal aliens arrested were arrested for sex offenses, noted 2% of an estimated 12 million illegals was about 240,000, and noted the average sex offender has multiple victims. She also noted the misogynistic background of many of the illegal immigrants, and the overrepresentation of young single males among the illegal immigrant population, as well as her conservative estimate of the number of illegals probably meant her estimate was on the low side. Ms. Schurman-Kauflin forgot to count male victims. Not counting jail rapes, about one victim in eight is male; almost all male victims not in prison are boys.

6. The source for most info is a CDC report titled "Summary of Notifiable Diseases – United States, 2003. The SARS source of disease info came from a 5/9/2006 Newsmax article by James Walsh.

7. The source is the 2007 Yearbook of Immigration Statistics.

8. Sources are the 2007 Yearbook of Immigration Statistics, and the article "The Impact of New Immigration on Young Native-Born Workers, 2005-2006."

9. The April 2006 Department of Homeland Security report "Detention and Removal of Illegal Aliens" (OIG-06-33) noted federal authorities released 280,000 illegal aliens in a three-year period, and also released 310,000 non-Mexican illegals from 2000 through 2005. The vast majority of them did not show up for court hearings. The Supreme Court, in their 2001 Zadvydas vs. Davis and Reno vs. Ma rulings, ruled officials could not incarcerate most illegal aliens indefinitely after securing a court order for their removal. In many cases, delays are due to the foot-dragging and non-cooperation of foreign governments who just might want these people in America. They more or less capped the detention at six months, and unimaginative federal prosecutors did not devise ways to organize the removal of aliens or use the loopholes allowed by the Supreme Court to deport these people. The report's authors noted the situation created a "mini amnesty" for aliens from China, India, and Iran.

10. Sources include testimony of U.S. Bureau of Customs and Border Protection acting commissioner Jayson Ahern before Congress (6/11/2009), Congressional Research Service's 5/13/2008 report "Border Security: Key Agencies and Their Missions" by Blas Nuñez-Neto, a 12/18/2008 U.S. Department of Homeland Security fact sheet titled "DHS End-of Year Accomplishments," and a 7/17/2008 "statement for the record" by former DHS Secretary Michael Chertoff.

SOME FINAL THOUGHTS

I farm part-time. It's a hard way to make a living. The vast majority of your ancestors earned their livings farming. They didn't have many options, until the Industrial Revolution provided factory jobs and farming machinery and greedy landlords ran many workers off the land. Our ancestors really did have to toil and sweat daily to make ends meet.

That was still true In the Ellis Island Era; most people even in the United States still earned their living by sweating. More people were farmers in the early 1900s than any other profession. The miners, loggers, and construction workers were also many in percentage of the work force. The steel mills and slaughterhouses employed many under conditions appalling by today's standards.

Women's trades were not easy either. Just ask the seamstresses who worked long hours and regularly got cheated out of their money and risked burning to death in firetrap buildings. Or ask the servant girls how long they worked and how little they made and how often they had to defend themselves from sexual assault. Or ask the female farmworkers of that era if they would prefer an office job of today to their farm labors in terms of pay, hours, and wear and tear on the body.

Because they were tough and independent-minded, our people in the Ellis Island Era demanded better performance from their politicians and bureaucrats than we demand today. Likewise, the immigrants themselves were used to hardships and were independent-minded enough to leave home and adopt our land as their own and assimilate. Half of my ancestors from Ireland and my wife's grandmother passed through Ellis Island along with millions of other people from the early 1890s through the end of the 1920s. My other ancestors who came to America (and hers) passed through Castle Garden.

The chapter on the growth of America is a sketch of how we as different types of people formed a Union and rose to greatness. Yes, there was a lot of wrongdoing in the process. Yet we are still head and shoulders above any other country that ever existed. Those who hate our way of life have nothing better to move to.

The chapters on immigration regulation and immigrant processing show the development of our laws and techniques for assuring decent people came to America to help it grow instead of allowing undesirables to come and leech off of America and work against America. No laws are perfect, but the goals of any politician who actually wants to serve America should be to limit immigration to the nation's actual needs, and to preserve the existing culture of America. We have the right to value our traditions and cultural practices, and we have the right to insist all of those who would live here do so as well. We don't _have_ to take in any immigrants who won't add to this nation. No other nation has dealt as charitably with systematic waves of immigration as our nation has done. Our people have been more generous in blood and treasure to other people around the globe than the people of any other country which ever existed.

The chapters on "white slavery" and on the investigations in the wake of the _Titanic_ sinking and the Triangle Fire showed that politicians of integrity and good will could accomplish something useful. We need more of these kinds of politicians, not less.

Most Ellis Island Era agents covered in this book thought about people, America, and God above of careerism. They cared about the safety of immigrants, about their ability to make their way in this country, and about their spiritual needs. They did not on the whole exclude aliens from America arbitrarily. And if their methods were paternalistic, Christian, and America-centric, so be it. That was who they were and what they did. And it worked fabulously.

They also cared about serving the people of America. They tried to keep out those who would pose a burden, an unfair competition, or a safety threat to Americans. They tried to include people as often as they could, as the 98 percent admission rate shows. They were not mean people, but conscientious and decent people.

There is a reason there is nothing like Ellis Island today. Those who come here legally get inspected and approved overseas. Political and commercial interests want it this way. There is no similar "quality control" backup screening like there used to be at Ellis Island and other immigration stations in America. Our State Department and Homeland Security people allow many spies, saboteurs, wage scale breakers, jihadists, and other undesirables into America. That doesn't count the millions who come in illegally across the Mexican and Canadian borders, or the millions who fly here on tourist visas, then overstay their visas. Today's immigration agents have much better crime fighting tools than those at Ellis Island did. But they face more hostile immigrants, immigration advocacy groups, and business interests. And they do not have the backing of the politicians when they try to do their jobs.

In the Ellis Island Era, our agents got little co-operation from foreign governments. Foreign politicians who wanted to get rid of people falsified their records or falsely certified them. They lied about the backgrounds of spies they sent here. Immigration agents at Ellis Island and other American immigration stations worked hard to determine the truth about would-be immigrants. They had to – the American people demanded it.

Politicians today run immigration for the benefit of their business donors who want cheap labor, and for their own perceived benefit of getting votes. Instead of men like William Williams and Henry Curran running things, there is a steady stream of careerist bureaucrats who help the politicians thwart the will of the people. The agent who tries to do his or her job properly is going to have more problems on the job than those who just punch the clock and obey their supervisors even when they are giving unethical orders. This fear of running into trouble on the job no doubt prevents many an immigration agent from making an arrest he should make, and prevents many an immigration employee from ensuring all checks are properly done on visa applicants when a supervisor screams she's not working fast enough.

The 9/11 Commission report "Entry of the 9/11 Hijackers into the United States" noted the following:

> Every visa application of the hijackers had missing or false information that was easy to refute. On this alone, they should not have gotten visas.

> Some hijackers had links to al-Qaeda that were easily verifiable if only our State Department people and intelligence community people had kept their databases current.

> A Saudi working with his government's passport agency helped his hijacker relatives get passports.

> American consular officials in Saudi Arabia averaged questioning applicants and issuing visas every two to three minutes. This was no real screening.

> Some hijackers had obviously doctored passports; American immigration agents didn't catch them.

> Many hijackers lied to American immigration agents to gain entry into America.

> Immigration agents in airports usually took only a minute or two per alien to evaluate alien travelers for admissibility. This was no real screening.

> When agents did hold up questionable aliens for secondary inspection, secondary inspectors allowed five of the six who were in on the hijacking and mass murder plot into the country.

> Many hijackers overstayed visas, didn't report to school on a student visa, or committed other immigration law violations that were easy to detect.

> <u>Business, government, and college educator pressures led immigration officials to soften the immigration entry inspection process, the overstay tracking process, and the student tracking process</u>.

The results? The 9/11 hijackers got in when Middle Eastern bureaucrats falsely vouched for them and our bureaucrats and agents wrongly let them in. They also were able to stay because immigration agents didn't screen them properly in America and American law enforcement agents did not track them down after they violated immigration laws. This laxity was in large part the result of top-down pressure from government officials, college officials, and corporate interests. Thanks to the Gilligan's Island approach, and not the Ellis Island approach, the hijackers were able to murder 3000 Americans.

A Puerto Rican inspector named José Melendez-Perez rejected the 20th would-be hijacker, Mohamed al-Kahtani. José Melendez-Perez, a Vietnam veteran, profiled Mohamed as a hit man. His co-workers thought he was risking his career to profile and deny entry to an arrogant Saudi – and it took a phone call to José's boss' boss at home on his day off to allow José's judgment to stand. Mohamed got a free ride back to the Middle East, courtesy of us taxpayers. Mohamed was evidently supposed to pilot Flight 93. There were only four hijackers on that plane; passengers overpowered the vermin and the plane crashed in a hilly rural area in Pennsylvania instead of in a city. Mohamed would wind up at the Guantanamo Bay terrorist prison.

*　　*　　*　　*　　*　　*　　*

On the feast of the Assumption (August 15) in 2007, my wife and I went up to my friend Greg the Sicilian's ancestral parish, Our Lady of the Most Holy Rosary Church on Murray Hill in Cleveland. The place was packed to overflowing with Italian Americans with roots in Cleveland's Little Italy. The walls of the church were light, and there were life-size painted statues of Jesus, Mary, John the Baptist, and other saints of the church. The choir sang in Italian, accompanied by a trumpeter. Despite the heat and the crowding, people were joyful to be together in their ancestral parish, worshiping God.

As I looked at the walls of the church, and the altar, I couldn't help but think of the immigrants of the Ellis Island Era. Cleveland has many such churches built by immigrants who came to work and be real Americans, but not throw away what they came from. In Cleveland, and throughout the Midwest, and in the Northeast, and even in the South and the Far West are many such churches, built by people with little money but plenty of substance.

In California and New Mexico and other states where the Spaniards went, you see similar churches built by the Spanish, the Mexicans, and the Native American Indians. In New Orleans and in South Bend, Indiana, and in other places with a French presence or a French past, you see similar churches built by the French, the Cajuns, and the Creoles. The people who built these churches and worshiped in them for generations would not tolerate a sermon of hatred against America.

America is like a table propped up by several legs of different diameters. There is a leg that represents our British European ancestors. There is a leg that represents our Spanish and French European ancestors, who established communities in the South and in the Southwest, and in some Northern states. There is a leg that represents our Irish, Italian, German, Jewish, Slavic, Scandinavian, and other European ancestors. There is a leg that represents our African ancestors, most of who were forced to come here. And there is a Native American leg, made up of our Native American Indian ancestors, our Inuit ancestors, and our Polynesian ancestors, who were overrun. These are the peoples who make America what it is.

Every real nation on Earth has a dominant culture. And it is the right of the people of each nation to embrace their culture and cherish it. It took our various peoples a couple of hundred years to make our traditions and our culture. The vast majority of us mongrels like what we have and would not trade with any other nation. That's why we tend not to leave this country.

Why should we Americans have to change our culture for the benefit of the many peoples from Asia and the Middle East who want to bring their own cultures, which in so many ways clash with the Euro-Afro-American Judeo-Christian culture that defines the people of the United States? Those so-called Americans who think our culture needs to adapt to theirs should first live in China, India, and the Middle East and see what happens to those who don't do as the natives do.

Except for the separatists, who should be deported, legal immigrants from Mexico and elsewhere in Latin America are by and large reasonable people. The illegals are the problem, simply because of their numbers and the large percentage of criminals and public assistance takers among them.

Most of the Asian and Middle Eastern aliens who have committed crimes in this country came here legally. This points to a flaw in our immigration screening processes. It also points to flaws in the Asian and Middle Eastern governments whose agents falsely certify these people. Of course, many of the crimes of these people serve their homelands.

Chinese military and industrial spies, and Indian techies came here on visas, and many of them have become residents and citizens. Yet they still steal and undermine this country's economy and national security. The Chinese have no problem selling us poisonous food and medical products, and they have no problem making poisonous toys for our children.

People from the Middle East also pose serious risks.

Many of the 9/11 murderers and the World Trade Center bombers got in "legally." So did many Moslems whose criminal acts you hear about routinely. The desire to do non-Moslems harm is in the blood of far too many of these people; their countrymen are doing far too little to help us ferret them out. The people of India can likewise murder in the name of their religion. They continue to do so in their homeland today.

These people have not assimilated much in another important way. Very few people from these lands have volunteered for military service relative to their numbers. Mexicans and other Hispanics and Filipinos at least serve in our armed forces in good proportions relative to their numbers.

Immigrants must be assimilable into America's traditions and institutions. They must become loyal Americans. They must not massively break our laws and defy our cultural standards. America is our house, and we have the right to determine who and how many can come here, and how they conduct themselves.

What would immigration today look like if immigrants had to meet Ellis Island standards? If the Ellis Island yardstick was used on immigrants today, many of them would not measure up.

This is not a judgment on the intelligence of the people of Asia or the Middle East. Many of them are highly intelligent; many of them are hard-working people. Of course, they have to be to survive in their homelands.

However, it is a simple recognition of human nature. They by and large do not view things the way we do. Nor do they want to. They prefer their religions, customs, and cultural practices. We prefer our own; very few Americans live in Asia or the Middle East by choice. We as peoples can agree to disagree.

Let those who prefer their ways stay at home and disagree with us *from there* instead of coming here and committing acts of violence, thievery, and espionage against us in our homeland to coerce us into their way of thinking. It's not our job to take in those who will harm us or loot us or drain us. Only the traitors and the stupidly or falsely charitable among us would disagree, for it is not their money and safety they propose to spend and degrade in allowing the criminals, the jihadists, the spies, the thieves, and the subscale laborers and techies into this country, it is ours!

Henry Curran, the cheerful soul who ran Ellis Island from 1923 to 1926, said the following about the immigration issue decades ago:

"Our country needed a rest from the task of assimilating so many millions of foreigners piling in here from every part of the world to become voting Americans five years from the day they came ashore from Ellis Island. The art of self-government is not acquired so easily. It is a long hard road. There must be a habit of it, a strong element of matured experience in it, if the composite sum of our American population is to succeed at it. We have done pretty well so far, but we are still an experiment, with only a hundred and fifty years of national life behind us – a tick of the clock, against the ages! And most of the immigrants were coming from countries where for centuries they had lived under the heel of dictators, knowing nothing of the obligations of self-government that must go hand in hand with its blessings – if self-government is to survive."

Curran's sage remarks referred to immigrants who were coming mostly from Europe. The immigrants from that continent had beliefs and cultural practices much closer to those of the people of the United States than the practices of the people of Asia and the Middle East are to the those of the people of the United States.

Curran also said, "Incidentally, it would be good to have enough jobs to go around among ourselves – if we ever get near that millennium again – without letting in more impecunious millions to compete with us for relief and for such jobs as we have." His words ring even truer today.

Frank Leahy, the great football coach at Notre Dame and World War Two veteran, wrote, "The American advantages have developed chiefly because we are blessed with the most successful form of government ever devised, and because in this great nation there are, proportionately speaking, more God-fearing and God-loving people than in any other section of the world. It is our duty to defend the qualities that have made our country superior. Not long ago, thousands of young Americans made the supreme sacrifice for the sake of a finer America and a better world. The least we can do is to vow solemnly that we will at all times strive diligently to make America the kind of nation they wanted it to be, for all time to come."

Leahy's exhortation is truer today, America's core values are under more attack now than they have ever been.

Leahy also said after World War Two, "All of the things that go together to make this country great must be continually defended from any attack." He listed faith in God, hard work, democracy, competitiveness, and the American Spirit (the can-do attitude we as a people used to have), as the things that made America the finest nation on earth.

Our ancestors were tougher people than we are. The men who fought World War Two were the last generation of men in this country who were physically tough and unafraid to speak their minds. And their women – who kept the home fires burning and the factories churning while they were away at war -- expected honesty, hard work, and manly behavior from them, not politically correct thought and metrosexual dress codes. We need to be more like them, not less.

You younger men and women and teenagers especially need to learn what is at stake and fight accordingly. Our nation's politicians are giving away your jobs and are taking away your money for decades to come to buy the votes of the selfish and the lazy in the generations ahead of you. If you don't force some change to this trend, you will be a beggar and a crime victim in your own land.

Too many of our political leaders have proven they are not our friends by the way they have mishandled the various aspects of immigration and trade and national security. This means you will have to force them to do right or force them out of office.

Using the Ellis Island yardstick for would-be immigrants, combined with the removal of all illegals and "legals" who act against us, and a tariff on imports that reflects our commitment to our American workforce, would be the greatest stimuli our economy could ever hope for. We outlawed slavery in 1865. We outlawed foreign contract labor undercutting our standards of living in the late 1800s. We had a tariff policy in the 1930s, 1940s, 1950s, and early 1960s that forbade imports from countries with servile labor. In those decades, we had a position of worldwide manufacturing dominance. There is no reason for us to export jobs to slave labor countries. There is no reason for us to subsidize the oppression of slave laborers by doing business with their government or corporate masters. There is no reason for us to import poor wages and working condition along with inferior products made by servile labor which may be toxic. There is no reason for us to admit immigrants who can't meet the same standards the Ellis Island Era immigrants had to meet.

We need to heed Frank Leahy's advice. We also need to heed the example of our ancestors, who worked to provide us with the wonderful nation we enjoy today. We should be grateful for the advances in safety and pay and liberty these people won for us, and we should not look down on them because their book learning wasn't what ours is. We should seek to defend and improve what these people provided us. And we should live our lives in a way that would make them proud of us, and our descendants grateful to us.

In this effort, to paraphrase the advice of a saint, pray as if everything depended on God, and work as if everything depended on you.

INDEX

Thanks, Bry and Greg, for your help and encouragement. God rest your souls!

ACKNOWLEDGEMENTS AND DEDICATIONS

The two people who deserve the most credit for this book are my brother Bryan Sherlock and my friend Greg the Sicilian aka Greg Shackel.

My brother Bryan, who died suddenly a few months ago, urged me to write this book, and he cheerfully reviewed it. But my younger brother also gave me a great example to follow. Bry was born three months premature, and suffered birth defects which included brain and motor nerve damage, and the loss of sight in one eye. Bryan was supposed to die at birth, then he was supposed to die any number of times as a boy. He was supposed to live as a shut-in. Mom and Dad told the doctors to pound sand. Bryan went to school and ran the streets with us.

Bryan underwent a shunt valve operation to relieve fluid pressure on his brain. Every time he grew so much, he had to undergo followup surgery to have the suction tube from his heart to the valve lengthened. Yet he graduated from high school. Bryan underwent a battery of tests after school; the results showed he read at the college level and did math at the eighth grade level. This proved Bryan was smarter than most members of Congress, for he knew you can't spend what you don't have!

What example did Bryan set? He dreamed, and then did. Bryan always wanted to be a park ranger. His handicaps disqualified him from taking peace officer training and firefighting training for the job, but he found a way in anyway. He earned an associate's degree in wildlife management and was able to work for county and state park systems in California as a maintenance man. Bryan did assist tourists, and assisted in making arrests. He pulled support duty in some major wildfires in California. During one, he rescued some horses by going into their barn and leading them to safety.

Bryan liked the way I discussed history and politics, and knew I wanted to write about these topics. He urged me to do so, just like he pursued his dream. So I did. Besides reading my work, Bryan had the pull to get me out to Angel Island with him and other staffers in 2006 well ahead of the rush of tourists.

Greg the Sicilian died of cancer a few months earlier, brave and tough to the end. I talked with him days before he reported for duty to Purgatory.

Greg dreamed of aviation, and pursued his dreams in the Navy as an aircraft mechanic. Greg was a patriot, and was proud of his service to his country. Greg's skills kept many a jet flying on the aircraft carrier that was his duty station. Greg won acclaim as a skilled aviation mechanic in the aviation firms smart enough to retain his services. The flying public benefits from the work of men like him.

Greg loved music and enjoyed success as a club band bassist. He never got the brass ring that led to big-time stardom, but he could make music and sing like a rock star. He helped people forget their troubles for a little bit while he performed. And he showed his Sicilian craftsmanship on stage as well – Greg made his guitars by hand, and they were beauties. He was self-assured enough to hang out with Pat Benatar after one of his gigs.

Not many guys can tell that story, and have it be true.

Greg also put his skills to work on a much more noble project – restoring World War Two aircraft so the public could appreciate the men who fought that war in the skies over Europe and the Pacific. It was a practical hands-on patriotism — like the juggler who juggled for Mary and Jesus' entertainment, Greg used his skills to pay tribute to the heroes. Greg also urged me to follow my dream, to write a book that told the unvarnished truth about America's problems, and do it in a way that would honor our ancestors and try to instigate positive reforms.

Barry Moreno, Jeff Dosik, and other staffers at the Ellis Island Immigration Museum deserve a great deal of credit for ensuring I checked credible documents. They patiently answered my questions, and provided a great deal of insight about Ellis Island and immigration in general. They also helped me line up the photos that grace this book. If you don't agree with my opinion, don't blame it on them. My point of view is my own.

My mother-in-law Mary Petros painted much of the art in this book. Her talent is self-evident. She is the Grandma Moses of Slavic America. My wife the Slavic Princess aka Agent 99 was mistress of design. She assisted in the researching and interviewing I did for this book, and in prepping the trip we took to Europe to do work for this book. She also painted for the book, drove me to complete the book, and made numerous suggestions for the book's improvement.

Marian the Librarian did a thorough reading and professional critique of this book. Madame M, Moose Morse, and Sister Nancy read the manuscript and made good suggestions. Black Mike, one of the few government people inside the Beltway who tells the truth, also offered sound advice. And the nuns and the lay teachers at my parish school, who so many years ago gave me a great education, and who reinforced the lessons in life Dad and Mom were teaching me, gave me the training I needed to put this book together.

Ultimately, I owe my thanks to those who fought in uniform for this nation so it could become and remain the greatest nation on earth. I also owe my thanks to Dad and Mom, and to the many worthy people like Dad and Mom who labored so hard through the centuries to make Christian society. I dedicate this book to my parents, my grandparents, my family and friends, and those in the military and the emergency professions. I also dedicate this book to Kim Bergalis, the pretty young woman who stood up to government officials and pressure groups who wanted to give spreaders of AIDS political protection. The vermin lyingly smeared her, but like Joan of Arc, she didn't run, but stood and fought them. Miss Kimberly died a hero and martyr; she died with her boots on.

I give a final dedication to you, my readers. May we look out for the interests of our nation and our families, not the interests of the greedy and powerful. May we serve God and obey Him. May God bless you all, every day, as long as you shall live.

ABOUT THE AUTHOR

Some say Kevin Sherlock never figured out what he wanted to be when he grew up. So he tried several careers.

Sherlock wanted to serve the nation. He attended the U.S. Military Academy in the 1970s, and earned a degree in engineering. Sherlock served as an Army officer in the late 1970s and early 1980s.

Sherlock wanted to write and engineer. He alternated between gigs as a technical writer and test engineer and gigs as a journalist in the 1980s.

For roughly 20 years, Sherlock has operated a technical publishing firm and a research service. For the last decade or so, he has also operated a small orchard and livestock farm. He can slaughter animals, harvest produce, and make reasonably potent wine and hard cider. Sherlock's Irish ancestors were farmers and livestock slaughterers, and his Czech ancestors were tailors, coopers, and bakers. His farming brought him an appreciation of the hard work of the many generations of his ancestors.

In the 1990s, Sherlock went back to college and studied chemistry, physiology, toxicology, and forensic science. Sherlock served an internship with a coroner's office in Ohio; he assisted at autopsies and did labwork to determine causes of death.

Sherlock has assisted lawyers in locating assets of white collar criminals who have cheated veterans and widows. He also wrote a book called How to be Your Own Detective, which was a guide to public records research for the average citizen. Morton Downey Jr. liked the book and had kind words for it on his radio show.

Sherlock believes in the Ten Commandments, the Baltimore Catechism, and the U.S. Constitution, especially the 2nd, 9th, 10th, 13th, and 21st Amendments.

Sherlock's engineering background leads him to apply science and numerical analysis to his research. His patriotism and his religion lead him to research if policies and powerful participants are right and just for the American people.

Sherlock also believes short of the direct intervention of God Himself, an alert and informed public is the best defense against the abuses of the powerful. An alert and informed public also contains the natural enemies of the politicians and other powerful interests who would unjustly limit their freedoms.